A FIRST COURSE IN OPTIMIZATION THEORY

A First Course in Optimization Theory introduces students to optimization theory and its use in economics and allied disciplines. The first of its three parts examines the existence of solutions to optimization problems in $\mathbb{R}^n$, and how these solutions may be identified. The second part explores how solutions to optimization problems change with changes in the underlying parameters, and the last part provides an extensive description of the fundamental principles of finite- and infinite-horizon dynamic programming.

Each chapter contains a number of detailed examples explaining both the theory and its applications for first-year master's and graduate students. "Cookbook" procedures are accompanied by a discussion of when such methods are guaranteed to be successful, and equally importantly, when they could fail. Each result in the main body of the text is also accompanied by a complete proof. A preliminary chapter and three appendices are designed to keep the book mathematically self-contained.

A FIRST COURSE
IN OPTIMIZATION THEORY

RANGARAJAN K. SUNDARAM
New York University

CAMBRIDGE
UNIVERSITY PRESS

CAMBRIDGE UNIVERSITY PRESS
Cambridge, New York, Melbourne, Madrid, Cape Town, Singapore, São Paulo, Delhi

Cambridge University Press
32 Avenue of the Americas, New York, NY 10013-2473, USA

www.cambridge.org
Information on this title: www.cambridge.org/9780521497701

First published 1996
13th printing 2008

Printed in the United States of America

A catalog record for this publication is available from the British Library.

ISBN 978-0-521-49719-0 hardback
ISBN 978-0-521-49770-1 paperback

To
my parents
and
to my grandmother Innumma

Contents

Preface   *page* xiii
Acknowledgements   xvii

1   Mathematical Preliminaries   1
    1.1   Notation and Preliminary Definitions   2
          1.1.1   Integers, Rationals, Reals, $\mathbb{R}^n$ 2
          1.1.2   Inner Product, Norm, Metric   4
    1.2   Sets and Sequences in $\mathbb{R}^n$ 7
          1.2.1   Sequences and Limits   7
          1.2.2   Subsequences and Limit Points   10
          1.2.3   Cauchy Sequences and Completeness   11
          1.2.4   Suprema, Infima, Maxima, Minima   14
          1.2.5   Monotone Sequences in $\mathbb{R}$ 17
          1.2.6   The Lim Sup and Lim Inf   18
          1.2.7   Open Balls, Open Sets, Closed Sets   22
          1.2.8   Bounded Sets and Compact Sets   23
          1.2.9   Convex Combinations and Convex Sets   23
          1.2.10   Unions, Intersections, and Other Binary Operations   24
    1.3   Matrices   30
          1.3.1   Sum, Product, Transpose   30
          1.3.2   Some Important Classes of Matrices   32
          1.3.3   Rank of a Matrix   33
          1.3.4   The Determinant   35
          1.3.5   The Inverse   38
          1.3.6   Calculating the Determinant   39
    1.4   Functions   41
          1.4.1   Continuous Functions   41
          1.4.2   Differentiable and Continuously Differentiable Functions   43

	1.4.3 Partial Derivatives and Differentiability	46
	1.4.4 Directional Derivatives and Differentiability	48
	1.4.5 Higher Order Derivatives	49
1.5	Quadratic Forms: Definite and Semidefinite Matrices	50
	1.5.1 Quadratic Forms and Definiteness	50
	1.5.2 Identifying Definiteness and Semidefiniteness	53
1.6	Some Important Results	55
	1.6.1 Separation Theorems	56
	1.6.2 The Intermediate and Mean Value Theorems	60
	1.6.3 The Inverse and Implicit Function Theorems	65
1.7	Exercises	66
2	**Optimization in $\mathbb{R}^n$**	**74**
2.1	Optimization Problems in $\mathbb{R}^n$	74
2.2	Optimization Problems in Parametric Form	77
2.3	Optimization Problems: Some Examples	78
	2.3.1 Utility Maximization	78
	2.3.2 Expenditure Minimization	79
	2.3.3 Profit Maximization	80
	2.3.4 Cost Minimization	80
	2.3.5 Consumption-Leisure Choice	81
	2.3.6 Portfolio Choice	81
	2.3.7 Identifying Pareto Optima	82
	2.3.8 Optimal Provision of Public Goods	83
	2.3.9 Optimal Commodity Taxation	84
2.4	Objectives of Optimization Theory	85
2.5	A Roadmap	86
2.6	Exercises	88
3	**Existence of Solutions: The Weierstrass Theorem**	**90**
3.1	The Weierstrass Theorem	90
3.2	The Weierstrass Theorem in Applications	92
3.3	A Proof of the Weierstrass Theorem	96
3.4	Exercises	97
4	**Unconstrained Optima**	**100**
4.1	"Unconstrained" Optima	100
4.2	First-Order Conditions	101
4.3	Second-Order Conditions	103
4.4	Using the First- and Second-Order Conditions	104

4.5 A Proof of the First-Order Conditions 106
4.6 A Proof of the Second-Order Conditions 108
4.7 Exercises 110

5 Equality Constraints and the Theorem of Lagrange 112
5.1 Constrained Optimization Problems 112
5.2 Equality Constraints and the Theorem of Lagrange 113
    5.2.1 Statement of the Theorem 114
    5.2.2 The Constraint Qualification 115
    5.2.3 The Lagrangean Multipliers 116
5.3 Second-Order Conditions 117
5.4 Using the Theorem of Lagrange 121
    5.4.1 A "Cookbook" Procedure 121
    5.4.2 Why the Procedure Usually Works 122
    5.4.3 When It Could Fail 123
    5.4.4 A Numerical Example 127
5.5 Two Examples from Economics 128
    5.5.1 An Illustration from Consumer Theory 128
    5.5.2 An Illustration from Producer Theory 130
    5.5.3 Remarks 132
5.6 A Proof of the Theorem of Lagrange 135
5.7 A Proof of the Second-Order Conditions 137
5.8 Exercises 142

6 Inequality Constraints and the Theorem of Kuhn and Tucker 145
6.1 The Theorem of Kuhn and Tucker 145
    6.1.1 Statement of the Theorem 145
    6.1.2 The Constraint Qualification 147
    6.1.3 The Kuhn–Tucker Multipliers 148
6.2 Using the Theorem of Kuhn and Tucker 150
    6.2.1 A "Cookbook" Procedure 150
    6.2.2 Why the Procedure Usually Works 151
    6.2.3 When It Could Fail 152
    6.2.4 A Numerical Example 155
6.3 Illustrations from Economics 157
    6.3.1 An Illustration from Consumer Theory 158
    6.3.2 An Illustration from Producer Theory 161
6.4 The General Case: Mixed Constraints 164
6.5 A Proof of the Theorem of Kuhn and Tucker 165
6.6 Exercises 168

7 Convex Structures in Optimization Theory   172
   7.1 Convexity Defined   173
        7.1.1 Concave and Convex Functions   174
        7.1.2 Strictly Concave and Strictly Convex Functions   176
   7.2 Implications of Convexity   177
        7.2.1 Convexity and Continuity   177
        7.2.2 Convexity and Differentiability   179
        7.2.3 Convexity and the Properties of the Derivative   183
   7.3 Convexity and Optimization   185
        7.3.1 Some General Observations   185
        7.3.2 Convexity and Unconstrained Optimization   187
        7.3.3 Convexity and the Theorem of Kuhn and Tucker   187
   7.4 Using Convexity in Optimization   189
   7.5 A Proof of the First-Derivative Characterization of Convexity   190
   7.6 A Proof of the Second-Derivative Characterization of Convexity   191
   7.7 A Proof of the Theorem of Kuhn and Tucker under Convexity   194
   7.8 Exercises   198

8 Quasi-Convexity and Optimization   203
   8.1 Quasi-Concave and Quasi-Convex Functions   204
   8.2 Quasi-Convexity as a Generalization of Convexity   205
   8.3 Implications of Quasi-Convexity   209
   8.4 Quasi-Convexity and Optimization   213
   8.5 Using Quasi-Convexity in Optimization Problems   215
   8.6 A Proof of the First-Derivative Characterization of Quasi-Convexity   216
   8.7 A Proof of the Second-Derivative Characterization of
        Quasi-Convexity   217
   8.8 A Proof of the Theorem of Kuhn and Tucker under Quasi-Convexity   220
   8.9 Exercises   221

9 Parametric Continuity: The Maximum Theorem   224
   9.1 Correspondences   225
        9.1.1 Upper- and Lower-Semicontinuous Correspondences   225
        9.1.2 Additional Definitions   228
        9.1.3 A Characterization of Semicontinuous Correspondences   229
        9.1.4 Semicontinuous Functions and Semicontinuous
               Correspondences   233
   9.2 Parametric Continuity: The Maximum Theorem   235
        9.2.1 The Maximum Theorem   235
        9.2.2 The Maximum Theorem under Convexity   237

9.3 An Application to Consumer Theory 240
    9.3.1 Continuity of the Budget Correspondence 240
    9.3.2 The Indirect Utility Function and Demand
          Correspondence 242
9.4 An Application to Nash Equilibrium 243
    9.4.1 Normal-Form Games 243
    9.4.2 The Brouwer/Kakutani Fixed Point Theorem 244
    9.4.3 Existence of Nash Equilibrium 246
9.5 Exercises 247

10 Supermodularity and Parametric Monotonicity 253
  10.1 Lattices and Supermodularity 254
    10.1.1 Lattices 254
    10.1.2 Supermodularity and Increasing Differences 255
  10.2 Parametric Monotonicity 258
  10.3 An Application to Supermodular Games 262
    10.3.1 Supermodular Games 262
    10.3.2 The Tarski Fixed Point Theorem 263
    10.3.3 Existence of Nash Equilibrium 263
  10.4 A Proof of the Second-Derivative Characterization of
      Supermodularity 264
  10.5 Exercises 266

11 Finite-Horizon Dynamic Programming 268
  11.1 Dynamic Programming Problems 268
  11.2 Finite-Horizon Dynamic Programming 268
  11.3 Histories, Strategies, and the Value Function 269
  11.4 Markovian Strategies 271
  11.5 Existence of an Optimal Strategy 272
  11.6 An Example: The Consumption–Savings Problem 276
  11.7 Exercises 278

12 Stationary Discounted Dynamic Programming 281
  12.1 Description of the Framework 281
  12.2 Histories, Strategies, and the Value Function 282
  12.3 The Bellman Equation 283
  12.4 A Technical Digression 286
    12.4.1 Complete Metric Spaces and Cauchy Sequences 286
    12.4.2 Contraction Mappings 287
    12.4.3 Uniform Convergence 289

12.5   Existence of an Optimal Strategy   291
       12.5.1   A Preliminary Result   292
       12.5.2   Stationary Strategies   294
       12.5.3   Existence of an Optimal Strategy   295
12.6   An Example: The Optimal Growth Model   298
       12.6.1   The Model   299
       12.6.2   Existence of Optimal Strategies   300
       12.6.3   Characterization of Optimal Strategies   301
12.7   Exercises   309

Appendix A   Set Theory and Logic: An Introduction   315
A.1   Sets, Unions, Intersections   315
A.2   Propositions: Contrapositives and Converses   316
A.3   Quantifiers and Negation   318
A.4   Necessary and Sufficient Conditions   320

Appendix B   The Real Line   323
B.1   Construction of the Real Line   323
B.2   Properties of the Real Line   326

Appendix C   Structures on Vector Spaces   330
C.1   Vector Spaces   330
C.2   Inner Product Spaces   332
C.3   Normed Spaces   333
C.4   Metric Spaces   336
       C.4.1   Definitions   336
       C.4.2   Sets and Sequences in Metric Spaces   337
       C.4.3   Continuous Functions on Metric Spaces   339
       C.4.4   Separable Metric Spaces   340
       C.4.5   Subspaces   341
C.5   Topological Spaces   342
       C.5.1   Definitions   342
       C.5.2   Sets and Sequences in Topological Spaces   343
       C.5.3   Continuous Functions on Topological Spaces   343
       C.5.4   Bases   343
C.6   Exercises   345

Bibliography   349
Index   351

Preface

This book developed out of a course I have taught since 1988 to first-year Ph.D. students at the University of Rochester on the use of optimization techniques in economic analysis. A detailed account of its contents is presented in Section 2.5 of Chapter 2. The discussion below is aimed at providing a broad overview of the book, as well as at emphasizing some of its special features.

An Overview of the Contents

The main body of this book may be divided into three parts. The first part, encompassing Chapters 3 through 8, studies optimization in n-dimensional Euclidean space, $\mathbb{R}^n$. Several topics are covered in this span. These include—but are not limited to— (i) the Weierstrass Theorem, and the existence of solutions to optimization problems; (ii) the Theorem of Lagrange, and necessary conditions for optima in problems with *equality* constraints; (iii) the Theorem of Kuhn and Tucker, and necessary conditions for optima in problems with *inequality* constraints; (iv) the role of *convexity* in obtaining *sufficient* conditions for optima in constrained optimization problems; and (v) the extent to which convexity can be replaced with *quasi*-convexity, while still obtaining sufficiency of the first-order conditions for global optima.

The second part of the book, comprised of Chapters 9 and 10, looks at the issue of *parametric variation* in optimization problems, that is, at the manner in which solutions to optimization problems respond to changes in the values of underlying parameters. Chapter 9 begins this exercise with the question of *parametric continuity*: under what conditions will solutions to optimization problems vary "continuously" with changes in the underlying parameters? An answer is provided in the centerpiece of this chapter, the Maximum Theorem. The strengthening of the Maximum Theorem that is obtained by adding convexity restrictions to the problem is also examined. Chapter 10 is concerned with *parametric monotonicity*, that is, with conditions under which increases in the values of parameters result in increases in the size of optimal

xiii

actions. The important concept of *supermodularity*, and its role in securing parametric monotonicity, is described here.

The third and final part of the book, consisting of Chapters 11 and 12, explores optimization theory in a *dynamic* environment. Chapter 11 discusses dynamic optimization in problems with a *finite* horizon. It establishes the existence of optimal strategies under suitable conditions, and details the method of *backwards induction* by which these strategies may be recovered. Chapter 12 focuses on the infinite-horizon problem, and derives the Bellman optimality equation for this case. The role of this equation in identifying optimal strategies is discussed, and the existence of optimal strategies is established under suitable conditions.

Prerequisites

In principle, this book is mathematically self-contained. There are four chapters (Chapter 1, and Appendices A, B, and C) devoted exclusively to providing the reader with a description of the mathematical results used in the body of the text. Of these, Appendix A is concerned with the basic rules of logic; among other things, it discusses the concept of *negation* and the importance of the order of quantifiers in forming a negation; the distinction between a *contrapositive* and a *converse*; and that between a *necessary* condition and a *sufficient* condition. It is vital that the reader have a mastery over this material before reading the rest of the text.

Chapter 1 presents a compendium of results from mathematical analysis and linear algebra that are used in the rest of the book. Strictly speaking, not all the contents of this chapter are required for a comprehension of the material that follows; rather, it suffices that the reader is familiar with a few topics such as continuous and differentiable functions on $\mathbb{R}^n$, closed, open, compact, and convex sets in $\mathbb{R}^n$, and definite and semidefinite matrices. However, the contents of Chapter 1 are invoked repeatedly in various *proofs* in the main body of the text. As such, a systematic knowledge of this material should significantly enhance understanding in the sequel.

It is presumed in Chapter 1 that the reader has at least an intuitive feel for what is meant by a "real number." Appendix B, which describes the construction of the real line from rational numbers, is aimed at readers who either lack this knowledge, or who wish to have a somewhat more formal introduction to the real number line. However, it is to be emphasized that Appendix B is genuinely only an "appendix"; a knowledge of its contents is by no means required at any point in the book.

The presentation in Chapter 1 also takes place solely in the context of Euclidean spaces, although many of the structures presented here (inner product, norm, metric, etc.) can be developed in more abstract vector spaces. Appendix C is aimed at readers who wish to see the outline of such a development. It defines abstract vector spaces, and describes four constructs on such spaces: inner product spaces, normed spaces, metric spaces, and toplogical spaces.

What Is Different About This Book?

In part, at least, this book owes its existence to a feeling of dissatisfaction with the available texts in this area. Many of the available texts concentrate on applications to the exclusion of theory. The cookbook approach they espouse is problematic for many reasons, not least because students do not obtain a clear understanding of even the assumptions underlying a particular result, let alone why those assumptions are required. At the other end of the spectrum, there are a number of books that are mathematically precise and detailed, but that do not elaborate on the use of the theory in *solving* optimization problems.

This book represents an attempt to avoid either of these pitfalls. The presentation has five features that aim at blending the theory with its applications. The first two features are directed at clarifying the theory itself; the next two concern the use of the theory in identifying solutions to given optimization problems; and the last involves *working* with both the theory and its application.

First, every result in the main body of the book is accompanied by a complete and detailed proof. To avoid disrupting the flow of material, these proofs are usually placed at the end of each chapter.

Second, following the statement of each important result, a number of examples are given that illustrate why the result would be invalid were any of the assumptions to be violated. Taken together with the proofs of the various results, these examples are designed to make the student appreciate the part played by each assumption in the overall result.

Third, each important result is also followed by a section discussing procedures for using the result in applications to actually locate an optimum. Where the results concerned are *sufficient* conditions, the discussion is relatively straightforward. However, where *necessary* conditions are involved (as in the Lagrange and Kuhn–Tucker Theorems), the "cookbook" procedures for using these results are not guaranteed to be uniformly successful. Consequently, the description of these procedures is also accompanied by a detailed discussion of when the procedure is guaranteed to be successful, and equally importantly, when it could fail.

Fourth, in each chapter, the use of the chapter's results in applications is illustrated through detailed worked-out examples based on well-known paradigms. Thus, for instance, the utility-maximization problem from consumer theory, and the cost-minimization problem from producer theory, are each used to describe the use of Lagrange's Theorem in solving equality-constrained optimization problems, while the two examples used to illustrate the use of the Maximum Theorem (and the

Maximum Theorem under Convexity) are taken from consumer theory, and game theory, respectively.

Finally, since the only real way to learn mathematics is to use it, there is a list of exercises provided at the end of each chapter. The exercises range from the very easy to the quite difficult. Some of the exercises emphasize the theory by, for example, requiring the students to find counterexamples to given statements. Others focus on applications, and ask students to detail optimization problems describing specific situations, and to solve them for given parametrizations.

Acknowledgements

No work of authorship is ever the accomplishment of one individual, and the present volume is no exception. It is a pleasure to be able to acknowledge the many people whose help and advice shaped this book.

Among the colleagues who gave generously of their time, Jeff Banks, John Boyd, and Prajit Dutta deserve special mention for their detailed suggestions on how and where the manuscript could be improved. Much valuable input also came from David Austen Smith, Sanjiv Das, Dhananjay Gode, Sreedhar Moorthy, Abon Mozumdar, Massoud Mussavian, and Jim Schummer.

I owe a very special debt to Tarık Kara, who introduced me to the magical world of TEX, guided me expertly through my early difficulties, helped me with the preparation of the end-of-chapter exercises, and developed all of the figures and illustrations that appear in this book.

Karl Shell provided a great deal of support and encouragement throughout this project, most notably in its early stages when I was still doubtful of the wisdom of continuing with it. In this context, I am also grateful to Beth Allen, Ron Jones, Mukul Majumdar, Andy McLennan, and especially Marti Subrahmanyam.

As chairman of the Department of Economics at the University of Rochester, Alan Stockman enabled me to alter my teaching schedule and get two valuable months off in the Fall of 1994. With Jess Benhabib's assistance, I spent these two months at the Department of Economics at New York University, and it was in this period that over a third of the manuscript was written. I am indebted to Alan and Jess for their respective roles in this regard.

Scott Parris and the rest of the Cambridge University Press team (especially Linda Johnson and Janis Bolster) were always helpful and prompt. It was a pleasure working with them.

Perhaps my greatest debt is to my wife, Urmilla, who bore the many late nights and weekends of my work on this manuscript with patience, and whose support on the home front was what, in the final analysis, made completion of this project possible.

1

Mathematical Preliminaries

This chapter lays the mathematical foundation for the study of optimization that occupies the rest of this book. It focuses on three main topics: the topological structure of Euclidean spaces, continuous and differentiable functions on Euclidean spaces and their properties, and matrices and quadratic forms. Readers familiar with real analysis at the level of Rudin (1976) or Bartle (1964), and with matrix algebra at the level of Munkres (1964) or Johnston (1984, Chapter 4), will find this chapter useful primarily as a refresher; for others, a systematic knowledge of its contents should significantly enhance understanding of the material to follow.

Since this is not a book in introductory analysis or linear algebra, the presentation in this chapter cannot be as comprehensive or as leisurely as one might desire. The results stated here have been chosen with an eye to their usefulness towards the book's main purpose, which is to develop a theory of optimization in Euclidean spaces. The selective presentation of proofs in this chapter reveals a similar bias. Proofs whose formal structure bears some resemblance to those encountered in the main body of the text are spelt out in detail; others are omitted altogether, and the reader is given the choice of either accepting the concerned results on faith or consulting the more primary sources listed alongside the result.

It would be inaccurate to say that this chapter does not presuppose any knowledge on the part of the reader, but it is true that it does not presuppose much. Appendices A and B aim to fill in the gaps and make the book largely self-contained. Appendix A reviews the basic rules of propositional logic; it is taken for granted throughout that the reader is familiar with this material. An intuitive understanding of the concept of an "irrational number," and of the relationship between rational and irrational numbers, suffices for this chapter and for the rest of this book. A formal knowledge of the real line and its properties will, however, be an obvious advantage, and readers who wish to acquaint themselves with this material may consult Appendix B.

The discussion in this chapter takes place solely in the context of Euclidean spaces. This is entirely adequate for our purposes, and avoids generality that we do not need. However, Euclidean spaces are somewhat special in that many of their properties (such as completeness, or the compactness of closed and bounded sets) do not carry over to more general metric or topological spaces. Readers wishing to view the topological structure of Euclidean spaces in a more abstract context can, at a first pass, consult Appendix C, where the concepts of inner product, norm, metric, and topology are defined on general vector spaces, and some of their properties are reviewed.

1.1 Notation and Preliminary Definitions

1.1.1 Integers, Rationals, Reals, $\mathbb{R}^n$

The notation we adopt is largely standard. The set of positive integers is denoted by $\mathbb{N}$, and the set of all integers by $\mathbb{Z}$:

$$\mathbb{N} = \{1, 2, 3, \ldots\}$$
$$\mathbb{Z} = \{\ldots, -2, -1, 0, 1, 2, \ldots\}.$$

The set of rational numbers is denoted by $\mathbb{Q}$:

$$\mathbb{Q} = \left\{ x \mid x = \frac{p}{q}, \ p, q \in \mathbb{Z}, q \neq 0 \right\}.$$

Finally, the set of all real numbers, both rational and irrational, is denoted by $\mathbb{R}$. As mentioned earlier, it is presumed that the reader has at least an intuitive understanding of the real line and its properties. Readers lacking this knowledge should first review Appendix B.

Given a real number $z \in \mathbb{R}$, its *absolute value* will be denoted $|z|$:

$$|z| = \begin{cases} z & \text{if } z \geq 0 \\ -z & \text{if } z < 0. \end{cases}$$

The *Euclidean distance* between two points x and y in $\mathbb{R}$ is defined as $|x - y|$, i.e., as the absolute value of their difference.

For any positive integer $n \in \mathbb{N}$, the n-fold Cartesian product of $\mathbb{R}$ will be denoted $\mathbb{R}^n$. We will refer to $\mathbb{R}^n$ as *n-dimensional Euclidean space*. When $n = 1$, we shall continue writing $\mathbb{R}$ for $\mathbb{R}^1$.

A point in $\mathbb{R}^n$ is a vector $x = (x_1, \ldots, x_n)$ where for each $i = 1, \ldots, n$, x_i is a real number. The number x_i is called the *i-th coordinate* of the vector x.

We use 0 to denote the real number 0 as well as the null vector $(0, \ldots, 0) \in \mathbb{R}^n$. This notation is ambiguous, but the correct meaning will usually be clear from the context.

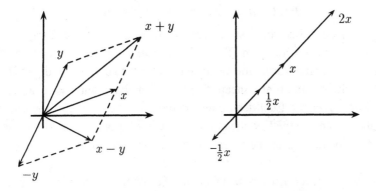

Fig. 1.1. Vector Addition and Scalar Multiplication in $\mathbb{R}^2$

Vector addition and scalar multiplication are defined in $\mathbb{R}^n$ as follows: for $x, y \in \mathbb{R}^n$ and $\alpha \in \mathbb{R}$,

$$x + y = (x_1 + y_1, \ldots, x_n + y_n)$$
$$\alpha x = (\alpha x_1, \ldots, \alpha x_n).$$

Figure 1.1 provides a graphical interpretation of vector addition and scalar mutiplication in $\mathbb{R}^2$.

Given any two n-vectors $x = (x_1, \ldots, x_n)$ and $y = (y_1, \ldots, y_n)$, we write

$$x = y, \quad \text{if } x_i = y_i, \quad i = 1, \ldots, n.$$
$$x \geq y, \quad \text{if } x_i \geq y_i, \quad i = 1, \ldots, n.$$
$$x > y, \quad \text{if } x \geq y \text{ and } x \neq y.$$
$$x \gg y, \quad \text{if } x_i > y_i, \quad i = 1, \ldots, n.$$

Note that

- $x \geq y$ does *not* preclude the possibility that $x = y$, and
- for $n > 1$, the vectors x and y need not be comparable under any of the categories above; for instance, the vectors $x = (2, 1)$ and $y = (1, 2)$ in $\mathbb{R}^2$ do not satisfy $x \geq y$, but neither is it true that $y \geq x$.

The *nonnegative* and *strictly positive* orthants of $\mathbb{R}^n$, denoted $\mathbb{R}^n_+$ and $\mathbb{R}^n_{++}$, respectively, are defined as

$$\mathbb{R}^n_+ = \{x \in \mathbb{R}^n \mid x \geq 0\},$$

and

$$\mathbb{R}^n_{++} = \{x \in \mathbb{R}^n \mid x \gg 0\}.$$

1.1.2 Inner Product, Norm, Metric

This subsection describes three structures on the space $\mathbb{R}^n$: the *Euclidean inner product* of two vectors x and y in $\mathbb{R}^n$, the *Euclidean norm* of a vector x in $\mathbb{R}^n$, and the *Euclidean metric* measuring the distance between two points x and y in $\mathbb{R}^n$. Each of these generalizes a familiar concept from $\mathbb{R}$. Namely, when $n = 1$, and x and y are just real numbers, the Euclidean inner product of x and y is just the product xy of the numbers x and y; the Euclidean norm of x is simply the absolute value $|x|$ of x; and the Euclidean distance between x and y is the absolute value $|x - y|$ of their difference.

Given $x, y \in \mathbb{R}^n$, the *Euclidean inner product* of the vectors x and y, denoted $x \cdot y$, is defined as:

$$x \cdot y = \sum_{i=1}^{n} x_i y_i.$$

We shall henceforth refer to the Euclidean inner product simply as the inner product.

Theorem 1.1 *The inner product has the following properties for any vectors x, y, $z \in \mathbb{R}^n$ and scalars $a, b \in \mathbb{R}$:*

1. *Symmetry: $x \cdot y = y \cdot x$.*
2. *Bilinearity: $(ax + by) \cdot z = ax \cdot z + by \cdot z$ and $x \cdot (ay + bz) = x \cdot ay + x \cdot bz$.*
3. *Positivity: $x \cdot x \geq 0$, with equality holding if and only if $x = 0$.*

Proof Symmetry and bilinearity are easy to verify from the definition of the inner product. To check that positivity holds, note that the square of a real number is always nonnegative, and can be zero if and only if the number is itself zero. It follows that as the sum of squared real numbers, $x \cdot x = \sum_{i=1}^{n} x_i^2$ is always nonnegative, and is zero if and only if $x_i = 0$ for each i, i.e., if and only if $x = 0$. $\square$

The inner product also satisfies a very useful condition called the *Cauchy–Schwartz inequality:*

Theorem 1.2 (Cauchy–Schwartz Inequality) *For any $x, y \in \mathbb{R}^n$ we have*

$$|x \cdot y| \leq (x \cdot x)^{1/2} (y \cdot y)^{1/2}.$$

Proof For notational ease, let $X = x \cdot x$, $Y = y \cdot y$, and $Z = x \cdot y$. Then, the result will be proved if we show that $XY \geq Z^2$, since the required inequality will follow simply by taking square roots on both sides.

If $x = 0$, then $Z = X = 0$, and the inequality holds trivially. Suppose, therefore, that $x \neq 0$. Note that by the positivity property of the inner product, we must then have $X > 0$. The positivity property also implies that for any scalar $a \in \mathbb{R}$, we have

$$
\begin{aligned}
0 \leq (ax + y) \cdot (ax + y) \\
= a^2 x \cdot x + 2ax \cdot y + y \cdot y \\
= a^2 X + 2aZ + Y.
\end{aligned}
$$

In particular, this inequality must hold for $a = -Z/X$. When this value of a is used in the equation above, we obtain

$$
\left(\frac{Z}{X}\right)^2 X - 2\left(\frac{Z}{X}\right) Z + Y = -\left(\frac{Z^2}{X}\right) + Y \geq 0,
$$

or $Y \geq Z^2/X$. Since $X > 0$, this in turn implies $XY \geq Z^2$, as required. □

The *Euclidean norm* (henceforth, simply the *norm*) of a vector $x \in \mathbb{R}^n$, denoted $\|x\|$, is defined as

$$
\|x\| = \left(\sum_{i=1}^{n} x_i^2\right)^{1/2}.
$$

The norm is related to the inner product through the identity

$$
\|x\| = (x \cdot x)^{1/2}
$$

for all $x \in \mathbb{R}^n$; in particular, the Cauchy–Schwartz inequality may be written as

$$
|x \cdot y| \leq \|x\| \|y\|.
$$

Our next result, which describes some useful properties of the norm, uses this obser-vation.

Theorem 1.3 *The norm satisfies the following properties at all x, $y \in \mathbb{R}^n$, and $a \in \mathbb{R}$:*

1. *Positivity:* $\|x\| \geq 0$, *with equality if and only if $x = 0$.*
2. *Homogeneity:* $\|ax\| = |a| \cdot \|x\|$.
3. *Triangle Inequality:* $\|x + y\| \leq \|x\| + \|y\|$.

Proof The positivity property of the norm follows from the positivity property of the inner product, and the fact that $\|x\| = (x \cdot x)^{1/2}$. Homogeneity obtains since

$$
\|ax\| = \left(\sum_{i=1}^{n} a^2 x_i^2\right)^{1/2} = \left(a^2 \sum_{i=1}^{n} x_i^2\right)^{1/2} = |a| \|x\|.
$$

The triangle inequality is a little trickier; we will need the Cauchy–Schwartz inequality to establish it. Observe that for any x and y in $\mathbb{R}^n$, we have

$$\|x + y\|^2 = (x + y) \cdot (x + y) = \|x\|^2 + 2x \cdot y + \|y\|^2.$$

By the Cauchy–Schwartz inequality, $x \cdot y \leq \|x\| \|y\|$. Substituting this in the previous equation, we obtain

$$\|x + y\|^2 \leq \|x\|^2 + 2\|x\| \|y\| + \|y\|^2 = (\|x\| + \|y\|)^2.$$

The proof is completed by taking square roots on both sides.   □

The *Euclidean distance* $d(x, y)$ between two vectors x and y in $\mathbb{R}^n$ is given by

$$d(x, y) = \left(\sum_{i=1}^{n} (x_i - y_i)^2 \right)^{1/2}.$$

The distance function d is called a *metric*, and is related to the norm $\| \cdot \|$ through the identity

$$d(x, y) = \|x - y\|$$

for all $x, y \in \mathbb{R}^n$.

Theorem 1.4 *The metric d satisfies the following properties at all $x, y, z \in \mathbb{R}^n$:*

1. *Positivity: $d(x, y) \geq 0$ with equality if and only if $x = y$.*
2. *Symmetry: $d(x, y) = d(y, x)$.*
3. *Triangle Inequality: $d(x, z) \leq d(x, y) + d(y, z)$ for all $x, y, z \in \mathbb{R}^n$.*

Proof The positivity property of the metric follows from the positivity property of the norm, and the observation that $d(x, y) = \|x - y\|$. Symmetry is immediate from the definition. The inequality $d(x, z) \leq d(x, y) + d(y, z)$ is the same as

$$\|x - z\| \leq \|x - y\| + \|y - z\|.$$

This is just the triangle inequality for norms, which we have already established.   □

The concepts of inner product, norm, and metric can be defined on any abstract vector space, and not just $\mathbb{R}^n$. In fact, the properties we have listed in Theorems 1.1, 1.3, and 1.4 are, in abstract vector spaces, defining characteristics of the respective concepts. Thus, for instance, an inner product on a vector space is *defined* to be any operator on that space that satisfies the three properties of symmetry, bilinearity, and positivity; while a norm on that space is defined to be any operator that meets the conditions of positivity, homogeneity, and the triangle inequality. For more on this, see Appendix C.

1.2 Sets and Sequences in $\mathbb{R}^n$

1.2.1 Sequences and Limits

A *sequence* in $\mathbb{R}^n$ is the specification of a point $x_k \in \mathbb{R}^n$ for each integer $k \in \{1, 2, \ldots\}$. The sequence is usually written as

$$x_1, x_2, x_3, \ldots$$

or, more compactly, simply as $\{x_k\}$. Occasionally, where notational clarity will be enhanced by this change, we will use superscripts instead of subscripts, and denote the sequence by $\{x^k\}$.

A sequence of points $\{x_k\}$ in $\mathbb{R}^n$ is said to *converge* to a limit x (written $x_k \to x$) if the distance $d(x_k, x)$ between x_k and x tends to zero as k goes to infinity, i.e., if for all $\epsilon > 0$, there exists an integer $k(\epsilon)$ such that for all $k \geq k(\epsilon)$, we have $d(x_k, x) < \epsilon$. A sequence $\{x_k\}$ which converges to a limit x is called a *convergent sequence*.

For example, the sequence $\{x_k\}$ in $\mathbb{R}$ defined by $x_k = 1/k$ for all k is a convergent sequence, with limit $x = 0$. To see this, let any $\epsilon > 0$ be given. Let $k(\epsilon)$ be any integer such that $k(\epsilon) > 1/\epsilon$. Then, for all $k > k(\epsilon)$, we have $d(x_k, 0) = d(1/k, 0) = 1/k < 1/k(\epsilon) < \epsilon$, so indeed, $x_k \to 0$.

Theorem 1.5 *A sequence can have at most one limit. That is, if $\{x_k\}$ is a sequence in $\mathbb{R}^n$ converging to a point $x \in \mathbb{R}^n$, it cannot also converge to a point $y \in \mathbb{R}^n$ for $y \neq x$.*

Proof This follows from a simple application of the triangle inequality. If $x_k \to x$ and $y \neq x$, then

$$d(x_k, y) \geq d(x, y) - d(x_k, x).$$

Since $d(x, y) > 0$ and $d(x_k, x) \to 0$, this inequality shows that $d(x_k, y)$ cannot go to zero as k goes to infinity, so $x_k \to y$ is impossible. □

A sequence $\{x_k\}$ in $\mathbb{R}^n$ is called a *bounded* sequence if there exists a real number M such that $\|x_k\| \leq M$ for all k. A sequence $\{x_k\}$ which is not bounded is said to be *unbounded*; that is, $\{x_k\}$ is an unbounded sequence if for any $M \in \mathbb{R}$, there exists $k(M)$ such that $|x_{k(M)}| > M$.

Theorem 1.6 *Every convergent sequence in $\mathbb{R}^n$ is bounded.*

Proof Suppose $x_k \to x$. Let $\epsilon = 1$ in the definition of convergence. Then, there exists $k(1)$ such that for all $k \geq k(1)$, $d(x_k, x) < 1$. Since $d(x_k, x) = \|x_k - x\|$, an application of the triangle inequality yields for any $k \geq k(1)$

$$
\begin{aligned}
\|x_k\| &= \|(x_k - x) + x\| \\
&\leq \|x_k - x\| + \|x\| \\
&< 1 + \|x\|.
\end{aligned}
$$

Now define M to be the maximum of the finite set of numbers

$$\{\|x_1\|, \ldots, \|x_{k(1)-1}\|, 1 + \|x\|\}.$$

Then, $M \geq \|x_k\|$ for all k, completing the proof. $\square$

While Theorem 1.5 established that a sequence can have at most one limit, Theorem 1.6 implies that a sequence may have *no* limit at all. Indeed, because every convergent sequence must be bounded, it follows that if $\{x_k\}$ is an unbounded sequence, then $\{x_k\}$ cannot converge. Thus, for instance, the sequence $\{x_k\}$ in $\mathbb{R}$ defined by $x_k = k$ for all k is a non-convergent sequence.[1]

However, unboundedness is not the only reason a sequence may fail to converge. Consider the following example: let $\{x_k\}$ in $\mathbb{R}$ be given by

$$
x_k =
\begin{cases}
\dfrac{1}{k}, & k = 1, 3, 5, \ldots \\[2ex]
1 - \dfrac{1}{k}, & k = 2, 4, 6, \ldots
\end{cases}
$$

This sequence is bounded since we have $|x_k| \leq 1$ for all k. However, it does not possess a limit. The reason here is that the odd terms of the sequence are converging to the point 0, while the even terms are converging to the point 1. Since a sequence can have only one limit, this sequence does not converge.

Our next result shows that convergence of a sequence $\{x^k\}$ in $\mathbb{R}^n$ is equivalent to convergence in each coordinate. This gives us an alternative way to establish convergence in $\mathbb{R}^n$. We use superscripts to denote the sequence in this result to avoid confusion between the k-th element x_k of the sequence, and the i-th coordinate x_i of a vector x.

Theorem 1.7 *A sequence $\{x^k\}$ in $\mathbb{R}^n$ converges to a limit x if and only if $x_i^k \to x_i$ for each $i \in \{1, \ldots, n\}$, where $x^k = (x_1^k, \ldots, x_n^k)$ and $x = (x_1, \ldots, x_n)$.*

---

[1] This may also be shown directly: for any fixed candidate limit x the distance $d(x_k, x) = |x - x_k| = |x - k|$ becomes unbounded as k goes to infinity. It follows that no $x \in \mathbb{R}$ can be a limit of this sequence, and therefore that it does not possess a limit.

Proof We will use the fact that the Euclidean distance between two points $x = (x_1, \ldots, x_n)$ and $y = (y_1, \ldots, y_n)$ in $\mathbb{R}^n$ can be written as

$$d(x, y) = \left(\sum_{i=1}^{n} |x_i - y_i|^2 \right)^{1/2},$$

where $|x_i - y_i|$ is the Euclidean distance between x_i and y_i in $\mathbb{R}$.

First, suppose that $x^k \to x$. We are to show that $x_i^k \to x_i$ for each i, i.e., that, given any i and $\epsilon > 0$, there exists $k_i(\epsilon)$ such that for $k \geq k_i(\epsilon)$, we have $|x_i^k - x_i| < \epsilon$.

So let $\epsilon > 0$ be given. By definition of $x^k \to x$, we know that there exists $k(\epsilon)$ such that $d(x^k, x) < \epsilon$ for all $k \geq k(\epsilon)$. Therefore, for $k \geq k(\epsilon)$ and any i, we obtain:

$$|x_i^k - x_i| = \left(|x_i^k - x_i|^2 \right)^{1/2} \leq \left(\sum_{j=1}^{n} |x_j^k - x_j|^2 \right)^{1/2} = d(x^k, x) < \epsilon.$$

Setting $k_i(\epsilon) = k(\epsilon)$ for each i, the proof that $x_i^k \to x_i$ for each i is complete.

Now, suppose that $\{x_i^k\}$ converges to x_i for each i. Let $\epsilon > 0$ be given. We will show that there is $k(\epsilon)$ such that $d(x^k, x) < \epsilon$ for all $k \geq k(\epsilon)$, which will establish that $x^k \to x$.

Define $\eta = \epsilon / \sqrt{n}$. For each i, there exists $k_i(\eta)$ such that for $k \geq k_i(\eta)$, we have $|x_i^k - x_i| < \eta$. Define $k(\epsilon)$ to be the maximum of the finite set of numbers $k_1(\eta), \ldots, k_n(\eta)$. Then, for $k \geq k(\epsilon)$, we have $|x_i^k - x_i| < \eta$ for all i, so

$$d(x^k, x) = \left(\sum_{i=1}^{n} |x_i^k - x_i|^2 \right)^{1/2} < \left(\sum_{i=1}^{n} \left[\frac{\epsilon}{\sqrt{n}} \right]^2 \right)^{1/2} = \epsilon,$$

which completes the proof. $\qquad \square$

Theorem 1.7 makes it easy to prove the following useful result:

Theorem 1.8 *Let $\{x^k\}$ be a sequence in $\mathbb{R}^n$ converging to a limit x. Suppose that for every k, we have $a \leq x^k \leq b$, where $a = (a_1, \ldots, a_n)$ and $b = (b_1, \ldots, b_n)$ are some fixed vectors in $\mathbb{R}^n$. Then, it is also the case that $a \leq x \leq b$.*

Proof The theorem will be proved if we show that $a_i \leq x_i \leq b_i$ for each $i \in \{1, \ldots, n\}$. Suppose that the result were false, so for some i, we had $x_i < a_i$ (say). Since $x^k \to x$, it is the case by Theorem 1.7 that $x_j^k \to x_j$ for each $j \in \{1, \ldots, n\}$; in particular, $x_i^k \to x_i$. But $x_i^k \to x_i$ combined with $x_i < a_i$ implies that for all large k, we must have $x_i^k < a_i$. This contradicts the hypothesis that $a_i \leq x_i^k \leq b_i$ for all k. A similar argument establishes that $x_i > b_i$ also leads to a contradiction. Thus, $a_i \leq x_i \leq b_i$, and the proof is complete. $\qquad \square$

1.2.2 Subsequences and Limit Points

Let a sequence $\{x_k\}$ in $\mathbb{R}^n$ be given. Let m be any rule that assigns to each $k \in \mathbb{N}$ a value $m(k) \in \mathbb{N}$. Suppose further that m is *increasing*, i.e., for each $k \in \mathbb{N}$, we have $m(k) < m(k+1)$. Given $\{x_k\}$, we can now define a new sequence $\{x_{m(k)}\}$, whose k-th element is the $m(k)$-th element of the sequence $\{x_k\}$. This new sequence is called a *subsequence* of $\{x_k\}$. Put differently, a subsequence of a sequence is any infinite subset of the original sequence that preserves the ordering of terms.

Even if a sequence $\{x_k\}$ is not convergent, it may contain subsequences that converge. For instance, the sequence $0, 1, 0, 1, 0, 1, \ldots$ has no limit, but the subsequences $0, 0, 0, \ldots$ and $1, 1, 1, \ldots$ which are obtained from the original sequence by selecting the odd and even elements, respectively, are both convergent.

If a sequence contains a convergent subsequence, the limit of the convergent subsequence is called a *limit point* of the original sequence. Thus, the sequence $0, 1, 0, 1, 0, 1, \ldots$ has two limit points 0 and 1. The following result is simply a restatement of the definition of a limit point:

Theorem 1.9 *A point x is a limit point of the sequence $\{x_k\}$ if and only if for any $\epsilon > 0$, there are infinitely many indices m for which $d(x, x_m) < \epsilon$.*

Proof If x is a limit point of $\{x_k\}$ then there must be a subsequence $\{x_{m(k)}\}$ that converges to x. By definition of convergence, it is the case that for any $\epsilon > 0$, all but finitely many elements of the sequence $\{x_{m(k)}\}$ must be within ϵ of x. Therefore, infinitely many elements of the sequence $\{x_k\}$ must also be within ϵ of x.

Conversely, suppose that for every $\epsilon > 0$, there are infinitely many m such that $d(x_m, x) < \epsilon$. Define a subsequence $\{x_{m(k)}\}$ as follows: let $m(1)$ be any m for which $d(x_m, x) < 1$. Now for $k = 2, 3, \ldots$ define successively $m(k)$ to be any m that satisfies (a) $d(x, x_m) < 1/k$, and (b) $m > m(k-1)$. This construction is feasible, since for each k, there are infinitely many m satisfying $d(x_m, x) < 1/k$. Moreover, the sequence $\{x_{m(k)}\}$ evidently converges to x, so x is a limit point of $\{x_k\}$. $\square$

If a sequence $\{x_k\}$ is convergent (say, to a limit x), then it is apparent that every subsequence of $\{x_k\}$ must converge to x. It is less obvious, but also true, that if *every* subsequence $\{x_{m(k)}\}$ of a given sequence $\{x_k\}$ converges to the limit x, then $\{x_k\}$ itself converges to x. We do not offer a proof of this fact here, since it may be easily derived as a consequence of other considerations. See Corollary 1.19 below.

In general, a sequence $\{x_k\}$ may have any number of limit points. For instance, *every* positive integer arises as a limit point of the sequence

$$1, 1, 2, 1, 2, 3, 1, 2, 3, 4, \ldots$$

Of course, it is also possible that *no* subsequence of a given sequence converges, so a given sequence may have no limit points at all. A simple example is the sequence $\{x_k\}$ in $\mathbb{R}$ defined by $x_k = k$ for all k: every subsequence of this sequence diverges to $+\infty$.

1.2.3 Cauchy Sequences and Completeness

A sequence $\{x_k\}$ in $\mathbb{R}^n$ is said to satisfy the *Cauchy criterion* if for all $\epsilon > 0$ there is an integer $k(\epsilon)$ such that for all $m, l \geq k(\epsilon)$, we have $d(x_m, x_l) < \epsilon$. Informally, a sequence $\{x_k\}$ satisfies the Cauchy criterion if, by choosing k large enough, the distance between any two elements x_m and x_l in the "tail" of the sequence

$$x_k, x_{k+1}, x_{k+2}, \ldots$$

can be made as small as desired. A sequence which satisfies the Cauchy criterion is called a *Cauchy sequence*.

An example of a Cauchy sequence is given by the sequence $\{x_k\}$ in $\mathbb{R}$ defined by $x_k = 1/k^2$ for all k. To check that this sequence does, in fact, satisfy the Cauchy criterion, let any $\epsilon > 0$ be given. Let $k(\epsilon)$ be any integer k that satisfies $k^2\epsilon > 2$. For $m, l \geq k(\epsilon)$, we have

$$d(x_m, x_l) = \left| \frac{1}{m^2} - \frac{1}{l^2} \right| \leq \left| \frac{1}{m^2} + \frac{1}{l^2} \right| \leq \left| \frac{1}{[k(\epsilon)]^2} + \frac{1}{[k(\epsilon)]^2} \right| = \frac{2}{[k(\epsilon)]^2},$$

and this last term is less than ϵ by choice of $k(\epsilon)$.

Our first result deals with the analog of Theorem 1.7 for Cauchy sequences. It establishes that a sequence in $\mathbb{R}^n$ is a Cauchy sequence if and only if each of the coordinate sequences is a Cauchy sequence in $\mathbb{R}$.

Theorem 1.10 *A sequence $\{x^k\}$ in $\mathbb{R}^n$ is a Cauchy sequence if and only if for each $i \in \{1, \ldots, n\}$, the sequence $\{x_i^k\}$ is a Cauchy sequence in $\mathbb{R}$.*

Proof Let $\{x^k\}$ be a Cauchy sequence in $\mathbb{R}^n$. We are to show that for any i and any $\epsilon > 0$, there is $k_i(\epsilon)$ such that for all $m, l \geq k_i(\epsilon)$, we have $|x_i^m - x_i^l| < \epsilon$. So let $\epsilon > 0$ and i be given. Since $\{x^k\}$ is a Cauchy sequence, there is $k(\epsilon)$ such that for all $m, l \geq k(\epsilon)$, we have $d(x^m, x^l) < \epsilon$. Therefore, for any $m, l \geq k(\epsilon)$, we have

$$|x_i^m - x_i^l| = \left(|x_i^m - x_i^l|^2 \right)^{1/2} \leq \left(\sum_{j=1}^{n} |x_j^m - x_j^l|^2 \right)^{1/2} = d(x^m, x^l) < \epsilon.$$

By setting $k_i(\epsilon) = k(\epsilon)$, the proof that $\{x_i^k\}$ is a Cauchy sequence for each i is complete.

Now suppose $\{x_i^k\}$ is a Cauchy sequence for each i. We are to show that for any $\epsilon > 0$, there is $k(\epsilon)$ such that $m, l \geq k(\epsilon)$ implies $d(x^m, x^l) < \epsilon$. So let $\epsilon > 0$ be given. Define $\eta = \epsilon/\sqrt{n}$. Since each $\{x_i^k\}$ is a Cauchy sequence, there exists $k_i(\eta)$ such that for all $m, l \geq k_i(\eta)$, we have $|x_i^m - x_i^l| < \eta$. Define $k(\epsilon) = \max\{k_1(\eta), \ldots, k_n(\eta)\}$. Then, for $m, l \geq k(\epsilon)$, we have

$$d(x^m, x^l) = \left(\sum_{i=1}^{n} |x_i^m - x_i^l|^2 \right)^{1/2} < \left(\sum_{i=1}^{n} \left[\frac{\epsilon}{\sqrt{n}} \right]^2 \right)^{1/2} = \epsilon,$$

and the proof is complete.   □

Observe that the important difference between the definition of a convergent sequence and that of a Cauchy sequence is that the limit of the sequence is explicitly involved in the former, but plays no role in the latter. Our next result shows, however, that the two concepts are intimately linked:

Theorem 1.11 *A sequence $\{x_k\}$ in $\mathbb{R}^n$ is a Cauchy sequence if and only if it is a convergent sequence, i.e., if and only if there is $x \in \mathbb{R}^n$ such that $x_k \to x$.*

Proof The proof that every convergent sequence must also be a Cauchy sequence is simple. Suppose $x_k \to x$. Let $\epsilon > 0$ be given. Define $\eta = \epsilon/2$. Since $x_k \to x$, there exists $k(\eta)$ such that for all $j \geq k(\eta)$, we have $d(x_j, x) < \eta$. It follows by using the triangle inequality that for all $j, l \geq k(\eta)$, we have

$$d(x_j, x_l) \leq d(x_j, x) + d(x_l, x) < \eta + \eta = \epsilon.$$

Thus, setting $k(\epsilon) = k(\eta)$, the proof that $\{x_k\}$ is a Cauchy sequence is complete.

The proof that every Cauchy sequence must converge unfortunately requires more apparatus than we have built up. In particular, it requires a formal definition of the notion of a "real number," and the properties of real numbers. Appendix B, which which presents such a formal description, proves that every Cauchy sequence in $\mathbb{R}$ must converge. An appeal to Theorem 1.10 then completes the proof.   □

Any metric space which has the property that every Cauchy sequence is also a convergent sequence is said to be *complete*. Thus, by Theorem 1.11, $\mathbb{R}^n$ is complete. It is important to note that not all metric spaces are complete (so the definition is not vacuous). For more on this, see Appendix C.

Even without appealing to the completeness of $\mathbb{R}^n$, it is possible to show that a Cauchy sequence must possess two properties that all convergent sequences must have: namely, that it must be bounded, and that it has at most one limit point.

Theorem 1.12 *Let $\{x_k\}$ be a Cauchy sequence in $\mathbb{R}^n$. Then,*

1. *$\{x_k\}$ is bounded.*
2. *$\{x_k\}$ has at most one limit point.*

Proof To see that every Cauchy sequence $\{x_k\}$ in $\mathbb{R}^n$ must be bounded, take $\epsilon = 1$ in the Cauchy criterion. Then, there exists an integer $k(1)$ such that for all $j, l \geq k(1)$, we have $d(x_j, x_l) < 1$. An application of the triangle inequality now implies for all $j > k(1)$ that

$$\begin{aligned}
\|x_j\| &= \|(x_j - x_{k(1)}) + x_{k(1)}\| \\
&\leq \|x_j - x_{k(1)}\| + \|x_{k(1)}\| \\
&< 1 + \|x_{k(1)}\|.
\end{aligned}$$

Let M be the maximum of the finite set of numbers

$$\{\|x_1\|, \ldots, \|x_{k(1)-1}\|, 1 + \|x_{k(1)}\|\}.$$

Then, by construction, $M \geq \|x_k\|$ for all k, and the proof is complete.

To see that a Cauchy sequence cannot have two or more limit points, suppose that x is a limit point of the Cauchy sequence $\{x_k\}$. We will show that $x_k \to x$. Let $\epsilon > 0$ be given, and let $\eta = \epsilon/2$. Since $\{x_k\}$ is Cauchy, there exists $k(\eta)$ such that $d(x_j, x_l) < \eta$ for all $j, l \geq k(\eta)$. Moreover, since x is a limit point of $\{x_k\}$, there are elements of the sequence $\{x_k\}$ that lie arbitrarily close to x; in particular, we can find $m \geq k(\eta)$ such that $d(x_m, x) < \eta$. Therefore, if $j \geq k(\eta)$,

$$\begin{aligned}
d(x_j, x) &\leq d(x_j, x_m) + d(x_m, x) \\
&\leq \eta + \eta \\
&= \epsilon.
\end{aligned}$$

Since $\epsilon > 0$ was arbitrary, this string of inequalities shows precisely that $x_k \to x$.
□

Finally, two Cauchy sequences $\{x_k\}$ and $\{y_k\}$ are said to be *equivalent* if for all $\epsilon > 0$, there is $k(\epsilon)$ such that for all $j \geq k(\epsilon)$ we have $d(x_j, y_j) < \epsilon$. We write this as $\{x_k\} \sim \{y_k\}$. It is easy to see that $\sim$ is, in fact, an equivalence relationship. It is reflexive ($\{x_k\} \sim \{x_k\}$) and symmetric ($\{x_k\} \sim \{y_k\}$ implies $\{y_k\} \sim \{x_k\}$). It is also transitive: $\{x_k\} \sim \{y_k\}$ and $\{y_k\} \sim \{z_k\}$ implies $\{x_k\} \sim \{z_k\}$. To see this, let $\epsilon > 0$ be given. Let $\eta = \epsilon/2$. Since $\{x_k\} \sim \{y_k\}$, there is $k_1(\eta)$ such that for all $k \geq k_1(\eta)$, we have $d(x_k, y_k) < \eta$. Similarly, there is $k_2(\eta)$ such that for all $k \geq k_2(\eta)$, $d(y_k, z_k) < \eta$. Let $k(\epsilon) = \max\{k_1(\eta), k_2(\eta)\}$. Then, for $k \geq k(\epsilon)$, we have $d(x_k, z_k) \leq d(x_k, y_k) + d(y_k, z_k) < \eta + \eta = \epsilon$, and we indeed have $\{x_k\} \sim \{z_k\}$.

Equivalent Cauchy sequences must have the same limit.[2] For, suppose $\{x_k\} \sim \{y_k\}$ and $x_k \to x$. Given $\epsilon > 0$, there is $k_1(\epsilon)$ such that $k \geq k_1(\epsilon)$ implies $d(x_k, x) < \epsilon/2$. There is also $k_2(\epsilon)$ such that $k \geq k_2(\epsilon)$ implies $d(x_k, y_k) < \epsilon/2$. Therefore, letting $k(\epsilon) = \max\{k_1(\epsilon), k_2(\epsilon)\}$, $k \geq k(\epsilon)$ implies $d(x, y_k) \leq d(x, x_k) + d(x_k, y_k) < \epsilon/2 + \epsilon/2 = \epsilon$, which states precisely that $y_k \to x$.

1.2.4 Suprema, Infima, Maxima, Minima

Let A be a nonempty subset of $\mathbb{R}$. The set of *upper bounds* of A, denoted $U(A)$, is defined as

$$U(A) = \{u \in \mathbb{R} \mid u \geq a \text{ for all } a \in A\}$$

while the set of *lower bounds* of A, denoted $L(A)$, is given by

$$L(A) = \{l \in \mathbb{R} \mid l \leq a \text{ for all } a \in A\}.$$

In general, $U(A)$ and/or $L(A)$ could be empty. For instance, if $A = \mathbb{N}$, the set of positive integers, then $U(A)$ is empty; if $A = \mathbb{Z}$, the set of all integers, then both $U(A)$ and $L(A)$ are empty. If $U(A)$ is nonempty, then A is said to be *bounded above*. If $L(A)$ is nonempty, then A is said to be *bounded below*.

The *supremum* of A, written sup A, is defined to be the *least upper bound* of A. Namely, if $U(A)$ is nonempty, then sup A is defined to be the unique point $a^* \in U(A)$ such that $a^* \leq u$ for all $u \in U(A)$. If $U(A)$ is empty, on the other hand, then A has no finite upper bounds, so, by convention, we set sup $A = +\infty$.

Similarly, the *infimum* of A, denoted inf A, is defined to be the *greatest lower bound* of A. That is, when $L(A)$ is nonempty, then inf A is the unique point $\hat{a} \in L(A)$ such that $\hat{a} \geq l$ for all $l \in L(A)$. If $L(A)$ is empty, then A admits no finite lower bounds, so, by convention, we set inf $A = -\infty$.

Theorem 1.13 *If $U(A)$ is nonempty, the supremum of A is well defined, i.e., there is $a^* \in U(A)$ such that $a^* \leq u$ for all $u \in U(A)$. Similarly, if $L(A)$ is nonempty, the infimum of A is well defined, i.e., there is $\hat{a} \in L(A)$ such that $\hat{a} \geq l$ for all $l \in L(A)$.*

Remark 1 By our conventions that sup $A = +\infty$ when $U(A)$ is empty and inf $A = -\infty$ when $L(A)$ is empty, this will establish that sup A and inf A are defined for any nonempty set $A \subset \mathbb{R}$. □

Remark 2 To avoid legitimate confusion, we should stress the point that some

---

[2] In fact, the procedure of constructing the real numbers from the rational numbers using Cauchy sequences of rationals (see Appendix B) *defines* a real number to be an equivalence class of Cauchy sequences of rational numbers.

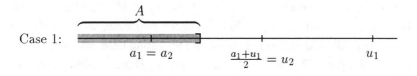

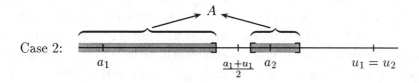

Fig. 1.2. Constructing the Supremum

authors (e.g., Apostol, 1967, or Bartle, 1964) take an axiomatic approach to the real line. In this approach, Theorem 1.13 is an *axiom*, indeed, a key axiom. Other authors adopt a constructive approach to the real line, building the real numbers from the rationals by using, for example, the method of Dedekind cuts (Rudin, 1976), or equivalent Cauchy sequences of rationals (Hewitt and Stromberg, 1965; Strichartz, 1982; Appendix B in this book). In this case, the result that bounded sets have well-defined suprema is genuinely a "theorem." We implicitly adopt the latter approach in this chapter. $\square$

Proof We prove that sup A is well defined whenever A is bounded above. A similar procedure can be employed to show that inf A is well-defined whenever A is bounded below. The details are left as an exercise.

So suppose A is bounded above and $U(A)$ is nonempty. We will construct two sequences $\{a_k\}$ and $\{u_k\}$ that have a common limit a^*. The sequence $\{a_k\}$ will consist entirely of points from A and will converge "upwards" to a^*, while the sequence $\{u_k\}$ will consist solely of points from $U(A)$, and will converge "downwards" to a^*. It will follow quite easily from the construction of these sequences that the common limit a^* is, in fact, sup A.

The required sequences are constructed using a divide-and-conquer procedure. Pick any point a_1 in A and any point u_1 in $U(A)$. Let $z_1 = (a_1 + u_1)/2$ be their midpoint. Of course, $a_1 \leq z_1 \leq u_1$. There are two possible cases: $z_1 \in U(A)$ and $z_1 \notin U(A)$. In case 1, where $z_1 \in U(A)$, set $a_2 = a_1$ and $u_2 = z_1$. In case 2, where $z_1 \notin U(A)$, there must exist some point $a \in A$ such that $a \geq z_1$.[3] In this case, let $a_2 = a$ and $u_2 = u_1$ (see Figure 1.2).

---

[3]Note that $z_1 \notin U(A)$ does *not* imply that $z_1 \in A$. For instance, if $A = [0, 1] \cup [3, 4]$ and $z_1 = 2$, then $z_1 \notin U(A)$ and $z_1 \notin A$.

Note that in either case we have $a_2 \in A$ and $u_2 \in U(A)$. Moreover, we must also have $a_1 \leq a_2$ and $u_1 \geq u_2$. Finally, in the first case, we have $d(a_2, u_2) = d(a_1, (a_1 + u_1)/2) = d(a_1, u_1)/2$, while in the second case, we have $d(a_2, u_2) = d(a, u_1) \leq d(a_1, u_1)/2$, since $a \geq (a_1 + u_1)/2$. Thus, in either case, we have $d(a_2, u_2) \leq d(a_1, u_1)/2$.

We iterate on this procedure. Let $z_2 = (a_2 + u_2)/2$ be the midpoint of a_2 and u_2. If $z_2 \in U(A)$, let $u_3 = z_2$ and $a_3 = a_2$. If $z_2 \notin U(A)$, then there must exist $a' \in A$ such that $a' \geq z_2$; in this case, set $a_3 = a'$ and $u_3 = u_2$. Then, it is once again true that the following three conditions hold in either case: first, we have $a_3 \in A$ and $u_3 \in U(A)$; second, $a_3 \geq a_2$ and $u_3 \leq u_2$; finally, $d(a_3, u_3) \leq d(a_2, u_2)/2 \leq d(a_1, u_1)/4$.

Continuing in this vein, we obtain sequences $\{a_k\}$ and $\{u_k\}$ such that

1. for each k, $a_k \in A$ and $u_k \in U(A)$;
2. $\{a_k\}$ is a nondecreasing sequence, and $\{u_k\}$ is a nonincreasing sequence; and
3. $d(a_k, u_k) \leq d(a_1, u_1)/2^k$.

Property 2 implies in particular that $\{a_k\}$ and $\{u_k\}$ are bounded sequences. It now follows from property 3 that $\{a_k\}$ and $\{u_k\}$ are equivalent Cauchy sequences, and, therefore, that they have the same limit a^*. We will show that $a^* = \sup A$, by showing first that $a^* \in U(A)$, and then that $a^* \leq u$ for all $u \in U(A)$.

Pick any $a \in A$. Since $u_k \in U(A)$ for each k, we have $u_k \geq a$ for each k, so $a^* = \lim_k u_k \geq a$. Since $a \in A$ was arbitrary, this inequality implies $a^* \in U(A)$. Now pick any $u \in U(A)$. Since $a_k \in A$ for each k, we must have $u \geq a_k$ for each k. Therefore, we must also have $u \geq \lim_k a_k = a^*$. Since $u \in U(A)$ was arbitrary, this inequality implies $u \geq a^*$ for all $u \in U(A)$.

Summing up, $a^* \in U(A)$ and $a^* \leq u$ for all $u \in U(A)$. By definition, this means $a^* = \sup A$, and the proof is complete. $\qquad \square$

The following result is an immediate consequence of the definition of the supremum. We raise it to the level of a theorem, since it is an observation that comes in handy quite frequently:

Theorem 1.14 *Suppose $\sup A$ is finite. Then, for any $\epsilon > 0$, there is $a(\epsilon) \in A$ such that $a(\epsilon) > \sup A - \epsilon$.*

Proof For notational ease, let $a^* = \sup A$. Suppose the theorem failed for some $\epsilon > 0$, that is, suppose there were $\epsilon > 0$ such that $a \leq a^* - \epsilon$ for all $a \in A$. Then, $a^* - \epsilon$ would be an upper bound of A. But this violates the definition of a^* as the *least* upper bound, since $a^* - \epsilon$ is obviously strictly smaller than a^*. $\qquad \square$

A similar result to Theorem 1.14 evidently holds for the infimum. It is left to the reader as an exercise to fill in the details.

Two concepts closely related to the supremum and the infimum are the *maximum* and the *minimum* of a nonempty set $A \subset \mathbb{R}$. The *maximum* of A, denoted max A, is defined as a point $z \in A$ such that $z \geq a$ for all $a \in A$. The *minimum* of A, denoted min A, is defined as a point $w \in A$ such that $w \leq a$ for all $a \in A$. By definition, the maximum must be an upper bound of A, and the minimum must be a lower bound of A. Therefore, we can equivalently define max $A = A \cap U(A)$, and min $A = A \cap L(A)$.

It is very important to point out that while sup A and inf A are always defined for any nonempty set A (they could be infinite), $A \cap U(A)$ and $A \cap L(A)$ could both be empty, so max A and min A need *not* always exist. This is true even if sup A and inf A are both finite. For instance, if $A = (0, 1)$, we have $U(A) = \{x \mid x \geq 1\}$ and $L(A) = \{x \mid x \leq 0\}$, so sup $A = 1$ and inf $A = 0$, but max A and min A do not exist. Indeed, it follows from the definition that if max A (resp. min A) is well defined, we must have max $A = $ sup A (resp. inf $A = $ min A), so that max A exists if, and only if, sup $A \in A$ (resp. min A exists if and only if inf $A \in A$).

1.2.5 Monotone Sequences in $\mathbb{R}$

A sequence $\{x_k\}$ in $\mathbb{R}$ is said to be a *monotone increasing* sequence if it is the case that

$$x_{k+1} \geq x_k \text{ for all } k.$$

It is *monotone decreasing* if

$$x_{k+1} \leq x_k \text{ for all } k.$$

We will also refer to monotone increasing sequences as *nondecreasing* sequences, and to monotone decreasing sequences as *nonincreasing* sequences.

Monotone sequences possess a particularly simple asymptotic (i.e., limiting) structure, and this is one of the reasons they are of special interest. To state the formal result requires one more definition.

Say that a sequence $\{x_k\}$ in $\mathbb{R}$ *diverges to* $+\infty$ (written $x_k \uparrow +\infty$) if for all positive integers $p \in \mathbb{N}$, there is $k(p)$ such that for all $k \geq k(p)$, we have $x_k \geq p$; and that $\{x_k\}$ *diverges to* $-\infty$ (written $x_k \downarrow -\infty$) if for any positive integer $p \in \mathbb{N}$, there exists $k(p)$ such that for all $k \geq k(p)$, we have $x_k \leq -p$.

Observe that while a sequence that diverges to $\pm\infty$ must necessarily be unbounded, the converse is not always true: the sequence $\{x_k\}$ defined by

$$x_k = \begin{cases} 1, & \text{if } k \text{ is odd} \\ k, & \text{if } k \text{ is even} \end{cases}$$

is an unbounded sequence but it does not diverge to $+\infty$ (why?). On the other hand, it is true that if $\{x_k\}$ is an unbounded sequence, it must contain at least one subsequence that diverges (to either $+\infty$ or $-\infty$).

The following result classifies the asymptotic behavior of monotone increasing sequences.

Theorem 1.15 *Let $\{x_k\}$ be a monotone increasing sequence in $\mathbb{R}$. If $\{x_k\}$ is unbounded, it must diverge to $+\infty$. If $\{x_k\}$ is bounded, it must converge to the limit x, where x is the supremum of the set of points $\{x_1, x_2, \ldots\}$.*

Proof First suppose that $\{x_k\}$ is an unbounded sequence. Then, for any $p \in \mathbb{R}$, there exists an integer $k(p)$ such that $x_{k(p)} \geq p$. Since $\{x_k\}$ is monotone increasing, it is now the case that for any $k \geq k(p)$, we have $x_k \geq x_{k(p)} \geq p$. This says precisely that $\{x_k\}$ diverges to $+\infty$.

Next suppose that $\{x_k\}$ is a bounded sequence. We will show that $x_k \to x$, where, as defined in the statement of the theorem, x is the supremum of the set of points $\{x_1, x_2, \ldots\}$. Let $\epsilon > 0$ be given. The proof will be complete if we show that there is $k(\epsilon)$ such that $d(x, x_k) < \epsilon$ for all $k \geq k(\epsilon)$.

Since x is the *least* upper bound of the set of points $\{x_1, x_2, \ldots\}$, $x - \epsilon$ is not an upper bound of this set. Therefore, there exists $k(\epsilon)$ such that $x_{k(\epsilon)} > x - \epsilon$. Since $\{x_k\}$ is monotone increasing, it follows that $x_k > x - \epsilon$ for all $k \geq k(\epsilon)$. On the other hand, since x is an upper bound, it is certainly true that $x \geq x_k$ for all k. Combining these statements, we have

$$x_k \in (x - \epsilon, x], \quad k \geq k(\epsilon),$$

which, of course, implies that $d(x_k, x) < \epsilon$ for all $k \geq k(\epsilon)$. $\qquad\square$

Since a sequence $\{x_k\}$ in $\mathbb{R}$ is monotone increasing if and only if $\{-x_k\}$ is monotone decreasing, Theorem 1.15 has the following immediate corollary:

Corollary 1.16 *Let $\{x_k\}$ be a monotone decreasing sequence in $\mathbb{R}$. If $\{x_k\}$ is unbounded, it must diverge to $-\infty$. If $\{x_k\}$ is bounded, it must converge to the limit x, where x is the infimum of the set of points $\{x_1, x_2, \ldots\}$.*

1.2.6 The Lim Sup and Lim Inf

We now define the important concepts of the "lim sup" and the "lim inf" of a real-valued sequence. Throughout this discussion, we will assume as a convention that the values $\pm\infty$ are allowed as "limit points" of a sequence of real numbers $\{x_k\}$ in the following sense: the sequence $\{x_k\}$ will be said to have the limit point $+\infty$ if

$\{x_k\}$ contains a subsequence $\{x_{m(k)}\}$ that diverges to $+\infty$, and to have the limit point $-\infty$ if $\{x_k\}$ contains a subsequence $\{x_{l(k)}\}$ that diverges to $-\infty$. In particular, if the sequence $\{x_k\}$ itself diverges to $+\infty$ (resp. $-\infty$), then we will refer to $+\infty$ (resp. $-\infty$) as the limit of the sequence $\{x_k\}$.

So let a sequence $\{x_k\}$ in $\mathbb{R}$ be given. The *lim sup* of the sequence $\{x_k\}$ is then defined as the limit as $k \to \infty$ of the sequence $\{a_k\}$ defined by

$$a_k = \sup\{x_k, x_{k+1}, x_{k+2}, \ldots\}$$

and is usually abbreviated as $\lim_{k\to\infty} \sup_{l\ge k} x_l$, or in more compact notation, as simply $\limsup_{k\to\infty} x_k$. To see that the lim sup is always well defined, note that there are only three possibilities that arise concerning the sequence $\{a_k\}$. First, it could be that $a_k = +\infty$ for some k, in which case $a_k = +\infty$ for all k. If this case is ruled out (so a_k is finite for each k), the sequence $\{a_k\}$ must satisfy $a_{k+1} \le a_k$ for all k, since a_{k+1} is the supremum over a smaller set; that is, $\{a_k\}$ must be a *nonincreasing* sequence in $\mathbb{R}$. By Corollary 1.16, this specifies the only two remaining possibilities: either $\{a_k\}$ is unbounded, in which case $a_k \downarrow -\infty$, or $\{a_k\}$ is bounded, in which case $\{a_k\}$ converges to a limit a in $\mathbb{R}$. In all three cases, therefore, the limit of a_k is well defined (given our convention that $\pm\infty$ may be limiting values), and this limit is, of course, $\limsup_{k\to\infty} x_k$. Thus, the lim sup of *any* real-valued sequence always exists.

In a similar vein, the *lim inf* of the sequence $\{x_k\}$ is defined as the limit as $k \to \infty$ of $\{b_k\}$, where

$$b_k = \inf\{x_k, x_{k+1}, x_{k+2}, \ldots\},$$

and is usually denoted $\lim_{k\to\infty} \inf_{l\ge k} x_l$, or just $\liminf_{k\to\infty} x_k$. Once again, either $b_k = -\infty$ for some k (in which case $b_k = -\infty$ for all k), or $\{b_k\}$ is a *nondecreasing* sequence in $\mathbb{R}$. Therefore, $\liminf_{k\to\infty} x_k$, is always well defined for any real-valued sequence $\{x_k\}$, although it could also take on infinite values.

The following result establishes two important facts: first, that the lim sup and lim inf of a sequence $\{x_k\}$ are themselves limit points of the sequence $\{x_k\}$, and second, that the lim sup is actually the supremum of the set of limit points of $\{x_k\}$, and the lim inf is the infimum of this set. This second part gives us an alternative interpretation of the lim sup and lim inf.

Theorem 1.17 *Let $\{x_k\}$ be a real-valued sequence, and let A denote the set of all limit points of $\{x_k\}$ (including $\pm\infty$ if $\{x_k\}$ contains such divergent subsequences). For notational convenience, let $a = \limsup_{k\to\infty} x_k$ and $b = \liminf_{k\to\infty} x_k$. Then:*

1. *There exist subsequences $m(k)$ and $l(k)$ of k such that $x_{m(k)} \to a$ and $x_{l(k)} \to b$.*
2. *$a = \sup A$ and $b = \inf A$.*

Remark   Note that the first part of the theorem does not follow from the second, since there exist sets which do not contain their suprema and infima.

Proof   We prove the results for the lim sup. The arguments for the lim inf are analogous; the details are left to the reader. We consider, in turn, the cases where a is finite, $a = +\infty$, and $a = -\infty$.

We first consider the case where a is finite. We will show that for any $\epsilon > 0$, an infinite number of terms of the sequence $\{x_k\}$ lie in the interval $(a - \epsilon, a + \epsilon)$. By Theorem 1.9, this will establish that a is a limit point of $\{x_k\}$.

Suppose that for some $\epsilon > 0$, only a finite number of the terms of the sequence $\{x_k\}$ lie in the interval $(a - \epsilon, a + \epsilon)$. We will show that a contradiction must result. If $x_k \in (a - \epsilon, a + \epsilon)$ for only finitely many k, there must exist K sufficiently large such that for all $k \geq K$,

$$x_k \notin (a - \epsilon, a + \epsilon).$$

We will show that for any $k \geq K$, we must now have $|a_k - a| \geq \epsilon$, where, as in the definition of the lim sup, $a_k = \sup\{x_k, x_{k+1}, \ldots\}$. This violates the definition of a as the limit of the sequence $\{a_k\}$, and provides the required contradiction.

So pick any $k \geq K$. For any $j \geq k$, there are only two possibilities: either $x_j \geq a + \epsilon$, or $x_j \leq a - \epsilon$. Therefore, a_k must satisfy either (i) $a_k \geq a + \epsilon$ (which happens if there exists at least one $j \geq k$ such that $x_j \geq a + \epsilon$), or (b) $a_k \leq a - \epsilon$ (which occurs if $x_j \leq a - \epsilon$ for all $j \geq k$). In either case, $|a_k - a| \geq \epsilon$, as required. This completes the proof that a is a limit point of $\{x_k\}$ when a is finite.

Now suppose $a = +\infty$. This is possible only if $a_k = +\infty$ for all k.[4] But $a_1 = +\infty$ implies

$$\sup\{x_1, x_2, \ldots\} = +\infty,$$

and from the definition of the supremum, this is possible only if for all positive integers p, there is $k(p)$ such that $x_{k(p)} \geq p$. Of course, this is the same as saying that there is a subsequence of $\{x_k\}$ which diverges to $+\infty$. It therefore follows that a is a limit point of $\{x_k\}$ in this case also.

Finally, suppose $a = -\infty$. This is possible only if the nonincreasing sequence $\{a_k\}$ is unbounded below, i.e., that for any positive integer p, there is $k(p)$ such that $a_k < -p$ for all $k \geq k(p)$. But a_k is the supremum of the set $\{x_k, x_{k+1}, \ldots\}$, so this implies in turn that for all $k \geq k(p)$, we must have $x_k < -p$. This states precisely that the sequence $\{x_k\}$ itself diverges to $-\infty$, so of course a is a limit point of $\{x_k\}$ in this case also. This completes the proof of part 1 that $a \in A$.

---

[4]If a_k is finite for some k, then a_j must also be finite for any $j > k$, because a_j is the supremum over a smaller set.

Part 2 will be proved if we can show that a is an upper bound of the set of limit points A: we have already shown that $a \in A$, and if a is also an upper bound of A, we must clearly have $a = \sup A$. If $a = +\infty$, it is trivial that $a \geq x$ must hold for all $x \in A$. If $a = -\infty$, we have shown that the sequence $\{x_k\}$ itself must diverge to $-\infty$, so A consists of only the point a, and vacuously therefore, $a \geq x$ for all $x \in A$.

This leaves the case where a is finite. Let $x \in A$. Then, by definition of A, there exists a subsequence $\{x_{m(k)}\}$ such that $x_{m(k)} \to x$. Now, $a_{m(k)}$ as the supremum of the set $\{x_{m(k)}, x_{m(k)+1}, x_{m(k)+2}, \ldots\}$ clearly satisfies $a_{m(k)} \geq x_{m(k)}$, and since $a_k \to a$, it is also evidently true that $a_{m(k)} \to a$. Therefore,

$$a = \lim_{k \to \infty} a_{m(k)} \geq \lim_{k \to \infty} x_{m(k)} = x,$$

and the proof is complete. □

It is a trivial consequence of Theorem 1.17 that $\limsup_{k \to \infty} x_k \geq \liminf_{k \to \infty} x_k$ for any sequence $\{x_k\}$. (This could also have been established directly from the definitions, since $a_k \geq b_k$ for each k.) Strict inequality is, of course, possible: the sequence $\{x_k\} = \{0, 1, 0, 1, 0, 1, \ldots\}$ has $\limsup_{k \to \infty} x_k = 1$ and $\liminf_{k \to \infty} x_k = 0$. Indeed, the only situation in which equality obtains is identified in the following result:

Theorem 1.18 *A sequence $\{x_k\}$ in $\mathbb{R}$ converges to a limit $x \in \mathbb{R}$ if and only if $\limsup_{k \to \infty} x_k = \liminf_{k \to \infty} x_k = x$. Equivalently, $\{x_k\}$ converges to x if and only if every subsequence of $\{x_k\}$ converges to x.*

Proof From the second part of Theorem 1.17, $\limsup_{k \to \infty} x_k$ is the supremum, and $\liminf_{k \to \infty} x_k$ the infimum, of the set of limit points of $\{x_k\}$. So $\limsup_{k \to \infty} x_k = \liminf_{k \to \infty} x_k$ implies that $\{x_k\}$ has only one limit point, and therefore that it converges. Conversely, if $\limsup_{k \to \infty} x_k > \liminf_{k \to \infty} x_k$, then the sequence $\{x_k\}$ has at least two limit points by the first part of Theorem 1.17. □

Finally, the following result is obtained by combining Theorems 1.18 and 1.7:

Corollary 1.19 *A sequence $\{x_k\}$ in $\mathbb{R}^n$ converges to a limit x if and only if every subsequence of x_k converges to x.*

The Exercises contain some other useful properties of the lim sup and lim inf.

1.2.7 Open Balls, Open Sets, Closed Sets

Let $x \in \mathbb{R}^n$. The *open ball* $B(x, r)$ with center x and radius $r > 0$ is given by

$$B(x, r) = \{y \in \mathbb{R}^n \mid d(x, y) < r\}.$$

In words, $B(x, r)$ is the set of points in $\mathbb{R}^n$ whose distance from x is *strictly* less than r. If we replace the strict inequality with a weak inequality ($d(x, y) \leq r$), then we obtain the *closed ball* $\bar{B}(x, r)$.

A set S in $\mathbb{R}^n$ is said to be *open* if for all $x \in S$, there is an $r > 0$ such that $B(x, r) \subset S$. Intuitively, S is open if given any $x \in S$, one can move a small distance away from x *in any direction* without leaving S.

A set S in $\mathbb{R}^n$ is said to be *closed* if its complement $S^c = \{x \in \mathbb{R}^n \mid x \notin S\}$ is open. An equivalent—and perhaps more intuitive—definition is provided by the following result, using the notion of convergent sequences. Roughly put, it says that a set S is closed if and only if any sequence formed by using only points of S cannot "escape" from S.

Theorem 1.20 *A set $S \subset \mathbb{R}^n$ is closed if and only if for all sequences $\{x_k\}$ such that $x_k \in S$ for each k and $x_k \to x$, it is the case that $x \in S$.*

Proof Suppose S is closed. Let $\{x_k\}$ be a sequence in S and suppose $x_k \to x$. We are to show that $x \in S$. Suppose $x \notin S$, i.e., $x \in S^c$. Then, since S is closed, S^c must be open, so there exists $r > 0$ such that $B(x, r) \subset S^c$. On the other hand, by definition of $x_k \to x$, there must exist $k(r)$ such that for all $k \geq k(r)$, we have $d(x_k, x) < r$, i.e., such that $x_k \in B(x, r) \subset S^c$. This contradicts the hypothesis that $\{x_k\}$ is a sequence in S, which proves the result.

Now suppose that for all sequences $\{x_k\}$ in S such that $x_k \to x$, we have $x \in S$. We will show that S must be closed. If S is not closed, then S^c is not open. For the openness of S^c to fail, there must exist a point $x \in S^c$ such that no open ball with center x is ever completely contained in S^c, i.e., such that every open ball with center x and radius $r > 0$ has at least one point $x(r)$ that is *not* in S^c. For $k = 1, 2, 3, \ldots$, define $r_k = 1/k$, and let $x_k = x(r_k)$. Then, by construction $x_k \notin S^c$ for each k, so $x_k \in S$ for each k. Moreover, since $x_k \in B(x, r_k)$ for each k, it is the case that $d(x_k, x) < r_k = 1/k$, so $x_k \to x$. But this implies that x must be in S, a contradiction. $\square$

Among the commonly encountered closed and open sets are the "closed unit interval" $[0,1]$ defined as $\{x \in \mathbb{R} \mid 0 \leq x \leq 1\}$, and the "open unit interval" $(0, 1)$ defined as $\{x \in \mathbb{R} \mid 0 < x < 1\}$. Observe that there exist sets that are neither open nor closed such as the intervals $[0, 1) = \{x \in \mathbb{R} \mid 0 \leq x < 1\}$, and $(0, 1] = \{x \in \mathbb{R} \mid 0 < x \leq 1\}$.

1.2.8 Bounded Sets and Compact Sets

A set S in $\mathbb{R}^n$ is said to be *bounded* if there exists $r > 0$ such that $S \subset B(0, r)$, that is, if S is completely contained in some open ball in $\mathbb{R}^n$ centered at the origin. For instance, the interval $(0, 1)$ is a bounded subset of $\mathbb{R}$, but the set of integers $\{1, 2, 3, \ldots\}$ is not.

A set $S \subset \mathbb{R}^n$ is said to be *compact* if for all sequences of points $\{x_k\}$ such that $x_k \in S$ for each k, there exists a subsequence $\{x_{m(k)}\}$ of $\{x_k\}$ and a point $x \in S$ such that $x_{m(k)} \to x$. In words, this definition is abbreviated as "a set is compact if every sequence contains a convergent subsequence." If $S \subset \mathbb{R}^n$ is compact, it is easy to see that S must be bounded. For, if S were unbounded, it would be possible to pick a sequence $\{x_k\}$ in S such that $\|x_k\| > k$, and such a sequence cannot contain a convergent subsequence (why?). Similarly, if S is compact, it must also be closed. If not, there would exist a sequence $\{x_k\}$ in S such that $x_k \to x$, where $x \notin S$. All subsequences of this sequence then also converge to x, and since $x \notin S$, the definition of compactness is violated. Thus, every compact set in $\mathbb{R}^n$ must be closed and bounded.

The following result establishes that the converse of this statement is also true. It is a particularly useful result since it gives us an easy way of identifying compact sets in $\mathbb{R}^n$.

Theorem 1.21 *A set $S \subset \mathbb{R}^n$ is compact if and only if it is closed and bounded.*

Proof See Rudin (1976, Theorem 2.41, p.40). $\qquad\qquad\qquad\qquad\qquad\square$

1.2.9 Convex Combinations and Convex Sets

Given any finite collection of points $x_1, \ldots, x_m \in \mathbb{R}^n$, a point $z \in \mathbb{R}^n$ is said to be a *convex combination* of the points $(x_1, \ldots, x_m)$ if there exists $\lambda \in \mathbb{R}^m$ satisfying (i) $\lambda_i \geq 0$, $i = 1, \ldots, m$, and (ii) $\sum_{i=1}^{m} \lambda_i = 1$, such that $z = \sum_{i=1}^{m} \lambda_i x_i$.

A set $S \subset \mathbb{R}^n$ is *convex* if the convex combination of any two points in S is also in S. Intuitively, S is convex if the straight line joining any two points in S is itself completely contained in S.

For example, the closed and open unit intervals $(0, 1)$ and $[0, 1]$ are both convex subsets of $\mathbb{R}$, while the unit disk

$$\mathcal{D} = \{x \in \mathbb{R}^2 \mid \|x\| \leq 1\}$$

is a convex subset of $\mathbb{R}^2$. On the other hand, the unit circle

$$\mathcal{C} = \{x \in \mathbb{R}^2 \mid \|x\| = 1\}$$

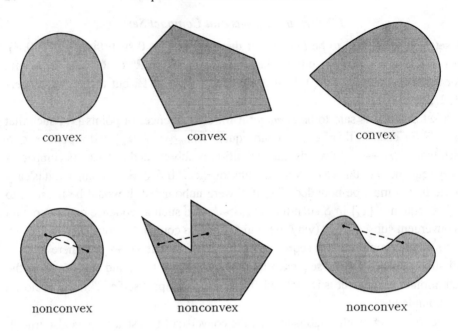

Fig. 1.3. Convex and Nonconvex Sets

is not a convex subset of $\mathbb{R}^2$ since $(-1, 0) \in \mathcal{C}$ and $(1, 0) \in \mathcal{C}$, but the convex combination $(0, 0) \notin \mathcal{C}$. Additional examples of convex and nonconvex sets are given in Figure 1.3.

1.2.10 Unions, Intersections, and Other Binary Operations

This section summarizes some important properties of open, closed, compact, and convex sets. While most of the properties listed here are used elsewhere in the book, some are presented solely for their illustrative value.

Some definitions first. A set A is said to *index* a collection of sets $\mathcal{S}$ in $\mathbb{R}^n$ if a set $S_\alpha \in \mathcal{S}$ is specified for each $\alpha \in A$, and each $S \in \mathcal{S}$ corresponds to some $\alpha \in A$. We will denote such a collection by $(S_\alpha)_{\alpha \in A}$, or when A is understood, simply by (S_α). When the index set A consists of a finite number of elements, we will call it a *finite index set*; if there are no restrictions on the number of elements in A, we will call it an *arbitrary index set*. If $B \subset A$, then the collection $(S_\beta)_{\beta \in B}$ is called a *subcollection* of $(S_\alpha)_{\alpha \in A}$. If B consists of only a finite number of elements, $(S_\beta)_{\beta \in B}$ is called a *finite subcollection*. For notational clarity, we will use $(S_\varphi)_{\varphi \in F}$ to denote a finite subcollection, and retain $(S_\beta)_{\beta \in B}$ to denote an arbitrary subcollection.

Given any collection of sets (S_α) indexed by A, recall that the *union* of the collection (S_α), denoted $\cup_{\alpha \in A} S_\alpha$, and the *intersection* of the collection (S_α), denoted

$\cap_{\alpha \in A} S_\alpha$, are defined as

$$\cup_{\alpha \in A} S_\alpha = \{x \in \mathbb{R}^n \mid x \in S_\alpha \text{ for some } \alpha \in A\}$$
$$\cap_{\alpha \in A} S_\alpha = \{x \in \mathbb{R}^n \mid x \in S_\alpha \text{ for all } \alpha \in A\}.$$

The following pair of identities, known as *DeMorgan's laws*, relates unions, intersections, and complementation.

Theorem 1.22 (DeMorgan's Laws) *Let A be an arbitrary index set, and let (G_α) be a collection of sets in $\mathbb{R}^n$ indexed by A. Then,*

1. $(\cup_{\alpha \in A} G_\alpha)^c = \cap_{\alpha \in A} G_\alpha^c$, *and*
2. $(\cap_{\alpha \in A} G_\alpha)^c = \cup_{\alpha \in A} G_\alpha^c.$

Proof We prove part 1 here. Part 2 may be established analogously, and is left as an exercise. We first show that each element of the set on the left-hand side (*LHS*) of (1) is also an element of the right-hand side (*RHS*), thereby establishing *LHS* $\subset$ *RHS*. Then, we show that *RHS* $\subset$ *LHS* also, completing the proof.

So suppose $x \in LHS$. Then, by definition, $x \notin G_\alpha$ for any $\alpha \in A$, so $x \in G_\alpha^c$ for all α, and, therefore $x \in RHS$. So $LHS \subset RHS$.

Now suppose $x \in RHS$. Then $x \in G_\alpha^c$ for all α, or $x \notin G_\alpha$ for any $\alpha \in A$. It follows that $x \in LHS$. Thus we also have $RHS \subset LHS$. □

The next set of results deals with conditions under which closedness and openness are preserved under unions and intersections.

Theorem 1.23 *Let A be an arbitrary index set. Suppose for each $\alpha \in A$, G_α is an open set. Then, $\cup_{\alpha \in A} G_\alpha$ is also open. That is, the arbitrary union of open sets is open.*

Proof Suppose $x \in \cup_{\alpha \in A} G_\alpha$. Then, $x \in G_\alpha$ for some α. Since G_α is open, there is $r > 0$ such that $B(x, r) \subset G_\alpha \subset \cup_{\alpha \in A} G_\alpha$. □

Theorem 1.24 *Let A be an arbitrary index set. Suppose for each $\alpha \in A$, H_α is a closed set. Then, $\cap_{\alpha \in A} H_\alpha$ is closed. That is, the arbitrary intersection of closed sets is closed.*

Proof By definition, $\cap_{\alpha \in A} H_\alpha$ is closed if and only if $(\cap_{\alpha \in A} H_\alpha)^c$ is open. By DeMorgan's laws, $(\cap_{\alpha \in A} H_\alpha)^c = \cup_{\alpha \in A} H_\alpha^c$. For each $\alpha \in A$, H_α^c is open since H_α is closed. Now use Theorem 1.23. □

Theorem 1.25 *Let $G_1, \ldots, G_l$ be open sets, where l is some positive integer. Then, $\cap_{i=1}^{l} G_i$ is open. That is, the* finite *intersection of open sets is open.*

Proof Let $x \in \cap_{i=1}^{l} G_i$. We will show that there is $r > 0$ such that $B(x, r) \subset \cap_{i=1}^{l} G_i$. Since x is an arbitrary point in the intersection, the proof will be complete.

Since x is in the intersection, we must have $x \in G_i$ for each i. Since G_i is open, there exists $r_i > 0$ such that $B(x, r_i) \subset G_i$. Let r denote the minimum of the finite set of numbers $r_1, \ldots, r_l$. Clearly, $r > 0$. Moreover, $B(x, r) \subset B(x, r_i)$ for each i, so $B(x, r) \subset G_i$ for each i. Therefore, $B(x, r) \subset \cap_{i=1}^{l} G_i$. $\square$

Theorem 1.26 *Let $H_1, \ldots, H_l$ be closed sets, where l is some positive integer. Then, $\cup_{i=1}^{l} H_i$ is closed. That is, the* finite *union of closed sets is closed.*

Proof This is an immediate consequence of Theorem 1.25 and DeMorgan's laws. $\square$

Unlike Theorems 1.23 and 1.24, neither Theorem 1.25 nor Theorem 1.26 is valid if we allow for arbitrary (i.e., possibly infinite) intersections and unions respectively. Consider the following counterexample:

Example 1.27 Let $A = \{1, 2, 3, \ldots\}$. For each $\alpha \in A$, let G_α be the open interval $(0, 1 + 1/\alpha)$, and H_α be the closed interval $[0, 1 - 1/\alpha]$. Then, $\cap_{\alpha \in A} G_\alpha = (0, 1]$, which is not open, while $\cup_{\alpha \in A} H_\alpha = [0, 1)$, which is not closed. $\square$

Since compact sets are necessarily closed, all of the properties we have identified here for closed sets also apply to compact sets. The next collection of results describes some properties that are special to compact sets. Given a subcollection $(S_\beta)_{\beta \in B}$ of a collection $(S_\alpha)_{\alpha \in A}$, say that the subcollection has a *nonempty intersection* if $\cap_{\beta \in B} S_\beta \neq \emptyset$.

Theorem 1.28 *Suppose $(S_\alpha)_{\alpha \in A}$ is a collection of compact sets in $\mathbb{R}^n$ such that every finite subcollection $(S_\varphi)_{\varphi \in F}$ has nonempty intersection. Then the entire collection has nonempty intersection, i.e., $\cap_{\alpha \in A} S_\alpha \neq \emptyset$.*

Proof See Rudin (1976, Theorem 2.36, p.38). $\square$

As an immediate corollary, we have the result that every nested sequence of compact sets has a nonempty intersection:

Corollary 1.29 *Suppose* $(S_k)_{k \in \mathbb{N}}$ *is a collection of compact sets in* $\mathbb{R}^n$ *that is nested, i.e., such that* $S_{k+1} \subset S_k$ *for each* k. *Then* $\cap_{k=1}^{\infty} S_k \neq \emptyset$.

Compactness is essential in Theorem 1.28 and Corollary 1.29. The following examples show that the results may fail if the sets are allowed to be noncompact.

Example 1.30 For $k \in \mathbb{N}$, let $S_k = [k, \infty)$. Then, S_k is noncompact for each k (it is closed but not bounded). The collection $(S_k)_{k \in \mathbb{N}}$ is clearly nested since $S_{k+1} \subset S_k$ for each k. However, $\cap_{k=1}^{\infty} S_k$ is empty. To see this, consider any $x \in \mathbb{R}$. If k is any integer larger than x, then $x \notin S_k$, so x cannot be in the intersection. $\square$

Example 1.31 Let $S_k = (0, 1/k)$, $k \in \mathbb{N}$. Once again, S_k is noncompact for each k (this time it is bounded but not closed). Since $1/k > 1/(k+1)$, the collection $(S_k)_{k \in \mathbb{N}}$ is evidently nested. But $\cap_{k=1}^{\infty} S_k$ is again empty. For if $x \in (0, 1)$, $x \notin S_k$ for any k satisfying $kx > 1$; while if $x \leq 0$ or $x \geq 1$, $x \notin S_k$ for any k. $\square$

Next, given sets S_1, S_2 in $\mathbb{R}^n$, define their *sum* $S_1 + S_2$ by:

$$S_1 + S_2 = \{x \in \mathbb{R}^n \mid x = x_1 + x_2, \ x_1 \in S_1, x_2 \in S_2\}.$$

Theorem 1.32 *If* S_1 *and* S_2 *are compact, so is* $S_1 + S_2$.

Proof Let $\{x_k\}$ be a sequence in $S_1 + S_2$. We will show that it has a convergent subsequence, i.e., that there is a point $x \in S_1 + S_2$ and a subsequence $l(k)$ of k such that $x_{l(k)} \to x$.

For each k, there must exist points $y_k \in S_1$ and $z_k \in S_2$ such that $x_k = y_k + z_k$. Since S_1 is compact, there is a subsequence $m(k)$ of k such that $y_{m(k)} \to y \in S_1$. Now $\{z_{m(k)}\}$, as a subsequence of $\{z_k\}$, itself defines a sequence in the compact set S_2. Thus, there must exist a further subsequence of $m(k)$ (denoted say, $l(k)$) such that $z_{l(k)} \to z \in S_2$. Since $l(k)$ is a subsequence of $m(k)$ and $y_{m(k)} \to y$, it is clearly the case that $y_{l(k)} \to y$. Therefore, $x_{l(k)} = y_{l(k)} + z_{l(k)}$ is a subsequence of $\{x_k\}$ that converges to $y + z$. Since $y \in S_1$ and $z \in S_2$, $(y + z) \in S_1 + S_2$, so we have shown the existence of the required subsequence. $\square$

The following example, which shows that the word "compact" in Theorem 1.32 cannot be replaced with "closed," provides another illustration of the power of compactness.

Example 1.33 Let $S_1 = \{(x, y) \in \mathbb{R}^2 \mid xy = 1\}$ and $S_2 = \{(x, y) \in \mathbb{R}^2 \mid xy = -1\}$ (see Figure 1.4). Then, S_1 and S_2 are closed. For each $k = 1, 2, 3, \ldots, (k, 1/k) \in S_1$ and $(-k, 1/k) \in S_2$, so $(0, 2/k) \in S_1 + S_2$. This sequence converges to $(0,0)$

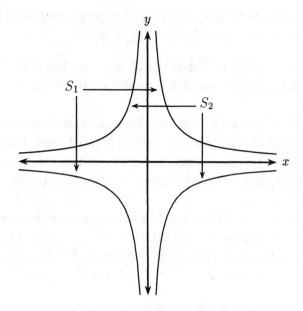

Fig. 1.4. The Sum of Closed Sets Need Not Be Closed

which cannot be in $S_1 + S_2$. To see this, observe that $(0, 0)$ can be in $S_1 + S_2$ if and only if there is a point of the form $(x, y) \in S_1$ such that $(-x, -y) \in S_2$. However, $xy = (-x)(-y)$, so $(x, y) \in S_1$ implies $(-x, -y) \in S_1$ also.   □

The next result describes a property that is *equivalent* to compactness. A definition is required first. A collection of *open* sets $(S_\alpha)_{\alpha \in A}$ in $\mathbb{R}^n$ is said to be an *open cover* of a given set $S \subset \mathbb{R}^n$, if

$$S \subset \cup_{\alpha \in A} S_\alpha.$$

The open cover $(S_\alpha)_{\alpha \in A}$ of S is said to admit a *finite subcover* if there exists a finite subcollection $(S_\varphi)_{\varphi \in F}$ such that

$$S \subset \cup_{\varphi \in F} S_\varphi.$$

It is an elementary matter to construct sets S in $\mathbb{R}^n$ and open covers $(S_\alpha)_{\alpha \in A}$ of S, such that $(S_\alpha)_{\alpha \in A}$ admits no finite subcover. Here are two examples:

Example 1.34 Let S be the closed unbounded interval $[0, \infty)$, and let $A = \mathbb{N}$. For $k \in \mathbb{N}$, define S_k be the open interval $(k-2, k+2)$. Clearly, $(S_k)_{k \in \mathbb{N}}$ is an open cover of S that has no finite subcover.   □

Example 1.35 Let S be the bounded open interval $(0, 1)$, and let $A = \mathbb{N}$. For $k \in \mathbb{N}$, let S_k be the open interval $(1/(k + 2), 1/k)$. A little reflection shows that $\cup_{k \in \mathbb{N}} S_k = (0, 1) = S$, and therefore that the collection $(S_k)_{k \in \mathbb{N}}$ is an open cover of S. The collection $(S_k)_{k \in \mathbb{N}}$, moreover, admits no finite subcover. For, suppose $\{k_1, \ldots, k_l\}$ is any finite subset of $\mathbb{N}$. Let $k^* = \max\{k_1, \ldots, k_l\}$. If x is such that $0 < x < 1/(k^* + 2)$, then $x \notin \cup_{j=1}^{l} S_{k_j}$, so the finite subcollection $(S_{k_j})_{j=1}^{l}$ does not cover S. $\square$

The following result states that examples such as these are impossible if (and only if) S is compact.

Theorem 1.36 *A set S in $\mathbb{R}^n$ is compact if and only if every open cover of S has a finite subcover.*

Proof See Rudin (1976, Theorem 2.41, p.40). $\square$

There is yet another property, called the *finite intersection property*, that is equivalent to compactness. This property is described in the Exercises.

Lastly, we turn to some of the properties of convex sets:

Theorem 1.37 *Suppose $(S_\alpha)_{\alpha \in A}$ is a collection of convex sets in $\mathbb{R}^n$. Then $\cap_{\alpha \in A} S_\alpha$ is also convex.*

Proof Let $S = \cap_{\alpha \in A} S_\alpha$. If $x_1, x_2 \in S$, then $x_1, x_2 \in S_\alpha$ for every $\alpha \in A$. Since each S_α is convex, any convex combination of x_1 and x_2 is in each S_α, and therefore in S. $\square$

Theorem 1.38 *Suppose S_1 and S_2 are convex sets in $\mathbb{R}^n$. Then $S_1 + S_2$ is convex.*

Proof Let $S = S_1 + S_2$. Pick any $x, y \in S$ and $\lambda \in (0, 1)$. Then, there exist points $x_1 \in S_1$ and $x_2 \in S_2$ such that $x = x_1 + x_2$; and points $y_1 \in S_1$ and $y_2 \in S_2$ such that $y = y_1 + y_2$. Since S_1 and S_2 are both convex, $\lambda x_1 + (1 - \lambda) y_1 \in S_1$ and $\lambda x_2 + (1 - \lambda) y_2 \in S_2$. Therefore,

$$[(\lambda x_1 + (1 - \lambda) y_1) + (\lambda x_2 + (1 - \lambda) y_2)] \in S.$$

But $\lambda x_1 + (1-\lambda) y_1 + \lambda x_2 + (1-\lambda) y_2 = \lambda(x_1 + x_2) + (1-\lambda)(y_1 + y_2) = \lambda x + (1-\lambda) y$, so $\lambda x + (1 - \lambda) y \in S$, as required. $\square$

On the other hand, the convexity of S_1 and S_2 obviously has no implications for $S_1 \cup S_2$. For instance, if $S_1 = [0, 1]$ and $S_2 = [2, 3]$, then S_1 and S_2 are both convex, but $S_1 \cup S_2$ is not.

1.3 Matrices

1.3.1 Sum, Product, Transpose

An $n \times m$ matrix A is an array

$$A = \begin{bmatrix} a_{11} & a_{12} & \cdots & a_{1m} \\ a_{21} & a_{22} & \cdots & a_{2m} \\ \vdots & \vdots & \ddots & \vdots \\ a_{n1} & a_{n2} & \cdots & a_{nm} \end{bmatrix}$$

where a_{ij} is a real number for each $i \in \{1, \ldots, n\}$ and $j \in \{1, \ldots, m\}$. We will frequently refer to a_{ij} as the (i, j)-th entry of the matrix A. In more compact notation, we write the matrix as $A = (a_{ij})$. The vector

$$[a_{i1}, \ldots, a_{im}]$$

is called the *i-th row* of the matrix A, and will be denoted A_i^r, $i = 1, \ldots, n$. The vector

$$\begin{bmatrix} a_{1j} \\ \vdots \\ a_{nj} \end{bmatrix}$$

is called the *j-th column* of the matrix A, and will be denoted A_j^c, $j = 1, \ldots, m$. Thus, an $n \times m$ matrix A has n rows and m columns, and may be represented variously as

$$A = \begin{bmatrix} a_{11} & \cdots & a_{1m} \\ \vdots & \ddots & \vdots \\ a_{n1} & \cdots & a_{nm} \end{bmatrix} = \begin{bmatrix} A_1^r \\ \vdots \\ A_n^r \end{bmatrix} = [A_1^c, \ldots, A_m^c].$$

If A and B are two $n \times m$ matrices, their *sum* $A + B$ is the $n \times m$ matrix whose (i, j)-th entry is $a_{ij} + b_{ij}$:

$$A + B = \begin{bmatrix} a_{11} + b_{11} & \cdots & a_{1m} + b_{1m} \\ \vdots & \ddots & \vdots \\ a_{n1} + b_{n1} & \cdots & a_{nm} + b_{nm} \end{bmatrix}.$$

Observe that $A + B$ is defined only if A and B have the same numbers of rows and columns.

If A is an $n \times m$ matrix and B is an $m \times k$ matrix, their *product* AB is the $n \times k$ matrix whose (i, j)-th entry is the inner product of the i-th row A_i^r of A and the j-th column B_j^c of B:

$$AB = \begin{bmatrix} A_1^r \cdot B_1^c & A_1^r \cdot B_2^c & \cdots & A_1^r \cdot B_k^c \\ A_2^r \cdot B_1^c & A_2^r \cdot B_2^c & \cdots & A_2^r \cdot B_k^c \\ \vdots & \vdots & \ddots & \vdots \\ A_n^r \cdot B_1^c & A_n^r \cdot B_2^c & \cdots & A_n^r \cdot B_k^c \end{bmatrix}.$$

Of course, for any $i \in \{1, \ldots, n\}$ and $j \in \{1, \ldots, k\}$, $A_i^r \cdot B_j^c = \sum_{l=1}^m a_{il}b_{lj}$. Note that for the product AB to be well-defined, the number of columns in A must be the same as the number of rows in B. Note also that the product AB is *not*, in general, the same as the product BA. Indeed, if A is an $n \times m$ matrix, and B is an $m \times k$ matrix, then AB is well-defined, but BA is not even defined unless $n = k$.

Theorem 1.39 *The matrix sum $A + B$ and product AB have the following properties:*

1. $A + B = B + A$.
2. *Addition is associative:* $(A + B) + C = A + (B + C)$.
3. *Multiplication is associative:* $(AB)C = A(BC)$.
4. *Multiplication distributes over addition:* $A(B + C) = AB + AC$.

Proof Immediate from the definitions. □

The *transpose* of a matrix A, denoted A', is the matrix whose (i, j)-th entry is a_{ji}. Thus, if A is an $n \times m$ matrix, A' is an $m \times n$ matrix.

For example, if A is the 3×2 matrix

$$\begin{bmatrix} a_{11} & a_{12} \\ a_{21} & a_{22} \\ a_{31} & a_{33} \end{bmatrix}$$

then A' is the 2×3 matrix

$$\begin{bmatrix} a_{11} & a_{21} & a_{31} \\ a_{12} & a_{22} & a_{32} \end{bmatrix}.$$

It is easy to check from the definitions that the transpose has the following properties with respect to the sum and product. (For the second property, note that the product $B'A'$ is well-defined whenever the product AB is well defined and vice versa.)

1. $(A + B)' = A' + B'$.
2. $(AB)' = B'A'$,

Finally, a word on notation. It is customary in linear algebra to regard vectors $x \in \mathbb{R}^n$ as *column vectors*, i.e., as $n \times 1$ matrices, and to write x' when one wishes to represent x as a *row vector*, i.e., as a $1 \times n$ matrix. In particular, under this convention, we would write $x'y$ to denote the inner product of the vectors x and y, rather than $x \cdot y$ as we have chosen to do. In an abuse of notation, we will continue to use $x \cdot y$ to denote the inner product, but will, in the context of matrix multiplication, regard x as a column vector. Thus, for instance, we will use Ax to denote the product of the $m \times n$ matrix A and the vector $x \in \mathbb{R}^n$. Similarly, we will use $x'A$ to denote the pre-multiplication of the $n \times k$ matrix A by the vector x.

1.3.2 Some Important Classes of Matrices

The object of this subsection is to single out some important classes of matrices. Properties of these matrices are highlighted in the succeeding sections on rank, determinants, and inverses.

Square Matrix

A *square matrix* is an $n \times m$ matrix A for which $n = m$ (i.e., the number of rows and columns are the same). The common value of n and m for a square matrix A is called the *order* of the matrix. Given a square matrix $A = (a_{ij})$ of order n, the elements a_{ii}, $i = 1, \ldots n$, are called the *diagonal entries* of A, and the elements a_{ij} for $i \neq j$ are called the *off-diagonal* elements.

Symmetric Matrix

A square matrix A of order n is called a *symmetric matrix* if for all $i, j \in \{1, \ldots, n\}$, we have $a_{ij} = a_{ji}$. Observe that A is a symmetric matrix if and only if it coincides with its transpose, i.e., if and only if we have $A = A'$.

Diagonal Matrix

A *diagonal matrix* D of order n is a square matrix of order n, all of whose off-diagonal entries are zero:

$$D = \begin{bmatrix} d_{11} & 0 & \cdots & 0 \\ 0 & d_{22} & \cdots & 0 \\ \vdots & \vdots & \ddots & \vdots \\ 0 & 0 & \cdots & d_{nn} \end{bmatrix}.$$

Note that every diagonal matrix is also symmetric.

Identity Matrix

The *identity matrix* of order n is a square $n \times n$ matrix whose diagonal entries are all equal to unity, and whose off-diagonal entries are all zero:

$$I = \begin{bmatrix} 1 & 0 & \cdots & 0 \\ 0 & 1 & \cdots & 0 \\ \vdots & \vdots & \ddots & \vdots \\ 0 & 0 & \cdots & 1 \end{bmatrix}.$$

The identity matrix is a diagonal matrix (and, therefore, also a symmetric matrix). In addition, it has the property that if A and B are any $k \times n$ and $n \times m$ matrices, then $AI = A$ and $IB = B$. In particular, therefore, $I^2 = I \times I = I$.

Lower-Triangular Matrix

A *lower triangular* matrix of order n is a square matrix D of order n which has the property that all the entries above the diagonal are zero:

$$D = \begin{bmatrix} d_{11} & 0 & \cdots & 0 \\ d_{21} & d_{22} & \cdots & 0 \\ \vdots & \vdots & \ddots & \vdots \\ d_{n1} & d_{n2} & \cdots & d_{nn} \end{bmatrix}.$$

Upper-triangular Matrix

An *upper-triangular* matrix of order n is a square matrix of order n which has the property that all the entries below the diagonal are zero:

$$D = \begin{bmatrix} d_{11} & d_{12} & \cdots & d_{1n} \\ 0 & d_{22} & \cdots & d_{2n} \\ \vdots & \vdots & \ddots & \vdots \\ 0 & 0 & \cdots & d_{nn} \end{bmatrix}.$$

Note that the transpose of an upper-triangular matrix is a lower-triangular matrix, and vice versa.

1.3.3 Rank of a Matrix

Let a finite collection of vectors $x_1, \ldots, x_k$ in $\mathbb{R}^n$ be given. The vectors $x_1, \ldots, x_k$ are said to be *linearly dependent* if there exist real numbers $\alpha_1, \ldots, \alpha_k$, with $\alpha_i \neq 0$ for some i, such that

$$\alpha_1 x_1 + \cdots + \alpha_k x_k = 0.$$

If, on the other hand, the only solution to $\alpha_1 x_1 + \cdots + \alpha_k x_k = 0$ is $\alpha_1 = \cdots = \alpha_k = 0$, the vectors $x_1, \ldots, x_k$ are said to be *linearly independent*.

For example, the vectors x, y, and z given by

$$x = \begin{bmatrix} 3 \\ 2 \end{bmatrix} \quad y = \begin{bmatrix} 7 \\ 6 \end{bmatrix} \quad z = \begin{bmatrix} 12 \\ 10 \end{bmatrix}$$

are linearly dependent since $x + 3y - 2z = 0$. On the other hand, the following vectors x, y, and z are obviously linearly independent:

$$x = \begin{bmatrix} 1 \\ 0 \\ 0 \end{bmatrix} \quad y = \begin{bmatrix} 0 \\ 1 \\ 0 \end{bmatrix} \quad z = \begin{bmatrix} 0 \\ 0 \\ 1 \end{bmatrix}.$$

Let A be an $n \times m$ matrix. Then, each of the n rows of A defines a vector in $\mathbb{R}^m$. The *row rank* of A, denoted $\rho^r(A)$, is defined to be the maximum number of linearly independent rows of A. That is, the row rank of A is k if the following conditions both hold:

1. There is some subset $(l_1, \ldots, l_k)$ of k distinct integers of the set $\{1, \ldots, n\}$ such that the set of vectors $A_{l_1}^r, \ldots, A_{l_k}^r$ are linearly independent.
2. For all selections of $(k + 1)$ distinct integers $(l_1, \ldots, l_{k+1})$ from $\{1, \ldots, n\}$, the vectors $A_{l_1}^r, \ldots, A_{l_{k+1}}^r$ are linearly dependent.

Note that if $k = n$, the second condition is redundant, since it is not possible to select $(n + 1)$ distinct integers from a set consisting of only n integers.

Similarly, each of the m columns of A defines a vector in $\mathbb{R}^n$, and the *column rank* of A, denoted $\rho^c(A)$, is defined as the maximum number of linearly independent columns in A. Since A is an $n \times m$ matrix, we must have $\rho^r(A) \leq n$ and $\rho^c(A) \leq m$. Among the most useful results in linear algebra is:

Theorem 1.40 *The row rank $\rho^r(A)$ of any $n \times m$ matrix A coincides with its column rank $\rho^c(A)$.*

Proof See Munkres (1964, Corollarly 7.3, p.27) or Johnston (1984, Chapter 4, p.115). □

In the sequel, we will denote this common value of $\rho^r(A)$ and $\rho^c(A)$ by $\rho(A)$. Note that since $\rho^r(A) \leq n$ and $\rho^c(A) \leq m$, we must have $\rho(A) \leq \min\{m, n\}$. An immediate consequence of Theorem 1.40, which we present as a corollary for emphasis, is that the rank of a matrix coincides with the rank of its transpose:

Corollary 1.41 *The rank $\rho(A)$ of any matrix A is equal to the rank $\rho(A')$ of its transpose A'.*

Our next result lists some important transformations of a matrix which leave its rank unchanged.

Theorem 1.42 *Let A be a given $n \times m$ matrix. If B is an $n \times m$ matrix obtained from A*

1. *by interchanging any two rows of A, or*
2. *by multiplying each entry in a given row by a nonzero constant α, or*
3. *by replacing a given row, say the i-th by itself plus a scalar multiple α of some other row, say the j-th,*

the rank $\rho(B)$ of B is the same as the rank $\rho(A)$ of A. The same result is true if the word "row" in each of the operations above is replaced by "column."

Proof See Munkres (1964, Theorem 5.1, p.15). □

The three operations described in Theorem 1.42 are termed the "elementary row operations." They play a significant role in solving systems of linear equations by the method of transforming the coefficient matrix to reduced row-echelon form (see Munkres, 1964, for details).

Finally, an $m \times n$ matrix A is said to be of *full rank* if $\rho(A) = \min\{m, n\}$. In particular, a square matrix A of order n is said to have full rank if $\rho(A) = n$.

Theorem 1.43 *Let A be an $m \times n$ matrix.*

1. *If B is any $n \times k$ matrix, then $\rho(AB) \leq \min\{\rho(A), \rho(B)\}$.*
2. *Suppose P and Q are square matrices of orders m and n, respectively, that are both of full rank. Then, $\rho(PA) = \rho(AQ) = \rho(PAQ) = \rho(A)$.*

Proof See Johnston (1984, Chapter 4, p.122). □

1.3.4 The Determinant

Throughout this subsection, it will be assumed that A is a square matrix of order n.

The *determinant* is a function that assigns to every square matrix A, a real number denoted $|A|$. The formal definition of this function is somewhat complicated. We present it in several steps.

Given the finite set of integers $\{1, \ldots, n\}$, a *permutation* of this set is a rewriting of these n integers in some order, say $j_1, \ldots, j_n$. Fix a permutation, and pick any j_i.

Count the number of integers that *follow* j_i in the ordering $j_1, \ldots, j_n$, but that *precede* it in the natural order $1, \ldots n$. This number is the *number of inversions caused by* j_i. When we determine the number of inversions caused by each j_i and sum them up, we obtain the *total number of inversions in the permutation* $j_1, \ldots, j_n$. If this total is an odd number, we call the permutation an *odd permutation*; if the total is even, we call the permutation an *even permutation*.

For example, consider the permutation $\{4, 2, 3, 1\}$ of the integers $\{1, 2, 3, 4\}$. The number of inversions caused by the number 4 in the permutation is 3, since all three numbers that follow it in the permutation also precede it in the natural ordering. The number 2 in the permutation causes only one inversion, since only the integer 1 follows it in the permutation and also precedes it in the natural ordering. Similarly, the number 3 also causes only one inversion, and, finally, the number 1 evidently causes no inversions. Thus, the total number of inversions in the permutation $\{4, 2, 3, 1\}$ is $3 + 1 + 1 = 5$, making it an odd permutation.

Now let an $n \times n$ matrix $A = (a_{ij})$ be given. Let $j_1, \ldots, j_n$ denote any permutation of the integers $\{1, \ldots, n\}$, and consider the vector $(a_{1j_1}, \ldots, a_{nj_n})$. Note that this vector consists of one entry from each row of A, and that no two entries lie in the same column. Take the product of these entries

$$a_{1j_1} a_{2j_2} \cdots a_{nj_n}.$$

Prefix a $+$ sign to this product if the permutation $j_1, \ldots, j_n$ is an odd permutation of $\{1, \ldots, n\}$, and a $-$ sign if the permutation is even.

When *all possible* such expressions $a_{1j_1} \cdots a_{nj_n}$ are written down (prefixed with the appropriate $\pm$ sign), the sum of these expressions gives us a number, which is the determinant of A, and which we have denoted $|A|$.

For example, given the 2×2 matrix

$$A = \begin{bmatrix} a_{11} & a_{12} \\ a_{21} & a_{22} \end{bmatrix}$$

we have $|A| = a_{11}a_{22} - a_{21}a_{12}$. The expression for the determinant of a 3×3 matrix is more complicated. If

$$A = \begin{bmatrix} a_{11} & a_{12} & a_{13} \\ a_{21} & a_{22} & a_{23} \\ a_{31} & a_{32} & a_{33} \end{bmatrix},$$

then

$$|A| = a_{11}a_{22}a_{33} - a_{11}a_{23}a_{32} - a_{12}a_{21}a_{33}$$
$$+ a_{12}a_{23}a_{31} + a_{13}a_{21}a_{32} - a_{13}a_{22}a_{31}.$$

For higher order matrices, the expressions get progressively messier: there are $4! = 24$ permutations of the set $\{1, 2, 3, 4\}$, so there are 24 expressions in the determinant of a 4×4 matrix, while the number for a 5×5 matrix is 120.

It is evident that the definition of the determinant we have provided is not of much use from a computational standpoint. In a later subsection, we offer some easier procedures for calculating determinants. These procedures are based on the following very useful properties:

Theorem 1.44 *Let A be a square matrix of order n.*

1. *If the matrix B is obtained from the matrix A by interchanging any two rows of A, then $|B| = -|A|$.*
2. *If B is obtained from A by multiplying each entry of some given row of A by the nonzero constant α, then $|B| = \alpha|A|$.*
3. *If B is obtained from A by replacing some row of A (say row i) by row i plus α times row j, then $|B| = |A|$.*
4. *If A has a row of zeros, then $|A| = 0$.*
5. *If A is a lower-triangular (or upper-triangular) matrix of order n, then the determinant of A is the product of the diagonal terms: $|A| = a_{11} \cdots a_{nn}$. In particular, the determinant of the identity matrix is unity: $|I| = 1$.*

Each of the first four properties remains valid if the word "row" is replaced by "column."

Proof See Munkres (1964, Chapter 8). □

The notion of the determinant is closely related to that of the rank of a matrix. To state this relationship requires one further definition. Given a (possibly nonsquare) $n \times m$ matrix B, any matrix obtained from B by deleting some of its rows and/or columns is called a *submatrix* of B. For instance, if

$$B = \begin{bmatrix} b_{11} & b_{12} & b_{13} \\ b_{21} & b_{22} & b_{23} \\ b_{31} & b_{32} & b_{33} \\ b_{41} & b_{42} & b_{43} \end{bmatrix}$$

then the following are all submatrices of B:

$$\begin{bmatrix} b_{21} \end{bmatrix} \qquad \begin{bmatrix} b_{31} & b_{33} \\ b_{41} & b_{43} \end{bmatrix} \qquad \begin{bmatrix} b_{11} & b_{12} & b_{13} \\ b_{21} & b_{22} & b_{23} \\ b_{31} & b_{32} & b_{33} \end{bmatrix}.$$

Of course, not all submatrices of B need be square. The following, for instance, is not:

$$\begin{bmatrix} b_{11} & b_{12} \\ b_{21} & b_{22} \\ b_{41} & b_{42} \end{bmatrix}.$$

Theorem 1.45 *Let B be an $n \times m$ matrix. Let k be the order of the largest square submatrix of B whose determinant is nonzero. Then, $\rho(B) = k$. In particular, the rows of B are linearly independent if and only if B contains some square submatrix of order n whose determinant is nonzero.*

Proof See Munkres (1964, Theorem 8.1). ☐

A special case of this result is that square matrices have full rank if and only if they have a non-zero determinant:

Corollary 1.46 *A square matrix A of order n has rank n if, and only if, $|A| \neq 0$.*

1.3.5 The Inverse

Let a square $n \times n$ matrix A be given. The *inverse of A*, denoted A^{-1}, is defined to be an $n \times n$ matrix B which has the property that $AB = I$.

Theorem 1.47 *Let A be an $n \times n$ matrix.*

1. *A necessary and sufficient condition for A to have an inverse is that A have rank n, or, equivalently, that $|A| \neq 0$.*
2. *If A^{-1} exists, it is unique, i.e., two different matrices B and C cannot both be the inverse of a given matrix A.*

Proof See Johnston (1984, Chapter 4). ☐

It is possible to describe a procedure for constructing the inverse of a square matrix A which satisfies the condition that $|A| \neq 0$. Consider first the $(n-1) \times (n-1)$ submatrix of A that is obtained when row i and column j are deleted. Denote the determinant of this submatrix by $|A(ij)|$. Define

$$C_{ij}(A) = (-1)^{i+j}|A(ij)|.$$

$C_{ij}(A)$ is called the (i, j)-th *cofactor* of A.

Now, construct an $n \times n$ matrix $C(A)$ whose (i, j)-th entry is $C_{ij}(A)$. The transpose of $C(A)$ is called the *adjoint of A*, and is denoted $\mathrm{Adj}(A)$:

$$\mathrm{Adj}(A) = \begin{bmatrix} C_{11}(A) & \cdots & C_{n1}(A) \\ \vdots & \ddots & \vdots \\ C_{1n}(A) & \cdots & C_{nn}(A) \end{bmatrix}.$$

Finally, when each element of $\mathrm{Adj}(A)$ is divided by $|A|$, the result is A^{-1}. Thus,

$$A^{-1} = \frac{1}{|A|}\mathrm{Adj}(A).$$

We list some useful properties of the inverse in our next result. In stating these properties, it is assumed in each case that the relevant inverse is well defined.

Theorem 1.48 *The inverse has the following properties:*

1. *The inverse of A^{-1} is A: $(A^{-1})^{-1} = A$.*
2. *The inverse of the transpose is the transpose of the inverse: $(A')^{-1} = (A^{-1})'$.*
3. *$(AB)^{-1} = B^{-1}A^{-1}$.*
4. *$|A^{-1}| = 1/|A|$.*
5. *The inverse of a lower- (resp. upper-) triangular matrix is also a lower- (resp. upper-) triangular matrix.*

Proof See Johnston (1984, Chapter 4, pp.133–135). □

1.3.6 Calculating the Determinant

We offer in this subsection two methods for calculating the determinant of a square matrix A. Each method is easier to use than directly following the definition of the determinant.

The first method is based on the observation that, from the definition of the determinant, the expression for $|A|$ for any given $n \times n$ matrix A can be written as

$$|A| = a_{11}C_{11}(A) + \cdots + a_{1n}C_{1n}(A).$$

Here, as in the previous subsection, $C_{ij}(A)$ is the (i, j)-th cofactor of the matrix A, i.e.,

$$C_{ij}(A) = (-1)^{i+j}|A(ij)|,$$

where $A(ij)$ is the $(n-1) \times (n-1)$ matrix obtained from A by deleting row i and column j.

This observation gives us a recursive method for computing the determinant, since it enables us to express the determinant of an $n \times n$ matrix A in terms of the determinants of the $(n-1) \times (n-1)$ submatrices $A(11), \ldots, A(1n)$. By reapplying the method, we can express the determinants of each of these $(n-1) \times (n-1)$ submatrices in terms of some of the $(n-2) \times (n-2)$ submatrices of these submatrices, and so on. Thus, for example, for a 3×3 matrix $A = (a_{ij})$, we obtain:

$$\begin{vmatrix} a_{11} & a_{12} & a_{13} \\ a_{21} & a_{22} & a_{23} \\ a_{31} & a_{32} & a_{33} \end{vmatrix} = a_{11} \begin{vmatrix} a_{22} & a_{23} \\ a_{32} & a_{33} \end{vmatrix} - a_{12} \begin{vmatrix} a_{21} & a_{23} \\ a_{31} & a_{33} \end{vmatrix} + a_{13} \begin{vmatrix} a_{21} & a_{22} \\ a_{31} & a_{32} \end{vmatrix}.$$

For example, if

$$A = \begin{bmatrix} 1 & 5 & 7 \\ 3 & 2 & 8 \\ 6 & 1 & 9 \end{bmatrix},$$

then, we have

$$|A| = 1(18-8) - 5(27-48) + 7(3-12) = 10 + 105 - 63 = 52.$$

Nothing in this method relies on using the *first* row of the matrix. Any row (or, for that matter, column) would do as well; in fact, we have

$$|A| = a_{i1}C_{i1} + \cdots + a_{in}C_{in}$$
$$= a_{1j}C_{1j} + \cdots + a_{nj}C_{nj}.$$

The second method is based on exploiting the following three properties of the determinant:

1. If B is obtained from A by interchanging any two rows (or columns), then $|B| = -|A|$.
2. If B is obtained from A by replacing any row i (resp. column i) by itself plus α times some other row j (resp. some other column j), then $|B| = |A|$.
3. If A is a (lower- or upper-) triangular matrix, then the determinant of A is the product of its diagonal elements.

Specifically, the idea is to repeatedly use properties 1 and 2 to convert a given matrix A into a triangular matrix B, and then use property 3. This method is easier to use than the earlier one on large matrices (say, order 4 or larger). Nonetheless, we illustrate its use through the same 3×3 matrix used to illustrate the earlier method:

$$A = \begin{bmatrix} 1 & 5 & 7 \\ 3 & 2 & 8 \\ 6 & 1 & 9 \end{bmatrix}.$$

We have:

$$
\begin{vmatrix} 1 & 5 & 7 \\ 3 & 2 & 8 \\ 6 & 1 & 9 \end{vmatrix} = \begin{vmatrix} 1 & 5 & 7 \\ 0 & -13 & -13 \\ 6 & 1 & 9 \end{vmatrix} = \begin{vmatrix} 1 & 5 & 7 \\ 0 & -13 & -13 \\ 0 & -29 & -33 \end{vmatrix} = \begin{vmatrix} 1 & 5 & 7 \\ 0 & -13 & -13 \\ 0 & 0 & -4 \end{vmatrix},
$$

where the second expression is obtained from the first by replacing row 2 by itself plus (-3) times row 1; the third is obtained from the second by replacing row 3 by itself plus (-6) times row 1; and, finally, the last expression is obtained from the third by replacing row 3 by itself plus $(-29/13)$ times row 2. Since the last is in triangular form, the determinant of A is seen to be given by $(1)(-13)(-4) = 52$.

1.4 Functions

Let S, T be subsets of $\mathbb{R}^n$ and $\mathbb{R}^l$, respectively. A *function* f from S to T, denoted $f: S \to T$, is a rule that associates with each element of S, one and only one element of T. The set S is called the *domain* of the function f, and the set T its *range*.

1.4.1 Continuous Functions

Let $f: S \to T$, where $S \subset \mathbb{R}^n$ and $T \subset \mathbb{R}^l$. Then, f is said to be *continuous* at $x \in S$ if for all $\epsilon > 0$, there is $\delta > 0$ such that $y \in S$ and $d(x, y) < \delta$ implies $d(f(x), f(y)) < \epsilon$. (Note that $d(x, y)$ is the distance between x and y in $\mathbb{R}^n$, while $d(f(x), f(y))$ is the distance in $\mathbb{R}^l$.) In the language of sequences, $f: S \to T$ is continuous at $x \in S$ if for all sequences $\{x_k\}$ such that $x_k \in S$ for all k, and $\lim_{k \to \infty} x_k = x$, it is the case that $\lim_{k \to \infty} f(x_k) = f(x)$.

Intuitively, f is continuous at x if the value of f at any point y that is "close" to x is a good approximation of the value of f at x. Thus, the identity function $f(x) = x$ for all $x \in \mathbb{R}$ is continuous at each $x \in \mathbb{R}$, while the function $f: \mathbb{R} \to \mathbb{R}$ given by

$$
f(x) = \begin{cases} 0, & x \le 0 \\ 1, & x > 0 \end{cases}
$$

is continuous everywhere except at $x = 0$. At $x = 0$, every open ball $B(x, \delta)$ with center x and radius $\delta > 0$ contains at least one point $y > 0$. At all such points, $f(y) = 1 > 0 = f(x)$, and this approximation does not get better, no matter how close y gets to x (i.e., no matter how small we take δ to be).

A function $f: S \to T$ is said to be *continuous on S* if it is continuous at *each* point in S.

Observe that if $f: S \subset \mathbb{R}^n \to \mathbb{R}^l$, then f consists of l "component functions" $(f^1, \ldots, f^l)$, i.e., there are functions $f^i: S \to \mathbb{R}$, $i = 1, \ldots, l$, such that for each $x \in S$, we have $f(x) = (f^1(x), \ldots, f^l(x))$. It is left to the reader as an exercise to show that f is continuous at $x \in S$ (resp. f is continuous on S) if and only if each f^i is continuous at x (resp. if and only if each f^i is continuous on S).

The following result gives us an equivalent characterization of continuity that comes in quite useful in practice:

Theorem 1.49 *A function $f: S \subset \mathbb{R}^n \to \mathbb{R}^l$ is continuous at a point $x \in S$ if and only if for all open sets $V \subset \mathbb{R}^l$ such that $f(x) \in V$, there is an open set $U \subset \mathbb{R}^n$ such that $x \in U$, and $f(z) \in V$ for all $z \in U \cap S$.*

Proof Suppose f is continuous at x, and V is an open set in $\mathbb{R}^l$ containing $f(x)$. Suppose, per absurdum, that the theorem was false, so for *any* open set U containing x, there is $y \in U \cap S$ such that $f(y) \notin V$. We will show a contradiction. For $k \in \{1, 2, 3, \ldots\}$, let U_k be the open ball with center x and radius $1/k$. Let $y_k \in U_k \cap S$ be such that $f(y_k) \notin V$. The sequence $\{y_k\}$ is clearly well defined, and since $y_k \in U_k$ for all k, we have $d(x, y_k) < 1/k$ for each k, so $y_k \to x$ as $k \to \infty$. Since f is continuous at x by hypothesis, we also have $f(y_k) \to f(x)$ as $k \to \infty$. However, $f(y_k) \notin V$ for any k, and since V is open, V^c is closed, so $f(x) = \lim_k f(y_k) \in V^c$, which contradicts $f(x) \in V$.

Now, suppose that for each open set V containing $f(x)$, there is an open set U containing x such that $f(y) \in V$ for all $y \in U \cap S$. We will show that f is continuous at x. Let $\epsilon > 0$ be given. Define V_ϵ to be the open ball in $\mathbb{R}^l$ with center $f(x)$ and radius ϵ. Then, there exists an open set U_ϵ containing x such that $f(y) \in V_\epsilon$ for all $y \in U_\epsilon \cap S$. Pick any $\delta > 0$ so that $B(x, \delta) \subset U_\epsilon$. Then, by construction, it is true that $y \in S$ and $d(x, y) < \delta$ implies $f(y) \in V_\epsilon$, i.e., that $d(f(x), f(y)) < \epsilon$. Since $\epsilon > 0$ was arbitrary, we have shown precisely that f is continuous at x. $\square$

As an immediate corollary, we have the following statement, which is usually abbreviated as: "a function is continuous if and only if the inverse image of every open set is open."

Corollary 1.50 *A function $f: S \subset \mathbb{R}^n \to \mathbb{R}^l$ is continuous on S if and only if for each open set $V \subset \mathbb{R}^l$, there is an open set $U \subset \mathbb{R}^n$ such that $f^{-1}(V) = U \cap S$, where $f^{-1}(V)$ is defined by*

$$f^{-1}(V) = \{x \in S \mid f(x) \in V\}.$$

In particular, if S is an open set in $\mathbb{R}^n$, f is continuous on S if and only if $f^{-1}(V)$ is an open set in $\mathbb{R}^n$ for each open set V in $\mathbb{R}^l$.

Finally, some observations. Note that continuity of a function f at a point x is a *local* property, i.e., it relates to the behavior of f near x, but tells us nothing about the

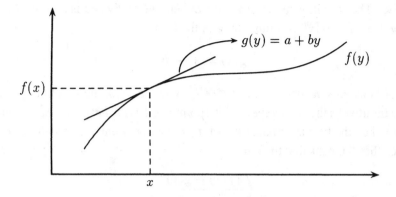

Fig. 1.5. The Derivative

behavior of f elsewhere. In particular, the continuity of f at x has *no* implications even for the continuity of f at points "close" to x. Indeed, it is easy to construct functions that are continuous at a given point x, but that are discontinuous at *every* other point in every neighborhood of x (see the Exercises). It is also important to note that, in general, functions need not be continuous at even a single point in their domain. Consider $f: \mathbb{R}_+ \to \mathbb{R}_+$ given by $f(x) = 1$, if x is a rational number, and $f(x) = 0$, otherwise. This function is discontinuous everywhere on $\mathbb{R}_+$.

1.4.2 Differentiable and Continuously Differentiable Functions

Throughout this subsection S will denote an open set in $\mathbb{R}^n$.

A function $f: S \to \mathbb{R}^m$ is said to be *differentiable* at a point $x \in S$ if there exists an $m \times n$ matrix A such that for all $\epsilon > 0$, there is $\delta > 0$ such that $y \in S$ and $\|x - y\| < \delta$ implies

$$\|f(x) - f(y) - A(x - y)\| < \epsilon \|x - y\|.$$

Equivalently, f is differentiable at $x \in S$ if

$$\lim_{y \to x} \left(\frac{\|f(y) - f(x) - A(y - x)\|}{\|y - x\|} \right) = 0.$$

(The notation "$y \to x$" is shorthand for "for all sequences $\{y_k\}$ such that $y_k \to x$.") The matrix A in this case is called the *derivative of f at x* and is denoted $Df(x)$. Figure 1.5 provides a graphical illustration of the derivative. In keeping with standard practice, we shall, in the sequel, denote $Df(x)$ by $f'(x)$ whenever $n = m = 1$, i.e., whenever $S \subset \mathbb{R}$ and $f: S \to \mathbb{R}$.

Remark   The definition of the derivative Df may be motivated as follows. An *affine function* from $\mathbb{R}^n$ to $\mathbb{R}^m$ is a function g of the form

$$g(y) = Ay + b,$$

where A is an $m \times n$ matrix, and $b \in \mathbb{R}^m$. (When $b = 0$, the function g is called *linear*.) Intuitively, the *derivative* of f at a point $x \in S$ is the *best affine approximation* to f at x, i.e., the best approximation of f around the point x by an affine function g. Here, "best" means that the ratio

$$\left(\frac{\|f(y) - g(y)\|}{\|y - x\|} \right)$$

goes to zero as $y \to x$. Since the values of f and g must coincide at x (otherwise g would hardly be a good approximation to f at x), we must have $g(x) = Ax + b = f(x)$, or $b = f(x) - Ax$. Thus, we may write this approximating function g as

$$g(y) = Ay - Ax + f(x) = A(y - x) + f(x).$$

Given this value for $g(y)$, the task of identifying the best affine approximation to f at x now amounts to identifying a matrix A such that

$$\left(\frac{\|f(y) - g(y)\|}{\|y - x\|} \right) = \left(\frac{\|f(y) - (A(y - x) + f(x))\|}{\|y - x\|} \right) \to 0 \quad \text{as} \quad y \to x.$$

This is precisely the definition of the derivative we have given.   □

If f is differentiable at all points in S, then f is said to be *differentiable on S*. When f is differentiable on S, the derivative Df itself forms a function from S to $\mathbb{R}^{m \times n}$. If $Df: S \to \mathbb{R}^{m \times n}$ is a continuous function, then f is said to be *continuously differentiable* on S, and we write f is C^1.

The following observations are immediate from the definitions. A function $f: S \subset \mathbb{R}^n \to \mathbb{R}^m$ is differentiable at $x \in S$ if and only if each of the m component functions $f^i: S \to \mathbb{R}$ of f is differentiable at x, in which case we have $Df(x) = (Df^1(x), \ldots, Df^m(x))$. Moreover, f is C^1 on S if and only if each f^i is C^1 on S.

The difference between differentiability and continuous differentiability is nontrivial. The following example shows that a function may be differentiable everywhere, but may still not be continuously differentiable.

Example 1.51   Let $f: \mathbb{R} \to \mathbb{R}$ be given by

$$f(x) = \begin{cases} 0 & \text{if } x = 0 \\ x^2 \sin(1/x^2) & \text{if } x \neq 0. \end{cases}$$

For $x \neq 0$, we have

$$f'(x) = 2x \sin\left(\frac{1}{x^2}\right) - \left(\frac{2}{x}\right) \cos\left(\frac{1}{x^2}\right).$$

Since $|\sin(\cdot)| \leq 1$ and $|\cos(\cdot)| \leq 1$, but $(2/x) \to \infty$ as $x \to 0$, it is clear that the limit as $x \to 0$ of $f'(x)$ is not well defined. However, $f'(0)$ does exist! Indeed,

$$f'(0) = \lim_{x \to 0}\left(\frac{f(x) - f(0)}{x - 0}\right) = \lim_{x \to 0} x \sin\left(\frac{1}{x^2}\right).$$

Since $|\sin(1/x^2)| \leq 1$, we have $|x \sin(1/x^2)| \leq |x|$, so $x \sin(1/x^2) \to 0$ as $x \to 0$. This means $f'(0) = 0$. Thus, f is not C^1 on $\mathbb{R}_+$. $\qquad\square$

This example notwithstanding, it is true that the derivative of an everywhere differentiable function f must possess a minimal amount of continuity. See the Intermediate Value Theorem for the Derivative in subsection 1.6.1 for details.

We close this subsection with a statement of two important properties of the derivative. First, given two functions $f: \mathbb{R}^n \to \mathbb{R}^m$ and $g: \mathbb{R}^n \to \mathbb{R}^m$, define their *sum* $(f + g)$ to be the function from $\mathbb{R}^n$ to $\mathbb{R}^m$ whose value at any $x \in \mathbb{R}^n$ is $f(x) + g(x)$.

Theorem 1.52 *If $f: \mathbb{R}^n \to \mathbb{R}^m$ and $g: \mathbb{R}^n \to \mathbb{R}^m$ are both differentiable at a point $x \in \mathbb{R}^n$, so is $(f + g)$ and, in fact,*

$$D(f + g)(x) = Df(x) + Dg(x).$$

Proof Obvious from the definition of differentiability. $\qquad\square$

Next, given functions $f: \mathbb{R}^n \to \mathbb{R}^m$ and $h: \mathbb{R}^k \to \mathbb{R}^n$, define their *composition* $f \circ h$ to be the function from $\mathbb{R}^k$ to $\mathbb{R}^m$ whose value at any $x \in \mathbb{R}^k$ is given by $f(h(x))$, that is, by the value of f evaluated at $h(x)$.

Theorem 1.53 *Let $f: \mathbb{R}^n \to \mathbb{R}^m$ and $h: \mathbb{R}^k \to \mathbb{R}^n$. Let $x \in \mathbb{R}^k$. If h is differentiable at x, and f is differentiable at $h(x)$, then $f \circ h$ is itself differentiable at x, and its derivative may be obtained throught the "chain rule" as:*

$$D(f \circ h)(x) = Df(h(x))Dh(x).$$

Proof See Rudin (1976, Theorem 9.15, p.214). $\qquad\square$

Theorems 1.52 and 1.53 are only one-way implications. For instance, while the differentiability of f and g at x implies the differentiability of $(f + g)$ at x, $(f + g)$ can be differentiable everywhere (even C^1) without f and g being differentiable anywhere. For an example, let $f: \mathbb{R} \to \mathbb{R}$ be given by $f(x) = 1$ if x is rational, and

$f(x) = 0$ otherwise, and let $g: \mathbb{R} \to \mathbb{R}$ be given by $g(x) = 0$ if x is rational, and $g(x) = 1$ otherwise. Then, f and g are discontinuous everywhere, so are certainly not differentiable anywhere. However, $(f + g)(x) = 1$ for all x, so $(f + g)'(x) = 0$ at all x, meaning $(f + g)$ is C^1. Similarly, the differentiability of $f \circ h$ has no implications for the differentiability of f at $h(x)$ or the differentiability of h at x.

1.4.3 Partial Derivatives and Differentiability

Let $f: S \to \mathbb{R}$, where $S \subset \mathbb{R}^n$ is an open set. Let e_j denote the vector in $\mathbb{R}^n$ that has a 1 in the j-th place and zeros elsewhere ($j = 1, \dots, n$). Then the j-th *partial derivative* of f is said to exist at a point x if there is a number $\partial f(x)/\partial x_j$ such that

$$\lim_{t \to 0} \left(\frac{f(x + te_j) - f(x)}{t} \right) = \frac{\partial f}{\partial x_j}(x).$$

Among the more pleasant facts of life are the following:

Theorem 1.54 *Let $f: S \to \mathbb{R}$, where $S \subset \mathbb{R}^n$ is open.*

1. *If f is differentiable at x, then all partials $\partial f(x)/\partial x_j$ exist at x, and $Df(x) = [\partial f(x)/\partial x_1, \dots, \partial f(x)/\partial x_n]$.*
2. *If all the partials exist and are continuous at x, then $Df(x)$ exists, and $Df(x) = [\partial f(x)/\partial x_1, \dots, \partial f(x)/\partial x_n]$.*
3. *f is C^1 on S if and only if all partial derivatives of f exist and are continuous on S.*

Proof See Rudin (1976, Theorem 9.21, p.219).   □

Thus, to check if f is C^1, we only need figure out if (a) the partial derivatives all exist on S, and (b) if they are all continuous on S. On the other hand, the requirement that the partials not only exist but be continuous at x is very important for the coincidence of the vector of partials with $Df(x)$. In the absence of this condition, all partials could exist at some point without the function itself being differentiable at that point. Consider the following example:

Example 1.55 Let $f : \mathbb{R}^2 \to \mathbb{R}$ be given by $f(0, 0) = 0$, and for $(x, y) \neq (0, 0)$,

$$f(x, y) = \frac{xy}{\sqrt{x^2 + y^2}}.$$

We will show that f has all partial derivatives everywhere (including at (0,0)), but that these partials are not continuous at (0,0). Then we will show that f is not differentiable at (0,0).

Since $f(x, 0) = 0$ for any $x \neq 0$, it is immediate that for all $x \neq 0$,

$$\frac{\partial f}{\partial y}(x, 0) = \lim_{\hat{y} \to 0} \frac{f(x, \hat{y}) - f(x, 0)}{\hat{y}} = \lim_{\hat{y} \to 0} \frac{x}{\sqrt{x^2 + \hat{y}^2}} = 1.$$

Similarly, at all points of the form $(0, y)$ for $y \neq 0$, we have $\partial f(0, y)/\partial x = 1$. However, note that

$$\frac{\partial f}{\partial x}(0, 0) = \lim_{x \to 0} \frac{f(x, 0) - f(0, 0)}{x} = \lim_{x \to 0} \frac{0 - 0}{x} = 0,$$

so $\partial f(0, 0)/\partial x$ exists at $(0, 0)$, but is not the limit of $\partial f(0, y)/\partial x$ as $y \to 0$. Similarly, we also have $\partial f(0, 0)/\partial y = 0 \neq 1 = \lim_{x \to 0} \partial f(x, 0)/\partial y$.

Suppose f were differentiable at $(0, 0)$. Then, the derivative $Df(0, 0)$ must coincide with the vector of partials at $(0,0)$ so we must have $Df(0, 0) = (0, 0)$. However, from the definition of the derivative, we must also have

$$\lim_{(x,y) \to (0,0)} \frac{\| f(x, y) - f(0, 0) - Df(0, 0) \cdot (x, y) \|}{\| (x, y) - (0, 0) \|} = 0,$$

but this is impossible if $Df(0, 0) = 0$. To see this, take any point (x, y) of the form (a, a) for some $a > 0$, and note that every neighborhood of $(0,0)$ contains at least one such point. Since $f(0, 0) = 0$, $Df(0, 0) = (0, 0)$, and $\| (x, y) \| = \sqrt{x^2 + y^2}$, it follows that

$$\frac{\| f(a, a) - f(0, 0) - Df(0, 0) \cdot (a, a) \|}{\| (a, a) - (0, 0) \|} = \frac{a^2}{2a^2} = \frac{1}{2},$$

so the limit of this fraction as $a \to 0$ cannot be zero. $\qquad\square$

Intuitively, the feature that drives this example is that in looking at the partial derivative of f with respect to (say) x at a point (x, y), we are moving along only the line through (x, y) parallel to the x-axis (see the line denoted l_1 in Figure 1.6). Similarly, the partial with derivative with respect to y involves holding the x variable fixed, and moving only on the line through (x, y) parallel to the y-axis (see the line denoted l_2 in Figure 1.6). On the other hand, in looking at the derivative Df, both the x and y variables are allowed to vary *simultaneously* (for instance, along the dotted curve in Figure 1.6).

Lastly, it is worth stressing that although a function must be continuous in order to be differentiable (this is easy to see from the definitions), there is no implication in the other direction whatsoever. Extreme examples exist of functions which are continuous on all of $\mathbb{R}$, but fail to be differentiable at even a single point (see, for example, Rudin, 1976, Theorem 7.18, p.154). Such functions are by no means pathological; they play, for instance, a central role in the study of Brownian motion

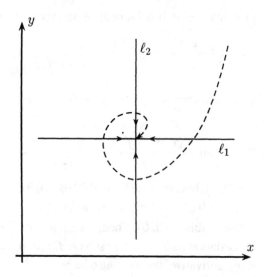

Fig. 1.6. Partial Derivatives and Differentiability

in probability theory (with probability one, a Brownian motion path is everywhere continuous and nowhere differentiable).

1.4.4 Directional Derivatives and Differentiability

Let $f: S \to \mathbb{R}$, where $S \subset \mathbb{R}^n$ is open. Let x be any point in S, and let $h \in \mathbb{R}^n$. The *directional derivative of f at x in the direction h* is defined as

$$\lim_{t \to 0+} \left(\frac{f(x + th) - f(x)}{t} \right)$$

when this limit exists, and is denoted $Df(x; h)$. (The notation $t \to 0+$ is shorthand for $t > 0, t \to 0$.)

When the condition $t \to 0+$ is replaced with $t \to 0$, we obtain what is sometimes called the "two-sided directional derivative." Observe that partial derivatives are a special case of two-sided directional derivatives: when $h = e_i$ for some i, the two-sided directional derivative at x is precisely the partial derivative $\partial f(x)/\partial x_i$.

In the previous subsection, it was pointed out that the existence of all partial derivatives at a point x is not sufficient to ensure that f is differentiable at x. It is actually true that not even the existence of *all* two-sided directional derivatives at x implies that f is differentiable at x (see the Exercises for an example). However, the following relationship in the reverse direction is easy to show and is left to the reader as an exercise.

Theorem 1.56 *Suppose f is differentiable at $x \in S$. Then, for any $h \in \mathbb{R}^n$, the (one-sided) directional derivative $Df(x; h)$ of f at x in the direction h exists, and, in fact, we have $Df(x; h) = Df(x) \cdot h$.*

An immediate corollary is:

Corollary 1.57 *If $Df(x)$ exists, then $Df(x; h) = -Df(x; -h)$.*

Remark   What is the relationship between $Df(x)$ and the *two-sided* directional derivative of f at x in an arbitrary direction h?

1.4.5 Higher Order Derivatives

Let f be a function from $S \subset \mathbb{R}^n$ to $\mathbb{R}$, where S is an open set. Throughout this subsection, we will assume that f is differentiable on all of S, so that the derivative $Df = [\partial f / \partial x_1, \ldots, \partial f / \partial x_n]$ itself defines a function from S to $\mathbb{R}^n$.

Suppose now that there is $x \in S$ such that the derivative Df is itself differentiable at x, i.e., such that for each i, the function $\partial f / \partial x_i \colon S \to \mathbb{R}$ is differentiable at x. Denote the partial of $\partial f / \partial x_i$ in the direction e_j at x by $\partial^2 f(x) / \partial x_j \partial x_i$, if $i \neq j$, and $\partial^2 f(x) / \partial x_i^2$, if $i = j$. Then, we say that f is *twice-differentiable* at x, with second derivative $D^2 f(x)$, where

$$D^2 f(x) = \begin{bmatrix} \dfrac{\partial^2 f(x)}{\partial x_1^2} & \cdots & \dfrac{\partial^2 f(x)}{\partial x_1 \partial x_n} \\ \vdots & \ddots & \vdots \\ \dfrac{\partial^2 f(x)}{\partial x_n \partial x_1} & \cdots & \dfrac{\partial^2 f(x)}{\partial x_n^2} \end{bmatrix}.$$

Once again, we shall follow standard practice and denote $D^2 f(x)$ by $f''(x)$ whenever $n = 1$ (i.e., if $S \subset \mathbb{R}$).

If f is twice-differentiable at each x in S, we say that f is twice-differentiable *on* S. When f is twice-differentiable on S, and for each $i, j = 1, \ldots, n$, the cross-partial $\partial^2 f / \partial x_i x_j$ is a *continuous* function from S to $\mathbb{R}$, we say that f is *twice continuously differentiable* on S, and we write f is C^2.

When f is C^2, the second-derivative $D^2 f$, which is also called the matrix of cross-partials (or the *hessian* of f at x), has the following useful property:

Theorem 1.58 *If $f \colon D \to \mathbb{R}^n$ is a C^2 function, $D^2 f$ is a symmetric matrix, i.e., we have*

$$\frac{\partial^2 f}{\partial x_i \partial x_j}(x) = \frac{\partial^2 f}{\partial x_j \partial x_i}(x)$$

for all $i, j = 1, \ldots, n$, and for all $x \in D$.

Proof See Rudin (1976, Corollary to Theorem 9.41, p.236).   □

For an example where the symmetry of $D^2 f$ fails because the cross-partials fail to be continuous, see the Exercises.

The condition that the partials should be continuous for $D^2 f$ to be a symmetric matrix can be weakened a little. In particular, for

$$\frac{\partial^2 f}{\partial x_j \partial x_k}(y) = \frac{\partial^2 f}{\partial x_k \partial x_j}(y)$$

to hold, it suffices just that (a) the partials $\partial f / \partial x_j$ and $\partial f / \partial x_k$ exist everywhere on D, and (b) that one of the cross-partials $\partial^2 f / \partial x_j \partial x_k$ or $\partial^2 f / \partial x_k \partial x_j$ exist everywhere on D and be continuous at y.

Still higher derivatives (third, fourth, etc.) may be defined for a function $f : \mathbb{R}^n \to \mathbb{R}$. The underlying idea is simple: for instance, a function is thrice-differentiable at a point x if all the component functions of its second-derivative $D^2 f$ (i.e., if all the cross-partial functions $\partial^2 f / \partial x_i \partial x_j$) are themselves differentiable at x; it is C^3 if all these component functions are continuously differentiable, etc. On the other hand, the notation becomes quite complex unless $n = 1$ (i.e., $f : \mathbb{R} \to \mathbb{R}$), and we do not have any use in this book for derivatives beyond the second, so we will not attempt formal definitions here.

1.5 Quadratic Forms: Definite and Semidefinite Matrices

1.5.1 Quadratic Forms and Definiteness

A *quadratic form* on $\mathbb{R}^n$ is a function g_A on $\mathbb{R}^n$ of the form

$$g_A(x) = x'Ax = \sum_{i,j=1}^{n} a_{ij} x_i x_j$$

where $A = (a_{ij})$ is any *symmetric* $n \times n$ matrix. Since the quadratic form g_A is completely specified by the matrix A, we henceforth refer to A itself as the quadratic form. Our interest in quadratic forms arises from the fact that if f is a C^2 function, and z is a point in the domain of f, then the matrix of second partials $D^2 f(z)$ defines a quadratic form (this follows from Theorem 1.58 on the symmetry property of $D^2 f$ for a C^2 function f).

A quadratic form A is said to be

1. *positive definite* if we have $x'Ax > 0$ for all $x \in \mathbb{R}^n$, $x \neq 0$.
2. *positive semidefinite* if we have $x'Ax \geq 0$ for all $x \in \mathbb{R}^n$, $x \neq 0$.
3. *negative definite* if we have $x'Ax < 0$ for all $x \in \mathbb{R}^n$, $x \neq 0$.
4. *negative semidefinite* if we have $x'Ax \leq 0$ for all $x \in \mathbb{R}^n$, $x \neq 0$.

The terms "nonnegative definite" and "nonpositive definite" are often used in place of "positive semidefinite" and "negative semidefinite" respectively.

For instance, the quadratic form A defined by

$$A = \begin{bmatrix} 1 & 0 \\ 0 & 1 \end{bmatrix}$$

is positive definite, since for any $x = (x_1, x_2) \in \mathbb{R}^2$, we have $x'Ax = x_1^2 + x_2^2$, and this quantity is positive whenever $x \neq 0$. On the other hand, consider the quadratic form

$$A = \begin{bmatrix} 1 & 0 \\ 0 & 0 \end{bmatrix}.$$

For any $x = (x_1, x_2) \in \mathbb{R}^2$, we have $x'Ax = x_1^2$, so $x'Ax$ can be zero even if $x \neq 0$. (For example, $x'Ax = 0$ if $x = (0, 1)$.) Thus, A is not positive definite. On the other hand, it is certainly true that we always have $x'Ax \geq 0$, so A is positive semidefinite.

Observe that there exist matrices A which are neither positive semidefinite nor negative semidefinite, and that do not, therefore, fit into any of the four categories we have identified. Such matrices are called *indefinite quadratic forms*. As an example of an indefinite quadratic form A, consider

$$A = \begin{bmatrix} 0 & 1 \\ 1 & 0 \end{bmatrix}.$$

For $x = (1, 1)$, $x'Ax = 2 > 0$, so A is not negative semidefinite. But for $x = (-1, 1)$, $x'Ax = -2 < 0$, so A is not positive semidefinite either.

Given a quadratic form A and any $t \in \mathbb{R}$, we have $(tx)'A(tx) = t^2 x'Ax$, so the quadratic form has the same sign along lines through the origin. Thus, in particular, A is positive definite (resp. negative definite) if and only if it satisfies $x'Ax > 0$ (resp. $x'Ax < 0$) for all x in the unit sphere $C = \{u \in \mathbb{R}^n \mid \|u\| = 1\}$. We will use this observation to show that if A is a positive definite (or negative definite) $n \times n$ matrix, so is any other quadratic form B which is sufficiently close to A:

Theorem 1.59 *Let A be a positive definite $n \times n$ matrix. Then, there is $\gamma > 0$ such that if B is any symmetric $n \times n$ matrix with $|b_{jk} - a_{jk}| < \gamma$ for all $j, k \in \{1, \ldots, n\}$, then B is also positive definite. A similar statement holds for negative definite matrices A.*

Proof We will make use of the Weierstrass Theorem, which is proved in Chapter 3 (see Theorem 3.1). The Weierstrass Theorem states that if $\mathcal{K} \subset \mathbb{R}^n$ is compact, and $f : \mathcal{K} \to \mathbb{R}$ is a continuous function, then f has both a maximum and a minimum on $\mathcal{K}$, i.e., there exist points k' and k^* in $\mathcal{K}$ such that $f(k') \geq f(k) \geq f(k^*)$ for all $k \in \mathcal{K}$.

Now, the unit sphere $\mathcal{C}$ is clearly compact, and the quadratic form A is continuous on this set. Therefore, by the Weierstrass Theorem, there is z in $\mathcal{C}$ such that for any $x \in \mathcal{C}$, we have

$$z'Az \leq x'Ax.$$

If A is positive definite, then $z'Az$ must be strictly positive, so there must exist $\epsilon > 0$ such that $x'Ax \geq \epsilon > 0$ for all $x \in \mathcal{C}$.

Define $\gamma = \epsilon/2n^2 > 0$. Let B be any symmetric $n \times n$ matrix, which is such that $|b_{jk} - a_{jk}| < \gamma$ for all $j, k = 1, \ldots, n$. Then, for any $x \in \mathcal{C}$,

$$
\begin{aligned}
|x'(B - A)x| = {} & \left| \sum_{j,k=1}^{n} (b_{jk} - a_{jk})x_j x_k \right| \\
\leq {} & \sum_{j,k=1}^{n} |b_{jk} - a_{jk}||x_j||x_k| \\
< {} & \gamma \sum_{j,k=1}^{n} |x_j||x_k| \\
< {} & \gamma n^2 = \epsilon/2.
\end{aligned}
$$

Therefore, for any $x \in \mathcal{C}$,

$$x'Bx = x'Ax + x'(B - A)x \geq \epsilon - \epsilon/2 = \epsilon/2$$

so B is also positive definite, and the desired result is established. □

A particular implication of this result, which we will use in Chapter 4 in the study of unconstrained optimization problems, is the following:

Corollary 1.60 *If f is a C^2 function such that at some point x, $D^2 f(x)$ is a positive definite matrix, then there is a neighborhood $B(x, r)$ of x such that for all $y \in B(x, r)$, $D^2 f(y)$ is also a positive definite matrix. A similar statement holds if $D^2 f(x)$ is, instead, a negative definite matrix.*

Finally, it is important to point out that Theorem 1.59 is no longer true if "positive definite" is replaced by "positive semidefinite." Consider, as a counterexample, the matrix A defined by

$$A = \begin{bmatrix} 1 & 0 \\ 0 & 0 \end{bmatrix}.$$

We have seen above that A is positive semidefinite (but not positive definite). Pick any $\gamma > 0$. Then, for $\epsilon = \gamma/2$, the matrix

$$B = \begin{bmatrix} 1 & 0 \\ 0 & -\epsilon \end{bmatrix}$$

satisfies $|a_{ij} - b_{ij}| < \gamma$ for all i, j. However, B is not positive semidefinite: for $x = (x_1, x_2)$, we have $x'Bx = x_1^2 - \epsilon x_2^2$, and this quantity can be negative (for instance, if $x_1 = 0$ and $x_2 \neq 0$). Thus, there is no neighborhood of A such that all quadratic forms in that neighborhood are also positive semidefinite.

1.5.2 Identifying Definiteness and Semidefiniteness

From a practical standpoint, it is of interest to ask: what restrictions on the structure of A are imposed by the requirement that A be a positive (or negative) definite quadratic form? We provide answers to this question in this section. The results we present are, in fact, *equivalence* statements; that is, quadratic forms possess the required definiteness or semidefiniteness property *if and only if* they meet the conditions we outline.

The first result deals with positive and negative definiteness. Given an $n \times n$ symmetric matrix A, let A_k denote the $k \times k$ submatrix of A that is obtained when only the first k rows and columns are retained, i.e., let

$$A_k = \begin{bmatrix} a_{11} & \cdots & a_{1k} \\ \vdots & \ddots & \vdots \\ a_{k1} & \cdots & a_{kk} \end{bmatrix}.$$

We will refer to A_k as the *k-th naturally ordered principal minor* of A.

Theorem 1.61 *An $n \times n$ symmetric matrix A is*

1. *negative definite if and only if $(-1)^k |A_k| > 0$ for all $k \in \{1, \ldots, n\}$.*
2. *positive definite if and only if $|A_k| > 0$ for all $k \in \{1, \ldots, n\}$.*

Moreover, a positive semidefinite quadratic form A is positive definite if and only if $|A| \neq 0$, while a negative semidefinite quadratic form is negative definite if and only if $|A| \neq 0$.

Proof See Debreu (1952, Theorem 2, p.296). □

A natural conjecture is that this theorem would continue to hold if the words "negative definite" and "positive definite" were replaced with "negative semidefinite" and "positive semidefinite," respectively, provided the strict inequalities were replaced with weak ones. *This conjecture is false.* Consider the following example:

Example 1.62 Let

$$A = \begin{bmatrix} 0 & 0 \\ 0 & 1 \end{bmatrix} \quad \text{and} \quad B = \begin{bmatrix} 0 & 0 \\ 0 & -1 \end{bmatrix}.$$

Then, A and B are both symmetric matrices. Moreover, $|A_1| = |A_2| = |B_1| = |B_2| = 0$, so if the conjecture were true, both A and B would pass the test for positive semidefiniteness, as well as the test for negative semidefiniteness. However, for any $x \in \mathbb{R}^2$, $x'Ax = x_2^2$ and $x'Bx = -x_2^2$. Therefore, A is positive semidefinite but not negative semidefinite, while B is negative semidefinite, but not positive semidefinite.

$\square$

Roughly speaking, the feature driving this counterexample is that, in both the matrices A and B, the zero entries in all but the (2,2)-place of the matrix make the determinants of order 1 and 2 both zero. In particular, no play is given to the sign of the entry in the (2,2)-place, which is positive in one case, and negative in the other. On the other hand, an examination of the expressions $x'Ax$ and $x'Bx$ reveals that in both cases, the sign of the quadratic form is determined precisely by the sign of the (2,2)-entry.

This problem points to the need to expand the set of submatrices that we consider, if we are to obtain an analog of Theorem 1.61 for positive and negative semidefiniteness. Let an $n \times n$ symmetric matrix A be given, and let $\pi = (\pi_1, \ldots, \pi_n)$ be a permutation of the integers $\{1, \ldots, n\}$. Denote by A^{π} the symmetric $n \times n$ matrix obtained by applying the permutation π to both the rows and columns of A:

$$A^{\pi} = \begin{bmatrix} a_{\pi_1 \pi_1} & \cdots & a_{\pi_1 \pi_n} \\ \vdots & \ddots & \vdots \\ a_{\pi_n \pi_1} & \cdots & a_{\pi_n \pi_n} \end{bmatrix}.$$

For $k \in \{1, \ldots, n\}$, let A_k^{π} denote the $k \times k$ symmetric submatrix of A^{π} obtained by retaining only the first k rows and columns:

$$A_k^{\pi} = \begin{bmatrix} a_{\pi_1 \pi_1} & \cdots & a_{\pi_1 \pi_k} \\ \vdots & \ddots & \vdots \\ a_{\pi_k \pi_1} & \cdots & a_{\pi_k \pi_k} \end{bmatrix}.$$

Finally, let Π denote the set of all possible permutations of $\{1, \ldots, n\}$.

Theorem 1.63 *A symmetric n × n matrix A is*

1. *positive semidefinite if and only if $|A_k^\pi| \geq 0$ for all $k \in \{1, \ldots, n\}$ and for all $\pi \in \Pi$.*

2. *negative semidefinite if and only if $(-1)^k |A_k^\pi| \geq 0$ for all $k \in \{1, \ldots, n\}$ and for all $\pi \in \Pi$.*

Proof See Debreu (1952, Theorem 7, p.298). $\square$

One final remark is important. The symmetry assumption is crucial to the validity of these results. If it fails, a matrix A might pass all the tests for (say) positive semidefiniteness without actually being positive semidefinite. Here are two examples:

Example 1.64 Let

$$A = \begin{bmatrix} 1 & -3 \\ 0 & 1 \end{bmatrix}.$$

Note that $|A_1| = 1$, and $|A_2| = (1)(1) - (-3)(0) = 1$, so A passes the test for positive definiteness. However, A is not a symmetric matrix, and is not, in fact, positive definite: we have $x'Ax = x_1^2 + x_2^2 - 3x_1x_2$ which is negative for $x = (1, 1)$. $\square$

Example 1.65 Let

$$A = \begin{bmatrix} 0 & 1 \\ 0 & 0 \end{bmatrix}.$$

There are only two possible permutations of the set $\{1, 2\}$, namely, $\{1, 2\}$ itself, and $\{2, 1\}$. This gives rise to four different submatrices, whose determinants we have to consider:

$$[a_{11}], \quad [a_{22}], \quad \begin{bmatrix} a_{11} & a_{12} \\ a_{21} & a_{22} \end{bmatrix}, \quad \text{and} \quad \begin{bmatrix} a_{22} & a_{21} \\ a_{12} & a_{11} \end{bmatrix}.$$

It is an easy matter to check that the determinants of all four of these are nonnegative, so A passes the test for positive semidefiniteness. However, A is not positive semidefinite: we have $x'Ax = x_1x_2$, which could be positive or negative. $\square$

1.6 Some Important Results

This section brings together some results of importance for the study of optimization theory. Subsection 1.6.1 discusses a class of results called "separation theorems" for convex sets in $\mathbb{R}^n$. Subsection 1.6.2 summarizes some important consequences of assuming the continuity and/or differentiability of real-valued functions defined on $\mathbb{R}^n$. Finally, Subsection 1.6.3 outlines two fundamental results known as the Inverse Function Theorem and the Implicit Function Theorem.

1.6.1 Separation Theorems

Let $p \neq 0$ be a vector in $\mathbb{R}^n$, and let $a \in \mathbb{R}$. The set H defined by

$$H = \{x \in \mathbb{R}^n \mid p \cdot x = a\}$$

is called a *hyperplane* in $\mathbb{R}^n$, and will be denoted $H(p, a)$.

A hyperplane in $\mathbb{R}^2$, for example, is simply a straight line: if $p \in \mathbb{R}^2$ and $a \in \mathbb{R}$, the hyperplane $H(p, a)$ is simply the set of points (x_1, x_2) that satisfy $p_1 x_1 + p_2 x_2 = a$. Similarly, a hyperplane in $\mathbb{R}^3$ is a plane.

A set $\mathcal{D}$ in $\mathbb{R}^n$ is said to be bounded by a hyperplane $H(p, a)$ if $\mathcal{D}$ lies entirely on one side of $H(p, a)$, i.e., if either

$$p \cdot x \leq a, \quad \text{for all } x \in \mathcal{D},$$

or

$$p \cdot x \geq a, \quad \text{for all } x \in \mathcal{D}.$$

If $\mathcal{D}$ is bounded by $H(p, a)$ and $\mathcal{D} \cap H(p, a) \neq \emptyset$, then $H(p, a)$ is said to be a *supporting hyperplane* for $\mathcal{D}$.

Example 1.66 Let $\mathcal{D} = \{(x, y) \in \mathbb{R}_+^2 \mid xy \geq 1\}$. Let p be the vector $(1, 1)$, and let $a = 2$. Then, the hyperplane

$$H(p, a) = \{(x, y) \in \mathbb{R}^2 \mid x + y = 2\}$$

bounds $\mathcal{D}$: if $xy \geq 1$ and $x, y \geq 0$, then we must have $(x + y) \geq (x + x^{-1}) \geq 2$. In fact, $H(p, a)$ is a supporting hyperplane for $\mathcal{D}$ since $H(p, a)$ and $\mathcal{D}$ have the point $(x, y) = (1, 1)$ in common. $\square$

Two sets $\mathcal{D}$ and $\mathcal{E}$ in $\mathbb{R}^n$ are said to be *separated* by the hyperplane $H(p, a)$ in $\mathbb{R}^n$ if $\mathcal{D}$ and $\mathcal{E}$ lie on opposite sides of $H(p, a)$, i.e., if we have

$$p \cdot y \;\leq\; a, \quad \text{for all } y \in \mathcal{D}$$
$$p \cdot z \;\geq\; a, \quad \text{for all } z \in \mathcal{E}.$$

If $\mathcal{D}$ and $\mathcal{E}$ are separated by $H(p, a)$ and one of the sets (say, $\mathcal{E}$) consists of just a single point x, we will indulge in a slight abuse of terminology and say that $H(p, a)$ separates the set $\mathcal{D}$ and the point x.

A final definition is required before we state the main results of this section. Given a set $\mathcal{X} \subset \mathbb{R}^n$, the *closure of* $\mathcal{X}$, denoted $\mathcal{X}^o$, is defined to be the intersection of all closed sets containing $\mathcal{X}$, i.e., if

$$\Delta(\mathcal{X}) = \{\mathcal{Y} \subset \mathbb{R}^n \mid \mathcal{X} \subset \mathcal{Y}\},$$

then

$$\mathcal{X}^o = \cap_{\mathcal{Y} \in \Delta(X)}\mathcal{Y}.$$

Intuitively, the closure of $\mathcal{X}$ is the "smallest" closed set that contains $\mathcal{X}$. Since the arbitrary intersection of closed sets in closed, $\mathcal{X}^o$ is closed for any set $\mathcal{X}^o$. Note that $\mathcal{X}^o = \mathcal{X}$ if and only if $\mathcal{X}$ is itself closed.

The following results deal with the separation of convex sets by hyperplanes. They play a significant role in the study of inequality-constrained optimization problems under convexity restrictions (see Chapter 7).

Theorem 1.67 *Let $\mathcal{D}$ be a nonempty convex set in $\mathbb{R}^n$, and let x^* be a point in $\mathbb{R}^n$ that is not in $\mathcal{D}$. Then, there is a hyperplane $H(p, a)$ in $\mathbb{R}^n$ with $p \neq 0$ which separates $\mathcal{D}$ and x^*. We may, if we desire, choose p to also satisfy $\| p \| = 1$.*

Proof We first prove the result for the case where $\mathcal{D}$ is a closed set. Then, using this result, we establish the general case. The proof will make use of the Weierstrass Theorem (see Theorem 3.1 in Chapter 3), which states that if $\mathcal{K} \subset \mathbb{R}^n$ is compact, and $f : \mathcal{K} \to \mathbb{R}$ is a continuous function, then f has both a maximum and a minimum on $\mathcal{K}$, i.e., there exist points k' and k^* in $\mathcal{K}$ such that $f(k') \geq f(k) \geq f(k^*)$ for all $k \in \mathcal{K}$.

So suppose $\mathcal{D}$ is a nonempty, closed, convex set in $\mathbb{R}^n$, and $x^* \notin \mathcal{D}$. We claim that there exists $y^* \in \mathcal{D}$ such that

$$d(x^*, y^*) \leq d(x^*, y), \qquad y \in \mathcal{D}.$$

Indeed, this is an easy consequence of the Weierstrass Theorem. Let $\bar{B}(x^*, r)$ denote the closed ball with center x^* and radius r. Pick $r > 0$ sufficiently large so that the set $Y = \bar{B}(x^*, r) \cap \mathcal{D}$ is nonempty. Since $\bar{B}(x^*, r)$ and $\mathcal{D}$ are both closed sets, so is Y. Since $\bar{B}(x^*, r)$ is bounded, and $Y \subset \bar{B}(x^*, r)$, Y is also bounded. Therefore, Y is compact. The function $f : Y \to \mathbb{R}$ defined by $f(y) = d(x^*, y)$ is clearly continuous on Y, since the Euclidean metric d is continuous. Thus, by the Weierstrass Theorem, there exists a minimum y^* of f on $\mathcal{Y}$, i.e., there exists y^* in Y such that

$$d(x^*, y^*) \leq d(x^*, y), \qquad y \in \mathcal{Y}.$$

If $y \in \mathcal{D}$ and $y \notin \mathcal{Y}$, then we must have $y \notin \bar{B}(x^*, r)$, so $d(x^*, y) > r$. Therefore, we have established, as required, that

$$d(x^*, y^*) \leq d(x^*, y), \qquad y \in \mathcal{D}.$$

Now let $p = y^* - x^*$ and let $a = p \cdot y^*$. We will show that the hyperplane $H(p, a)$ separates $\mathcal{D}$ and x^*. To this end, note first that

$$\begin{aligned}
p \cdot x^* &= (y^* - x^*) \cdot x^* \\
&= -(y^* - x^*) \cdot (y^* - x^*) + y^* \cdot (y^* - x^*) \\
&= -\|p\|^2 + a \\
&< a.
\end{aligned}$$

To complete the proof of the theorem for the case where $\mathcal{D}$ is closed, we will now show that $p \cdot y \geq a$ for all $y \in \mathcal{D}$. Pick any $y \in \mathcal{D}$. Since $y^* \in \mathcal{D}$ and $\mathcal{D}$ is convex, it is the case that for all $\lambda \in (0, 1)$, the point $y(\lambda) = \lambda y + (1 - \lambda)y^*$ is also in $\mathcal{D}$. By definition of y^*, we then have

$$d(x^*, y^*) \leq d(x^*, y(\lambda)).$$

By expanding the terms in this inequality, we obtain

$$\begin{aligned}
\|x^* - y^*\|^2 &\leq \|x^* - y(\lambda)\|^2 \\
&= \|x^* - \lambda y - (1 - \lambda)y^*\|^2 \\
&= \|\lambda(x^* - y) + (1 - \lambda)(x^* - y^*)\|^2 \\
&= \lambda^2 \|x^* - y\|^2 + 2\lambda(1 - \lambda)(x^* - y) \cdot (x^* - y^*) \\
&\quad + (1 - \lambda)^2 \|x^* - y^*\|^2.
\end{aligned}$$

Rearranging terms, this gives us

$$0 \leq \lambda^2 \|x^* - y\|^2 + 2\lambda(1 - \lambda)(x^* - y) \cdot (x^* - y^*) - \lambda(2 - \lambda)\|x^* - y^*\|^2.$$

Dividing both sides by $\lambda > 0$, we get

$$0 \leq \lambda \|x^* - y\|^2 + 2(1 - \lambda)(x^* - y) \cdot (x^* - y^*) - (2 - \lambda)\|x^* - y^*\|^2.$$

Taking limits as $\lambda \to 0$, and dividing the result by 2, results in the inequality

$$\begin{aligned}
0 &\leq (x^* - y) \cdot (x^* - y^*) - \|x^* - y^*\|^2 \\
&= (x^* - y^*) \cdot (x^* - y - x^* + y^*) \\
&= (x^* - y^*) \cdot (y^* - y).
\end{aligned}$$

Rearranging terms once again, and using the definitional relations $p = (y^* - x^*)$ and $p \cdot y^* = a$, we finally obtain

$$p \cdot y = (y^* - x^*) \cdot y \geq (y^* - x^*) \cdot y^* = a.$$

Thus, we have shown that there is a hyperplane $H(p, a)$ that separates $\mathcal{D}$ and x^* when $\mathcal{D}$ is closed. It remains to be shown that we may, without loss of generality, take $\|p\|$ to be unity. Suppose $\|p\| \neq 1$. We will show the existence of $(\tilde{p}, \tilde{a})$ such that $H(\tilde{p}, \tilde{a})$ also separates $\mathcal{D}$ and x^*, and which further satisfies $\|\tilde{p}\| = 1$. Since $p \neq 0$, we have $\|p\| > 0$. Define $\tilde{p} = p/\|p\|$ and $\tilde{a} = a/\|p\|$. Then, we have $\|\tilde{p}\| = 1$ and

$$\tilde{p} \cdot x^* = \frac{p \cdot x^*}{\|p\|} < \frac{a}{\|p\|} = \tilde{a},$$

while for $y \in \mathcal{D}$, we also have

$$\tilde{p} \cdot y = \frac{p \cdot y}{\|p\|} \geq \frac{a}{\|p\|} = \tilde{a}.$$

Thus, $H(\tilde{p}, \tilde{a})$ also separates $\mathcal{D}$ and x^*, as required, and we have shown that the vector p in the separating hyperplane may be taken to have unit norm without loss of generality. This completes the proof of the theorem for the case where $\mathcal{D}$ is closed.

Now, suppose $\mathcal{D}$ is not closed. Let $\mathcal{D}^o$ denote the closure of $\mathcal{D}$. As the closure of a convex set, $\mathcal{D}^o$ is also convex. If $x^* \notin \mathcal{D}^o$, then by the arguments we have just given, there exists a hyperplane that separates the closed set $\mathcal{D}^o$ and x^*. Since $\mathcal{D} \subset \mathcal{D}^o$, this implies $\mathcal{D}$ and x^* can be separated.

Finally, suppose $x^* \notin \mathcal{D}$, but $x^* \in \mathcal{D}^o$. Then, for any $r > 0$, there must exist a point $x(r) \in B(x, r)$ such that $x(r) \notin \mathcal{D}^o$. Therefore, there exists $p(r) \in \mathbb{R}^n$ with $\|p(r)\| = 1$ such that

$$p(r) \cdot x^* \leq p(r) \cdot y, \qquad y \in \mathcal{D}^o.$$

Pick a sequence $\{r_k\}$ with $r_k > 0$ and $r_k \to 0$. For notational ease, let $p_k = p(r_k)$ and $x_k = x(r(k))$. Since $\|p_k\| = 1$ for all k, each p_k lies in the compact set

$$\mathcal{C} = \{z \in \mathbb{R}^n \mid \|z\| = 1\}.$$

Therefore, there is a subsequence $m(k)$ of k, and a point $p \in \mathcal{C}$ such that $p(m(k)) \to p$. Since we have

$$p_{m(k)} \cdot x_{m(k)} \leq p_{m(k)} \cdot y, \qquad y \in \mathcal{D}^o,$$

and the inner product is continuous, by taking limits as $k \to \infty$, we obtain

$$p \cdot x^* \leq p \cdot y, \qquad y \in \mathcal{D}^o.$$

Since $\mathcal{D} \subset \mathcal{D}^o$, this implies

$$p \cdot x^* \leq p \cdot y, \qquad y \in \mathcal{D}.$$

If we define $a = p \cdot x^*$, we have shown that the hyperplane $H(p, a)$ separates $\mathcal{D}$ and x^*. □

Theorem 1.68 *Let D and $\mathcal{E}$ be convex sets in $\mathbb{R}^n$ such that $D \cap \mathcal{E} = \emptyset$. Then, there exists a hyperplane $H(p, a)$ in $\mathbb{R}^n$ which separates D and $\mathcal{E}$. We may, if we desire, choose p to also satisfy $\|p\| = 1$.*

Proof Let $\mathcal{F} = D + (-\mathcal{E})$, where, in obvious notation, $-\mathcal{E}$ is the set

$$\{y \in \mathbb{R}^n \mid -y \in \mathcal{E}\}.$$

By Theorem 1.38, the convexity of D and $\mathcal{E}$ implies that $\mathcal{F}$ is also convex. We claim that $0 \notin \mathcal{F}$. If we had $0 \in \mathcal{F}$, then there would exist points $x \in D$ and $y \in \mathcal{E}$ such that $x - y = 0$. But this implies $x = y$, so $x \in D \cap \mathcal{E}$, which contradicts the assumption that $D \cap \mathcal{E}$ is empty. Therefore, $0 \notin \mathcal{F}$.

By Theorem 1.67, there exists $p \in \mathbb{R}^n$ such that

$$p \cdot 0 \leq p \cdot z, \qquad z \in \mathcal{F}.$$

This is the same thing as

$$p \cdot y \leq p \cdot x, \qquad x \in D, y \in \mathcal{E}.$$

It follows that $\sup_{y \in \mathcal{E}} p \cdot y \leq \inf_{x \in D} p \cdot x$. If $a \in [\sup_{y \in \mathcal{E}} p \cdot y, \inf_{x \in D} p \cdot x]$, the hyperplane $H(p, a)$ separates D and $\mathcal{E}$.

That p can also be chosen to satisfy $\|p\| = 1$ is established in the same way as in Theorem 1.67, and is left to the reader as an exercise. $\qquad\square$

1.6.2 The Intermediate and Mean Value Theorems

The Intermediate Value Theorem asserts that a continuous real function on an interval assumes all intermediate values on the interval. Figure 1.7 illustrates the result.

Theorem 1.69 (Intermediate Value Theorem) *Let $D = [a, b]$ be an interval in $\mathbb{R}$ and let $f: D \to \mathbb{R}$ be a continuous function. If $f(a) < f(b)$, and if c is a real number such that $f(a) < c < f(b)$, then there exists $x \in (a, b)$ such that $f(x) = c$. A similar statement holds if $f(a) > f(b)$.*

Proof See Rudin (1976, Theorem 4.23, p.93). $\qquad\square$

Remark It might appear at first glance that the intermediate value property actually *characterizes* continuous functions, i.e., that a function $f: [a, b] \to \mathbb{R}$ is continuous if and only if for any two points $x_1 < x_2$ and for any real number c lying between $f(x_1)$ and $f(x_2)$, there is $x \in (x_1, x_2)$ such that $f(x) = c$. The Intermediate Value

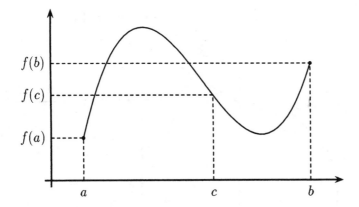

Fig. 1.7. The Intermediate Value Theorem

Theorem shows that the "only if" part is true. It is left to the reader to show that the converse, namely the "if" part, is actually false. (Hint: Use Example 1.51.) □

We have seen in Example 1.51 that a function may be differentiable everywhere, but may fail to be continuously differentiable. The following result (which may be regarded as an Intermediate Value Theorem for the derivative) states, however, that the derivative must still have some minimal continuity properties, viz., that the derivative must assume all intermediate values. In particular, it shows that the derivative f' of an everywhere differentiable function f cannot have jump discontinuities.

Theorem 1.70 (Intermediate Value Theorem for the Derivative) *Let $D = [a, b]$ be an interval in $\mathbb{R}$, and let $f: D \rightarrow \mathbb{R}$ be a function that is differentiable everywhere on D. If $f'(a) < f'(b)$, and if c is a real number such that $f'(a) < c < f'(b)$, then there is a point $x \in (a, b)$ such that $f'(x) = c$. A similar statement holds if $f'(a) > f'(b)$.*

Proof See Rudin (1976, Theorem 5.12, p.108). □

It is very important to emphasize that Theorem 1.70 does *not* assume that f is a C^1 function. Indeed, if f were C^1, the result would be a trivial consequence of the Intermediate Value Theorem, since the derivative f' would then be a continuous function on D.

The next result, the Mean Value Theorem, provides another property that the derivative must satisfy. A graphical representation of this result is provided in Figure 1.8. As with Theorem 1.70, it is assumed only that f is everywhere differentiable on its domain D, and not that it is C^1.

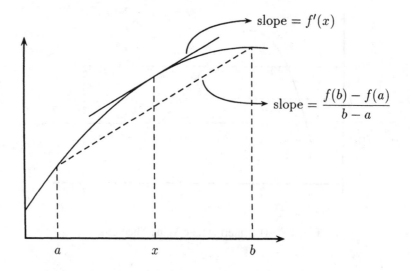

Fig. 1.8. The Mean Value Theorem

Theorem 1.71 (Mean Value Theorem) *Let $D = [a, b]$ be an interval in $\mathbb{R}$, and let $f : D \to \mathbb{R}$ be a continuous function. Suppose f is differentiable on (a, b). Then, there exists $x \in (a, b)$ such that*

$$f(b) - f(a) = (b - a) f'(x).$$

Proof   See Rudin (1976, Theorem 5.10, p.108).   □

The following generalization of the Mean Value Theorem is known as Taylor's Theorem. It may be regarded as showing that a many-times differentiable function can be approximated by a polynomial. The notation $f^{(k)}(z)$ is used in the statement of Taylor's Theorem to denote the k-th derivative of f evaluated at the point z. When $k = 0$, $f^{(k)}(x)$ should be interpreted simply as $f(x)$.

Theorem 1.72 (Taylor's Theorem) *Let $f : D \to \mathbb{R}$ be a C^m function, where D is an open interval in $\mathbb{R}$, and $m \geq 0$ is a nonnegative integer. Suppose also that $f^{m+1}(z)$ exists for every point $z \in D$. Then, for any $x, y \in D$, there is $z \in (x, y)$ such that*

$$f(y) = \sum_{k=0}^{m} \left(\frac{f^{(k)}(x)(y - x)^k}{k!} \right) + \frac{f^{m+1}(z)(y - x)^{m+1}}{(m + 1)!}.$$

Proof   See Rudin (1976, Theorem 5.15, p.110).   □

Each of the results stated in this subsection, with the obvious exception of the Intermediate Value Theorem for the Derivative, also has an n-dimensional version. We state these versions here, deriving their proofs as consequences of the corresponding result in $\mathbb{R}$.

Theorem 1.73 (The Intermediate Value Theorem in $\mathbb{R}^n$) *Let $D \subset \mathbb{R}^n$ be a convex set, and let $f: D \to \mathbb{R}$ be continuous on D. Suppose that a and b are points in D such that $f(a) < f(b)$. Then, for any c such that $f(a) < c < f(b)$, there is $\hat{\lambda} \in (0, 1)$ such that $f((1 - \hat{\lambda})a + \hat{\lambda}b) = c$.*

Proof We derive this result as a consequence of the Intermediate Value Theorem in $\mathbb{R}$. Let $g: [0, 1] \to \mathbb{R}$ be defined by $g(\lambda) = f((1 - \lambda)a + \lambda b)$, $\lambda \in [0, 1]$. Since f is a continuous function, g is evidently continuous on $[0,1]$. Moreover, $g(0) = f(a)$ and $g(1) = f(b)$, so $g(0) < c < g(1)$. By the Intermediate Value Theorem in $\mathbb{R}$, there exists $\hat{\lambda} \in (0, 1)$ such that $g(\hat{\lambda}) = c$. Since $g(\hat{\lambda}) = f((1 - \hat{\lambda})a + \hat{\lambda}b)$, we are done. $\qquad\qquad\square$

An n-dimensional version of the Mean Value Theorem is similarly established:

Theorem 1.74 (The Mean Value Theorem in $\mathbb{R}^n$) *Let $D \subset \mathbb{R}^n$ be open and convex, and let $f: S \to \mathbb{R}$ be a function that is differentiable everywhere on D. Then, for any $a, b \in D$, there is $\hat{\lambda} \in (0, 1)$ such that*

$$f(b) - f(a) = Df((1 - \hat{\lambda})a + \hat{\lambda}b) \cdot (b - a).$$

Proof For notational ease, let $z(\lambda) = (1 - \lambda)a + \lambda b$. Define $g: [0, 1] \to \mathbb{R}$ by $g(\lambda) = f(z(\lambda))$ for $\lambda \in [0, 1]$. Note that $g(0) = f(a)$ and $g(1) = f(b)$. Since f is everywhere differentiable by hypothesis, it follows that g is differentiable at all $\lambda \in [0, 1]$, and in fact, $g'(\lambda) = Df(z(\lambda)) \cdot (b - a)$. By the Mean Value Theorem for functions of one variable, therefore, there is $\lambda' \in (0, 1)$ such that

$$g(1) - g(0) = g'(\lambda')(1 - 0) = g'(\lambda').$$

Substituting for g in terms of f, this is precisely the statement that

$$f(b) - f(a) = Df(z(\lambda')) \cdot (b - a).$$

The theorem is proved. $\qquad\qquad\square$

Finally, we turn to Taylor's Theorem in $\mathbb{R}^n$. A complete statement of this result requires some new notation, and is also irrelevant for the remainder of this book. We confine ourselves, therefore, to stating two special cases that are useful for our purposes.

Theorem 1.75 (Taylor's Theorem in $\mathbb{R}^n$) *Let $f \colon D \to \mathbb{R}$, where D is an open set in $\mathbb{R}^n$. If f is C^1 on D, then it is the case that for any $x, y \in D$, we have*

$$f(y) = f(x) + Df(x)(y - x) + R_1(x, y),$$

where the remainder term $R_1(x, y)$ has the property that

$$\lim_{y \to x} \left(\frac{R_1(x, y)}{\|x - y\|} \right) = 0.$$

If f is C^2, this statement can be strengthened to

$$f(y) = f(x) + Df(x)(y - x) + \frac{1}{2}(y - x)' D^2 f(x)(y - x) + R_2(x, y),$$

where the remainder term $R_2(x, y)$ has the property that

$$\lim_{y \to x} \left(\frac{R_2(x, y)}{\|x - y\|^2} \right) = 0.$$

Proof Fix any $x \in D$, and define the function $F(\cdot)$ on D by

$$F(y) = f(x) + Df(x) \cdot (y - x).$$

Let $h(y) = f(y) - F(y)$. Since f and F are C^1, so is h. Note that $h(x) = Dh(x) = 0$. The first-part of the theorem will be proved if we show that

$$\frac{h(y)}{\|y - x\|} \to 0 \text{ as } y \to x,$$

or, equivalently, if we show that for any $\epsilon > 0$, there is $\delta > 0$ such that

$$\|y - x\| < \delta \text{ implies } |h(y)| < \epsilon \|x - y\|.$$

So let $\epsilon > 0$ be given. By the continuity of h and Dh, there is $\delta > 0$ such that

$$|y - x| < \delta \text{ implies } |h(y)| < \epsilon \text{ and } \|Dh(y)\| < \epsilon.$$

Fix any y satisfying $|y - x| < \delta$. Define a function g on [0,1] by

$$g(t) = h[(1 - t)x + ty].^5$$

Then, $g(0) = h(x) = 0$. Moreover, g is C^1 with $g'(t) = Dh[(1 - t)x + ty](y - x)$.

Now note that $|(1 - t)x + ty - x| = t|(y - x)| < \delta$ for all $t \in [0, 1]$, since $|x - y| < \delta$. Therefore, $\|Dh[(1 - t)x + ty]\| < \epsilon$ for all $t \in [0, 1]$, and it follows that $|g'(t)| \leq \epsilon \|y - x\|$ for all $t \in [0, 1]$.

---

[5] We are implicitly assuming here that $g(\cdot)$ is well-defined, i.e., that $(1 - t)x + ty \in D$ for all $t \in [0, 1]$. This assumption is without loss of generality. To see this, note that since D is open and $x \in D$, there is $r > 0$ such that $B(x, r) \subset D$. By shrinking δ if need be, we can ensure that $\delta < r$. Then it is evidently the case that for all y satisfying $\|y - x\| < \delta$, the line segment joining y and x (i.e., the set of points $(1 - t)x + ty$ for $t \in [0, 1]$) is completely contained in D.

By Taylor's Theorem in $\mathbb{R}$, there is $t^* \in (0, 1)$ such that

$$g(1) = g(0) + g'(t^*)(1 - 0) = g'(t^*).$$

Therefore,

$$|h(y)| = |g(1)| = |g'(t^*)| \leq \epsilon |y - x|.$$

Since y was an arbitrary point satisfying $|y - x| < \delta$, the first part of the theorem is proved.

The second part may be established analogously. The details are left as an exercise. $\quad\square$

1.6.3 The Inverse and Implicit Function Theorems

We now state two results of much importance especially for "comparative statics" exercises. The second of these results (the Implicit Function Theorem) also plays a central role in proving Lagrange's Theorem on the first-order conditions for equality-constrained optimization problems (see Chapter 5 below). Some new terminology is, unfortunately, required first.

Given a function $f: A \to B$, we say that the function f maps A *onto* B, if for any $b \in B$, there is some $a \in A$ such that $f(a) = b$. We say that f is a *one-to-one* function if for any $b \in B$, there is at most one $a \in A$ such that $f(a) = b$. If $f: A \to B$ is both one-to-one and onto, then it is easy to see that there is a (*unique*) function $g: B \to A$ such that $f(g(b)) = b$ for all $b \in B$. (Note that we also have $g(f(a)) = a$ for all $a \in A$.) The function g is called the *inverse function* of f.

Theorem 1.76 (Inverse Function Theorem) *Let $f: S \to \mathbb{R}^n$ be a C^1 function, where $S \subset \mathbb{R}^n$ is open. Suppose there is a point $y \in S$ such that the $n \times n$ matrix $Df(y)$ is invertible. Let $x = f(y)$. Then:*

1. *There are open sets U and V in $\mathbb{R}^n$ such that $x \in U$, $y \in V$, f is one-to-one on V, and $f(V) = U$.*
2. *The inverse function $g: U \to V$ of f is a C^1 function on U, whose derivative at any point $\hat{x} \in U$ satisfies*

$$Dg(\hat{x}) = \left(Df(\hat{y})\right)^{-1}, \quad \text{where} \quad f(\hat{y}) = x.$$

Proof See Rudin (1976, Theorem 9.24, p.221). $\quad\square$

Turning now to the Implicit Function Theorem, the question this result addresses may be motivated by a simple example. Let $S = \mathbb{R}^2_{++}$, and let $f: S \to \mathbb{R}$ be defined by $f(x, y) = xy$. Pick any point $(\bar{x}, \bar{y}) \in S$, and consider the "level set"

$$C(\bar{x}, \bar{y}) = \{(x, y) \in S \mid f(x, y) = f(\bar{x}, \bar{y})\}.$$

If we now define the function $h: \mathbb{R}_{++} \to \mathbb{R}$ by $h(y) = f(\bar{x}, \bar{y})/y$, we have

$$f(h(y), y) \equiv f(\bar{x}, \bar{y}), \quad y \in \mathbb{R}_{++}.$$

Thus, the values of the x-variable on the level set $C(\bar{x}, \bar{y})$ can be represented explicitly in terms of the values of the y-variable on this set, through the function h.

In general, an exact form for the original function f may not be specified—for instance, we may only know that f is an increasing C^1 function on $\mathbb{R}^2$—so we may not be able to solve for h explicitly. The question arises whether at least an *implicit* representation of the function h would exist in such a case.

The Implicit Function Theorem studies this problem in a general setting. That is, it looks at level sets of functions f from $S \subset \mathbb{R}^m$ to $\mathbb{R}^k$, where $m > k$, and asks when the values of some of the variables in the domain can be represented in terms of the others, on a given level set. Under very general conditions, it proves that at least a *local* representation is possible.

The statement of the theorem requires a little more notation. Given integers $m \geq 1$ and $n \geq 1$, let a typical point in $\mathbb{R}^{m+n}$ be denoted by (x, y), where $x \in \mathbb{R}^m$ and $y \in \mathbb{R}^n$. For a C^1 function F mapping some subset of $\mathbb{R}^{m+n}$ into $\mathbb{R}^n$, let $DF_y(x, y)$ denote that portion of the derivative matrix $DF(x, y)$ corresponding to the last n variables. Note that $DF_y(x, y)$ is an $n \times n$ matrix. $DF_x(x, y)$ is defined similarly.

Theorem 1.77 (Implicit Function Theorem) *Let $F: S \subset \mathbb{R}^{m+n} \to \mathbb{R}^n$ be a C^1 function, where S is open. Let (x^*, y^*) be a point in S such that $DF_y(x^*, y^*)$ is invertible, and let $F(x^*, y^*) = c$. Then, there is a neighborhood $U \subset \mathbb{R}^m$ of x^* and a C^1 function $g: U \to \mathbb{R}^n$ such that (i) $(x, g(x)) \in S$ for all $x \in U$, (ii) $g(x^*) = y^*$, and (iii) $F(x, g(x)) \equiv c$ for all $x \in U$. The derivative of g at any $x \in U$ may be obtained from the chain rule:*

$$Dg(x) = (DF_y(x, y))^{-1} \cdot DF_x(x, y).$$

Proof See Rudin (1976, Theorem 9.28, p.224). □

1.7 Exercises

1. Show that equality obtains in the Cauchy–Schwartz inequality if and only if the vectors x and y are collinear (i.e., either $x = ay$ for some $a \in \mathbb{R}$ or $y = bx$ for some $b \in \mathbb{R}$). (Note: This is a difficult question. Prove the result for *unit vectors*

first, i.e., for vectors x and y which satisfy $x \cdot x = y \cdot y = 1$. Then reduce the general case to this one.)

2. Suppose a real-valued sequence $\{x_k\}$ satisfies $x_k > 0$ for all k, and x is any limit point of the sequence $\{x_k\}$. Under what further conditions on $\{x_k\}$ can we assert that $x > 0$?

3. Let $\{x_k\}$, $\{y_k\}$ be sequences in $\mathbb{R}^n$ such that $x_k \to x$ and $y_k \to y$. For each k, let $z_k = x_k + y_k$, and let $w_k = x_k \cdot y_k$. Show that $z_k \to (x + y)$ and $w_k \to x \cdot y$.

4. Give an example of a sequence $\{x_k\}$ which has exactly n limit points, where $n \in \{1, 2, \ldots\}$.

5. Give an example of a nonconvergent real-valued sequence $\{x_k\}$ such that $\{x_k\}$ contains at least one convergent subsequence, and every convergent subsequence of $\{x_k\}$ converges to the limit $x = 0$.

6. Let $x, y \in \mathbb{R}^n$. Show that for any sequences $\{x_k\}$, $\{y_k\}$ such that $x_k \to x$ and $y_k \to y$, we have $\lim_{k \to \infty} d(x_k, y_k) = d(x, y)$, where d is the Euclidean metric on $\mathbb{R}^n$.

7. Provide a formal proof that if a sequence $\{x_k\}$ converges to a limit x, then every subsequence of $\{x_k\}$ also converges to x.

8. Show that $\lim \sup_k x_k = -\lim \inf_k (-x_k)$ for any sequence $\{x_k\}$ in $\mathbb{R}$.

9. Given two sequences $\{a_k\}$ and $\{b_k\}$ in $\mathbb{R}$, show that

$$\lim_{k} \sup (a_k + b_k) \leq \lim_{k} \sup a_k + \lim_{k} \sup b_k$$

$$\lim_{k} \inf (a_k + b_k) \geq \lim_{k} \inf a_k + \lim_{k} \inf b_k.$$

Give examples where the strict inequalities obtain.

10. Let $\{a_k\}$ and $\{b_k\}$ be two real-valued sequences such that $a_k, b_k \geq 0$ for all k. What is the relationship between $\lim \sup_k (a_k b_k)$ and $(\lim \sup_k a_k)(\lim \sup_k b_k)$? What if $a_k, b_k \leq 0$ for all k?

11. Let $\{x_k\}$ be a real-valued sequence, and $\alpha \in \mathbb{R}$. When is it the case that $\lim \sup_k (\alpha a_k) = \alpha \lim \sup_k a_k$?

12. In each of the following cases, give an example of a real-valued sequence $\{x_k\}$ meeting the stated properties:

   (a) $\lim \sup_k x_k = \lim \inf_k x_k = +\infty$.
   (b) $\lim \sup_k x_k = +\infty$ and $\lim \inf_k x_k = -\infty$.
   (c) $\lim \sup_k x_k = +\infty$ and $\lim \inf_k x_k = 0$.
   (d) $\lim \sup_k x_k = 0$ and $\lim \inf_k x_k = -\infty$.

   or show that no such sequence can exist.

13. Find the lim sup and the lim inf of each of the following sequences:

    (a) $x_k = (-1)^k$, $k = 1, 2, \ldots$
    (b) $x_k = k(-1)^k$, $k = 1, 2, \ldots$
    (c) $x_k = (-1)^k + 1/k$, $k = 1, 2, \ldots$
    (d) $x_k = 1$ if k is odd, and $x_k = -k/2$ if k is even, $k = 1, 2, \ldots$

14. Find the lim sup and lim inf of the following sequence: $1,1,2,1,2,3,1,2,3,4, \ldots$

15. Let $\{x_k\}$ be a bounded sequence of real numbers. Let $S \subset \mathbb{R}$ be the set which consists only of members of the sequence $\{x_k\}$, i.e., $x \in S$ if and only if $x = x_k$ for some k. What is the relationship between $\limsup_k x_k$ and $\sup S$?

16. Find the supremum, infimum, maximum, and minimum of the set X in each of the following cases:

    (a) $X = \{x \in [0, 1] \mid x \text{ is irrational}\}$.
    (b) $X = \{x \mid x = 1/n, \ n = 1, 2, \ldots\}$.
    (c) $X = \{x \mid x = 1 - 1/n, \ n = 1, 2, \ldots\}$.
    (d) $X = \{x \in [0, \pi] \mid \sin x > 1/2\}$.

17. Prove that the "closed interval" $[0,1]$ is, in fact, a closed set, and that the "open interval" $(0,1)$ is, in fact, an open set. Prove also that $[0,1)$ and $(0,1]$ are neither open nor closed.

18. Consider the set $\mathbb{Z}_+ = \{0, 1, 2, \ldots\}$ of nonnegative integers viewed as a subset of $\mathbb{R}$. Is it closed, open, or neither?

19. Is $\mathbb{R}^n$ viewed as a subset of itself an open set? Is it a closed set? Explain your answer.

20. Give an example of an open set in $\mathbb{R}$ that is not convex.

21. Give an example of a compact set in $\mathbb{R}$ that is not convex.

22. A set $X \subset \mathbb{R}^n$ is said to be *connected* if there do not exist two nonempty open sets X_1 and X_2 such that $X_1 \cap X_2 = \emptyset$ and $X_1 \cup X_2 \supset X$. Show that every connected set in $\mathbb{R}$ must be convex. Give an example of a connected set in $\mathbb{R}^2$ that is not convex.

23. Let $X \subset \mathbb{R}$ be an open set. Show that if a finite number of points $\{x_1, \ldots, x_l\}$ are removed from X, the remaining set is still open. Is this true if we remove a countable infinity of points $\{x_1, x_2, \ldots\}$ from X?

24. Let A_n be the interval $(0, 1/n)$. Provide a formal proof that $\cap_{n=1}^{\infty} A_n$ is empty.

25. Let $B \subset \mathbb{R}^2$ be as follows:

$$B = \left\{ (x, y) \in \mathbb{R}^2 : y = \sin \frac{1}{x}, \ x > 0\} \cup \{(0, 0) \right\}.$$

Is B closed? open? bounded? compact?

26. Let $A \subset \mathbb{R}^2$ be defined as

$$A = \{(x, y) \in \mathbb{R}^2 : 1 < x < 2 \text{ and } y = x\}.$$

Is A open? bounded? compact?

27. Let $A = [-1, 0)$ and $B = (0, 1]$. Examine whether each of the following statements is true or false.

(a) $A \cup B$ is compact;
(b) $A + B = \{x + y : x \in A, \ y \in B\}$ is compact;
(c) $A \cap B$ is compact.

28. Let $A \subset \mathbb{R}^n$ be given. Show that there is a smallest closed set, $\overline{A}$, which contains A, i.e., $\overline{A}$ is a closed set containing A and if C is a closed set containing A then $A \subseteq \overline{A} \subseteq C$. The set $\overline{A}$ is called the *closure* of A.

29. Let $A \subset \mathbb{R}^2$. Let $B \subset \mathbb{R}$ be defined by

$$B = \{x \in \mathbb{R} \mid \text{there is } y \in \mathbb{R} \text{ such that } (x, y) \in A\}.$$

B is called the projection of A onto the x-axis.

(a) If A is a closed set in $\mathbb{R}^2$, is B necessarily a closed set in $\mathbb{R}$?
(b) If A is an open set in $\mathbb{R}^2$, is B necessarily an open set in $\mathbb{R}$?

30. Given two subsets A and B of $\mathbb{R}$, recall that their *Cartesian product $A \times B \subset \mathbb{R}^2$* is defined as

$$A \times B = \{(a, b) \mid a \in A, b \in B\}.$$

Give an example of a set $X \subset \mathbb{R}^2$ that *cannot* be expressed as the Cartesian product of sets $A, B \subset \mathbb{R}$.

31. Give an example of an infinite collection of compact sets whose union is bounded but not compact.

32. Let $A = \{1, 1/2, 1/3, \ldots, 1/n, \ldots\} \cup \{0\}$. Is A closed? Is it compact?

33. Give an example of a countably infinite collection of bounded sets whose union is bounded and an example where the union is unbounded.

34. Say that a set S in $\mathbb{R}^n$ has the *finite intersection property* if the following condition holds: given an arbitrary collection of *closed* sets $(S_\alpha)_{\alpha \in A}$ in $\mathbb{R}^n$, it is the case that whenever every finite subcollection $(S_\alpha)_{\alpha \in F}$ has nonempty intersection with S, then the entire collection has nonempty intersection with S, i.e., whenever

$$\cap_{\alpha \in F} S_\alpha \cap S \neq \emptyset$$

for every finite subset F of A, then we also have

$$\cap_{\alpha \in A} S_\alpha \cap S \neq \emptyset.$$

Show that the finite intersection property is *equivalent* to compactness, i.e., that a set S is compact if and only if it has the finite intersection property.

35. Show that a set $S \subset \mathbb{R}$ is convex if, and only if, it is an interval, i.e., it is of the form $[a, b]$, $[a, b)$, $(a, b]$, or (a, b). (We do not preclude the possibility that $a = -\infty$ and/or $b = +\infty$.)

36. Show that if $S \subset \mathbb{R}^n$ is convex (i.e., the convex combination of any two points in S is also in S), then the convex combination of any finite collection of points from S is also in S.

37. Give an example of a bounded and convex set $S \subset \mathbb{R}$ such that $\sup S \in S$ but $\inf S \notin S$.

38. Let A and B be 2×2 matrices. Identify general conditions on the entries (a_{ij}) and (b_{ij}) under which $AB = BA$. Using these conditions, find a numerical example of such matrices A and B.

39. Let A be a given $n \times n$ nonsingular matrix, and let αA be the matrix whose (i, j)-th element is $\alpha a_{ij}, i, j = 1, \ldots, n$. What is the relationship, if any, between $(\alpha A)^{-1}$ and A^{-1}?

40. Find the rank of each of the following matrices by finding the size of the largest submatrix which has a nonzero determinant:

$$A = \begin{bmatrix} 3 & 6 & 4 & 8 \\ 2 & 7 & 1 & 9 \\ 4 & 2 & 5 & 0 \end{bmatrix} \quad B = \begin{bmatrix} 18 & 2 \\ 7 & -4 \\ 6 & 11 \end{bmatrix} \quad C = \begin{bmatrix} -5 & 8 & 11 & 0 \\ 13 & 3 & 0 & 2 \\ 10 & 0 & -6 & 2 \end{bmatrix}.$$

41. Using the first method described in subsection 1.3.6, find the determinant of each of the following three matrices. Verify that you get the same answers if you use the second method.

$$A = \begin{bmatrix} -1 & 3 & 2 \\ 6 & -2 & 3 \\ 7 & 10 & 0 \end{bmatrix} \quad B = \begin{bmatrix} 13 & 4 & 1 \\ 0 & 4 & 1 \\ -7 & 2 & 3 \end{bmatrix} \quad C = \begin{bmatrix} -4 & 4 & 12 \\ 3 & -3 & -9 \\ 8 & 2 & 6 \end{bmatrix}.$$

42. Find the inverse of the following matrices:

$$A = \begin{bmatrix} 6 & 13 & 4 \\ 8 & 15 & 2 \\ 7 & 14 & 3 \end{bmatrix} \quad B = \begin{bmatrix} 15 & 24 & 12 \\ 10 & 16 & 10 \\ 2 & 3 & 1 \end{bmatrix} \quad C = \begin{bmatrix} 1 & 0 & 2 \\ 0 & 8 & 3 \\ 11 & 4 & 0 \end{bmatrix}.$$

43. Let S be a finite set. Show that any function $f: S \to \mathbb{R}^n$ is continuous on S. What if S is countably infinite?

44. Let f be a function from $\mathbb{R}^n$ to $\mathbb{R}^m$. For $B \subset \mathbb{R}^m$, define $f^{-1}(B)$ by $f^{-1}(B) = \{x \in \mathbb{R}^n \mid f(x) \in B\}$. Show that for any subsets A_1, A_2 of $\mathbb{R}^n$ and B_1, B_2 of $\mathbb{R}^m$:

    (a) $f(A_1 \cap A_2) \subseteq f(A_1) \cap f(A_2)$.
    (b) $f(A_1 \cup A_2) = f(A_1) \cup f(A_2)$.
    (c) $f^{-1}(B_1 \cup B_2) = f^{-1}(B_1) \cup f^{-1}(B_2)$.
    (d) $f^{-1}(B_1^c) = [f^{-1}(B_1)]^c$.
    (e) $f^{-1}(B_1 \cap B_2) = f^{-1}(B_1) \cap f^{-1}(B_2)$.
    (f) $A_1 \subseteq f^{-1}(f(A_1))$.
    (g) $f(f^{-1}(B_1)) \subseteq B_1$.

45. Let $f : \mathbb{R}^n \to \mathbb{R}$ be continuous at a point $p \in \mathbb{R}^n$. Assume $f(p) > 0$. Show that there is an open ball $B \subseteq \mathbb{R}^n$ such that $p \in B$, and for all $x \in B$, we have $f(x) > 0$.

46. Suppose $f: \mathbb{R}^n \to \mathbb{R}$ is a continuous function. Show that the set

$$\{x \in \mathbb{R}^n \mid f(x) = 0\}$$

is a closed set.

47. Let $f: \mathbb{R} \to \mathbb{R}$ be defined by

$$f(x) = \begin{cases} 1 & \text{if } 0 \le x \le 1 \\ 0 & \text{otherwise} . \end{cases}$$

Find an open set O such that $f^{-1}(O)$ is not open and find a closed set C such that $f^{-1}(C)$ is not closed.

48. Give an example of a function $f: \mathbb{R} \to \mathbb{R}$ which is continuous at exactly two points (say, at 0 and 1), or show that no such function can exist.

49. Show that it is possible for two functions $f: \mathbb{R} \to \mathbb{R}$ and $g: \mathbb{R} \to \mathbb{R}$ to be discontinuous, but for their product $f \cdot g$ to be continuous. What about their composition $f \circ g$?

50. Let $f: \mathbb{R} \to \mathbb{R}$ be a function which satisfies

$$f(x + y) = f(x)f(y) \quad \text{for all } x, y \in \mathbb{R}.$$

Show that if f is continuous at $x = 0$, then it is continuous at every point of $\mathbb{R}$. Also show that if f vanishes at a single point of $\mathbb{R}$, then f vanishes at every point of $\mathbb{R}$.

51. Let $f : \mathbb{R}_+ \to \mathbb{R}$ be defined by

$$f(x) = \begin{cases} 0, & x = 0 \\ x \sin(1/x), & x \ne 0. \end{cases}$$

Show that f is continuous at 0.

52. Let D be the unit square $[0, 1] \times [0, 1]$ in $\mathbb{R}^2$. For $(s, t) \in D$, let $f(s, t)$ be defined by

$$f(s, 0) = 0, \quad \text{for all } s \in [0, 1],$$

and for $t > 0$,

$$f(s, t) = \begin{cases} \dfrac{2s}{t} & s \in \left[0, \dfrac{t}{2}\right] \\[2mm] 2 - \dfrac{2s}{t} & s \in \left(\dfrac{t}{2}, t\right] \\[2mm] 0 & s \in (t, 1]. \end{cases}$$

(Drawing a picture of f for a fixed t will help.) Show that f is a *separately continuous* function, i.e., for each fixed value of t, f is continuous as a function of s, and for each fixed value of s, f is continuous in t. Show also that f is not *jointly continuous* in s and t, i.e., show that there exists a point $(s, t) \in D$ and a sequence (s_n, t_n) in D converging to (s, t) such that $\lim_{n \to \infty} f(s_n, t_n) \neq f(s, t)$.

53. Let $f : \mathbb{R} \to \mathbb{R}$ be defined as

$$f(x) = \begin{cases} x & \text{if } x \text{ is irrational} \\ 1 - x & \text{if } x \text{ is rational}. \end{cases}$$

Show that f is continuous at $1/2$ but discontinuous elsewhere.

54. Let $f : \mathbb{R}^n \to \mathbb{R}$ and $g : \mathbb{R} \to \mathbb{R}$ be continuous functions. Define $h : \mathbb{R}^n \to \mathbb{R}$ by $h(x) = g[f(x)]$. Show that h is continuous. Is it possible for h to be continuous even if f and g are not?

55. Show that if a function $f : \mathbb{R} \to \mathbb{R}$ satisfies

$$|f(x) - f(y)| \leq M(|x - y|)^a$$

for some fixed $M > 0$ and $a > 1$, then f is a constant function, i.e., $f(x)$ is identically equal to some real number b at all $x \in \mathbb{R}$.

56. Let $f : \mathbb{R}^2 \to \mathbb{R}$ be defined by $f(0, 0) = 0$, and for $(x, y) \neq (0, 0)$,

$$f(x, y) = \frac{xy}{\sqrt{x^2 + y^2}}.$$

Show that the two-sided directional derivative of f evaluated at $(x, y) = (0, 0)$ exists in *all* directions $h \in \mathbb{R}^2$, but that f is not differentiable at $(0, 0)$.

57. Let $f: \mathbb{R}^2 \to \mathbb{R}$ be defined by $f(0, 0) = 0$, and for $(x, y) \neq (0, 0)$,

$$f(x, y) = \frac{xy(x^2 - y^2)}{x^2 + y^2}.$$

Show that the cross-partials $\partial^2 f(x, y)/\partial x \partial y$ and $\partial^2 f(x, y)/\partial y \partial x$ exist at all $(x, y) \in \mathbb{R}^2$, but that these partials are not continuous at $(0, 0)$. Show also that

$$\frac{\partial^2 f}{\partial x \partial y}(0, 0) \neq \frac{\partial^2 f}{\partial y \partial x}(0, 0).$$

58. Show that an $n \times n$ symmetric matrix A is a positive definite matrix if and only if $-A$ is a negative definite matrix. ($-A$ refers to the matrix whose (i, j)-th entry is $-a_{ij}$.)

59. Prove the following statement or provide a counterexample to show it is false: if A is a positive definite matrix, then A^{-1} is a negative definite matrix.

60. Give an example of matrices A and B which are each negative semidefinite, but not negative definite, and which are such that $A + B$ is negative definite.

61. Is it possible for a symmetric matrix A to be simultaneously negative semidefinite *and* positive semidefinite? If yes, give an example. If not, provide a proof.

62. Examine the definiteness or semidefiniteness of the following quadratic forms:

$$A = \begin{bmatrix} 0 & 0 & 1 \\ 0 & 1 & 0 \\ 1 & 0 & 0 \end{bmatrix} \qquad A = \begin{bmatrix} 1 & 2 & 3 \\ 2 & 4 & 6 \\ 3 & 6 & 0 \end{bmatrix}$$

$$A = \begin{bmatrix} 1 & 0 & 1 \\ 0 & 1 & 0 \\ 1 & 0 & 1 \end{bmatrix} \qquad A = \begin{bmatrix} -1 & 2 & -1 \\ 2 & -4 & 2 \\ -1 & 2 & -1 \end{bmatrix}.$$

63. Find the hessians $D^2 f$ of each of the following functions. Evaluate the hessians at the specified points, and examine if the hessian is positive definite, negative definite, positive semidefinite, negative semidefinite, or indefinite:

   (a) $f: \mathbb{R}^2 \to \mathbb{R}$, $f(x) = x_1^2 + \sqrt{x_2}$, at $x = (1, 1)$.
   (b) $f: \mathbb{R}^2 \to \mathbb{R}$, $f(x) = (x_1 x_2)^{1/2}$, at an arbitrary point $x \in \mathbb{R}^2_{++}$.
   (c) $f: \mathbb{R}^2 \to \mathbb{R}$, $f(x) = (x_1 x_2)^2$, at an arbitrary point $x \in \mathbb{R}^2_{++}$.
   (d) $f: \mathbb{R}^3_+ \to \mathbb{R}$, $f(x) = \sqrt{x_1} + \sqrt{x_2} + \sqrt{x_3}$, at $x = (2, 2, 2)$.
   (e) $f: \mathbb{R}^3_+ \to \mathbb{R}$, $f(x) = \sqrt{x_1 x_2 x_3}$, at $x = (2, 2, 2)$.
   (f) $f: \mathbb{R}^3_+ \to \mathbb{R}$, $f(x) = x_1 x_2 + x_2 x_3 + x_3 x_1$, at $x = (1, 1, 1)$.
   (g) $f: \mathbb{R}^3_+ \to \mathbb{R}$, $f(x) = ax_1 + bx_2 + cx_3$ for some constants $a, b, c \in \mathbb{R}$, at $x = (2, 2, 2)$.

2

Optimization in $\mathbb{R}^n$

This chapter constitutes the starting point of our investigation into optimization theory. Sections 2.1 and 2.2 introduce the notation we use to represent abstract optimization problems and their solutions. Section 2.3 then describes a number of examples of optimization problems drawn from economics and its allied disciplines, which are invoked at various points throughout the book to illustrate the use of the techniques we develop to identify and characterize solutions to optimization problems. Finally, Sections 2.4 and 2.5 describe the chief questions of interest that we examine over the next several chapters, and provide a roadmap for the rest of the book.

2.1 Optimization Problems in $\mathbb{R}^n$

An *optimization problem in $\mathbb{R}^n$*, or simply an *optimization problem*, is one where the values of a given function $f \colon \mathbb{R}^n \to \mathbb{R}$ are to be maximized or minimized over a given set $\mathcal{D} \subset \mathbb{R}^n$. The function f is called the *objective function*, and the set $\mathcal{D}$ the *constraint set*. Notationally, we will represent these problems by

$$\text{Maximize } f(x) \text{ subject to } x \in \mathcal{D},$$

and

$$\text{Minimize } f(x) \text{ subject to } x \in \mathcal{D},$$

respectively. Alternatively, and more compactly, we shall also write

$$\max\{f(x) \mid x \in \mathcal{D}\},$$

and

$$\min\{f(x) \mid x \in \mathcal{D}\}.$$

Problems of the first sort are termed *maximization problems* and those of the second sort are called *minimization problems*. A *solution* to the problem max$\{f(x) \mid x \in \mathcal{D}\}$ is a point x in $\mathcal{D}$ such that

$$f(x) \geq f(y) \quad \text{for all } y \in \mathcal{D}.$$

We will say in this case that f attains a maximum on $\mathcal{D}$ at x, and also refer to x as a *maximizer* of f on $\mathcal{D}$.

Similarly,[1] a solution to the problem min$\{f(x) \mid x \in \mathcal{D}\}$ is a point z in $\mathcal{D}$ such that

$$f(z) \leq f(y) \quad \text{for all } y \in \mathcal{D}.$$

We say in this case that f attains a minimum on $\mathcal{D}$ at z, and also refer to z as a *minimizer* of f on $\mathcal{D}$.

The set of *attainable values* of f on $\mathcal{D}$, denoted $f(\mathcal{D})$, is defined by

$$f(\mathcal{D}) = \{w \in \mathbb{R} \mid \text{there is } x \in \mathcal{D} \text{ such that } f(x) = w\}.$$

We will also refer to $f(\mathcal{D})$ as the *image of $\mathcal{D}$ under f*. Observe that f attains a maximum on $\mathcal{D}$ (at some x) if and only if the set of real numbers $f(\mathcal{D})$ has a well-defined maximum, while f attains a minimum on $\mathcal{D}$ (at some z) if and only if $f(\mathcal{D})$ has a well-defined minimum. (This is simply a restatement of the definitions.)

The following simple examples reveal two important points: first, that in a given maximization problem, a solution may fail to exist (that is, the problem may have no solution at all), and, second, that even if a solution does exist, it need not necessarily be unique (that is, there could exist more than one solution). Similar statements obviously also hold for minimization problems.[2]

Example 2.1 Let $\mathcal{D} = \mathbb{R}_+$ and $f(x) = x$ for $x \in \mathcal{D}$. Then, $f(\mathcal{D}) = \mathbb{R}_+$ and sup $f(\mathcal{D}) = +\infty$, so the problem max$\{f(x) \mid x \in \mathcal{D}\}$ has no solution. $\quad\square$

Example 2.2 Let $\mathcal{D} = [0, 1]$ and let $f(x) = x(1 - x)$ for $x \in \mathcal{D}$. Then, the problem of maximizing f on $\mathcal{D}$ has exactly one solution, namely the point $x = 1/2$. $\quad\square$

Example 2.3 Let $\mathcal{D} = [-1, 1]$ and $f(x) = x^2$ for $x \in \mathcal{D}$. The problem of maximizing f on $\mathcal{D}$ now has two solutions: $x = -1$ and $x = 1$. $\quad\square$

In the sequel, therefore, we will not talk of *the* solution of a given optimization problem, but of a *set* of solutions of the problem, with the understanding that this

---

[1] It frequently happens through this text that definitions or results stated for maximization problems have an exact analog in the context of minimization problems. Rather than spell this analog out on each occasion, we shall often leave it to the reader to fill in the missing details.

[2] In this context, see Theorem 2.4 below.

set could, in general, be empty. The set of all maximizers of f on $\mathcal{D}$ will be denoted $\arg\max\{f(x) \mid x \in \mathcal{D}\}$:

$$\arg\max\{f(x) \mid x \in \mathcal{D}\} = \{x \in \mathcal{D} \mid f(x) \geq f(y) \text{ for all } y \in \mathcal{D}\}.$$

The set $\arg\min\{f(x) \mid x \in \mathcal{D}\}$ of minimizers of f on $\mathcal{D}$ is defined analogously.

We close this section with two elementary, but important, observations, which we state in the form of theorems for ease of future reference. The first shows that every maximization problem may be represented as a minimization problem, and *vice versa*. The second identifies a transformation of the optimization problem under which the solution set remains unaffected.

Theorem 2.4 *Let* $-f$ *denote the function whose value at any x is* $-f(x)$. *Then x is a maximum of f on $\mathcal{D}$ if and only if x is a minimum of* $-f$ *on $\mathcal{D}$; and z is a minimum of f on $\mathcal{D}$ if and only if z is a maximum of* $-f$ *on $\mathcal{D}$.*

Proof The point x maximizes f over $\mathcal{D}$ if and only if $f(x) \geq f(y)$ for all $y \in \mathcal{D}$, while x minimizes $-f$ over $\mathcal{D}$ if and only if $-f(x) \leq -f(y)$ for all $y \in \mathcal{D}$. Since $f(x) \geq f(y)$ is the same as $-f(x) \leq -f(y)$, the first part of the theorem is proved. The second part of the theorem follows from the first simply by noting that $-(-f) = f$. $\qquad\qquad\square$

Theorem 2.5 *Let* $\varphi: \mathbb{R} \to \mathbb{R}$ *be a strictly increasing function, that is, a function such that*

$$x > y \text{ implies } \varphi(x) > \varphi(y).$$

Then x is a maximum of f on $\mathcal{D}$ if and only if x is also a maximum of the composition $\varphi \circ f$ on $\mathcal{D}$; and z is a minimum of f on $\mathcal{D}$ if and only if z is also a minimum of $\varphi \circ f$ on $\mathcal{D}$.

Remark As will be evident from the proof, it suffices that φ be a strictly increasing function on just the set $f(\mathcal{D})$, i.e., that φ only satisfy $\varphi(z_1) > \varphi(z_2)$ for all $z_1, z_2 \in f(\mathcal{D})$ with $z_1 > z_2$. $\qquad\qquad\square$

Proof We deal with the maximization problem here; the minimization problem is left as an exercise. Suppose first that x maximizes f over $\mathcal{D}$. Pick any $y \in \mathcal{D}$. Then, $f(x) \geq f(y)$, and since φ is strictly increasing, $\varphi(f(x)) \geq \varphi(f(y))$. Since $y \in \mathcal{D}$ was arbitrary, this inequality holds for all $y \in \mathcal{D}$, which states precisely that x is a maximum of $\varphi \circ f$ on $\mathcal{D}$.

Now suppose that x maximizes $\varphi \circ f$ on $\mathcal{D}$, so $\varphi(f(x)) \geq \varphi(f(y))$ for all $y \in \mathcal{D}$. If x did not also maximize f on $\mathcal{D}$, there would exist $y^* \in \mathcal{D}$ such that $f(y^*) > f(x)$.

Since φ is a strictly increasing function, it follows that $\varphi(f(y^*)) > \varphi(f(x))$, so x does not maximize $\varphi \circ f$ over $\mathcal{D}$, a contradiction, completing the proof. $\qquad\square$

2.2 Optimization Problems in Parametric Form

It is often the case that optimization problems are presented in what is called *parametric form*, that is, the objective function and/or the feasible set depend on the value of a parameter θ in some set of feasible parameter values Θ. Indeed, all of the examples of optimization problems presented in Section 2.3 below belong to this class. Although we do not study parametrized optimization problems until Chapter 9, it is useful to introduce at this point the notation we shall use to represent these problems in the abstract. We will denote by Θ the set of all parameters of interest, with θ denoting a typical parameter configuration in Θ. Given a particular value $\theta \in \Theta$, the objective function and the feasible set of the optimization problem under θ will be denoted $f(\cdot, \theta)$ and $\mathcal{D}(\theta)$, respectively. Thus, if the optimization problem is a maximization problem, it will be written as

$$\max\{f(x, \theta) \mid x \in \mathcal{D}(\theta)\},$$

while the corresponding minimization problem will be denoted

$$\min\{f(x, \theta) \mid x \in \mathcal{D}(\theta)\}.$$

Notice that although our notation is general enough to allow both f and $\mathcal{D}$ to depend in a non-trivial way on θ, it also admits as a special case the situation where θ affects the shape of only the objective function or only the constraint set. More generally, it allows for the possibility that θ is a vector of parameters, some of which affect only the objective function, and others only the constraint set.

The set of *maximizers* of $f(\cdot, \theta)$ on $\mathcal{D}(\theta)$ will typically depend in a non-trivial way on θ. It would be consistent with our notation for the unparametrized case to denote this set by

$$\arg\max\{f(x, \theta) \mid x \in \mathcal{D}(\theta)\}.$$

However, the set of maximizers is itself an object of considerable interest in parametrized optimization problems (see Section 2.4 below), and a less cumbersome notation will be valuable. We shall use $\mathcal{D}^*(\theta)$ to denote this set:

$$\begin{aligned} D^*(\theta) &= \arg\max\{f(x, \theta) \mid x \in \mathcal{D}(\theta)\} \\ &= \{x \in \mathcal{D}(\theta) \mid f(x, \theta) \geq f(z, \theta) \text{ for all } z \in \mathcal{D}(\theta)\}. \end{aligned}$$

Similarly, we let $\mathcal{D}_*(\theta)$ denote the set of minimizers of $f(\cdot, \theta)$ on $\mathcal{D}(\theta)$.

Lastly, we will denote by $f^*(\theta)$ and $f_*(\theta)$, respectively, the *supremum* and *infimum* of the objective function given the parameter configuration θ. That is, if

$$f(\mathcal{D}(\theta)) = \{y \in \mathbb{R} \mid y = f(x, \theta) \text{ for some } x \in D(\theta)\}$$

represents the set of attainable values of $f(\cdot, \theta)$ on $\mathcal{D}(\theta)$, then

$$f^*(\theta) = \sup f(\mathcal{D}(\theta))$$

and

$$f_*(\theta) = \inf f(\mathcal{D}(\theta)).$$

We call f^* the *value function* of the problem $\max\{f(x, \theta) \mid x \in \mathcal{D}(\theta)\}$, and the function f_* the *value function* of the minimization problem $\min\{f(x, \theta) \mid x \in \mathcal{D}(\theta)\}$. We shall, in the sequel, refer to these functions as the *maximized value function* and the *minimized value function*, respectively.[3] Observe that if $\mathcal{D}^*(\theta)$ is nonempty for some θ, then we must have $\sup f(\mathcal{D}(\theta)) = f(x^*, \theta) = f(x', \theta)$ for any x^* and x' in $\mathcal{D}^*(\theta)$, so in this case, we may also write

$$f^*(\theta) = f(x^*, \theta) \text{ for any } x^* \in \mathcal{D}^*(\theta).$$

A similar remark is valid for $f_*(\theta)$ when $\mathcal{D}_*(\theta)$ is nonempty.

2.3 Optimization Problems: Some Examples

Economics and its allied disciplines are rich in decision problems that can be cast as optimization problems. This section describes simple versions of several of these problems. Many of these examples are invoked elsewhere in the book to illustrate the use of the techniques we shall develop. All of the examples presented in this section are also optimization problems in parametric form. This is pointed out explicitly in some cases, but in others we leave it to the reader to identify the parameters of interest.

2.3.1 Utility Maximization

A basic, but typical, model in consumer theory concerns a single agent who consumes n commodities in nonnegative quantities. Her *utility* from consuming $x_i \geq 0$ units of commodity i ($i = 1, \ldots, n$) is given by $u(x_1, \ldots, x_n)$, where $u \colon \mathbb{R}^n_+ \to \mathbb{R}$ is the agent's *utility function*. The agent has an income of $I \geq 0$, and faces the price vector $p = (p_1, \ldots, p_n)$, where $p_i \geq 0$ denotes the unit price of the i-th commodity.

---

[3] There is a slight abuse of terminology here. Since $f^*(\theta)$ is defined through the supremum, the "maximized value function" could be well defined even if a maximum does not exist.

Her *budget set* (i.e., the set of feasible or affordable consumption bundles, given her income I and the prices p) is denoted $\mathcal{B}(p, I)$, and is given by

$$\mathcal{B}(p, I) = \{x \in \mathbb{R}_+^n \mid p \cdot x \leq I\}.$$

The agent's objective is to maximize the level of her utility over the set of affordable commodity bundles, i.e., to solve:

Maximize $u(x)$ subject to $x \in \mathcal{B}(p, I)$.

The utility maximization problem is a typical example of an optimization problem in parametric form. When the price vector p and/or the income I change, so too does the feasible set[4] $\mathcal{B}(p, I)$, and therefore, the underlying optimization problem. Thus, p and I parametrize this problem. Since prices and income are usually restricted to taking on nonnegative values, the range of possible values for these parameters is $\mathbb{R}_+^n \times \mathbb{R}_+$.

Of course, depending on the purpose of the investigation, p and I may not be the only—or even the primary—parameters of interest. For instance, we may wish to study the problem when the utility function is restricted to being in the *Cobb–Douglas* class:

$$u(x_1, \ldots x_n) = x_1^{a_1} \cdots x_n^{a_n}, \qquad a_i > 0 \text{ for all } i.$$

In particular, our objective may be to examine how the solutions to the problem change as the vector of "weights" $a = (a_1, \ldots, a_n)$ changes, for a *given* level of prices and income. The vector a would then constitute the *only* parameter of interest.

2.3.2 Expenditure Minimization

The expenditure minimization problem represents the flip side of utility maximization. The problem takes as given a price vector $p \in \mathbb{R}_+^n$, and asks: what is the *minimum* amount of income needed to give a utility-maximizing consumer a utility level of at least $\bar{u}$, where $\bar{u}$ is some fixed utility level (possibly corresponding to some given commodity bundle). Thus, the constraint set in this problem is the set

$$X(\bar{u}) = \{x \in \mathbb{R}_+^n \mid u(x) \geq \bar{u}\}.$$

The objective is to solve:

Minimize $p \cdot x$ subject to $x \in X(\bar{u})$.

---

[4] Well, almost. The feasible set will change as long as prices and income do not change in the same proportion.

2.3.3 Profit Maximization

Producer theory in economics studies the decision-making processes of firms. A canonical, if simple, model involves a firm which produces a single output using n inputs through the production relationship $y = g(x_1, \ldots, x_n)$, where x_i denotes the quantity of the i-th input used in the production process, y is the resultant output, and $g \colon \mathbb{R}^n_+ \to \mathbb{R}_+$ is the firm's *production function* or *technology*. The unit price of input i is $w_i \geq 0$. When the firm produces y units of output, the unit price it can obtain is given by $p(y)$, where $p \colon \mathbb{R}_+ \to \mathbb{R}_+$ is the market *(inverse-)demand curve*.[5] Inputs may be used in any nonnegative quantities. Thus, the set of feasible input combinations is $\mathbb{R}^n_+$. Letting w denote the input price vector $(w_1, \ldots, w_n)$, and x the input vector $(x_1, \ldots, x_n)$, the firm's objective is to choose an input mix that will maximize its level of profits, that is, which solves

$$\text{Maximize } p(g(x))g(x) - w \cdot x \text{ subject to } x \in \mathbb{R}^n_+.$$

The profit maximization problem is another typical example of an optimization problem in parametric form. The input price vector w, which affects the shape of the objective function, evidently parametrizes the problem, but there could also be other parameters of interest, such as those affecting the demand curve $p(\cdot)$, or the technology $g(\cdot)$. For example, in the case of a competitive firm, we have $p(y) = \bar{p}$ for all $y \geq 0$, where $\bar{p} > 0$ is given. In this case, the value of $\bar{p}$ is obviously important for the objective function; $\bar{p}$, therefore, constitutes a parameter of the problem.

2.3.4 Cost Minimization

The cost minimization problem for a firm is similar to the expenditure minimization problem for a consumer. The aim is to identify the mix of inputs that will minimize the cost of producing at least $\bar{y}$ units of output, given the production function $g \colon \mathbb{R}^n_+ \to \mathbb{R}_+$ and the input price vector $w = (w_1, \ldots, w_n) \in \mathbb{R}^n_+$. Thus, the set of feasible input choices is

$$F(\bar{y}) = \{x \in \mathbb{R}^n_+ \mid g(x) \geq \bar{y}\},$$

and the problem is to solve

$$\text{Minimize } w \cdot x \text{ subject to } x \in F(\bar{y}).$$

Implicitly, this formulation of the cost-minimization problem presumes that a "free disposal" condition holds, i.e., that any excess amount produced may be costlessly discarded. If there is a nonzero cost of disposal, this should also be built into the objective function.

---

[5]If the firm operates in a competitive environment, we usually assume that $p(y) = \bar{p}$ for all $y \geq 0$ for some fixed $\bar{p}$, i.e., that the firm has no influence over market prices.

2.3.5 Consumption-Leisure Choice

A simple model of the labor-supply decision process of households may be obtained from the utility maximization problem by making the income level I also an object of choice. That is, it is assumed that the agent begins with an *endowment* of $H \geq 0$ units of "time," and faces a wage rate of $w \geq 0$. By choosing to work for L units of time, the agent can earn an income of wL; thus, the maximum possible income is wH, while the minimum is zero. The agent also gets utility from *leisure*, i.e., from the time not spent working. Thus, the agent's utility function takes the form $u(x_1, \ldots, x_n, l)$, where x_i represents the consumption of commodity i, and $l = H - L$ is the amount of leisure enjoyed. Letting $p = (p_1, \ldots, p_n) \in \mathbb{R}^n_+$ denote the price vector for the n consumption goods, the set of feasible leisure-consumption bundles for the agent is, therefore, given by:

$$F(p, w) = \{(x, l) \in \mathbb{R}^{n+1}_+ \mid p \cdot x \leq w(H - l), \ l \leq H\}.$$

The agent's maximization problem may now be represented as:

Maximize $u(x, l)$ subject to $(x, l) \in F(p, w)$.

2.3.6 Portfolio Choice

The portfolio selection problem in finance involves a single agent who faces S possible *states of the world*, one of which will be realized as the "true state." The agent has a utility function $U : \mathbb{R}^S_+ \to \mathbb{R}$ defined across these states: if the income the agent will have in state s is y_s, $s = 1, \ldots, S$, his utility is given by $U(y_1, \ldots, y_S)$.

If the true state of the world is revealed as s, the agent will have an *endowment* of $\omega_s \in \mathbb{R}_+$; this represents the agent's initial income in state s. Let $\omega = (\omega_1, \ldots, \omega_S)$ represent the initial endowment vector of the agent.

Before the true state is revealed, the agent may shift income from one state to another by buying and selling *securities*. There are N securities available. One unit of security i costs $p_i \geq 0$ and pays an income of z_{is} if state s occurs.

A *portfolio* is a vector of securities $\phi = (\phi_1, \ldots, \phi_N) \in \mathbb{R}^N$. If the agent selects the portfolio ϕ, then his income from the securities in state s is $\sum_{i=1}^N \phi_i z_{is}$; thus, his overall income in state s is

$$y_s(\phi) = \omega_s + \sum_{i=1}^N \phi_i z_{is}.$$

Letting $y(\phi) = (y_1(\phi), \ldots, y_S(\phi))$, it follows that the agent's utility from choosing the portfolio ϕ is $U(y(\phi))$.

A portfolio ϕ is *affordable* if the amount made from the sales of securities is sufficient to cover the purchases of securities, i.e., if $p \cdot \phi \leq 0$. It leads to a *feasible consumption policy* if income is nonnegative in all states, i.e., if $y_s(\phi) \geq 0$ for all s. A portfolio is *feasible* if it is both affordable and leads to a feasible consumption policy. Thus, the set of all feasible portfolios is

$$\Phi(p, \omega) = \{\phi \in \mathbb{R}^n \mid p \cdot \phi \leq 0 \text{ and } y(\phi) \geq 0\}.$$

The agent's problem is to select the portfolio that maximizes his utility from among the set of all feasible portfolios:

$$\text{Maximize } U(y(\phi)) \text{ subject to } \phi \in \Phi(p, \omega).$$

As with the earlier examples, the portfolio selection problem is also one in parametric form. In this case, the parameters of interest include the initial endowment vector ω, the security price vector p, and the security payoffs (z_{ij}). Of course, once again, these need not be the only parameters of interest. For instance, the agent's utility function may be of the *expected utility* form

$$U(y_1, \ldots, y_S) = \sum_{i=1}^{S} \pi_i u(y_i),$$

where π_i represents the (agent's subjective) probability of state i occurring, and $u(y_i)$ is the utility the agent obtains from having an income of y_i in state i. In this case, the probability vector $\pi = (\pi_1, \ldots, \pi_S)$ also forms part of the parameters of interest; so too may any parameters that affect the form of $u(\cdot)$.

2.3.7 Identifying Pareto Optima

The notion of a *Pareto optimum* is fundamental to many areas of economics. An economic outcome involving many agents is said to be *Pareto optimal* if it is not possible to readjust the outcome in a manner that makes some agent better off, without making at least one of the other agents worse off.

The identification and characterization of Pareto optimal outcomes is a matter of considerable interest in many settings. A simple example involves allocating a given total supply of resource $\omega \in \mathbb{R}_+^n$ between two agents. Agent i's utility from receiving the allocation $x_i \in \mathbb{R}_+^n$ is $u_i(x_i)$, where $u_i : \mathbb{R}_+^n \to \mathbb{R}$ is agent i's utility function. An allocation (x_1, x_2) is *feasible* if $x_1, x_2 \geq 0$ and $x_1 + x_2 \leq \omega$. Let $F(\omega)$ be the set of all feasible outcomes:

$$F(\omega) = \{(x_1, x_2) \in \mathbb{R}_+^n \times \mathbb{R}_+^n \mid x_1 + x_2 \leq \omega\}.$$

A feasible allocation is *Pareto optimal* if there does not exist another feasible allocation (x_1', x_2') such that

$$u_i(x_i') \geq u_i(x_i), \text{ for } i = 1, 2,$$

with strict inequality for at least one i.

There are several alternative methods for identifying a Pareto optimal allocation. One is to use a "weighted" utility function. Pick any $\alpha \in (0, 1)$, and let $U(x_1, x_2, \alpha)$ be defined by

$$U(x_1, x_2, \alpha) = \alpha u_1(x_1) + (1 - \alpha)u_2(x_2).$$

Now consider the optimization problem

Maximize $U(x_1, x_2, \alpha)$ subject to $(x_1, x_2) \in F(\omega)$.

Observe that the weight $\alpha \in (0, 1)$ is a parameter of this optimization problem, as is the total endowment vector ω. It is not very hard to see that every solution (x_1^*, x_2^*) to this weighted utility maximization problem must define a Pareto optimal outcome. For, if (x_1^*, x_2^*) were a solution, but were not Pareto optimal, there would exist $(x_1', x_2') \in F(\omega)$ such that $u_1(x_i') \geq u_i(x_i^*)$ with at least one strict inequality. But this would imply

$$\begin{aligned} U(x_1', x_2', \alpha) &= \alpha u_1(x_1') + (1 - \alpha)u_2(x_2') \\ &> \alpha u_1(x_1^*) + (1 - \alpha)u_2(x_2^*) \\ &= U(x_1^*, x_2^*, \alpha), \end{aligned}$$

which contradicts the fact that (x_1^*, x_2^*) is a maximum of the weighted utility maximization problem.

2.3.8 *Optimal Provision of Public Goods*

As opposed to private consumption goods, a *public good* in economics is defined as a good which has the characteristic that one agent's consumption of the good does not affect other agents' ability to also consume it. A central problem in public finance concerns the optimal provision of public goods. A simple version of this problem involves a setting with n agents, a single public good, and a single private good ("money"). The initial total endowment of the private good is $\omega > 0$, and that of the public good is zero. The private good can either be used in the production of the public good, or it can be allocated to the agents for consumption by them. If $x \geq 0$ is the amount of the private good used in production of the public good, then the amount of the public good produced is $h(x)$, where $h : \mathbb{R}_+ \to \mathbb{R}_+$. Letting x_i denote the allocation of the private good to agent i, the set of feasible combinations of private consumption and public good provision that can be achieved is, therefore,

$$\Phi(\omega) = \{(x_1, \ldots, x_n, y) \in \mathbb{R}_+^{n+1} \mid \text{there is } x \in \mathbb{R}_+ \text{ such that}$$
$$y = h(x) \text{ and } x + x_1 + \cdots + x_n \leq \omega\}.$$

The utility of any agent i depends on her own consumption x_i of the private good, and on the level y of provision of the public good, and is denoted $u_i(x_i, y)$. A *social welfare function* is a function $W(u_1, \ldots, u_n)$ that takes as its arguments the utility levels of the n agents. (For instance, W could be a weighted utility function $\alpha_1 u_1 + \cdots + \alpha_n u_n$ as in the previous subsection.) The public goods provision problem typically takes as given some social welfare function W, and aims to find the combination of private consumption levels $(x_1, \ldots, x_n)$ and public good provision y that is feasible and that maximizes W, i.e., that solves

$$\text{Maximize } W[u_1(x_1, y), \ldots, u_n(x_n, y)] \text{ subject to } (x_1, \ldots, x_n, y) \in \Phi(\omega).$$

2.3.9 Optimal Commodity Taxation

A second question of interest in public finance is determining the *optimal* rate at which different commodities should be taxed to raise a given amount of money. It is taken for granted that consumers will react to tax changes in a manner that maximizes their utility under the new tax regime. Thus, the study of optimal taxation begins with the utility maximization problem of a typical consumer.

There are n goods in the model, indexed by i. The (pre-tax) prices of the n commodities are given by the vector $p = (p_1, \ldots, p_n)$. Given a tax per unit of τ_i on the i-th commodity, the gross price vector faced by the consumer is $p + \tau$, where $\tau = (\tau_1, \ldots \tau_n)$. Thus, if I represents the consumer's income, and $u \colon \mathbb{R}^n_+ \to \mathbb{R}$ the consumer's utility function, the consumer solves

$$\text{Maximize } u(x) \text{ subject to } x \in \mathcal{B}(p + \tau, I) = \{x \in \mathbb{R}^n_+ \mid (p + \tau) \cdot x \leq I\}.$$

Assume that a unique solution exists to this problem for each choice of values of the parameter vector (p, τ, I),[6] and denote this solution by $x(p + \tau, I)$. That is, $x(p + \tau, I)$ is the commodity bundle that maximizes $u(x)$ over $\mathcal{B}(p + \tau, I)$. Further, let $v(p + \tau, I)$ be the maximized value of the utility function given (p, τ, I), i.e., $v(p + \tau, I) = u(x(p + \tau, I))$.

Now suppose the government has a given revenue requirement of R. The optimal commodity taxation problem is to determine the tax vector τ that will (a) raise at least the required amount of money, and (b) make the consumer best-off amongst all plans that will also raise at least R in tax revenue. That is, suppose that the tax authority chooses the tax vector τ. Then, the consumer will choose the commodity bundle $x(p + \tau, I)$, so this will result in a total tax revenue of $\tau \cdot x(p + \tau, I)$. Thus, the set of *feasible* tax vectors is

$$T(p, I) = \{\tau \in \mathbb{R}^n \mid \tau \cdot x(p + \tau, I) \geq R\}.$$

---

[6]It is possible to describe a suitable set of regularity conditions on u under which such existence and uniqueness may be guaranteed, but this is peripheral to our purposes here.

The tax rate of τ gives the optimally reacting consumer a maximized utility of $v(p + \tau, I)$. Thus, the optimal commodity taxation problem is to solve

$$\text{Maximize } v(p + \tau, I) \text{ subject to } \tau \in T(p, I).$$

2.4 The Objectives of Optimization Theory

Optimization theory has two main objectives. The first is to identify a set of conditions on f and $\mathcal{D}$ under which the *existence* of solutions to optimization problems is guaranteed. An important advantage to be gained from having such conditions is that the case-by-case verification of existence of solutions in applications can be avoided. In particular, given a parametrized family of optimization problems, it will be possible to identify restrictions on parameter values which ensure existence of solutions. On the other hand, to be of use in a wide variety of applications, it is important that the identified conditions be as general as possible. This makes the "existence question" non-trivial.

The second objective of optimization theory is more detailed and open-ended: it lies in obtaining a *characterization* of the set of optimal points. Broad categories of questions of interest here include the following:

1. The identification of conditions that every solution to an optimization problem *must* satisfy, that is, of conditions that are *necessary* for an optimum point.
2. The identification of conditions such that *any* point that meets these conditions is a solution, that is, of conditions that are *sufficient* to identify a point as being optimal.
3. The identification of conditions that ensure only a single solution exists to a given optimization problem, that is, of conditions that guarantee *uniqueness* of solutions.
4. A general theory of *parametric variation* in a parametrized family of optimization problems. For instance, given a family of optimization problems of the form $\max\{f(x, \theta) \mid x \in \mathcal{D}(\theta)\}$, we are interested in

    (a) the identification of conditions under which the solution set $\mathcal{D}^*(\theta)$ varies "continuously" with θ, that is, conditions which give rise to *parametric continuity*; and

    (b) in problems where the parameters θ and actions x have a natural ordering,[7] the identification of conditions under which an increase in the value of θ also leads to an increase in the value of the optimal action x^*, that is, of conditions that lead to *parametric monotonicity*.

---

[7] For instance, θ could be a real number representing a variable such as "income" or "price," and x could represent consumption levels.

These questions, and related ones, form the focus of the next several chapters of this book. As is perhaps to be expected, further hypotheses on the structure of the underlying optimization problems are required before many of them can be tackled. For instance, the notion of *differentiability* plays a central role in the identification of necessary conditions for optima, while the key concept in obtaining sufficient conditions is *convexity*. The next section elaborates further on this point.

2.5 A Roadmap

Chapter 3 begins our study of optimization with an examination of the fundamental question of *existence*. The main result of this chapter is the Weierstrass Theorem, which provides a general set of conditions under which optimization problems are guaranteed to have both maxima and minima. We then describe the use of this result in applications, and, in particular, illustrate how it could come in handy even in problems where the given structure violates the conditions of the theorem.

Chapters 4 through 6 turn to a study of *necessary conditions* for optima using differentiability assumptions on the underlying problem. Since differentiability is only a local property, the results of these chapters all pertain only to *local optima*, i.e., of points that are optima in some neighborhood, but not necessarily on all of the constraint set. Formally, we say that x is a local maximum of f on $\mathcal{D}$ if there is $r > 0$ such that x is a maximum of f on the set $B(x, r) \cap \mathcal{D}$. Local minima are defined similarly. Of course, every optimum of f on $\mathcal{D}$ is also a local optimum of f on $\mathcal{D}$. To distinguish between points that are only local optima and those that are optima on all of $\mathcal{D}$, we will refer to the latter as *global optima*.

Chapter 4 looks at the simplest case, where local optima occur in the *interior* of the feasible set $\mathcal{D}$, i.e., at a point where it is possible to move away from the optimum in any direction by at least a small amount without leaving $\mathcal{D}$. The main results here pertain to *necessary conditions* that must be met by the derivatives of the objective function at such points. We also provide *sufficient conditions* on the derivatives of the objective function that identify specific points as being *local optima*.

Chapters 5 and 6 examine the case where some or all of the constraints in $\mathcal{D}$ could matter at an optimal point. Chapter 5 focuses on the classical case where $\mathcal{D}$ is specified implicitly using *equality constraints*, i.e., where there are functions $g_i \colon \mathbb{R}^n \to \mathbb{R}$, $i = 1, \ldots, k$, such that

$$\mathcal{D} = \{x \in \mathbb{R}^n \mid g_i(x) = 0, \ i = 1, \ldots, k\}.$$

The main result of this chapter is the *Theorem of Lagrange*, which describes necessary conditions that must be met at all local optima of such problems. Analogous to the results for interior optima, we also describe conditions that are *sufficient* to identify specific points as being local optima. The remainder of the chapter focusses on using the theory in applications. We describe a "cookbook" procedure for using the necessary conditions of the Theorem of Lagrange in finding solutions to equality-constrained optimization problems. The procedure will not always work, since the conditions of the theorem are only necessary, and not also sufficient. Nonetheless, the procedure is quite successful in practice, and the chapter explores why this is the case, and, importantly, when the procedure could fail.

Chapter 6 moves on to *inequality-constrained* optimization problems, that is, where the constraint set is specified using functions $h_i \colon \mathbb{R}^n \to \mathbb{R}$, $i = 1, \ldots, l$, as

$$\mathcal{D} = \{x \in \mathbb{R}^n \mid h_i(x) \geq 0, \ i = 1, \ldots, l\}.$$

The centerpiece of this chapter is the *Theorem of Kuhn and Tucker*, which describes necessary conditions for optima in such problems. The remainder of the analysis in this chapter is, in some sense, isomorphic to that of Chapter 5. We discuss a cookbook procedure for using the Theorem of Kuhn and Tucker in applications. As with the cookbook procedure for solving equality-constrained problems, this one is also not guaranteed to be successful, and once again, for the same reason (namely, because the conditions of the relevant theorem are only necessary, and not also sufficient.) Nonetheless, this procedure also works well in practice, and the chapter examines when the procedure will definitely succeed and when it could fail.

Chapters 7 and 8 turn to a study of *sufficient conditions*, that is, conditions that, when met, will identify specific points as being global optima of given optimization problems. Chapter 7 presents the notion of *convexity*, that is, of convex sets, and of concave and convex functions, and examines the continuity, differentiability, and curvature properties of such functions. It also provides easy-to-use tests for identifying concave and convex functions in practice. The most important results of this chapter, however, pertain to the use of convexity in optimization theory. We show that the same first-order conditions that were proved, in earlier chapters, to be *necessary* for *local optima*, are also, under convexity conditions, *sufficient* for *global optima*.

Although these results are very strong, the assumption of convexity is not an unrestrictive one. In Chapter 8, therefore, a weakening of this condition, called *quasiconvexity*, is studied. The weakening turns out to be substantial; quasi-concave and quasi-convex functions fail to possess many of the strong properties that characterize concave and convex functions. However, it is again possible to give tests for identifying such functions in practice. This is especially useful because our main result of this chapter shows that, under quasi-convexity, the first-order necessary conditions for local optima are "almost" sufficient for global optima; that is, they are sufficient whenever some mild additional regularity conditions are met.

Chapters 9 and 10 address questions that arise from the study of parametric families of optimization problems. Chapter 9 examines the issue of *parametric continuity*: under what conditions on the primitives will the solutions to such problems vary *continuously* with the parameters θ? Of course, continuity in the solutions will not obtain without continuity in the primitives, and this requires a notion of continuity for a map such as $\mathcal{D}(\theta)$ which takes *points* $\theta \in \Theta$ into *sets* $\mathcal{D}(\theta) \subset \mathbb{R}^n$. The study of such point-to-set maps, called *correspondences* is the starting point of this chapter. With a satisfactory notion of continuity for correspondences in hand, Chapter 9 presents one of the major results of optimization theory, the *Maximum Theorem*. Roughly speaking, the Maximum Theorem states that the continuity properties of the primitives are inherited, but not in their entirety, by the solutions. A second result, the *Maximum Theorem under Convexity*, studies the impact of adding convexity assumptions on the primitives.

Chapter 10 looks at the problem of *parametric monotonicity*. It introduces the key notion of *supermodularity* of a function, which has become, in recent years, a valuable tool for the study of incomplete-information problems in economics. It is shown that, under some regularity conditions on the problem, supermodularity of the objective function suffices to yield monotonicity of optimal actions in the parameter.

Chapters 11 and 12 introduce the reader to the field of *dynamic programming*, i.e., of multiperiod decision problems, in which the decisions taken in any period affect the decision-making environment in all future periods. Chapter 11 studies dynamic programming problems with finite horizons. It is shown that under mild continuity conditions, an optimal strategy exists in such problems. More importantly, it is shown that the optimal strategies can be recovered by the process of *backwards induction*, that is, by begining in the last period of the problem and working backwards to the first period.

Chapter 12 looks at dynamic programming problems with an infinite horizon. Such problems are more complex than the corresponding finite-horizon case, since they lack a "last" period. The key to finding a solution turns out to be the *Bellman Equation*, which is essentially a statement of dynamic consistency. Using this equation, we show that a solution to the problem can be shown to exist under just continuity and boundedness conditions; and the solution itself obtained using a rather simple procedure. A detailed presentation of the neoclassical model of economic growth illustrates the use of these results; more importantly, it also demonstrates how convexity conditions can be worked into dynamic programming problems to obtain a sharp characterization of the solution.

2.6 Exercises

1. Is Theorem 2.5 valid if φ is only required to be *nondecreasing* (i.e., if $x > y$ implies $\varphi(x) \geq \varphi(y)$) instead of strictly increasing? Why or why not?

2. Give an example of an optimization problem with an infinite number of solutions.

3. Let $\mathcal{D} = [0, 1]$. Describe the set $f(\mathcal{D})$ in each of the following cases, and identify sup $f(\mathcal{D})$ and inf $f(\mathcal{D})$. In which cases does f attain its supremum? What about its infimum?

   (a) $f(x) = 1 + x$ for all $x \in \mathcal{D}$.
   (b) $f(x) = 1$, if $x < 1/2$, and $f(x) = 2x$ otherwise.
   (c) $f(x) = x$, if $x < 1$, and $f(1) = 2$.
   (d) $f(0) = 1$, $f(1) = 0$, and $f(x) = 3x$ for $x \in (0, 1)$.

4. Let $\mathcal{D} = [0, 1]$. Suppose $f : \mathcal{D} \to \mathbb{R}$ is *increasing* on $\mathcal{D}$, i.e., for $x, y \in \mathcal{D}$, if $x > y$, then $f(x) > f(y)$. [Note that f is not assumed to be continuous on $\mathcal{D}$.] Is $f(\mathcal{D})$ a compact set? Prove your answer, or provide a counterexample.

5. Find a function $f : \mathbb{R} \to \mathbb{R}$ and a collection of sets $S_k \subset \mathbb{R}$, $k = 1, 2, 3, \ldots$, such that f attains a maximum on each S_k, but not on $\cap_{k=1}^{\infty} S_k$.

6. Give an example of a function $f : [0, 1] \to \mathbb{R}$ such that $f([0, 1])$ is an open set.

7. Give an example of a set $\mathcal{D} \subset \mathbb{R}$ and a continuous function $f : \mathcal{D} \to \mathbb{R}$ such that f attains its maximum, but not a minimum, on $\mathcal{D}$.

8. Let $\mathcal{D} = [0, 1]$. Let $f : \mathcal{D} \to \mathbb{R}$ be an increasing function on $\mathcal{D}$, and let $g : \mathcal{D} \to \mathbb{R}$ be a decreasing function on $\mathcal{D}$. (That is, if $x, y \in \mathcal{D}$ with $x > y$ then $f(x) > f(y)$ and $g(x) < g(y)$.) Then, f attains a minimum and a maximum on $\mathcal{D}$ (at 0 and 1, respectively), as does g (at 1 and 0, respectively). Does $f + g$ necessarily attain a maximum and minimum on $\mathcal{D}$?

3

Existence of Solutions: The Weierstrass Theorem

We begin our study of optimization with the fundamental question of *existence:* under what conditions on the objective function f and the constraint set $\mathcal{D}$ are we *guaranteed* that solutions will always exist in optimization problems of the form $\max\{f(x) \mid x \in \mathcal{D}\}$ or $\min\{f(x) \mid x \in \mathcal{D}\}$? Equivalently, under what conditions on f and $\mathcal{D}$ is it the case that the set of attainable values $f(\mathcal{D})$ contains its supremum and/or infimum?

Trivial answers to the existence question are, of course, always available: for instance, f is guaranteed to attain a maximum and a minimum on $\mathcal{D}$ if $\mathcal{D}$ is a finite set. On the other hand, our primary purpose in studying the existence issue is from the standpoint of applications: we would like to avoid, to the maximum extent possible, the need to verify existence on a case-by-case basis. In particular, when dealing with parametric families of optimization problems, we would like to be in a position to describe restrictions on parameter values under which solutions always exist. All of this is possible only if the identified set of conditions possesses a considerable degree of generality.

The centerpiece of this chapter, the Weierstrass Theorem, describes just such a set of conditions. The statement of the theorem, and a discussion of its conditions, is the subject of Section 3.1. The use of the Weierstrass Theorem in applications is examined in Section 3.2. The chapter concludes with the proof of the Weierstrass Theorem in Section 3.3.

3.1 The Weierstrass Theorem

The following result, a powerful theorem credited to the mathematician Karl Weierstrass, is the main result of this chapter:

Theorem 3.1 (The Weierstrass Theorem) *Let $\mathcal{D} \subset \mathbb{R}^n$ be compact, and let $f: \mathcal{D} \to \mathbb{R}$ be a continuous function on $\mathcal{D}$. Then f attains a maximum and a minimum* on $\mathcal{D}$, i.e., there exist points z_1 and z_2 in $\mathcal{D}$ such that

$$f(z_1) \geq f(x) \geq f(z_2), \qquad x \in \mathcal{D}.$$

Proof See Section 3.3. □

It is of the utmost importance to realize that the Weierstrass Theorem only provides *sufficient* conditions for the existence of optima. The theorem has nothing to say about what happens if these conditions are not met, and, indeed, in general, nothing can be said, as the following examples illustrate. In each of Examples 3.2–3.4, only a single condition of the Weierstrass Theorem is violated, yet maxima and minima fail to exist in each case. In the last example, *all* of the conditions of the theorem are violated, yet both maxima and minima exist.

Example 3.2 Let $\mathcal{D} = \mathbb{R}$, and $f(x) = x^3$ for all $x \in \mathbb{R}$. Then f is continuous, but $\mathcal{D}$ is not compact (it is closed, but not bounded). Since $f(\mathcal{D}) = \mathbb{R}$, f evidently attains neither a maximum nor a minimum on $\mathcal{D}$. □

Example 3.3 Let $\mathcal{D} = (0, 1)$ and $f(x) = x$ for all $x \in (0, 1)$. Then f is continuous, but $\mathcal{D}$ is again noncompact (this time it is bounded, but not closed). The set $f(\mathcal{D})$ is the open interval $(0, 1)$, so, once again, f attains neither a maximum nor a minimum on $\mathcal{D}$. □

Example 3.4 Let $\mathcal{D} = [-1, 1]$, and let f be given by

$$f(x) = \begin{cases} 0, & \text{if } x = -1 \text{ or } x = 1 \\ x, & \text{if } -1 < x < 1. \end{cases}$$

Note that $\mathcal{D}$ is compact, but f fails to be continuous at just the two points -1 and 1. In this case, $f(\mathcal{D})$ is the open interval $(-1, 1)$; consequently, f fails to attain either a maximum or a minimum on $\mathcal{D}$. □

Example 3.5 Let $\mathcal{D} = \mathbb{R}_{++}$, and let $f: \mathcal{D} \to \mathbb{R}$ be defined by

$$f(x) = \begin{cases} 1, & \text{if } x \text{ is rational} \\ 0, & \text{otherwise.} \end{cases}$$

Then $\mathcal{D}$ is not compact (it is neither closed nor bounded), and f is discontinuous at every single point in $\mathbb{R}$ (it "chatters" back and forth between the values 0 and 1). Nonetheless, f attains a maximum (at every rational number) and a minimum (at every irrational number). □

To restate the point: if the conditions of the Weierstrass Theorem are met, a maximum and a minimum are guaranteed to exist. On the other hand, if one or more of the theorem's conditions fails, maxima and minima may or may not exist, depending on the specific structure of the problem in question.

As one might perhaps anticipate from Examples 3.2 through 3.5, the proof of the Weierstrass Theorem presented in Section 3.3 proceeds in two steps. First, it is shown that, under the stated conditions, $f(\mathcal{D})$ must be a compact set. Since compact sets in $\mathbb{R}$ are necessarily also bounded, the unboundedness problem of Example 3.2, where $\sup f(\mathcal{D}) = +\infty$ and $\inf f(\mathcal{D}) = -\infty$, cannot arise. Second, it is shown that if A is a compact set in $\mathbb{R}$, $\max A$ and $\min A$ are always well-defined; in particular, the possibility of $f(\mathcal{D})$ being a bounded set that fails to contain its sup and inf, as in Examples 3.3 and 3.4, is also precluded. Since $f(\mathcal{D})$ has been shown to be compact in step 1, the proof is complete.

3.2 The Weierstrass Theorem in Applications

Perhaps the most obvious use of the Weierstrass Theorem arises in the context of optimization problems in parametric form: the theorem makes it possible for us to identify restrictions on parameter values that will guarantee existence of solutions in such problems, by simply identifying the subset of the parameter space on which the required continuity and compactness conditions are satisfied. The following example illustrates this point using the framework of subsection 2.3.1.

Example 3.6 Consider the utility maximization problem

$$\text{Maximize } u(x) \text{ subject to } x \in \mathcal{B}(p, I) = \{x \in \mathbb{R}^n_+ \mid p \cdot x \le I\},$$

where the price vector $p = (p_1, \ldots, p_n)$ and income I are given. As is usual, we shall restrict prices and income to taking on nonnegative values, so the parameter set Θ in this problem is given by $\mathbb{R}^n_+ \times \mathbb{R}_+$.

It is assumed throughout this example that the utility function $u: \mathbb{R}^n_+ \to \mathbb{R}$ is continuous on its domain. By the Weierstrass Theorem, a solution to the utility maximization problem will always exist as long as the budget set $\mathcal{B}(p, I)$ is compact. We will show that compactness of this set obtains as long as $p \gg 0$; thus, a solution to the utility maximization problem is guaranteed to exist for all $(p, I) \in \tilde{\Theta}$, where $\tilde{\Theta} \subset \Theta$ is defined by

$$\tilde{\Theta} = \{(p, I) \in \Theta \mid p \gg 0\}.$$

So suppose that $(p, I) \in \tilde{\Theta}$. Observe that even if the agent spent her entire income I on commodity j, her consumption of this commodity cannot exceed I/p_j. Therefore, if we define

$$\xi = \max\left\{\frac{I}{p_1}, \ldots, \frac{I}{p_n}\right\},$$

it is the case that for any $x \in \mathcal{B}(p, I)$, we have $0 \leq x \leq (\xi, \ldots, \xi)$. It follows that $\mathcal{B}(p, I)$ is bounded.

To see that $\mathcal{B}(p, I)$ is also closed, let $\{x^k\}$ be a sequence in $\mathcal{B}(p, I)$, and suppose $x^k \to x$. We are to show that $x \in \mathcal{B}(p, I)$, i.e., that $x \geq 0$ and $0 \leq p \cdot x \leq I$. The first of these inequalities is easy: since $x^k \geq 0$ for all k, and $x^k \to x$, Theorem 1.8 implies $x \geq 0$. To see that $0 \leq p \cdot x \leq I$, pick any $j \in \{1, \ldots, n\}$. Since $x^k \to x$, we have $x_j^k \to x_j$ by Theorem 1.7. Therefore, $p_j x_j^k \to p_j x_j$ for each j, and summing over j, we obtain

$$p \cdot x^k = \sum_{j=1}^n p_j x_j^k \to \sum_{j=1}^n p_j x_j = p \cdot x.$$

Since the sequence of real numbers $p \cdot x^k$ satisfies $0 \leq p \cdot x^k \leq I$ for each k, another appeal to Theorem 1.8 yields $0 \leq p \cdot x \leq I$. Thus, $x \in \mathcal{B}(p, I)$, and $\mathcal{B}(p, I)$ is closed.

As a closed and bounded subset of $\mathbb{R}^n$, it follows that $\mathcal{B}(p, I)$ is compact. Since $p \in \mathbb{R}^n_{++}$ and $I \geq 0$ were arbitrary, we are done. $\qquad\square$

A similar, but considerably simpler, argument works for the problem described in subsection 2.3.7:

Example 3.7 In subsection 2.3.7, we described how a weighted utility function can be used to identify a Pareto-optimal division of a given quantity of resources between two agents. The optimization exercise here is

Maximize $\alpha u_1(x_1) + (1 - \alpha)u_2(x_2)$ subject to $(x_1, x_2) \in F(\omega)$,

where $F(\omega) = \{(x_1, x_2) \in \mathbb{R}^n_+ \times \mathbb{R}^n_+ \mid x_1 + x_2 \leq \omega\}$ represents the set of possible divisions, and u_i is agent i's utility function, $i = 1, 2$. The parameters of this problem are $\alpha \in (0, 1)$ and $\omega \in \mathbb{R}^n_+$; thus, the space Θ of possible parameter values is given by $(0, 1) \times \mathbb{R}^n_+$.

It is easy to see that $F(\omega)$ is compact for any $\omega \in \mathbb{R}^n_+$. Moreover, the weighted utility function $\alpha u_1(x_1) + (1 - \alpha)u_2(x_2)$ is continuous as a function of (x_1, x_2) whenever the underlying utility functions u_1 and u_2 are continuous on $\mathbb{R}^n_+$. Thus, provided only that the utility functions u_1 and u_2 are continuous functions, the Weierstrass Theorem assures us of the existence of a solution to this family of optimization problems *for every possible choice of parameters* $(\alpha, \omega) \in \Theta$. $\qquad\square$

Unlike these problems, natural formulations of some economic models involve feasible action sets that are noncompact for all feasible parameter values. At first blush, it might appear that the Weierstrass Theorem does not have anything to say in these models. However, it frequently happens that such problems may be reduced to equivalent ones with compact action sets, to which the Weierstrass Theorem *is* applicable. A typical example of this situation is the cost minimization problem outlined in subsection 2.3.4:

Example 3.8 Recall that the cost minimization involves finding the cheapest mix of inputs through which a firm may produce (at least) $y > 0$ units of output, given the input price vector $w \in \mathbb{R}^n_+$, and technology $g: \mathbb{R}^n_+ \to \mathbb{R}$. We will suppose throughout this example that g is a continuous function on $\mathbb{R}^n_+$. The problem is to minimize the (obviously continuous) objective function $w \cdot x$ over the feasible action set

$$F(y) = \{x \in \mathbb{R}^n_+ \mid g(x) \geq y\}.$$

This feasible set is unbounded—and therefore noncompact—for many popularly used forms for g, including the linear technology

$$g(x) = a_1 x_1 + \cdots + a_n x_n, \qquad a_i > 0 \text{ for all } i$$

and members of the *Cobb–Douglas* family

$$g(x) = x_1^{a_1} \cdots x_n^{a_n}, \qquad a_i > 0 \text{ for all } i.$$

Thus, despite the continuity of the objective function, a direct appeal to the Weierstrass Theorem is precluded.

However, for a suitable range of parameter values, it is possible in this problem to "compactify" the action set, and thus to bring it within the ambit of the Weierstrass Theorem. Specifically, one can show that, whenever the input price vector w satisfies $w \gg 0$, it is possible to define a *compact* subset $\bar{F}(y)$ of $F(y)$, such that attention may be restricted to $\bar{F}(y)$ *without any attendant loss of generality*. Consider the following procedure. Let $\bar{x} \in \mathbb{R}^n_+$ be any vector that satisfies $g(\bar{x}) \geq y$. (We presume that at least one such vector exists; otherwise the set of feasible actions is empty, and the problem is trivial.) Let $\bar{c} = w \cdot \bar{x}$. Define for $i = 1, \ldots, n$,

$$\xi_i = \frac{2\bar{c}}{w_i}.$$

Then, the firm will never use more than ξ_i units of input i: if it does so, then—no matter what the quantities of the other inputs used—this will result in total cost strictly exceeding $\bar{c}$. On the other hand, the required output level can be produced at a total cost of $\bar{c}$ by using the input vector $\bar{x}$. It follows that we may, without loss, restrict attention to the set of actions

$$\bar{F}(y) = \{x \in \mathbb{R}^n_+ \mid g(x) \geq y, \; x_i \leq \xi_i \text{ for all } i\}.$$

This restricted set $\bar{F}(y)$ is clearly bounded. The continuity of g implies it is also closed. To see this, let x^k be any sequence in $\bar{F}(y)$, and let $x^k \to x$. Then, $g(x^k) \geq y$ for each k, which implies by the continuity of g that

$$g(x) = \lim_{k \to \infty} g(x^k) \geq y.$$

Moreover, $x^k \geq 0$ for all k implies $x \geq 0$ by Theorem 1.8. Therefore, $x \in \bar{F}(y)$, so $\bar{F}(y)$ is closed. An appeal to the Weierstrass Theorem now shows the existence of a solution to the problem of minimizing $w \cdot x$ over $\bar{F}(y)$, and, therefore, to the problem of minimizing $w \cdot x$ over $F(y)$.[1] $\square$

Like the cost minimization problem, the expenditure minimization problem of subsection 2.3.2 also involves an action space that is unbounded for most popularly used forms for the utility function. However, a construction similar to the one described here can also be employed to show that, under suitable conditions, the action space can be compactified, so that a solution to the expenditure minimization problem does exist (see the Exercises).

Finally, the Weierstrass Theorem can also be used in conjunction with other results to actually *identify* an optimal point. We demonstrate its value in this direction in the succeeding chapters, where we present *necessary* conditions that every solution to an optimization problem must satisfy. By themselves, these necessary conditions are not enough to identify an optimum, since they are, in general, not also sufficient; in particular, there may exist points that are not optima that meet these conditions, and indeed, there may exist points meeting the necessary conditions without optima even existing.

On the other hand, if the primitives of the problem also meet the compactness and continuity conditions of the Weierstrass Theorem, a solution *must* exist. By definition, moreover, the solution must satisfy the necessary conditions. It follows that one of the points satisfying the necessary conditions must, in fact, be the solution. Therefore, a solution can be found merely by evaluating the objective function at each point

[1] For some forms of the production function g, the necessary compactification could have been achieved by a simpler argument. For instance, it is apparent that when g is linear, the firm will never produce an output level strictly greater than the minimum required level y. (Otherwise, costs could be reduced by using less of some input and producing exactly y.) So attention may be restricted to the set $\{x \in \mathbb{R}^n_+ \mid g(x) = y\}$, which in this case is compact. However, the set $\{x \in \mathbb{R}^n_+ \mid g(x) = y\}$ is noncompact for many forms of g (for instance, when g is a member of the Cobb–Douglas family), so, unlike the method outlined in the text, merely restricting attention to this set will not always work.

that satisfies the necessary conditions, and choosing the point that maximizes (or, as required, minimizes) the value of the objective on this set. Since the set of points at which the necessary conditions are met is typically quite small, this procedure is not very difficult to carry out.

3.3 A Proof of the Weierstrass Theorem

The following lemmata, when combined, prove the Weierstrass Theorem. The first shows that, under the theorem's assumptions, $f(\mathcal{D})$ must be a compact set, so, in particular, the problem of unboundedness cannot arise. The second completes the proof by showing that if $A \subset \mathbb{R}$ is a compact set, max A and min A are both well defined, so the "openness" problem is also precluded.

Lemma 3.9 *If $f: \mathcal{D} \to \mathbb{R}$ is continuous on $\mathcal{D}$, and $\mathcal{D}$ is compact, then $f(\mathcal{D})$ is also compact.*

Proof Pick any sequence $\{y_k\}$ in $f(\mathcal{D})$. The lemma will be proved if we can show that $\{y_k\}$ must have a convergent subsequence, i.e., there is a subsequence $\{y_{m(k)}\}$ of $\{y_k\}$ and a point $y \in f(\mathcal{D})$ such that $y_{m(k)} \to y$.

For each k, pick $x_k \in \mathcal{D}$ such that $f(x_k) = y_k$. (For each k, at least one such point x_k must exist by definition of $f(\mathcal{D})$; if more than one exists, pick any one.) This gives us a sequence $\{x_k\}$ in $\mathcal{D}$. Since $\mathcal{D}$ is compact, there is a subsequence $\{x_{m(k)}\}$ of $\{x_k\}$, and a point $x \in \mathcal{D}$ such that $x_{m(k)} \to x$.

Define $y = f(x)$, and $y_{m(k)} = f(x_{m(k)})$. By construction, $\{y_{m(k)}\}$ is a subsequence of the original sequence $\{y_k\}$. Moreover, since $x \in \mathcal{D}$, it is the case that $y = f(x) \in f(\mathcal{D})$. Finally, since $x_{m(k)} \to x$ and f is a continuous function, $y_{m(k)} = f(x_{m(k)}) \to f(x) = y$, completing the proof. $\square$

Lemma 3.10 *If $A \subset \mathbb{R}$ is compact, then $\sup A \in A$ and $\inf A \in A$, so the maximum and minimum of A are well defined.*

Proof Since A is bounded, $\sup A \in \mathbb{R}$. For $k = 1, 2, \ldots$, let N_k represent the interval $(\sup A - 1/k, \sup A]$, and let $A_k = N_k \cap A$. Then A_k must be nonempty for each k. (If not, we would have an upper-bound of A that was strictly smaller than $\sup A$, which is impossible.) Pick any point from A_k, and label it x_k.

We claim that $x_k \to \sup A$ as $k \to \infty$. This follows simply from the observation that since $x_k \in (\sup A - 1/k, \sup A]$ for each k, it must be the case that $d(x_k, \sup A) < 1/k$. Therefore, $d(x_k, \sup A) \to 0$ with k, establishing the claim.

But $x_k \in A_k \subset A$ for each k, and A is a closed set, so the limit of the sequence $\{x_k\}$ must be in A, establishing one part of the result. The other part, that $\inf A \in A$ is established analogously. $\square$

The Weierstrass is an immediate consequence of these lemmata. $\square$

3.4 Exercises

1. Prove the following statement or provide a counterexample: if f is a continuous function on a bounded (but not necessarily closed) set $\mathcal{D}$, then $\sup f(\mathcal{D})$ is finite.

2. Suppose $\mathcal{D} \subset \mathbb{R}^n$ is a set consisting of a finite number of points $\{x_1, \ldots, x_p\}$. Show that any function $f: \mathcal{D} \to \mathbb{R}$ has a maximum and a minimum on $\mathcal{D}$. Is this result implied by the Weierstrass Theorem? Explain your answer.

3. Call a function $f: \mathbb{R}^n \to \mathbb{R}$ *nondecreasing* if $x, y \in \mathbb{R}^n$ with $x \geq y$ implies $f(x) \geq f(y)$. Suppose f is a nondecreasing, but not necessarily continuous, function on $\mathbb{R}^n$, and $\mathcal{D} \subset \mathbb{R}^n$ is compact. Show that if $n = 1$, f always has a maximum on $\mathcal{D}$. Show also that if $n > 1$, this need no longer be the case.

4. Give an example of a compact set $\mathcal{D} \subset \mathbb{R}^n$ and a continuous function $f: \mathcal{D} \to \mathbb{R}$ such that $f(\mathcal{D})$ consists of precisely k points where $k \geq 2$. Is this possible if $\mathcal{D}$ is also convex? Why or why not?

5. Let $f: \mathbb{R}_+ \to \mathbb{R}$ be continuous on $\mathbb{R}_+$. Suppose that f also satisfies the conditions that $f(0) = 1$ and $\lim_{x \to \infty} f(x) = 0$. Show that f must have a maximum on $\mathbb{R}_+$. What about a minimum?

6. Let C be a compact subset of $\mathbb{R}$. Let $g: C \to \mathbb{R}$ and $f: \mathbb{R} \to \mathbb{R}$ be a continuous function. Does the composition $f \circ g$ have a maximum on C?

7. Let $g: \mathbb{R} \to \mathbb{R}$ be a function (not necessarily continuous) which has a maximum and minimum on $\mathbb{R}$. Let $f: \mathbb{R} \to \mathbb{R}$ be a function which is continuous on the range of g. Does $f \circ g$ necessarily have a maximum on $\mathbb{R}$? Prove your answer, or provide a counterexample.

8. Use the Weierstrass Theorem to show that a solution exists to the expenditure minimization problem of subsection 2.3.2, as long as the utility function u is continuous on $\mathbb{R}^n_+$ and the price vector p satisfies $p \gg 0$. What if one of these conditions fails?

9. Consider the profit maximization problem of subsection 2.3.3. For simplicity, assume that the inverse-demand curve facing the firm is constant, i.e., that $p(y) = p > 0$ for all output levels $y \geq 0$. Assume also that the technology g is continuous on $\mathbb{R}^n_+$, and that the input price vector w satisfies $w \gg 0$. Are these assumptions

sufficient to guarantee the existence of a solution to the profit maximization problem? Why or why not?

10. Show that the budget set $F(p, w) = \{(x, l) \in \mathbb{R}_+^{n+1} \mid p \cdot x \leq w(H - l), \ l \leq H\}$ in the consumption-leisure choice problem of subsection 2.3.5 is compact if and only if $p \gg 0$.

11. Consider the portfolio selection problem of subsection 2.3.6. The problem is said to admit *arbitrage*, if there is some portfolio $\phi \in \mathbb{R}^N$ such that $p \cdot \phi \leq 0$ and $Z'\phi > 0$, where $p = (p_1, \ldots, p_N)$ is the vector of security prices, and $Z = (z_{ij})$ is the $N \times S$ matrix of security payoffs. (In words, the problem admits arbitrage if it is possible to create a portfolio at nonpositive cost, whose payoffs are nonnegative in all states, and are strictly positive in some states.) Suppose that the utility function $U: \mathbb{R}_+^S \rightarrow \mathbb{R}$ in this problem is continuous and strictly increasing on $\mathbb{R}_+^S$ (that is, $y, y' \in \mathbb{R}_+^S$ with $y > y'$ implies $U(y) > U(y')$.) Show that a solution exists to the utility maximization problem if and only if there is no arbitrage.

12. Under what conditions (if any) on the primitives does the problem of the optimal provision of public goods (see subsection 2.3.8) meet the continuity and compactness conditions of the Weierstrass Theorem?

13. A monopolist faces a downward sloping inverse-demand curve $p(x)$ that satisfies $p(0) < \infty$ and $p(x) \geq 0$ for all $x \in \mathbb{R}_+$. The cost of producing x units is given by $c(x) \geq 0$ where $c(0) = 0$. Suppose $p(\cdot)$ and $c(\cdot)$ are both continuous on $\mathbb{R}_+$. The monopolist wishes to maximize $\pi(x) = xp(x) - c(x)$ subject to the constraint $x \geq 0$.

   (a) Suppose there is $x^* > 0$ such that $p(x^*) = 0$. Show that the Weierstrass Theorem can be used to prove the existence of a solution to this problem.

   (b) Now suppose instead there is $x' > 0$ such that $c(x) \geq xp(x)$ for all $x \geq x'$. Show, once again, that the Weierstrass Theorem can be used to prove existence of a solution.

   (c) What about the case where $p(x) = \bar{p}$ for all x (the demand curve is infinitely elastic) and $c(x) \rightarrow \infty$ as $x \rightarrow \infty$?

14. A consumer, who lives for two periods, has the utility function $v(c(1), c(2))$, where $c(t) \in \mathbb{R}_+^n$ denotes the consumer's consumption bundle in period t, $t = 1, 2$. The price vector in period t is given by $p(t) \in \mathbb{R}_+^n$, $p(t) = (p_1(t), \ldots, p_n(t))$. The consumer has an initial wealth of W_0, but has no other income. Any amount not spent in the first period can be saved and used for the second period. Savings earn interest at a rate $r \geq 0$. (Thus, a dollar saved in period 1 becomes $\$(1 + r)$ in period 2.)

(a) Assume the usual nonnegativity constraints on consumption and set up the consumer's utility-maximization problem.

(b) Show that the feasible set in this problem is compact if and only if $p(1) \gg 0$ and $p(2) \gg 0$.

15. A fishery earns a profit of $\pi(x)$ from catching and selling x units of fish. The firm owns a pool which currently has y_1 fish in it. If $x \in [0, y_1]$ fish are caught this period, the remaining $i = y_1 - x$ fish will grow to $f(i)$ fish by the beginning of the next period, where $f \colon \mathbb{R}_+ \to \mathbb{R}_+$ is the *growth* function for the fish population. The fishery wishes to set the volume of its catch in each of the next three periods so as to maximize the sum of its profits over this horizon. That is, it solves:

$$\text{Maximize } \pi(x_1) + \pi(x_2) + \pi(x_3)$$

$$\begin{aligned}
\text{subject to } \ x_1 &\leq y_1 \\
x_2 &\leq y_2 = f(y_1 - x_1) \\
x_3 &\leq y_3 = f(y_2 - x_2)
\end{aligned}$$

and the nonnegativity constraints that $x_t \geq 0$, $t = 1, 2, 3$.

Show that if π and f are continuous on $\mathbb{R}_+$, then the Weierstrass Theorem may be used to prove that a solution exists to this problem. (This is immediate if one can show that the continuity of f implies the compactness of the set of feasible triples (x_1, x_2, x_3).)

4

Unconstrained Optima

4.1 "Unconstrained" Optima

We now turn to a study of optimization theory under assumptions of differentiability. Our principal objective here is to identify *necessary* conditions that the derivative of f must satisfy at an optimum. We begin our analysis with an examination of what are called "unconstrained" optima. The terminology, while standard, is somewhat unfortunate, since unconstrained does not literally mean the absence of constraints. Rather, it refers to the more general situation where the constraints have no bite at the optimal point, that is, a situation in which we can move (at least) a small distance away from the optimal point in any direction without leaving the feasible set.[1]

Formally, given a set $\mathcal{D} \subset \mathbb{R}^n$, we define the *interior* of $\mathcal{D}$ (denoted int $\mathcal{D}$) by

$$\text{int } \mathcal{D} = \{x \in \mathcal{D} \mid \text{there is } r > 0 \text{ such that } B(x, r) \subset \mathcal{D}\}.$$

A point x where f achieves a maximum will be called an *unconstrained maximum* of f if $x \in \text{int } \mathcal{D}$. Unconstrained minima are defined analogously.

One observation is important before proceeding to the analysis. The concepts of maxima and minima are *global* concepts, i.e., they involve comparisons between the value of f at a particular point x and *all other feasible points* $z \in \mathcal{D}$. On the other hand, differentiability is a *local* property: the derivative of f at a point x tells us something about the behavior of f in a neighborhood of x, but nothing at all about the behavior of f elsewhere on $\mathcal{D}$. Intuitively, this suggests that if there exists an open set $X \subset \mathcal{D}$ such that x is a maximum of f on X (but maybe not on all of $\mathcal{D}$), the behavior of f at x would be similar to the behavior of f at a point z which is an unconstrained maximum of f on all of $\mathcal{D}$. (Compare the behavior of f at x^* and y^* in Figure 4.1.) This motivates the following definitions:

---

[1]The term "interior optimum" is sometimes used to represent what we have called an "unconstrained optimum." While this alternative term is both more descriptive and less misleading, it is not as popular, at least in the context of optimization theory. Consequently, we stick to "unconstrained optimum."

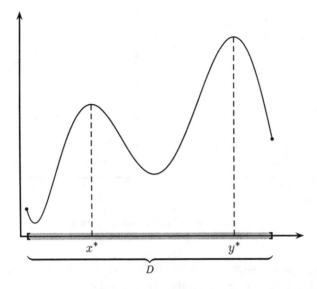

Fig. 4.1. Global and Local Optima

- A point $x \in \mathcal{D}$ is a *local maximum* of f on $\mathcal{D}$ if there is $r > 0$ such that $f(x) \geq f(y)$ for all $y \in \mathcal{D} \cap B(x, r)$.
- A point $x \in \mathcal{D}$ is an *unconstrained local maximum* of f on $\mathcal{D}$ if there is $r > 0$ such that $B(x, r) \subset \mathcal{D}$, and $f(x) \geq f(y)$ for all $y \in B(x, r)$.

To maintain a distinction between the concepts, we will sometimes refer to a point x which is a maximum of f on all of $\mathcal{D}$ as a *global maximum*. Local and global minima of f on $\mathcal{D}$ are defined analogously.

The next two sections classify the behavior of the derivatives of f at unconstrained local maxima and minima. Section 4.2 deals with "first-order" conditions, namely, the behavior of the first derivative Df of f around an optimal point x^*, while Section 4.3 presents "second-order" conditions, that is, those relating to the behavior of the second derivative $D^2 f$ of f around the optimum x^*.

4.2 First-Order Conditions

Our first result states that the derivative of f must be zero at every unconstrained local maximum or minimum. At an intuitive level, this result is easiest to see in the one-dimensional case: suppose x^* were a local maximum (say), and $f'(x^*) \neq 0$. Then, if $f'(x^*) > 0$, it would be possible to increase the value of f by moving a small amount to the right of x^*, while if $f'(x^*) < 0$, the same conclusion could be obtained by moving a small amount to the left of x^* (see Figure 4.2); at an

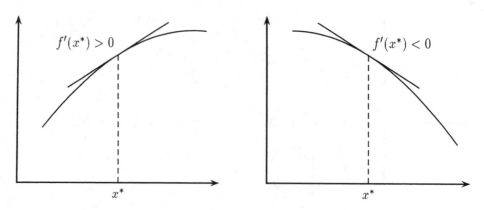

Fig. 4.2. First-Order Conditions in $\mathbb{R}$

unconstrained point x^*, such moves would be feasible, and this would violate the definition of a local maximum. A similar argument shows that $f'(x^*)$ must be zero at a local minimum x^*.

Theorem 4.1 *Suppose $x^* \in int\, \mathcal{D} \subset \mathbb{R}^n$ is a local maximum of f on $\mathcal{D}$, i.e., there is $r > 0$ such that $B(x^*, r) \subset \mathcal{D}$ and $f(x^*) \geq f(x)$ for all $x \in B(x^*, r)$. Suppose also that f is differentiable at x^*. Then $Df(x^*) = 0$. The same result is true if, instead, x^* were a local minimum of f on $\mathcal{D}$.*

Proof See Section 4.5. □

It must be emphasized that Theorem 4.1 only provides a *necessary* condition for an unconstrained local optimum. The condition is in no way also *sufficient*; that is, the theorem does *not* state that if $Df(x^*) = 0$ for some x^* in the interior of the feasible set, then x^* must be either an unconstrained local maximum or an unconstrained local minimum. In point of fact, it need be neither. Consider the following example:

Example 4.2 Let $\mathcal{D} = \mathbb{R}$, and let $f: \mathbb{R} \to \mathbb{R}$ be given by $f(x) = x^3$ for $x \in \mathbb{R}$. Then, we have $f'(0) = 0$, but 0 is neither a local maximum nor a local minimum of f on $\mathbb{R}$. For, any open ball around 0 must contain a point $x > 0$ and a point $z < 0$, and, of course, $x > 0$ implies $f(x) = x^3 > 0 = f(0)$, while $z < 0$ implies $f(z) = z^3 < 0 = f(0)$. □

In the sequel, we will refer to any point x^* that satisfies the first-order condition $Df(x^*) = 0$ as a *critical point of f on $\mathcal{D}$*. To restate the point made by Theorem 4.1

and Example 4.2, every unconstrained local optimum must be a critical point, but there could exist critical points that are neither local maxima nor local minima.

4.3 Second-Order Conditions

The first-order conditions for unconstrained local optima do not distinguish between *maxima* and *minima*. To obtain such a distinction in the behavior of f at an optimum, we need to examine the behavior of the second derivative $D^2 f$ of f. A preliminary definition first:

- A local maximum x of f on $\mathcal{D}$ is called a *strict local maximum* if there is $r > 0$ such that $f(x) > f(y)$ for all $y \in B(x, r) \cap D$, $y \neq x$.

Strict local minima are defined analogously. The following theorem classifies the behavior of $D^2 f$ at unconstrained local optima.

Theorem 4.3 *Suppose f is a C^2 function on $\mathcal{D} \subset \mathbb{R}^n$, and x is a point in the interior of $\mathcal{D}$.*

1. *If f has a local maximum at x, then $D^2 f(x)$ is negative semidefinite.*
2. *If f has a local minimum at x, then $D^2 f(x)$ is positive semidefinite.*
3. *If $Df(x) = 0$ and $D^2 f(x)$ is negative definite at some x, then x is a strict local maximum of f on $\mathcal{D}$.*
4. *If $Df(x) = 0$ and $D^2 f(x)$ is positive definite at some x, then x is a strict local minimum of f on $\mathcal{D}$.*

Proof See Section 4.6. □

Observe that unlike Theorem 4.1, the conditions of Theorem 4.3 are not all necessary conditions. In particular, while parts 1 and 2 of Theorem 4.3 do identify necessary conditions that the second derivative $D^2 f$ must satisfy at local optima, parts 3 and 4 are actually *sufficient* conditions that identify specific points as being local optima. Unfortunately, these necessary and sufficient conditions are not the same: while the necessary conditions pertain to *semidefiniteness* of $D^2 f$ at the optimal point, the sufficient conditions require *definiteness* of this matrix. This is problematic from the point of view of applications. Suppose we have a critical point x^* at which $D^2 f(x^*)$ is negative semidefinite (say), but not negative definite. Then, Part 3 of Theorem 4.3 does not allow us to conclude that x^* must be a local maximum. On the other hand, we cannot rule out the possibility of x^* being a local maximum either, because by Part 1 of the theorem, $D^2 f(x^*)$ need only be negative semidefinite at a local maximum x^*.

This situation could be improved if we could either strengthen parts 1 and 2 of the theorem to

$D^2 f(x)$ must be negative definite at a local maximum x, and positive definite at a local minimum x,

or strengthen parts 3 and 4 of the theorem to

If $Df(x) = 0$ and $D^2 f(x)$ is negative semidefinite (resp. positive semidefinite), then x is a (possibly non-strict) local maximum (resp. local minimum) of f on $\mathcal{D}$.

However, such strengthening is impossible, as the following examples demonstrate. The first example shows that parts 1 and 2 of the theorem cannot be improved upon, while the second does the same for parts 3 and 4.

Example 4.4 Let $\mathcal{D} = \mathbb{R}$, and let $f : \mathbb{R} \to \mathbb{R}$ and $g : \mathbb{R} \to \mathbb{R}$ be defined by $f(x) = x^4$ and $g(x) = -x^4$, respectively, for all $x \in \mathbb{R}$. Since $x^4 \geq 0$ everywhere, and $f(0) = g(0) = 0$, it is clear that 0 is a global minimum of f on $\mathcal{D}$, and a global maximum of g on $\mathcal{D}$. However, $f''(0) = g''(0) = 0$, so viewed as 1×1 matrices, $f''(0)$ is positive semidefinite, but not positive definite, while $g''(0)$ is negative semidefinite, but not negative definite. $\square$

Example 4.5 As is Example 4.2, let $\mathcal{D} = \mathbb{R}$, and let $f : \mathbb{R} \to \mathbb{R}$ be given by $f(x) = x^3$ for all $x \in \mathbb{R}$. Then, $f'(x) = 3x^2$ and $f''(x) = 6x$, so $f'(0) = f''(0) = 0$. Thus, $f''(0)$, viewed as a 1×1 matrix, is both positive semidefinite and negative semidefinite (but not either positive definite or negative definite). If parts 3 and 4 of Theorem 4.3 only required semidefiniteness, $f''(0)$ would pass both tests; however, 0 is neither a local maximum nor a local minimum of f on $\mathcal{D}$. $\square$

4.4 Using the First- and Second-Order Conditions

Taken by itself, the first-order condition of Theorem 4.1 is of limited use in computing solutions to optimization problems for at least two reasons. First, the condition applies only to the cases where the optimum occurs at an interior point of the feasible set, whereas in most applications, some or all of the constraints will tend to matter. Second, the condition is only a *necessary* one: as evidenced by Example 4.2, it is possible for a point x to meet the first-order condition without x being either a local maximum or a local minimum, and, indeed, without an optimum even existing.

Even if Theorem 4.1 is combined with the second-order conditions provided by Theorem 4.3, a material improvement in the situation does not result. Parts 1 and 2 of Theorem 4.3 also provide only *necessary* conditions, and the function of Example 4.5 passes both of these conditions at $x = 0$, although 0 is not even a local maximum or local minimum. While parts 3 and 4 do provide *sufficient* conditions, these are sufficient for all local optima, and not just for global optima. Thus, the second-order conditions can at most help ascertain if a point is a *local* optimum; they cannot help determine if a critical point is a global optimum or not.[2] In particular, global optima might fail to exist altogether (though several critical points, including local optima, may exist), but the first- or second-order conditions will not help spot this problem. Consider the following example:

Example 4.6 Let $\mathcal{D} = \mathbb{R}$, and let $f: \mathcal{D} \to \mathbb{R}$ be given by

$$f(x) = 2x^3 - 3x^2.$$

It is easily checked that f is a C^2 function on $\mathbb{R}$, and that there are precisely two points at which $f'(x) = 0$: namely, at $x = 0$ and $x = 1$. Invoking the second-order conditions, we get $f''(0) = -6$, while $f''(1) = +6$. Thus, the point 0 is a strict local maximum of f on $\mathcal{D}$, while the point 1 is a strict local minimum of f on $\mathcal{D}$.

However, there is nothing in the first- or second-order conditions that will help determine whether these points are *global* optima. In fact, they are not: global optima do not exist in this problem, since $\lim_{x \to +\infty} f(x) = +\infty$, and $\lim_{x \to -\infty} f(x) = -\infty$. □

On the other hand, in problems in which it is known *a priori* that a solution[3] does exist (say, because the problem meets the conditions of the Weierstrass Theorem), Theorem 4.1 can, sometimes, come in handy in computing the solution. The simplest case where this is true is where the problem at hand is known to have an *unconstrained* solution. In this case, the set $\mathcal{N}^*$ of all points that meet the first-order conditions must contain this unconstrained optimum point (denoted, say, x^*); moreover, since x^* is an optimum on all of the feasible set, it must certainly be an optimum on $\mathcal{N}^*$. Thus, by solving for $\mathcal{N}^*$ and finding the point that optimizes the objective function over $\mathcal{N}^*$, the solution to the problem may be identified.

More generally, even if it is not known that the optimum must be in the interior of the feasible set, a modified version of this procedure can be successfully employed, provided the set of boundary points of the feasible set is "small" (say, is a finite set). To wit, the optimum must either occur in the interior of the feasible set, or on its boundary. Since it must satisfy the first-order conditions in the former case, it suffices, in order to identify the optimum, to compare the optimum value of the objective function on the boundary, with those points in the interior that meet the first-order conditions. The point that optimizes f over this restricted set is the optimum we are seeking. Here is a simple example of a situation where this procedure works:

---

[2] Second-order conditions can also help to rule out candidate critical points. For instance, a critical point cannot be a global maximum if it passes the test for a strict local minimum.

[3] A "solution," as always, refers to a *global* maximum or minimum, whichever is the object of study in the specific problem at hand.

Example 4.7 Consider the problem of maximizing $f(x) = 4x^3 - 5x^2 + 2x$ over the unit interval [0,1]. Since [0,1] is compact, and f is continuous on this interval, the Weierstrass Theorem shows that f has a maximum on this interval. There are two possibilities: either the maximum occurs at one of the boundary points 0 or 1, or it is an unconstrained maximum. In the latter case, it must meet the first-order conditions: $f'(x) = 12x^2 - 10x + 2 = 0$. The only points that satisfy this condition are $x = 1/2$ and $x = 1/3$. Evaluating f at the four points 0, 1/3, 1/2, and 1 shows that $x = 1$ is the point where f is maximized on [0,1]. An identical procedure also shows that $x = 0$ is the point where f is minimized on [0,1].   □

In most economic applications, however, the set of boundary points is quite large, so carrying out the appropriate comparisons is a non-trivial task. For example, in the utility maximization problem of subsection 2.3.1, the entire line segment

$$\{x \mid p \cdot x = I, x \geq 0\}$$

is part of the boundary of the budget set $\mathcal{B}(p, I) = \{x \mid p \cdot x \leq I, x \geq 0\}$. Nonetheless, this procedure is indicative of how *global optima* may be identified by combining knowledge of the existence of a solution with first-order necessary conditions for *local* optima. We will return to this point again in the next two chapters.

It bears stressing that the *a priori* knowledge of existence of an optimum is important if the first-order conditions (or, more generally, *any* set of necessary conditions) are to be used successfully in locating an optimum. If such knowledge is lacking, then, as in Example 4.6, the set of points satisfying the necessary conditions may fail to contain the global optimum, because no global optimum may exist.

Finally, it must be stated that the limited importance given in this section to the use of second-order conditions in locating optima is deliberate. The value of second-order conditions is often exaggerated. As we have seen, if a solution is known to exist, then it may be identified simply by comparing the value of the objective function at the points that satisfy the first-order conditions. The only role the second-order conditions can play here is, perhaps, to cut down on the number of points at which the comparison has to be carried out; for instance, if we are seeking a maximum of f, then all critical points can be ruled out that also satisfy the second-order conditions for a strict local minimum. On the other hand, if *a priori* knowledge of existence of a solution is lacking, then as Example 4.6 shows, the most that second-order conditions can do is to help identify *local* optima, and this is evidently of limited value.

4.5 A Proof of the First-Order Conditions

We provide two proofs of Theorem 4.1. The first illustrates the technique of "bootstrapping," a technique that we employ repeatedly in this book. That is, we first prove the result for a special case, and then use this result to establish the general case. The second proof, which is shorter, establishes the result by appealing to properties of the directional derivative (see Chapter 1).

First Proof We proceed in two steps. First, we establish the result for the case $n = 1$, i.e., when $\mathcal{D}$ is a subset of $\mathbb{R}$. Then we use this to prove that the result holds for any $n > 1$. Our proofs only cover local *maxima*. The case of local *minima* can be proved analogously; the details are left to the reader.

Case 1: $n = 1$

Since f is assumed differentiable at x^*, it is the case that for any sequence $y_k \to x^*$, we have

$$\lim_{k \to \infty} \left(\frac{f(y_k) - f(x^*)}{y_k - x^*} \right) = f'(x^*).$$

Consider two sequences $\{y_k\}$ and $\{z_k\}$ such that (a) $y_k < x^*$ for all k, $y_k \to x^*$, and (b) $z_k > x^*$ for all k, $z_k \to x^*$. For sufficiently large k, we must have $y_k, z_k \in B(x^*, \epsilon)$, so for all large k, $f(x^*) \geq f(y_k)$ and $f(x^*) \geq f(z_k)$. Therefore, for all large k,

$$\frac{f(y_k) - f(x^*)}{y_k - x^*} \geq 0 \geq \frac{f(z_k) - f(x^*)}{z_k - x^*}.$$

Taking limits as k goes to infinity along the y_k sequence establishes $f'(x^*) \geq 0$, while taking limits along the z_k sequence establishes $f'(x^*) \leq 0$. These can hold simultaneously only if $f'(x^*) = 0$, which establishes the desired result.

Case 2: $n > 1$

Suppose f has a local maximum at $x^* \in \mathcal{D} \subset \mathbb{R}^n$, and that f is differentiable at x^*. We will show that $\partial f(x^*)/\partial x_i = 0$ for any i. By the hypothesis that $Df(x^*)$ exists, we must have $Df(x^*) = [\partial f(x^*)/\partial x_1, \ldots, \partial f(x^*)/\partial x_n]$, so this will complete the proof.

For $i = 1, \ldots, n$, let $e_i \in \mathbb{R}^n$ be the i-th unit vector, i.e., the vector with a 1 in the i-th place and zeros elsewhere. Fix any i, and define a function g on $\mathbb{R}$ by

$$g(t) = f(x^* + te_i).$$

Note that $g(0) = f'(x^*)$. Moreover, for any sequence $t_k \to 0$, we have for each k,

$$\frac{g(t_k) - g(0)}{t_k} = \frac{f(x^* + t_k e_i) - f(x^*)}{t_k}$$

and the right-hand side (RHS) of this expression converges to $\partial f(x^*)/\partial x_i$ as $k \to \infty$. Therefore, g is differentiable at 0, and $g'(0) = \partial f(x^*)/\partial x_i$.

Now, $d(x^* + te_i, x^*) = \|x^* + te_i - x^*\| = |t|$, so for t sufficiently close to zero, we must have $(x + te_i) \in U$. Therefore, for sufficiently small $|t|$,

$$g(t) = f(x^* + te_i) \leq f(x^*) = g(0),$$

implying that g has a local maximum at $t = 0$. By case 1, this means we must have $g'(0) = 0$, and the proof is complete.   □

Second Proof Once again, we prove the result for local *maxima*. The case of local minima may be handled analogously. So suppose x^* is a local maximum of f on $\mathcal{D}$, i.e., there is $r > 0$ such that $f(x^*) \geq f(y)$ for all $y \in B(x^*, r)$. Suppose also that f is differentiable at x^*.

Recall from Chapter 1 that the differentiability of f at x^* implies that the (one-sided) directional derivative $Df(x^*; h)$ exists for any $h \in \mathbb{R}^n$, with, in fact, $Df(x^*; h) = Df(x^*) \cdot h$ (see Theorem 1.56). We will show that $Df(x^*; h) = 0$ for all $h \in \mathbb{R}^n$. This will establish the desired result since $Df(x^*) \cdot h = 0$ can hold for all h only if $Df(x^*) = 0$.

First, we claim that $Df(x^*; h) \leq 0$ for any $h \in \mathbb{R}^n$. Suppose this were not true for some h, so $Df(x^*; h) > 0$. From the definition of $Df(x^*; h)$, we now have

$$Df(x^*; h) = \lim_{t \to 0+} \frac{f(x^* + th) - f(x^*)}{t} > 0.$$

Therefore, for all $t > 0$ sufficiently small, it is the case that $(f(x^* + th) - f(x^*)) > 0$. However, for $t < r/\|h\|$, we also have $d(x + th, x) = t\|h\| < r$, so $(x + th) \in B(x^*, r)$. Since x is a maximum on $B(x^*, r)$, this implies $f(x^* + th) \leq f(x^*)$, a contradiction which establishes the claim.

Now, pick any $h \in \mathbb{R}^n$, and let $h_1 = h$, $h_2 = -h$. Since $h_1, h_2 \in \mathbb{R}^n$, we must then have $Df(x^*; h_1) = Df(x^*) \cdot h_1 = Df(x^*) \cdot h \leq 0$, and $Df(x^*; h_2) = Df(x^*) \cdot h_2 = -Df(x^*) \cdot h \leq 0$. But $Df(x^*) \cdot h \leq 0$ and $-Df(x^*) \cdot h \leq 0$ are possible simultaneously only if $Df(x^*; h) = 0$. Since h was chosen arbitrarily, we have $Df(x^*) \cdot h = 0$ for all h.   □

4.6 A Proof of the Second-Order Conditions

As with the first proof of Theorem 4.1, we adopt a two-step procedure to prove Theorem 4.3. We first prove the result for the case where $n = 1$ (i.e., $\mathcal{D} \subset \mathbb{R}$), and then using this result to prove the general case.

Case 1: n = 1

When $n = 1$, the second-derivative $f''(x)$ of f at x is simply a real number. Therefore, Parts 1 and 2 of the theorem will be proved if we prove Parts 3 and 4. For, suppose Parts 3 and 4 are true. Suppose further that x is a local maximum, so $f'(x) = 0$. If

$f''(x) \not< 0$, we must have $f''(x) > 0$. But this will imply by Part 4 that x is actually a *strict local minimum*, which is a contradiction because a *strict* local minimum cannot also be a local maximum.

We prove Part 3 here. Part 4 may be proved by a completely analogous procedure. Suppose x is in the interior of $\mathcal{D}$ and satisfies $f'(x) = 0$ and $f''(x) < 0$. Since $f''(x) < 0$, the first derivative f' must be strictly decreasing in a neighborhood (denoted, say, $B(x, r)$) of x. Since $f'(x) = 0$, a point $z \in B(x, r)$ must satisfy $f'(z) > 0$ if $z < x$, and $f'(z) < 0$ if $z > x$. In turn, these signs of f' mean that f is strictly increasing to the left of x (i.e., $f(x) > f(z)$ if $z \in B(x, r), z < x$) and strictly decreasing to the right of x (i.e., $f(x) > f(z)$ if $z \in B(x, r), z > x$). This states precisely that x is a strict local maximum.

Case 2: $n > 1$

When $n > 1$, Parts 3 and 4 are no longer the contrapositives of Parts 1 and 2, respectively, since the failure of an $n \times n$ matrix to be positive definite does not make it negative semidefinite. So a proof of Parts 1 and 2 will not suffice to establish Parts 3 and 4, and vice versa.

We prove Part 1 first. Let x be an unconstrained local maximum of f on $\mathcal{D}$. We have to show that for any z in $\mathbb{R}^n$, $z \neq 0$, we have $z'D^2 f(x)z \geq 0$.

Pick any z in $\mathbb{R}^n$. Define the real-valued function g by $g(t) = f(x + tz)$. Note that $g(0) = f(x)$. For $|t|$ sufficiently small, $(x + tz)$ will belong to the neighborhood of x on which x is a local maximum of f. It follows that there is some $\epsilon > 0$ such that $g(0) \geq g(t)$ for all $t \in (-\epsilon, \epsilon)$, i.e., that 0 is a local maximum of g. By case 1, therefore, we must have $g''(0) \leq 0$. On the other hand, it follows from the definition of g that $g''(t) = z'D^2 f(x + tz)z$, so that $z'D^2 f(x)z = g''(0) \leq 0$, as desired. This proves Part 1. Part 2 is proved similarly and is left to the reader.

To see Part 3, suppose $Df(x) = 0$ and $D^2 f(x)$ is negative definite. Since f is C^2, by Corollary 1.60, there exists $\epsilon > 0$ such that $D^2 f(w)$ is negative definite for all $w \in B(x, \epsilon)$. Fix ϵ. We will show that $f(x) > f(w)$ for all $w \in B(x, \epsilon), w \neq x$.

Let $S = \{z \in \mathbb{R}^n \mid \|z\| = 1\}$. Define $B = \{y \in \mathbb{R}^n \mid y = x + tz, \ z \in S, \ |t| < \epsilon\}$. We claim that $B = B(x, \epsilon)$.

To see this, first note that for any $y = x + tz \in B$, $d(x, y) = \|x + tz - x\| = |t| \cdot \|z\| = |t| < \epsilon$, so certainly $B \subset B(x, \epsilon)$. On the other hand, pick any $w \in B(x, \epsilon)$. Define $t \doteq d(x, w) = \|x - w\|$, and $z = (w - x)/t$. Then, since $w \in B(x, \epsilon)$, we have $0 \leq t < \epsilon$, and of course, $\|z\| = \|w - x\|/\|w - x\| = 1$, so $z \in S$. By construction, $tz = w - x$ or $x + tz = w$. This establishes $B(x, \epsilon) \subset B$. Therefore, $B(x, \epsilon) = B$, as claimed.

We will prove that x is a strict local maximum of f on B. Fix any $z \in S$. Let $g(t) = f(x + tz)$, $t \in (-\epsilon, \epsilon)$. Since $(x + tz) \in B = B(x, \epsilon)$, it is the case that $D^2 f(x + tz)$ is negative definite for $|t| < \epsilon$. The usual argument shows that

$g'(0) = 0$. Moreover, $g''(t) = z'D^2(f(x+tz)z$, which is strictly negative for $|t| < \epsilon$. This implies that the point 0 is a strict maximum of g on the interval $|t| < \epsilon$. In turn, this means that $f(x) > f(x + tz)$ for all $|t| < \epsilon$.

Since z was arbitrary, this inequality holds for any $z \in S$ on $|t| < \epsilon$. This states precisely that $f(x) > f(w)$ for all $w \in B(x, \epsilon)$, proving Part 3. Part 4 is proved analogously.   □

4.7 Exercises

1. Is Theorem 4.1 valid if $x^* \notin \text{int } \mathcal{D}$? If yes, provide a proof. If not, a counterexample.

2. Find all the critical points (i.e., points where $f'(x) = 0$) of the function $f \colon \mathbb{R} \to \mathbb{R}$, defined as $f(x) = x - x^2 - x^3$ for $x \in \mathbb{R}$. Which of these points can you identify as local maxima or minima using the second-order test? Are any of these *global* optima?

3. Suppose $x \in \text{int } \mathcal{D}$ is a local minimum of f on $\mathcal{D}$. Suppose also that f is differentiable at x. Prove, without appealing to Theorem 4.1, that $Df(x) = 0$.

4. Find and classify the critical points (local maximum, local minimum, neither) of each of the following functions. Are any of the local optima also global optima?

   (a) $f(x, y) = 2x^3 + xy^2 + 5x^2 + y^2$.
   (b) $f(x, y) = e^{2x}(x + y^2 + 2y)$.
   (c) $f(x, y) = xy(a - x - y)$.
   (d) $f(x, y) = x \sin y$.
   (e) $f(x, y) = x^4 + x^2y^2 - y$.
   (f) $f(x, y) = x^4 + y^4 - x^3$.
   (g) $f(x, y) = \dfrac{x}{1 + x^2 + y^2}$.
   (h) $f(x, y) = (x^4/32) + x^2y^2 - x - y^2$.

5. Find the maximum and minimum values of

$$f(x, y) = 2 + 2x + 2y - x^2 - y^2$$

   on the set $\{(x, y) \in \mathbb{R}_+^2 \mid x + y = 9\}$ by representing the problem as an unconstrained optimization problem in one variable.

6. Let $f \colon \mathbb{R} \to \mathbb{R}$ have a local maximum at x^*. Show that the following inequalities (called the "generalized first-order conditions") hold regardless of whether f is assumed differentiable or not:

$$\liminf_{y \uparrow x^*} \left(\frac{f(x^*) - f(y)}{x^* - y} \right) \geq 0, \quad \text{and} \quad \limsup_{y \downarrow x^*} \left(\frac{f(x^*) - f(y)}{x^* - y} \right) \leq 0.$$

(The expression $y \uparrow x$ is shorthand for $y < x$ and $y \to x$, while $y \downarrow x$ is shorthand for $y > x$ and $y \to x$.) Explain whether the "lim sup" and "lim inf" in these inequalities can be replaced with a plain "limit." Examine also whether the weak inequalities can be replaced with strict ones, if x^* is instead a *strict* local maximum.

7. Suppose $f: \mathbb{R} \to \mathbb{R}$ has a local maximum at x that is not a strict local maximum. Does this imply that f is constant in some neighborhood of x? Prove your answer or provide a counterexample.

8. Let $f: \mathbb{R}_+ \to \mathbb{R}_+$ be a C^1 function that satisfies $f(0) = 0$ and $\lim_{x \to \infty} f(x) = 0$. Suppose there is only a single point $x \in \mathbb{R}_+$ at which $f'(x) = 0$. Show that x must be a global maximum of f on $\mathbb{R}$.

9. Let $\varphi: \mathbb{R} \to \mathbb{R}$ be a strictly increasing C^2 function. Let $\mathcal{D}$ be an open set in $\mathbb{R}^n$ and let $f: \mathcal{D} \to \mathbb{R}$ also be a C^2 function. Finally, suppose that f has a strict local maximum at $x^* \in \mathcal{D}$, and that $D^2 f(x^*)$ is negative definite. Use Theorem 4.3 to show that the composition $\varphi \circ f$ also has a strict local maximum at x^*.

10. Let $f: \mathbb{R}^n \to \mathbb{R}$ be a C^1 function, and let $g = -f$. Fix any x, and show that the quadratic form $D^2 g(x)$ is positive definite if and only if $D^2 f(x)$ is negative definite.

5

Equality Constraints and the Theorem of Lagrange

It is not often that optimization problems have unconstrained solutions. Typically, some or all of the constraints will matter. Over this chapter and the next, we examine necessary conditions for optima in such a context.

If the constraints do bite at an optimum x, it is imperative, in order to characterize the behavior of the objective function f around x, to have some knowledge of what the constraint set looks like in a neighborhood of x. Thus, a first step in the analysis of constrained optimization problems is to require some additional structure of the constraint set $\mathcal{D}$, beyond just that it be some subset of $\mathbb{R}^n$. The structure that we shall require, and the order in which our analysis will proceed, is the subject of the following section.

5.1 Constrained Optimization Problems

It is assumed in the sequel that the constraint set $\mathcal{D}$ has the form

$$\mathcal{D} = U \cap \{x \in \mathbb{R}^n \mid g(x) = 0, \ h(x) \geq 0\},$$

where $U \subset \mathbb{R}^n$ is open, $g: \mathbb{R}^n \to \mathbb{R}^k$, and $h: \mathbb{R}^n \to \mathbb{R}^l$. We will refer to the functions $g = (g_1, \ldots, g_k)$ as *equality constraints*, and to the functions $h = (h_1, \ldots, h_l)$ as *inequality constraints*.[1]

This specification for the constraint set $\mathcal{D}$ is very general, much more so than might appear at first sight. Many problems of interest in economic theory can be written in this form, including all of the examples outlined in Section 2.3. Nonnegativity constraints are, for instance, easily handled: if a problem requires that $x \in \mathbb{R}^n_+$, this may be accomplished by defining the functions $h_j: \mathbb{R}^n \to \mathbb{R}$

$$h_j(x) = x_j, \qquad j = 1, \ldots, n,$$

---

[1] Note that we do not preclude the possibility that U could simply be all of $\mathbb{R}^n$, that is, that $\mathcal{D}$ can be expressed using only the inequality and equality constraints.

and using the n inequality constraints

$$h_j(x) \geq 0, \qquad j = 1, \ldots, n.$$

More generally, requirements of the form $\alpha(x) \geq a$, $\beta(x) \leq b$, or $\psi(x) = c$ (where a, b, and c are constants), can all be expressed in the desired form by simply writing them as $\alpha(x) - a \geq 0$, $b - \beta(x) \geq 0$, or $c - \psi(x) = 0$.

Thus for instance, the budget set $\mathcal{B}(p, I) = \{x \in \mathbb{R}^n_+ \mid p \cdot x \leq I\}$ of the utility maximization problem of subsection 2.3.1 can be represented using $(n+1)$ inequality constraints. Indeed, if we define $h_j(x) = x_j$ for $j = 1, \ldots, n$, and

$$h_{n+1}(x) = I - p \cdot x,$$

then it follows that $\mathcal{B}(p, I)$ is the set

$$\{x \in \mathbb{R}^n \mid h_j(x) \geq 0, \ j = 1, \ldots, n + 1\}.$$

As mentioned above, our analysis of constrained optimization problems in this book comes in three parts. In this chapter, we study the case where all the constraints are equality constraints, i.e., where the constraint set $\mathcal{D}$ can be represented as

$$\mathcal{D} = U \cap \{x \mid g(x) = 0\},$$

where $U \subset \mathbb{R}^n$ is open, and $g \colon \mathbb{R}^n \to \mathbb{R}^k$. In the sequel, we shall refer to these as *equality-constrained optimization problems*.

Then, in Chapter 6, we study the complementary case where all the constraints are inequality constraints, i.e., the constraint set has the form

$$\mathcal{D} = U \cap \{x \mid h(x) \geq 0\},$$

where $U \subset \mathbb{R}^n$ is open, and $h \colon \mathbb{R}^n \to \mathbb{R}^l$. We label these *inequality-constrained optimization problems*. Finally, in Section 6.4, we combine these results into the general case of *mixed constraints*, where the specification of $\mathcal{D}$ may involve both equality and inequality constraints:

$$\mathcal{D} = U \cap \{x \in \mathbb{R}^n \mid g(x) = 0, h(x) \geq 0\}.$$

5.2 Equality Constraints and the Theorem of Lagrange

The Theorem of Lagrange provides a powerful characterization of local optima of equality-constrained optimization problems in terms of the behavior of the objective function f and the constraint functions g at these points. The conditions the theorem describes may be viewed as the first-order necessary conditions for local optima in these problems. The statement of the theorem, and a discussion of some of its components, is the subject of this section.

5.2.1 Statement of the Theorem

To state the Theorem of Lagrange, it is necessary to recall two pieces of notation from Chapter 1. First, that $\rho(A)$ denotes the rank of a matrix A; and, second, that the derivative $D\xi(x)$ of a function $\xi \colon \mathbb{R}^n \to \mathbb{R}^p$ is the $p \times n$ matrix whose (i, j)-th entry is

$$\frac{\partial \xi_i}{\partial x_j}(x), \quad i = 1, \ldots, p, \quad j = 1, \ldots, n.$$

Theorem 5.1 (The Theorem of Lagrange) *Let $f \colon \mathbb{R}^n \to \mathbb{R}$, and $g_i \colon \mathbb{R}^n \to \mathbb{R}^k$ be C^1 functions, $i = 1, \ldots, k$. Suppose x^* is a local maximum or minimum of f on the set*

$$\mathcal{D} = U \cap \{x \mid g_i(x) = 0, \ i = 1, \ldots, k\},$$

where $U \subset \mathbb{R}^n$ is open. Suppose also that $\rho(Dg(x^*)) = k$. Then, there exists a vector $\lambda^* = (\lambda_1^*, \ldots, \lambda_k^*) \in \mathbb{R}^k$ such that

$$Df(x^*) + \sum_{i=1}^{k} \lambda_i^* Dg_i(x^*) = 0.$$

Proof   See Section 5.6 below.   □

Remark   In the sequel, if a pair (x^*, λ^*) satisfies the twin conditions that $g(x^*) = 0$ and $Df(x^*) + \sum_{i=1}^{k} \lambda_i^* Dg_i(x^*) = 0$, we will say that (x^*, λ^*) meets the first-order conditions of the Theorem of Lagrange, or that (x^*, λ^*) meets the first-order necessary conditions in equality-constrained optimization problems.   □

It must be stressed that the Theorem of Lagrange only provides *necessary* conditions for local optima x^*, and, at that, only for those local optima x^* which also meet the condition that $\rho(Dg(x^*)) = k$. These conditions are not asserted to be *sufficient*; that is, the theorem does *not* claim that if there exist (x, λ) such that $g(x) = 0$, and $Df(x) + \sum_{i=1}^{k} \lambda_i Dg_i(x) = 0$, then x must either be a local maximum or a local minimum, even if x also meets the rank condition $\rho(Dg(x)) = k$. Indeed, it is an easy matter to modify Example 4.2 slightly to show that these conditions *cannot* be sufficient:

Example 5.2   Let f and g be functions on $\mathbb{R}^2$ defined by $f(x, y) = x^3 + y^3$ and $g(x, y) = x - y$. Consider the equality-constrained optimization problem of maximizing and minimizing $f(x, y)$ over the set $\mathcal{D} = \{(x, y) \in \mathbb{R}^2 \mid g(x, y) = 0\}$.

Let (x^*, y^*) be the point $(0, 0)$, and let $\lambda^* = 0$. Then, $g(x^*, y^*) = 0$, so (x^*, y^*) is a feasible point. Moreover, since $Dg(x, y) = (1, -1)$ for any (x, y), it is clearly the case that $\rho(Dg(x^*, y^*)) = 1$. Finally, since $Df(x, y) = (3x^2, 3y^2)$, we have

$$Df(x^*, y^*) + \lambda^* Dg(x^*, y^*) = (0, 0) + 0 \cdot (1, -1) = (0, 0).$$

Thus, if the conditions of the Theorem of Lagrange were also sufficient, then (x^*, y^*) would be either a local maximum or a local minimum of f on $\mathcal{D}$. It is, quite evidently, neither: we have $f(x^*, y^*) = 0$, but for every $\epsilon > 0$, it is the case that $(-\epsilon, -\epsilon) \in \mathcal{D}$ and $(\epsilon, \epsilon) \in \mathcal{D}$, so $f(-\epsilon, -\epsilon) = -2\epsilon^3 < 0 = f(x^*, y^*)$, while $f(\epsilon, \epsilon) = 2\epsilon^3 > 0 = f(x^*, y^*)$. $\qquad\square$

In the subsections that follow, we focus on two aspects of the Theorem of Lagrange. Subsection 5.2.2 examines the importance of the rank condition that $\rho(Dg(x^*)) = k$, while subsection 5.2.3 sketches an interpretation of the vector $\lambda^* = (\lambda_1^*, \ldots, \lambda_k^*)$ whose existence the theorem asserts.

5.2.2 The Constraint Qualification

The condition in the Theorem of Lagrange that the rank of $Dg(x^*)$ be equal to the number of constraints k is called the *constraint qualification under equality constraints*. It plays a central role in the proof of the theorem; essentially, it ensures that $Dg(x^*)$ contains an invertible $k \times k$ submatrix, which may be used to define the vector λ^* (for details, see Section 5.6 below).

More importantly, it turns out to be the case that if the constraint qualification is violated, then the conclusions of the theorem may also fail. That is, if x^* is a local optimum at which $\rho(Dg(x^*)) < k$, then there need not exist a vector λ^* such that $Df(x^*) + \sum_{i=1}^{k} \lambda_i^* Dg_i(x^*) = 0$. The following example, which involves seemingly well-behaved objective and constraint functions, illustrates this point:

Example 5.3 Let $f: \mathbb{R}^2 \to \mathbb{R}$ and $g: \mathbb{R}^2 \to \mathbb{R}$ be given by $f(x, y) = -y$, and $g(x, y) = y^3 - x^2$, respectively. Consider the equality-constrained optimization problem

Maximize $f(x, y)$ subject to $(x, y) \in \mathcal{D} = \{(x', y') \in \mathbb{R}^2 \mid g(x', y') = 0\}$.

Since $x^2 \geq 0$ for any real number x, and the constraint requires that $y^3 = x^2$, we must have $y \geq 0$ for any $(x, y) \in \mathcal{D}$; moreover, $y = 0$ if and only if $x = 0$. It easily follows that f attains a unique global maximum on $\mathcal{D}$ at the origin $(x, y) = (0, 0)$. At this global—and, therefore, also local—maximum, $Dg(x, y) = (0, 0)$, so $\rho(Dg(0, 0)) = 0 < 1$. Thus, the constraint qualification is violated. Moreover, $Df(x, y) = (0, -1)$ at any (x, y), which means that there cannot exist any $\lambda \in \mathbb{R}$ such that $Df(0, 0) + \lambda Dg(0, 0) = (0, 0)$. Thus, the conclusions of the Theorem of Lagrange also fail. $\qquad\square$

5.2.3 The Lagrangean Multipliers

The vector $\lambda^* = (\lambda_1^*, \ldots, \lambda_k^*)$ described in the Theorem of Lagrange is called the vector of *Lagrangean multipliers* corresponding to the local optimum x^*. The i-th multiplier λ_i^* measures, in a sense, the sensitivity of the value of the objective function at x^* to a small relaxation of the i-th constraint g_i. We demonstrate this interpretation of λ^* under some assumptions designed to simplify the exposition.

We begin with a clarification of the notion of the "relaxation" of a constraint. To this end, we will suppose in the rest of this subsection that the constraint functions g are given in parametric form as

$$g(x; c) = g(x) + c,$$

where $c = (c_1, \ldots, c_k)$ is a vector of constants. This assumption enables a formal definition of the concept we need: a relaxation of the i-th constraint may now be thought of as an increase in the value of the constant c_i.

Now, let C be some open set of feasible values of c. Suppose that for each $c \in C$, there is a global optimum,[2] denoted $x^*(c)$, of f on the constraint set

$$\mathcal{D} = U \cap \{x \in \mathbb{R}^n \mid g(x; c) = 0\}.$$

Suppose further that, for each $c \in C$, the constraint qualification holds at $x^*(c)$, so there exists $\lambda^*(c) \in \mathbb{R}^k$ such that

$$Df(x^*(c)) + \sum_{i=1}^{k} \lambda_i^*(c) Dg_i(x^*(c)) = 0.$$

Finally, suppose that $x^*(\cdot)$ is a differentiable function on C, that is, that the optimum changes smoothly with changes in the underlying parameters. Let

$$F(c) = f(x^*(c))$$

be the value of the objective function at the optimum given the parameter c. Since f is C^1 and $x^*(\cdot)$ has been assumed to be differentiable on C, $F(\cdot)$ is also differentiable on C. We will show that

$$DF(c) = \lambda^*(c),$$

that is, that $\partial F(c)/\partial c_i = \lambda_i^*(c)$. In words, this states precisely that $\lambda_i^*(c)$ represents the sensitivity of the objective function at $x^*(c)$ to a small relaxation in the i-th constraint.

First, note that from the definition of $F(\cdot)$, we have

$$DF(c) = Df(x^*(c))Dx^*(c),$$

---

[2]Everything in the sequel remains valid if $x^*(c)$ is just a local maximum of f on $\mathcal{D}$.

where $Dx^*(c)$ is the $n \times k$ matrix whose (i, j)-th entry is $\partial x_i^*(c)/\partial c_j$. By the first-order conditions at each c, we also have

$$Df(x^*(c)) = -\sum_{i=1}^{k} \lambda_i^*(c) Dg_i(x^*(c)).$$

By combining the last two expressions, we obtain

$$DF(c) = -\left(\sum_{i=1}^{k} \lambda_i^*(c) Dg_i(x^*(c)) \right) Dx^*(c) = -\sum_{i=1}^{k} \lambda_i^*(c) Dg_i(x^*(c)) Dx^*(c).$$

Since $x^*(c)$ must be feasible at all c, it must identically be true for each i and for all c that $g_i(x^*(c)) + c_i = 0$. Differentiating with respect to c, and rearranging, we obtain

$$Dg_i(x^*(c)) Dx^*(c) = -e_i,$$

where e_i is the i-th unit vector in $\mathbb{R}^k$, that is, the vector that has a 1 in the i-th place and zeros elsewhere. It follows that

$$DF(c) = -\sum_{i=1}^{k} \lambda_i^*(c)(-e_i) = \lambda^*(c),$$

and the proof is complete.

An economic interpretation of the result we have just derived bears mention. Since $\lambda_i^*(c) = \partial f(x^*(c))/\partial x_i$, a small relaxation in constraint i will raise the maximized value of the objective function by $\lambda_i^*(c)$. Therefore, $\lambda_i^*(c)$ also represents the maximum amount the decision-maker will be willing to pay for a marginal relaxation of constraint i, and is the marginal value or the "shadow price" of constraint i at c.

5.3 Second-Order Conditions

The Theorem of Lagrange gives us the first-order necessary conditions for optimization problems with equality constraints. In this section, we describe *second-order* conditions for such problems. As in the unconstrained case, these conditions pertain only to *local* maxima and minima, since differentiability is only a local property.

So consider the problem of maximizing or minimizing $f: \mathbb{R}^n \to \mathbb{R}$ over the set $\mathcal{D} = U \cap \{x \mid g(x) = 0\}$, where $g: \mathbb{R}^n \to \mathbb{R}^k$, and $U \subset \mathbb{R}^n$ is open. We will assume in this subsection that f and g are both C^2 functions. The following notation will come in handy: given any $\lambda \in \mathbb{R}^k$, define the function L on $\mathbb{R}^n$ by

$$L(x; \lambda) = f(x) + \sum_{i=1}^{k} \lambda_i g_i(x).$$

Note that the second derivative $D^2 L(x; \lambda)$ of $L(\cdot; \lambda)$ with respect to the x-variables is the $n \times n$ matrix defined by

$$D^2 L(x; \lambda) = D^2 f(x) + \sum_{i=1}^{k} \lambda_i D^2 g_i(x).$$

Since f and g are both C^2 functions of x, so is $L(\cdot; \lambda)$ for any given value of $\lambda \in \mathbb{R}^k$. Thus, $D^2 L(x; \lambda)$ is a symmetric matrix and defines a quadratic form on $\mathbb{R}^n$.

Theorem 5.4 *Suppose there exist points $x^* \in \mathcal{D}$ and $\lambda^* \in \mathbb{R}^k$ such that $\rho(Dg(x^*)) = k$, and $Df(x^*) + \sum_{i=1}^{k} \lambda_i^* Dg_i(x^*) = 0$. Define*

$$\mathcal{Z}(x^*) = \{z \in \mathbb{R}^n \mid Dg(x^*)z = 0\},$$

and let $D^2 L^*$ denote the $n \times n$ matrix $D^2 L(x^*; \lambda^*) = D^2 f(x^*) + \sum_{i=1}^{k} \lambda_i^* D^2 g_i(x^*)$.

1. *If f has a local maximum on $\mathcal{D}$ at x^*, then $z' D^2 L^* z \leq 0$ for all $z \in \mathcal{Z}(x^*)$.*
2. *If f has a local minimum on $\mathcal{D}$ at x^*, then $z' D^2 L^* z \geq 0$ for all $z \in \mathcal{Z}(x^*)$.*
3. *If $z' D^2 L^* z < 0$ for all $z \in \mathcal{Z}(x^*)$ with $z \neq 0$, then x^* is a strict local maximum of f on $\mathcal{D}$.*
4. *If $z' D^2 L^* z > 0$ for all $z \in \mathcal{Z}(x^*)$ with $z \neq 0$, then x^* is a strict local minimum of f on $\mathcal{D}$.*

Proof   See Section 5.7 below. $\square$

There are obvious similarities between this result and the corresponding one for unconstrained maximization problems (Theorem 4.3). As there, parts 1 and 2 of this theorem are *necessary* conditions that must be satisfied by all local maxima and minima, respectively, while parts 3 and 4 are *sufficient* conditions that identify specific points as being local maxima or minima.

There are also two very important differences. First, the second-order conditions are not stated in terms of only the second derivative $D^2 f(x^*)$ of f at x^*. Rather, we add the "correction term" $\sum_{i=1}^{k} \lambda_i^* D^2 g_i(x^*)$, and state these second-order conditions in terms of $D^2 L(x^*; \lambda^*) = D^2 f(x^*) + \sum_{i=1}^{k} \lambda_i^* D^2 g_i(x^*)$. Second, the stated properties of the quadratic form $D^2 L(x^*; \lambda^*)$ do not have to hold on all of $\mathbb{R}^n$, but only on the subset of $\mathbb{R}^n$ defined by $\mathcal{Z}(x^*)$.

The last observation motivates our next result. In Chapter 1, we have seen that the definiteness of a symmetric $n \times n$ matrix A can be completely characterized in terms of the submatrices of A. We now turn to a related question: the characterization of the definiteness of A on only the set $\{z \neq 0 \mid Bz = 0\}$, where B is a $k \times n$ matrix of rank k. Such a characterization would give us an alternative way to check for the conditions of Theorem 5.4 by simply using the substitution $A = D^2 L^*$ and $B = Dg(x^*)$.

Some notation first. For $l \in \{1, \ldots, n\}$, let A_l denote the $l \times l$ submatrix of A obtained by retaining only the first l rows and columns of A:

$$A_l = \begin{bmatrix} a_{11} & \cdots & a_{1l} \\ \vdots & \ddots & \vdots \\ a_{l1} & \cdots & a_{ll} \end{bmatrix}.$$

Similarly, for $l \in \{1, \ldots n\}$, let B_{kl} denote the $k \times l$ matrix obtained from B by retaining only the first l columns of B:

$$B_{kl} = \begin{bmatrix} b_{11} & \cdots & b_{1l} \\ \vdots & \ddots & \vdots \\ b_{k1} & \cdots & b_{kl} \end{bmatrix}.$$

When $k = l$, we shall denote B_{kl} simply by B_k.

Next, given any permutation π of the first n integers,[3] let A^π denote the $n \times n$ symmetric matrix obtained from A by applying the permutation π to both its rows and columns,

$$A^\pi = \begin{bmatrix} a_{\pi_1 \pi_1} & \cdots & a_{\pi_1 \pi_n} \\ \vdots & \ddots & \vdots \\ a_{\pi_1 \pi_n} & \cdots & a_{\pi_n \pi_n} \end{bmatrix}$$

and let B^π denote the $k \times n$ matrix obtained by applying the permutation π to only the columns of B:

$$B = \begin{bmatrix} b_{1\pi_1} & \cdots & b_{1\pi_n} \\ \vdots & \ddots & \vdots \\ b_{k\pi_1} & \cdots & b_{k\pi_n} \end{bmatrix}.$$

In an obvious extension of this notation, A_l^π will be the $l \times l$ submatrix obtained from A^π by retaining only the first l rows and l columns of A^π, and B_{kl}^π will denote the $k \times l$ submatrix of B^π obtained by retaining only the first l columns of B^π.

Finally, given any $l \in \{1, \ldots, n\}$, let C_l be the $(k+l) \times (k+l)$ matrix obtained by "bordering" the submatrix A_l by the submatrix B_{kl} in the following manner:

$$C_l = \begin{bmatrix} 0_k & B_{kl} \\ B'_{kl} & A_l \end{bmatrix},$$

---

[3] Recall from Chapter 1 that a permutation π of the integers $\{1, \ldots, n\}$ is simply a reordering of the integers. The notation π_k is used to denote the new integer in the position k under the ordering π. Thus, for instance, if we represent the permutation $\{2, 1, 3\}$ of the set $\{1, 2, 3\}$ by π, we have $\pi_1 = 2$, $\pi_2 = 1$, and $\pi_3 = 3$.

where 0_k is a null $k \times k$ matrix, and B'_{kl} is the transpose of B_{kl}. In full notation, we have

$$C_l = \begin{bmatrix} 0 & \cdots & 0 & b_{11} & \cdots & b_{1l} \\ \vdots & \ddots & \vdots & \vdots & \ddots & \vdots \\ 0 & \cdots & 0 & b_{k1} & \cdots & b_{kl} \\ b_{11} & \cdots & b_{k1} & a_{11} & \cdots & a_{1l} \\ \vdots & \ddots & \vdots & \vdots & \ddots & \vdots \\ b_{1l} & \cdots & b_{kl} & a_{l1} & \cdots & a_{ll} \end{bmatrix}.$$

Denote by C_l^π the matrix obtained similarly when A is replaced by A^π and B by B^π.

The following result shows that the behavior of the quadratic form $x'Ax$ on the set $\{z \neq 0 \mid Bz = 0\}$ can, in turn, be completely characterized by the behavior of the bordered matrices C_l. For this result, we will assume that $|B_k| \neq 0$. Since we have assumed that $\rho(B) = k$, the matrix B must contain some $k \times k$ submatrix whose determinant is nonzero; an assumption that this submatrix is the one consisting of the first k rows and columns involves no loss of generality.

Theorem 5.5 *Let A be a symmetric $n \times n$ matrix, and B a $k \times n$ matrix such that $|B_k| \neq 0$. Define the bordered matrices C_l as described above. Then,*

1. *$x'Ax \geq 0$ for every x such that $Bx = 0$ if and only if for all permutations π of the first n integers, and for all $r \in \{k+1, \ldots, n\}$, we have $(-1)^k|C_r^\pi| \geq 0$.*
2. *$x'Ax \leq 0$ for all x such that $Bx = 0$ if and only if for all permutations π of the first n integers, and for all $r \in \{k+1, \ldots, n\}$, we have $(-1)^r|C_r^\pi| \geq 0$.*
3. *$x'Ax > 0$ for all $x \neq 0$ such that $Bx = 0$ if and only if for all $r \in \{k+1, \ldots, n\}$, we have $(-1)^k|C_r| > 0$.*
4. *$x'Ax < 0$ for all $x \neq 0$ such that $Bx = 0$ if and only if for all $r \in \{k+1, \ldots, n\}$, we have $(-1)^r|C_r| > 0$.*

Proof See Debreu (1952, Theorem 4, p.297, Theorem 5, p.298, and Theorems 9 and 10, p.299).   □

Note the important difference between parts 1 and 3 of Theorem 5.5 on the one hand, and parts 2 and 4 on the other. In parts 1 and 3, the term -1 is raised to the fixed power k, so that the signs of the determinants $|C_r|$ are required to all be the same; in parts 2 and 4, the term -1 is raised to the power r, so the signs of the determinants $|C_r|$ are required to alternate.

When $A = D^2L^*$ and $B = Dg(x^*)$, the matrices C_r are called "bordered hessians." This term arises from the fact that C_r is constructed by bordering a $r \times r$ submatrix of the hessian D^2L^*, with terms obtained from the matrix $Dg(x^*)$.[4]

---

[4]Recall from Chapter 1 that the second derivative D^2h of a C^2 function h is called the hessian of h.

The use of the second-order conditions in applications is illustrated in Section 5.5 below, where we work out examples based on economic problems. Subsection 5.5.1 illustrates the use of Theorem 5.4 in the context of a utility maximization problem, while subsection 5.5.2 does likewise for Theorem 5.5 in the context of a cost minimization problem.

5.4 Using the Theorem of Lagrange

5.4.1 A "Cookbook" Procedure

Let an equality-constrained optimization problem of the form

$$\text{Maximize } f(x) \text{ subject to } x \in \mathcal{D} = U \cap \{x \mid g(x) = 0\}$$

be given, where $f: \mathbb{R}^n \to \mathbb{R}$, and $g: \mathbb{R}^n \to \mathbb{R}^k$ are C^1 functions, and $U \subset \mathbb{R}^n$ is open. We describe here a "cookbook" procedure for using the Theorem of Lagrange to solve this maximization problem. This procedure, which we shall call the *Lagrangean method*, involves three steps.

In the first step, we set up a function $L: \mathcal{D} \times \mathbb{R}^k \to \mathbb{R}$, called the *Lagrangean*, defined by:

$$L(x, \lambda) = f(x) + \sum_{i=1}^{k} \lambda_i g_i(x).$$

The vector $\lambda = (\lambda_1, \ldots, \lambda_k) \in \mathbb{R}^k$ is called the vector of *Lagrange multipliers*.

As the second step in the procedure, we find the set of all critical points of $L(x, \lambda)$ for which $x \in U$, i.e., all points (x, λ) at which $DL(x, \lambda) = 0$ and $x \in U$. Since $x \in \mathbb{R}^n$ and $\lambda \in \mathbb{R}^k$, the condition that $DL(x, \lambda) = 0$ results in a system of $(n + k)$ equations in the $(n + k)$ unknowns:

$$\frac{\partial L}{\partial x_j}(x, \lambda) = 0, \quad j = 1, \ldots, n$$

$$\frac{\partial L}{\partial \lambda_i}(x, \lambda) = 0, \quad i = 1, \ldots, k.$$

Let M be the set of all solutions to these equations for which $x \in U$:

$$M = \{(x, \lambda) \mid x \in U, \ DL(x, \lambda) = 0\}.$$

As the third and last step in the procedure, we evaluate f at each point x in the set

$$\{x \in \mathbb{R}^n \mid \text{there is } \lambda \text{ such that } (x, \lambda) \in M\}.$$

In practice, the values of x which maximize f over this set are also usually the solutions to the equality-constrained maximization problem we started with.

The steps to be followed for a minimization problem are identical to the ones for a maximization problem, with the sole difference that at the last step, we select the value of x that *minimizes* f over the set $\{x \mid$ there is λ such that $(x, \lambda) \in M\}$.

5.4.2 Why the Procedure Usually Works

It is important to understand why the Lagrangean method typically succeeds in identifying the desired optima, and equally importantly, when it may fail. The key to both questions lies in the following property of the set of critical points of L:

The set of all critical points of L contains the set of all local maxima and minima of f on $\mathcal{D}$ at which the constraint qualification is met. That is, if $\hat{x}$ is any local maximum or minimum of f on $\mathcal{D}$, and if the constraint qualification holds at $\hat{x}$, then there exists $\hat{\lambda}$ such that $(\hat{x}, \hat{\lambda})$ is a critical point of L.

Indeed, this is an immediate consequence of the definition of L. For (x, λ) to be a critical point of L, we must have

$$\frac{\partial L}{\partial \lambda_i}(x, \lambda) \;=\; g_i(x) \;=\; 0,$$

for $i = 1, \ldots, k$, as well as

$$\frac{\partial L}{\partial x_j}(x, \lambda) \;=\; \frac{\partial f}{\partial x_j}(x) + \sum_{i=1}^{k} \lambda_i \frac{\partial g_i}{\partial x_j}(x) \;=\; 0$$

for $i = 1, \ldots, n$. Thus, (x, λ) is a critical point of L *if and only if* it meets the first-order conditions of the Theorem of Lagrange, i.e., it satisfies both $g(x) = 0$ as well as $Df(x) + \sum_{i=1}^{k} \lambda_i Dg_i(x) = 0$.

Now, suppose $\hat{x}$ is a local optimum, and the constraint qualification holds at $\hat{x}$. Then, we must certainly have $g(\hat{x}) = 0$, since $\hat{x}$ must be feasible. By the Theorem of Lagrange, there also exists $\hat{\lambda}$ such that $Df(\hat{x}) + \sum_{i=1}^{k} \hat{\lambda}_i Dg_i(\hat{x}) = 0$. This states precisely that $(\hat{x}, \hat{\lambda})$ must be a critical point of L, and establishes the claimed property.

A particular implication of this property is the following, which we state in the form of a proposition for ease of future reference:

Proposition 5.6 *Suppose the following two conditions hold:*

1. *A global optimum x^* (i.e., a global maximum or, as required, a global minimum) exists to the given problem.*

2. *The constraint qualification is met at x^*.*

Then, there exists λ^* such that (x^*, λ^*) is a critical point of L.

It follows that under the two conditions of this proposition, the Lagrangean method will succeed in identifying the optimum x^*. Indirectly, the conditions of this proposition also explain why the Lagrangean method usually works in practice. In most applications, the existence of a solution is not a problem, and neither typically is the constraint qualification. In particular, it is often possible to verify existence *a priori*, say, by an appeal to the Weierstrass Theorem. Although it is not, in general, possible to do likewise for the constraint qualification (since this depends on the properties of Dg at the unknown optimal point x^*), it is quite often the case that the constraint qualification holds *everywhere* on the feasible set $\mathcal{D}$, so this is not a problem either. (The utility-maximization problem is a typical case in point. See subsection 5.5.1 below.)

5.4.3 When It Could Fail

Unfortunately, when the conditions of Proposition 5.6 fail to hold, the procedure could also fail to identify global optima. This subsection provides a number of examples to illustrate this point.

First, if an optimum exists but the constraint qualification is not met at the optimum, then the optimum need not appear as part of a critical point of L. Of course, this does not imply that L will have no critical points; the conditions of the Theorem of Lagrange are only necessary, so many critical points could exist. The following examples illustrate these points. In each example, a unique global maximum exists, and in each case the constraint qualification fails at this optimum. In the first example, this results in a situation where there are no solutions at all to the equations that define the critical points of L; in the second example, on the other hand, multiple solutions exist to these equations, but the problem's unique maximum is not one of these.

Example 5.7 As in Example 5.3, let f and g be functions on $\mathbb{R}^2$ given by $f(x, y) = -y$ and $g(x, y) = y^3 - x^2$, respectively. We saw earlier that the unique global maximum of f on $\mathcal{D} = \{(x, y) \mid g(x, y) = 0\}$ is at $(x, y) = (0, 0)$, but that the constraint qualification fails at this point; and, consequently, that there is no λ such that $Df(0, 0) + \lambda Dg(0, 0) = 0$. Evidently, then, there is no choice of λ for which the point $(0, 0, \lambda)$ turns up as a solution to the critical points of the Lagrangean L in this problem.

Indeed, the critical points of L in this problem admit no solution at all: if we define $L(x, y, \lambda) = f(x, y) + \lambda g(x, y) = -y + \lambda(y^3 - x^2)$, the critical points of L are the solutions (x, y, λ) to the following system of equations:

$$-2\lambda x = 0$$
$$-1 + 3\lambda y^2 = 0$$
$$-x^2 + y^3 = 0.$$

For the first equation to be satisfied, we must have $x = 0$ or $\lambda = 0$. If $\lambda = 0$, the second equation cannot be satisfied. If $x = 0$, the third equation implies $y = 0$, and once again the second equation cannot be satisfied. □

Example 5.8 Let f and g be functions on $\mathbb{R}^2$ defined by $f(x, y) = 2x^3 - 3x^2$, and $g(x, y) = (3 - x)^3 - y^2$, respectively. Consider the problem of maximizing f over the set $\mathcal{D} = \{(x, y) \in \mathbb{R}^2 \mid g(x, y) = 0\}$.

Since the constraint requires that $(3 - x)^3 = y^2$, and since $y^2 \geq 0$, it is easy to see that the largest value of x on the feasible set is $x = 3$ which occurs at $y = 0$. A little calculation also shows that f is nonpositive for x in the interval $(-\infty, \frac{3}{2}]$, and is strictly positive and strictly increasing for $x > \frac{3}{2}$.[5] It follows from these statements that f attains a global maximum on $\mathcal{D}$ at the point $(x, y) = (3, 0)$. Note that since $Dg(x, y) = (-3(3 - x)^2, -2y)$, we have $Dg(3, 0) = (0, 0)$, so the constraint qualification fails at this unique global maximum. We will show that, as a consequence, the cookbook procedure will fail to identify this point.

The Lagrangean L for this problem has the form $L(x, y, \lambda) = 2x^3 - 3x^2 + \lambda((3 - x)^3 - y^2)$, so the critical points of L are the solutions (x, y, λ) to

$$6x^2 - 6x - 3\lambda(3 - x)^2 = 0$$

$$-2\lambda y = 0$$

$$(3 - x)^3 - y^2 = 0.$$

For the second condition to be met, we must have $\lambda = 0$ or $y = 0$. If $y = 0$, then the third condition implies $x = 3$, but $x = 3$ violates the first condition. This leaves the case $\lambda = 0$, and it is easily checked that there are precisely two solutions that arise in this case, namely, $(x, y, \lambda) = (0, \sqrt{27}, 0)$ and $(x, y, \lambda) = (1, \sqrt{8}, 0)$. In particular, the unique global maximum of the problem $(x, y) = (3, 0)$ does not turn up as part of a solution to the critical points of L. □

Alternatively, even if the constraint qualification holds *everywhere* on the constraint set $\mathcal{D}$, the cookbook procedure may fail to identify the optimum, for the simple reason that an optimum may not exist. In this case, the optimum evidently cannot turn up as part of a critical point of L, although, once again, L may have many critical points. The following examples illustrate this point. In both examples, global optima do not exist. In the first example, it is also true that L has no critical points at all; in the second example, however, multiple solutions exist to the equations that define the critical points of L.

---

[5]It is evident that f is negative when $x < 0$ because, in this case, $2x^3 < 0$ and $-3x^2 < 0$. Since $f'(x) = 6x^2 - 6x$, a simple calculation shows that f is strictly decreasing on the interval $(0, 1)$ and is strictly increasing for $x > 1$. Since $f(0) = f(3/2) = 0$, the claim in the text obtains.

Example 5.9 Consider the problem of maximizing and minimizing $f(x, y) = x^2 - y^2$ subject to the single constraint $g(x, y) = 1 - x - y = 0$. Observe that $Dg(x, y) = (-1, -1)$ at any (x, y), so $\rho(Dg(x, y)) = 1$ everywhere, and the constraint qualification holds everywhere on the feasible set. Let $L(x, y, \lambda) = f(x, y) + \lambda g(x, y)$. The critical points of L are the solutions (x, y, λ) to:

$$2x - \lambda = 0$$
$$-2y - \lambda = 0$$
$$1 - x - y = 0.$$

If $\lambda \neq 0$, then the first two equations imply that $x = -y$, but this violates the third equation. If $\lambda = 0$, then from the first two equations, we have $x = y = 0$, so again the third equation cannot be met. Thus, there are no solutions to the critical points of L.

Since the constraint qualification holds everywhere, it must be the case that global maxima and minima fail to exist in this problem (otherwise, by Proposition 5.6, such points must arise as critical points of L), and, indeed, it is easy to see that this is the case. For any $x \in \mathbb{R}$, the point $(x, 1 - x)$ is in the feasible set of the problem. Moreover, $f(x, 1 - x) = x^2 - (1 - x)^2$, so by taking x large and positive, f can be made arbitrarily large, while by taking $-x$ large and positive, f can be made arbitrarily negative. □

Example 5.10 Let f and g be functions on $\mathbb{R}^2$ defined respectively by

$$f(x, y) = \frac{1}{3}x^3 - \frac{3}{2}y^2 + 2x,$$

and $g(x, y) = x - y$. Consider the problem of maximizing and minimizing f on the set $\mathcal{D} = \{(x, y) \mid g(x, y) = 0\}$. Since $Dg(x, y) = (1, -1)$ at all (x, y), we have $\rho(Dg(x, y)) = 1$ at all (x, y) and the constraint qualification holds everywhere on the feasible set. If we set up the Lagrangean $L(x, y) = f(x, y) + \lambda g(x, y)$, the critical points of L are the solutions (x, y, λ) to

$$x^2 + 2 + \lambda = 0$$
$$-3y - \lambda = 0$$
$$x - y = 0.$$

This system of equations has two solutions: $(x, y, \lambda) = (2, 2, -6)$ and $(x, y, \lambda) = (1, 1, -3)$.

Evaluating f at these two points, we get $f(1, 1) = 5/6$ and $f(2, 2) = 2/3$, so if we were following the cookbook Lagrangean procedure, we would pick $(1, 1)$ as the point where f is maximized on $\mathcal{D}$, and $(2, 2)$ as the point where f is minimized on

$\mathcal{D}$. Indeed, the second-order conditions confirm these points, in the sense that $(1, 1)$ passes the test for a strict local maximum, while $(2, 2)$ passes the test for a strict local minimum.[6]

However, neither of these points is a global optimum of the problem. In fact, the problem has no solutions, since $f(x, 0) \to +\infty$ as $x \to +\infty$, and $f(x, 0) \to -\infty$ as $x \to -\infty$. $\qquad\qquad\qquad\qquad\qquad\qquad\qquad\qquad\qquad\qquad\qquad\qquad\qquad\square$

The examples of this subsection add a word of caution regarding the blind use of the Lagrangean method in solving equality-constrained problems. In many applications, as we pointed out earlier, it is possible to verify *a priori* both the existence of a solution, and the constraint qualification condition, and in such cases the method works well. Sometimes, however, such *a priori* knowledge may not be available, and this could be problematic, whether or not solutions to the critical points of the Lagrangean exist.

To elaborate, the critical points of the Lagrangean could fail to have a solution for two very different reasons. First, as in Example 5.7, this could occur because although an optimum exists, the constraint qualification is violated at that point; alternatively, as in Example 5.9, this could be the case because an optimum does not even exist. Therefore, the absence of a solution to the critical points of the Lagrangean does not enable us to draw any conclusions about the existence, or nonexistence, of global optima.[7]

On the other hand, it is also possible that while solutions do exist to the critical points of L, none of these is the desired optimum point. Again, this could be because, although an optimum exists, the constraint qualification is violated at that point (as in Example 5.8); or because an optimum does not exist (as in Example 5.10).[8] Thus, even the existence of solutions to the critical points of L does not, in general, enable us to make inferences about the existence, or nonexistence, of optima.

---

[6]To see this, note that

$$D^2 L(x, y) = \begin{bmatrix} 2x & 0 \\ 0 & -3 \end{bmatrix}.$$

Note also that, since $Dg(x, y) = (1, -1)$ at all (x, y), the set

$$\mathcal{Z}(x, y) = \{z \in \mathbb{R}^2 \mid Dg(x, y)z = 0\}$$

is simply the set $\{z \in \mathbb{R}^2 \mid z = (w, w), \; w \in \mathbb{R}\}$, which is independent of (x, y). Denote this set by just $\mathcal{Z}$. To show that a point (x, y) is a strict local maximum (resp. strict local minimum) of f on $\mathcal{D}$, it suffices by Theorem 5.4 to show that $z' D^2 L(x, y)z$ is strictly negative (resp. strictly positive) for $z \in \mathcal{Z}$ with $z \neq 0$. At $(x, y) = (1, 1)$ and $z = (w, w) \in \mathcal{Z}$, we have $z' D^2 L(x, y)z = -w^2 < 0$ for all $w \neq 0$, while for $(x, y) = (2, 2)$, we have $z' D^2 L(x, Y)z = w^2 > 0$ for all $w \neq 0$. The claimed results are proved.

[7]An exception to this statement arises when the constraint qualification is known to hold *everywhere* on the constraint set $\mathcal{D}$. In this case, if a global optimum exists, it must turn up as part of a critical point of L; thus, if no critical points of L exist, it must be the case that the problem admits no solution.

[8]Note the important point that, as evidenced by Example 5.10, the second-order conditions are of limited help in resolving this problem. Even if a critical point of L could be shown to be a local maximum (say), this would not establish it to be a global maximum.

5.4.4 A Numerical Example

We close this section with an illustration of the use of the Lagrangean method on a simple numerical example. Consider the problem of maximizing and minimizing $f(x, y) = x^2 - y^2$ subject to the single constraint $g(x, y) = 1 - x^2 - y^2 = 0$. The constraint set

$$\mathcal{D} = \{(x, y) \in \mathbb{R}^2 \mid x^2 + y^2 = 1\}$$

is simply the unit circle in $\mathbb{R}^2$.

We will first show that the two conditions of Proposition 5.6 (namely, existence of global optima, and the constraint qualification) are both met, so the critical points of the Lagrangean L will, in fact, contain the set of global maxima and global minima. That solutions exist is easy to see: f is a continuous function on $\mathcal{D}$, and $\mathcal{D}$ is evidently compact, so an appeal to the Weierstrass Theorem yields the desired conclusion. To check the constraint qualification, note that the derivative of the constraint function g at any $(x, y) \in \mathbb{R}^2$ is given by $Dg(x, y) = (2x, 2y)$. Since x and y cannot be zero simultaneously on $\mathcal{D}$ (otherwise, $x^2 + y^2 = 1$ would fail), we must have $\rho(Dg(x, y)) = 1$ at all $(x, y) \in \mathcal{D}$. Therefore, the constraint qualification holds everywhere on $\mathcal{D}$.

Now set up the Lagrangean $L(x, y, \lambda) = x^2 - y^2 + \lambda(1 - x^2 - y^2)$. The critical points of L are the solutions $(x, y, \lambda) \in \mathbb{R}^3$ to

$$2x - 2\lambda x = 0$$
$$-2y - 2\lambda y = 0$$
$$x^2 + y^2 = 1.$$

From the first equation we have $2x(1 - \lambda) = 0$, while from the second, we have $2y(1 + \lambda) = 0$. If $\lambda \neq \pm 1$, these can hold only if $x = y = 0$, but this violates the third equation. So $\lambda = \pm 1$. It easily follows that there are only four possible solutions:

$$(x, y, \lambda) = \begin{cases} (+1, 0, +1) \\ (-1, 0, +1) \\ (0, +1, -1) \\ (0, -1, -1) \end{cases}.$$

Evaluating f at these four points, we see that $f(1, 0, 1) = f(-1, 0, 1) = 1$, while $f(0, 1, -1) = f(0, -1, -1) = 0$. Since the critical points of L contain the global maxima and minima of f on $\mathcal{D}$, the first two points must be *global maximizers* of f on $\mathcal{D}$, while the latter two are *global minimizers* of f on $\mathcal{D}$.

5.5 Two Examples from Economics

We now present two familiar examples drawn from consumer theory and producer theory, respectively, namely, those of utility maximization and cost minimization. The presentation here achieves two purposes:

1. As with most problems in economic theory, these problems are characterized by *inequality*, rather than *equality* constraints. We show that, under suitable conditions, it may be possible to reduce such problems to *equivalent* equality-constrained problems, and thereby to bring them within the framework of the Theorem of Lagrange.
2. We demonstrate the use of the Lagrangean L in determining the solution to the transformed equality-constrained maximization problems. In particular, we show how to

   (a) use the critical points of L to identify candidate optimal points in the reduced equality-constrained problem;
   (b) use the second-order conditions to determine if a critical point of L is a local optimum; and, finally,
   (c) combine the Weierstrass Theorem and the Theorem of Lagrange to identify *global* optima of the reduced, and thereby the original, problem.

Of course, the phrase "under suitable conditions" is important for the transformation of inequality-constrained problems into equality-constrained ones. See the remarks at the end of this section.

5.5.1 An Illustration from Consumer Theory

The utility-maximization example we consider here involves a consumer who consumes two goods, and whose utility from consuming an amount x_i of commodity $i = 1, 2$, is given by $u(x_1, x_2) = x_1 x_2$. The consumer has an income $I > 0$, and the price of commodity i is $p_i > 0$. The problem is to solve:

$$\max\{x_1 x_2 \mid I - p_1 x_1 - p_2 x_2 \geq 0, \ x_1 \geq 0, x_2 \geq 0\}.$$

We proceed with the analysis in three steps:

Step 1: Reduction to an Equality-Constrained Problem

As stated, this utility-maximization problem is not an equality-constrained one. We begin by transforming it in a manner that will facilitate use of the Lagrangean method. To this end, note that the budget set

$$\mathcal{B}(p, I) = \{(x_1, x_2) \mid I - p_1 x_1 - p_2 x_2 \geq 0, \ x_1 \geq 0, x_2 \geq 0\}$$

is a compact set. The utility function $u(x_1, x_2) = x_1 x_2$ is evidently continuous on this set, so by the Weierstrass Theorem a solution (x_1^*, x_2^*) does exist to the given maximization problem.

Now, if either $x_1 = 0$ or $x_2 = 0$, then $u(x_1, x_2) = 0$. On the other hand, the consumption point $(\bar{x}_1, \bar{x}_2) = (I/2p_1, I/2p_2)$, which divides the available income $I > 0$ equally between the two commodities, is a feasible consumption point, which satisfies $u(\bar{x}_1, \bar{x}_2) = \bar{x}_1 \bar{x}_2 > 0$. Since any solution (x_1^*, x_2^*) must satisfy $u(x_1^*, x_2^*) \geq u(\bar{x}_1, \bar{x}_2)$, it follows that any solution (x_1^*, x_2^*) must satisfy $x_i^* > 0$, $i = 1, 2$. Moreover, any solution must also meet the income constraint with equality (i.e., we must have $p_1 x_1^* + p_2 x_2^* = I$) or total utility could be increased.

Combining these observations, we see that (x_1^*, x_2^*) is a solution to the original problem *if and only if* it is a solution to the problem

$$\max\{x_1 x_2 \mid p_1 x_1 + p_2 x_2 = I, \ x_1, x_2 > 0\}.$$

The constraint set of this reduced problem, denoted, say, $\mathcal{B}^*(p, I)$, can equivalently be written as

$$\mathcal{B}^*(p, I) = \mathbb{R}^2_{++} \cap \{(x_1, x_2) \mid I - p_1 x_1 - p_2 x_2 = 0\},$$

and by setting $U = \mathbb{R}^2_{++}$ and $g(x_1, x_2) = I - p_1 x_1 - p_2 x_2$, we are now within the setting of the Theorem of Lagrange.

Step 2: Obtaining the Critical Points of L

We set up the Lagrangean

$$L(x_1, x_2, \lambda) = x_1 x_2 + \lambda(I - p_1 x_1 - p_2 x_2).$$

The critical points of L are the solutions $(x_1^*, x_2^*, \lambda) \in \mathbb{R}^2_{++} \times \mathbb{R}$ to:

$$x_2 - \lambda p_1 = 0$$
$$x_1 - \lambda p_2 = 0$$
$$I - p_1 x_1 - p_2 x_2 = 0.$$

If $\lambda = 0$, this system of equations has no solutions, since we must then have $x_1 = x_2 = 0$ from the first and second equations, but this violates the third equation. So suppose $\lambda \neq 0$. From the first two equations, we then have $\lambda = x_1/p_2 = x_2/p_1$, so $x_1 = p_2 x_2/p_1$. Using this in the third equation, we see that the *unique* solution to this set of equations is given by $x_1^* = I/2p_1$, $x_2^* = I/2p_2$, and $\lambda^* = I/2p_1 p_2$.

Step 3: Classifying the Critical Points of L

As a first step in classifying the single critical point of L, we show how the second-order conditions may be used to check that (x_1^*, x_2^*) is a strict local maximum of u on $\mathcal{B}^*(p, I)$. We begin by noting that $Dg(x_1^*, x_2^*) = (-p_1, -p_2)$ so the set

$$\mathcal{Z}(x^*) = \{z \in \mathbb{R}^2 \mid Dg(x^*)z = 0\}$$

is simply

$$\mathcal{Z}(x^*) = \left\{ z \in \mathbb{R}^2 \mid z_1 = -\frac{p_2 z_2}{p_1} \right\}.$$

Defining $D^2 L^* = D^2 u(x^*) + \lambda^* D^2 g(x^*)$, we have

$$D^2 L^* = \begin{bmatrix} 0 & 1 \\ 1 & 0 \end{bmatrix} + \lambda^* \begin{bmatrix} 0 & 0 \\ 0 & 0 \end{bmatrix} = \begin{bmatrix} 0 & 1 \\ 1 & 0 \end{bmatrix}.$$

So for any $z \in \mathbb{R}^2$, we have $z' D^2 L^* z = 2z_1 z_2$. In particular, for any $z \in \mathcal{Z}(x^*)$ with $z \neq 0$, we have $z' D^2 L^* z = -2 p_2 z_2^2 / p_1 < 0$. Thus, by Theorem 5.4, (x_1^*, x_2^*) is a strict local maximum of u on $\mathcal{B}^*(p, I)$.

However, we can actually show the stronger result that (x_1^*, x_2^*) is a *global* maximum of u on $\mathcal{B}^*(p, I)$ by showing that the conditions of Proposition 5.6 are met. First, note that a solution (i.e., a global maximum) does exist in the problem

$$\max\{x_1, x_2 \mid (x_1, x_2) \in \mathcal{B}^*(p, I)\},$$

by the arguments given in Step 1. Second, note that the single constraint

$$g(x_1, x_2) = I - p_1 x_1 - p_2 x_2$$

of this problem satisfies $Dg(x_1, x_2) = (-p_1, -p_2)$ everywhere on $\mathcal{B}^*(p, I)$. Since $p_1, p_2 > 0$ by hypothesis, we have $\rho(Dg(x_1, x_2)) = 1$ at all $(x_1, x_2) \in \mathcal{B}^*(p, I)$. In particular, the constraint qualification holds at the global maximum. Therefore, by Proposition 5.6, the global maximum must be part of a critical point of the Lagrangean L in this problem. There is a unique critical point, with associated x-values (x_1^*, x_2^*), so these x-values must represent the problem's global maximum.

5.5.2 An Illustration from Producer Theory

We now turn to the cost-minimization problem faced by a firm, which uses two inputs x_1 and x_2 to produce a single output y through the production function $y = g(x_1, x_2)$. The unit prices of x_1 and x_2 are $w_1 \geq 0$ and $w_2 \geq 0$ respectively. The firm wishes to find the cheapest input combination for producing $\bar{y}$ units of output, where $\bar{y} \geq 0$ is given. Let $X(\bar{y})$ denote the set of feasible input combinations:

$$X(\bar{y}) = \{(x_1, x_2) \in \mathbb{R}^2 \mid x_1 x_2 = \bar{y}, x_1 \geq 0, x_2 \geq 0\}.$$

The firm's optimization problem is:

$$\text{Minimize } w_1 x_1 + w_2 x_2 \text{ subject to } (x_1, x_2) \in X(\bar{y}).$$

We will assume throughout that $w_1 > 0$ and $w_2 > 0$ (otherwise, it is apparent that a solution cannot exist). Once again, we proceed in three steps.

Step 1: Reduction to an equality-constrained problem

In this problem, this first step is trivial. If $x_1 = 0$ or $x_2 = 0$, we have $x_1 x_2 = 0$, so the inequality constraints have no bite, and the constraint set is actually given by

$$X^*(\bar{y}) = \mathbb{R}^2_{++} \cap \{(x_1, x_2) \in \mathbb{R}^2 \mid x_1 x_2 = \bar{y}\}.$$

Setting $f(x_1, x_2) = w_1 x_1 + w_2 x_2$, $g(x_1, x_2) = \bar{y} - x_1 x_2$, and $U = \mathbb{R}^2_{++}$, we are in the framework of the Theorem of Lagrange.

Step 2: Obtaining the Critical Points of L

Define the Lagrangean $L(x_1, x_2, \lambda) = f(x_1, x_2) + \lambda g(x_1, x_2) = w_1 x_1 + w_2 x_2 + \lambda(\bar{y} - x_1 x_2)$. The critical points of L are the solutions to:

$$w_1 - \lambda x_2 = 0$$

$$w_2 - \lambda x_1 = 0$$

$$\bar{y} - x_1 x_2 = 0.$$

From the first (or the second) equation, λ cannot be zero. Therefore, from the first two equations we have

$$\frac{w_1}{w_2} = \frac{x_2}{x_1} \text{ or } x_2 = \frac{w_1 x_1}{w_2}.$$

Substituting this into the third equation, we obtain the unique solution

$$x_1^* = \left(\frac{w_2 \bar{y}}{w_1}\right)^{1/2}, \quad x_2^* = \left(\frac{w_1 \bar{y}}{w_2}\right)^{1/2}, \quad \text{and } \lambda^* = \left(\frac{w_1 w_2}{\bar{y}}\right)^{1/2}.$$

Step 3: Classifying the Critical Points of L

Once again, we begin with a demonstration that (x_1^*, x_2^*) is a strict local minimum of $f(x_1, x_2) = w_1 x_1 + w_2 x_2$ on $X^*(\bar{y})$. This time, we employ Theorem 5.5 to achieve this end. First, note that

$$Dg(x_1^*, x_2^*) = (-x_2^*, -x_1^*).$$

Next, note that the matrix $D^2 L^* = D^2 f(x^*) + \lambda^* \cdot D^2 g(x^*)$ is given by

$$D^2 L^* = \begin{bmatrix} 0 & 0 \\ 0 & 0 \end{bmatrix} + \lambda^* \begin{bmatrix} 0 & -1 \\ -1 & 0 \end{bmatrix} = \begin{bmatrix} 0 & -\lambda^* \\ -\lambda^* & 0 \end{bmatrix}.$$

By Theorem 5.4, if we show that $z' D^2 L^* z > 0$ for all $z \neq 0$ such that $D^2 g(x^*) \cdot z = 0$, then we would have established that x^* is a strict local minimum of f on $\mathcal{D}$. By Theorem 5.5, showing that $z' D^2 L^* z > 0$ for all $z \neq 0$ such that $Dg(x^*)z = 0$ is the same as showing that the determinant of the following matrix is negative:

$$C_1 = \begin{bmatrix} 0 & Dg(x^*) \\ Dg(x^*)' & D^2 L^* \end{bmatrix}.$$

Substituting for $Dg(x^*)$ and D^2L^*, we obtain:

$$C_1 = \begin{bmatrix} 0 & -x_2^* & -x_1^* \\ -x_2^* & 0 & -\lambda^* \\ -x_1^* & -\lambda^* & 0 \end{bmatrix}.$$

Some simple calculation shows that $|C_1| = -2\lambda^* x_1^* x_2^* < 0$, as required. Thus, (x_1^*, x_2^*) is a strict local minimum of f on $\mathcal{D}$.

As in the utility-maximization problem, however, we can show the stronger result that (x_1^*, x_2^*) is a *global* minimum of f on $X^*(\bar{y})$, by proving that the problem meets the conditions of Proposition 5.6. The existence issue is a little trickier, because the feasible action set $X^*(\bar{y})$ is noncompact. However, as explained in Chapter 3, we can reduce the problem to one with a compact action set as follows. Let $(\hat{x}_1, \hat{x}_2) = ((\bar{y})^{1/2}, (\bar{y})^{1/2})$. Note that $\hat{x}_1 \hat{x}_2 = \bar{y}$, so $(\hat{x}_1, \hat{x}_2) \in X^*(\bar{y})$. Define $\hat{c} = w_1 \hat{x}_1 + w_2 \hat{x}_2$. Let $\bar{x}_1 = 2\hat{c}/w_1$ and $\bar{x}_2 = 2\hat{c}/w_2$. Then, it is clear that the firm will never use more than $\bar{x}_i$ units of input i, since the total cost from doing so will strictly exceed $\hat{c}$ (no matter what the quantity of the other input used), while the input combination $(\hat{x}_1, \hat{x}_2)$ can produce the desired output at a cost of $\hat{c}$. Thus, we may, without loss, restrict the feasible action set to

$$\bar{X}(\bar{y}) = \{(x_1, x_2) \in \mathbb{R}^2 \mid x_1 x_2 = \bar{y}, \ x_i \in [0, \bar{x}_i], i = 1, 2\},$$

so that $f(x_1, x_2) = w_1 x_1 + w_2 x_2$ achieves a global minimum on $X^*(\bar{y})$ if and only if it achieves a global minimum on $\bar{X}(\bar{y})$. Since $\bar{X}(\bar{y})$ is evidently compact, and f is continuous on this set, a minimum certainly exists on $\bar{X}(\bar{y})$ by the Weierstrass Theorem; therefore, a minimum of f on $X^*(\bar{y})$ also exists.

That the constraint qualification condition is met is easier to see. The problem's single constraint $g(x_1, x_2) = \bar{y} - x_1 x_2$ satisfies $Dg(x_1, x_2) = (-x_2, -x_1)$, and since neither x_1 nor x_2 can be zero on $X^*(\bar{y})$ (otherwise, $x_1 x_2 = \bar{y} > 0$ is violated), we have $\rho(Dg(x_1, x_2)) = 1$ everywhere on $X^*(\bar{y})$. In particular, the constraint qualification must hold at the global minimum.

Since both conditions of Proposition 5.6 are met, the global minimum must turn up as part of the solution to the critical points of L. Since only a single solution exists to these critical points, it follows that the point (x_1^*, x_2^*) is, in fact, a global minimum of f on $\mathcal{D}$.

5.5.3 Remarks

At the beginning of this section, it was mentioned that the reduction of inequality-constrained problems to equality-constrained ones was possible only under suitable conditions. The purpose of this subsection is to emphasize this point through three examples, which demonstrate the danger of attempting such a reduction by ignoring nonnegativity constraints, when ignoring these constraints may not be a legitimate option. In the first two examples, the problems that arise take on the form of inconsistent equations defining the critical points of the Lagrangean. In the last example, the Lagrangean admits a unique solution, but this is not the solution to the problem.

Example 5.11 Consider a utility maximization problem as in subsection 5.5.1, but where the utility function $u(x_1, x_2) = x_1 x_2$ is replaced with $v(x_1, x_2) = x_1 + x_2$. That is, we are to solve

$$\text{Maximize } x_1 + x_2 \text{ subject to } (x_1, x_2) \in \mathcal{B}(p, I).$$

It is still true that the utility function is continuous and the budget set is compact, so the Weierstrass Theorem guarantees us a maximum. It also remains true that any maximum (x_1^*, x_2^*) must satisfy $I - p_1 x_1^* - p_2 x_2^* = 0$. Nonetheless, it is not possible to set up the problem as an equality-constrained maximization problem, since the constraints $x_1 \geq 0$ and $x_2 \geq 0$ can no longer be replaced with $x_1 > 0$ and $x_2 > 0$. Indeed, it is obvious upon inspection that the solution to the problem is

$$(x_1^*, x_2^*) = \begin{cases} (I/p_1, 0), & \text{if } p_1 < p_2 \\ (0, I/p_2), & \text{if } p_1 > p_2 \end{cases}$$

and that any $(x_1, x_2) \in \mathbb{R}^2_+$ that satisfies $p_1 x_1 + p_2 x_2 = I$ is optimal when $p_1 = p_2$. Thus, the constraints $x_i \geq 0$ "bite" when $p_1 \neq p_2$.

If we had ignored this problem, and attempted to use the Lagrangean method to solve this problem, the following system of equations would have resulted:

$$1 - \lambda p_1 = 0$$
$$1 - \lambda p_2 = 0$$
$$p_1 x_1 + p_2 x_2 = I.$$

The first two equations are in contradiction except when $p_1 = p_2$, which is the only case when the nonnegativity constraints do not bite. Thus, except in this case, the Lagrangean method fails to identify a solution.   □

A similar problem can also arise in the cost-minimization exercise, as the next example demonstrates.

Example 5.12 Suppose that in the problem of subsection 5.5.2, the production function were modified to the linear function $g(x_1, x_2) = x_1 + x_2$. A little reflection shows that, in this case, the solution to the problem is given by

$$(x_1, x_2) = \begin{cases} (\bar{y}, 0) & \text{if } w_1 < w_2 \\ (0, \bar{y}) & \text{if } w_1 > w_2 \end{cases}$$

and that any pair $(x_1, x_2) \in X(\bar{y})$ is optimal when $w_1 = w_2$. Thus, when $w_1 \neq w_2$, the nonnegativity constraints matter in a nontrivial sense. If these constraints are ignored and the problem is represented as an equality-constrained problem, the Lagrangean has the form

$$L(x_1, x_2, \lambda) = w_1 x_1 + w_2 x_2 + \lambda(x_1 + x_2 - y),$$

and the critical points of L are the solutions to

$$w_1 + \lambda = 0$$
$$w_2 + \lambda = 0$$
$$x_1 + x_2 = y.$$

The first two equations are consistent if and only if $w_1 = w_2$. Thus, if $w_1 \neq w_2$, the Lagrangean method will not work. $\qquad\qquad\square$

Finally, the following example shows that even if the equations that define the critical points of L do have a solution, the solution need not be the solution to the problem if the reduction of the original inequality-constrained problem to an equality-constrained one is not legitimate.

Example 5.13 We consider the problem of identifying Pareto-optimal divisions of a given amount of resources between two agents, as described in subsection 2.3.7. Suppose there are two commodities, and the endowment vector $\omega \in \mathbb{R}^2_{++}$ consists of x units of the first resource and y units of the second resource. Let x_i and y_i denote respectively the amounts of resources x and y that are allocated to agent i, $i = 1, 2$. Agent i's utility from receiving the allocation (x_i, y_i) is assumed to be given by $u(x_i, y_i) = x_i y_i$. Given a weight $\alpha \in (0, 1)$, the problem is to solve

Maximize $[\alpha x_1 y_1 + (1 - \alpha)x_2 y_2]$ subject to $(x_1, x_2, y_1, y_2) \in F(x, y)$,

where

$$F(x, y) = \{(x_1, y_1, x_2, y_2) \in \mathbb{R}^4_+ \mid x_1 + x_2 \leq x, \ y_1 + y_2 \leq y\}.$$

An optimum evidently exists in this problem, since the feasible set is compact and the objective function is continuous. Moreover, it is also apparent that at the optimum, both resources must be fully allocated; that is, we must have $x_1 + x_2 = x$ and $y_1 + y_2 = y$. If we ignore the nonnegativity constraints in this problem, and write it as an equality-constrained problem with only the resource constraints, the Lagrangean for the problem is

$$L(x_1, x_2, y_1, y_2, \lambda_x, \lambda_y) = \alpha x_1 y_1 + (1 - \alpha)x_2 y_2$$
$$+ \lambda_x(x - x_1 - x_2) + \lambda_y(y - y_1 - y_2).$$

The critical points of L are the solutions to:

$$\alpha y_1 - \lambda_x = 0$$
$$(1 - \alpha)y_2 - \lambda_x = 0$$
$$\alpha x_1 - \lambda_y = 0$$
$$(1 - \alpha)x_2 - \lambda_y = 0$$
$$x - x_1 - x_2 = 0$$
$$y - y_1 - y_2 = 0.$$

A simple computation shows that these equations admit the unique solution

$$\begin{aligned}
x_1^* &= (1 - \alpha)x & y_1^* &= (1 - \alpha)y \\
x_2^* &= \alpha x & y_2^* &= \alpha y \\
\lambda_x^* &= \alpha(1 - \alpha)y & \lambda_y^* &= \alpha(1 - \alpha)x.
\end{aligned}$$

However, it is easy to show that these values do not identify a solution to the maximization problem. When they are substituted into the objective function, we obtain

$$\alpha x_1^* y_1^* + (1 - \alpha)x_2^* y_2^* = \alpha(1 - \alpha)x(1 - \alpha)y + (1 - \alpha)\alpha x \alpha y$$
$$= \alpha(1 - \alpha)xy.$$

On the other hand, if the entire available vector of resources is given over to a single agent (say, agent 1), then the objective function has the value $\alpha x y$. Since $\alpha \in (0, 1)$, this is strictly larger than $\alpha(1 - \alpha)xy$.

The problem here, as in the earlier examples, is that the nonnegativity constraints bite at the optimum: viz., it can be shown that the solution to the problem is to turn over all the resources to agent 1 if $\alpha > 1/2$, to agent 2 if $\alpha < 1/2$, and to give it all to any one of the agents if $\alpha = 1/2$. □

5.6 A Proof of the Theorem of Lagrange

The following notational simplification will aid greatly in the proof of Theorem 5.1:

1. We shall assume, without loss of generality, that the $k \times k$ submatrix of $Dg(x^*)$ that has full rank is the $k \times k$ submatrix consisting of the first k rows and k columns.

2. We will denote the first k coordinates of a vector $x \in \mathcal{D}$ by w, and the last $(n-k)$ coordinates by z, i.e., we write $x = (w, z)$. In particular, we shall write (w^*, z^*) to denote the local optimum x^*.

3. We will denote by $Df_w(w, z)$, the derivative of f at (w, z) with respect to the w variables alone, and by $Df_z(w, z)$, the derivative of f at (w, z) with respect to the z variables alone. $Dg_w(w, z)$ and $Dg_z(w, z)$ are defined similarly. Note that the dimensions of the matrices $Df_w(w, z)$, $Df_z(w, z)$, $Dg_w(w, z)$, and $Dg_z(w, z)$, are, respectively, $1 \times k$, $1 \times (n-k)$, $k \times k$, and $k \times (n-k)$.

4. We shall treat the vector λ^* in $\mathbb{R}^k$, whose existence we are to show, as a $1 \times k$ matrix.[9] Thus, for instance, we will write $\lambda^* Dg(x^*)$ to represent $\sum_{i=1}^{k} \lambda_i^* Dg_i(x^*)$.

In this notation, we are given the data that (w^*, z^*) is a local maximum[10] of f on $\mathcal{D} = U \cap \{(w, z) \in \mathbb{R}^n \mid g(w, z) = 0\}$; and that $\rho(Dg_w(w^*, z^*)) = k$. We are to prove that there exists λ^* such that

$$Df_w(w^*, z^*) + \lambda^* Dg_w(w^*, z^*) = 0$$
$$Df_z(w^*, z^*) + \lambda^* Dg_z(w^*, z^*) = 0.$$

As a first step, note that since $\rho(Dg_w(w^*, z^*)) = k$, the Implicit Function Theorem (see Theorem 1.77 in Chapter 1) shows that there exists an open set V in $\mathbb{R}^{n-k}$ containing z^*, and a C^1 function $h: V \to \mathbb{R}^k$ such that $h(z^*) = w^*$ and $g(h(z), z) \equiv 0$ for all $z \in V$. Differentiating the identity $g(h(z), z) \equiv 0$ with respect to z by using the chain rule, we obtain

$$Dg_w(h(z), z)Dh(z) + Dg_z(h(z), z) = 0.$$

At $z = z^*$, we have $h(z^*) = w^*$. Since $Dg_w(w^*, z^*)$ is invertible by assumption, this implies

$$Dh(z^*) = -[Dg_w(w^*, z^*)]^{-1} Dg_z(w^*, z^*).$$

Now define λ^* by

$$\lambda^* = -Df_w(w^*, z^*)[Dg_w(w^*, z^*)]^{-1}.$$

We will show that λ^* so defined meets the required conditions. Indeed, it follows from the very definition of λ^* that when both sides are postmultiplied by $Dg_w(w^*, z^*)$, we obtain

$$\lambda^* Dg_w(w^*, z^*) = -Df_w(w^*, z^*)[Dg_w(w^*, z^*)]^{-1} Dg_w(w^*, z^*)$$
$$= -Df_w(w^*, z^*),$$

---

[9] As we mentioned in Chapter 1, it is customary to treat vectors as *column* vectors, and to use the transpose to represent them as row vectors. We are not following this rule here.

[10] We assume in this proof that x^* is a local maximum; the proof for a local minimum follows identical steps, with obvious changes.

which is the same as

$$Df_w(w^*, z^*) + \lambda^* Dg_w(w^*, z^*) = 0.$$

Thus, it remains only to be shown that

$$Df_z(w^*, z^*) + \lambda^* Dg_z(w^*, z^*) = 0.$$

To this end, define the function $F: V \to \mathbb{R}$ by $F(z) = f(h(z), z)$. Since f has a local maximum at $(w^*, z^*) = (h(z^*), z^*)$, it is immediate that F has a local maximum at z^*. Since V is open, z^* is an unconstrained local maximum of F, and the first-order conditions for an unconstrained maximum now imply that $DF(z^*) = 0$, or that

$$Df_w(w^*, z^*)Dh(z^*) + Df_z(w^*, z^*) = 0.$$

Substituting for $Dh(z^*)$, we obtain

$$-Df_w(w^*, z^*)[Dg_w(w^*, z^*)]^{-1} Dg_z(w^*, z^*) + Df_z(w^*, z^*) = 0,$$

which, from the definition of λ, is the same as

$$Df_z(w^*, z^*) + \lambda^* Dg_z(w^*, z^*) = 0.$$

Theorem 5.1 is proved. ☐

5.7 A Proof of the Second-Order Conditions

We prove parts 1 and 3 of Theorem 5.4 here. Parts 2 and 4 are proved analogously. The details are left as an exercise to the reader.

Proof of Part 1 of Theorem 5.4

We will prove Part 1 of Theorem 5.4 for the case where there is just a single constraint, i.e., where $g: \mathbb{R}^n \to \mathbb{R}$. The general case follows exactly along the same lines, except that notation gets considerably more involved.[11] The proof we will present is a direct extension of the proof of the first-order necessary conditions provided in Section 5.6. In particular, we will use the notation introduced there, adapted to the case $k = 1$. That is:

- We will denote a typical point $x \in \mathbb{R}^n$ by (w, z), where $w \in \mathbb{R}$ and $z \in \mathbb{R}^{n-1}$. The point x^* will be denoted (w^*, z^*).

---

[11] Specifically, the added complication derives from the fact that when there is only a single constraint g, the second-derivative $D^2 g$ is an $n \times n$ matrix, while in the general case where $g = (g_1, \ldots, g_k)$, Dg is itself an $n \times k$ matrix, so $D^2 g = D(Dg)$ is an array of dimensions $n \times k \times n$. A typical entry in this array is $\partial^2 g_i(x)/\partial x_j \partial x_l$, where $i = 1, \ldots, k$, and $j, l = 1, \ldots, n$.

- We will denote by $Df_w(w, z)$ and $Df_z(w, z)$ the derivatives of f with respect to the w-variable and the z-variables. The terms Dg_w and Dg_z are defined similarly. Of course, we have $Df = (Df_w, Df_z)$ and $Dg = (Dg_w, Dg_z)$.
- We will assume, without loss of generality, that the 1×1 submatrix of $Dg(w^*, z^*)$ that has full rank is $Dg_w(w^*, z^*)$. By the Implicit Function Theorem, there is a neighborhood V of $z^* \in \mathbb{R}^{n-1}$, and a C^1 function $h: V \to \mathbb{R}$ such that $h(z^*) = w^*$, and $g(h(z), z) = 0$ for all $z \in V$.

In an extension of this notation to second-derivatives, we define $D^2 f_{ww}$ to be the derivative of Df_w with respect to the w-variable; $D^2 f_{wz}$ to be the derivative of Df_w with respect to the z-variables; and $D^2 f_{zz}$ to be the derivative of Df_z with respect to the z-variables. The terms $D^2 g_{ww}$, $D^2 g_{wz}$, and $D^2 g_{zz}$ are defined analogously.[12] Finally, for notational ease, we will simply use the superscript "*" to denote evaluation of the derivatives of f and g at $x^* = (w^*, z^*)$. So, for instance, Df^* will denote $Df(w^*, z^*)$, $D^2 f_{ww}^*$ will denote $D^2 f_{ww}(w^*, z^*)$, $D^2 g_{wz}^*$ will denote $D^2 g_{wz}(w^*, z^*)$, etc.

In this notation, we are given that f and g are C^2 functions mapping $\mathbb{R}^n$ into $\mathbb{R}$; that (w^*, z^*) is a local maximum of f on the set

$$D = U \cap \{(w, z) \in \mathbb{R}^n \mid g(w, z) = 0\},$$

and that $\rho(Dg_w(w^*, z^*)) = 1$, where $U \subset \mathbb{R}^n$ is open. We have shown in Section 5.6 under these conditions, that if

$$\lambda^* = -Df_w^*[Dg_w^*]^{-1},$$

then

$$Df(x^*) + \lambda^* Dg(x^*) = \begin{bmatrix} Df_w^* + \lambda^* Dg_w^* \\ Df_z^* + \lambda^* Dg_z^* \end{bmatrix} = 0.$$

We are now ready to show that, if $D^2 L^*$ denotes the $n \times n$ quadratic form $D^2 f(w^*, z^*) + \lambda^* D^2 g(w^*, z^*)$, we have

$$x' D^2 L^* x \leq 0 \text{ for all } x \in \mathcal{Z}^* = \{x \in \mathbb{R}^n \mid Dg(w^*, z^*)x = 0\}.$$

As a first step, note that since $g(h(z), z) = 0$ for all $z \in V$, we have

$$Dg_w(w, z)Dh(z) + Dg_z(w, z) = 0$$

---

[12]Note that, in full notation, we have

$$D^2 f = \begin{bmatrix} D^2 f_{ww} & D^2 f_{wz} \\ (D^2 f_{wz})' & D^2 f_{zz} \end{bmatrix}, \text{ and } D^2 g = \begin{bmatrix} D^2 g_{ww} & D^2 g_{wz} \\ (D^2 g_{wz})' & D^2 g_{zz} \end{bmatrix}.$$

for all (w, z). Differentiating again with respect to z, and suppressing notation on (w, z), we obtain

$$(Dh)'[D^2 g_{ww} Dh + D^2 g_{wz}] + Dg_w D^2 h + (Dh)' D^2 g_{wz} + D^2 g_{zz} = 0.$$

Evaluating these expressions at (w^*, z^*), and using the assumption that $Dg_w^* \neq 0$, we obtain

$$Dh^* = -[Dg_w^*]^{-1} Dg_z^*,$$
$$D^2 h^* = -[Dg_w^*]^{-1} \left((Dh^*)' D^2 g_{ww}^* Dh^* + 2(Dh^*)' D^2 g_{wz}^* + D^2 g_{zz}^* \right).$$

Now, define $F: V \to \mathbb{R}$ by $F(z) = f(h(z), z)$. Since f has a local maximum at (w^*, z^*), it is easy to see that F has a local maximum on V at z^*. Therefore, we must have $z' D^2 F(z^*) z \leq 0$ for all $z \in \mathbb{R}^n$. Since $DF(z) = Df_w(h(z), z) Dh(z) + Df_z(h(z), z)$ at all $z \in V$, we have

$$D^2 F(z^*) = (Dh^*)' D^2 f_{ww}^* Dh^* + 2(Dh^*)' D^2 f_{wz}^* + Df_w^* D^2 h^* D^2 f_{zz}^*.$$

Substituting for $D^2 h^*$, using the fact that $\lambda^* = -Df_w^* [Dg_w^*]^{-1}$, and writing $D^2 L_{ww}^*$ for $D^2 f_{ww}^* + \lambda^* D^2 g_{ww}^*$, etc., we obtain

$$DF(z^*) = (Dh^*)' D^2 L_{ww}^* Dh^* + 2(Dh^*)' D^2 L_{wz}^* + D^2 L_{zz}^*,$$

where $Dh^* = -[Dg_w^*]^{-1} Dg_z^*$. Since $D^2 F(z^*)$ is a negative semidefinite quadratic form, we have shown that the expression on the right-hand side of this equation is also a negative semidefinite quadratic form on $\mathbb{R}^n$, i.e., we must have

$$(Dh^* \xi)' D^2 L_{ww}^* Dh^* \xi + 2(Dh^* \xi)' D^2 L_{wz}^* + \xi' D^2 L_{zz}^* \xi \leq 0$$

for all $\xi \in \mathbb{R}^n$. In more compact matrix notation, we can write this as

$$[Dh^* \xi, \xi] \begin{bmatrix} D^2 L_{ww}^* & D^2 L_{wz}^* \\ (D^2 L_{wz}^*)' & D^2 L_{zz}^* \end{bmatrix} \begin{bmatrix} Dh^* \xi \\ \xi \end{bmatrix} \leq 0$$

for all $\xi \in \mathbb{R}^n$. To complete the proof, we will now show that this is precisely the same thing as the negative definiteness of $D^2 L^*$* on the set $\mathcal{Z}^*$. Indeed, this is immediate: note that since $Dg(w^*, z^*) = (Dg_w(w^*, z^*), Dg_z(w^*, z^*))$, it is the case that $(\omega, \xi) \in \mathcal{Z}^*$ if and only if $Dg_w^* \omega + Dg_z^* \xi = 0$, i.e., if and only if

$$\omega = -[Dg_w^*]^{-1} Dg_z^* \xi = Dh^* \xi.$$

Therefore, $D^2 L^*$ is negative semidefinite on $\mathcal{Z}^*$ if and only if for all $\xi \in \mathbb{R}^n$, we have

$$[Dh^* \xi, \xi] \begin{bmatrix} D^2 L_{ww}^* & D^2 L_{wz}^* \\ (D^2 L_{wz}^*)' & D^2 L_{zz}^* \end{bmatrix} \begin{bmatrix} Dh^* \xi \\ \xi \end{bmatrix} \leq 0.$$

The result is proved.

Proof of Part 3 of Theorem 5.4

The sufficient conditions given in Part 3 of Theorem 5.4 may be established by reversing the arguments used in proving the necessary conditions of Part 1. That is, we begin with the condition that D^2L^* is negative definite on the set $\mathcal{Z}^*$, show that this implies that the second derivative $D^2F(z^*)$ of the function $F(z) = f(h(z), z)$ is negative definite on $\mathbb{R}^n$, and use this to conclude that f has a strict local maximum at (w^*, z^*). This is a relatively straightforward procedure, so we do not fill in the details here. Instead, we offer an alternative method of establishing Part 3, which uses a completely different approach.

We revert to the notation of Theorem 5.4, and drop the simplifying assumption that $k = 1$. We are given that x^* satisfies $\rho(Dg(x^*)) = k$, and that there exists $\lambda^* \in \mathbb{R}^k$ such that the following two conditions are met:

$$Df(x^*) + \sum_{i=1}^{k} \lambda_i^* Dg_i(x^*) = 0,$$

$$x'D^2L^*x < 0 \quad \text{for all } 0 \neq x \in \mathcal{Z}^* = \{v \in \mathbb{R}^n \mid Dg(x^*)v = 0\}.$$

We are to show that x^* is a strict local maximum of f on $\mathcal{D}$, i.e., that there exists $r > 0$ such that $f(x^*) > f(x)$ for all $x \in B(x^*, r) \cap \mathcal{D}$.

We use a *reductio ad absurdum* approach. Suppose that under the stated conditions, the conclusion of the theorem were *not* true. Then, it is the case that for all $r > 0$, there exists $x(r) \in B(x^*, r) \cap \mathcal{D}$ such that $x(r) \neq x^*$ and $f(x(r)) \geq f(x^*)$. Pick any sequence $r_l > 0$, $r_l \downarrow 0$, and let $x_l = x(r_l)$. We shall use the sequence $\{x_l\}$ to show that there must exist at least one point $y \in \mathbb{R}^n$ with the following properties:

1. $y \neq 0$.
2. $Dg(x^*)y = 0$.
3. $y'D^2L^*y \geq 0$.

This will furnish the required contradiction, since, by hypothesis, we must have $y'D^2L^*y < 0$ for all $y \neq 0$ such that $Dg(x^*)y = 0$. Taylor's Theorem, which was described in Chapter 1 (see Theorem 1.75), will play a central role in this process.

Define a sequence $\{y_l\}$ in $\mathbb{R}^n$ by

$$y_l = \frac{x_l - x^*}{\|x_l - x^*\|}.$$

Since $x_l \neq x^*$ for any l, the sequence $\{y_l\}$ is well-defined. Moreover, we have $\|y_l\| = 1$ for all l, so the sequence $\{y_l\}$ lies in the unit circle C^{n-1} in $\mathbb{R}^n$:

$$C^{n-1} = \{y' \in \mathbb{R}^n \mid \|y'\| = 1\}.$$

As a closed and bounded subset of $\mathbb{R}^n$, C^{n-1} is compact, so the sequence $\{y_l\}$ admits a convergent subsequence $\{y_{m(l)}\}$ converging to a point $y \in C^{n-1}$. Observe that since we must have $\|y\| = 1$, it is certainly the case that $y \neq 0$.

We will now show that $Dg(x^*)y = 0$. Using a first-order Taylor series expansion of g around x^*, we have

$$g(x_{m(l)}) = g(x^*) + Dg(x^*)(x_{m(l)} - x^*) + R_1(x_{m(l)}, x^*).$$

By definition of x^*, and by choice of $x_{m(l)}$, we must have $g(x^*) = g(x_{m(l)}) = 0$. Therefore,

$$0 = \frac{Dg(x^*)(x_{m(l)} - x^*)}{\|x_{m(l)} - x^*\|} + \frac{R(x_{m(l)}, x^*)}{\|x_{m(l)} - x^*\|} = Dg(x^*)y_{m(l)} + \frac{R(x_{m(l)}, x^*)}{\|x_{m(l)} - x^*\|}.$$

By Taylor's Theorem, we must have $R(x_{m(l)}, x^*)/\|x_{m(l)} - x^*\| \to 0$ as $x_{m(l)} \to x^*$. Therefore, taking limits as $l \to \infty$, and noting that $y_{m(l)} \to z$, we obtain

$$0 = Dg(x^*)y.$$

Finally, to complete the proof, we will show that $y'D^2L^*y \geq 0$. For notational ease, let $L(\cdot)$ denote $L(\cdot; \lambda^*)$. Since $L(\cdot)$ is C^2, a second-order Taylor series expansion around x^* yields

$$L(x_{m(l)}) = L(x^*) + DL(x^*)(x_{m(l)} - x^*)$$
$$+ \frac{1}{2}(x_{m(l)} - x^*)'D^2L(x^*)(x_{m(l)} - x^*) + R_2(x_{m(l)}, x^*).$$

Now, we also have

1. $DL(x^*) = Df(x^*) + \sum_{i=1}^{k} \lambda_i^* Dg_i(x^*) = 0$.
2. $D^2L(x^*) = D^2L^*$.
3. $L(x_{m(l)}) = f(x_{m(l)}) + \sum_{i=1}^{k} \lambda_i^* g_i(x_{m(l)}) = f(x_{m(l)})$, since $g(x_{m(l)}) = 0$ by choice of $x_{m(l)}$.
4. $L(x^*) = f(x^*) + \sum_{i=1}^{k} \lambda_i^* g_i(x^*) = f(x^*)$, since $g(x^*) = 0$ by definition of x^*.

Substituting these into the Taylor expansion of $L(\cdot)$, we obtain

$$f(x_{m(l)}) = f(x^*) + (x_{m(l)} - x^*)'D^2L^*(x_{m(l)} - x^*) + R(x_{m(l)}, x^*).$$

Rearranging terms, dividing through by $\|x_{m(l)} - x^*\|^2$, and using the fact that

$$y_{m(l)} = \frac{x_{m(l)} - x^*}{\|x_{m(l)} - x^*\|},$$

we see that

$$\frac{f(x_{m(l)}) - f(x^*)}{\|x_{m(l)} - x^*\|^2} = y_{m(l)}'D^2L^*y_{m(l)} + \frac{R_2(x_{m(l)}, x^*)}{\|x_{m(l)} - x^*\|^2}.$$

By the definition of the sequence $\{x_l\}$, the left-hand side of this equation must be nonnegative at each l. Since $R_2(x_{m(l)}, x^*)/\|x_{m(l)} - x^*\|^2 \to 0$ as $x_{m(l)} \to x^*$, taking limits as $l \to \infty$ now results in

$$0 \leq y' D^2 L^* y,$$

as required.   □

5.8 Exercises

1. Find the maximum and minimum of $f(x, y) = x^2 - y^2$ on the unit circle $x^2 + y^2 = 1$ using the Lagrange multipliers method. Using the substitution $y^2 = 1 - x^2$, solve the same problem as a single variable unconstrained problem. Do you get the same results? Why or why not?

2. Show that the problem of maximizing $f(x, y) = x^3 + y^3$ on the constraint set $\mathcal{D} = \{(x, y) \mid x + y = 1\}$ has no solution. Show also that if the Lagrangean method were used on this problem, the critical points of the Lagrangean have a unique solution. Is the point identified by this solution either a local maximum or a (local or global) minimum?

3. Find the maxima and minima of the following functions subject to the specified constraints:

   (a) $f(x, y) = xy$ subject to $x^2 + y^2 = 2a^2$.
   (b) $f(x, y) = 1/x + 1/y$ subject to $(1/x)^2 + (1/y)^2 = (1/a)^2$.
   (c) $f(x, y, z) = x + y + z$ subject to $(1/x) + (1/y) + (1/z) = 1$.
   (d) $f(x, y, z) = xyz$ subject to $x + y + z = 5$ and $xy + xz + yz = 8$.
   (e) $f(x, y) = x + y$ for $xy = 16$.
   (f) $f(x, y, z) = x^2 + 2y - z^2$ subject to $2x - y = 0$ and $x + z = 6$.

4. Maximize and minimize $f(x, y) = x + y$ on the lemniscate $(x^2 - y^2)^2 = x^2 + y^2$.

5. Consider the problem:

   $$\min \quad x^2 + y^2 \quad \text{subject to } (x - 1)^3 - y^2 = 0.$$

   (a) Solve the problem geometrically.
   (b) Show that the method of Lagrange multipliers does not work in this case. Can you explain why?

6. Consider the following problem where the objective function is quadratic and the constraints are linear:

   $$\max_{x} \quad c'x + \frac{1}{2}x' Dx \quad \text{subject to } Ax = b$$

where c is a given n-vector, D is a given $n \times n$ symmetric, negative definite matrix, and A is a given $m \times n$ matrix.

(a) Set up the Lagrangean and obtain the first-order conditions.

(b) Solve for the optimal vector x^* as a function of A, b, c, and D.

7. Solve the problem

$$\max f(x) = x'Ax \quad \text{subject to} \quad x \cdot x = 1$$

where A is a given symmetric matrix.

8. A firm's inventory of a certain homogeneous commodity, $I(t)$, is depleted at a constant rate per unit time dI/dt, and the firm reorders an amount x of the commodity, which is delivered immediately, whenever the level of inventory is zero. The annual requirement for the commodity is A, and the firm orders the commodity n times a year where

$$A = nx.$$

The firm incurs two types of inventory costs: a *holding cost* and an *ordering cost*. The average stock of inventory is $x/2$, and the cost of holding one unit of the commodity is C_h, so $C_h x/2$ is the holding cost. The firm orders the commodity, as stated above, n times a year, and the cost of placing one order is C_o, so $C_o n$ is the ordering cost. The total cost is then:

$$C = C_h \frac{x}{2} + C_o n.$$

(a) In a diagram show how the inventory level varies over time. Prove that the average inventory level is $x/2$.

(b) Minimize the cost of inventory, C, by choice of x and n subject to the constraint $A = nx$ using the Lagrange multiplier method. Find the optimal x as a function of the parameters C_o, C_h, and A. Interpret the Lagrange multiplier.

9. Suppose the utility function in subsection 5.5.1 is modified to

$$u(x_1, x_2) = x_1^\alpha + x_2^\beta,$$

where $\alpha, \beta > 0$. Under what circumstances, if any, can the problem now be reduced to an equality-constrained optimization problem?

10. Consider the cost-minimization problem of subsection 5.5.2, but with the production function g modified to

$$g(x_1, x_2) = x_1^2 + x_2^2.$$

(a) Let $y = 1$. Represent the set $\{(x_1, x_2) \in \mathbb{R}_+^2 \mid x_1^2 + x_2^2 \geq y\}$ in a diagram, and argue using this diagram that the solution to the problem is

$$(x_1^*, x_2^*) = \begin{cases} (1, 0), & \text{if } w_1 < w_2 \\ (0, 1), & \text{if } w_1 > w_2 \end{cases}$$

with either $(1, 0)$ or $(0, 1)$ being optimal if $w_1 = w_2$.

(b) Show that if the nonnegativity constraints are ignored and the Lagrangean method is employed, the method fails to identify the solution, regardless of the values of w_1 and w_2.

11. Consider the problem of maximizing the utility function

$$u(x, y) = x^{1/2} + y^{1/2}$$

on the budget set $\{(x, y) \in \mathbb{R}_+^2 \mid px + y = 1\}$. Show that if the nonnegativity constraints $x \geq 0$ and $y \geq 0$ are ignored, and the problem is written as an equality-constrained one, the resulting Lagrangean has a unique critical point. Does this critical point identify a solution to the problem? Why or why not?

6

Inequality Constraints and the Theorem of Kuhn and Tucker

Building on the analysis of the previous chapter, we now turn to a study of optimization problems defined by *inequality* constraints. The constraint set will now be assumed to have the form

$$\mathcal{D} = U \cap \{x \in \mathbb{R}^n \mid h_i(x) \geq 0, \ i = 1, \ldots, l\},$$

where $U \subset \mathbb{R}^n$ is open, and $h_i \colon \mathbb{R}^n \to \mathbb{R}, \ i = 1, \ldots, l$. The centerpiece of this chapter is the Theorem of Kuhn and Tucker, which describes necessary conditions for local optima in such problems. Following the description of the theorem—and of its use in locating optima in inequality-constrained problems—we show that the Theorem of Lagrange may be combined with the Theorem of Kuhn and Tucker to obtain necessary conditions for local optima in the general case of optimization problems defined by *mixed* constraints, where the constraint set takes the form

$$\mathcal{D} = U \cap \{x \in \mathbb{R}^n \mid g_j(x) = 0, \ j = 1, \ldots k, \ h_i(x) \geq 0, \ i = 1, \ldots, l\}.$$

6.1 The Theorem of Kuhn and Tucker

The Theorem of Kuhn and Tucker provides an elegant characterization of the behavior of the objective function f and the constraint functions h_i at local optima of inequality-constrained optimization problems. The conditions it describes may be viewed as the first-order necessary conditions for local optima in these problems. The statement of the theorem, and a discussion of some of its components, is the subject of this section.

6.1.1 Statement of the Theorem

In the statement of the theorem, as elsewhere in the sequel, we say that an inequality constraint $h_i(x) \geq 0$ is *effective* at a point x^* if the constraint holds with equality at

x^*, that is, we have $h_i(x^*) = 0$. We will also use the expression $|E|$ to denote the *cardinality* of a finite set E, i.e., the number of elements in the set E.

Theorem 6.1 (Theorem of Kuhn and Tucker) *Let $f \colon \mathbb{R}^n \to \mathbb{R}$ and $h_i \colon \mathbb{R}^n \to \mathbb{R}$ be C^1 functions, $i = 1, \ldots, l$. Suppose x^* is a local maximum of f on*

$$\mathcal{D} = U \cap \{x \in \mathbb{R}^n \mid h_i(x) \geq 0, \ i = 1, \ldots, l\},$$

where U is an open set in $\mathbb{R}^n$. Let $E \subset \{1, \ldots, l\}$ denote the set of effective constraints at x^*, and let $h_E = (h_i)_{i \in E}$. Suppose $\rho(Dh_E(x^*)) = |E|$. Then, there exists a vector $\lambda^* = (\lambda_1^*, \ldots, \lambda_l^*) \in \mathbb{R}^l$ such that the following conditions are met:

> *[KT-1]* $\lambda_i^* \geq 0$ *and* $\lambda_i^* h_i(x^*) = 0$ *for $i = 1, \ldots, l$.*

> *[KT-2]* $Df(x^*) + \displaystyle\sum_{i=1}^{l} \lambda_i^* Dh_i(x^*) = 0.$

Proof See Section 6.5.[1]   □

Although we have stated the Theorem of Kuhn and Tucker for local *maxima*, the theorem is easily extended to cover local *minima*. For, if x^* were a local minimum of f on $\mathcal{D}$, x^* would be a local maximum of $-f$ on $\mathcal{D}$. Since $D(-f) = -Df$, we have the following:

Corollary 6.2 *Suppose f and $\mathcal{D}$ are defined as in Theorem 6.1, and x^* is a local minimum of f on $\mathcal{D}$. Let E be the set of effective constraints at x^*, let $h_E = (h_i)_{i \in E}$, and suppose that $\rho(Dh_E(x^*)) = |E|$. Then, there exists $\lambda^* \in \mathbb{R}^l$ such that*

> *[KT-1']* $\lambda_i^* \geq 0$ *and* $\lambda_i^* h_i(x^*) = 0$ *for all i.*

> *[KT-2']* $Df(x^*) - \displaystyle\sum_{i=1}^{l} \lambda_i^* Dh_i(x^*) = 0.$

Proof Follows immediately from Theorem 6.1.   □

Remark In the sequel, we will say that a pair (x^*, λ^*) meets the first-order necessary conditions for a maximum (or that it meets the Kuhn–Tucker first-order conditions for a maximum) in a given inequality-constrained maximization problem, if (x^*, λ^*) satisfies $h(x^*) \geq 0$ as well as conditions [KT-1] and [KT-2] of Theorem 6.1. Similarly,

---

[1] With the (important) exception of the nonnegativity of the vector λ, the conclusions of the Theorem of Kuhn and Tucker can be derived from the Theorem of Lagrange. Indeed, this constitutes the starting point of our proof of the Theorem of Kuhn and Tucker in Section 6.5.

we will say that (x^*, λ^*) meets the first-order necessary conditions for a minimum (or that it meets the Kuhn–Tucker first-order conditions for a minimum) if it satisfies $h(x^*) \geq 0$ as well as conditions [KT-1'] and [KT-2'] of Corollary 6.2. □

Condition [KT-1] in Theorem 6.1 (which is the same as condition [KT-1'] in Corollary 6.2) is called the condition of "complementary slackness." The terminology arises simply from the observation that by the feasibility of x^*, we must have $h_i(x^*) \geq 0$ for each i; therefore, for $\lambda_i^* h_i(x^*) = 0$ to hold alongside $\lambda_i^* \geq 0$, we must have $\lambda_i^* = 0$ if $h_i(x^*) > 0$, and $h_i(x^*) = 0$ if $\lambda_i^* > 0$. That is, if one inequality is "slack" (not strict), the other cannot be.

It must be stressed that the Theorem of Kuhn and Tucker provides conditions that are only *necessary* for local optima, and at that, only for local optima that meet the constraint qualification. These conditions are not claimed to be *sufficient* to identify a point as being a local optimum, and indeed, it is easy to construct examples to show that the conditions *cannot* be sufficient. Here is a particularly simple one:

Example 6.3 Let $f: \mathbb{R} \to \mathbb{R}$ and $g: \mathbb{R} \to \mathbb{R}$ be defined by $f(x) = x^3$ and $g(x) = x$, respectively. Consider the problem of maximizing f on the set $\mathcal{D} = \{x \in \mathbb{R} \mid g(x) \geq 0\}$.

Let $x^* = \lambda^* = 0$. Then, x^* is evidently in the feasible set, and the problem's single constraint is effective at x^*. Moreover, $g'(x) = 1$ for all x, so the constraint qualification holds at all x, and, in particular, at x^*. Finally, note that

$$f'(x^*) + \lambda^* g'(x^*) = 0.$$

Thus, if the conditions of the Theorem of Kuhn and Tucker were also sufficient, x^* would be a local maximum of f on $\mathcal{D}$. However, f is strictly increasing at $x^* = 0$, so quite evidently x^* cannot be such a local maximum. □

This example notwithstanding, the Theorem of Kuhn and Tucker turns out to be quite useful in practice in identifying optima of inequality-constrained problems. Its use in this direction is explored in Sections 6.2 and 6.3 below.

In the subsections that follow, we elaborate on two aspects of the Theorem of Kuhn and Tucker. Subsection 6.1.2 discusses the importance of the rank condition that $\rho(Dh_E(x^*)) = |E|$. Subsection 6.1.3 then sketches an interpretation of the vector λ^*, whose existence the theorem asserts.

6.1.2 The Constraint Qualification

As with the analogous condition in the Theorem of Lagrange, the condition in the Theorem of Kuhn and Tucker that the rank of $Dh_E(x^*)$ be equal to $|E|$ is called the *constraint qualification*. This condition plays a central role in the proof of the theorem (see Section 6.5 below). Moreover, if the constraint qualification fails, the theorem itself could fail. Here is an example to illustrate this point:

Example 6.4 Let $f: \mathbb{R}^2 \to \mathbb{R}$ and $h: \mathbb{R}^2 \to \mathbb{R}$ be given by $f(x, y) = -(x^2 + y^2)$ and $h(x, y) = (x - 1)^3 - y^2$, respectively. Consider the problem of maximizing f on the set

$$\mathcal{D} = \{(x, y) \in \mathbb{R}^2 \mid h(x, y) \geq 0\}.$$

A solution to this problem can be obtained by inspection: the function f reaches a maximum at the point where $(x^2 + y^2)$ reaches a minimum. Since the constraint requires $(x - 1)^3 \geq y^2$, and $y^2 \geq 0$ for all y, the smallest absolute value of x on $\mathcal{D}$ is $x = 1$, which occurs when $y = 0$; and, of course, the smallest absolute value of y on $\mathcal{D}$ is $y = 0$. It follows that f is maximized at $(x^*, y^*) = (1, 0)$. Note that the problem's single constraint is effective at this point.

At this global maximum of f on $\mathcal{D}$, we have $Dh(x^*, y^*) = (3(x^* - 1)^2, 2y^*) = (0, 0)$, so $\rho(Dh(x^*, y^*)) = 0 < 1$, and the constraint qualification fails. On the other hand, we have $Df(x^*, y^*) = (-2x^*, -2y^*) = (-2, 0)$, so there cannot exist $\lambda \geq 0$ such that $Df(x^*, y^*) + \lambda Dh(x^*, y^*) = (0, 0)$. Therefore, the conclusions of the Theorem of Kuhn and Tucker also fail. □

6.1.3 The Kuhn–Tucker Multipliers

The vector λ^* in the Theorem of Kuhn and Tucker is called the vector of *Kuhn–Tucker multipliers* corresponding to the local maximum x^*. As with the Lagrangean multipliers, the Kuhn–Tucker multipliers may also be thought of as measuring the sensitivity of the objective function at x^* to relaxations of the various constraints. Indeed, this interpretation is particularly intuitive in the context of inequality constraints. To wit, if $h_i(x^*) > 0$, then the i-th constraint is already slack, so relaxing it further will not help raise the value of the objective function in the maximization exercise, and λ_i^* must be zero. On the other hand, if $h_i(x^*) = 0$, then relaxing the i-th constraint may help increase the value of the maximization exercise, so we have $\lambda_i \geq 0$.[2]

For a more formal demonstration of this interpretation of λ, we impose some simplifying assumptions in a manner similar to those used in Chapter 5. First, we will assume throughout this discussion that the constraint functions h_i are all given

---

[2]The reason we have $\lambda_i \geq 0$ in this case, and not the strict inequality $\lambda_i > 0$, is also intuitive: another constraint, say the j-th, may have also been binding at x^*, and it may not be possible to raise the objective function without simultaneously relaxing constraints i and j.

in parametric form as

$$h_i(x; c) = h_i(x) + c_i.$$

Under this assumption, we can define a relaxation of the i-th constraint as a "small" increase in the value of the parameter c_i.

Let $C \subset \mathbb{R}^l$ be some open set of feasible values for the parameters $(c_1, \ldots, c_l)$. Suppose that for each $c \in C$, there is a global maximum $x^*(c)$ of f on the constraint set

$$\mathcal{D}(c) = U \cap \{x \in \mathbb{R}^n \mid h_i(x) + c_i \geq 0, \ i = 1, \ldots, l\}.$$

Suppose further that the constraint qualification holds at each $c \in C$, so there exists $\lambda^*(c) \geq 0$ such that

$$Df(x^*(c)) + \sum_{i=1}^{l} \lambda_i^*(c) Dh_i(x^*(c)) = 0.$$

Finally, suppose that $\lambda^*(\cdot)$ and $x^*(\cdot)$ are C^1 functions of the parameters c on the set C.

Define $F: C \to \mathbb{R}$ by

$$F(c) = f(x^*(c)).$$

The demonstration will be complete if we show that $\partial F(c)/\partial c_i = \lambda_i, i = 1, \ldots, l$.

Pick any $c \in C$. Suppose i is such that $h_i(x^*(c)) + c_i > 0$. Pick any $\hat{c}_i$ such that $\hat{c}_i < c_i$ and

$$h_i(x^*(c)) + \hat{c}_i > 0.$$

Consider the constraint set $\mathcal{D}(c_{-i}, \hat{c}_i)$ which results when the parameter c_i in constraint i is replaced by $\hat{c}_i$. Since $\hat{c}_i < c_i$, we must have

$$\mathcal{D}(c_{-i}, \hat{c}_i) \subset \mathcal{D}(c).$$

Since $x^* = x^*(c)$ is a local maximum of f on the larger constraint set $\mathcal{D}(c)$, and since $x^*(c) \in \mathcal{D}(c_{-i}, \hat{c}_i)$ by choice of $\hat{c}_i$, it follows that $x^*(c)$ is also a maximum of f on the constraint set $\mathcal{D}(c_{-i}, \hat{c}_i)$. Therefore,

$$F(c_{-i}, \hat{c}_i) = f(x^*(c)) = F(c).$$

It follows immediately that $\partial F(c)/\partial c_i = 0$. On the other hand, it is also the case that $h_i(x^*(c)) + c_i > 0$ implies by the Kuhn–Tucker complementary slackness conditions that $\lambda_i^*(c) = 0$. Therefore, we have shown that if constraint i is slack at c, we must have

$$\frac{\partial F}{\partial c_i}(c) = \lambda_i^*(c).$$

It remains to be shown that this relationship also holds if i is an *effective* constraint at c, i.e., if constraint i holds with equality. This may be achieved by adapting the argument used in subsection 5.2.3 of Chapter 5. The details are left to the reader.

6.2 Using the Theorem of Kuhn and Tucker

6.2.1 A "Cookbook" Procedure

The cookbook procedure for using the Theorem of Kuhn and Tucker to solve an inequality-constrained optimization problem involves essentially the same steps as those in using the Theorem of Lagrange in solving equality-constrained problems: namely, we form a "Lagrangean" L, then we compute its critical points, and finally, we evaluate the objective at each critical point and select the point at which the objective is optimized.

There are, however, some important differences in the details. One of these arises from the fact that the conclusions of the Kuhn–Tucker Theorem differ for local *maxima* and local *minima*. This necessiates a difference in the steps to be followed in solving maximization problems, from those to be used in solving minimization problems. These differences are minor; nonetheless, for expositional ease, we postpone discussion of the minimization problem to the end of this subsection, and focus on *maximization* problems of the form

$$\text{Maximize } f(x) \text{ subject to } x \in \mathcal{D} = U \cap \{x \mid h(x) \geq 0\}.$$

As the first step in the procedure for solving this problem, we form a function $L: \mathbb{R}^n \times \mathbb{R}^l \to \mathbb{R}$, which we shall continue calling the Lagrangean, defined by:

$$L(x, \lambda) = f(x) + \sum_{i=1}^{l} \lambda_i h_i(x).$$

The second step in the procedure is to find all solutions (x, λ) to the following set of equations:

$$\frac{\partial L}{\partial x_j}(x, \lambda) = 0, \quad j = 1, \ldots, n,$$

$$\frac{\partial L}{\partial \lambda_i}(x, \lambda) \geq 0, \quad \lambda_i \geq 0, \quad \lambda_i \frac{\partial L}{\partial \lambda_i}(x, \lambda) = 0, \quad i = 1, \ldots, l.$$

Any solution to this system of equations will be called a "critical point" of L. It is important to note that the equations that define the critical points of L differ from the corresponding ones in equality-constrained problems, in particular with respect to the λ-derivatives. Let M denote the set of all critical points of L for which $x \in U$:

$$M = \{(x, \lambda) \mid (x, \lambda) \text{ is a critical point of } L \text{ and } x \in U\}.$$

As the third and last step, we compute the value of f at each x in the set

$$\{x \mid \text{there is } \lambda \text{ such that } (x, \lambda) \in M\}.$$

In practice, the value of x that maximizes f over this set is typically also the solution to the original maximization problem.

The reason this procedure works well in practice, and the conditions that may cause its failure, are explored in the following subsections. But first, some notes on inequality-constrained *minimization* problems. Suppose the original problem is to solve

$$\text{Minimize } f(x) \text{ subject to } x \in \mathcal{D} = U \cap \{x \mid h(x) \geq 0\}.$$

Two routes are open to us. First, since x minimizes f over $\mathcal{D}$ if, and only if, x maximizes $-f$ over $\mathcal{D}$, we could simply rewrite the problem as a maximization problem with the objective function given by $-f$, and use the procedure listed above.

The alternative route is to modify the definition of the Lagrangean to

$$\mathcal{L}(x, \lambda) = f(x) - \sum_{i=1}^{l} \lambda_i h_i(x),$$

and follow the same remaining steps as listed for the maximization problem. That is, in the second step, we find the set $\mathcal{M}$ of all the points (x, λ) which satisfy $x \in U$ as well as

$$\frac{\partial \mathcal{L}}{\partial x_j}(x, \lambda) = 0, \quad j = 1, \ldots, n,$$

$$\frac{\partial \mathcal{L}}{\partial \lambda_i}(x, \lambda) \geq 0, \quad \lambda_i \geq 0, \quad \lambda_i \frac{\partial \mathcal{L}}{\partial \lambda_i}(x, \lambda) = 0, \quad i = 1, \ldots, l.$$

Lastly, we evaluate f at each point x in the set $\{x \mid \text{there is } \lambda \text{ such that } (x, \lambda) \in \mathcal{M}\}$. The value of x that minimizes f over this set is typically also a global minimum of the original problem.

6.2.2 Why the Procedure Usually Works

As earlier with the Theorem of Lagrange, it is not very hard to see why this method is usually successful. We discuss the reasons in the context of inequality-constrained *maximization* problems here. With the appropriate modifications, the same arguments also hold for minimization problems.

The key, once again, lies in a property of the Lagrangean L:

The set of critical points of L contains the set of all local maxima of f on $\mathcal{D}$ at which the constraint qualification is met. That is, if x is a local maximum of f on $\mathcal{D}$, and the constraint qualification is satisfied at x, then there must exist λ such that (x, λ) is a critical point of L.

As earlier, this is an immediate consequence of the definition of L and its critical points. Since we have

$$\frac{\partial L}{\partial \lambda_i}(x, \lambda) = h_i(x)$$

$$\frac{\partial L}{\partial x_j}(x, \lambda) = \frac{\partial f}{\partial x_j}(x) + \sum_{i=1}^{l} \lambda_i \frac{\partial h_i}{\partial x_j}(x),$$

a pair (x, λ) can be a critical point of L if and only if it satisfies the following conditions:

$$h_i(x) \geq 0, \quad \lambda_i \geq 0, \quad \lambda_i h_i(x) = 0, \ i = 1, \ldots, l.$$

$$Df(x) + \sum_{i=1}^{l} \lambda_i Dh_i(x) = 0.$$

Equivalently, (x, λ) is a critical point of L if and only if it satisfies the Kuhn–Tucker first-order conditions for a maximum, i.e., it satisfies $h(x) \geq 0$ as well as conditions [KT-1] and [KT-2] of Theorem 6.1.

Now, suppose x^* is a local maximum of f on $\mathcal{D}$, and the constraint qualification holds at x^*. Since x^* is feasible, it must satisfy $h(x^*) \geq 0$. By the Theorem of Kuhn and Tucker, there must also exist λ^* such that (x^*, λ^*) satisfies conditions [KT-1] and [KT-2] of Theorem 6.1. This says precisely that (x^*, λ^*) must be a critical point of L, establishing the claimed property.

A special case of this property is:

Proposition 6.5 *Suppose the following conditions hold:*

1. *A global maximum x^* exists to the given inequality-constrained problem.*
2. *The constraint qualification is met at x^*.*

Then, there exists λ^* such that (x^*, λ^*) is a critical point of L.

It follows that, under the conditions of Proposition 6.5, the procedure we have outlined above will succeed in identifying the maximum x^*. Since neither the existence of solutions nor the constraint qualification is usually a problem in applications, Proposition 6.5 also provides an indirect explanation of why this procedure is quite successful in practice.

6.2.3 When It Could Fail

Unfortunately, the failure of either condition of Proposition 6.5 could also lead to failure of this procedure in identifying global optima. This subsection provides a number of examples to illustrate this point.

First, even if an optimum does exist, the constraint qualification may fail at the optimum, and as a consequence, the optimum may not turn up as part of a solution to the equations defining the critical points of L. It is very important to understand that this does *not* imply that L will possess no critical points. In each of Examples 6.6 and 6.7, a unique global maximum exists to the stated problem, and in each case the constraint qualification fails at the optimum. In Example 6.6, this results in a situation where L fails to have any critical points. This is not, however, the case in Example 6.7, where L possesses multiple critical points, although the problem's unique maximum is not amongst these.

Example 6.6 As in Example 6.4, let f and h be C^2 functions on $\mathbb{R}^2$ defined by $f(x, y) = -(x^2 + y^2)$, and $h(x, y) = (x - 1)^3 - y^2$, respectively. We have seen in Example 6.4 that the unique global maximum of f on $\mathcal{D}$ is achieved at $(x, y) = (1, 0)$, but that the constraint qualification fails at this point; and that, as a consequence, there is no $\lambda \in \mathbb{R}_+$ such that $(1, 0, \lambda)$ meets the conclusions of the Theorem of Kuhn and Tucker. Evidently, then, there is no value of λ for which the point $(1, 0, \lambda)$ arises as a critical point of $L(x, y) = f(x, y) + \lambda h(x, y)$, and the cookbook procedure fails to identify this unique global optimum.

Indeed, there are *no* solutions to the equations that define the critical points of L in this problem. These equations are given by:

$$-2x + 3\lambda(x - 1)^2 = 0$$

$$-2y - 2\lambda y = 0$$

$$(x - 1)^3 - y^2 \geq 0, \quad \lambda \geq 0, \quad \lambda((x - 1)^3 - y^2) = 0.$$

If $y \neq 0$, then the second equation implies $\lambda = -1$, which violates the third equation. So we must have $y = 0$. If λ is also zero, then from the first equation, we have $x = 0$, but $x = y = 0$ violates $(x - 1)^3 - y^2 \geq 0$. On the other hand, if $\lambda > 0$, then—since $y = 0$—the complementary slackness condition implies $(x - 1)^3 = 0$, or $x = 1$, but this violates the first equation. $\square$

Example 6.7 Let f and g be functions on $\mathbb{R}$ defined by $f(x) = 2x^3 - 3x^2$ and $g(x) = (3 - x)^3$, respectively. Consider the problem of maximizing f over the set $\mathcal{D} = \{x \mid g(x) \geq 0\}$.

Since $(3 - x)^3 \geq 0$ if and only if $3 - x \geq 0$, the constraint set is just the interval $(-\infty, 3]$. A simple calculation shows that f is nonpositive for $x \leq \frac{3}{2}$, and is strictly positive and strictly increasing for $x > \frac{3}{2}$. Therefore, the unique global maximum of f on $\mathcal{D}$ occurs at the point $x^* = 3$. At this point, however, we have $g'(x^*) = -3(3 - x^*)^2 = 0$, so the constraint qualification fails. We will show that, as a consequence, the procedure we have outlined will fail to identify x^*.

Form the Lagrangean $L(x, \lambda) = f(x) + \lambda g(x)$. The critical points of L are the solutions to

$$6x^2 - 6x - 3\lambda(3 - x)^2 = 0,$$

$$\lambda \geq 0, \ (3 - x)^3 \geq 0, \ \lambda(3 - x)^3 = 0.$$

For the complementary slackness condition to hold, we must have either $\lambda = 0$ or $x = 3$. A simple calculation shows that if $\lambda = 0$, there are precisely two solutions to these equations, namely $(x, \lambda) = (0, 0)$ and $(x, \lambda) = (1, 0)$. As we have seen, neither $x = 0$ nor $x = 1$ is a global maximum of the problem. On the other hand, if $x = 3$, the first equation cannot be satisfied, since $6x^2 - 6x - 3\lambda(3-x)^2 = 6x^2 - 6x = 36 \neq 0$. So the unique global maximum x^* is not part of a solution to the critical points of L.

□

Alternatively, even if the constraint qualification holds everywhere on the feasible set, the procedure may still fail to identify global optima, because global optima may simply not exist. In this case, the equations that define the critical points of L may have no solutions; alternatively, there may exist solutions to these equations which are not global, or maybe even local, optima. Consider the following examples:

Example 6.8 Let f and g be C^1 functions on $\mathbb{R}$ defined by $f(x) = x^2 - x$, and $g(x) = x$, respectively. Consider the problem of maximizing f over the set $\mathcal{D} = \{x \mid g(x) \geq 0\}$. Note that since $g'(x) = 1$ everywhere, the constraint qualification holds everywhere on $\mathcal{D}$.

Define $L(x, \lambda) = f(x) + \lambda g(x)$. The critical points of L are the solutions (x, λ) to

$$2x - 1 + \lambda = 0,$$

$$x \geq 0, \ \lambda \geq 0, \ \lambda x = 0.$$

This system of equations admits two solutions: $(x, \lambda) = (0, 1)$, and $(x, \lambda) = (\frac{1}{2}, 0)$. However, neither point is a solution to the given maximization problem: for instance, at $x = 2$ (which is a feasible point), we have $f(x) = 3$, while $f(0) = 0$ and $f(\frac{1}{2}) = -\frac{1}{4}$. Indeed, the given problem has no solution at all, since the feasible set is all of $\mathbb{R}_+$, and $f(x) \uparrow \infty$ as $x \uparrow \infty$.

□

Example 6.9 Let f and g be functions on $\mathbb{R}^2$ defined by $f(x, y) = x + y$ and $g(x, y) = xy - 1$, respectively. Consider the problem of maximizing f over the feasible set

$$\mathcal{D} = \{(x, y) \in \mathbb{R}^2 \mid g(x, y) \geq 0\}.$$

This problem evidently has no solution: for any real number $x \geq 1$, the vector (x, x) is in $\mathcal{D}$, and $f(x, x) = 2x$, which is increasing and unbounded in x. We will show that, nonetheless, a unique solution exists to the critical points of the Lagrangean in this problem.

The Lagrangean L has the form $L(x, y, \lambda) = x + y + \lambda(xy - 1)$. The critical points of L are the solutions (x, y, λ) to

$$1 + \lambda y = 0$$

$$1 + \lambda x = 0$$

$$\lambda \geq 0, \ xy \geq 1, \ \lambda(1 - xy) = 0.$$

A simple calculation shows that the vector $(x, y, \lambda) = (-1, -1, 1)$ satisfies all these conditions (and is, in fact, the unique solution to these equations). As we have seen, this point does not define a solution to the given problem. □

These examples suggest that caution should be employed in using the cookbook technique in solving inequality-constrained optimization problems. If one can verify existence of global optima and the constraint qualification *a priori*, then the method works well in identifying the optima. On the other hand, in situations where answers to these questions are not available *a priori*, problems arise.

First, the Lagrangean L may fail to have any critical points for two very different reasons. On the one hand, this may be because the problem itself does not have a solution (Example 6.8). On the other hand, this situation can arise even when a solution does exist, since the constraint qualification may be violated at the optimum (witness Example 6.6). Thus, the absence of critical points of L does not enable us to draw any conclusions about the existence or non-existence of solutions to the given problem.

Second, even if the Lagrangean L has one or more critical points, this set of critical points need not contain the solution. Once again, this may be because no solution exists to the problem (as in Example 6.9), or because a solution does exist, but one at which the constraint qualification is violated (cf. Example 6.7). Thus, even the presence of critical points of L does not enable us to draw conclusions about the existence of solutions to the given problem.

6.2.4 A Numerical Example

Let $g(x, y) = 1 - x^2 - y^2$. Consider the problem of maximizing $f(x, y) = x^2 - y$ over the set

$$\mathcal{D} = \{(x, y) \mid g(x, y) \geq 0\}.$$

We will first argue that both conditions of Proposition 6.5 are satisfied, so the cookbook procedure must succeed in identifying the optimum. The feasible set $\mathcal{D}$ in this problem is just the closed unit disk in $\mathbb{R}^2$, which is evidently compact. Since the objective function is continuous on $\mathcal{D}$, a maximum exists by the Weierstrass Theorem, so the first of the two conditions of Proposition 6.5 is satisfied. To see that the second condition is also met, note that at any point where the problem's single constraint is effective (that is, at any (x, y) where we have $x^2 + y^2 = 1$), we must have either $x \neq 0$ or $y \neq 0$. Since $Dg(x, y) = (-2x, -2y)$ at all (x, y), it follows that at all points where g is effective, we must have $\rho(Dg(x, y)) = 1$. Thus, the constraint qualification holds if the optimum occurs at a point (x, y) where $g(x, y) = 0$. If the optimum occurs at a point (x, y) where $g(x, y) > 0$, then the set of effective constraints is empty. Since the constraint qualification pertains only to effective constraints, it holds vacuously in this case also. Thus, the second of the two conditions of Proposition 6.5 is also met.

Now set up the Lagrangean $L(x, y, \lambda) = x^2 - y + \lambda(1 - x^2 - y^2)$. The critical points of L are the solutions (x, y, λ) to

$$2x - 2\lambda x = 0$$

$$-1 - 2\lambda y = 0$$

$$\lambda \geq 0, \quad (1 - x^2 - y^2) \geq 0, \quad \lambda(1 - x^2 - y^2) = 0.$$

For the first equation to hold, we must have $x = 0$ or $\lambda = 1$. If $\lambda = 1$, then from the second equation, we must have $y = -\frac{1}{2}$, while from the third equation, we must have $x^2 + y^2 = 1$. This gives us two critical points of L, which differ only in the value of x:

$$(x, y, \lambda) = \left(\pm \frac{\sqrt{3}}{2}, -\frac{1}{2}, 1 \right).$$

Note that at either of these critical points, we have $f(x, y) = \frac{3}{4} + \frac{1}{2} = \frac{5}{4}$.

This leaves the case $x = 0$. If we also have $\lambda = 0$, then the second equation cannot be satisfied, so we must have $\lambda > 0$. This implies from the third equation that $x^2 + y^2 = 1$, so $y = \pm 1$. Since $y = 1$ is inconsistent with a positive value for λ from the second equation, the only possible critical point in this case is

$$(x, y, \lambda) = \left(0, -1, \frac{1}{2} \right).$$

At this critical point, we have $f(0, -1) = 1 < \frac{5}{4}$, which means this point cannot be a solution to the original maximization problem. Since there are no other critical points, and we know that any global maximum of f on $\mathcal{D}$ must arise as part of a critical point of L, it follows that there are exactly two solutions to the given optimization problem, namely the points $(x, y) = (\sqrt{3/4}, -1/2)$ and $(x, y) = (-\sqrt{3/4}, -1/2)$.

$\square$

6.3 Illustrations from Economics

In this section, we present two examples drawn from economics, which illustrate the use of the procedure outlined in the previous section in finding solutions to inequality-constrained optimization problems. The first example, presented in subsection 6.3.1, considers a utility maximization problem. The second example, presented in subsection 6.3.2, describes a cost minimization problem.

The presentation in this section serves a twofold purpose:

1. It explains the process of checking for the constraint qualification condition in the presence of multiple inequality constraints. Unlike the case with equality-constrained problems where this process is relatively straightforward, there is the additional complication here that the constraint qualification depends on the precise subset of constraints that are effective at the *unknown* optimal point. Thus, the only way, in general, to check that the constraint qualification will hold at the optimal point is to take all possible locations of the optimal point, and demonstrate that the condition will hold at each of these locations.[3]
2. It details a method by which the critical points of L may be identified from the equations that define these points. This process is again more complicated than the corresponding situation in equality-constrained optimization problems, since a part of the equations (namely, the complementary slackness conditions) are not specified in the form of *in*equalities.

As a practical matter, these examples make an important point: that, whenever this is possible, it is better to solve an inequality-constrained optimization problem by reducing it to an equality-constrained one, since calculating the critical points of the Lagrangean in the latter class of problems is a significantly easier task.

Some comments on the examples themselves are also important. The two examples presented in this section share some common features. Most notably, in each case the formulations considered are such that the problem cannot be reduced to an equality-constrained problem. However, they are also designed to illustrate different aspects of solving inequality-constrained optimization problems. For instance, the set of critical points of the Lagrangean in the first example is very sensitive to the relationship between the parameters of the problem, whereas this dependence is

---

[3]"All possible locations of the optimal point" does *not* mean the entire feasible set, since it may be possible to use the structure of the specific problem at hand to rule out certain portions of the feasible set. See the examples that follow in this section.

much less pronounced in the second example. On the other hand, every critical point in the first example also identifies a solution of the problem; in contrast, the second example always has at least one critical point that is *not* a solution.

6.3.1 An Illustration from Consumer Theory

In this subsection, we consider the problem of maximizing the utility function $u(x_1, x_2) = x_1 + x_2$ on the budget set

$$\mathcal{B}(p, I) = \{(x_1, x_2) \mid I - p_1 x_1 - p_2 x_2 \geq 0, \ x_1 \geq 0, x_2 \geq 0\},$$

where I, p_1, and p_2 are all strictly positive terms. There are three inequality constraints that define this problem:

$$h_1(x_1, x_2) = x_1 \geq 0$$

$$h_2(x_1, x_2) = x_2 \geq 0$$

$$h_3(x_1, x_2) = I - p_1 x_1 - p_2 x_2 \geq 0.$$

As we have seen in Subsection 5.5.3, the nonnegativity constraints h_1 and h_2 cannot be ignored, so this problem cannot be reduced to an equality-constrained one. We will show that it can be solved through the procedure outlined in Section 6.2.

We begin by showing that both conditions of Proposition 6.5 are met. The budget set $\mathcal{B}(p, I)$ is evidently compact, since prices and income are all strictly positive, and the utility function is continuous on this set. An appeal to the Weierstrass Theorem yields the existence of a maximum in this problem, so one of the two requirements of Proposition 6.5 is satisfied.

To check that the other requirement is also met, we first identify all possible combinations of constraints that can, in principle, be effective at the optimum. Since there are three inequality constraints, there are a total of eight different combinations to be checked: namely, $\emptyset$, h_1, h_2, h_3, (h_1, h_2), (h_1, h_3), (h_2, h_3), and (h_1, h_2, h_3). Of these, the last can be ruled out, since $h_1 = h_2 = 0$ implies $h_3 > 0$. Moreover, since the utility function is strictly increasing in both arguments, it is obvious that all available income must be used up at the optimal point, so we must have $h_3 = 0$. Therefore, there are only three possible values for the set h_E of effective constraints at the optimum, namely, $h_E = (h_1, h_3)$, $h_E = (h_2, h_3)$, and $h_E = h_3$. We will show that the constraint qualification holds in each of these cases.

If the optimum occurs at a point where only the first and third constraints are effective and $h_E = (h_1, h_3)$, we have

$$Dh_E(x_1, x_2) = \begin{bmatrix} 1 & 0 \\ -p_1 & -p_2 \end{bmatrix}$$

at any (x_1, x_2). Since p_1 and p_2 are strictly positive by hypothesis, this matrix has full rank, so the constraint qualification will hold at such a point. A similar computation shows that if the optimum occurs at a point where only the second and third constraints are effective, the constraint qualification will be met. Finally, if the third constraint is the only effective one at the optimum and $h_E = h_3$, we have $Dh_E(x_1, x_2) = (-p_1, -p_2)$, and once again the positivity of the prices implies that there are no problems here.

In summary, the optimum in this problem must occur at a point where $h_3 = 0$, but no matter where on this set the optimum lies (i.e., no matter which other constraints are effective at the optimum), the constraint qualification must hold. Therefore, the second condition of Proposition 6.5 is also satisfied, and the critical points of the Lagrangean must contain the global maxima of the problem.

The Lagrangean for this problem is:

$$L(x, \lambda) = x_1 + x_2 + \lambda_1 x_1 + \lambda_2 x_2 + \lambda_3 (I - p_1 x_1 - p_2 x_2).$$

The critical points of the Lagrangean are the solutions $(x_1, x_2, \lambda_1, \lambda_2, \lambda_3)$ to the following system of equations:

1. $1 + \lambda_1 - \lambda_3 p_1 = 0.$
2. $1 + \lambda_2 - \lambda_3 p_2 = 0.$
3. $\lambda_1 \geq 0, \quad x_1 \geq 0, \quad \lambda_1 x_1 = 0.$
4. $\lambda_2 \geq 0, \quad x_2 \geq 0, \quad \lambda_2 x_2 = 0.$
5. $\lambda_3 \geq 0, \quad I - p_1 x_1 - p_2 x_2 \geq 0, \quad \lambda_3 (I - p_1 x_1 - p_2 x_2) = 0.$

To solve for all the critical points of this system, we adopt the following procedure. We fix a subset C of $\{h_1, h_2, h_3\}$, and examine if there are any critical points in which only the constraints in the set C hold with equality. Then, we vary C over all possible subsets of $\{h_1, h_2, h_3\}$, and thereby obtain all the critical points.

In general, this procedure would be somewhat lengthy, since there are 8 possible values for C: namely, $\emptyset, \{h_1\}, \{h_2\}, \{h_3\}, \{h_1, h_2\}, \{h_1, h_3\}, \{h_2, h_3\}$, and $\{h_1, h_2, h_3\}$. However, as we have already mentioned, the optimum in this problem must occur at a point where $h_3 = 0$, so it suffices to find the set of critical points of L at which $h_3 = 0$. Moreover, as also mentioned, the case $C = \{h_1, h_2, h_3\}$ has no solutions because $h_1 = h_2 = 0$ implies $h_3 > 0$. Thus, there are just three cases to be considered: $\{h_3\}$, $\{h_2, h_3\}$, and $\{h_1, h_3\}$. We examine each of these cases in turn.

Case 1: $C = \{h_3\}$

Since only constraint 3 is assumed to hold with equality in this case, we must have $x_1 > 0$ and $x_2 > 0$. By the complementary slackness conditions, this implies we must also have $\lambda_1 = \lambda_2 = 0$. Substituting this into the first two equations that define the critical points of L, we obtain

$$\lambda_3 p_1 = \lambda_3 p_2 = 1.$$

These conditions make sense only if $p_1 = p_2$. Thus, we retain this case as a possible solution only if the parameters happen to satisfy $p_1 = p_2$. Otherwise, it is discarded.

In the event that p_1 and p_2 are equal to a common value $p > 0$, we must evidently have $\lambda_3 = 1/p$. It is now easily seen that, when $p_1 = p_2 = p$, there are infinitely many critical points of L that satisfy $x_1 > 0$ and $x_2 > 0$. Indeed, any point $(x_1, x_2, \lambda_1, \lambda_2, \lambda_3)$ is a critical point provided

$$\lambda_1 = \lambda_2 = 0, \ \ \lambda_3 = 1/p, \ \ x_1 \in (0, I/p), \ \text{and} \ x_2 = (I - px_1)/p.$$

Note that at all these critical points, we have $u(x_1, x_2) = I/p$.

Case 2: $C = \{h_2, h_3\}$

Since $h_2 = h_3 = 0$ translates to $x_2 = 0$ and $I - p_1 x_1 - p_2 x_2 = 0$, we must have $x_1 = I/p > 0$ in this case. Therefore, by the complementary slackness condition, we must have $\lambda_1 = 0$. Of course, we must also have $\lambda_2 \geq 0$. Substituting these into the first two equations that define the critical points of L, we obtain

$$\lambda_3 p_1 = 1 \leq 1 + \lambda_2 = \lambda_3 p_2.$$

Therefore, such a critical point can exist only if $p_1 \leq p_2$. Assuming this inequality to be true, it is seen that the unique critical point of L at which $h_2 = h_3 = 0$ is

$$(x_1, x_2, \lambda_1, \lambda_2, \lambda_3) = \left(\frac{I}{p_1}, 0, 0, \frac{p_2}{p_1} - 1, \frac{1}{p_1} \right).$$

The value of the objective function at this critical point is given by $u(x_1, x_2) = I/p_1$.

Case 3: $C = \{h_1, h_3\}$

This is similar to Case 2. It is possible as a critical point of L only if $p_1 \geq p_2$. The unique critical point of L in this case is given by:

$$(x_1, x_2, \lambda_1, \lambda_2, \lambda_3) = \left(0, \frac{I}{p_2}, \frac{p_1}{p_2} - 1, 0, \frac{1}{p_2} \right).$$

The value of the objective function at this critical point is given by $u(x_1, x_2) = I/p_2$.

Summing up, we have the following:

- If $p_1 > p_2$, there is exactly one critical point of L (namely, that arising in Case 3), whose associated x-values are $(x_1, x_2) = (0, I/p_2)$.
- If $p_1 < p_2$, L has only a single critical point (namely, that arising in Case 2), and this has the associated x-values $(x_1, x_2) = (I/p_1, 0)$.

• If $p_1 = p_2 = p$, L has infinitely many critical points (viz., all of the critical points arising in each of the three cases). The set of x-values that arises in this case is $\{(x_1, x_2) \mid x_1 + x_2 = I/p, \ x_1 \geq 0, \ x_2 \geq 0\}$.

We have already shown that for any $p_1 > 0$ and $p_2 > 0$, the critical points of L must contain the solution of the problem. Since L has a unique critical point when $p_1 > p_2$, it follows that this critical point also identifies the problem's global maximum for this parameter configuration; that is, the unique solution to the problem when $p_1 > p_2$ is $(x_1, x_2) = (0, I/p_2)$. Similarly, the unique solution to the problem when $p_1 < p_2$ is $(x_1, x_2) = (I/p_1, 0)$. Finally, when $p_1 = p_2 = p$, there are infinitely many critical points of L, but at all of these we have $u(x_1, x_2) = I/p$. Therefore, *each* of these values of (x_1, x_2) defines a global maximum of the problem in this case.

6.3.2 An Illustration from Producer Theory

The problem we consider in this section is the one of minimizing $w_1 x_1 + w_2 x_2$ over the feasible set

$$\mathcal{D} = \{(x_1, x_2) \in \mathbb{R}_+^2 \mid x_1^2 + x_2^2 \geq y\}.$$

The constraint set of this problem is defined through three inequality constraints, namely

$$h_1(x_1, x_2) = x_1 \geq 0$$

$$h_2(x_1, x_2) = x_2 \geq 0$$

$$h_3(x_1, x_2) = x_1^2 + x_2^2 - y \geq 0.$$

As usual, we shall assume that all the parameters of the problem—namely, w_1, w_2, and y—are strictly positive.

Once again, we begin our analysis with a demonstration that both conditions of Proposition 6.5 are satisfied. The existence of solutions may be demonstrated in many ways, for instance, by compactifying the feasible action set in the manner described in Example 3.8. The details are omitted.

To check that the constraint qualification will hold at the optimum, we first identify all possible combinations of the constraints that can, in principle, hold with equality at the optimum. Since there are three constraints, there are eight cases to be checked: $\emptyset$, h_1, h_2, h_3, (h_1, h_2), (h_1, h_3), (h_2, h_3), and (h_1, h_2, h_3). Of these, the last can be ruled out since $h_1 = h_2 = 0$ implies $x_1^2 + x_2^2 = 0$, whereas the constraint set requires $x_1^2 + x_2^2 \geq y$. It is also apparent that, since w_1 and w_2 are strictly positive, we must have $h_3 = 0$ at the optimum (i.e., total production $x_1 + x_2^2$ must exactly equal y), or costs could be reduced by reducing output. This means there are only three possible descriptions of the set h_E of effective constraints at the optimum: $h_E = h_3$, $h_E = (h_1, h_3)$, and $h_E = (h_2, h_3)$. We will show that in each case, the constraint qualification must hold.

First, consider the case $h_E = (h_1, h_3)$. Since h_1 and h_3 are effective, we have $x_1 = 0$ and $x_1^2 + x_2^2 = y$, so $x_2 = \sqrt{y}$. Therefore,

$$Dh_E(x_1, x_2) = \begin{bmatrix} 1 & 0 \\ 2x_1 & 2x_2 \end{bmatrix} = \begin{bmatrix} 1 & 0 \\ 0 & 2\sqrt{y} \end{bmatrix}.$$

Since this matrix evidently has the required rank, it follows that if the optimum occurs at a point where h_1 and h_3 are the only effective constraints, the constraint qualification will be met.

An identical argument, with the obvious changes, shows that the constraint qualification is not a problem if the optimum happens to occur at a point where h_2 and h_3 are effective. This leaves the case $h_E = h_3$. In this case, we have

$$Dh_E(x_1, x_2) = (2x_1, 2x_2).$$

Since we are assuming that only h_3 holds with equality, we must have $x_1, x_2 > 0$, so $\rho(Dh_E(x_1, x_2)) = |E| = 1$ as required.

Summing up, the optimum must occur at a point where $h_3 = 0$, but no matter where on this set the optimum occurs, the constraint qualification will be met. It follows that the set of critical points of the Lagrangean must contain the solution(s) of the problem.

The Lagrangean L in this problem has the form

$$L(x_1, x_2, \lambda_1, \lambda_2, \lambda_3) = -w_1 x_1 - w_2 x_2 + \lambda_1 x_1 + \lambda_2 x_2 + \lambda_3 (x_1^2 + x_2^2 - y).$$

Note that we have implicitly set the problem up as a maximization problem, with objective $-w_1 x_1 - w_2 x_2$. The critical points of L are the solutions $(x_1, x_2, \lambda_1, \lambda_2, \lambda_3)$ to the following system of equations:

1. $-w_1 + \lambda_1 + 2\lambda_3 x_1 = 0$.
2. $-w_2 + \lambda_2 + 2\lambda_3 x_2 = 0$.
3. $\lambda_1 \geq 0, \quad x_1 \geq 0, \quad \lambda_1 x_1 = 0$.
4. $\lambda_2 \geq 0, \quad x_2 \geq 0, \quad \lambda_2 x_2 = 0$.
5. $\lambda_3 \geq 0, \quad x_1^2 + x_2^2 - y \geq 0, \quad \lambda_3 (x_1^2 + x_2^2 - y) = 0$.

As in subsection 6.3.1, we fix a subset C of $\{h_1, h_2, h_3\}$ and find the set of all possible solutions to these equations when only the constraints in C hold with equality. As C ranges over all possible subsets of $\{h_1, h_2, h_3\}$, we obtain the set of all critical points of L.

Once again, this process is simplified by the fact that we do not have to consider all possible subsets C. First, as we have mentioned, h_3 must be effective at an optimum, so it suffices to find all critical points of L at which $h_3 = 0$. Second, the case $C = \{h_1, h_2, h_3\}$ is ruled out, since $h_1 = h_2 = 0$ violates the third constraint that $h_3 \geq 0$. This results in three possible values for C, namely, $C = \{h_3\}$, $C = \{h_2, h_3\}$, and $C = \{h_1, h_3\}$. We consider each of these in turn.

Case 1: $C = \{h_3\}$

Since we must have $x_1 > 0$ and $x_2 > 0$ in this case, the complementary slackness conditions imply $\lambda_1 = \lambda_2 = 0$. Substituting these values into the first two equations that define the critical points of L, we obtain

$$2\lambda_3 x_1 = w_1$$

$$2\lambda_3 x_2 = w_2.$$

Dividing the first equation by the second, this implies

$$x_1 = \left(\frac{w_1}{w_2}\right) x_2.$$

By hypothesis, we also have $h_3 = 0$ or $x_1^2 + x_2^2 = y$. Therefore, we have

$$x_1 = \left(\frac{w_1^2 y}{w_1^2 + w_2^2}\right)^{1/2}, \quad x_2 = \left(\frac{w_2^2 y}{w_1^2 + w_2^2}\right)^{1/2}, \quad \lambda_3 = \left(\frac{w_1^2 + w_2^2}{y}\right)^{1/2}.$$

Combined with $\lambda_1 = \lambda_2 = 0$, this represents the unique critical point of L in which $h_1 > 0$, $h_2 > 0$, and $h_3 = 0$. Note that the value of the objective function $-w_1 x_1 - w_2 x_2$ at this critical point is

$$-w_1 x_1 - w_2 x_2 = -(w_1^2 + w_2^2)^{1/2} y^{1/2}.$$

Case 2: $C = \{h_2, h_3\}$

In this case, we have $x_1 > 0$ (and, in fact, $x_1 = \sqrt{y}$, since $h_2 = h_3 = 0$ implies $x_2 = 0$ and $x_1^2 + x_2^2 - y = 0$). Therefore, we must also have $\lambda_1 = 0$. Substituting $x_1 = \sqrt{y}$ and $\lambda_1 = 0$ into the first of the equations that define the critical points of L, we obtain

$$2\lambda_3 x_1 - w_1 = 2\lambda_3 \sqrt{y} - w_1 = 0,$$

or $\lambda_3 = w_1/2\sqrt{y}$. Finally, substituting $x_2 = 0$ into the second equation defining the critical points of L, we get $\lambda_2 = w_2$. Thus, the unique critical point of L which satisfies $h_2 = h_3 = 0$ is

$$(x_1, x_2, \lambda_1, \lambda_2, \lambda_3) = (\sqrt{y}, 0, 0, w_2, w_1/\sqrt{y}).$$

The value of the objective function $(-w_1 x_1 - w_2 x_2)$ at this critical point is $-w_1 y^{1/2}$.

$$\textit{Case 3: } C = \{h_1, h_3\}$$

This is the same as Case 2, with the obvious changes. The unique critical point of L that falls in this case is

$$(x_1, x_2, \lambda_1, \lambda_2, \lambda_3) = (0, \sqrt{y}, w_1, 0, w_2/\sqrt{y}),$$

and the value of the objective function $(-w_1 x_1 - w_2 x_2)$ at this critical point is $-w_2 y^{1/2}$.

Summing up, L has three critical points, and the values taken by the objective function at these three points are $-(w_1^2 + w_2^2)^{1/2} y^{1/2}$, $-w_1 y^{1/2}$, and $-w_2 y^{1/2}$. Now, we have already established that the set of critical points of L in this problem contains the solution(s) to the problem; and, therefore, that the point(s) that maximize the value of the objective function among the set of critical points must be the solution(s) to the problem. All that remains now is to compare the value of the objective function at the three critical points.

Since $w_1 > 0$ and $w_2 > 0$, it is always the case that $(w_1^2 + w_2^2)^{1/2} > w_1$ and, therefore, that

$$-(w_1^2 + w_2^2)^{1/2} y^{1/2} < -w_1 y^{1/2}.$$

We may, as a consequence, ignore the first value of the objective function, and the point that it represents. Comparing the value of the objective function at the remaining two points, it can be seen that

- When $w_1 < w_2$, then the larger of the two values is $-w_1 y^{1/2}$, which arises at $(x_1, x_2) = (y^{1/2}, 0)$. Therefore, the problem has a unique solution when $w_1 < w_2$, namely $(y^{1/2}, 0)$.

- When $w_1 < w_2$, then the larger of the two values is $-w_1 y^{1/2}$, which arises at $(x_1, x_2) = (0, y^{1/2})$. Therefore, the problem has a unique solution when $w_1 > w_2$, namely $(0, y^{1/2})$.

- When w_1 and w_2 have a common value $w > 0$, then these two values of the objective function coincide. Therefore, if $w_1 = w_2$, the problem has two solutions, namely $(y^{1/2}, 0)$ and $(0, y^{1/2})$.

6.4 The General Case: Mixed Constraints

A constrained optimization problem with *mixed constraints* is a problem where the constraint set $\mathcal{D}$ has the form

$$\mathcal{D} = U \cap \{x \in \mathbb{R}^n \mid g(x) = 0, \ h(x) \geq 0\},$$

where $U \subset \mathbb{R}^n$ is open, $g: \mathbb{R}^n \to \mathbb{R}^k$, and $h: \mathbb{R}^n \to \mathbb{R}^l$. For notational ease, define $\varphi_i: \mathbb{R}^n \to \mathbb{R}^{k+l}$, where

$$\varphi_i = \begin{cases} g_i, & \text{if } i \in \{1, \ldots, k\} \\ h_{i-k}, & \text{if } i \in \{k+1, \ldots, k+l\}. \end{cases}$$

The following theorem is a simple consequence of combining the Theorem of Lagrange with the Theorem of Kuhn and Tucker:

Theorem 6.10 *Let $f: \mathbb{R}^n \to \mathbb{R}$, and $\varphi_i: \mathbb{R}^n \to \mathbb{R}$, $i = 1, \ldots, l+k$ be C^1 functions. Suppose x^* maximizes f on*

$$\mathcal{D} \; = \; U \cap \{x \in \mathbb{R}^n \mid \varphi_i(x) = 0, \; i = 1, \ldots, k, \; \varphi_j(x) \geq 0, \; j = k+1, \ldots, k+l\},$$

where $U \subset \mathbb{R}^n$ is open. Let $E \subset \{1, \ldots, k+l\}$ denote the set of effective constraints at x^*, and let $\varphi_E = (\varphi_i)_{i \in E}$. Suppose $\rho((D\varphi_E(x^*)) = |E|$. Then, there exists $\lambda \in \mathbb{R}^{l+k}$ such that

1. *$\lambda_j \geq 0$ and $\lambda_j \varphi_j(x^*) = 0$ for $j \in \{k+1, \ldots, k+l\}$.*
2. *$Df(x^*) + \sum_{i=1}^{k+l} \lambda_i D\varphi_i(x^*) \; = \; 0$.*

6.5 A Proof of the Theorem of Kuhn and Tucker

Let x^* be a local maximum of f on the set

$$\mathcal{D} \; = \; U \cap \{x \in \mathbb{R}^n \mid h(x) \geq 0\},$$

where $h = (h_1, \ldots, h_l)$ is a C^1 function from $\mathbb{R}^n$ to $\mathbb{R}^l$, and $U \subset \mathbb{R}^n$ is open. Let E be the set of effective constraints at x^*, and suppose that $\rho(Dh_E(x^*)) = |E|$, where $h_E = (h_i)_{i \in E}$. We are to show that there is $\lambda \in \mathbb{R}^l$ such that

1. $\lambda_i \geq 0$, and $\lambda_i h_i(x^*) = 0$, $i = 1, \ldots, l$.
2. $Df(x^*) + \sum_{i=1}^l \lambda_i Dh_i(x^*) = 0$.

With the important exception of the nonnegativity of the vector λ, the Theorem of Kuhn and Tucker can be derived as a consequence of the Theorem of Lagrange. To simplify notation in the proof, we will denote $|E|$ by k; we will also assume that the effective constraints at x^* are the first k constraints:

$$h_i(x^*) = 0, \quad i = 1, \ldots, k$$
$$h_i(x^*) > 0, \quad i = k+1, \ldots l.$$

There is, of course, no loss of generality in this assumption, since this may be achieved simply by renumbering constraints.

For each $i \in \{1, \ldots, l\}$, define

$$V_i = \{x \in \mathbb{R}^n \mid h_i(x) > 0\}.$$

Let $V = \cap_{i=k+1}^{l} V_i$. By the continuity of h_i, V_i is open for each i, and so, therefore, is V. Now, let $D^* \subset D$ be the *equality*-constrained set defined through k equality constraints and given by

$$D^* = U \cap V \cap \{x \in \mathbb{R}^n \mid h_i(x) = 0, \ i = 1, \ldots, k\}.$$

By construction, we have $x^* \in \mathcal{D}^*$. Since x^* is a local maximum of f on $\mathcal{D}$, it is certainly a local maximum of f on D^*. Moreover, we have $\rho(Dh_E(x^*)) = k$, by hypothesis. Therefore, by the Theorem of Lagrange, there exists a vector $\mu = (\mu_1, \ldots, \mu_k) \in \mathbb{R}^k$ such that

$$Df(x^*) + \sum_{i=1}^{k} \mu_i Dh_i(x^*) = 0.$$

Now define $\lambda \in \mathbb{R}^l$ by

$$\lambda_i = \begin{cases} \mu_i, & i = 1, \ldots, k \\ 0, & i = k+1, \ldots, l. \end{cases}$$

We will show that the vector λ satisfies the properties stated in the theorem.

First, observe that for $i = k+1, \ldots, l$, we have $\lambda_i = 0$, and, therefore, $\lambda_i Dh_i(x^*) = 0$. Therefore,

$$Df(x^*) + \sum_{i=1}^{l} \lambda_i Dh_i(x^*) = Df(x^*) + \sum_{i=1}^{k} \lambda_i Dh_i(x^*)$$

$$= Df(x^*) + \sum_{i=1}^{k} \mu_i Dh_i(x^*)$$

$$= 0,$$

which establishes one of the desired properties.

Now, for any $i \in \{1, \ldots, k\}$, we have $h_i(x^*) = 0$, so certainly it is the case that $\lambda_i h_i(x^*) = 0$ for $i \in \{1, \ldots, k\}$. For $i \in \{k+1, \ldots, l\}$, we have $\lambda_i = 0$, so it is also the case that $\lambda_i h_i(x^*) = 0$ for $i \in \{k+1, \ldots, l\}$. Summing up, we have as required

$$\lambda_i h_i(x^*) = 0, \qquad i = 1, \ldots, l.$$

It remains to be shown that $\lambda \geq 0$. Since $\lambda_i = 0$ for $i = k+1, \ldots, l$, we are required only to show that $\lambda_i \geq 0$ for $i = 1, \ldots, k$. We will establish that $\lambda_1 \geq 0$. A similar argument will establish that $\lambda_i \geq 0$ for $i = 2, \ldots, k$.

To this end, define for $x \in \mathbb{R}^n$ and $\eta \in \mathbb{R}$, the function $H = (H_1, \ldots, H_k)$ from $\mathbb{R}^{n+1}$ to $\mathbb{R}^k$ by

$$H_1(x, \eta) = h_1(x) - \eta$$
$$H_i(x, \eta) = h_i(x), \quad i = 2, \ldots, k.$$

Let $DH_x(x, \eta)$ denote the $k \times n$ derivative matrix of H with respect to the x variables alone, and $DH_\eta(x, \eta)$ denote the $k \times 1$ derivative vector of H with respect to η. For future reference, we note that since $h_E = (h_1, \ldots, h_k)$, we have $DH_x(x, \eta) = Dh_E(x)$; we also have $DH_\eta(x, \eta) = (-1, 0, \ldots, 0)$ at any (x, η).

By the definition of H, we have $H(x^*, 0) = 0$. Moreover, $\rho(DH_x(x^*, 0)) = \rho(Dh_E(x^*)) = k$. Therefore, by the Implicit Function Theorem (see Chapter 1, Theorem 1.77), there is a neighborhood N of zero, and a C^1 function $\xi \colon N \to \mathbb{R}^n$, such that $\xi(0) = x^*$, and

$$H(\xi(\eta), \eta) = 0, \quad \eta \in N.$$

Differentiating this expression using the chain rule, and evaluating at $\xi(0) = x^*$, we obtain

$$DH_x(x^*, 0) D\xi(0) + DH_\eta(x^*, 0) = 0.$$

Since $DH_x(x, \eta) = Dh_E(x)$ and $DH_\eta(x, \eta) = (-1, 0, \ldots, 0)$ at any (x, η), this implies in turn

$$Dh_E(x^*) D\xi(0) = (1, 0, \ldots, 0).$$

or, equivalently, that

$$Dh_1(x^*) D\xi(0) = 1$$
$$Dh_i(x^*) D\xi(0) = 0, \quad i = 2, \ldots, k.$$

Since $\lambda_i = 0$ for $i = k + 1, \ldots, l$, we now have

$$Df(x^*) D\xi(0) = -\left(\sum_{i=1}^{l} \lambda_i Dh_i(x^*) \right) D\xi(0)$$

$$= -\left(\sum_{i=1}^{k} \lambda_i Dh_i(x^*) D\xi(0) \right)$$

$$= -\lambda_1.$$

To complete the proof, we will show that

$$Df(x^*) D\xi(0) \leq 0.$$

To this end, we first show that there is $\eta^* > 0$ such that for all $\eta \in [0, \eta^*)$, we must have $\xi(\eta) \in \mathcal{D}$, where $\mathcal{D}$ is the constraint set of the original problem.

If $\eta > 0$, then $H_i(\xi(\eta)) = 0$ for $i = 1, \ldots, k$, and from the definition of the functions H_i, this means

$$h_1(\xi(\eta)) = \eta > 0,$$

and

$$h_i(\xi(\eta)) = 0, \quad i = 2, \ldots, k.$$

For $i = k+1, \ldots, l$, we have $h_i(\xi(0)) = h_i(x^*) > 0$. Since both $h_i(\cdot)$ and $\xi(\cdot)$ are continuous, it follows that by choosing η sufficiently small (say, $\eta \in (0, \eta^*)$), we can also ensure that

$$h_i(\xi(\eta)) > 0, \quad i = k+1, \ldots, l.$$

Finally, by shrinking the value of η^* if need be, we can evidently ensure that $\xi(\eta) \in U$ for all $\eta \in [0, \eta^*)$. Thus, there is $\eta^* > 0$ such that $\xi(\eta) \in \mathcal{D}$ for $\eta \in [0, \eta^*)$, as claimed.

Now, since $\xi(0) = x^*$ is a local maximum of f on $\mathcal{D}$, and $\xi(\eta)$ is in the feasible set for $\eta \in [0, \eta^*)$, it follows that for $\eta > 0$ and sufficiently close to zero, we must have

$$f(x^*) \geq f(\xi(\eta)).$$

Therefore,

$$\left(\frac{f(\xi(0)) - f(\xi(\eta))}{\eta} \right) \leq 0,$$

for all $\eta > 0$ and sufficiently small. Taking limits as $\eta \downarrow 0$, we obtain

$$Df(\xi(0)) D\xi(0) \leq 0,$$

or $Df(x^*) D\xi(0) \leq 0$. The proof is complete. $\qquad \square$

6.6 Exercises

1. Solve the following maximization problem:

$$\text{Maximize} \quad \ln x + \ln y$$

$$\text{subject to} \quad x^2 + y^2 = 1$$

$$x, y \geq 0.$$

2. A firm produces two outputs y and z using a single input x. The set of attainable output levels $H(x)$ from an input use of x, is given by

$$H(x) = \{(y, z) \in \mathbb{R}_+^2 \mid y^2 + z^2 \leq x\}.$$

The firm has available to it a maximum of one unit of the input x. Letting p_y

and p_z denote the prices of the two outputs, determine the firm's optimal output mix.

3. A consumer has income $I > 0$, and faces a price vector $p \in \mathbb{R}_{++}$ for the three commodities she consumes. All commodities must be consumed in nonnegative amounts. Moreover, she must consume at least two units of commodity 2, and cannot consume more than one unit of commodity 1. Assuming $I = 4$ and $p = (1, 1, 1)$, calculate the optimal consumption bundle if the utility function is given by $u(x_1, x_2, x_3) = x_1 x_2 x_3$. What if $I = 6$ and $p = (1, 2, 3)$?

4. Let $T \geq 1$ be some finite integer. Solve the following maximization problem:

$$\text{Maximize} \quad \sum_{t=1}^{T} \left(\frac{1}{2}\right)^t \sqrt{x_t}$$

$$\text{subject to} \quad \sum_{t=1}^{T} x_t \leq 1$$

$$x_t \geq 0, \ t = 1, \ldots, T.$$

5. A firm produces an output y using two inputs x_1 and x_2 as $y = \sqrt{x_1 x_2}$. Union agreements obligate the firm to use at least one unit of x_1 in its production process. The input prices of x_1 and x_2 are given by w_1 and w_2, respectively. Assume that the firm wishes to minimize the cost of producing $\bar{y}$ units of output.

   (a) Set up the firm's cost-minimization problem. Is the feasible set closed? Is it compact?

   (b) Does the cookbook Lagrangean procedure identify a solution of this problem? Why or why not?

6. A firm manufactures two outputs y_1 and y_2 using two inputs x_1 and x_2. The production function $f: \mathbb{R}_+^2 \to \mathbb{R}_+^2$ is given by

$$(y_1, y_2) = f(x_1, x_2) = (x_1^{1/2}, x_1^{1/2} x_2^{1/3}).$$

Let p_i denote the unit price of y_i, and w_i that of x_i. Describe the firm's optimization problem and derive the equations that define the critical points of the Lagrangean L. Calculate the solution when $p_1 = p_2 = 1$ and $w_1 = w_2 = 2$.

7. A consumer with a utility function given by $u(x_1, x_2) = \sqrt{x_1} + x_1 x_2$ has an income of 100. The unit prices of x_1 and x_2 are 4 and 5, respectively.

   (a) Compute the utility-maximizing commodity bundle, if consumption must be nonnegative.

   (b) Now suppose the consumer were offered the following option. By paying a lump sum of a to the government, the consumer can obtain coupons which will enable him to purchase commodity 1 at a price of 3. (The price of commodity 2 remains unchanged.) For what values of a will the consumer accept this offer? For what values of a is he indifferent between accepting the offer and not accepting it?

8. An agent allocates the H hours of time available to her between labor (l) and leisure ($H - l$). Her only source of income is from the wages she obtains by working. She earns w per hour of labor; thus, if she works $l \in [0, H]$ hours, her total income is wl. She spends her income on food (f) and entertainment (e), which cost p and q per unit respectively. Her utility function is given by $u(f, e, l)$ and is increasing in f and e, and is *decreasing* in l.

   (a) Describe the consumer's utility maximization problem.
   (b) Describe the equations that define the critical points of the Lagrangean L.
   (c) Assuming $H = 16$, $w = 3$, and $p = q = 1$, find the utility-maximizing consumption bundle if $u(f, e, l) = f^{1/3}e^{1/3} - l^2$.

9. An agent who consumes three commodities has a utility function given by

$$u(x_1, x_2, x_3) = x_1^{1/3} + \min\{x_2, x_3\}.$$

   Given an income of I, and prices of p_1, p_2, p_3, describe the consumer's utility maximization problem. Can the Weierstrass and/or Kuhn–Tucker theorems be used to obtain and characterize a solution? Why or why not?

10. A firm has contracted with its union to hire at least L^* units of labor at a wage rate of w_1 per unit. Any amount of additional labor may be hired at a rate of w_2 per unit, where $w_1 > w_2$. Assume that labor is the only input used by the firm in its production process, and that the production function is given by $f: \mathbb{R}_+ \to \mathbb{R}_+$, where f is C^1 and concave. Given that the output sells at a price of p, describe the firm's maximization problem. Derive the equations that define the critical points of the Lagrangean L in this problem. Do the critical points of L identify a solution of the problem?

11. A firm produces the output y using two inputs x_1 and x_2 in nonnegative quantities through the production relationship

$$y = g(x_1, x_2) = x_1^{1/4}x_2^{1/4}.$$

   The firm obtains a price of $p_y > 0$ per unit of y that it sells. It has available an inventory of K_1 units of the input x_1 and K_2 units of the input x_2. More units of x_1 and x_2 may be purchased from the market at the unit prices of $p_1 > 0$ and $p_2 > 0$, respectively. Alternatively, the firm can also sell any unused amount of its inputs to the market at these prices.

   (a) Describe the firm's profit-maximization problem, and derive the equations that define the critical points of the Lagrangean L.

(b) Assuming $p_y = p_1 = p_2 = 1$, $K_1 = 4$, and $K_2 = 0$, solve for the firm's optimal level of output y.

(c) Assume again that $p_y = p_1 = p_2 = 1$, but suppose now that the values of K_1 and K_2 are interchanged, i.e., we have $K_1 = 0$ and $K_2 = 4$. Is the firm's new optimal output level different from the old level? Why or why not?

12. A firm produces a single output y using three inputs x_1, x_2, and x_3 in nonnegative quantities through the relationship

$$y = g(x_1, x_2, x_3) = x_1(x_2 + x_3).$$

The unit price of y is $p_y > 0$, while that of the input x_i is $w_i > 0$, $i = 1, 2, 3$.

(a) Describe the firm's profit-maximization problem, and derive the equations that define the critical points of the Lagrangean L in this problem.

(b) Show that the Lagrangean L has multiple critical points for any choice of $(p_y, w_1, w_2, w_3, w_4) \in \mathbb{R}^4_{++}$.

(c) Show that none of these critical points identifies a solution of the profit-maximization problem. Can you explain why this is the case?

7

Convex Structures in Optimization Theory

The notion of *convexity* occupies a central position in the study of optimization theory. It encompasses not only the idea of *convex sets*, but also of *concave* and *convex functions* (see Section 7.1 for definitions). The attractiveness of convexity for optimization theory arises from the fact that when an optimization problem meets suitable convexity conditions, the same first-order conditions that we have shown in previous chapters to be *necessary* for *local optima*, also become *sufficient* for *global optima*. Indeed, even more is true. When the convexity conditions are tightened to what are called *strict convexity* conditions, we get the additional bonus of *uniqueness* of the solution.

The importance of such results, especially from a computational standpoint, is obvious. Of course, such a marked strengthening of our earlier analysis does not come free. As we show in Section 7.2, the assumption of convexity is a strong one. A function that is concave or convex must necessarily be *continuous* everywhere on the interior of its domain. It must also possess strong *differentiability* properties; for instance, all directional derivatives of such a function must exist at all points in the domain. Finally, an assumption of convexity imposes strong *curvature* restrictions on the underlying function, in the form of properties that must be met by its first- and second-derivatives.

These results indicate that an assumption of convexity is not an innocuous one, but, viewed from the narrow standpoint of this book, the restrictive picture they paint is perhaps somewhat exaggerated. For one thing, we continue to assume in studying constrained optimization problems that all the functions involved are (at least) continuously differentiable. Continuous differentiability is a much greater degree of smoothness than can be obtained from just an assumption of convexity; thus, the continuity and differentiability properties of concave and convex functions, which appear very strong when viewed in isolation, certainly do not imply any increased restrictiveness on this problem's structure. Although the same cannot be said of the curvature implications of convexity, even these are not very significant in *economic*

172

applications, since they are often justifiable by an appeal to such considerations as diminishing marginal utility, or diminishing marginal product.

7.1 Convexity Defined

Recall from Chapter 1 that a set $\mathcal{D} \subset \mathbb{R}^n$ is called *convex* if the convex combination of any two points in $\mathcal{D}$ is itself in $\mathcal{D}$, that is, if for all x and y in $\mathcal{D}$ and all $\lambda \in (0, 1)$, it is the case that $\lambda x + (1 - \lambda)y \in \mathcal{D}$. Building on this definition, we introduce in subsection 7.1.1 two classes of functions called *concave functions* and *convex functions*.

Concave and convex functions play an important role in the study of *maximization* and *minimization* problems, respectively. Their significance arises primarily from the fact that in problems with a convex constraint set and a concave objective function, the first-order conditions are both necessary and sufficient to identify global maxima; while in problems with a convex constraint set and a convex objective function, the first-order conditions are necessary and sufficient to identify global minima.[1]

Motivated by this, we will say in the sequel that a maximization problem is a *convex maximization problem* if the constraint set is convex and the objective function is concave. A minimization problem will similarly be said to be a *convex minimization problem* if the constraint set is convex, and the objective function is convex. More generally, we will say that an optimization problem is a *convex optimization problem*, or has a *convex environment*, if it is either a convex maximization problem, or a convex minimization problem. Thus, our use of the word "convexity" encompasses the entire collective of convex sets, and concave and convex functions.

Following our definition of concave and convex functions in subsection 7.1.1, we define the more restricted notions of *strictly concave* and *strictly convex* functions in subsection 7.1.2. In addition to possessing all the desirable properties of concave and convex functions, respectively, strictly concave and strictly convex functions also possess the remarkable feature that they guarantee *uniqueness* of solutions. That is, a convex maximization problem with a strictly concave objective function can have at most one solution, as can a convex minimization problem with a strictly convex objective function. In an obvious extension of the terminology introduced earlier, we will say that a maximization problem is a strictly convex maximization problem if it is a convex maximization problem, and the objective function is strictly concave. Strictly convex minimization problems are similarly defined.

---

[1] As always, some additional regularity conditions may have to be met.

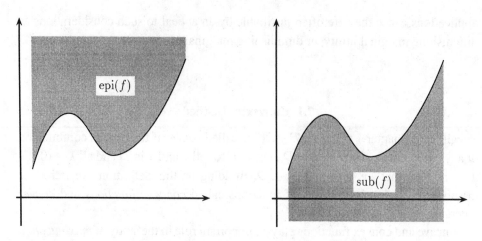

Fig. 7.1. The Epigraph and Subgraph

7.1.1 Concave and Convex Functions

Let $f: \mathcal{D} \subset \mathbb{R}^n \to \mathbb{R}$. Through the rest of this chapter, it will be assumed that $\mathcal{D}$ is a convex set.

The *subgraph* of f and the *epigraph* of f, denoted sub f and epi f, are defined by:

$$\text{sub } f \;=\; \{(x, y) \in \mathcal{D} \times \mathbb{R} \mid f(x) \geq y\}$$

$$\text{epi } f \;=\; \{(x, y) \in \mathcal{D} \times \mathbb{R} \mid f(x) \leq y\}.$$

Intuitively, the subgraph of a function is the area lying *below* the graph of a function, while the epigraph of a function is the area lying *above* the graph of the function. Figure 7.1 illustrates these concepts.

A function f is said to be *concave* on $\mathcal{D}$ if sub f is a convex set, and to be *convex* on $\mathcal{D}$ if epi f is a convex set.

Theorem 7.1 *A function $f: \mathcal{D} \to \mathbb{R}$ is concave on $\mathcal{D}$ if and only if for all $x, y \in \mathcal{D}$ and $\lambda \in (0, 1)$, it is the case that*

$$f[\lambda x + (1 - \lambda)y] \;\geq\; \lambda f(x) + (1 - \lambda)f(y).$$

Similarly, $f: \mathcal{D} \to \mathbb{R}$ is convex if and only if for all $x, y \in \mathcal{D}$ and $\lambda \in (0, 1)$, it is the case that

$$f[\lambda x + (1 - \lambda)y] \;\leq\; \lambda f(x) + (1 - \lambda)f(y).$$

Proof First, suppose f is concave, i.e., sub f is a convex set. Let x and y be arbitrary points in $\mathcal{D}$. Then, $(x, f(x)) \in$ sub f and $(y, f(y)) \in$ sub f. Since sub f is a convex set, it is the case that for any $\lambda \in (0, 1)$

$$(\lambda x + (1 - \lambda)y, \lambda f(x) + (1 - \lambda)f(y)) \in \text{ sub } f.$$

By definition of sub f, a point (w, z) is in sub f only if $f(w) \geq z$. Therefore,

$$f[\lambda x + (1 - \lambda)y] \geq \lambda f(x) + (1 - \lambda)f(y),$$

as required.

Now, suppose it is the case that for all $x, y \in \mathcal{D}$, and all $\lambda \in (0, 1)$, it is the case that

$$f[\lambda x + (1 - \lambda)y] \geq \lambda f(x) + (1 - \lambda)f(y).$$

We will show that sub f is a convex set, i.e., that if (w_1, z_1) and (w_2, z_2) are arbitrary points in sub f, and $\lambda \in (0, 1)$, then $(\lambda w_1 + (1 - \lambda)w_2, \lambda z_1 + (1 - \lambda)z_2)$ is also in sub f.

By definition of sub f, we must have $f(w_1) \geq z_1$ and $f(w_2) \geq z_2$. By hypothesis, if $\lambda \in (0, 1)$, we must also have

$$f[\lambda w_1 + (1 - \lambda)w_2] \geq \lambda f(w_1) + (-\lambda)f(w_2).$$

Therefore, we have $f[\lambda w_1 + (1 - \lambda)w_2] \geq \lambda z_1 + (1 - \lambda)z_2$, or

$$(\lambda w_1 + (1 - \lambda)w_2, \lambda z_1 + (1 - \lambda)z_2) \in \text{ sub } f.$$

This completes the proof for concave functions. The result for convex functions is proved along analogous lines. $\qquad\square$

The notions of concavity and convexity are neither exhaustive nor mutually exclusive; that is, there are functions that are neither concave nor convex, and functions that are both concave and convex. As an example of a function of the former sort, consider $f: \mathbb{R} \to \mathbb{R}$ defined by $f(x) = x^3$ for $x \in \mathbb{R}$. Let $x = -2$ and $y = 2$. For $\lambda = 1/4$, we have

$$f[\lambda x + (1 - \lambda)y] = f(1) = 1 < 4 = \lambda f(x) + (1 - \lambda)f(y),$$

so f is not concave. On the other hand, for $\lambda = 3/4$, we have

$$f[\lambda x + (1 - \lambda)y] = f(-1) = -1 > -4 = \lambda f(x) + (1 - \lambda)f(y),$$

so f is not convex either.

For an example of a function that is both concave and convex, pick any $a \in \mathbb{R}^n$ and $b \in \mathbb{R}$. Consider the function $f : \mathbb{R}^n \to \mathbb{R}$ defined by $f(x) = a \cdot x + b$. For any x and y in $\mathbb{R}^n$, and any $\lambda \in (0, 1)$, we have

$$
\begin{aligned}
f[\lambda x + (1 - \lambda)y] &= a \cdot [\lambda x + (1 - \lambda)y] + b \\
&= \lambda(a \cdot x + b) + (1 - \lambda)(a \cdot y + b) \\
&= \lambda f(x) + (1 - \lambda)f(y),
\end{aligned}
$$

and it follows that f has the required properties.[2] Such functions, which are both concave and convex, are termed *affine*.[3]

7.1.2 Strictly Concave and Strictly Convex Functions

A concave function $f : \mathcal{D} \to \mathbb{R}$ is said to be *strictly concave* if for all $x, y \in \mathcal{D}$ with $x \neq y$, and all $\lambda \in (0, 1)$, we have

$$
f[\lambda x + (1 - \lambda)y] > \lambda f(x) + (1 - \lambda)f(y).
$$

Similarly, a convex function $f : \mathcal{D} \to \mathbb{R}$ is said to be *strictly convex* if for all $x, y \in \mathcal{D}$ with $x \neq y$, and for all $\lambda \in (0, 1)$, we have

$$
f[\lambda x + (1 - \lambda)y] < \lambda f(x) + (1 - \lambda)f(y).
$$

It is trivial to give examples of functions that are concave, but not strictly concave, or convex, but not strictly convex. Any affine function, for instance, is both concave and convex, but is neither strictly concave nor strictly convex. On the other hand, the function $f : \mathbb{R}_{++} \to \mathbb{R}$ defined by

$$
f(x) = x^\alpha
$$

is strictly concave if $0 < \alpha < 1$, and is strictly convex if $\alpha > 1$. At the "knife-edge" point $\alpha = 1$, the function is both concave and convex, but is neither strictly concave nor strictly convex.

Our last result of this section is an immediate consequence of the definitions of concavity and convexity. Its most important implication is that it enables us, in the sequel, to concentrate solely on concave functions, whenever this is convenient for expositional reasons. The analogous statements for convex functions in such cases are easily derived, and are left to the reader.

Theorem 7.2 *A function $f : \mathcal{D} \to \mathbb{R}$ is concave on $\mathcal{D}$ if and only if the function $-f$ is convex on $\mathcal{D}$. It is strictly concave on $\mathcal{D}$ if and only if f is strictly convex on $\mathcal{D}$.*

---

[2]Indeed, it can be shown that if a function on $\mathbb{R}^n$ is both concave and convex on $\mathbb{R}^n$, then it *must* have the form $f(x) = a \cdot x + b$ for some a and b.

[3]The term "linear" is usually reserved for affine functions which also satisfy $f(0) = 0$.

7.2 Implications of Convexity

This section is divided into three parts which examine, respectively, the continuity, differentiability, and curvature properties that obtain from an assumption of convexity. Our main results here are that:

- Every concave or convex function must also be continuous on the interior of its domain (subsection 7.2.1).
- Every concave or convex function must possess minimal differentiability properties (subsection 7.2.2). Among other things, every directional derivative must be well-defined at all points in the domain of a concave or convex function.
- The concavity or convexity of an everywhere differentiable function f can be completely characterized in terms of the behavior of its derivative Df, and the concavity or convexity of a C^2 function f can be completely characterized in terms of the behavior of its second derivative $D^2 f$ (subsection 7.2.3).

Several other useful properties of concave and convex functions are listed in the Exercises.

With the exception of Theorem 7.9, which is used in the proof of Theorem 7.15, none of the results of this section play any role in the sequel, so readers who are in a hurry (and who are willing to accept on faith that convexity has strong implications) may wish to skip this section altogether. The statement of one result, however, may be worth spending some time on, on account of its practical significance: Theorem 7.10 in subsection 7.2.3 describes a test for identifying when a C^2 function is concave or convex, and this test is almost always easier to use in applications than the original definition.

7.2.1 Convexity and Continuity

Our main result in this subsection is that a concave function must be continuous everywhere on its domain, except perhaps at boundary points.

Theorem 7.3 *Let $f: \mathcal{D} \to \mathbb{R}$ be a concave function. Then, if $\mathcal{D}$ is open, f is continuous on $\mathcal{D}$. If $\mathcal{D}$ is not open, f is continuous on the interior of $\mathcal{D}$.*

Proof We will prove that if $\mathcal{D}$ is open and f is concave on $\mathcal{D}$, then f must be continuous on $\mathcal{D}$. Since int $\mathcal{D}$ is always open for any set $\mathcal{D}$, and since the concavity of f on $\mathcal{D}$ also implies its concavity on int $\mathcal{D}$, this result will also prove that even if $\mathcal{D}$ is not open, f must be continuous on the interior of $\mathcal{D}$.

So suppose $\mathcal{D}$ is open and $x \in \mathcal{D}$. Let $x_k \to x$, $x_k \in \mathcal{D}$ for all k. Since $\mathcal{D}$ is open, there is $r > 0$, such that $B(x, r) \subset D$. Pick α such that $0 < \alpha < r$. Let $A \subset B(x, r)$

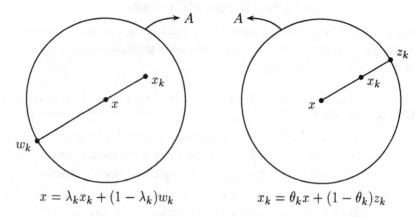

$$x = \lambda_k x_k + (1 - \lambda_k) w_k \qquad\qquad x_k = \theta_k x + (1 - \theta_k) z_k$$

Fig. 7.2. Convexity and Continuity

be defined by $A = \{z \mid \|z - x\| = \alpha\}$. Pick K large enough so that for all $k \geq K$, we have $\|x_k - x\| < \alpha$. Since $x_k \to x$, such a K exists.

Then, for all $k \geq K$, there is $z_k \in A$ such that $x_k = \theta_k x + (1 - \theta_k) z_k$ for some $\theta_k \in (0, 1)$ (see Figure 7.2). Since $x_k \to x$, and $\|z_k - x\| = \alpha > 0$ for all k, it is the case that $\theta_k \to 1$. Therefore, by the concavity of f,

$$f(x_k) = f(\theta_k x + (1 - \theta_k) z_k) \geq \theta_k f(x) + (1 - \theta_k) f(z_k).$$

Taking limits, we now have

$$\liminf_{k \to \infty} f(x_k) \ \geq \ f(x).$$

Secondly, it is also true that for all $k \geq K$, there is $w_k \in A$ and $\lambda_k \in (0, 1)$ such that $x = \lambda_k x_k + (1 - \lambda_k) w_k$ (see Figure 7.2). Once again, exploiting the concavity of f, we have

$$f(x) = f(\lambda_k x_k + (1 - \lambda_k) w_k) \geq \lambda_k f(x_k) + (1 - \lambda_k) f(w_k).$$

Since λ_k must go to 1 as $k \to \infty$, by taking limits we obtain

$$f(x) \ \geq \ \limsup_{k \to \infty} f(x_k).$$

We have already established that $\liminf_k f(x_k) \geq f(x)$. Therefore, we must have $\lim_{k \to \infty} f(x_k) = f(x)$, and the proof is complete. □

The conclusions of Theorem 7.3 cannot be strengthened to obtain continuity on all of $\mathcal{D}$; that is, the continuity of f could fail at the boundary points of $\mathcal{D}$. Consider the following example:

Example 7.4 Define $f : [0, 1] \to \mathbb{R}$ by

$$f(x) = \begin{cases} \sqrt{x}, & \text{if } 0 < x < 1 \\ -1, & \text{if } x = 0, 1. \end{cases}$$

Then, f is concave (in fact, *strictly* concave) on $[0, 1]$, but is discontinuous at the boundary points 0 and 1. □

7.2.2 Convexity and Differentiability

As with continuity, the assumption of convexity also carries strong implications for the *differentiability* of the function involved. We examine some of these implications in this subsection. We begin by establishing properties of concave functions of one variable. Then we use these properties in a bootstrapping argument to derive analogous results for concave functions defined on $\mathbb{R}^n$.

Theorem 7.5 *Let $g : \mathcal{D} \to \mathbb{R}$ be concave, where $\mathcal{D} \subset \mathbb{R}$ is open and convex. Let x_1, x_2, and x_3 be points in $\mathcal{D}$ satisfying $x_1 < x_2 < x_3$. Then,*

$$\frac{g(x_2) - g(x_1)}{x_2 - x_1} \geq \frac{g(x_3) - g(x_1)}{x_3 - x_1} \geq \frac{g(x_3) - g(x_2)}{x_3 - x_2}.$$

If g is strictly concave, these inequalities become strict.

Remark Figure 7.3 describes the content of Theorem 7.5 in a graph. □

Proof Define $\alpha = (x_2 - x_1)/(x_3 - x_1)$. Then $\alpha \in (0, 1)$, and some simple calculations show that $(1 - \alpha) = (x_3 - x_2)/(x_3 - x_1)$, and that $\alpha x_3 + (1 - \alpha)x_1 = x_2$. Since g is concave, we have

$$g[\alpha x_3 + (1 - \alpha)x_1] \geq \alpha g(x_3) + (1 - \alpha)g(x_1),$$

with strict inequality if g is strictly concave. Therefore,

$$g(x_2) \geq \frac{x_2 - x_1}{x_3 - x_1} g(x_3) + \frac{x_3 - x_2}{x_3 - x_1} g(x_1)$$

with strict inequality if g is strictly concave. Rearranging this expression, we finally obtain

$$\frac{g(x_2) - g(x_1)}{x_2 - x_1} \geq \frac{g(x_3) - g(x_1)}{x_3 - x_1},$$

with strict inequality if g is strictly concave. This establishes one of the required inequalities. The other inequalities may be obtained in a similar way. □

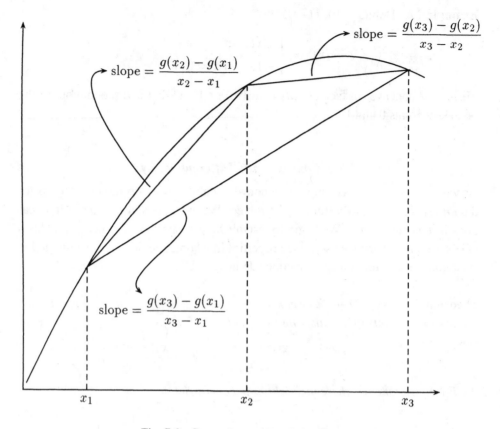

Fig. 7.3. Concavity and Declining Slopes

Theorem 7.5 implies, in particular, that if $g: \mathbb{R} \to \mathbb{R}$ is a concave function, and x is any point in $\mathbb{R}$, the difference quotient

$$\frac{g(x + b) - g(x)}{b}$$

is nonincreasing in b for $b > 0$. Therefore, allowing $+\infty$ as a limiting value, the limit of this expression exists as $b \to 0+$. It is now easy to establish that a concave function on $\mathbb{R}$ must possess all its directional derivatives:

Theorem 7.6 *If $g: \mathbb{R} \to \mathbb{R}$ is concave then all (one-sided) directional derivatives of g exist at all points x in $\mathbb{R}$, although some of these may have infinite values.*

Proof Fix any x and y in $\mathbb{R}$. First, suppose $y > 0$. Then,

$$\left(\frac{g(x + ty) - g(x)}{t} \right) = \left(\frac{g(x + ty) - g(x)}{ty} \right) y.$$

Since $y > 0$, it is the case that $ty > 0$ whenever $t > 0$; therefore, $ty \to 0+$ if and only if $t \to 0+$. Letting $b = ty$, we have

$$\lim_{t \to 0+} \left(\frac{g(x + ty) - g(x)}{t} \right) = y \cdot \lim_{b \to 0+} \left(\frac{g(x + b) - g(x)}{b} \right).$$

We have already established as a consequence of Theorem 7.5 that the limit of the second expression on the right-hand side exists as $b \to 0+$. Therefore, the directional derivative of x exists in any direction $y > 0$.

Now suppose $y < 0$. Then, we have

$$\left(\frac{g(x + ty) - g(x)}{t} \right) = \left(\frac{g(x + ty) - g(x)}{-ty} \right)(-y).$$

Since $y < 0$, we have $-ty > 0$ whenever $t > 0$; therefore, $-ty \to 0+$ if and only if $t \to 0+$. Letting $b = -ty$, we have

$$\lim_{t \to 0+} \left(\frac{g(x + ty) - g(x)}{t} \right) = (-y) \cdot \lim_{b \to 0+} \left(\frac{g(x + b) - g(x)}{b} \right).$$

Since the limit on the right-hand side is known to be well-defined, we have shown that the directional derivative of g at x exists in any direction $y < 0$ also.

Finally, if $y = 0$, the directional derivative at x in the direction y trivially exists since

$$\left(\frac{g(x + ty) - g(x)}{t} \right) = \left(\frac{g(x) - g(x)}{t} \right) = 0,$$

and this completes the proof. □

An n-dimensional analogue of this result is now easy to establish:

Theorem 7.7 *Let $\mathcal{D} \subset \mathbb{R}^n$ be open and convex. Then, if $f : \mathcal{D} \to \mathbb{R}$ is concave, f possesses all directional derivatives at all points in $\mathcal{D}$. (These derivatives could be infinite.)*

Proof Let $x \in D$ and $h \in \mathbb{R}^n$ be arbitrary. Define $g(t) = f(x + th)$, $t \geq 0$. Since $\mathcal{D}$ is open, g is well-defined in a neighborhood of zero. Note that

$$\frac{f(x + th) - f(x)}{t} = \frac{g(t) - g(0)}{t}.$$

Moreover, for any $\alpha \in (0, 1)$,

$$g[\alpha t + (1 - \alpha)t'] = f[\alpha(x + th) + (1 - \alpha)(x + t'h)]$$
$$\geq \alpha f(x + th) + (1 - \alpha) f(x + t'h)$$
$$= \alpha g(t) + (1 - \alpha)g(t'),$$

so g is concave on $\mathbb{R}_+$. By Theorem 7.6, therefore, the difference quotient

$$\left(\frac{g(t) - g(0)}{t} \right)$$

is nondecreasing as $t \to 0+$, so the limit as $t \to 0+$ of $(g(t) - g(0))/t$ exists, although it could be infinite. From the definition of g, this limit is $Df(x; h)$. Since $x \in \mathcal{D}$ and $y \in \mathbb{R}^n$ were arbitrary, we are done.   □

A natural question that arises from Theorem 7.7 is whether, or to what extent, convexity actually implies full differentiability of a function. The answer to this question, unfortunately, requires a knowledge of the concept of Lebesgue measure on $\mathbb{R}^n$. For readers unfamiliar with measure theory, an interpretation of the result is given following the statement of the theorem.

Theorem 7.8 *Let $\mathcal{D}$ be an open and convex set in $\mathbb{R}^n$, and let $f: \mathcal{D} \to \mathbb{R}$ be concave. Then f is differentiable everywhere on $\mathcal{D}$, except possibly at a set of points of Lebesgue measure zero. Moreover, the derivative Df of f is continuous at all points where it exists.*

Proof See Fenchel (1953, p.87).   □

Remark A property which holds everywhere on a subset of $\mathbb{R}^n$, except possibly on a set of Lebesgue measure zero, is also said to hold "almost everywhere" on that subset (or, more accurately, "almost everywhere with respect to the Lebesgue measure"). In this terminology, Theorem 7.8 would be stated as: a concave or convex function defined on an open subset of $\mathbb{R}^n$ must be differentiable almost everywhere on its domain.   □

The following discussion is aimed at readers who are unfamiliar with measure theory. It attempts to provide an intuitive idea of what is meant by a set of Lebesgue measure zero. A more formal description may be found in Royden (1963) or Billingsley (1978). Define a *cylinder* in $\mathbb{R}^n$ to be a set E of the form

$$E = \{(x_1, \ldots, x_n) \mid a_i < x_i \le b_i, \ i = 1, \ldots, n\},$$

where $a = (a_1, \ldots, a_n)$ and $b = (b_1, \ldots, b_n)$ are given vectors satisfying $a \ll b$. The Lebesgue measure of this cylinder, denoted $\mu(E)$ say, is defined as

$$\mu(E) = (b_1 - a_1)(b_2 - a_2) \cdots (b_n - a_n).$$

Observe that the Lebesgue measure is a natural generalization of the familiar "measures" of length in $\mathbb{R}$, area in $\mathbb{R}^2$, and volume in $\mathbb{R}^3$. A cylinder in $\mathbb{R}$ is simply an interval $(a, b]$, and its Lebesgue measure is $(b - a)$, which is the same as the interval's length. Similarly, a cylinder in $\mathbb{R}^2$ is a rectangle, whose Lebesgue measure corresponds to our usual notion of the rectangle's area, while a cylinder in $\mathbb{R}^3$ is a cube, whose Lebesgue measure corresponds to our usual notion of volume.

In an intuitive sense, a set of Lebesgue measure zero may be thought of as a set that can be covered using cylinders whose combined Lebesgue measure can be made arbitrarily small. That is, a set $X \subset \mathbb{R}^n$ has Lebesgue measure zero if it is true that given any $\epsilon > 0$, there is a collection of cylinders $E_1, E_2, \ldots$ in $\mathbb{R}^n$ such that $X \subset \cup_{i=1}^{\infty} E_i$ and

$$\sum_{i=1}^{\infty} \mu(E_i) < \epsilon.$$

For instance, the rationals $\mathbb{Q}$ constitute a set of measure zero in $\mathbb{R}$. To see this, take any enumeration $\{r_1, r_2, \ldots\}$ of the rationals (recall that the rationals are a countable set), and any $\epsilon > 0$. Pick η such that $0 < \eta < \epsilon$. For each k, define r_k^- and r_k^+ by

$$r_k^- = r_k - \left(\frac{1}{2}\right)^{k+1} \eta, \quad r_k^+ = r_k + \left(\frac{1}{2}\right)^{k+1} \eta$$

and let E_k be the interval $(r_k^-, r_k^+]$. Note that

$$\mu(E_k) = 2\left(\frac{1}{2}\right)^{k+1} \eta = \left(\frac{1}{2}\right)^{k} \eta.$$

We now have $r_k \in E_k$ for each k, so $\mathbb{Q} \subset \cup_{k=1}^{\infty} E_k$. Moreover,

$$\sum_{k=1}^{\infty} \mu(E_k) = \sum_{k=1}^{\infty} \left(\frac{1}{2}\right)^{k} \eta = \eta < \epsilon,$$

so we have covered the rationals by cylinders of total measure less than ϵ. Since ϵ was arbitrary, we are done.

7.2.3 Convexity and the Properties of the Derivative

In this section, we establish the implications of convexity for the behavior of the derivative. Our first result provides a complete characterization of the concavity or convexity of an everywhere differentiable function f using its first derivative Df:

Theorem 7.9 *Let $\mathcal{D}$ be an open and convex set in $\mathbb{R}^n$, and let $f: \mathcal{D} \to \mathbb{R}$ be differentiable on $\mathcal{D}$. Then, f is concave on $\mathcal{D}$ if and only if*

$$Df(x)(y - x) \geq f(y) - f(x) \quad \text{for all } x, y \in D,$$

while f is convex on D if and only if

$$Dfx)(y - x) \leq f(y) - f(x) \quad \text{for all } x, y \in D.$$

Proof See Section 7.5. □

The concavity or convexity of a C^2 function can also be characterized using its *second* derivative, as our next result shows. The result also provides a sufficient condition for identifying strictly concave and strictly convex functions, and is of especial interest from a computational standpoint as we explain shortly.

Theorem 7.10 *Let $f: D \to \mathbb{R}$ be a C^2 function, where $D \subset \mathbb{R}^n$ is open and convex. Then,*

1. *f is concave on D if and only if $D^2 f(x)$ is a negative semidefinite matrix for all $x \in D$.*
2. *f is convex on D if and only if $D^2 f(x)$ is a positive semidefinite matrix for all $x \in D$.*
3. *If $D^2 f(x)$ is negative definite for all $x \in D$, then f is strictly concave on D.*
4. *If $D^2 f(x)$ is positive definite for all $x \in D$, then f is strictly convex on D.*

Proof See Section 7.6. □

It is very important to note that parts 3 and 4 of Theorem 7.10 are only one-way implications. The theorem does *not* assert the *necessity* of these conditions, and, indeed, it is easy to see that the conditions cannot be necessary. Consider the following example:

Example 7.11 Let $f: \mathbb{R} \to \mathbb{R}$ and $g: \mathbb{R} \to \mathbb{R}$ be defined by $f(x) = -x^4$ and $g(x) = x^4$, respectively. Then, f is strictly concave on $\mathbb{R}$, while g is strictly convex on $\mathbb{R}$. However, $f'(0) = g'(0) = 0$, so, viewed as 1×1 matrices, $f'(0)$ is not negative definite, while $g'(0)$ is not positive definite. □

Our next example demonstrates the significance of Theorem 7.10 from a practical standpoint.

Example 7.12 Let $f: \mathbb{R}^2_{++} \to \mathbb{R}$ be defined by

$$f(x, y) = x^a y^b, \qquad a, b > 0.$$

For given a and b, this function is concave if, for any (x, y) and $(\hat{x}, \hat{y})$ in $\mathbb{R}^2_{++}$ and any $\lambda \in (0, 1)$, we have

$$[\lambda x + (1 - \lambda)\hat{x}]^a [\lambda y + (1 - \lambda)\hat{y}]^b \leq \lambda x^a y^b + (1 - \lambda)\hat{x}^a \hat{y}^b,$$

while it is convex on $\mathbb{R}^2_{++}$ if for all x and y in $\mathbb{R}^2_{++}$ and all $\lambda \in (0, 1)$, we have

$$[\lambda x + (1 - \lambda)\hat{x}]^a [\lambda y + (1 - \lambda)\hat{y}]^b \geq \lambda x^a y^b + (1 - \lambda)\hat{x}^a \hat{y}^b.$$

Compare checking for the convexity properties of f by using these inequalities to checking for the convexity properties of f using the second derivative test provided by Theorem 7.10. The latter only requires us to identify the definiteness of the following matrix:

$$D^2 f(x, y) = \begin{bmatrix} a(a - 1)x^{a-2}y^b & abx^{a-1}y^{b-1} \\ abx^{a-1}y^{b-1} & b(b - 1)x^a y^{b-2} \end{bmatrix}.$$

The determinant of this matrix is $ab(1 - a - b)x^{2a-2}y^{2b-2}$, which is positive if $a + b < 1$, zero if $a + b = 1$, and negative if $a + b > 1$. Since the diagonal terms are negative whenever $a, b < 1$, it follows that f is a strictly concave function if $a + b < 1$, that it is a concave function if $a + b = 1$, and that it is neither concave nor convex when $a + b > 1$. $\qquad\square$

7.3 Convexity and Optimization

This section is divided into three parts. In subsection 7.3.1, we point out some simple, but strong, implications of assuming a convex structure in abstract optimization problems. Subsection 7.3.2 then deals with sufficiency of first-order conditions for unconstrained optima. Finally, in subsection 7.3.3, we present one of the main results of this section, Theorem 7.16, which shows that under a mild regularity condition, the Kuhn–Tucker first-order conditions are both necessary and sufficient to identify optima of convex inequality-constrained optimization problems.

All results in this section are stated in the context of *maximization* problems. Each has an exact analogue in the context of *minimization* problems; it is left to the reader to fill in the details.

7.3.1 Some General Observations

This section presents two results which indicate the importance of convexity for optimization theory. The first result (Theorem 7.13) establishes that in convex optimization problems, all local optima must also be global optima; and, therefore, that to find a global optimum in such problems, it always suffices to locate a local optimum. The second result (Theorem 7.14) shows that if a *strictly* convex optimization problem admits a solution, the solution must be *unique*.

Theorem 7.13 *Suppose $\mathcal{D} \subset \mathbb{R}^n$ is convex, and $f: \mathcal{D} \to \mathbb{R}$ is concave. Then,*

1. *Any local maximum of f is a global maximum of f.*
2. *The set $\arg\max\{f(x) \mid x \in \mathcal{D}\}$ of maximizers of f on $\mathcal{D}$ is either empty or convex.*

Proof Suppose f admits a local maximum x that is not also a global maximum. Since x is a local maximum, there is $r > 0$ such that $f(x) \geq f(y)$ for all $y \in B(x, r) \cap D$. Since x is not a global maximum, there is $z \in D$ such that $f(z) > f(x)$. Since $\mathcal{D}$ is convex, $(\lambda x + (1 - \lambda)z) \in \mathcal{D}$ for all $\lambda \in (0, 1)$. Pick λ sufficiently close to unity so that $(\lambda x + (1 - \lambda)z) \in B(x, r)$. By the concavity of f,

$$f[\lambda x + (1 - \lambda)z] \geq \lambda f(x) + (1 - \lambda)f(z) > f(x),$$

since $f(z) > f(x)$. But $\lambda x + (1 - \lambda)z$ is in $B(x, r)$ by construction, so $f(x) \geq f[\lambda x + (1 - \lambda)z]$, a contradiction. This establishes Part 1.

To see Part 2, suppose x_1 and x_2 are both maximizers of f on $\mathcal{D}$. Then, we have $f(x_1) = f(x_2)$. Further, for $\lambda \in (0, 1)$, we have

$$f[\lambda x_1 + (1 - \lambda)x_2] \geq \lambda f(x_1) + (1 - \lambda)f(x_2) = f(x_1),$$

and this must hold with equality or x_1 and x_2 would not be maximizers. Thus, the set of maximizers must be convex, completing the proof. $\square$

Theorem 7.14 *Suppose $\mathcal{D} \subset \mathbb{R}^n$ is convex, and $f: \mathcal{D} \to \mathbb{R}$ is strictly concave. Then $\arg\max\{f(x) \mid x \in \mathcal{D}\}$ either is empty or contains a single point.*

Proof Suppose $\arg\max\{f(x) \mid x \in \mathcal{D}\}$ is nonempty. We will show it must contain a single point.

We have already shown in Theorem 7.13 that $\arg\max\{f(x) \mid x \in \mathcal{D}\}$ must be convex. Suppose this set contains two distinct points x and y. Pick any $\lambda \in (0, 1)$ and let $z = \lambda x + (1 - \lambda)y$. Then, z must also be a maximizer of f, so we must have $f(z) = f(x) = f(y)$. However, by the strict concavity of f,

$$f(z) = f[\lambda x + (1 - \lambda)y] > \lambda f(x) + (1 - \lambda)f(y) == f(x),$$

a contradiction. $\square$

7.3.2 Convexity and Unconstrained Optimization

The following result shows that the first-order condition for unconstrained optima (i.e., the condition that $Df(x) = 0$) is both necessary and sufficient to identify global unconstrained maxima, when such maxima exist.

Theorem 7.15 *Let $D \subset \mathbb{R}^n$ be convex, and $f: D \rightarrow \mathbb{R}$ be a concave and differentiable function on D. Then, x is an unconstrained maximum of f on D if and only if $Df(x) = 0$.*

Proof We have shown in Chapter 4 that the condition $Df(x) = 0$ must hold whenever x is any unconstrained local maximum. It must evidently also hold, therefore, if x is an unconstrained global maximum.

The reverse implication (which requires the concavity of f) is actually an immediate consequence of Theorem 7.9. For, suppose x and y are any two points in D. Theorem 7.9 states that, by the concavity of f, we must have

$$f(y) - f(x) \leq Df(x)(y - x).$$

If $Df(x) = 0$, the right-hand side of this equation is also zero, so the equation states precisely that $f(x) \geq f(y)$. Since $y \in D$ was arbitrary, x is a global maximum of f on D. $\qquad\square$

7.3.3 Convexity and the Theorem of Kuhn and Tucker

The following result, perhaps the most important of this entire section, states that the first-order conditions of the Theorem of Kuhn and Tucker are both *necessary and sufficient* to identify optima of convex inequality-constrained optimization problems, provided a mild regularity condition is met.

Theorem 7.16 (The Theorem of Kuhn and Tucker under Convexity) *Let f be a concave C^1 function mapping U into $\mathbb{R}$, where $U \subset \mathbb{R}^n$ is open and convex. For $i = 1, \ldots, l$, let $h_i: U \rightarrow \mathbb{R}$ also be concave C^1 functions. Suppose there is some $\bar{x} \in U$ such that*

$$h_i(\bar{x}) > 0, \qquad i = 1, \ldots, l.$$

Then x^* maximizes f over

$$D = \{x \in U \mid h_i(x) \geq 0, \ i = 1, \ldots, l\}$$

if and only if there is $\lambda^* \in \mathbb{R}^k$ such that the Kuhn–Tucker first-order conditions hold:

$$[KT\text{-}1] \quad Df(x^*) + \sum_{i=1}^{l} \lambda_i^* Dh_i(x^*) = 0.$$

$$[KT\text{-}2] \quad \lambda^* \geq 0, \; \sum_{i=1}^{l} \lambda_i^* h_i(x^*) = 0.$$

Proof See Section 7.7.   □

The condition that there exist a point $\bar{x}$ at which $h_i(\bar{x}) > 0$ for all i is called *Slater's condition*. There are two points about this condition that bear stressing.

First, Slater's condition is used only in the proof that [KT-1] and [KT-2] are *necessary* at an optimum. It plays no role in proving *sufficiency*. That is, the conditions [KT-1] and [KT-2] are sufficient to identify an optimum when f and the functions h_i are all concave, regardless of whether Slater's condition is satisfied or not.

Second, the necessity of conditions [KT-1] and [KT-2] at any local maximum was established in Theorem 6.1, but under a different hypothesis, namely, that the rank condition described in Theorem 6.1 held. Effectively, the necessity part of Theorem 7.16 states that this rank condition can be replaced with the combination of Slater's condition and concave constraint functions. However, *both* parts of this combination are important: just as the necessity of [KT-1] and [KT-2] could fail if the rank condition is not met, the necessity of [KT-1] and [KT-2] could also fail if *either* Slater's condition *or* the concavity of the functions h_i fails. Consider the following examples:

Example 7.17 Let f and h be functions on $\mathbb{R}$ defined by $f(x) = x$ and $h(x) = -x^2$ for all $x \in \mathbb{R}$. Then f and h are concave functions. However, the constraint set

$$\mathcal{D} = \{x \in \mathbb{R} \mid h(x) \geq 0\}$$

consists of exactly the one point 0; thus, there is no point $x \in \mathcal{D}$ such that $h(x) > 0$, and Slater's condition is violated. Evidently, the maximum of f on $\mathcal{D}$ must occur at 0. Since $f'(0) = 1$ and $h'(0) = 0$, there is no λ^* such that $f'(0) + \lambda^* g'(0) = 0$, and [KT-1] fails at this optimum.   □

Example 7.18 As in Example 6.4, let $f: \mathbb{R}^2 \to \mathbb{R}$ and $h: \mathbb{R}^2 \to \mathbb{R}$ be defined by $f(x, y) = -x^2 - y^2$ and $h(x, y) = (x-1)^3 - y^2$, respectively. Consider the problem of maximizing f on the set

$$\mathcal{D} = \{(x, y) \in \mathbb{R}^2 \mid h(x, y) \geq 0\}.$$

Note that while Slater's condition is met in this problem (for instance, $h(x, y) = 1 > 0$ at $(x, y) = (2, 0)$), h is not concave on $\mathcal{D}$. As a consequence, the conditions [KT-1] and [KT-2] fail to be necessary; indeed, we have shown in Example 6.4 that the unique global maximum of f on $\mathcal{D}$ occurs at $(x^*, y^*) = (1, 0)$, but that there is no $\lambda^* \in \mathbb{R}$ such that $Df(x^*, y^*) + \lambda^* Dg(x^*, y^*) = 0$. Thus, [KT-1] fails at this optimal point. $\qquad\square$

The point of Example 7.18 is to stress that Slater's condition cannot, by itself, replace the rank condition of Theorem 6.1. Rather, this is possible only if the functions h_i are all also concave.

7.4 Using Convexity in Optimization

The results of the previous section are of obvious importance in solving optimization problems. The purpose of this section is to highlight by repetition their value in this direction. We focus on inequality-constrained problems of the sort

Maximize $f(x)$ subject to $x \in \mathcal{D} = \{z \in U \mid h_i(z) \geq 0, \ i = 1, \ldots, l\}$,

where the functions f and h_i are all concave C^1 functions on the open and convex set $U \subset \mathbb{R}^n$. Recall that the Lagrangean for this problem is the function $L: U \times \mathbb{R}^l \to \mathbb{R}$ defined by

$$L(x, \lambda) = f(x) + \sum_{i=1}^{l} \lambda_i h_i(x),$$

and the critical points of L are the points $(x, \lambda) \in U \times \mathbb{R}^l$ that satisfy the following conditions:

$$Df(x) + \lambda_i Dh_i(x) = 0,$$

$$\lambda_i \geq 0, \ h_i(x) \geq 0, \ \lambda_i h_i(x) = 0, \ i = 1, \ldots, l.$$

Of course, as we have seen in Section 6.2, a point (x, λ) is a critical point of L if and only if $x \in \mathcal{D}$ and (x, λ) meets [KT-1] and [KT-2].

First, we consider the case where Slater's condition is met. In this case, Theorem 7.16 has the powerful implication that the cookbook procedure for using the Theorem of Kuhn and Tucker (outlined in Section 6.2) can be employed "blindly," that is, without regard to whether the conditions of Proposition 6.5 are met or not. Two factors give rise to, and strengthen, this implication. First, the concavity of the functions f and h_i together with Slater's condition imply that the first-order conditions [KT-1] and [KT-2] are necessary at any optimum. So, if an optimum exists at all, it must satisfy these conditions, and must, therefore, turn up as part of a critical point of the Lagrangean L. Second, since [KT-1] and [KT-2] are also sufficient for a maximum, it is the case that *every* critical point identifies a solution to the problem. Summing up:

- If L has no critical points, then no solution exists to the given problem.
- If (x^*, λ^*) is a critical point of L, then x^* is a solution of the problem.

In particular, the last step outlined in the cookbook procedure of Section 6.2 (viz., comparing the values of f at the different critical points of L), can be ignored: since each of these points identifies a global maximum, the value of f at all these points must, perforce, be the same.

The situation is less rosy if Slater's condition is not met. In this case, it remains true that every critical point of L identifies a solution to the problem, since the conditions [KT-1] and [KT-2] are still sufficient for a solution. On the other hand, [KT-1] and [KT-2] are no longer necessary, so the absence of a critical point of L does not enable us to conclude that no solution exists to the problem. In Example 7.17, for instance, we have seen that Slater's condition fails; and although the Lagrangean L admits no critical points, a solution to the problem does exist. This points to a potentially serious problem in cases where the existence of solutions cannot be verified *a priori*; however, its practical significance is much diminished by the fact that the failure of Slater's condition happens only in rare cases.

Finally, a small point. When the constraint functions h_i are all concave, the constraint set $\mathcal{D}$ is a convex set. Thus, if the objective function f happens to be *strictly* concave, there can exist at most one solution to the problem by Theorem 7.14. From an applications standpoint, this observation implies that if we succeed in unearthing a single critical point of the Lagrangean, we need not search for any others, since the problem's unique solution is already identified.

7.5 A Proof of the First-Derivative Characterization of Convexity

We prove Theorem 7.9 for the case where f is concave. The result for convex f then follows simply by noting that $D(-f) = -Df$, and appealing to Theorem 7.2.

So suppose first that f is concave. We have

$$Df(x)(y-x) = \lim_{t \to 0+} \frac{f(x + t(y - x)) - f(x)}{t} = \lim_{t \to 0+} \frac{f(ty + (1 - t)x) - f(x)}{t}.$$

When $t \in (0, 1)$, the concavity of f implies $f(ty + (1 - t)x) \geq tf(y) + (1 - t)f(x)$, so by choosing $t > 0, t \to 0$, we have

$$Df(x)(y - x) \geq \lim_{t \to 0+} \frac{tf(y) + (1 - t)f(x) - f(x)}{t} = f(y) - f(x),$$

and the result is proved.

Now, suppose that for all x_1 and x_2 in $\mathcal{D}$ we have

$$Df(x_1)(x_2 - x_1) \geq f(x_2) - f(x_1).$$

Pick any x and y in $\mathcal{D}$, and any $\lambda \in (0, 1)$. We will show that we must have

$$f[\lambda x + (1 - \lambda)y] \leq \lambda f(x) + (1 - \lambda)f(y),$$

which will establish that f is concave on $\mathcal{D}$. For expositional convenience, define

$$z = \lambda x + (1 - \lambda)y,$$
$$w = x - z = (1 - \lambda)(x - y).$$

Note that we have

$$y = z - \left(\frac{\lambda}{1 - \lambda}\right)w.$$

By hypothesis, we also have

$$f(x) - f(z) \leq Df(z)(x - z) = Df(z)w,$$

and

$$f(y) - f(z) \leq Df(z)(y - z) = \left(\frac{\lambda}{1 - \lambda}\right)Df(z)w.$$

Multiplying the first equation by $[\lambda/(1 - \lambda)]$, and adding the two equations, we obtain

$$\left(\frac{\lambda}{1 - \lambda}\right)f(x) + f(y) - \left(\frac{1}{1 - \lambda}\right)f(z) \leq 0.$$

Rearranging terms after multiplying through by $(1 - \lambda)$, we have

$$\lambda f(x) + 1 - \lambda)f(y) \leq f(z) = f[\lambda x + (1 - \lambda)y],$$

which completes the proof. $\qquad\square$

7.6 A Proof of the Second-Derivative Characterization of Convexity

For expositional convenience, we prove Theorem 7.10 for the case where the domain $\mathcal{D}$ of f is all of $\mathbb{R}^n$. With minor changes, the proof is easily adapted to include the case where $\mathcal{D}$ is an arbitrary open and convex subset of $\mathbb{R}^n$. The proof requires the following preliminary result:

Lemma 7.19 *Let* $f \colon \mathbb{R}^n \to \mathbb{R}$. *Given any x and h in $\mathbb{R}^n$, define the function* $\varphi_{x,h}(\cdot)$ *by* $\varphi_{x,h}(t) = f(x + th)$, $t \in \mathbb{R}$. *Then,*

1. *f is concave on $\mathbb{R}^n$ if and only if the function $\varphi_{x,h}(\cdot)$ is concave in t for each fixed $x, h \in \mathbb{R}^n$.*

2. *If $\varphi_{x,h}(\cdot)$ is strictly concave in t for each fixed x, $h \in \mathbb{R}^n$ with $h \neq 0$, then f is strictly concave on $\mathbb{R}^n$.*

Proof of Lemma 7.19 First suppose that f is concave on $\mathbb{R}^n$. Fix any x and h in $\mathbb{R}^n$. For any pair of real numbers t and t', and any $\alpha \in (0,1)$, we have

$$
\begin{aligned}
\varphi_{x,h}(\alpha t + (1-\alpha)t') &= f(x + \alpha th + (1-\alpha)t'h) \\
&= f(\alpha(x+th) + (1-\alpha)(x+t'h)) \\
&\geq \alpha f(x+th) + (1-\alpha)f(x+t'h) \\
&= \alpha\varphi_{x,h}(t) + (1-\alpha)\varphi_{x,h}(t'),
\end{aligned}
$$

so $\varphi_{x,h}(\cdot)$ is indeed concave in t.

Next, suppose for any x and h in $\mathbb{R}^n$, $\varphi_{x,h}(\cdot)$ is concave in t. Pick any $z_1, z_2 \in \mathbb{R}^n$ and any $\alpha \in (0,1)$. Let $z(\alpha) = \alpha z_1 + (1-\alpha)z_2$. In order to prove that f is concave, we are required to show that $f(z(\alpha)) \geq \alpha f(z_1) + (1-\alpha)f(z_2)$ for any $\alpha \in (0,1)$.

Consider the function $\varphi_{x,h}(\cdot)$ where $x = z_1$, and $h = z_2 - z_1$. Note that $\varphi_{x,h}(0) = f(z_1)$ and $\varphi_{x,h}(1) = f(z_2)$. Moreover, $\varphi_{x,h}(\alpha) = f(z_1 + \alpha(z_2 - z_1)) = f((1-\alpha)z_1 + \alpha z_2)$. Since $\varphi_{x,h}(\cdot)$ is concave by hypothesis, we have for any $\alpha \in (0,1)$

$$
\begin{aligned}
f((1-\alpha)z_1 + \alpha z_2) &= \varphi_{x,h}(\alpha) \\
&= \varphi_{x,h}((1-\alpha)0 + \alpha 1) \\
&\geq (1-\alpha)\varphi_{x,h}(0) + \alpha\varphi_{x,h}(1) \\
&= (1-\alpha)f(z_1) + (1-\alpha)f(z_2),
\end{aligned}
$$

which completes the proof that f is concave.

The proof of Part 2 of the lemma is left as an exercise to the reader. $\square$

Proof of Theorem 7.10 It is easy to see that for any C^2 function $g: \mathbb{R}^n \to \mathbb{R}$, the matrix of cross-partials $D^2 g(x)$ at a point x, is negative semidefinite (resp. negative definite) if and only if $D^2 h(x)$ is positive semidefinite (resp. positive definite). Therefore, Parts 2 and 4 of the theorem will be proved if we prove Parts 1 and 3. We concentrate on establishing Parts 1 and 3 here. Once again, we resort to a bootstrapping argument; we establish the theorem first for the case $n = 1$ (i.e., $f: \mathbb{R} \to \mathbb{R}$), and then use this to prove the general case.

Case 1: $n = 1$

Suppose first that $f: \mathbb{R} \to \mathbb{R}$ is a C^2 concave function. We will show that $D^2 f$ is negative semidefinite at all $x \in \mathcal{D}$, i.e., that $f''(x) \leq 0$ at all $x \in \mathcal{D}$.

Let $x, y \in \mathbb{R}$ and suppose $x < y$. Pick sequences $\{x_k\}$ and $\{y_k\}$ in $\mathbb{R}$ so that for each k we have $x < x_k < y_k < y$, and $x_k \to x$, $y_k \to y$. By repeating the arguments of Theorem 7.5, it is seen that the following inequalities hold at each k:

$$\frac{f(x) - f(x_k)}{x - x_k} \geq \frac{f(x_k) - f(y_k)}{x_k - y_k} \geq \frac{f(y_k) - f(y)}{y_k - y}.$$

When $k \to \infty$ the left-most term in this expression converges to $f'(x)$, while the right-most term converges to $f'(y)$, so we must have $f'(x) \geq f'(y)$. Since x and y were arbitrary points that satisfied $x < y$, this says f' is a nonincreasing function on $\mathbb{R}$. If f' is nonincreasing, its derivative f'' must satisfy $f''(x) \leq 0$ at all $x \in \mathbb{R}$, which is precisely the statement that f'' is negative semidefinite at all x.

Now suppose $f:\mathbb{R} \to \mathbb{R}$ satisfies $f''(x) \leq 0$ at all $x \in \mathbb{R}$. We will show that f is concave on $\mathbb{R}$, completing the proof of Part 1 of the theorem for the case $n = 1$. Pick any x and y in $\mathbb{R}$ and assume, without loss of generality, that $x < y$. Pick any $\lambda \in (0, 1)$, and let $z = \lambda x + (1-\lambda)y$. We are to show that $f(z) \geq \lambda f(x) + (1-\lambda)f(y)$.

By the Mean Value Theorem (see Theorem 1.71 in Chapter 1), there exist points w_1 and w_2 such that $w_1 \in (x, z)$, $w_2 \in (z, y)$, and

$$\frac{f(x) - f(z)}{x - z} = f'(w_1) \quad \text{and} \quad \frac{f(z) - f(y)}{z - y} = f'(w_2).$$

Since $w_1 < w_2$ and $f'' \leq 0$, we must have $f'(w_1) \geq f'(w_2)$. Using this in the expression above, we obtain

$$\frac{f(x) - f(z)}{x - z} \geq \frac{f(z) - f(y)}{z - y}.$$

Cross-multiplying and rearranging terms, we finally obtain,

$$f(z) \geq \frac{y - z}{y - x} f(x) + \frac{z - x}{y - x} f(y).$$

Since $z = \lambda x + (1 - \lambda)y$, we have $\lambda = (y - z)/(y - x)$ and $1 - \lambda = (z - x)/(y - x)$. Substituting in the inequality above, the proof of the concavity of f is complete. This establishes Part 1 of the theorem for the case $n = 1$.

Note that if we had $f''(x) < 0$, then we would have also had $f'(w_1) > f'(w_2)$, so all the inequalities in the above argument become strict. In particular, retracing the steps (but with the strict inequality) establishes that f is then strictly concave, completing the proof of Part 3 of the theorem for the case $n = 1$.

Case 2: $n > 1$

We now turn to the general case where $f:\mathbb{R}^n \to \mathbb{R}$ for some $n \geq 1$. Lemma 7.19 will be repeatedly invoked in this step.

We begin with Part 1. Suppose first that f is concave. Pick any x and h in $\mathbb{R}^n$. We are required to show that $h' D^2 f(x)h \leq 0$. Define $\varphi_{x,h}(t) = f(x + th)$. Since f is C^2 by hypothesis, so is $\varphi_{x,h}(\cdot)$, and in fact, we have $\varphi'_{x,h}(t) = Df(x + th) \cdot h$, and

$\varphi''_{x,h}(t) = h' D^2 f(x + th)h$. Moreover, by Lemma 7.19, $\varphi_{x,h}(\cdot)$ is concave in t, so we have $\varphi''_{x,h}(t) \leq 0$ for all t, by the result established for concave functions of one variable. Therefore, $h' D^2 f(x + th)h \leq 0$ for all t, and in particular, $h' D^2 f(x)h \leq 0$, as required.

Now suppose that $D^2 f(z)$ is negative semidefinite at all z. We will show that f is concave by showing that for any x and h in $\mathbb{R}^n$, the function $\varphi_{x,h}(t) = f(x + th)$ is concave in t. Indeed, since f is C^2, we again have $\varphi'_{x,h}(t) = Df(x + th) \cdot h$, and $\varphi''_{x,h}(t) = h' D^2 f(x + th)h$. Since $D^2 f$ is negative semidefinite at all points, it is the case that $h' D^2 f(x + th)h \leq 0$. Therefore, $\varphi''_{x,h}(t) \leq 0$ everywhere, so by the result established for concave functions of one variable, $\varphi_{x,h}(\cdot)$ is concave. Since x and h were arbitrary, an appeal to Lemma 7.19 establishes that f is also concave, completing the proof of Part 1 of the theorem.

To see Part 3, suppose that $D^2 f(z)$ were negative definite at all z. Pick any x and h in $\mathbb{R}^n$ with $h \neq 0$. Let $\varphi_{x,h}(t) = f(x + th)$. As above, the twice-continuous differentiability of f implies the same property for $\varphi_{x,h}(\cdot)$, and we have $\varphi''_{x,h}(t) = h' D^2 f(x + th)h$ for any t. Since $h \neq 0$ and $D^2 f$ is negative definite everywhere, it follows that $\varphi''_{x,h}(t) < 0$ at all t. From the result established in the case $n = 1$, it follows that $\varphi_{x,h}(\cdot)$ is strictly concave in t. Since x and $h \neq 0$ were arbitrary, Lemma 7.19 implies that f is also strictly concave. $\qquad \square$

7.7 A Proof of the Theorem of Kuhn and Tucker under Convexity

We first present a result that can be viewed as an abstract version of Theorem 7.16. Then, we will use this result to prove Theorem 7.16.

A definition first. Let $x \in \mathcal{D} \subset \mathbb{R}^n$, and $y \in \mathbb{R}^n$. We will say that *y points into $\mathcal{D}$ at x* if there is $\omega > 0$ such that for all $\eta \in (0, \omega)$, we have $(x + \eta y) \in \mathcal{D}$.

Theorem 7.20 *Suppose $f: \mathcal{D} \to \mathbb{R}$ is concave, where $\mathcal{D} \subset \mathbb{R}^n$ is convex. Then x^* maximizes f over $\mathcal{D}$ if, and only if, $Df(x^*; y) \leq 0$ for all y pointing into $\mathcal{D}$ at x^*.*

Proof Suppose x^* maximizes f over $\mathcal{D}$. Let y point into $\mathcal{D}$ at x^*. Then, for all $\eta > 0$ such that $(x^* + \eta y) \in \mathcal{D}$, we have $f(x^*) \geq f(x^* + \eta y)$ since x^* is a maximizer. Subtracting $f(x^*)$ from both sides, dividing by η and taking limits as $\eta \to 0+$ establishes necessity.[4]

Conversely, suppose $Df(x^*; y) \leq 0$ for all y pointing into $\mathcal{D}$ at x^*. If x^* does not maximize f over $\mathcal{D}$, there exists $z \in \mathcal{D}$ with $f(z) > f(x^*)$. Let $y = z - x^*$. Then, $x^* + y = z$, so by taking $\omega = 1$, it follows from the convexity of $\mathcal{D}$ that y points

---

[4]Note that, as with all necessary conditions, the concavity of f and the convexity of $\mathcal{D}$ played no role here.

into $\mathcal{D}$ at x^*. But for $\eta \in (0, 1)$,

$$f(x^* + \eta(z - x^*)) \geq (1 - \eta)f(x^*) + \eta f(z)$$
$$= f(x^*) + \eta(f(z) - f(x^*))$$

by concavity of f. Thus,

$$\frac{f(x^* + \eta(z - x^*)) - f(x^*)}{\eta} \geq f(z) - f(x^*) > 0.$$

But the left-hand side tends to $Df(x^*; y)$ as $\eta \to 0+$ and this implies $Df(x^*; y) > 0$. By hypothesis, on the other hand, $Df(x^*; y) \leq 0$ since y points into $\mathcal{D}$ at x^*, a contradiction establishing the theorem. $\qquad\square$

We begin our proof of Theorem 7.16 by demonstrating the sufficiency of the conditions [KT-1] and [KT-2] when f and the functions h_i are all concave. (As we have already mentioned, Slater's condition plays no part in proving sufficiency.) Our proof will use the fact that if a function $\phi: U \to \mathbb{R}$ is differentiable at a point x, then the directional derivative $D\phi(x; h)$ exists at all $h \in \mathbb{R}^n$, and, in fact, $D\phi(x; h) = D\phi(x)h$.

So suppose that there exists $\lambda^* \in \mathbb{R}_+^k$ such that [KT-1] and [KT-2] hold. Let

$$\mathcal{D}_i = \{x \in U \mid h_i(x) \geq 0\}.$$

Suppose $x_1, x_2 \in \mathcal{D}_i$. Pick any $\lambda \in (0, 1)$, and let $z = \lambda x_1 + (1 - \lambda)x_2$. Then, $z \in U$ since U is convex. Moreover, $h_i(z) \geq \lambda h_i(x_1) + (1 - \lambda)h_i(x_2) \geq 0$, so $z \in \mathcal{D}_i$. Thus, $\mathcal{D}_i$ is convex for each i. This implies $\mathcal{D} = \cap_{i=1}^l \mathcal{D}_i$ is also convex. Since f is concave, all that remains to be shown now is that $Df(x^*)y \leq 0$ for all y pointing into $\mathcal{D}$ at x^*, and we can then appeal to Theorem 7.20.

So suppose y points into $\mathcal{D}$ at x^*. Fix y. We will show that for each $i = 1, \ldots, l$, we have $\lambda_i^* Dh_i(x^*)y \geq 0$. First, note that by definition of y, there is $\epsilon > 0$ such that for all $t \in (0, \epsilon)$, we have $(x^* + ty) \in \mathcal{D}$. This implies $h_i(x^* + ty) \geq 0$ for all i, for all $t \in (0, \epsilon)$.

Pick any i. There are two possibilities: $h_i(x^*) > 0$, and $h_i(x^*) = 0$. In the first case, $\lambda_i^* = 0$ by condition [KT-2], so certainly, $\lambda_i^* Dh_i(x^*)y \geq 0$. Now, consider the case $h_i(x^*) = 0$. By hypothesis, we have $h_i(x^* + ty) \geq 0$ for all $t \in (0, \epsilon)$, so we also have

$$\frac{h_i(x^* + ty) - h_i(x^*)}{t} \geq 0$$

for all $t \in (0, \epsilon)$. Taking limits as $t \downarrow 0$, we obtain $Dh_i(x^*)y \geq 0$. Since $\lambda_i^* \geq 0$, we finally obtain $\lambda_i^* Dh_i(x^*)y \geq 0$ in this case also. It now follows that

$$Df(x^*)y = -\sum_{i=1}^{l}\lambda_i^* Dh_i(x^*)y \leq 0.$$

Since y was an arbitrary vector pointing into $\mathcal{D}$ at x^*, this inequality holds for all such y. By Theorem 7.20, x^* is then a maximum of f on $\mathcal{D}$, completing the proof of the sufficiency of [KT-1] and [KT-2].

We now turn to necessity. Unlike the sufficiency part, Slater's condition will play an important role here. So suppose that x^* is a maximum of f on the given constraint set $\mathcal{D}$. We are to show the existence of λ^* such that [KT-1] and [KT-2] hold. Define the function $L: U \times \mathbb{R}_+^l \to \mathbb{R}$ by

$$L(x, \lambda) = f(x) + \sum_{i=1}^{l}\lambda_i h_i(x).$$

To prove the result, we will show that there is $\lambda^* \in \mathbb{R}_+^l$ which satisfies

$$\lambda_i^* h_i(x^*) = 0, \qquad i = 1, \ldots, l,$$

as well as[5]

$$L(x, \lambda^*) \leq L(x^*, \lambda^*), \qquad x \in U.$$

Since $\lambda^* \geq 0$, the first of these conditions establishes [KT-2]. The second condition states that x^* is a maximum of $L(\cdot, \lambda^*)$ on U. Since U is open and convex, and $L(\cdot, \lambda^*)$ is concave in x, x^* can be a maximum of L on U if and only if $DL_x(x^*, \lambda^*) = 0$, i.e., if and only if

$$Df(x^*) + \sum_{i=1}^{l}\lambda_i^* Dh_i(x^*) = 0.$$

Thus, [KT-1] must also hold, and the proof will be complete.

We will utilize a separation theorem to derive the required point λ^*. To this end, define the sets $\mathcal{X}$ and $\mathcal{Y}$ by

$$\mathcal{X} = \{(w, z) \in \mathbb{R} \times \mathbb{R}^n \mid w \leq f(x), \; z \leq h(x) \text{ for some } x \in U\},$$

and

$$\mathcal{Y} = \{(w, z) \in \mathbb{R} \times \mathbb{R}^n \mid w > f(x^*), z \gg 0\}.$$

We claim that $\mathcal{X} \cap \mathcal{Y}$ is empty. For if there were a point (w, z) in this intersection,

[5]One can actually show that the following stronger "saddle-point condition" is met at (x^*, λ^*):

$$L(x, \lambda^*) \leq L(x^*, \lambda^*) \leq L(x^*, \lambda), \qquad x \in U, \; \lambda \in \mathbb{R}_+^l.$$

we would have the existence of an x in U such that $f(x) \geq w > f(x^*)$ and $0 \ll z \leq h(x)$, so the point x is feasible and dominates x^*. This contradicts the presumed optimality of x^*. Thus, $\mathcal{X}$ and $\mathcal{Y}$ have no points in common, as claimed.

It is also true that $\mathcal{X}$ and $\mathcal{Y}$ are convex sets. The convexity of $\mathcal{Y}$ is obvious. The convexity of $\mathcal{X}$ follows from the concavity of f and the constraint functions h_i.

By Theorem 1.68, there is a vector $(p, q) \in \mathbb{R} \times \mathbb{R}^n$, $(p, q) \neq 0$, such that

$$pw + q \cdot z \leq pu + q \cdot v, \qquad (w, z) \in \mathcal{X}, \ (u, v) \in \mathcal{Y}.$$

From the definition of $\mathcal{Y}$, we must have $(p, q) \geq 0$. For, if some coordinate was negative, by taking the corresponding coordinate of (u, v) positive and large, the sum $pu + q \cdot v$ could be made arbitrarily negative. It would not, then, be possible to satisfy the inequality required by the separation.

Now, by taking a sequence $(u_m, v_m) \in \mathcal{Y}$ converging to the boundary point $(f(x^*), 0)$, it also follows from the separation inequality and the definition of $\mathcal{X}$ that

$$pf(x) + q \cdot h(x) \leq pf(x^*), \qquad x \in U.$$

We have already established that $(p, q) \geq 0$. We now claim that $p = 0$ leads to a contradiction. If $p = 0$, then from the last inequality, we must have

$$q \cdot h(x) \leq 0, \qquad x \in U.$$

But $p = 0$ combined with $(p, q) \geq 0$ and $(p, q) \neq 0$ implies $q > 0$ (i.e., that $q = (q_1, \ldots, q_l)$ has at least one positive coordinate). By Slater's condition, there is $\bar{x} \in U$ such that $h(\bar{x}) \gg 0$. Together with $q > 0$, this means $q \cdot h(\bar{x}) > 0$, a contradiction. Therefore, we cannot have $p = 0$.

Now define

$$\lambda^* = \frac{1}{p}q = \left(\frac{q_1}{p}, \ldots, \frac{q_l}{p} \right) \geq 0.$$

We then have

$$f(x) + \sum_{i=1}^{l} \lambda_i^* h_i(x) \leq f(x^*), \qquad x \in U.$$

If we take $x = x^*$ in this expression, we obtain $\sum_{i=1}^{l} \lambda_i^* h_i(x^*) \leq 0$. On the other hand, we also have $h(x^*) \geq 0$, and $\lambda^* \geq 0$, so $\sum_{i=1}^{l} \lambda_i^* h_i(x^*) \geq 0$. Together, these inequalities imply

$$\sum_{i=1}^{l} \lambda_i^* h_i(x^*) = 0,$$

and, therefore, that for all $x \in U$,

$$L(x, \lambda^*) = f(x) + \sum_{i=1}^{l} \lambda_i^* h_i(x)$$

$$\leq f(x^*)$$

$$= f(x^*) + \sum_{i=1}^{l} \lambda_i^* h_i(x^*)$$

$$= L(x^*, \lambda^*).$$

The proof is complete.[6]   □

7.8 Exercises

1. Define $f \colon \mathbb{R}^2 \to \mathbb{R}$ by $f(x, y) = ax^2 + by^2 + 2cxy + d$. For what values of a, b, c, and d is f concave?

2. Let $f \colon \mathbb{R}^n_{++} \to \mathbb{R}$ be defined by

$$f(x_1, \ldots, x_n) = \log(x_1^\alpha \cdots x_n^\alpha)$$

   where $\alpha > 0$. Is f concave?

3. Let $f \colon \mathbb{R}^n_+ \to \mathbb{R}$ be a concave function satisfying $f(0) = 0$. Show that for all $k \geq 1$ we have $kf(x) \geq f(kx)$. What happens if $k \in [0, 1)$?

4. Let $\mathcal{D} = \{(x, y) \in \mathbb{R}^2 \mid x^2 + y^2 \leq 1\}$ be the unit disk in $\mathbb{R}^2$. Give an example of a concave function $f \colon \mathcal{D} \to \mathbb{R}$ such that f is discountinuous at *every* boundary point of $\mathcal{D}$.

5. Show that the linear function $f \colon \mathbb{R}^n \to \mathbb{R}$ defined by $f(x) = a \cdot x - b$, $a \in \mathbb{R}^n$, $b \in \mathbb{R}$ is both convex and concave on $\mathbb{R}^n$. Conversely, show that if $f \colon \mathbb{R}^n \to \mathbb{R}$ is both convex and concave, then it is a linear function.

6. Let $\{f_1, f_2, \ldots, f_n\}$ be a set of convex functions from $\mathbb{R}^n$ to $\mathbb{R}$. Show that the nonnegative linear combination

$$f(x) = \alpha_1 f_1(x) + \cdots + \alpha_n f_n(x) \qquad \alpha_1, \ldots, \alpha_n \geq 0$$

   is convex. Is this still true for any linear combination of convex functions?

---

[6]To see that (x^*, λ^*) is actually a saddle point of L as claimed in the earlier footnote, note that since $\sum_{i=1}^{l} \lambda_i h_i(x^*) = 0$, we also have $\sum_{i=1}^{l} \lambda_i h_i(x^*) \geq \sum_{i=1}^{l} \lambda_i^* h_i(x^*)$. Therefore,

$$L(x^*, \lambda^*) = f(x^*) + \sum_{i=1}^{l} \lambda_i^* h_i(x^*) \leq f(x^*) + \sum_{i=1}^{l} \lambda_i h_i(x) = L(x^*, \lambda).$$

7. Show that a function $f: \mathbb{R}^n \to \mathbb{R}$ is convex if and only if for each $x_1, x_2 \in \mathbb{R}^n$, the function $\varphi: [0, 1] \to \mathbb{R}$ defined by

$$\varphi(\lambda) = f[\lambda x_1 + (1 - \lambda)x_2]$$

is convex on $[0, 1]$. Is the above statement still true if we replace convex with concave?

8. Let $\{f_i : i \in I\}$ be a set (finite or infinite) of functions from a convex set $\mathcal{D} \subseteq \mathbb{R}^n$ to $\mathbb{R}$ which are convex and bounded on $\mathcal{D}$. Show that the function, f, defined as

$$f(x) = \sup_{i \in I} f_i(x)$$

is a convex function on $\mathcal{D}$. What about the function g, defined as

$$g(x) = \inf_{i \in I} f_i(x)?$$

Is g convex? Why or why not?

9. Let $\mathcal{D} \subset \mathbb{R}^n$ be a convex set. Let $f: \mathcal{D} \to \mathbb{R}$ be a differentiable function. Show that the following are equivalent:

   (a) f is concave on $\mathcal{D}$.
   (b) $f(y) - f(x) \leq Df(x)(y - x)$ for all $x, y \in \mathcal{D}$.
   (c) $[Df(y) - Df(x)](y - x) \leq 0$ for all $x, y \in \mathcal{D}$.

10. Let $f: \mathbb{R}^n \to \mathbb{R}$ be concave. Let A be an $n \times m$ matrix, and let $b \in \mathbb{R}^n$. Consider the function $h: \mathbb{R}^m \to \mathbb{R}$ defined by

$$h(x) = f[Ax + b], \quad x \in \mathbb{R}^m.$$

Is h concave? Why or why not?

11. Let f and g be concave functions on $\mathbb{R}$. Give an example to show that their composition $f \circ g$ is not necessarily concave. Show also that if f is an *increasing* concave function and g is any concave function, then $f \circ g$ will also be concave. What if instead, g were increasing and concave, and f were simply concave?

12. Let f and g be concave functions on $\mathbb{R}$. Is the product function $f \cdot g$ concave on $\mathbb{R}$? Prove your answer, or provide a counterexample.

13. Let $f: [0, 2] \to \mathbb{R}$ be defined by

$$f(x) = \begin{cases} x, & x \in [0, 1] \\ 2 - x, & x \in (1, 2]. \end{cases}$$

Show that f is concave on $[0, 2]$. Observe that $x^* = 1$ is a global maximizer of f. Let V be the set of all y that point into $[0,2]$ at x^*. Show that $Df(x^*; y) \leq 0$ for all $y \in V$.

14. Repeat problem 13 if $f(x) = x$, and if $f(x) = x(1 - x)$.

15. Describe a set of conditions on the parameters p and I under which the budget set $\mathcal{B}(p, I)$ of the utility-maximization problem of subsection 2.3.1 meets Slater's condition.

16. Under what conditions on p and w does the constraint set $F(p, w)$ of the consumption-leisure choice problem of subsection 2.3.5 meet Slater's condition?

17. Identify a set of conditions on the parameters p and ω of the portfolio choice problem of subsection 2.3.6 under which the constraint set $\Phi(p, \omega)$ of the problem satisfies Slater's condition.

18. Find a set of sufficient conditions on the technology g under which the constraint set of the cost-minimization problem of subsection 2.3.4 meets Slater's condition.

19. Let T be any positive integer. Consider the following problem:

$$\text{Maximize} \quad \sum_{t=1}^{T} u(c_t)$$

$$\text{subject to} \quad c_1 + x_1 \leq x$$
$$c_t + x_t \leq f(x_{t-1}), \ t = 2, \ldots, T$$
$$c_t, x_t \geq 0, \ t = 1, \ldots, T$$

where $x \in \mathbb{R}_+$, and u and f are nondecreasing continuous functions from $\mathbb{R}_+$ into itself. Derive the Kuhn–Tucker first-order conditions for this problem, and explain under what circumstances these conditions are sufficient.

20. A firm produces an output y using two inputs x_1 and x_2 as $y = \sqrt{x_1 x_2}$. The firm is obligated to use at least one unit of x_1 in its production process. The input prices of x_1 and x_2 are given by w_1 and w_2, respectively. Assume that the firm wishes to minimize the cost of producing $\bar{y}$ units of output.

    (a) Set up the firm's cost-minimization problem. Is the feasible set closed? compact? convex?

    (b) Describe the Kuhn–Tucker first-order conditions. Are they sufficient for a solution? Why or why not?

21. Describe conditions on f under which the first-order conditions in the following optimization problem are sufficient:

$$\text{Maximize} \quad pf(x_1, \ldots, x_n) - w_1 x_1 - \cdots - w_n x_n$$
$$\text{subject to} \quad x_i \geq 0, \ i = 1, \ldots, n.$$

22. A firm has contracted with its union to hire at least L^* units of labor at a wage rate of w_1 per unit. Any amount of additional labor may be hired at a rate of w_2 per unit, where $w_1 > w_2$. Assume that labor is the only input used by the firm in its production process, and that the production function is given by $f: \mathbb{R}_+ \to \mathbb{R}_+$, where f is C^1 and concave. Given that the output sells at a price of p, describe the firm's maximization problem. Derive the Kuhn–Tucker first-order conditions. Are these necessary for a solution? Are they sufficient?

23. A firm uses two inputs, labor (l) and raw material (m), to produce a single output y. The production function is given by $y = f(l, m)$. The output sells for a price of p, while labor has a unit cost of w. The firm has in its stock 4 units of the raw material m. Additional units may be purchased from the market at a price of c. The firm can also sell part or all of its own raw material stock in the market at the price c.

    (a) Set up the firm's profit-maximization problem, and derive the Kuhn–Tucker first-order conditions. Describe under what conditions on f, these conditions are sufficient.

    (b) Let $p = w = m = 1$, and let $f(l, m) = l^{1/3}m^{1/3}$. Calculate the firm's optimal choice of actions.

24. A firm produces an output y using a single input l through the production function $y = f(l)$. The output is sold at a constant price of p. The firm is a monopsonist in the labor market: if it offers a wage of w, then it can hire $\lambda(w)$ units of labor, where $\lambda(0) = 0$, $\lambda'(w) > 0$ at all $w \geq 0$, and $\lambda(w) \uparrow \infty$ as $w \uparrow \infty$. Assume the usual nonnegativity conditions.

    (a) Describe the firm's profit-maximization problem, and write down the Kuhn–Tucker first-order conditions for a maximum.

    (b) Explain under what further assumptions on $f(\cdot)$ and $\lambda(\cdot)$ these first-order conditions are also sufficient. (Specify the most general conditions you can think of.)

25. An agent who consumes three commodities has a utility function given by

$$u(x_1, x_2, x_3) = x_1^{1/3} + \min\{x_2, x_3\}.$$

Given an income of I, and prices of p_1, p_2, p_3, write down the consumer's utility-maximization problem. Can the Weierstrass and/or Kuhn–Tucker theorems be used to obtain and characterize a solution? Why or why not?

26. An agent consumes two commodities x and y. His utility function is given by $u(x, y) = x + \ln(1 + y)$, where $\ln(z)$ denotes the natural logarithm of z. The prices of the two commodities are given by $p_x > 0$ and $p_y > 0$. The consumer

has an income of $I > 0$. Assuming consumption of either commodity must be nonnegative, find the consumer's utility-maximizing commodity bundle.

27. A consumer with a fixed income of $I > 0$ consumes two commodities. If he purchases q_i units of commodity i ($i = 1, 2$), the price he pays is $p_i(q_i)$, where $p_i(\cdot)$ is a strictly increasing C^1 function. The consumer's utility function is given by $u(q_1, q_2) = \ln q_1 + \ln q_2$.

   (a) Describe the consumer's utility maximization problem. Does the Weierstrass Theorem apply to yield existence of a maximum? Write down the Kuhn–Tucker first-order conditions for a maximum.

   (b) Under what conditions on $p_1(\cdot)$ and $p_2(\cdot)$ are these conditions also sufficient? (Specify the most general conditions you can think of.)

   (c) Suppose $p_1(q_1) = \sqrt{q_1}$ and $p_2(q_2) = \sqrt{q_2}$. Are the sufficient conditions you have given met by this specification? Calculate the optimal consumption bundle in this case.

8

Quasi-Convexity and Optimization

The previous chapter showed that convexity carries powerful implications for optimization theory. However, from the point of view of applications, convexity is often also quite restrictive as an assumption. For instance, such a commonly used utility function as the Cobb–Douglas function

$$u(x_1, \ldots, x_n) = x_1^{\alpha_1} \cdots x_n^{\alpha_n}$$

is not concave unless $\sum_{i=1}^{n} \alpha_i \leq 1$. In this chapter, we examine optimization under a weakening of the condition of convexity, which is called *quasi-convexity*.

Quasi-concave and quasi-convex functions fail to exhibit many of the sharp properties that distinguish concave and convex functions. A quasi-concave function may, for instance, be discontinuous on the interior of its domain. A local maximum of a quasi-concave function need not also be a global maximum of the function. Perhaps more significantly, first-order conditions are *not*, in general, sufficient to identify global optima of quasi-convex optimization problems.

Nonetheless, quasi-concave and quasi-convex functions do possess enough structure to be of value for optimization theory. Most importantly, it turns out that the Kuhn–Tucker first-order conditions are "almost" sufficient to identify optima of inequality-constrained optimization problems under quasi-convexity restrictions; more precisely, the first-order conditions are sufficient provided the optimum occurs at a point where an additional regularity condition is also met. The result cannot, unfortunately, be strengthened to obtain unconditional sufficiency of the first-order conditions: it is easy to construct examples of otherwise well-behaved quasi-convex optimization problems where the regularity condition fails, and as a consequence, the first-order conditions do not suffice to identify optima. However, the regularity condition is not a very restrictive one, and is satisfied in many models of economic interest.

Finally, it must be mentioned that technical expedience is not the only, or even the primary, ground for the significance of quasi-convex structures in economic analysis. As Arrow and Enthoven (1961) demonstrate, the quasi-concavity of a function turns out to be, under certain conditions, the precise mathematical expression of the economic concept of a *diminishing marginal rate of substitution*. The latter is an assumption that is frequently imposed on economic models, and is usually justified by an appeal to economic considerations alone. That such functions also yield sufficiency of the first-order conditions can be viewed as simply an added bonus.

8.1 Quasi-Concave and Quasi-Convex Functions

Throughout this chapter, $\mathcal{D}$ will denote a convex set in $\mathbb{R}^n$. Let $f: \mathcal{D} \to \mathbb{R}$. The *upper-contour set* of f at $a \in \mathbb{R}$, denoted $U_f(y)$, is defined as

$$U_f(a) = \{x \in \mathcal{D} \mid f(x) \geq a\},$$

while the *lower-contour set* of f at $a \in \mathbb{R}$, denoted $L_f(a)$, is defined as

$$L_f(a) = \{x \in \mathcal{D} \mid f(x) \leq a\}.$$

The function f is said to be *quasi-concave* on $\mathcal{D}$ if $U_f(a)$ is a convex set for each a. It is said to be *quasi-convex* on $\mathcal{D}$ if $L_f(a)$ is a convex set for each a.

As with concave and convex functions, it is also true in the case of quasi-concave and quasi-convex functions that a strong relationship exists between the value of a function at two points x and y, and the value of the function at a convex combination $\lambda x + (1 - \lambda) y$:

Theorem 8.1 *A function $f: \mathcal{D} \to \mathbb{R}$ is quasi-concave on $\mathcal{D}$ if and only if for all $x, y \in \mathcal{D}$ and for all $\lambda \in (0, 1)$, it is the case that*

$$f[\lambda x + (1 - \lambda) y] \geq \min\{f(x), f(y)\}.$$

The function f is quasi-convex on $\mathcal{D}$ if and only if for all $x, y \in \mathcal{D}$ and for all $\lambda \in (0, 1)$, it is the case that

$$f[\lambda x + (1 - \lambda) y] \leq \max\{f(x), f(y)\}.$$

Proof First, suppose that f is quasi-concave, i.e., that $U_f(a)$ is a convex set for each $a \in \mathbb{R}$. Let $x, y \in \mathcal{D}$ and $\lambda \in (0, 1)$. Assume, without loss of generality, that $f(x) \geq f(y)$. Letting $f(y) = a$, we have $x, y \in U_f(a)$. By the convexity of $U_f(a)$, we have $\lambda x + (1 - \lambda) y \in U_f(a)$, which means

$$f[\lambda x + (1 - \lambda) y] \geq f(y) \geq a = f(y) = \min\{f(x), f(y)\}.$$

Now, suppose we have $f[\lambda x + (1 - \lambda)y] \geq \min\{f(x), f(y)\}$ for all $x, y \in \mathcal{D}$ and for all $\lambda \in (0, 1)$. Let $a \in \mathbb{R}$. If $U_f(a)$ is empty or contains only one point, it is evidently convex, so suppose it contains at least two points x and y. Then $f(x) \geq a$ and $f(y) \geq a$, so $\min\{f(x), f(y)\} \geq a$. Now, for any $\lambda \in (0, 1)$, we have $f[\lambda x + (1 - \lambda)y] \geq \min\{f(x), f(y)\}$ by hypothesis, and so $\lambda x + (1 - \lambda)y \in U_f(a)$. Since a was arbitrary, the proof is complete for the case of quasi-concave functions.

An analogous argument shows that the claimed result is also true in the case of quasi-convex functions. □

A quasi-concave function $f: \mathcal{D} \to \mathbb{R}$ is said to be *strictly quasi-concave* if the defining inequality can be made strict, i.e., if for all $x, y \in \mathcal{D}$ with $x \neq y$, and for all $\lambda \in (0, 1)$, we have

$$f[\lambda x + (1 - \lambda)y] > \min\{f(x), f(y)\}.$$

A *strictly quasi-convex* function is similarly defined.

In the sequel, we will use the term "quasi-convexity" to encompass the concepts of convex sets, and of quasi-concave and quasi-convex functions. In an obvious extension of the terminology we defined in the previous chapter, we will say that a maximization problem is a *quasi-convex maximization problem* if it has a convex constraint set and a quasi-concave objective function. A *quasi-convex minimization problem* will, similarly, refer to a minimization problem with a convex constraint set and a quasi-convex objective function. A *quasi-convex optimization problem* will refer to a problem that is either a quasi-convex maximization problem, or a quasi-convex minimization problem.

Finally, the following observation, which relates quasi-concave and quasi-convex functions, enables us to focus solely on quasi-*concave* functions, wherever this simplifies the exposition. Deriving analogous results for quasi-*convex* functions using Theorem 8.2 is then a straightforward task, and will be left to the reader as an exercise.

Theorem 8.2 *The function $f: \mathcal{D} \to \mathbb{R}$ is quasi-concave on $\mathcal{D}$ if and only if $-f$ is quasi-convex on $\mathcal{D}$. It is strictly quasi-concave on $\mathcal{D}$ if and only if $-f$ is strictly quasi-convex on $\mathcal{D}$.*

8.2 Quasi-Convexity as a Generalization of Convexity

It is a simple matter to show that the set of all quasi-concave functions contains the set of all concave functions, and that the set of all quasi-convex functions contains the set of all convex functions:

Theorem 8.3 *Let $f: \mathcal{D} \subset \mathbb{R}^n \to \mathbb{R}$. If f is concave on $\mathcal{D}$, it is also quasi-concave on $\mathcal{D}$. If f is convex on $\mathcal{D}$, it is also quasi-convex on $\mathcal{D}$.*

Proof Suppose f is concave. Then, for all $x, y \in \mathcal{D}$ and $\lambda \in (0, 1)$, we have

$$f[\lambda x + (1 - \lambda)y] \geq \lambda f(x) + (1 - \lambda)f(y)$$
$$\geq \lambda \min\{f(x), f(y)\} + (1 - \lambda)\min\{f(x), f(y)\}$$
$$= \min\{f(x), f(y)\},$$

so f is also quasi-concave. A similar argument establishes that if f is convex, it is also quasi-convex.   □

The converse of this result is false, as the following example shows:

Example 8.4 Let $f: \mathbb{R} \to \mathbb{R}$ be any nondecreasing function on $\mathbb{R}$. Then, f is both quasi-concave and quasi-convex on $\mathbb{R}$. To see this, pick any x and y in $\mathbb{R}$, and any $\lambda \in (0, 1)$. Assume, without loss of generality, that $x > y$. Then, $x > \lambda x + (1 - \lambda)y > y$. Since f is nondecreasing, we have

$$f(x) \geq f[\lambda x + (1 - \lambda)y] \geq f(y).$$

Since $f(x) = \max\{f(x), f(y)\}$, the first inequality shows that f is quasi-convex on $\mathbb{R}$. Since $f(y) = \min\{f(x), f(y)\}$, the second inequality shows that f is quasi-concave on $\mathbb{R}$.

Since it is always possible to choose a nondecreasing function f that is neither concave nor convex on $\mathbb{R}$ (for instance, take $f(x) = x^3$ for all $x \in \mathbb{R}$), we have shown that not every quasi-concave function is concave, and not every quasi-convex function is convex.   □

The next result elaborates on the relationship between concave and quasi-concave functions. It also raises a very important question regarding the value of quasi-convexity for optimization theory. This is discussed after the proof of the theorem.

Theorem 8.5 *If $f: \mathcal{D} \to \mathbb{R}$ is quasi-concave on $\mathcal{D}$, and $\phi: \mathbb{R} \to \mathbb{R}$ is a monotone nondecreasing function, then the composition $\phi \circ f$ is a quasi-concave function from $\mathcal{D}$ to $\mathbb{R}$. In particular, any monotone transform of a concave function results in a quasi-concave function.*

Proof Pick any x and y in $\mathcal{D}$, and any $\lambda \in (0, 1)$. We will show that

$$\phi(f[\lambda x + (1 - \lambda)y]) \geq \min\{\phi(f(x)), \phi(f(y))\},$$

which will complete the proof. Indeed, this is immediate. Since f is quasi-concave by hypothesis, we have

$$f[\lambda x + (1 - \lambda)y] \geq \min\{f(x), f(y)\}.$$

Since ϕ is nondecreasing, this implies

$$\phi(f[\lambda x + (1 - \lambda)y]) \geq \phi(\min\{f(x), f(y)\}) = \min\{\phi(f(x)), \phi(f(y))\}.$$

The proof is complete.   □

A natural question that arises is whether the converse of the second part of Theorem 8.5 is also true, that is, whether every quasi-concave function is a monotone transformation of some concave function. This question is significant in light of Theorem 2.5, which states that if φ is any strictly increasing function on $\mathbb{R}$, then a point x^* maximizes a given function f over a given constraint set $\mathcal{D}$ if and only if x^* maximizes the composition $\varphi \circ f$ over $\mathcal{D}$.[1] If it turned out that every quasi-concave function could be obtained as a strictly increasing transformation of some concave function, then any optimization problem with a quasi-concave objective could be converted to an equivalent problem with a concave objective. Thus, quasi-convexity would have nothing to add to convexity, at least from the point of view of optimization theory.

It turns out, however, that this concern is without foundation: there do exist functions which are quasi-concave, but which are *not* obtainable as a strictly increasing transformation of a concave function. A particularly simple example of such a function is presented in Example 8.1 below. Thus, the notion of quasi-concavity is a genuine generalization of the notion of concavity.

Example 8.6 Let $f : \mathbb{R}_+ \to \mathbb{R}$ be defined by

$$f(x) = \begin{cases} 0, & x \in [0, 1] \\ (x - 1)^2, & x > 1. \end{cases}$$

Figure 8.1 illustrates this function. Evidently, f is a nondecreasing, and therefore quasi-concave, function on $\mathbb{R}_+$. Note that f is constant in x for $x \in [0, 1]$, and is strictly increasing in x for $x > 1$.

Suppose there existed a concave function g and a strictly increasing function φ such that $\varphi \circ g \equiv f$. We will show that a contradiction must result.

We claim first that g must be constant on the interval $[0, 1]$. To see this, suppose there existed x and y in $[0, 1]$ such that $g(x) \neq g(y)$, say $g(x) > g(y)$. Then, since φ is strictly increasing, we must also have $\varphi(g(x)) > \varphi(g(y))$. This contradicts the requirement that $\varphi \circ g$ be constant on $[0, 1]$.

Next we claim that g is strictly increasing in x for $x > 1$. For, suppose there existed points x and y such that $x > y > 1$, and such that $g(x) \leq g(y)$. Then,

---

[1] Note that Theorem 2.5 requires the transforming function φ to be *strictly increasing*, not just nondecreasing. Indeed, the equivalence claimed in the theorem would be false if φ were only nondecreasing. For instance, if φ was a constant function, then it would also be nondecreasing, and evidently every point in the domain would now maximize $\varphi \circ f$ over $\mathcal{D}$; clearly, not every point need be a maximizer of f on $\mathcal{D}$.

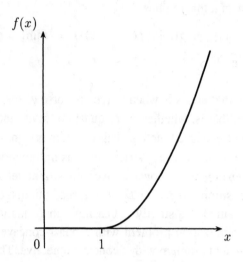

Fig. 8.1. A Quasi-Concave Function That Is Not a Monotone Transform of a Concave Function

$\varphi(g(x)) \leq \varphi(g(y))$. This contradicts the requirement that $\varphi \circ g$ be strictly increasing in x for $x > 1$.

But if g is constant on the interval $[0, 1]$, it has a local maximum at every $z \in (0, 1)$. These local maxima are not global maxima, since g is increasing for $x > 1$. This contradicts Theorem 7.13, which shows that every local maximum of a concave function must also be a global maximum.   □

Arrow and Enthoven (1961) provide a richer, but also more complicated, example to illustrate this point. They consider the function $f \colon \mathbb{R}_+^2 \to \mathbb{R}$ given by

$$f(x, y) = (x - 1) + [(1 - x)^2 + 4(x + y)]^{1/2}.$$

Note that f is a strictly increasing function on $\mathbb{R}_+^2$, i.e., we have $\partial f(x, y)/\partial x \geq 0$ and $\partial f(x, y)/\partial y \geq 0$ at all $(x, y) \in \mathbb{R}_+^2$. Moreover, the "indifference curve" of f at k, i.e., the locus of points $(x, y) \in \mathbb{R}_+^2$ such that $f(x, y) = k$, is the straight line

$$4y + (4 + 2k)x = k^2 + 2k.$$

(This indifference curve is graphed in Figure 8.2.) Since f is strictly increasing, the upper-contour set $U_f(k)$ consists of all points $(x, y) \in \mathbb{R}_+^2$ lying "above" (i.e., to the northeast of) this straight line, and so is clearly convex. Thus, f is quasi-concave.

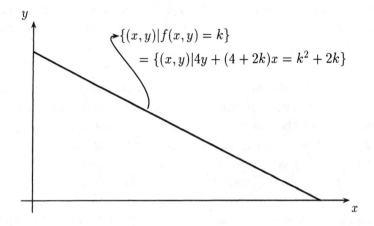

Fig. 8.2. The Arrow–Enthoven Example: An Indifference Curve

To prove that f cannot be a strict monotone transform of a concave function is significantly more difficult. We leave it to the reader as an exercise.

8.3 Implications of Quasi-Convexity

Quasi-concave and quasi-convex functions do not enjoy many of the properties that come with convexity. For instance, unlike concave and convex functions,

1. Quasi-concave and quasi-convex functions are not necessarily continuous in the interior of their domains;
2. Quasi-concave functions can have local maxima that are not global maxima, and quasi-convex functions can have local minima that are not global minima;
3. First-order conditions are not sufficient to identify even *local* optima under quasi-convexity.

The following example illustrates all of these points:

Example 8.7 Let $f: \mathbb{R} \to \mathbb{R}$ be defined by

$$f(x) = \begin{cases} x^3, & x \in [0, 1] \\ 1, & x \in (1, 2] \\ x^3, & x > 2. \end{cases}$$

Since f is a nondecreasing function, it is both quasi-concave and quasi-convex on $\mathbb{R}$. Clearly, f has a dicontinuity at $x = 2$. Moreover, f is constant on the open interval $(1, 2)$, so every point in this interval is a local maximum of f as well as a local minimum of f. However, no point in $(0, 1)$ is either a global maximum or a global minimum. Finally, $f'(0) = 0$, although 0 is evidently neither a local maximum, nor a local mimimum. $\square$

Another significant distinction between convexity and quasi-convexity arises from the fact that a strictly concave function cannot be even weakly convex, and a strictly convex function cannot be even weakly concave. In contrast, a strictly quasi-concave function may well be strictly quasi-convex also: a simple modification of Example 8.4 shows that if f is any strictly increasing function on $\mathbb{R}$ (i.e., if $x > y$ implies $f(x) > f(y)$), then f is both strictly quasi-concave and strictly quasi-convex on $\mathbb{R}$.

However, as with concave and convex functions, the derivatives of quasi-concave and quasi-convex functions do possess a good deal of structure. In particular, it is possible to provide analogs of Theorems 7.9 and 7.10, which characterized the convexity properties of functions using their first- and second-derivatives, respectively. Here is the first result in this direction:

Theorem 8.8 *Let $f: \mathcal{D} \to \mathbb{R}$ be a C^1 function where $\mathcal{D} \subset \mathbb{R}^n$ is convex and open. Then f is a quasi-concave function on $\mathcal{D}$ if and only if it is the case that for any $x, y \in \mathcal{D}$,*

$$f(y) \geq f(x) \implies Df(x)(y - x) \geq 0.$$

Proof See Section 8.6. $\square$

It is also possible to give a second-derivative test for quasi-convexity along the lines of Theorem 7.10 for concave and convex functions. Let a C^2 function f defined on some open domain $\mathcal{D} \subset \mathbb{R}^n$ be given, and let $x \in \mathcal{D}$. For $k = 1, \ldots n$, let $C_k(x)$ be the $(k + 1) \times (k + 1)$ matrix defined by

$$C_k(x) = \begin{bmatrix} 0 & \dfrac{\partial f}{\partial x_1}(x) & \cdots & \dfrac{\partial f}{\partial x_k}(x) \\[2ex] \dfrac{\partial f}{\partial x_1}(x) & \dfrac{\partial^2 f}{\partial x_1^2}(x) & \cdots & \dfrac{\partial^2 f}{\partial x_1 \partial x_k}(x) \\[2ex] \vdots & \vdots & \ddots & \vdots \\[2ex] \dfrac{\partial f}{\partial x_k}(x) & \dfrac{\partial^2 f}{\partial x_k \partial x_1}(x) & \cdots & \dfrac{\partial^2 f}{\partial x_k^2}(x) \end{bmatrix}.$$

Theorem 8.9 *Let* $f: \mathcal{D} \to \mathbb{R}$ *be a* C^2 *function, where* $\mathcal{D} \subset \mathbb{R}^n$ *is open and convex. Then:*

1. *If* f *is quasi-concave on* $\mathcal{D}$, *we have* $(-1)^k |C_k(x)| \geq 0$ *for* $k = 1, \ldots, n$.
2. *If* $(-1)^k |C_k(x)| > 0$ *for all* $k \in \{1, \ldots, n\}$, *then* f *is quasi-concave on* $\mathcal{D}$.

Proof See Section 8.7. $\qquad\qquad\qquad\qquad\qquad\qquad\qquad\qquad\qquad\qquad\square$

There is one very important difference between Theorem 8.9 and the corresponding result for concave functions, Theorem 7.10. In Theorem 7.10, a *weak* inequality (viz., the negative semidefiniteness of $D^2 f$) was both necessary and sufficient to establish concavity. In the current result, the weak inequality is necessary for quasi-concavity, but the sufficient condition involves a strict inequality. The following example shows that the weak inequality is *not* sufficient to identify quasi-convexity, so Theorem 8.9 cannot be made into a perfect analog of Theorem 7.10.[2]

Example 8.10 Let $f: \mathbb{R}^2_+ \to \mathbb{R}$ be given by

$$f(x, y) = (x - 1)^2 (y - 1)^2, \quad (x, y) \in \mathbb{R}^2_+.$$

Then, we have $Df(x, y) = (2(x - 1)(y - 1)^2, 2(x - 1)^2(y - 1))$, and

$$D^2 f(x, y) = \begin{bmatrix} 2(y - 1)^2 & 4(x - 1)(y - 1) \\ 4(x - 1)(y - 1) & 2(x - 1)^2 \end{bmatrix}.$$

Therefore,

$$C_1(x, y) = \begin{bmatrix} 0 & 2(x - 1)(y - 1)^2 \\ 2(x - 1)(y - 1)^2 & 2(y - 1)^2 \end{bmatrix},$$

and

$$C_2(x, y) = \begin{bmatrix} 0 & 2(x - 1)(y - 1)^2 & 2(x - 1)^2(y - 1) \\ 2(x - 1)(y - 1)^2 & 2(y - 1)^2 & 4(x - 1)(y - 1) \\ 2(x - 1)^2(y - 1) & 4(x - 1)(y - 1) & 2(x - 1)^2 \end{bmatrix}.$$

---

[2] There is also another difference between the two results. In Theorem 7.10, the strict inequality (the negative definiteness of $D^2 f$) was shown to be sufficient for *strict* concavity. In Theorem 8.9, the strict inequality is claimed to be sufficient only for quasi-concavity and not for *strict* quasi-concavity. We leave it to the reader to check whether, or under what conditions, strict quasi-concavity results from the strict inequality.

A pair of simple calculations now yields

$$|C_1(x, y)| = -4(x - 1)^2(y - 1)^4 \le 0, \quad (x, y) \in \mathbb{R}^2_+$$
$$|C_2(x, y)| = 16(x - 1)^4(y - 1)^4 \ge 0, \quad (x, y) \in \mathbb{R}^2_+$$

with equality holding in either case if and only if $x = 1$ or $y = 1$. Thus, if weak inequalities were also sufficient to establish quasi-concavity, f would have to be quasi-concave. However, f is not quasi-concave: we have $f(0, 0) = f(2, 2) = 1$, but for $\lambda = \frac{1}{2}$,

$$f[\lambda(0, 0) + (1 - \lambda)(2, 2)] = f(1, 1) = 0 < 1 = \min\{f(0, 0), f(2, 2)\}.$$

Thus, the sufficient condition of Theorem 8.9 cannot be strengthened to allow for weak inequalities.   □

As with the second-derivative test provided by Theorem 7.10 for convexity, the test given in Theorem 8.9 is also of considerable practical value. The following example illustrates this point.

Example 8.11 Let $f: \mathbb{R}^2_{++} \to \mathbb{R}$ be defined by

$$f(x, y) = x^a y^b, \quad a, b > 0.$$

We have seen in Example 7.12 that this function is strictly concave on $\mathbb{R}^2_{++}$ if $a + b < 1$, that it is concave on $\mathbb{R}^2_{++}$ if $a + b = 1$, and that it is neither concave nor convex on $\mathbb{R}^2_{++}$ if $a + b > 1$. We will show using Theorem 8.9 that it is quasi-concave on $\mathbb{R}^2_{++}$ for all $a, b > 0$. Note that to show this directly from the definition of quasi-concavity would require us to prove that the following inequality holds for all distinct (x, y) and $(\hat{x}, \hat{y})$ in $\mathbb{R}^2_{++}$ and for all $\lambda \in (0, 1)$:

$$(\lambda x + (1 - \lambda)\hat{x})^a (\lambda y + (1 - \lambda)\hat{y})^b \ge \min\{x^a y^b, \hat{x}^a \hat{y}^b\}.$$

In contrast, if we appeal to Theorem 8.9, we only have to show that $|C_1(x, y)| < 0$ and $|C_2(x, y)| > 0$, where

$$C_1(x, y) = \begin{bmatrix} 0 & ax^{a-1}y^b \\ ax^{a-1}y^b & a(a-1)x^{a-2}y^b \end{bmatrix},$$

and

$$C_2(x, y) = \begin{bmatrix} 0 & ax^{a-1}y^b & bx^a y^{b-1} \\ ax^{a-1}y^b & a(a-1)x^{a-2}y^b & abx^{a-1}y^{b-1} \\ bx^a y^{b-1} & abx^{a-1}y^{b-1} & b(b-1)x^a y^{b-2} \end{bmatrix}.$$

A simple calculation shows that $|C_1(x, y)| = -a^2 x^{2(a-1)} y^{2b}$, which is strictly negative for all $(x, y) \in \mathbb{R}^2_{++}$, while

$$|C_2(x, y)| = x^{3a-2} y^{3b-2} (a^b + b^2 a),$$

which is strictly positive for all $(x, y) \in \mathbb{R}^2_{++}$. The quasi-concavity of f on $\mathbb{R}^2_{++}$ is established. $\qquad\Box$

8.4 Quasi-Convexity and Optimization

We have already seen that local maxima of quasi-concave functions need not, in general, also be global maxima. When the function involved is *strictly* quasi-concave, however, a sharp result is valid:

Theorem 8.12 *Suppose* $f: \mathcal{D} \to \mathbb{R}$ *be strictly quasi-concave where* $\mathcal{D} \subset \mathbb{R}^n$ *is convex. Then, any local maximum of* f *on* $\mathcal{D}$ *is also a global maximum of* f *on* $\mathcal{D}$. *Moreover, the set* $\arg\max\{f(x) \mid x \in \mathcal{D}\}$ *of maximizers of* f *on* $\mathcal{D}$ *is either empty or a singleton.*

Proof Suppose x is a local maximum of f on $\mathcal{D}$, so there exists $r > 0$ such that $f(x) \geq f(y)$ for all $y \in B(x, r) \cap D$. If x were not a global maximum of f on $\mathcal{D}$, there must be $z \in \mathcal{D}$ such that $f(z) > f(x)$. Let $y(\lambda) = \lambda x + (1 - \lambda)z$. Note that $y(\lambda) \in \mathcal{D}$ because $\mathcal{D}$ is convex. By the strict quasi-concavity of f, we have

$$f(y(\lambda)) > \min\{f(x), f(z)\} = f(x),$$

for any $\lambda \in (0, 1)$. But for $\lambda > 1 - r/d(x, z), d(x, y(\lambda)) < r$, so $y(\lambda) \in B(x, r) \cap D$, which contradicts the hypothesis that x is a local maximum, and establishes one part of the result.

To see the other part, let x and y both be maximizers of f on $\mathcal{D}$. Pick any $\lambda \in (0, 1)$ and let $z = \lambda x + (1 - \lambda)y$. Since $\mathcal{D}$ is convex, $z \in \mathcal{D}$. Since f is strictly quasi-concave, $f(z) = f(\lambda x + (1 - \lambda)y) > \min\{f(x)f(y)\} = f(x) = f(y)$, and this contradicts the hypothesis that x and y are maximizers. $\qquad\Box$

A similar result to Theorem 8.12 is true for strictly quasi-convex functions in minimization problems. It is left to the reader to provide details. The most significant part of Theorem 8.12 for optimization is that, as with strict concavity, strict quasi-concavity also implies *uniqueness* of the solution.

Perhaps the most important result concerning quasi-concave functions in optimization theory is the following. It shows that the Kuhn–Tucker first-order conditions are "almost" sufficient to identify the global optimum of an inequality-constrained maximization problem, if all the functions involved are quasi-concave:

Theorem 8.13 (The Theorem of Kuhn and Tucker under Quasi-Convexity) *Let f and h_i (i = 1, ..., k) be C^1 quasi-concave functions mapping $U \subset \mathbb{R}^n$ into $\mathbb{R}$, where U is open and convex. Define*

$$\mathcal{D} = \{x \in U \mid h_i(x) \geq 0, \ i = 1, \ldots, k\}.$$

Suppose there exist $x^* \in \mathcal{D}$ and $\lambda \in \mathbb{R}^k$ such that the Kuhn–Tucker first-order conditions are met:

$$[\textit{KT-1}] \quad Df(x^*) + \sum_{i=1}^{k} \lambda_i \, Dh_i(x^*) = 0.$$

$$[\textit{KT-2}] \quad \lambda_i \geq 0, \ \lambda_i h_i(x^*) = 0, \ i = 1, \ldots, k.$$

Then, x^* maximizes f over $\mathcal{D}$ provided at least one of the following conditions holds:

$$[\textit{QC-1}] \quad Df(x^*) \neq 0.$$

$$[\textit{QC-2}] \quad f \text{ is concave.}$$

Proof See Section 8.8. □

It is very important to note that Theorem 8.13 does *not* assert that the first-order conditions of the Kuhn–Tucker theorem are sufficient under quasi-concavity, *unless one of the conditions [QC-1] or [QC-2] holds*. Indeed, if [QC-1] and [QC-2] both fail, it is easy to construct examples where the Kuhn–Tucker first-order conditions do *not* identify a maximum point, even though all the other conditions of Theorem 8.13 are met. Consider the following:

Example 8.14 Let $f: \mathbb{R} \to \mathbb{R}$ and $h: \mathbb{R} \to \mathbb{R}$ be quasi-concave C^1 functions given by

$$f(x) = \begin{cases} x^3, & x < 0 \\ 0, & 0 \leq x \leq 1 \\ (x-1)^2, & x > 1 \end{cases}$$

and $h(x) = x$ for all $x \in \mathbb{R}$, respectively. Consider the problem of maximizing f over the inequality-constrained set $\mathcal{D} = \{x \in \mathbb{R} \mid h(x) \geq 0\}$. Note that f is not concave,[3] so condition [QC-2] does not hold in this problem.

We claim that for any point $x^* \in [0, 1]$, there is $\lambda^* \geq 0$ such that the pair (x^*, λ^*) meets the Kuhn–Tucker first-order conditions. At any such point, [QC-1] fails, since $f'(x^*) = 0$. Indeed, pick any point $x^* \in [0, 1]$ and set $\lambda^* = 0$. Then,

[3]In fact, we have established in Example 8.6 that f cannot even be a strictly increasing transformation of a concave function.

since $x^* \in [0, 1]$, we have $f'(x^*) = 0$. Since $\lambda^* = 0$, we also have $\lambda^* h'(x^*) = 0$. Therefore,

$$f'(x^*) + \lambda^* h'(x^*) = 0,$$

and [KT-1] holds. Moreover, it is clearly true that for any $x^* \in [0, 1]$, we have $h(x^*) \geq 0$ and $\lambda^* h(x^*) = 0$, so [KT-2] also holds. Thus, (x^*, λ^*) meets the Kuhn–Tucker first-order conditions.

However, it is evident that no $x^* \in [0, 1]$ can be a solution to the problem: since f is unbounded on the feasible set $\mathbb{R}_+$, a solution to the problem does not exist. □

It is also important to note that Theorem 8.13 only provides *sufficient* conditions that identify an optimum. It does not assert these conditions are *necessary*, and indeed, they are not unless the constraint qualification is met at x^*, or, as in Theorem 7.16, the functions h_i are all concave and Slater's condition holds.

8.5 Using Quasi-Convexity in Optimization Problems

Theorem 8.13 is of obvious value in solving optimization problems of the form

Maximize $f(x)$ subject to $x \in \mathcal{D} = \{z \in \mathbb{R}^n \mid h_i(z) \geq 0, \ i = 1, \ldots, l\}$,

where f and h_i are quasi-concave C^1 functions, $i = 1, \ldots, l$. A simple three-step procedure may be employed.

1. Set up the Lagrangean $L(x, \lambda) = f(x) + \sum_{i=1}^{l} \lambda_i h_i(x)$.
2. Calculate the set of critical points of L, i.e., the set of points (x, λ) at which the following conditions hold:

$$Df(x) + \sum_{i=1}^{k} \lambda_i Dh_i(x) = 0,$$

$$h_i(x) \geq 0, \ \lambda \geq 0, \ \lambda_1 h_i(x) = 0, \quad i = 1, \ldots, l.$$

   Of course, the set of critical points of L is the same as the set of points (x, λ) that satisfy $h(x) \geq 0$ as well as the first-order conditions [KT-1] and [KT-2].
3. Identify the critical points (x, λ) of L which also satisfy $Df(x) \neq 0$. At any such point (x, λ), condition [QC-1] of Theorem 8.13 is satisfied, so x must be a solution to the given maximization problem.

As an alternative to appealing to condition [QC-1] in step 3, it might be easier in some problems to use condition [QC-2] that f is concave. Indeed, it may be possible to use [QC-2] even if f is not itself concave, if f happens to at least be an increasing transformation of a concave function. In this case, the given problem can be transformed into an equivalent one with a concave objective function, and

[QC-2] can be used to obtain sufficiency of the first-order conditions in the trans-formed problem. Formally, we *begin* in this case by checking the following condition, that we call [QC-2']:

[QC-2'] f is a strictly increasing transform of a C^1 concave function $\hat{f}$.[4]

If [QC-2'] holds, the given optimization problem is equivalent to the following one in which the objective function is the concave function $\hat{f}$:

Maximize $\hat{f}(x)$ subject to $x \in \mathcal{D} = \{z \in \mathbb{R}^n \mid h_i(z) \geq 0, \ i = 1, \ldots, l\}$.

The concavity of $\hat{f}$ in this transformed problem implies that condition [QC-2] of Theorem 8.13 is met. If we now set up the Lagrangean

$$\hat{L}(x, \lambda) = \hat{f}(x) + \sum_{i=1}^{l} \lambda_i h_i(x),$$

it follows from Theorem 8.13 that every critical point of $\hat{L}$ will identify a solution to the transformed problem, and, therefore, also to the original problem.

Of course, if it turns out that [QC-2'] is inapplicable to the given problem, and there is also no critical point (x, λ) of the Lagrangean L at which $Df(x) \neq 0$, then it is not possible to appeal to Theorem 8.13. As we have seen, it is possible under these circumstances that a point may meet the Kuhn–Tucker first-order conditions, and still not be a solution to the problem.

8.6 A Proof of the First-Derivative Characterization of Quasi-Convexity

First, suppose f is quasi-concave on $\mathcal{D}$, and let $x, y \in \mathcal{D}$ be such that $f(y) \geq f(x)$. Let $t \in (0, 1)$. Since f is quasi-concave, we have

$$f(x + t(y - x)) = f((1 - t)x + ty) \geq \min\{f(x), f(y)\} = f(x).$$

Therefore, it is the case that for all $t \in (0, 1)$:

$$\frac{f(x + t(y - x)) - f(x)}{t} \geq 0.$$

As $t \to 0+$, the LHS of this expression converges to $Df(x)(y - x)$, so $Df(x)(y - x) \geq 0$, establishing one part of the result.

Now suppose that for all $x, y \in \mathcal{D}$ such that $f(y) \geq f(x)$, we have $Df(x)(y - x) \geq 0$. Pick any $x, y \in \mathcal{D}$, and suppose without loss of generality that $f(x) = \min\{f(x), f(y)\}$. We will show that for any $t \in [0, 1]$, we must also

---

[4]Note that this condition does not exclude the possibility that f is itself concave. For, if f is itself concave, we can simply let $\hat{f} = f$, and take φ to be the identity function $\varphi(x) = x$ for all x. Then φ is a strictly increasing function, and $\hat{f}$ is concave, and, of course, we now have $f = \varphi \circ \hat{f}$.

have $f[(1 - t)x + ty] \geq \min\{f(x), f(y)\}$, establishing the quasi-concavity of f. For notational simplicity, let $z(t) = (1 - t)x + ty$.

Define $g(t) = f[x + t(y - x)]$. Note that $g(0) = f(x) \leq f(y) = g(1)$; and that g is C^1 on $[0, 1]$ with $g'(t) = Df[x + t(y - x)](y - x)$. We will show that if $t^* \in (0, 1)$ is *any* point such that $f[z(t^*)] \leq f(x)$ (i.e., such that $g(t^*) \leq g(0)$), we must have $g'(t^*) = 0$. This evidently precludes the possibility of having any point $\hat{t} \in (0, 1)$ such that $g(\hat{t}) < g(0)$, and the desired result is established.

So suppose that $t^* \in (0, 1)$ and we have $f(x) \geq f[z(t^*)]$. Then, by hypothesis, we must also have $Df[z(t^*)](x - z(t^*)) = -t^* Df[z(t^*)](y - x) \geq 0$. Since $t > 0$, this implies $g'(t^*) \leq 0$. On the other hand, since it is also true that $f(y) \geq f(x)$, we have $f(y) \geq f[z(t^*)]$, so we must also have $Df[z(t^*)](y - z(t^*)) = (1 - t^*)Df[z(t^*)](y - x) \geq 0$. Since $t^* < 1$, this implies in turn that $g'(t^*) \geq 0$. It follows that $g'(t^*) = 0$. $\qquad\square$

8.7 A Proof of the Second-Derivative Characterization of Quasi-Convexity

We prove Part 1 of the theorem first. Suppose f is a quasi-concave and C^2 function on the open and convex set $\mathcal{D} \subset \mathbb{R}^n$. Pick any $x \in \mathcal{D}$. If $Df(x) = 0$, then we have $|C_k(x)| = 0$ for each k, since the first row of this matrix is null. This evidently implies $(-1)^k |C_k(x)| \geq 0$ for all k, so Part 1 of the theorem is true in this case.

Now suppose $Df(x) \neq 0$. Define g by $g(y) = Df(x)(x - y)$ for $y \in \mathbb{R}^n$, and consider the problem of maximizing f over the constraint set

$$A[x] = \{y \in \mathbb{R}^n \mid g(y) \geq 0\}.$$

Since the constraint function is linear, $A[x]$ is a convex set. Since the objective function f is quasi-concave by hypothesis, Theorem 8.13 states that any point (y, λ) meeting the Kuhn–Tucker first-order conditions identifies a solution to the problem, provided $Df(y) \neq 0$. We will show that for $\lambda = 1$, the pair (x, λ) meets the Kuhn–Tucker first-order conditions. Since we are assuming that $Df(x) \neq 0$, this means x is a global maximum of f on $A[x]$. Indeed, since $Dg(y) = -Df(x)$ at each y, we have at $(y, \lambda) = (x, 1)$,

$$Df(y) + \lambda Dg(y) = Df(x) + (-Df(x)) = 0.$$

Since $\lambda = 1$, it also satisfies $\lambda \geq 0$. Finally, at $y = x$, we have $g(y) = 0$, so $\lambda g(y) = 0$. Thus, x is a global maximum of f on $A[x]$.

Now define the subset $A'[x]$ of $A[x]$ by

$$A'[x] = \{y \in \mathbb{R}^n \mid g(y) = 0\}.$$

Since $x \in A'[x]$, and x maximizes f over all of $A[x]$, it also maximizes f over $A'[x]$. Since $Dg(x) = Df(x) \neq 0$, we must have $\rho(Dg(x)) = 1$. Since the constraint qualification is met, x must meet the second-order *necessary* conditions provided in Theorem 5.4, that is, it must be the case that the quadratic form $D^2 f(x) + \lambda D^2 g(x)$ is negative semidefinite on the set $\{z \mid Dg(x)z = 0\}$. By Theorem 5.5, a necessary condition for this negative semidefiniteness to obtain is that the determinants of the submatrices M_k derived from the following matrix by retaining only the first $(k+1)$ rows and columns should have the same sign as $(-1)^k$, $k = 1, \ldots, n$:

$$M = \begin{bmatrix} 0 & Dg(x) \\ Dg(x)' & D^2 f(x) + \lambda D^2 g(x) \end{bmatrix}.$$

Since $D^2 g(x) = 0$, and $Dg(x) = -Df(x)$, the matrix M_k is precisely $C_k(x)$. Thus, we must have $(-1)^k |C_k(x)| \geq 0$ for $k = 2, \ldots, n$, and this establishes the first part of the theorem.

The second part of the theorem will be proved using a three-step procedure. Fix an arbitrary point x in $\mathcal{D}$, and, as earlier, let $g(y) = Df(x)(x - y)$.

- In Step 1, we will show that x is itself a strict local maximum of f on the constraint set

$$A'[x] = \{y \in \mathcal{D} \mid g(y) = 0\}.$$

- In Step 2, we will show that x is actually a global maximum of f on the constraint set

$$A[x] = \{y \in \mathcal{D} \mid g(y) \geq 0\}.$$

- Finally, we will show in Step 3 that if y is any other point in $\mathcal{D}$, and $\lambda \in (0, 1)$, then $f[\lambda x + (1 - \lambda)y] \geq \min\{f(x), f(y)\}$. Since x was chosen arbitrarily, the proof of the quasi-concavity of f is complete.

So fix $x \in \mathcal{D}$. We will show that x is a strict local maximum of f on $A'[x]$ by showing (a) that the constraint qualification is met at x, (b) that there is λ such that (x, λ) meets the first-order conditions of the Theorem of Lagrange, and (c) that (x, λ) also meets the second-order conditions of Theorems 5.4 and 5.5 for a strict local maximum.

First, note that since $(-1)^k |C_k(x)| > 0$ at each k, we cannot have $Df(x) = 0$. Since $Dg(y) = -Df(x)$ at any $y \in \mathbb{R}^n$, and $Df(x) \neq 0$, we must have $\rho(Dg(y)) = 1$ at all y, and, in particular, $\rho(Dg(x)) = 1$. This establishes (a). Moreover, for $\lambda = 1$, the pair (x, λ) is a critical point of the Lagrangean $L(y) = f(y) + \lambda g(y)$, since $DL(x) = Df(x) + \lambda Dg(x) = Df(x) - Df(x) = 0$. This establishes (b). Finally, note that since g is linear, we have $D^2 L(x) = D^2 f(x)$. From the definition of g, it now follows that the condition

$$(-1)^k |C_k(x)| > 0, \quad k = 1, \ldots, n,$$

is exactly the same as the second-order condition required under Theorems 5.4 and 5.5. This establishes (c), proving that x is a strict local maximum of f on $A'[x]$, and completing Step 1.

We turn to Step 2. Pick any $y \in A[x]$. We will show that $f(x) \geq f(y)$. Since y was chosen arbitrarily in $A[x]$, Step 2 will be complete. Let $x(t) = tx + (1-t)y$, and define the function F on $[0, 1]$ by

$$F(t) = f(x(t)).$$

Note that $F(0) = f(y)$, $F(1) = f(x)$, and that F is C^1 on $[0, 1]$ with $F'(t) = Df(x(t))(x-y)$. Let A denote the set of minimizers of F on $[0,1]$, and let $t^* = \inf A$. We claim that $t^* = 0$.

Suppose $t^* \neq 0$. We will show the existence of a contradiction. If $t^* \in (0, 1)$, then we must, of course, have $F'(t^*) = 0$ since t^* is an interior minimum of F on $[0, 1]$; and this implies we must have

$$Df(x(t^*))(x - y) = 0.$$

If $t^* = 1$, then we must have $F'(t^*) \leq 0$, or t^* could not be a minimum of F. Therefore, we must have $Df(x(t^*))(x - y) \leq 0$. However, at $t^* = 1$ we also have $x(t^*) = x$, and since y is in $A[x]$, we must have $g(y) = Df(x)(x - y) \geq 0$. Combining these inequalities, we see that in this case also, we must have

$$Df(x(t^*))(x - y) = 0.$$

Now pick any $\eta \in (0, t^*)$. Observe that $x(t^* - \eta) - x(t^*) = -\eta(x - y)$, which implies that

$$Df(x(t^*))[x(t^* - h) - x(t^*)] = 0.$$

By Step 1, $Df(x(t^*))[x(t^* - h) - x(t^*)] = 0$ implies that $x(t^*)$ is a strict local *maximum* of f on the constraint set

$$A'[x(t^*)] = \{y \in \mathbb{R}^n \mid Df(x(t^*))[x(t^*) - y] = 0\}.$$

Since $x(t^* - \eta) \in A'[x(t^*)]$ for $\eta \in (0, t^*)$, this means that for $\eta > 0$ but sufficiently small, we must have $f(x(t^*)) > f(x(t^* - \eta))$. This contradicts the definition of $x(t^*)$ as the smallest minimizer of F on $[0,1]$, and shows that $t^* \in (0, 1]$ is impossible. Therefore, we must have $t^* = 0$. Step 2 is now complete, since $t^* = 0$ implies $F(1) \geq F(0)$, which is the same as $f(x) \geq f(y)$.

This leaves Step 3. Pick any $y \in \mathcal{D}$ and any $\lambda \in (0, 1)$, and let $z = \lambda x + (1 - \lambda)y$. Observe that

$$Df(z)z = \lambda Df(z)x + (1 - \lambda)Df(z)y \geq \min\{Df(z)x, Df(z)y\}.$$

Suppose first that $Df(z)x \leq Df(z)y$. Then, $Df(z)z \geq Df(z)x$ implies $Df(z)(z - x) \geq 0$. Therefore, $x \in A[z]$, where, of course,

$$A[z] = \{w \in \mathbb{R}^n \mid Df(z)(z - w) \geq 0\},$$

By Step 2, z maximizes f over $A[z]$, so we must have $f(z) \geq f(x)$.

Now suppose $Df(z)y \leq Df(z)x$. Then, we must have $Df(z)(z - y) \geq 0$, so $y \in A[z]$. Since z maximizes f over $A[z]$, in this case we must have $f(z) \geq f(y)$.

Thus, we must have either $f(z) \geq f(x)$ or $f(z) \geq f(y)$. This implies that $f(z) \geq \min\{f(x), f(y)\}$, so the proof is complete.   □

8.8 A Proof of the Theorem of Kuhn and Tucker under Quasi-Convexity

We begin the proof of Theorem 8.13 by noting the simple fact that when h_i is quasi-concave, the set $\mathcal{D}_i = \{x \mid h_i(x) \geq 0\}$ is a convex set, and so then is the feasible set $\mathcal{D} = \cap_{i=1}^k \mathcal{D}_i$. We now claim that

Lemma 8.15 *Under the hypotheses of the theorem, it is the case that for any $y \in \mathcal{D}$, we have $Df(x^*)(y - x^*) \leq 0$.*

Proof of Lemma 8.15 By hypothesis, we have

$$Df(x^*)(y - x^*) = -\sum_{i=1}^k \lambda_i Dh_i(x^*)(y - x^*).$$

The lemma will be established if we can show that the sum on the right-hand side is nonpositive. We will prove that this is the case, by proving that for each $i \in \{1, \ldots, k\}$, it is the case that $\lambda_i Dh_i(x^*)(y - x^*) \geq 0$.

So pick any $y \in \mathcal{D}$, and any $i \in \{1, \ldots, k\}$. By definition, we must have $h_i(x^*) \geq 0$. Suppose first that $h_i(x^*) > 0$. Then, we must have $\lambda_i = 0$ by the Kuhn–Tucker first-order conditions, and it follows that $\lambda_i Dh_i(x^*)(y - x^*) = 0$. Next suppose $h_i(x^*) = 0$. Since $\mathcal{D}$ is convex, $(x^* + t(y - x^*)) = ((1 - t)x^* + ty) \in \mathcal{D}$ for all $t \in (0, 1)$, and therefore, we have $h_i(x^* + t(y - x^*)) \geq 0$. It follows that for $t \in (0, 1)$, we also have

$$0 \leq \frac{h_i(x^* + t(y - x^*))}{t} = \frac{h_i(x^* + t(y - x^*)) - h_i(x^*)}{t},$$

and taking limits as $t \to 0+$ establishes that $Dh_i(x^*)(y - x^*) \geq 0$. Since $\lambda_i \geq 0$, we finally obtain $\lambda_i Dh_i(x^*)(y - x^*) \geq 0$ in this case also. Thus, for any $i \in \{1, \ldots, k\}$, we must have $\lambda_i Dh_i(x^*)(y - x^*) \geq 0$, and the lemma is proved.   □

We return now to the proof of Theorem 8.13. We will show that the theorem is true under each of the two identified conditions, [QC-1] $Df(x^*) \neq 0$, and [QC-2] f is concave.

Case 1: [QC-1] $Df(x^*) \neq 0$

Since $Df(x^*) \neq 0$, there is $w \in \mathbb{R}^n$ such that $Df(x^*)w < 0$. Let $z = x^* + w$. Note that we then have $Df(x^*)(z - x^*) < 0$.

Now pick any $y \in \mathcal{D}$. For $t \in (0, 1)$, let

$$y(t) = (1 - t)y + tz \quad \text{and} \quad x(t) = (1 - t)x^* + tz.$$

Fix any $t \in (0, 1)$. Then we have

$$Df(x^*)(x(t) - x^*) = t Df(x^*)(z - x^*) < 0,$$
$$Df(x^*)(y(t) - x(t)) = (1 - t)Df(x^*)(y - x^*) \leq 0,$$

where the inequality in the first expression follows from the definition of z, and that in the second inequality obtains from Lemma 8.15. When these inequalities are summed, we have

$$Df(x^*)(y(t) - x^*) < 0,$$

implying, by Theorem 8.8, that $f(y(t)) < f(x^*)$. Since this holds for any $t \in (0, 1)$, taking limits as $t \to 1$, we have $f(y) \leq f(x^*)$. Since $y \in \mathcal{D}$ was chosen arbitrarily, this states precisely that x^* is a global maximum of f on $\mathcal{D}$.

Case 2: [QC-2] f is concave

By repeating the arguments used in the proof of the Theorem of Kuhn and Tucker under Convexity (Theorem 7.16), it is readily established that $Df(x^*)y \leq 0$ for all y pointing into $\mathcal{D}$ at x^*. Since f is concave and $\mathcal{D}$ is convex, the optimality of x^* is now a consequence of Theorem 7.20. $\qquad\square$

8.9 Exercises

1. Let f and g be real-valued functions on $\mathbb{R}$. Define the function $h: \mathbb{R}^2 \to \mathbb{R}$ by

$$h(x, y) = f(x) + g(y).$$

   Show that if f and g are both strictly concave functions on $\mathbb{R}$, then h is a strictly concave function on $\mathbb{R}^2$. Give an example to show that if f and g are both strictly quasi-concave functions on $\mathbb{R}$, then h need *not* be a strictly quasi-concave function on $\mathbb{R}^2$.

2. Give an example of a strictly quasi-concave function $f: \mathbb{R}^2_+ \to \mathbb{R}$ which is also strictly quasi-convex, or show that no such example is possible.

3. We have seen in this chapter that if $f: \mathbb{R} \to \mathbb{R}$ is a nondecreasing function, then f is both quasi-concave and quasi-convex on $\mathbb{R}$. Is this true if f is instead non-*increasing*?

4. Let $f_1, \ldots f_l$ be functions mapping $\mathcal{D} \subset \mathbb{R}^n$ into $\mathbb{R}$, where $\mathcal{D}$ is convex. Let $a_1, \ldots, a_l$ be nonnegative numbers. Show that if for each $i \in \{1, \ldots, l\}$, f_i is concave, then so is f, where f is defined by

$$f(x) = \sum_{i=1}^{l} a_i f_i(x), \qquad x \in \mathcal{D}.$$

   Give an example to show that if each f_i is only quasi-concave, then f need not be quasi-concave.

5. Let $f: \mathcal{D} \to \mathbb{R}$, where $\mathcal{D} \subset \mathbb{R}^n$ is convex. Suppose f is a strictly quasi-concave function. If f is also a concave function, is it necessarily *strictly* concave? Why or why not?

6. Let $g: \mathbb{R}^n \to \mathbb{R}$ be quasi-concave, and let $f: \mathbb{R} \to \mathbb{R}$ be a nondecreasing function. Show that $h(x) = f[g(x)]$ is also quasi-concave.

7. Show that the "Cobb–Douglas" utility function $u: \mathbb{R}^2_+ \to \mathbb{R}$ defined by

$$u(x_1, x_2) = x_1^{\alpha} x_2^{\beta}, \quad \alpha, \beta > 0,$$

   (a) is concave if $\alpha + \beta \leq 1$.
   (b) is quasi-concave, but not concave, if $\alpha + \beta > 1$.

   Show also that $h(x_1, x_2) = \log(u(x_1, x_2))$ is concave for any value of $\alpha > 0$ and $\beta > 0$.

8. Show that the function $f: \mathcal{D} \subset \mathbb{R}^2 \to \mathbb{R}$ defined by $f(x, y) = xy$ is quasi-concave if $\mathcal{D} = \mathbb{R}^2_+$, but not if $\mathcal{D} = \mathbb{R}^2$.

9. Give an example of a function $u: \mathbb{R}^2_+ \to \mathbb{R}$ such that u is strictly increasing and strictly quasi-concave on $\mathbb{R}^2_+$. [Note: Strictly increasing means that if $x \geq x'$ and $x \neq x'$ then $u(x) > u(x')$. This rules out Cobb–Douglas type functions of the form $u(x, y) = x^a y^b$ for $a, b > 0$: since $u(0, y) = u(x, 0) = 0$ for all (x, y), so u cannot be strictly increasing.]

10. Describe a continuous quasi-concave function $u: \mathbb{R}^2_+ \to \mathbb{R}$ such that for all $c \in \mathbb{R}$, the *lower*-contour set $L_u(c) = \{x \in \mathbb{R}^2_+ \mid u(x) \leq c\}$ is a convex set. Would such an example be possible if u were required to be *strictly* quasi-concave? Why or why not?

11. A consumer gets utility not only out of the two goods that he consumes, but also from the income he has left over after consumption. Suppose the consumer's utility function is given by $u(c_1, c_2, m)$ where c_i denotes the quantity consumed

of commodity i, and $m \geq 0$ is the left-over income. Suppose further that u is strictly increasing in each of the three arguments. Assuming that the consumer has an income of $I > 0$, that the price of commodity i is $p_i > 0$, and that all the usual nonnegativity constraints hold, answer the following questions:

(a) Set up the consumer's utility maximization problem, and describe the Kuhn–Tucker first-order conditions.

(b) Explain under what further assumptions, if any, these conditions are also sufficient for a maximum.

9

Parametric Continuity: The Maximum Theorem

The notion of a *parametric family of optimization problems* was defined in Section 2.2 of Chapter 2. To recall the basic notation, such a family is defined by a *parameter space* $\Theta \subset \mathbb{R}^l$, and the specification for each $\theta \in \Theta$ of two objects: a constraint set $\mathcal{D}(\theta) \subset \mathbb{R}^n$ and an objective function $f(\cdot, \theta)$ defined on $\mathcal{D}(\theta)$. We will assume throughout this chapter that we are dealing with *maximization* problems; that is, that the problem in question is to solve at each $\theta \in \Theta$,

$$\text{Maximize } f(x) \text{ subject to } x \in \mathcal{D}(\theta).$$

Deriving the corresponding results for *minimization* problems is a routine exercise and is left to the reader. As in Chapter 2, we will denote by $f^*(\theta)$ the *maximized value function* which describes the supremum of attainable rewards under the parameter configuration θ; and by $\mathcal{D}^*(\theta)$ the set of maximizers in the problem at θ. That is,

$$f^*(\theta) = \sup\{f(x, \theta) \mid x \in D(\theta)\}$$
$$\mathcal{D}^*(\theta) = \arg\max\{f(x, \theta) \mid x \in D(\theta)\}.$$

We will sometimes refer to the pair $(f^*, \mathcal{D}^*)$ as the *solutions* of the given family of parametric optimization problems.

In this chapter, we examine the issue of *parametric continuity*: under what conditions do $f^*(\cdot)$ and $\mathcal{D}^*(\cdot)$ vary *continuously* with the underlying parameters θ? At an intuitive level, it is apparent that for continuity in the solutions to obtain, some degree of continuity must be present in the primitives $f(\cdot, \cdot)$ and $\mathcal{D}(\cdot)$ of the problem. Being precise about this requires, first of all, a notion of continuity for a map such as $\mathcal{D}(\cdot)$ which takes *points* $\theta \in \Theta$ into *sets* $\mathcal{D}(\theta) \subset \mathbb{R}^n$. Our analysis in this chapter begins in Section 9.1 with the study of such point-to-set maps, which are called *correspondences*.[1]

---

[1] Note also that the set of solutions $\mathcal{D}^*(\theta)$ will not, in general, be single-valued. Thus, the question of when this set varies continuously with θ also requires a notion of continuity for point-to-set maps.

Section 9.2 is the centerpiece of this chapter. In subsection 9.2.1, we prove one of the major results of optimization theory, the *Maximum Theorem*. Roughly speaking, the Maximum Theorem states that continuity in the primitives is inherited by the solutions, but not in its entirety; that is, some degree of continuity in the problem is inevitably lost in the process of optimization. In subsection 9.2.2, we then examine the effect of placing *convexity* restrictions on the primitives, in addition to the continuity conditions required by the Maximum Theorem. We label the result derived here, the *Maximum Theorem under Convexity*. We show here that, analogous to the continuity results of the Maximum Theorem, the convexity structure of the primitives is also inherited by the solutions, but, again, not in its entirety.

Finally, Sections 9.3 and 9.4 present two detailed worked-out examples, designed to illustrate the use of the material of Section 9.2.

9.1 Correspondences

Let Θ and S be subsets of $\mathbb{R}^l$ and $\mathbb{R}^n$, respectively. A *correspondence* Φ from Θ to S is a map that associates with each element $\theta \in \Theta$ a (nonempty) subset $\Phi(\theta) \subset S$. To distinguish a correspondence notationally from a function, we will denote a correspondence Φ from Θ to S by $\Phi: \Theta \to P(S)$, where $P(S)$ denotes the *power set* of S, i.e., the set of all nonempty subsets of S.

In subsection 9.1.1 below, we explore some definitions of continuity for a correspondence, based on "natural" generalizations of the corresponding definition for functions. Some additional structures on correspondences are then provided in subsection 9.1.2. In subsection 9.1.3, the various definitions are related to each other and characterized. Finally, the definitions for correspondences and functions are compared in subsection 9.1.4.

9.1.1 Upper- and Lower-Semicontinuous Correspondences

Any function f from Θ to S may also be viewed as a single-valued correspondence from Θ to S. Thus, an intuitively appealing consideration to keep in mind in defining a notion of continuity for correspondences is that the definition be consistent with the definition of continuity for functions; that is, we would like the two definitions to coincide when the correspondence in question is single-valued. Recall that a function $f: \Theta \to S$ is continuous at a point $\theta \in \Theta$ if and only if for all open sets V such that $f(\theta) \in V$, there is an open set U containing θ such that for all $\theta' \in \Theta \cap U$, we have $f(\theta') \in V$. In extending this definition to a notion of continuity for correspondences $\Phi: \Theta \to P(S)$, a problem arises: there are at least two ways to replace the condition that

$$f(\cdot) \in V$$

with a condition appropriate for correspondences: namely, one can require either that

$$\Phi(\cdot) \subset V,$$

or that

$$\Phi(\cdot) \cap V \neq \emptyset.$$

These two conditions coincide when Φ is single-valued everywhere (for, in this case, $\Phi(\cdot) \subset V$ if and only if $\Phi(\cdot) \cap V \neq \emptyset$), but this is evidently not true if Φ is not single-valued. This leads us to two different notions of continuity for correspondences.

First, a correspondence $\Phi \colon \Theta \to P(S)$ is said to be *upper-semicontinuous* or *usc* at a point $\theta \in \Theta$ if for all open sets V such that $\Phi(\theta) \subset V$, there exists an open set U containing θ, such that $\theta' \in U \cap \Theta$ implies $\Phi(\theta') \subset V$. We say that Φ is *usc on* Θ if Φ is usc at each $\theta \in \Theta$.

Second, the correspondence Φ is said to be *lower-semicontinuous* or *lsc* at $\theta \in \Theta$ if for all open sets V such that $V \cap \Phi(\theta) \neq \emptyset$, there exists an open set U containing θ such that $\theta' \in U \cap \Theta$ implies $V \cap \Phi(\theta') \neq \emptyset$. The correspondence Φ is said to be *lsc on* Θ if it is lsc at each $\theta \in \Theta$.

Combining these definitions, the correspondence $\Phi \colon \Theta \to P(S)$ is said to be *continuous* at $\theta \in \Theta$ if Φ is *both* usc and lsc at θ. The correspondence Φ is *continuous on* Θ if Φ is continuous at each $\theta \in \Theta$.

The following examples illustrate these definitions. The first presents an example of a correspondence that is usc but not lsc, the second describes one that is lsc but not usc, and the third one that is both usc and lsc, and, therefore, continuous.

Example 9.1   Let $\Theta = S = [0, 2]$. Define $\Phi \colon \Theta \to P(S)$ by

$$\Phi(\theta) = \begin{cases} \{1\}, & 0 \leq \theta < 1 \\ S, & 1 \leq \theta \leq 2. \end{cases}$$

This correspondence is graphed in Figure 9.1. It is not very difficult to see that Φ is both usc and lsc at all $\theta \neq 1$. For, suppose $\theta < 1$. Let $\epsilon = (1 - \theta)/2$. Let U be the open interval $(\theta - \epsilon, \theta + \epsilon)$. Then, for all $\theta' \in U \cap \Theta$, we have $\Phi(\theta') = \Phi(\theta)$. Therefore, if V is any open set such that $\Phi(\theta) \subset V$, we also have $\Phi(\theta') \subset V$ for all $\theta' \in U \cap \Theta$; while if V is any open set such that $V \cap \Phi(\theta) \neq \emptyset$, we also have $V \cap \Phi(\theta') \neq \emptyset$ for all $\theta' \in U \cap \Theta$. Therefore, Φ is both usc and lsc at all $\theta < 1$. A similar argument establishes that it is both usc and lsc at all $\theta > 1$.

At $\theta = 1$, if V is any open set containing $\Phi(1) = [0, 2]$, then V contains $\Phi(\theta')$ for all $\theta' \in \Theta$, so Φ is clearly usc at $\theta = 1$. However, Φ is not lsc at $\theta = 1$. To see this, consider the open interval $V = (\frac{3}{2}, \frac{5}{2})$. Clearly, V has a nonempty intersection with $\Phi(1)$, but an empty intersection with $\Phi(\theta)$ for all $\theta < 1$. Since any open set

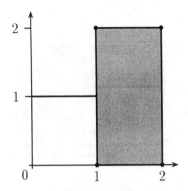

Fig. 9.1. A Correspondence That Is Usc, But Not Lsc

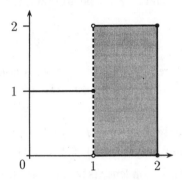

Fig. 9.2. A Correspondence That Is Lsc, But Not Usc

U containing $\theta = 1$ must also contain at least one point $\theta' < 1$, it follows that for this choice of V, there is no open set U containing $\theta = 1$ which is also such that $\Phi(\theta') \cap V \neq \emptyset$ for all $\theta' \in U \cap \Theta$. Therefore, Φ is not lsc at $\theta = 1$. $\qquad \square$

Example 9.2 Let $\Theta = S = [0, 2]$. Define $\Phi: \Theta \to P(S)$ by

$$\Phi(\theta) = \begin{cases} \{1\}, & 0 \leq \theta \leq 1 \\ T, & 1 < \theta \leq 2. \end{cases}$$

A graphical illustration of Φ is provided in Figure 9.2. The same argument as in the earlier example establishes that Φ is both usc and lsc at all $\theta \neq 1$. At $\theta = 1$, $\Phi(\theta)$ can have a nonempty intersection with an open set V if and only if $1 \in V$. Since we also have $1 \in \Phi(\theta')$ for all $\theta' \in \Theta$, it follows that Φ is lsc at 1.

However, Φ is not usc at $\theta = 1$: the open interval $V = (\frac{2}{3}, \frac{4}{3})$ contains $\Phi(1)$, but fails to contain $\Phi(\theta')$ for any $\theta' > 1$. $\qquad \square$

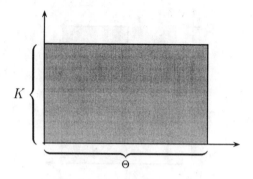

Fig. 9.3. A Continuous Correspondence

Example 9.3 Let $\Theta \subset \mathbb{R}^l$ and $S \subset \mathbb{R}^n$ be arbitrary, and let K be any subset of S. Define $\Phi: \Theta \to P(S)$ by

$$\Phi(\theta) = K, \quad \theta \in \Theta.$$

Figure 9.3 presents this correspondence in a graph. A correspondence such as Φ is called a "constant-valued" or simply a "constant" correspondence. Pick any open set V, and any $\theta \in \Theta$. Then,

- $\Phi(\theta) \subset V$ if and only if $\Phi(\theta') \subset V$ for all $\theta' \in \Theta$, and
- $\Phi(\theta) \cap V \neq \emptyset$ if and only if $\Phi(\theta') \neq \emptyset$ for all $\theta' \in \Theta$.

It follows that a constant correspondence is both usc and lsc at all points in its domain.

$\square$

9.1.2 Additional Definitions

In this subsection, we define some additional concepts pertaining to correspondences. These are extremely useful in applications, but are also of help in understanding and characterizing the definitions of semicontinuity given above.

So let $\Theta \subset \mathbb{R}^n$ and $S \subset \mathbb{R}^l$. A correspondence $\Phi: \Theta \to P(S)$ is said to be

1. *closed-valued* at $\theta \in \Theta$ if $\Phi(\theta)$ is a closed set;
2. *compact-valued* at $\theta \in \Theta$ if $\Phi(\theta)$ is a compact set; and
3. *convex-valued* at $\theta \in \Theta$ if $\Phi(\theta)$ is a convex set.

If a correspondence Φ is closed-valued (resp. compact-valued, convex-valued) at all $\theta \in \Theta$, then we will simply say that Φ is a closed-valued (resp. compact-valued, convex-valued) correspondence.

The *graph* of a correspondence $\Phi: \Theta \to P(S)$, denoted $\mathrm{Gr}(\Phi)$, is defined as

$$\mathrm{Gr}(\Phi) = \{(\theta, s) \in \Theta \times S \mid s \in \Phi(\theta)\}.$$

Note that $\mathrm{Gr}(\Phi)$ is a subset of $\mathbb{R}^n \times \mathbb{R}^l$, since $\Theta \subset \mathbb{R}^n$ and $S \subset \mathbb{R}^l$.

The correspondence Φ is said to be a *closed correspondence* or a *closed-graph correspondence* if Gr(Φ) is a closed subset of $\mathbb{R}^n \times \mathbb{R}^l$, that is, if it is the case that for all sequences $\{\theta_m\}$ in Θ such that $\theta_m \to \theta \in \Theta$,

$$s_m \in \Phi(\theta_m), \ s_m \to s \text{ implies } s \in \Phi(\theta).$$

Similarly, Φ is said to have a *convex graph* if Gr(Φ) is a convex subset of $\mathbb{R}^n \times \mathbb{R}^l$, i.e., if for any θ and θ' in Θ, and any $s \in \Phi(\theta)$ and $s' \in \Phi(\theta')$, it is the case that

$$\lambda s + (1 - \lambda)s' \in \Phi[\lambda\theta + (1 - \lambda)\theta'], \quad \lambda \in (0, 1).$$

Note that a closed-graph correspondence is necessarily closed-valued, but the converse is not true. Similarly, every correspondence with a convex graph is also convex-valued, but the converse is again false. Here is an example illustrating both points:

Example 9.4 Let $\Theta = T = [0, 1]$, and define Φ by

$$\Phi(\theta) = \begin{cases} \{\theta\}, & 0 \le \theta < 1 \\ \{0\}, & \theta = 1. \end{cases}$$

Clearly, $\Phi(\theta)$ is compact and convex for each $\theta \in \Theta$, so Φ is both convex-valued and compact-valued. It does not have a closed graph since the sequence $\{\theta_m, s_m\}$ defined by $\theta_m = s_m = 1 - \frac{1}{m}$ is in the graph of Φ, but this sequence converges to $(1, 1)$, which is not in the graph of Φ. Nor does Φ have a convex graph since $(\theta, s) = (0, 0)$ and $(\theta', s') = (1, 0)$ are both in the graph of Φ, but the convex combination $(\frac{1}{2}, 0) = \frac{1}{2}(\theta, s) + \frac{1}{2}(\theta', s')$ is not in the graph of Φ. $\square$

9.1.3 A Characterization of Semicontinuous Correspondences

We present in this subsection a number of results that characterize semicontinuous correspondences. The discussion here is based on the excellent summary of Hildenbrand (1974).

Some preliminary definitions will help simplify the exposition. Given a set $X \subset \mathbb{R}^k$ and a subset A of X, we will say that A *is open in* X if there exists an open set U in $\mathbb{R}^k$ such that $A = X \cap U$. We will also say that the subset B of X is *closed in* X if the set $\{x \in X \mid x \notin B\}$ is open in X. (The set $\{x \in X \mid x \notin B\}$ is called the *complement of B in X*. Abusing notation, we will denote this set by B^c.) Thus, for instance, the set $[0, a)$ is open in the closed unit interval $[0, 1]$ for any $a \in [0, 1)$, while the set $(0, 1)$ is closed in itself.

Let a correspondence $\Phi : \Theta \to P(S)$ be given, where $\Theta \subset \mathbb{R}^n$ and $S \subset \mathbb{R}^l$. Let W be any set in $\mathbb{R}^l$. Define the *upper inverse* of W under Φ, denoted $\Phi_+^{-1}(W)$, by

$$\Phi_+^{-1}(W) = \{\theta \in \Theta \mid \Phi(\theta) \subset W\},$$

and the *lower inverse* of W under Φ, denoted simply $\Phi^{-1}(W)$, by

$$\Phi^{-1}(W) = \{\theta \in \Theta \mid \Phi(\theta) \cap W \neq \emptyset\}.$$

Observe that the definitions of lower- and upper-inverses coincide with each other, as well as with the definition of the inverse of a function, when the correspondence is single-valued.

Proposition 9.5 *The following conditions are equivalent:*

1. Φ *is usc on* Θ.
2. $\Phi_+^{-1}(G)$ *is open in* Θ *for every* G *that is open in* S.
3. $\Phi^{-1}(F)$ *is closed in* Θ *for every* F *closed in* S.

Proof We prove the following series of implications:

$$1 \Rightarrow 2 \Rightarrow 3 \Rightarrow 2 \Rightarrow 1.$$

So suppose first that Condition 1 holds. If Condition 2 fails, there is an open set G in S such that the set $\Phi_+^{-1}(G)$ is not open in Θ. Therefore, there is $\theta \in \Phi_+^{-1}(G)$ such that for each $\epsilon > 0$, there is $\theta'(\epsilon) \in B(s, \epsilon) \cap \Theta$ such that $\Phi(\theta'(\epsilon))$ is not contained in G. But then Φ is not usc at θ, so Condition 1 also fails.

Next we show that Condition 2 holds if and only if Condition 3 holds. Given any two sets E and F, define $E - F$ to be the set $E \cap F^c$, that is $E - F$ is the set of elements of E that are *not* in F. Now, for all $A \subset T$,

$$\begin{aligned}
\Phi_+^{-1}(T - A) &= \{\theta \in \Theta \mid \Phi(\theta) \subset T - A\} \\
&= \{\theta \in \Theta \mid \Phi(\theta) \cap A = \emptyset\} \\
&= \Theta - \{\theta \in \Theta \mid \Phi(\theta) \cap A \neq \emptyset\} \\
&= \Theta - \Phi^{-1}(A).
\end{aligned}$$

The desired result obtains since a set H is open in Θ (resp. S) if and only if $\Theta - H$ is closed in Θ (resp. $S - H$ is closed in S).

It remains to be shown that Condition 2 implies Condition 1. Suppose Condition 2 holds. Let $\theta \in \Theta$, and let V be any open set containing $\Phi(\theta)$. By Condition 2, the set $W = \Phi_+^{-1}(V)$ is open in Θ. W is nonempty, since $\theta \in W$. Therefore, if U is any open set such that $U \cap \Theta = W$,[2] we have $\theta \in U$ and $\Phi(\theta') \subset V$ for all $\theta' \in U \cap \Theta$, which states precisely that Φ is usc at θ. Since θ was arbitrary, we are done. $\square$

Proposition 9.6 *The following conditions are equivalent:*

1. Φ *is lsc.*

[2]Such a set must exist since W is open in Θ.

2. $\Phi_+^{-1}(F)$ *is closed for every F that is closed in S.*
3. $\Phi^{-1}(G)$ *is open for every G that is open in S.*

Proof This result may be proved in a manner similar to the proof of Proposition 9.5. The details are left as an exercise. $\qquad\square$

Proposition 9.7 *Let $\Phi\colon \Theta \to P(S)$ be a compact-valued, usc correspondence. Then, if $K \subset \Theta$ is compact, so is $\Phi(K) = \{t \in T \mid t \in \Phi(\theta)\ \text{for some}\ \theta \in K\}$. That is, compact-valued usc correspondences preserve compactness.*

Proof We will use the characterization of compactness provided in Theorem 1.36 of Chapter 1, that a set $E \subset \mathbb{R}^n$ is compact if and only if every open cover of E has a finite subcover.

Let $(V_\alpha)_{\alpha\in A}$ be an open cover of $\Phi(K)$. Pick any $\theta \in \Theta$. Then, $\Phi(\theta) \subset \Phi(K) \subset \cup_{\alpha\in A}V_\alpha$. Since $\Phi(\theta)$ is compact by hypothesis, there exists a finite subcollection $B_\theta \subset A$ such that $\Phi(\theta) \subset \cup_{\beta\in B_\theta}V_\beta$. Let $V_\theta = \cup_{\beta\in B_\theta}V_\beta$. As the union of open sets, V_θ is open.

By Proposition 9.5, the set $W_\theta = \Phi_+^{-1}(V_\theta)$ is open in Θ. Trivially, $\theta \in W_\theta$. Therefore, we have $K \subset \cup_{\theta\in K}W_\theta$, which means that $\cup_{\theta\in K}W_\theta$ is an open cover of the compact set K. Therefore, there exist finitely many indices $\theta_1, \ldots, \theta_l \in K$ such that

$$K \subset \cup_{i=1}^{l}W_{\theta_i} = \cup_{i=1}^{l}\Phi_+^{-1}(V_{\theta_i}).$$

Therefore, the collection $(V_{\theta_i})_{i=1}^{l}$ is an open cover of $\Phi(K)$. Since each V_{θ_i} contains only finitely many elements of $(V_\alpha)_{\alpha\in A}$, it follows that $(V_{\theta_i})_{i=1}^{l}$ is a finite subcover of the open cover $(V_\alpha)_{\alpha\in A}$.

We have shown that an arbitrary open cover of $\Phi(K)$ must have a finite subcover, which is precisely the statement that $\Phi(K)$ is compact. $\qquad\square$

Proposition 9.8 *Let $\Phi\colon \Theta \to P(S)$ be a compact-valued correspondence. Then, Φ is usc at $\theta \in \Theta$ if and only if for all sequences $\theta_p \to \theta \in \Theta$ and for all sequences $s_p \in \Phi(\theta_p)$, there is a subsequence $s_{k(p)}$ of s_p such that $s_{k(p)}$ converges to some $s \in \Phi(\theta)$.*

Proof Suppose Φ is usc at $\theta \in \Theta$. Suppose also that $\theta_p \to \theta$, and $s_p \in \Phi(\theta_p)$ for all p. We are required to show that (i) there exists a convergent subsequence $s_{k(p)}$ of s_p, and (ii) the limit s of this subsequence is in $\Phi(\theta)$. The set $K = \{\theta\}\cup\{\theta_1, \theta_2, \theta_3, \ldots\}$ is clearly compact. Therefore, by Proposition 9.7, so is $\Phi(K)$. Hence, $\{s_p\}$ is a sequence in a compact set, and possesses a convergent subsequence, denoted (say) $s_{k(p)}$. This proves (i). Let $s = \lim_{p\to\infty}s_{k(p)}$. If $s \notin \Phi(\theta)$, then there is a closed neighborhood

$\bar{G} \supset \Phi(\theta)$ such that $s \notin \bar{G}$. But $\Phi(\theta_p) \subset \bar{G}$ for sufficiently large p, so $s_{k(p)} \in \bar{G}$, and since $s_{k(p)} \to t$, we must have $s \in \bar{G}$ after all, a contradiction. This proves (ii).

Conversely, suppose that for all $\theta_p \to s$ and for all $s_p \in \Phi(\theta_p)$, there is $s_{k(p)}$ converging to some $s \in \Phi(\theta)$. Suppose also that Φ is compact-valued. Suppose Φ is not usc at some $\theta \in \Theta$, that is, there exists an open set V containing $\Phi(\theta)$ such that for all open sets U containing θ, there exists $\theta' \in U \cap \Theta$ such that $\Phi(\theta')$ is not contained in V. For $m = 1, 2, \ldots$, let U_m be the open ball $B(\theta, \frac{1}{m})$ around θ, and let $\theta_m \in U_m \cap \Theta$ be such that $\Phi(\theta_m)$ is not contained in V. Pick any point $s_m \in \Phi(\theta_m)$ with $s_m \notin V$. By construction, it is the case that $\theta_m \to \theta$. Since $s_m \in \Phi(\theta_m)$ for each m, it is true by hypothesis that there is a subsequence $s_{k(m)}$ of s_m and $s \in \Phi(\theta)$ such that $s_{k(m)} \to s$. But $s_m \notin V$ for each m, and V is open. Therefore, $s \notin V$, which contradicts the assumption that $\Phi(\theta) \subset V$. □

Proposition 9.9 *Suppose the correspondence* $\Phi \colon \Theta \to P(S)$ *is lsc at* θ, *and* $s \in \Phi(\theta)$. *Then, for all sequences* $\theta_m \to \theta$, *there is* $s_m \in \Phi(\theta_m)$ *such that* $s_m \to s$.

Conversely, let $\Phi \colon \Theta \to P(S)$, *and let* $\theta \in \Theta$, $s \in \Phi(\theta)$. *Suppose that for all sequences* $\theta_m \to \theta$, *there is a subsequence* $k(m)$ *of* m, *and* $s_{k(m)} \in \Phi(\theta_{k(m)})$ *such that* $s_{k(m)} \to s$. *Then,* Φ *is lsc at* θ.

Proof Suppose Φ is lsc at θ. Let $s \in \Phi(\theta)$, and let $\{\theta_m\}$ be a sequence in Θ such that $\theta_m \to \theta$. For $p = 1, 2, \ldots$, let $B(s, \frac{1}{p})$ denote the open ball in $\mathbb{R}^l$ with center s and radius $\frac{1}{p}$. Since Φ is lsc at θ, it is the case that for each p, there exists an open set U_p containing θ such that $\Phi(\theta') \cap B(s, \frac{1}{p}) \neq \emptyset$ for each $\theta' \in U_p \cap \Theta$. Since $\theta_m \to \theta$, it is the case that for each p, there exists $m(p)$ such that $\theta_m \in U_p$ for all $m \geq m(p)$. Obviously, the sequence $m(p)$ can be chosen to be increasing, i.e., to satisfy $m(p+1) > m(p)$ for all p. Now, if m is such that $m(p) \leq m < m(p+1)$, define s_m to be any point in the set $\Phi(\theta_m) \cap B(t, \frac{1}{p})$. Since $m \geq m(p)$ implies $\theta_m \in U_p$, it follows from the definition of U_p that this intersection is nonempty. By construction, the distance between s_m and s goes to zero as $m \to \infty$. This proves the first result.

Now suppose that for all $s \in \Phi(\theta)$ and for all sequences $\theta_m \to \theta$, there is a subsequence $\{\theta_{k(m)}\}$ of $\{\theta_m\}$ and $s_{k(m)} \in \Phi(\theta_{k(m)})$ such that $s_{k(m)} \to s$. Suppose Φ is not lsc at θ. Then, there is an open set V such that $V \cap \Phi(\theta) \neq \emptyset$, and such that for all open sets U containing θ, there is $\theta' \in U \cap \Theta$ such that $\Phi(\theta') \cap V = \emptyset$. For $p = 1, 2, \ldots$, let U_p be the open ball $B(\theta, \frac{1}{p})$ with center θ and radius $\frac{1}{p}$. Let $\theta_p \in U_p$ be any point such that $\Phi(\theta_p) \cap V = \emptyset$. Pick any $s \in \Phi(\theta) \cap V$. By hypothesis in this case, there is a subsequence $k(p)$ and $s_{k(p)} \in \Phi(\theta_{k(p)})$ such that $s_{k(p)} \to s$. Since V is open, and $s \in V$, it must be the case that $s_{k(p)} \in V$ for all p sufficiently large. But this contradicts the definition of θ_p as a point where $\Phi(\theta_p) \cap V = \emptyset$. □

We close this section with an important warning. It is not uncommon in the economics literature to *define* an upper-semicontinuous correspondence as one with a closed graph. Such a definition is legitimate provided the range space S of the correspondence is compact, and the correspondence itself is compact-valued, for, as Proposition 9.8 then shows, a correspondence is usc if and only if it has a closed graph. However, in general, the link between usc and closed-graph correspondences is weak: it is *not* the case that usc correspondences necessarily have closed graphs, nor is it true that all closed-graph correspondences are usc (indeed, even if they are also compact-valued). Consider the following examples:

Example 9.10 (An upper-semicontinuous correspondence that does not have a closed graph) Let $\Theta = S = [0, 1]$, and let $\Phi(\theta) = (0, 1)$ for all $\theta \in \Theta$. Then, Φ is usc (and, in fact, continuous) on Θ since it is a constant correspondence, but $\mathrm{Gr}(\Phi)$ is not closed. Indeed, Φ is not even closed-valued. $\square$

Example 9.11 (A compact-valued, closed-graph correspondence that is not usc) Let $\Theta = S = \mathbb{R}_+$. Define $\Phi \colon \Theta \to P(S)$ by

$$\Phi(\theta) = \begin{cases} \{0\}, & \theta = 0 \\ \{0, 1/s\}, & \theta > 0. \end{cases}$$

It is easily checked that $\mathrm{Gr}(\Phi)$ is a closed subset of $\mathbb{R}_+^2$. Evidently, Φ is also a compact-valued correspondence. However, Φ is not usc at $\theta = 0$: if V is any bounded open set containing $\Phi(0) = \{0\}$, then V cannot contain $\Phi(\theta)$ for any θ which is positive, but sufficiently close to 0. $\square$

9.1.4 Semicontinuous Functions and Semicontinuous Correspondences

We have mentioned above that when Φ is single-valued at each $\theta \in \Theta$, it can be viewed as a *function* from Θ to S. This section explores further the relationship between the continuity of a single-valued correspondence, and the continuity of the same map when it is viewed as a function. The following preliminary result is immediate from the definitions, and was, indeed, used to motivate the concept of semicontinuity.

Theorem 9.12 *A single-valued correspondence that is semicontinuous (whether usc or lsc) is continuous when viewed as a function. Conversely, every continuous function, when viewed as a single-valued correspondence, is both usc and lsc.*

There are notions of upper- and lower-semicontinuity for functions also, and somewhat unfortunately, the terminology is misleading.[3] We elaborate on this below.

A function $f: \mathcal{D} \subset \mathbb{R}^n \to \mathbb{R}$ is said to be *upper-semicontinuous* or usc at $x \in \mathcal{D}$ if for all sequences $x_k \to x$, $\limsup_{k \to \infty} f(x_k) \leq f(x)$. The function f is said to be *lower-semicontinuous* or lsc at x if $-f$ is usc at x, i.e., if $\liminf_{k \to \infty} f(x_k) \geq f(x)$.

A semicontinuous (usc or lsc) function need not be a continuous function; indeed, a function is continuous (if and) only if it is *both* usc and lsc. The importance of semicontinuous functions for optimization theory lies in the following generalization of the Weierstrass Theorem:

Theorem 9.13 (Generalized Weierstrass Theorem) *Let $\mathcal{D} \subset \mathbb{R}^n$ be compact and $f: \mathcal{D} \to \mathbb{R}$.*

1. *If f is usc on $\mathcal{D}$, it attains its supremum on $\mathcal{D}$, i.e., there is $z_1 \in \mathcal{D}$ such that $f(z_2) \geq f(x)$ for all $x \in \mathcal{D}$.*
2. *If f is lsc on $\mathcal{D}$, it attains its infimum on $\mathcal{D}$, i.e., there exists $z_2 \in \mathcal{D}$ such that $f(z_2) \leq f(x)$ for all $x \in \mathcal{D}$.*

Proof Suppose f is usc on $\mathcal{D}$. Let $a = \sup f(\mathcal{D})$. By definition of the supremum, there must exist a sequence $\{a_p\}$ in $f(\mathcal{D})$ such that $a_p \to a$. Since $a_p \in f(\mathcal{D})$ for each n, there must be $x_p \in \mathcal{D}$ such that $f(x_p) = a_p$, and $f(x_p) \to a$. Since $\mathcal{D}$ is compact, there must exist a subsequence $x_{k(p)}$ of x_p and $z_1 \in \mathcal{D}$ such that $x_{k(p)} \to z_1$. Obviously, $f(x_{k(p)}) \to a$, and since f is usc, we must have $f(z_1) \geq \limsup_{n \to \infty} f(x_{k(p)}) = a$, so by the definition of a, $f(z_1) = a$, which establishes Part 1. Since f is usc if and only if $-f$ is lsc, Part 2 is also proved. □

Since a continuous function is both lsc and usc, it easily follows that a correspondence which is single-valued and usc is *both* usc and lsc, when viewed as a function. However, a function which is only usc but not lsc (or only lsc and not usc) is neither lsc nor usc when viewed as a single-valued correspondence. This is quite easy to see. Suppose that f were, for instance, usc, but not lsc. Then, there must exist a point x and a sequence $x_p \to x$ such that $f(x) > \lim_p f(x_p)$. Let $\epsilon = f(x) - \lim_p f(x_p)$. Take the open ball $(f(x) - \epsilon/2, f(x) + \epsilon/2)$ around $f(x)$. This open ball does not contain $f(x_p)$ for any large n, so, viewed as a single-valued correspondence, f is neither lsc nor usc.

---

[3]Perhaps on this account, it is not uncommon in the economics literature to use the adjective "hemicontinuous" when referring to correspondences, and to reserve "semicontinuous" for functions. Since very little of this book involves semicontinuous functions, we continue to use "semicontinuous" in both cases.

9.2 Parametric Continuity: The Maximum Theorem

This section describes the two main results of this chapter. In subsection 9.2.1, we present one of the fundamental results of optimization theory, the *Maximum Theorem*. This is followed in subsection 9.2.2 by an examination of the problem, when additional convexity conditions are imposed on the family of optimization problems.[4] Throughout this section, it will be assumed that $\Theta \subset \mathbb{R}^l$ and $S \subset \mathbb{R}^n$, where l and n are arbitrary positive integers.

9.2.1 The Maximum Theorem

The Maximum Theorem is essentially a statement that if the primitives of a parametric family of optimization problems possess a sufficient degree of continuity, then the solutions will also be continuous, albeit not to the same degree.

Theorem 9.14 (The Maximum Theorem) *Let $f: S \times \Theta \to \mathbb{R}$ be a continuous function, and $\mathcal{D}: \Theta \to P(S)$ be a compact-valued, continuous correspondence. Let $f^*: \Theta \to \mathbb{R}$ and $\mathcal{D}^*: \Theta \to P(S)$ be defined by*

$$f^*(\theta) = \max\{f(x,\theta) \mid x \in \mathcal{D}(\theta)\}$$
$$\mathcal{D}^*(\theta) = \arg\max\{f(x,\theta) \mid x \in \mathcal{D}(\theta)\} = \{x \in \mathcal{D}(\theta) \mid f(x,\theta) = f^*(\theta)\}.$$

Then f^* is a continuous function on Θ, and $\mathcal{D}^*$ is a compact-valued, upper-semicontinuous correspondence on Θ.

Proof We will appeal to Propositions 9.8 and 9.9. So let $\theta \in \Theta$, and let θ_m be a sequence in Θ converging to θ. Pick $x_m \in \mathcal{D}^*(\theta_m)$. By Proposition 9.8, there exists a subsequence $x_{k(m)}$ of x_m such that $x_{k(m)} \to x \in \mathcal{D}(\theta)$. The theorem will be proved if we can show that $f(x,\theta) = f^*(\theta)$, for this will establish not only the continuity of f^* at θ, but also (by Proposition 9.8) the upper-semicontinuity of the correspondence $\mathcal{D}^*$ at θ.

Since f is continuous on $\Theta \times S$, it is the case that $f(x_{k(m)}, \theta_{k(m)}) \to f(x,\theta)$. Suppose there were $x^* \in \mathcal{D}(\theta)$ such that $f(x^*,\theta) > f(x,\theta)$. We show a contradiction must result.

Since $\mathcal{D}$ is lsc at θ, $x^* \in \mathcal{D}(\theta)$, and $x_{k(m)} \to x$, there is, by Proposition 9.9, a further subsequence $l(m)$ of $k(m)$ and $x^*_{l(m)} \in \mathcal{D}(\theta_{l(m)})$ such that $x^*_{l(m)} \to x^*$. It follows from the continuity of f that

$$\lim_{m\to\infty} f(x^*_{l(m)}, \theta_{l(m)}) = f(x^*,\theta) > f(x,\theta) = \lim_{m\to\infty} f(x_{l(m)}, \theta_{l(m)}).$$

[4]The mathematics literature on parametric optimization contains a large number of related results, which examine the consequences of weakening or otherwise altering the hypotheses of the Maximum Theorem. For details, the reader is referred to Berge (1963) or Bank, et al. (1983).

But this means that for all sufficiently large m, we must have

$$f(x_{l(m)}^*, \theta_{l(m)}) > f(x_{l(m)}, \theta_{l(m)}),$$

and therefore, $x_{l(m)} \notin \mathcal{D}^*(\theta_{l(m)})$, a contradiction.   □

It is important to reiterate that although we assume full continuity in the primitives of the problem, the Maximum Theorem claims only that *upper*-semicontinuity of the optimal action correspondence will result, and not *lower*-semicontinuity. This raises two questions. First, is it possible, under the theorem's hypotheses, to strengthen the conclusions and obtain *full* continuity of $\mathcal{D}^*$? Alternatively, is it possible to obtain the same set of conclusions under a weaker hypothesis, namely, that $\mathcal{D}$ is only *upper*-semicontinuous, and not necessarily also *lower*-semicontinuous, on Θ? The following examples show, respectively, that the answer to each of these questions is in the negative.

Example 9.15 Let $\Theta = [0, 1]$ and $S = [1, 2]$. Define $f: S \times \Theta \to \mathbb{R}$ and $\mathcal{D}: \Theta \to P(S)$ by

$$f(x, \theta) = x^\theta, \qquad (x, \theta) \in S \times \Theta$$

and $\mathcal{D}(\theta) = [1, 2]$ for all $\theta \in \Theta$. Note that $\mathcal{D}(\cdot)$ is continuous and compact-valued on Θ, while f is continuous on $S \times \Theta$.

For $\theta > 0$, f is strictly increasing on S, so we have

$$\mathcal{D}^*(\theta) = \{2\}, \qquad \theta > 0.$$

At $\theta = 0$, however, f is identically equal to unity on $\mathcal{D}(\theta)$, so

$$\mathcal{D}^*(\theta) = [1, 2], \qquad \theta = 0.$$

Clearly, $\mathcal{D}^*(\theta)$ is usc, but not lsc, at $\theta = 0$.   □

Example 9.16 Let $S = \Theta = [0, 1]$. Define $f: S \times \Theta \to \mathbb{R}$ and $\mathcal{D}: \Theta \to P(S)$ by

$$f(x, \theta) = x, \qquad (x, \theta) \in S \times \Theta,$$

and

$$\mathcal{D}(\theta) = \begin{cases} [0, 1], & \theta = 0, \\ \{0\}, & \theta > 0. \end{cases}$$

Trivially, f is continuous on $S \times \Theta$. The correspondence $\mathcal{D}(\cdot)$ is continuous and compact-valued everywhere on Θ except at $\theta = 0$, where it is usc, but not lsc. We have

$$f^*(\theta) = \begin{cases} 1, & \theta = 0, \\ 0, & \theta > 0. \end{cases}$$

$$\mathcal{D}^*(\theta) = \begin{cases} \{1\}, & \theta = 0, \\ \{0\}, & \theta > 0. \end{cases}$$

Both conclusions of the Maximum Theorem fail: f^* is not continuous at $\theta = 0$, and $\mathcal{D}^*$ is not usc (or, for that matter, lsc) at $\theta = 0$. □

Finally, a small note. The joint continuity of f in (x, θ), i.e., the continuity of f on $S \times \Theta$, is important for the validity of the Maximum Theorem. This hypothesis cannot be replaced with one of *separate continuity*, i.e., that $f(\cdot, \theta)$ is continuous on S for each fixed θ, and that $f(x, \cdot)$ is continuous on Θ for each fixed x. For an example, see the Exercises.

9.2.2 The Maximum Theorem under Convexity

The purpose of this subsection is to highlight some points regarding the Maximum Theorem under convexity restrictions on the underlying problem. We retain the notation of the previous subsection. We will prove the following result:

Theorem 9.17 (The Maximum Theorem under Convexity) *Suppose f is a continuous function on $S \times \Theta$ and $\mathcal{D}$ is a compact-valued continuous correspondence on Θ. Let*

$$f^*(\theta) = \max\{f(x, \theta) \mid x \in \mathcal{D}(\theta)\}$$
$$\mathcal{D}^*(\theta) = \arg\max\{f(x, \theta) \mid x \in \mathcal{D}(\theta)\} = \{x \in \mathcal{D}(\theta) \mid f(x, \theta) = f^*(\theta)\}.$$

Then:

1. *f^* is a continuous function on Θ, and $\mathcal{D}^*$ is a usc correspondence on Θ.*
2. *If $f(\cdot, \theta)$ is concave in x for each θ, and $\mathcal{D}$ is convex-valued (i.e., $\mathcal{D}(\theta)$ is a convex set for each θ), then $\mathcal{D}^*$ is a convex-valued correspondence. When "concave" is replaced by "strictly concave," then $\mathcal{D}^*$ is a single-valued usc correspondence, hence a continuous function.*
3. *If f is concave on $S \times \Theta$, and $\mathcal{D}$ has a convex graph, then f^* is a concave function, and $\mathcal{D}^*$ is a convex-valued usc correspondence. If "concave" is replaced by "strictly concave," then f^* is also strictly concave, and $\mathcal{D}^*$ is single-valued everywhere, and therefore, a continuous function.*

Proof Part 1 is just the statement of the Maximum Theorem. To see Part 2, suppose $x, \bar{x} \in \mathcal{D}^*(\theta)$. Let $x' = \lambda x + (1 - \lambda)\bar{x}$ for some $\lambda \in (0, 1)$. Since $\mathcal{D}(\theta)$ is convex, $x' \in \mathcal{D}(\theta)$. Then,

$$
\begin{aligned}
f(x', \theta) &= f[\lambda x + (1 - \lambda)\bar{x}, \theta] \\
&\geq \lambda f(x, \theta) + (1 - \lambda) f(\bar{x}, \theta) \\
&= \lambda f^*(\theta) + (1 - \lambda) f^*(\theta) \\
&= f^*(\theta),
\end{aligned}
$$

so, by the definition of f^*, we must also have $x' \in \mathcal{D}^*(s)$. If f is strictly concave, then, since $\mathcal{D}(\theta)$ is a convex set, $f(\cdot, \theta)$ has a unique maximizer, so $\mathcal{D}^*$ must be single-valued. This completes the proof of Part 2.

Finally, to see Part 3, let $\theta, \bar{\theta} \in \Theta$, and let $\theta' = \lambda\theta + (1 - \lambda)\bar{\theta}$ for some $\lambda \in (0, 1)$. Pick any $x \in \mathcal{D}^*(\theta)$, and $\bar{x} \in \mathcal{D}(\bar{\theta})$. Let $x' = \lambda x + (1 - \lambda)\bar{x}$. Then, since $x \in \mathcal{D}(\theta)$ and $\bar{x} \in \mathcal{D}(\bar{\theta})$, and $\mathcal{D}(\cdot)$ has a convex graph, we must have $x' \in \mathcal{D}(\theta')$. Since x' is feasible, but not necessarily optimal at θ', we have by the concavity of f,

$$
\begin{aligned}
f^*(\theta') &\geq f(x', \theta') \\
&= f(\lambda x + (1 - \lambda)\bar{x}, \lambda\theta + (1 - \lambda)\bar{\theta}) \\
&\geq \lambda f(x, \theta) + (1 - \lambda) f(\bar{x}, \bar{\theta}) \\
&= \lambda f^*(\theta) + (1 - \lambda) f^*(\bar{\theta}).
\end{aligned}
$$

This establishes the concavity of f^*. If f is strictly concave, then the second inequality in this string becomes strict, proving strict concavity of f^*. $\quad\square$

Once again, simple examples show that the result cannot be strengthened. For instance, Part 2 of the theorem assumes that f is concave and $\mathcal{D}$ is convex-valued; while the convex-valuedness of $\mathcal{D}$ is inherited by $\mathcal{D}^*$, the theorem makes no claim regarding the concavity of f^*. In fact, the hypotheses of Part 2 are insufficient to obtain concavity of f^*; the stronger assumption made in Part 3 that $\mathcal{D}$ has a convex *graph* is needed. Here is an example:

Example 9.18 Let $S = \Theta = [0, 1]$. Define $f: S \times \Theta \to \mathbb{R}$ and $\mathcal{D}: \Theta \to P(S)$ by $f(x, \theta) = x$ for all $(x, \theta) \in S \times \Theta$, and $\mathcal{D}(\theta) = [0, \theta^2]$. Then, f is concave on S for each fixed θ,[5] and $\mathcal{D}(\cdot)$ is convex-valued for each θ. Note, however, that $\mathcal{D}(\cdot)$ does not have a convex graph. Since f is strictly increasing on S for each θ, we have

$$
\mathcal{D}^*(\theta) = \{\theta^2\}, \qquad \theta \in \Theta,
$$

---

[5]In fact, f is concave on $S \times \Theta$.

and, therefore,

$$f^*(\theta) = \theta^2, \qquad \theta \in \Theta.$$

Clearly, f^* is not concave on Θ. □

Similarly, although Part 3 of the theorem assumes that $\mathcal{D}(\cdot)$ has a convex graph, the theorem does not claim that $\mathcal{D}^*$ also has a convex graph. As the following example reveals, such a claim would be false.

Example 9.19 Let $S = \Theta = [0, 1]$. Define $f \colon S \times \Theta \to \mathbb{R}$ and $\mathcal{D} \colon \Theta \to P(S)$ by

$$f(x, \theta) = \sqrt{x}, \qquad (x, \theta) \in S \times \Theta,$$

and

$$\mathcal{D}(\theta) = [0, \sqrt{\theta}], \qquad \theta \in \Theta.$$

Then, f is concave on $S \times \Theta$, and is, in fact, strictly concave on S for each fixed θ, while $\mathcal{D}(\cdot)$ has a convex graph. Since f is strictly increasing on S for each fixed θ, we have

$$\mathcal{D}^*(\theta) = \{\sqrt{\theta}\}, \qquad \theta \in \Theta.$$

The graph of $\mathcal{D}^*(\cdot)$ is clearly not convex. □

The point of the examples of this subsection—as also of the examples of the previous subsection—is simply that it is not possible to obtain all the properties of the primitives in the solutions: inevitably, some properties are lost in the process of optimization itself.

Finally, we note that since the maximization of quasi-concave functions over convex sets also results in a convex set of maximizers, and since strictly quasi-concave functions also have unique maxima, we have the following obvious corollary of Theorem 9.17:

Corollary 9.20 *Let $f \colon S \times \Theta \to \mathbb{R}$ be continuous, and $\mathcal{D} \colon \Theta \to P(S)$ be continuous and compact-valued. Define f^* and $\mathcal{D}^*$ as in Theorem 9.17.*

1. *Suppose $f(\cdot, \theta)$ is quasi-concave in x for each θ, and $\mathcal{D}$ is convex-valued on Θ. Then, $\mathcal{D}^*$ is a convex-valued usc correspondence.*

2. *If "quasi-concave" is replaced by "strictly quasi-concave," $\mathcal{D}^*$ is single-valued everywhere on Θ, and hence defines a continuous function.*

9.3 An Application to Consumer Theory

This section is devoted to examining an application of the Maximum Theorem and the Maximum Theorem under convexity to the problem of utility maximization subject to a budget constraint. The objective is to examine under what conditions it is that maximized utility varies *continuously* with changes in underlying parameters (i.e., the prices and income), and how optimal demand varies as these parameters change.

There are l commodities in the model, which may be consumed in nonnegative amounts. We will assume that the price of each commodity is always strictly positive so $\mathbb{R}^l_{++}$ will represent our price space. Similarly, income will also be assumed to be strictly positive always, so $\mathbb{R}_{++}$ will represent the space of possible income levels. Define $\Theta = \mathbb{R}^l_{++} \times \mathbb{R}_{++}$. The set Θ will serve as our *parameter space*; a typical element of Θ will be represented by (p, I).

Let $S = \mathbb{R}^l_+$ be the set of all possible consumption bundles. Let $u: S \to \mathbb{R}$ be a continuous utility function. The *budget correspondence* $\mathcal{B}: \Theta \to P(S)$ is given by:

$$\mathcal{B}(p, I) = \{x \in \mathbb{R}^l_+ \mid p \cdot x \leq I\}.$$

Now, define the *indirect utility function* $v(\cdot)$ and the *demand correspondence* $x(\cdot)$ by:

$$v(p, I) = \max\{u(x) \mid x \in \mathcal{B}(p, I)\}$$
$$x(p, I) = \{x \in \mathcal{B}(p, I) \mid u(x) = v(p, I)\}.$$

The function $v(\cdot)$ and the correspondence $x(\cdot)$ form the objects of our study in this section. We proceed in two steps. First in subsection 9.4.1, we establish that the budget correspondence $\mathcal{B}$ is a compact-valued continuous correspondence on Θ. Then, in subsection 9.4.2, we examine the properties of v and x in the parameters (p, I), especially when additional convexity restrictions are placed on the primitives.

9.3.1 Continuity of the Budget Correspondence

We will prove the following result:

Theorem 9.21 *The correspondence $\mathcal{B}: \Theta \to P(S)$ is a continuous, compact-valued and convex-valued correspondence.*

Proof Compact-valuedness is obvious, since prices are assumed to be strictly positive. Convex-valuedness is also obvious. The continuity of $\mathcal{B}$ is established through the following lemmata:

Lemma 9.22 $\mathcal{B}: \Theta \to P(S)$ *is usc.*

Proof Let $V \subset \mathbb{R}^l$ be an open set such that $\mathcal{B}(p, I) \subset V$. Define an ϵ-neighborhood $N_\epsilon(p, I)$, of (p, I) in Θ by

$$N_\epsilon(p, I) = \{(p', I') \in \mathbb{R}^l_{++} \times \mathbb{R}_{++} \mid \|p - p'\| + |I - I'| < \epsilon\}.$$

Suppose $\mathcal{B}$ is not usc at (p, I). Then, for all $\epsilon > 0$, there is (p', I') in $N_\epsilon(p, I)$ such that $\mathcal{B}(p', I')$ is not contained in V, i.e., there exists x' such that $x' \in \mathcal{B}(p', I')$, $x' \notin V$. We will show a contradiction must occur.

Choose a sequence $\epsilon(n) \to 0$, and let $(p_n, I_n) \in N_{\epsilon(n)}(p, I)$, with $x_n \in \mathcal{B}(p_n, I_n)$ but $x_n \notin V$. We will first argue that the $\{x_n\}$ sequence contains a convergent subsequence, by showing that the sequence lies in a compact set.

Since $p \gg 0$, there is $\eta > 0$ such that $p_i > 2\eta, i = 1, \ldots, l$. Since $p_n \to p$, we have $p_{in} \to p_i$ for each $i = 1, \ldots, l$. Therefore, there is n^* such that for all $n \geq n^*$, we have

$$p_{in} > \eta, \qquad i = 1, \ldots, l.$$

Since $I_n \to I$, we can also ensure, by taking n^* large enough, that $I_n \leq 2I$ for $n \geq n^*$. Now, at any $n \geq n^*$, η is a lower bound for the price of commodity i, since $p_{in} > \eta$. Moreover, $2I$ is an upper bound on the income at n. It follows that for $n \geq n^*$, we have $x_n \in M$, where M is the compact set defined by

$$M = \left\{x \in \mathbb{R}^l_+ \mid \eta \sum_{i=1}^{l} x_i \leq 2I\right\}.$$

Therefore, there is a subsequence of $\{x_n\}$, which we shall continue to denote by $\{x_n\}$ for notational simplicity, along which $\{x_n\}$ converges to a limit x.

Since $x_n \geq 0$ for all n, we also have $x \geq 0$. Moreover, $p_n \cdot x_n \to p \cdot x$, and since $p_n \cdot x_n \leq I_n$ for each n and $I_n \to I$, we also have $p \cdot x \leq I$. Therefore, $x \in \mathcal{B}(p, I)$, and since $\mathcal{B}(p, I) \subset V$, by hypothesis, we have $x \in V$.

However, $x_n \notin V$ for any n, and V is an open set. Therefore, we also have $x \notin V$, a contradiction. This establishes Lemma 9.22. $\qquad \square$

Lemma 9.23 $\mathcal{B}: \Theta \to P(S)$ *is lsc.*

Proof Let $(p, I) \in \Theta$ and V be an open set such that $V \cap \mathcal{B}(p, I) \neq \emptyset$. Let x be a point in this intersection. Then $p \cdot x \leq I$. Since V is open, $\delta x \in V$ for $\delta < 1, \delta$ close to 1. Let $\bar{x} = \delta x$. Then, $p \cdot \bar{x} < p \cdot x \leq I$. Suppose there is no neighborhood of $(p, I) \in \Theta$ such that $\mathcal{B}(p', I') \cap V \neq \emptyset$ for all (p', I') in the neighborhood. Take a sequence $\epsilon(n) \to 0$, and pick $(p_n, I_n) \in N_{\epsilon(n)}(p, I)$ such that $\mathcal{B}(p_n, I_n) \cap V = \emptyset$. Now $(p_n.\bar{x} - I_n) \to (p.\bar{x} - I) < 0$, so for n sufficiently large, $\bar{x} \in \mathcal{B}(p_n, I_n) \subset V^c$, a contradiction. $\qquad \square$

By Lemmata 9.22 and 9.23, $\mathcal{B}$ is a continuous correspondence. The theorem is established.   □

9.3.2 The Indirect Utility Function and Demand Correspondence

The properties of $v(\cdot)$ and $x(\cdot)$ that we shall prove in this subsection are summed up in the following theorem:

Theorem 9.24 *The indirect utility function $v(\cdot)$ and the demand correspondence $x(\cdot)$ have the following properties on Θ:*

1. *$v(\cdot)$ is a continuous function on Θ, and $x(\cdot)$ is a compact-valued usc correspondence on Θ.*
2. *$v(\cdot)$ is nondecreasing in I for fixed p, and is nonincreasing in p for fixed I.*
3. *If u is concave, then $v(\cdot)$ is quasi-convex in p for fixed I, and is concave in I for fixed p; further, $x(\cdot)$ is a convex-valued correspondence.*
4. *If u is strictly concave, then $x(\cdot)$ is a continuous function.*

Proof We have already shown that $\mathcal{B}$ is a continuous and compact-valued correspondence on Θ. Since u is continuous on S by hypothesis, and u does not depend on (p, I), u is certainly continuous on $\Theta \times S$. Then, by the Maximum Theorem, $v(\cdot)$ is a continuous function on Θ, and $x(\cdot)$ is a compact-valued usc correspondence on Θ. This establishes Part 1.

That $v(p, I)$ is nonincreasing in p for fixed I is easily seen: if there are (p, I) and (p', I) in Θ such that $p \geq p'$, then $\mathcal{B}(p, I) \subset \mathcal{B}(p'I)$. Thus, any consumption level that is feasible at (p, I) is also feasible at (p', I), and it follows that we must have $v(p', I) \geq v(p, I)$. The other part of Part 2—that v is nondecreasing in I (i.e., that more income cannot hurt)—is similarly established.

Now, suppose u is concave. We will first show using the Maximum Theorem under Convexity that $v(\cdot)$ must be concave in I for fixed p. We will use the notation $\mathcal{B}(\bar{p}, \cdot)$ to denote that p is fixed at the value $\bar{p}$, and only the parameter I is allowed to vary. Note that since $\mathcal{B}$ is continuous in (p, I), it is also continuous in I for fixed p.

We claim that $\mathcal{B}(\bar{p}, \cdot)$ has a *convex graph* in I. To see this, pick any I, I' in $\mathbb{R}_{++}$, and let $x \in \mathcal{B}(\bar{p}, I)$ and $x' \in \mathcal{B}(\bar{p}, I')$. Pick any $\lambda \in (0, 1)$. Let $x(\lambda) = \lambda x + (1-\lambda)x'$, and $I(\lambda) = \lambda I + (1 - \lambda)I'$. We have to show that $x(\lambda)$ is in $\mathcal{B}(\bar{p}, I(\lambda))$. But this is immediate since

$$
\begin{aligned}
\bar{p} \cdot x(\lambda) &= \bar{p} \cdot (\lambda x) + \bar{p} \cdot ((1 - \lambda)x') \\
&= \lambda \bar{p} \cdot x + (1 - \lambda)\bar{p} \cdot x' \\
&\leq \lambda I + (1 - \lambda)I' \\
&= I(\lambda).
\end{aligned}
$$

Since u is concave in x and is independent of I, it is certainly jointly concave in (x, I). Thus, $v(\bar{p}, I) = \max\{u(x) \mid x \in \mathcal{B}(\bar{p}, I)\}$ is concave in I by the Maximum Theorem under Convexity. This completes the proof of the first part of Part 3.

The proof of the second part—the quasi-convexity of v in p, for each fixed value of I—is left as an exercise to the reader. Finally, since $\mathcal{B}(p, I)$ is compact and convex for each (p, I), it is immediate that $x(p, I)$ is a convex set for each (p, I). This completes the proof of Part 3.

Finally, suppose u is *strictly* concave. Since $\mathcal{B}(p, I)$ is a convex set, $x(p, I)$ is single-valued for each (p, I), and is thus a continuous function. $\qquad\square$

Remark It is left to the reader to check that if p is also allowed to vary, the graph of $\mathcal{B}$ could fail to be convex in the parameters. In particular, Part 3 of the theorem cannot be strengthened. It is also left to the reader to examine if it is true that when u is strictly concave, v is *strictly* concave in I for fixed p, i.e., if Part 4 can be strengthened.

9.4 An Application to Nash Equilibrium

9.4.1 Normal-Form Games

Unlike perfectly competitive markets in which no single agent has any market power, and monopoly in which one agent has all the market power, game theory attempts to study social situations in which there are many agents, each of whom has some effect on the overall outcome. In this section, we introduce the notion of *normal-form games*, and describe the notions of mixed strategies and a Nash equilibrium.

A normal-form game (henceforth, simply game) is specified by:

1. A finite set of *players* N. A generic player is indexed by i.
2. For each $i \in N$, a *strategy set* or *action set* S_i, with typical element s_i.
3. For each $i \in N$, a *payoff function* or *reward function* $r_i \colon S_1 \times \cdots \times S_n \to \mathbb{R}$.

We will confine our attention in this section to the case where S_i is a *finite* set for each i. Elements of S_i are also called the *pure strategies* of player i. The set of *mixed strategies* available to player i is simply the set of all probability distributions on S_i, and is denoted Σ_i, i.e.,

$$\Sigma_i = \left\{ \sigma_i \colon S_i \to [0, 1] \mid \sum_{s_i \in S_i} \sigma_i(s_i) = 1 \right\}.$$

A mixed strategy σ_i for player i is interpreted as a strategy under which player i will play the pure action $s_i \in S_i$ with probability $\sigma_i(s_i)$. One of the most important reasons we allow players to use mixed strategies is that the resulting strategy set

Σ_i is *convex*, and convexity of the set of available strategies for each player plays a critical role in proving existence of equilibrium. (Note that S_i is not convex, since it is a finite set.)

The following shorthand notation will be useful. In statements pertaining to i, let the index $-i$ denote "everyone-but-i." Let $S = \times_{i \in N} S_i$, and for any $i \in N$, let $S_{-i} = \times_{j \neq i} S_j$. For any $s_{-i} \in S_{-i}$ and $\hat{s}_i \in S_i$, $(\hat{s}_i, s_{-i})$ will represent the obvious vector in S. Similarly, let $\Sigma = \times_{i \in N} \Sigma_i$, and let $\Sigma_{-i} = \times_{j \neq i} \Sigma_i$. Observe that (a) S is a finite set, and (b) Σ is a convex set. Observe also that Σ is strictly smaller than the set of probability measures on S (why?).

Given a vector $\sigma = (\sigma_1, \ldots, \sigma_n) \in \Sigma$, the pure-action profile $\theta = (s_1, \ldots s_n) \in S$ occurs with probability $\sigma_1(s_1) \times \cdots \times \sigma_n(s_n)$. Thus, player i receives a reward of $r_i(s)$ with probability $\sigma_1(s_1) \times \cdots \times \sigma_n(s_n)$. Assuming that players seek to maximize *expected reward*, we extend the payoff functions to Σ by defining for each i, and for any $\sigma = (\sigma_1, \ldots, \sigma_n) \in \Sigma$,

$$r_i(\sigma) = \sum_{s \in S} (r_i(s)\sigma_1(s_1) \cdots \sigma_n(s_n)) .$$

It is left to the reader to verify that r_i so defined is a continuous function on Σ for each i.

Given any $\sigma \in \Sigma$, we define $\hat{\sigma}_i \in \Sigma_i$ to be player i's *best response to σ* if

$$r_i(\hat{\sigma}_i, \sigma_{-i}) \geq r_i(\tilde{\sigma}_i, \sigma_{-i}), \quad \text{for all } \tilde{\sigma}_i \in \Sigma_i.$$

The set of all best responses of player i to σ is denoted $BR_i(\sigma)$. Observe that $BR_i(\sigma)$ only depends on σ_{-i} and not on the i-th coordinate of σ. Notationally, however, it is much easier to write BR_i as depending on the entire vector σ.

A *Nash equilibrium* of the game is a strategy vector $\sigma^* = (\sigma_1^*, \ldots, \sigma_n^*) \in \Sigma$ such that for each $i \in N$ we have $\sigma_i^* \in BR_i(\sigma_*)$.

The existence of at least one Nash equilibrium in every finite game is proved below. A technical digression is required first in the form of the Brouwer/Kakutani Fixed Point Theorem.

9.4.2 The Brouwer/Kakutani Fixed Point Theorem

Given a set X and a function f mapping X into itself, a point $x \in X$ is said to be a *fixed point* of f if it is the case that $f(x) = x$.

Example 9.25 Let $X = [0, 1]$, and let $f: X \to X$ be defined by $f(x) = x^2$. Then, f has two fixed points on X, namely, the points 0 and 1. □

The definition of fixed points for functions generalizes in a natural way to a definition of fixed points for correspondences Φ from X into itself: a point $x \in X$ is said to be a fixed point of $\Phi: X \to P(X)$ if it is the case that $x \in \Phi(x)$, that is, if it is the case that the image of x under Φ contains x. Note that when Φ is single-valued, this is precisely the definition of a fixed point for a function.

The following result provides sufficient conditions for a correspondence to possess a fixed point:

Theorem 9.26 (Kakutani's Fixed Point Theorem) *Let $X \subset \mathbb{R}^n$ be compact and convex. If $\Phi: X \to P(X)$ is a usc correspondence that has nonempty, compact, and convex values, then Φ has a fixed point.*

Proof See Smart (1974). □

While the condition that Φ be nonempty-valued is of obvious importance, the other conditions (that it be usc, compact- and convex-valued) are also critical. Moreover, neither the compactness nor the convexity of X can be dispensed with. Simple examples show that if any of these conditions are not satisfied, a fixed point may not exist:

Example 9.27 Let $X = [0, 2]$, and let Φ be defined by

$$\Phi(x) = \begin{cases} \{2\}, & x \in [0, 1) \\ \{0, 2\}, & x = 1 \\ \{0\}, & x \in (1, 2]. \end{cases}$$

Then, X is compact and convex, and Φ is nonempty-valued and usc. However, Φ is not convex-valued at 1, and evidently Φ possesses no fixed point. □

Example 9.28 Let $X = [0, 1]$, and let Φ be defined by

$$\Phi(x) = \begin{cases} \{1\}, & x = 0 \\ \{0\}, & x \neq 0. \end{cases}$$

Then, X is compact and convex, and Φ is nonempty-valued and convex-valued. However, Φ is not usc; it also fails to have a fixed point. □

Example 9.29 Let $X = \mathbb{R}$. Define Φ by $\Phi(x) = [x + 1, x + 3]$. Then, X is convex, Φ is nonempty-valued, convex-valued, and usc (in fact, continuous). However, X is not compact, and Φ fails to possess a fixed point. □

Example 9.30 Let $X = [0, 1] \cup [2, 3]$. Let Φ be given by

$$\Phi(x) = \begin{cases} \{2\}, & x \in [0, 1] \\ \{1\}, & x \in [2, 3]. \end{cases}$$

Then, X is compact, Φ is nonempty-valued, convex-valued, and usc (in fact, continuous), but X is not convex, and Φ does not have a fixed point.   □

In closing this section, it should be noted that Kakutani's Theorem is a generalization of an earlier fixed point theorem that was proved by L.E.J. Brouwer in 1912 for functions:

Theorem 9.31 (Brouwer's Fixed Point Theorem) *Let $X \subset \mathbb{R}^n$ be compact and convex, and $f: X \to X$ a continuous function. Then f has a fixed point.*

Proof See Smart (1974).   □

9.4.3 Existence of Nash Equilibrium

We shall now show that every finite game has at least one Nash equilibrium.

Theorem 9.32 *Every finite game $\Gamma = \{N, (S_i, r_i)_{i \in N}\}$ has a Nash equilibrium point.*

Proof Recall that for any $\sigma \in \Sigma$, $BR_i(\sigma) \subset \Sigma_i$ denotes the set of best responses of player i to σ. BR_i evidently defines a correspondence from Σ to Σ_i. Thus, defining $BR = \times_{i \in N} BR_i$, we obtain a correspondence BR from Σ into itself. By definition, a Nash equilibrium is simply a fixed point of this correspondence. Thus, the theorem will be proved if we can show that BR and Σ satisfy all the conditions of the Kakutani fixed point theorem. That Σ does so is immediate (why is compactness apparent?).

Lemma 9.33 Σ *is convex and compact.*

We will now show that BR has all the properties required by the Kakutani Fixed Point Theorem.

Lemma 9.34 BR *is nonempty-valued, convex-valued, and usc on Σ.*

Proof We show that BR_i is nonempty-valued, convex-valued, and usc for each i. This will obviously establish the result.

Pick any $\sigma \in \Sigma$ and $i \in N$. Then, player i solves:

$$\max\{r_i(\sigma_i', \sigma_{-i}) \mid \sigma_i' \in \Sigma_i\}.$$

This is simply a parametric family of optimization problems in which:

- The parameter space is given by Σ.
- The action space is given by Σ_i.
- For $\sigma_i' \in S_i$ and $\sigma = (\sigma_i, \sigma_{-i}) \in \Sigma$, the reward $f(\sigma_i', \sigma)$ is given by $r_i(\sigma_i, \sigma_{-i})$.
- The correspondence of feasible actions $\mathcal{D}$ is given by $\mathcal{D}(\sigma) = \Sigma_i$ for all $\sigma \in \Sigma$.

Since Σ_i is compact and convex, the feasible action correspondence is continuous, compact-valued, and convex-valued. Since r_i is continuous on $\Sigma_i \times \Sigma_{-i}$, it follows from the Maximum Theorem that

$$BR_i(\sigma) = \arg\max\{r_i(\hat{\sigma}_i, \sigma_{-i}) \mid \hat{\sigma}_i \in \Sigma_i\}$$

is a nonempty-valued, compact-valued, usc correspondence from Σ into itself.

It remains to be shown that BR_i is convex-valued. Define for any $\hat{s}_i \in S_i$ and $\sigma_{-i} \in \Sigma_{-i}$,

$$r_i(\hat{s}_i, \sigma_{-i}) = r_i(\hat{s}_i, s_{-i}) \prod_{j \neq i} \sigma_j(s_j).$$

Then, for any $\hat{\sigma}_i \in \Sigma_i$ and $\sigma_{-i} \in \Sigma_{-i}$,

$$r_i(\hat{\sigma}_i, \sigma_{-i}) = \sum_{s_i \in S_i} r_i(s_i, \sigma_{-i}) \sigma_i(s_i).$$

It follows that r_i is linear (so concave) on Σ_i. By the Maximum Theorem under Convexity, BR_i is also convex-valued, and this completes the proof. $\square$

The existence of a Nash equilibrium in every finite game now follows from Kakutani's fixed point theorem. $\square$

Remark The existence of a Nash equilibrium in *pure strategies* can be shown under the following modified set of assumptions: for each i (i) S_i is a compact and convex set, and (ii) r_i is quasi-concave on S_i for every fixed $s_{-i} \in S_{-i}$. The arguments involve essentially a repetition of those above, except that mixed strategies are not used at any point (so the best-response correspondence maps $S_1 \times \cdots \times S_n$ into itself). The details are left to the reader. $\square$

9.5 Exercises

1. Let $S = \Theta = \mathbb{R}_+$. Determine, in each of the following cases, whether $\Phi\colon \Theta \to P(S)$ is usc and/or lsc at each $\theta \in \Theta$:

   (a) $\Phi(\theta) = [0, \theta]$, $\quad \theta \in \Theta$.
   (b) $\Phi(\theta) = [0, \theta)$, $\quad \theta \in \Theta$.
   (c) $\Phi(\theta) = (0, \theta]$, $\quad \theta \in \Theta$.

(d) $\Phi(\theta) = (0, \theta)$ if $\theta > 0$, and $\Phi(0) = \{0\}$.

2. Let $\Phi \colon \mathbb{R} \to P(\mathbb{R})$ be defined as

$$\Phi(x) = [-|x|, |x|], \quad x \in \mathbb{R}.$$

Determine if Φ is usc and/or lsc on $\mathbb{R}$.

3. Let $\Phi \colon \mathbb{R}_+ \to P(\mathbb{R})$ be defined as

$$\Phi(x) = \begin{cases} [0, 1/x] & \text{if } x > 0 \\ \{0\} & \text{if } x = 0. \end{cases}$$

Determine if Φ is usc and/or lsc on $\mathbb{R}_+$.

4. Let $\Phi \colon \mathbb{R}_+ \to P(\mathbb{R})$ be defined by

$$\Phi(x) = \begin{cases} \{1/x\} & \text{if } x > 0 \\ \{0\} & \text{if } x = 0. \end{cases}$$

Determine if Φ is usc and/or lsc on $\mathbb{R}_+$.

5. Let $\Phi \colon \mathbb{R} \to P(\mathbb{R})$ be defined by

$$\Phi(x) = \begin{cases} [0, 1] & \text{if } x \neq 0 \\ (0, 1) & \text{if } x = 0. \end{cases}$$

Determine if Φ is usc and/or lsc on $\mathbb{R}$.

6. Let $\Phi \colon \mathbb{R} \to P(\mathbb{R})$ be defined by

$$\Phi(x) = \begin{cases} (0, 1) & \text{if } x \neq 0 \\ [0, 1] & \text{if } x = 0. \end{cases}$$

Determine if Φ is usc and/or lsc on $\mathbb{R}$.

7. Define the correspondence $\Phi \colon \mathbb{R}_+ \to P(\mathbb{R}_+)$ as

$$\Phi(x) = [x, \infty), \quad x \in \mathbb{R}_+.$$

Is this correspondence usc on $\mathbb{R}_+$? Is it lsc? Does it have a closed graph?

8. Let $I = [0, 1]$, and let the correspondence $\Phi \colon I \to P(I)$ be defined by

$$\Phi(x) = \{0, x\}, \quad x \in I.$$

Is this correspondence usc on I? Is it lsc? Does it have a closed graph?

9. Let $X = Y = [0, 1]$, and $f \colon X \to Y$ be defined by

$$f(x) = \begin{cases} x & \text{if } x \in (0, 1] \\ 1 & \text{if } x = 0. \end{cases}$$

Examine if f is an upper-semicontinuous and/or lower-semicontinuous function on X. Does f attain a minimum on X?

10. Let $X = Y = [0, 1]$, and $f: X \to Y$ be defined by

$$f(x) = \begin{cases} x & \text{if } x \in [0, 1) \\ 0 & \text{if } x = 1. \end{cases}$$

Determine if (a) f is an upper-semicontinuous function on X, and (b) if it attains a maximum on X.

11. Let $X = Y = [0, 1]$ and $f: X \to Y$ be defined by

$$f(x) = \begin{cases} 1 & \text{if } x \text{ is irrational} \\ 0 & \text{if } x \text{ is rational.} \end{cases}$$

Examine if f is an upper-semicontinuous and/or lower-semicontinuous function on X.

12. Let $f: \mathbb{R}_+ \times \mathbb{R}_+ \to \mathbb{R}$ be defined by

$$f(a, x) = (x - 1) - (x - a)^2, \quad (a, x) \in \mathbb{R}_+^2.$$

Define the correspondence $\mathcal{D}: \mathbb{R}_+ \to P(\mathbb{R}_+)$ by

$$\mathcal{D}(a) = \{y \in \mathbb{R}_+ : y \le a\}, \quad a \in \mathbb{R}_+.$$

Let

$$f^*(a) = \max\{f(a, x) \mid x \in \mathcal{D}(a)\}.$$

Let $\mathcal{D}^*(a)$ be the set of maximizers of $f(\cdot, a)$ on $\mathcal{D}(a)$. Do the hypotheses of the Maximum Theorem hold for this problem? Verify, through direct calculation, whether the conclusions of the Maximum Theorem hold.

13. Let $S = [0, 2]$, and $\Theta = [0, 1]$. Let $f: S \times \Theta \to \mathbb{R}$ be defined by

$$f(, \theta) = \begin{cases} 0 & \text{if } \theta = 0 \\ x/\theta & \text{if } \theta > 0 \text{ and } x \in [0, \theta) \\ 2 - (x/\theta) & \text{if } \theta > 0 \text{ and } x \in [\theta, 2\theta] \\ 0 & \text{if } x > 2\theta. \end{cases}$$

Let the correspondence $\mathcal{D}: \Theta \to P(S)$ be defined by

$$\mathcal{D}(\theta) = \begin{cases} [0, 1 - 2\theta] & \text{if } \theta \in [0, 1/2) \\ [0, 2 - 2\theta] & \text{if } \theta \in [1/2, 1]. \end{cases}$$

(a) Do f and $\mathcal{D}$ meet all the conditions of the Maximum Theorem? If yes, prove your claim. If no, list all the conditions you believe are violated and explain precisely why you believe each of them is violated.

(b) Let $\mathcal{D}^*: \Theta \to P(S)$ be given by

$$\mathcal{D}^*(t) = \{x \in \mathcal{D}(\theta) \mid f(x, \theta) \geq f(x', \theta) \text{ for all } x \in \mathcal{D}(\theta)\}.$$

Is it the case that $\mathcal{D}^*(\theta) \neq \emptyset$ for each $\theta \in \Theta$? If so, determine whether $\mathcal{D}^*$ is usc and/or lsc on Θ.

14. Repeat the last problem with the definition of $\mathcal{D}$ changed to

$$\mathcal{D}(\theta) = \begin{cases} [0, 1 - 2\theta] & \text{if } \theta \in [0, 1/2) \\ [0, 2\theta - 1] & \text{if } \theta \in [1/2, 1]. \end{cases}$$

15. Let $f: S \times \Theta \to \mathbb{R}$ be a continuous function, and $\mathcal{D}: \Theta \to P(S)$ be a continuous compact-valued correspondence, where $S \subset \mathbb{R}^n$, $\Theta \subset \mathbb{R}^l$. Suppose the correspondence $\mathcal{D}$ is *monotonic* in the sense that if $\theta, \theta' \in \Theta$, then

$$\theta \geq \theta' \implies \mathcal{D}(\theta) \supset \mathcal{D}(\theta').$$

That is, all actions feasible at a value of θ are also feasible at all larger values of θ.

(a) Show that $f^*(\cdot)$ must then be nondecreasing on Θ.

(b) Examine under what additional conditions f will be strictly increasing on Θ.

(c) Give an example to show that if $\mathcal{D}$ is not monotone, then f^* need not be nondecreasing on Θ.

16. Let $S = \Theta = [0, 1]$. Define $\mathcal{D}: \Theta \to P(S)$ by $\mathcal{D}(\theta) = [0, \theta]$ for all $\theta \in S$. Give an example of a function $f: S \times \Theta \to \mathbb{R}$ such that $f^*(\theta) = \max\{f(x, \theta) \mid x \in \mathcal{D}(\theta)\}$ fails to be continuous at only the point $\theta = 1/2$, or show that no such example is possible.

17. Let $S = \Theta = \mathbb{R}_+$. Describe a continuous function $f: S \times \Theta \to \mathbb{R}$ and a continuous, compact-valued correspondence $\mathcal{D}: \Theta \to P(S)$ that possess the following properties (or show that no such example is possible):

(a) $\mathcal{D}$ is an increasing correspondence on Θ, that is, $\theta > \theta'$ implies $\mathcal{D}(\theta) \supset \mathcal{D}(\theta')$.

(b) There are points $\theta_1, \theta_2, \theta_3$ in Θ such that $\theta_1 > \theta_2 > \theta_3$, but $f^*(\theta_1) > f^*(\theta_3) > f^*(\theta_2)$, where $f^*(\theta) = \max\{f(x) \mid x \in \mathcal{D}(\theta)\}$.

18. Provide examples to show that Part 2 of the Maximum Theorem under Convexity is not necessarily true if $\mathcal{D}$ is not convex-valued, or if f is not necessarily concave.

19. Provide an example to show that Part 3 of the Maximum Theorem under Convexity is not necessarily true if the graph of $\mathcal{D}$ fails to be convex.

20. Given an example of a function $f: S \times \Theta \to \mathbb{R}$ and a correspondence $\mathcal{D}: \Theta \to P(S)$ such that f is not continuous on $S \times \Theta$, $\mathcal{D}$ is not continuous on Θ, but f^* is a continuous function on Θ, and $\mathcal{D}^*$ is an upper-semicontinuous correspondence on Θ, where f^* and $\mathcal{D}^*$ are obtained from f and $\mathcal{D}$ as in the Maximum Theorem.

21. Suppose we were *minimizing* $f(x, \theta)$ over $x \in \mathcal{D}(\theta)$, where f and $\mathcal{D}$ meet all the conditions of the Maximum Theorem. What can one say about the *minimized value function*

$$f_*(\theta) = \max\{f(x, \theta) \mid x \in \mathcal{D}(\theta)\},$$

and the correspondence of minimizers

$$\mathcal{D}_*(\theta) = \arg\min\{f(x, \theta) \mid x \in \mathcal{D}(\theta)\}?$$

22. Suppose that in the statement of the Maximum Theorem, the hypothesis on f was weakened to require only the *upper*-semicontinuity of f on $S \times \Theta$, rather than full continuity. Assume that the other conditions of the theorem remain unchanged.

    (a) Prove that the maximized value function f^* will also now be an upper-semicontinuous function on Θ.

    (b) Give an example to show that $\mathcal{D}^*$ may fail to be usc on Θ.

23. Let $\{N, (S_i, r_i)_{i \in N}\}$ be a normal-form game in which for each i, S_i is a convex and compact set, and r_i is a continuous concave function on S. Show that this game has a Nash equilibrium in pure strategies, i.e., that there is $s^* \in S$ such that $r_i(s^*) \geq r_i(\hat{s}_i, s^*_{-i})$ for any $\hat{s}_i \in S_i$ and any $i \in N$.

24. Show that the result of the previous question holds even if r_i is only quasi-concave on S_i for each fixed $s_{-i} \in S_{-i}$.

25. Find all the Nash equilibria of each the following games:

	L_2	R_2
L_1	(4, 4)	(0, 5)
R_1	(5, 0)	(1, 1)

	L_2	R_2
L_1	(2, 1)	(0, 0)
R_1	(0, 0)	(1, 2)

	L_2	R_2
L_1	(1, 1)	(0, 0)
R_1	(0, 0)	(0, 0)

	L_2	R_2
L_1	(3, 3)	(1, 1)
R_1	(1, 1)	(2, 2)

	L_2	R_2
L_1	(8, 8)	(0, 7)
R_1	(7, 0)	(7, 7)

	L_2	M_2	R_2
L_1	(10, 10)	(10, 6)	(10, 1)
M_1	(6, 10)	(14, 14)	(8, 2)
R_1	(1, 10)	(2, 8)	(10, 10)

	L_2	M_2	R_2
L_1	(4, 6)	(0, 0)	(6, 4)
M_1	(0, 0)	(4, 6)	(0, 0)
R_1	(6, 4)	(0, 0)	(4, 6)

	L_2	M_2	R_2
L_1	(4, 10)	(2, 10)	(8, 10)
M_1	(4, 4)	(8, 3)	(2, 10)
R_1	(4, 7)	(3, 7)	(10, 5)

10

Supermodularity and Parametric Monotonicity

This chapter examines the issue of *parametric monotonicity*. The objective is to identify conditions on the primitives of parametric families of optimization problems under which the optimal action correspondence $\mathcal{D}^*(\cdot)$ varies *monotonically* with the parameter θ, that is, under which increases in the parameter θ result in increases in the optimal actions.

Implicit in the very question of parametric monotonicity is the idea of an order structure on the parameter space Θ and the action space S. In subsection 10.1.1 below, we identify the structure we will require these spaces to have. This is followed in subsection 10.1.2 by the definition of the two key conditions of *supermodularity* and *increasing differences* that will be placed on the objective function.

Section 10.2 then presents the main result of this chapter, a set of sufficient conditions on the primitives of a parametric family of optimization problems under which parametric monotonicity obtains. A rough summary of this result is as follows. Suppose $S \subset \mathbb{R}^n$ and $\Theta \subset \mathbb{R}^l$. Let $D^2 f(x, \theta)$ represent the $(n+l) \times (n+l)$ matrix of second-partials of the objective function f:

$$
D^2 f(x, \theta) = \begin{bmatrix} \dfrac{\partial^2 f}{\partial x_i^2}(x, \theta) & \cdots & \dfrac{\partial^2 f}{\partial x_1 \partial \theta_l}(x, \theta) \\ \vdots & \ddots & \vdots \\ \dfrac{\partial^2 f}{\partial \theta_l \partial x_1}(x, \theta) & \cdots & \dfrac{\partial^2 f}{\partial \theta_l^2}(x, \theta) \end{bmatrix}.
$$

Then, under some technical regularity conditions, optimal actions increase in the parameter vector θ whenever all the *off-diagonal* terms in the matrix $D^2 f(x, \theta)$ are nonnegative. The remarkable part of the result is that it involves no restrictions on the *diagonal* terms of this matrix; in particular, there are no convexity assumptions required.

Finally, Section 10.3 provides an example illustrating the value of the results of this chapter.

10.1 Lattices and Supermodularity

Recall our basic notation that, given any two vectors $x = (x_1, \ldots, x_m)$ and $y = (y_1, \ldots, y_m)$ in $\mathbb{R}^m$, we have

$$
\begin{aligned}
x &= y, & &\text{if } x_i = y_i,\ i = 1, \ldots, m \\
x &\geq y, & &\text{if } x_i \geq y_i,\ i = 1, \ldots, m \\
x &> y, & &\text{if } x \geq y \text{ and } x \neq y \\
x &\gg y, & &\text{if } x_i > y_i,\ i = 1, \ldots, m.
\end{aligned}
$$

Except in the case $m = 1$, the ordering given by "$\geq$" on $\mathbb{R}^m$ is incomplete. Nonetheless, this ordering suffices to define the restrictions that we will need to obtain parametric monotonicity. We do this in two stages. In subsection 10.1.1, we discuss the conditions we will require the action space S to satisfy. Then, in subsection 10.1.2, we describe the assumptions that will be placed on the objective function f.

10.1.1 Lattices

Given two points x and y in $\mathbb{R}^m$, we define the *meet* of x and y, denoted $x \wedge y$, to be the coordinate-wise minimum of x and y:

$$
x \wedge y = (\min\{x_1, y_1\}, \ldots, \min\{x_m, y_m\}).
$$

In corresponding fashion, the *join* of x and y, denoted $x \vee y$, is defined to be the coordinate-wise maximum of the points x and y:

$$
x \vee y = (\max\{x_1, y_1\}, \ldots, \max\{x_m, y_m\}).
$$

It is always true that $x \vee y \geq x$; equality occurs if and only if $x \geq y$. Similarly, it is always true that $x \wedge y \leq x$, with equality if and only if $x \leq y$. In particular, it is the case that

$$
\begin{aligned}
x \not\geq y &\Rightarrow (x \vee y) > x \\
x \not\leq y &\Rightarrow (x \wedge y) < x.
\end{aligned}
$$

These elementary observations will come in handy in the proof of parametric monotonicity in Section 10.2.

A set $X \subset \mathbb{R}^m$ is said to be a *sublattice* of $\mathbb{R}^m$ if the meet and join of any two points in X is also in X. That is, X is a sublattice of $\mathbb{R}^m$ if

$$
x, y \in X \implies \{(x \wedge y) \in X \text{ and } (x \vee y) \in X\}.
$$

For instance, any interval in $\mathbb{R}$ is a sublattice of $\mathbb{R}$, while the unit square

$$I = \{(x, y) \in \mathbb{R}^2 \mid 0 \leq x \leq 1, \ 0 \leq y \leq 1\}$$

and the hyperplane

$$H = \{(x, y) \in \mathbb{R}^2 \mid x = y\}$$

are sublattices of $\mathbb{R}^2$. On the other hand, the hyperplane

$$H' = \{(x, y) \in \mathbb{R}^2 \mid x + y = 1\}$$

is not a sublattice of $\mathbb{R}^2$: we have $(1, 0) \in H'$ and $(0, 1) \in H'$, but the meet $(0, 0)$ and the join $(1, 1)$ of these two points are not contained in H'.

A sublattice $X \subset \mathbb{R}^m$ is said to be a *compact sublattice* in $\mathbb{R}^m$ if X is also a compact set in the Euclidean metric. Thus, any compact interval is a compact sublattice in $\mathbb{R}$, while the unit square I^2 is a compact sublattice in $\mathbb{R}^2$. On the other hand, the open interval $(0, 1)$ is a noncompact sublattice of $\mathbb{R}$, while the set $\mathbb{R}_+^m$ is a noncompact sublattice of $\mathbb{R}^m$.

A point $x^* \in X$ is said to be a *greatest element* of a sublattice X if it is the case that $x^* \geq x$ for all $x \in X$. A point $\hat{x} \in X$ is said to be a *least element* of a sublattice X if it is the case that $\hat{x} \leq x$ for all $x \in X$.

It is an elementary matter to construct sublattices that admit no greatest and/or least element. For example, consider the open unit square I^o in $\mathbb{R}^2$:

$$I^o = \{(x, y) \in \mathbb{R}^2 \mid 0 < x < 1, \ 0 < y < 1\}.$$

The following result offers sufficient conditions for a sublattice in $\mathbb{R}^m$ to admit a greatest element; it plays an important role in the proof of our main result in Section 10.2:

Theorem 10.1 *Suppose X is a nonempty, compact sublattice of $\mathbb{R}^m$. Then, X has a greatest element and a least element.*

Proof See Birkhoff (1967). $\square$

10.1.2 Supermodularity and Increasing Differences

Let S and Θ be subsets of $\mathbb{R}^n$ and $\mathbb{R}^l$, respectively. We will assume, through the rest of this chapter, that S and Θ are both sublattices.

A function $f \colon S \times \Theta \to \mathbb{R}$ is said to be *supermodular in* (x, θ) if it is the case that for all $z = (x, \theta)$ and $z' = (x', \theta')$ in $S \times \Theta$, we have

$$f(z) + f(z') \leq f(z \vee z') + f(z \wedge z').$$

If the inequality becomes strict whenever z and z' are not comparable under the ordering $\geq$, then f is said to be *strictly supermodular* in (x, θ).[1]

Example 10.2 Let $S = \Theta = \mathbb{R}_+$, and let $f: S \times \Theta \to \mathbb{R}$ be given by

$$f(x, \theta) = x\theta.$$

Pick any (x, θ) and (x', θ') in $S \times \Theta$, and assume without loss that $x \geq x'$. Suppose first that $\theta \geq \theta'$. Then, $(x, \theta) \vee (x', \theta') = (x, \theta)$ and $(x, \theta) \wedge (x', \theta') = (x', \theta')$. Therefore, it is trivially the case that

$$f(x, \theta) + f(x', \theta') \leq f[(x, \theta) \vee (x', \theta')] + f[(x, \theta) \wedge (x', \theta')].$$

Now suppose, alternatively, that $\theta < \theta'$. Then, $(x, \theta) \vee (x', \theta') = (x, \theta')$ and $(x, \theta) \wedge (x', \theta') = (x', \theta)$. Therefore,

$$f((x, \theta) \vee (x', \theta')) + f((x, \theta) \wedge (x', \theta')) = x\theta' + x'\theta.$$

Now, $(x\theta' + x'\theta) - (x\theta + x'\theta') = x(\theta' - \theta) - x'(\theta' - \theta) = (x - x')(\theta' - \theta) \geq 0$, so it is true in this case also that

$$f(x, \theta) + f(x', \theta') \leq f((x, \theta) \vee (x', \theta')) + f((x, \theta) \wedge (x', \theta')).$$

Therefore, $f(x, \theta) = x\theta$ is supermodular on $S \times \Theta$. In fact, since strict inequality holds whenever $x < x'$ and $\theta > \theta'$ (or $x > x'$ and $\theta > \theta'$), f is *strictly* supermodular on $S \times \Theta$. $\qquad\square$

Supermodularity of f in (x, θ) is the key notion that goes into obtaining parametric monotonicity. It turns out, however, that two implications of supermodularity, which are summarized in Theorem 10.3 below, are all we really need. A definition is required before we can state the exact result.

A function $f: S \times \Theta \to \mathbb{R}$ is said to satisfy *increasing differences in* (x, θ) if for all pairs (x, θ) and (x', θ') in $S \times \Theta$, it is the case that $x \geq x'$ and $\theta \geq \theta'$ implies

$$f(x, \theta) - f(x', \theta) \geq f(x, \theta') - f(x', \theta').$$

If the inequality becomes strict whenever $x > x'$ and $\theta > \theta'$, then f is said to satisfy *strictly increasing differences in* (x, θ).

In words, f has increasing differences in (x, θ) if the difference

$$f(x, \theta) - f(x', \theta)$$

between the values of f evaluated at the larger action x and the lesser action x' is itself an increasing function of the parameter θ.

---

[1] If z and z' are comparable under $\geq$ (i.e., if either $z \geq z'$ or $z' \geq z$), then a simple computation shows that both sides of the defining inequality are equal to $f(z) + f(z')$, so a strict inequality is impossible.

Theorem 10.3 *Suppose* $f: S \times \Theta \to \mathbb{R}$ *is supermodular in* (x, θ). *Then:*

1. f *is supermodular in* x *for each fixed* θ, *i.e., for any fixed* $\theta \in \Theta$, *and for any* x *and* x' *in* S, *we have* $f(x, \theta) + f(x', \theta) \leq f(x \vee x', \theta) + f(x \wedge x', \theta)$.
2. f *satisfies increasing differences in* (x, θ).

Proof Part 1 is trivial. To see Part 2, pick any $z = (x, \theta)$ and $z' = (x', \theta')$ that satisfy $x \geq x'$ and $\theta \geq \theta'$. Let $w = (x, \theta')$ and $w' = (x', \theta)$. Then, $w \vee w' = z$ and $w \wedge w' = z'$. Since f is supermodular on $S \times \Theta$,

$$f(w) + f(w') \leq f(z) + f(z').$$

Rearranging, and using the definitions of w and w', this is the same as

$$f(x, \theta) - f(x, \theta') \geq f(x', \theta) - f(x', \theta'),$$

so f satisfies increasing differences also, as claimed. $\square$

A partial converse to Part 2 of Theorem 10.3 is valid. This converse is somewhat peripheral to our purposes here; consequently, in the interests of expositional continuity, we postpone its statement and proof to Section 10.4 below (see Theorem 10.12). Perhaps the most significant aspect of Theorem 10.12 is that it makes for an easy proof of the following very useful result concerning when a twice-differentiable function is supermodular:

Theorem 10.4 *Let* Z *be an open sublattice of* $\mathbb{R}^m$. *A* C^2 *function* $h: Z \to \mathbb{R}$ *is supermodular on* Z *if and only if for all* $z \in Z$, *we have*

$$\frac{\partial^2 h}{\partial z_i \partial z_j}(z) \geq 0, \qquad i, j = 1, \ldots, m, \ i \neq j.$$

Proof See Section 10.4. $\square$

Theorem 10.4 is of particular interest from a computational standpoint: it becomes easy to check for supermodularity of a C^2 function. The following example illustrates this point, using a generalization of the function of Example 10.2:

Example 10.5 Let $S \subset \mathbb{R}_+^2$ and $\Theta \subset \mathbb{R}_+$. Let $f: S \times \Theta \to \mathbb{R}$ be given by

$$f((x, y), \theta) = xy\theta.$$

By a process a little more painful than that employed in Example 10.2, it can be shown that f meets the inequality required to be supermodular in (x, y, θ). For a simpler procedure to verify this, note that

$$\frac{\partial^2 f}{\partial x \partial y}(x, y, \theta) = \theta, \quad \frac{\partial^2 f}{\partial x \partial \theta}(x, y, \theta) = y, \quad \text{and} \quad \frac{\partial^2 f}{\partial y \partial \theta}(x, y, \theta) = x.$$

Since x, y, and θ are all nonnegative, these cross-partials are all nonnegative, so f is supermodular in (x, y, θ) by Theorem 10.4. $\qquad \square$

10.2 Parametric Monotonicity

To get an intuitive feel for the role played by the condition of increasing differences in obtaining parametric monotonicity, consider the following problem in the special case where $S \subset \mathbb{R}$ (i.e., where x is a scalar):

$$\text{Maximize } f(x, \theta) \text{ subject to } x \in S.$$

Suppose that a solution exists for all $\theta \in \Theta$ (for instance, suppose that $f(\cdot, \theta)$ is continuous on S for each fixed θ, and that S is compact). Pick any two points θ_1 and θ_2 in Θ, and suppose that $\theta_1 > \theta_2$. Let x_1 and x_2 be points that are optimal at θ_1 and θ_2, respectively. Since x_2 need not be optimal at θ_1 nor x_1 at θ_2, we have

$$f(x_1, \theta_1) - f(x_2, \theta_1) \geq 0$$
$$\geq f(x_1, \theta_2) - f(x_2, \theta_2).$$

Suppose f satisfies strictly increasing differences. Suppose further that although $\theta_1 > \theta_2$, parametric monotonicity fails, and we have $x_1 \not\geq x_2$. Since x is a scalar variable, we must then have $x_1 < x_2$. Therefore, the vectors (x_2, θ_1) and (x_1, θ_2) satisfy $x_2 > x_1$ and $\theta_1 > \theta_2$. By strictly increasing differences, this implies

$$f(x_2, \theta_1) - f(x_1, \theta_1) > f(x_2, \theta_2) - f(x_1, \theta_2),$$

which is in direct contradiction to the weak inequalities we obtained above. Thus, we must have $x_1 \geq x_2$, and since x_1 and x_2 were arbitrary selections from the sets of optimal actions at θ_1 and θ_2, respectively, we have shown that if S is a subset of $\mathbb{R}$, the condition of strictly increasing differences suffices by itself to obtain monotonicity of optimal actions in the parameter.

Theorem 10.6 *Suppose that the optimization problem*

$$\text{Maximize } f(x, \theta) \text{ subject to } x \in S$$

has at least one solution for each $\theta \in \Theta$. Suppose also that f satisfies strictly increasing differences in (x, θ). Finally, suppose that $S \subset \mathbb{R}$. Then optimal actions are monotone increasing in the parameter θ.

The arguments leading to Theorem 10.6 do not extend to the case where $S \subset \mathbb{R}^n$ for $n \geq 2$, since now the failure of x_1 and x_2 to satisfy $x_1 \geq x_2$ does not imply that $x_1 < x_2$. Thus, additional assumptions will be needed in this case. The appropriate condition is, it turns out, that of *supermodularity in x*. The following result is the centerpiece of this chapter:

Theorem 10.7 *Let S be a compact sublattice of $\mathbb{R}^n$, Θ be a sublattice of $\mathbb{R}^l$, and $f: S \times \Theta \to \mathbb{R}$ be a continuous function on S for each fixed θ. Suppose that f satisfies increasing differences in (x, θ), and is supermodular in x for each fixed θ. Let the correspondence $\mathcal{D}^*$ from Θ to S be defined by*

$$\mathcal{D}^*(\theta) = \arg\max\{f(x, \theta) \mid x \in S\}.$$

1. *For each $\theta \in \Theta$, $\mathcal{D}^*(\theta)$ is a nonempty compact sublattice of $\mathbb{R}^n$, and admits a greatest element, denoted $x^*(\theta)$.*
2. *$x^*(\theta_1) \geq x^*(\theta_2)$ whenever $\theta_1 > \theta_2$.*
3. *If f satisfies strictly increasing differences in (x, θ), then $x_1 \geq x_2$ for any $x_1 \in \mathcal{D}(\theta_1)$ and $x_2 \in \mathcal{D}(\theta_2)$, whenever $\theta_1 > \theta_2$.*

Proof Since f is continuous on S for each fixed θ and S is compact, $\mathcal{D}^*(\theta)$ is nonempty for each θ. Fix θ and suppose $\{x_p\}$ is a sequence in $\mathcal{D}^*(\theta)$ converging to $x \in S$. Then, for any $y \in S$, we have

$$f(x_p, \theta) \geq f(y, \theta)$$

by the optimality of x_p. Taking limits as $p \to \infty$, and using the continuity of $f(\cdot, \theta)$, we obtain

$$f(x, \theta) \geq f(y, \theta),$$

so $x \in \mathcal{D}^*(\theta)$. Therefore, $\mathcal{D}^*(\theta)$ is closed, and as a closed subset of the compact set S, it is also compact. Let x and x' be distinct elements of $\mathcal{D}^*(\theta)$. If $x \wedge x' \notin \mathcal{D}^*(\theta)$, we must have

$$f(x \wedge x', \theta) < f(x, \theta) = f(x', \theta).$$

Supermodularity in x then implies

$$f(x' \vee x, \theta) > f(x, \theta) = f(x', \theta),$$

which contradicts the presumed optimality of x and x' at θ. A similar argument also establishes that $x \vee x' \in \mathcal{D}^*(\theta)$. Thus, $\mathcal{D}^*(\theta)$ is a sublattice of $\mathbb{R}^n$, and as a nonempty, compact sublattice of $\mathbb{R}^n$, admits a greatest element $x^*(\theta)$. This completes the proof of Part 1.

Now, let θ_1 and θ_2 be given with $\theta_1 > \theta_2$. Let $x_1 \in \mathcal{D}^*(\theta_1)$ and $x_2 \in \mathcal{D}^*(\theta_2)$. Then, we have

$$0 \leq f(x_1, \theta_1) - f(x_1 \vee x_2, \theta_1) \qquad \text{(by optimality of } x_1 \text{ at } \theta_1)$$

$$\leq f(x_1 \wedge x_2, \theta_1) - f(x_2, \theta_1) \qquad \text{(by supermodularity in } x)$$

$$\leq f(x_1 \wedge x_2, \theta_2) - f(x_2, \theta_2) \qquad \text{(by increasing differences in } (x, \theta))$$

$$\leq 0 \qquad \text{(by optimality of } x_2 \text{ at } \theta_2),$$

so equality holds at every point in this string.

Now, suppose $x_1 = x^*(\theta_1)$ and $x_2 = x^*(\theta_2)$. Since equality holds at all points in the string, it is the case that $x_1 \vee x_2$ is also an optimal action at θ_1. If it were not true that $x_1 \geq x_2$, then we would have $x_1 \vee x_2 > x_1$, and this contradicts the definition of x_1 as the greatest element of $\mathcal{D}^*(\theta_1)$. Thus, we must have $x_1 \geq x_2$, and this establishes Part 2 of the theorem.

To see Part 3, suppose that x_1 and x_2 are arbitrary selections from $\mathcal{D}^*(\theta_1)$ and $\mathcal{D}^*(\theta_2)$, respectively. Suppose we did not have $x_1 \geq x_2$. Then, we must have $x_1 \vee x_2 > x_1$ and $x_1 \wedge x_2 < x_2$. If f satisfies strictly increasing differences, then, since $\theta_1 > \theta_2$, we have

$$f(x_2, \theta_1) - f(x_1 \wedge x_2, \theta_1) > f(x_2, \theta_2) - f(x_1 \wedge x_2, \theta_2),$$

so the third inequality in the string becomes strict, contradicting the equality. $\quad\square$

Theorem 10.7 effectively assumes a constant feasible action correspondence $\mathcal{D}$ with $\mathcal{D}(\theta) = S$ for all θ. The only significant role this assumption plays in the proof is in ensuring the feasibility of the action $x_1 \vee x_2$ at θ_1, and the feasibility of the action $x_1 \wedge x_2$ at θ_2. To wit, the proof used the fact that optimality of x_1 at θ_1 implied the inequality

$$f(x_1, \theta_1) - f(x_1 \vee x_2, \theta_1) \geq 0,$$

and that the optimality of x_2 at θ_2 implied the inequality

$$f(x_1 \wedge x_2, \theta_2) - f(x_2, \theta_2) \geq 0.$$

If the feasible correspondence $\mathcal{D}$ is allowed to be nonconstant, and if $x_1 \vee x_2 \notin \mathcal{D}(\theta_1)$ (say), then we could not conclude from the optimality of x_1 at θ_1 that the first of these inequalities holds, since x_1 only maximizes f over $\mathcal{D}(\theta_1)$. On the other hand, if we directly assume a condition that implies the feasibility of $x_1 \vee x_2$ at $\mathcal{D}(\theta_1)$ and $x_1 \wedge x_2$ at $\mathcal{D}(\theta_2)$, then we can obtain a generalization of Theorem 10.7 to the case where $\mathcal{D}$ is nonconstant:

Corollary 10.8 *Suppose S, Θ, and f meet the conditions of Theorem 10.7. Suppose also that $\mathcal{D}: \Theta \rightarrow P(S)$ satisfies the following conditions:*

1. *For all $\theta \in \Theta$, $\mathcal{D}(\theta)$ is a compact sublattice of Θ.*
2. *For all θ_1 and θ_2 in Θ, and for all $x_1 \in \mathcal{D}(\theta_1)$ and $x_2 \in \mathcal{D}(\theta_2)$,*

$$\theta_1 \geq \theta_2 \text{ implies } x_1 \vee x_2 \in \mathcal{D}(\theta_1) \text{ and } x_1 \wedge x_2 \in \mathcal{D}(\theta_2).$$

Then, if $\mathcal{D}^*(\theta) = \arg \max\{f(x, \theta) \mid x \in \mathcal{D}(\theta)\}$, both conclusions of Theorem 10.7 hold.

The conditions on $\mathcal{D}$ given in Corollary 10.8 are less forbidding than they might appear at first sight. For instance, if $S = \Theta = \mathbb{R}_+$, the correspondence

$$\mathcal{D}(\theta) = [0, \theta]$$

satisfies them. More generally, if $S = \Theta = \mathbb{R}^l_+$, the correspondence

$$\mathcal{D}(\theta) = \{x \in S \mid 0 \leq x \leq \theta\}$$

also meets the conditions of Corollary 10.8.

On the other hand, these conditions are also sufficiently restrictive that many interesting applications are precluded. Consider, for instance, the utility maximization problem

$$\text{Maximize } u(x) \text{ subject to } x \in \mathcal{B}(p, I) = \{z \in \mathbb{R}^n_+ \mid p \cdot z \leq I\}.$$

Letting $x(p, I)$ denote a solution to this problem at the parameters (p, I), a question of some interest is whether, or under what conditions, "own-price" effects on optimal demand are negative, that is, whether $x_i(p, I)$ is nonincreasing in the parameter p_i.

It is easy to put this question into the framework of Corollary 10.8 by writing $-p_i$, rather than p_i, as the parameter of interest. Then, a nonincreasing own-price effect is the same thing as the optimal demand for commodity i being non*decreasing* in the parameter $-p_i$, and this is exactly the manner in which the conclusions of Corollary 10.8 are stated.

Unfortunately, Corollary 10.8 cannot help us obtain an answer. Suppressing the dependence on the remaining parameters, the correspondence of feasible actions $\mathcal{B}(-\hat{p}_i)$ is given by

$$\mathcal{B}(-\hat{p}_i) = \left\{x \in \mathbb{R}^n_+ \mid \hat{p}_i x_i + \sum_{j \neq i} p_j x_j \leq I\right\}.$$

It is easy to check that this correspondence does not meet the conditions of Corollary 10.8; indeed, $\mathcal{B}(\cdot)$ is not even a sublattice of $\mathbb{R}^n$.

10.3 An Application to Supermodular Games

This section offers an application of the theory of the previous section to a class of n-person games known as *supermodular games*. For further examples along these lines, the reader is referred to Vives (1990), Milgrom and Roberts (1990), Fudenberg and Tirole (1990), or Topkis (1995).

10.3.1 Supermodular Games

Recall from Section 9.4 that an n-person normal-form game is specified by a strategy set S_i and a payoff function $r_i \colon S_1 \times \S_n \to \mathbb{R}$ for each player i, $i = 1, \dots, n$. As earlier, we will write S for $\times_{i=1}^n S_i$, and S_{-i} to denote the strategy sets of "everyone-but-i:" $S_{-i} = \times_{j \neq i} S_j$. The notation $(\hat{s}_i, s_{-i})$ will be used to denote the obvious vector in S.

An n-person game is said to be a *supermodular game* if for each i, S_i is a sublattice of some Euclidean space, and $r_i \colon S \to \mathbb{R}$ is supermodular in s_i for each fixed s_{-i}, and satisfies increasing differences in (s_i, s_{-i}). The game is said to be *strictly supermodular* if r_i has strictly increasing differences in (s_i, s_{-i}) and is strictly supermodular in s_i for each fixed s_{-i}.

Example 10.9 A typical example of a supermodular game is the Bertrand oligopoly model with linear demand curves. In this example, players $i = 1, \dots, n$, are firms in an oligopolistic market. The firms' products are substitutes, but not perfect substitutes in the eyes of consumers. Thus, each firm has some degree of market power. It is assumed that firms compete by setting prices so as to maximize (own) profit. Suppose the demand curves are given by the following information: if the vector of prices chosen by the n firms is $p = (p_1, \dots, p_n)$, the demand that arises for firm i's product is

$$q_i(p) = \alpha_i - \beta_i p_i + \sum_{j \neq i} \gamma_{ij} p_j,$$

where β and $(\gamma_{ij})_{j \neq i}$ are strictly positive parameters.[2] Suppose further that it costs firm i a total of $c_i q_i$ to produce q_i units, where $c_i > 0$. Then, firm i's payoff from setting the price p_i, given the choices p_{-i} of the other firms, is

$$r_i(p_i, p_{-i}) = (p_i - c_i) q_i(p_i, p_{-i}).$$

A simple calculation shows that r_i satisfies increasing differences in (p_i, p_{-i}). Since p_i is unidimensional, r_i also satisfies supermodularity in p_i for each p_{-i}. Finally, the strategy space S_i for firm i is simply $\mathbb{R}_+$, the set of all possible prices

---

[2] The positive coefficient on p_j for $j \neq i$ captures the fact that an increase in the price of product j causes some consumers to move to the substitute offered by i; the positive coefficient on p_i reflects the demand that will be lost (or that will move to other firms) if i raises prices.

firm i may charge. Since this is evidently a sublattice of $\mathbb{R}$, the game we have described here is a supermodular game. $\qquad\square$

10.3.2 The Tarski Fixed Point Theorem

As is almost always the case, the existence of Nash equilibrium in the class of supermodular games will also be proved through the use of a fixed point theorem. The relevant theorem in this case is the fixed point theorem due to Tarski, which deals with fixed points of monotone functions on lattices.

Theorem 10.10 (Tarski's Fixed Point Theorem) *Let X be a nonempty compact sublattice of $\mathbb{R}^m$. Let $f\colon X \to X$ be a nondecreasing function, i.e., $x, y \in X$ with $x \geq y$ implies $f(x) \geq f(y)$. Then, f has a fixed point on X.*

Proof See Tarski (1955). $\qquad\square$

There are at least three features of the Tarski fixed point theorem that are worth stressing:

1. Unlike the great majority of fixed point theorems, the Tarski Fixed Point Theorem does not require *convexity* of the set X.
2. Equally unusually, the theorem does not require the map f to be *continuous*, but merely to be nondecreasing.
3. The theorem is valid for nondecreasing functions f, but (somewhat unintuitively) is false for non*increasing* functions f. Indeed, it is an elementary task to construct examples of nonincreasing functions from the compact sublattice [0,1] into itself that do not have a fixed point; we leave this as an exercise.

10.3.3 Existence of Nash Equilibrium

The following result is an easy consequence of Theorem 10.7 on parametric monotonicity and Tarski's Fixed Point Theorem.

Theorem 10.11 *Suppose an n-player supermodular game has the property that for each $i \in \{1, \ldots, n\}$, S_i is compact and r_i is continuous on S_i for each fixed s_{-i}. Then, the game has a Nash equilibrium.*

Proof Given $s \in S$, player solves[3]

$$\text{Maximize } f(\hat{s}_i, s_{-i}) \text{ subject to } \hat{s}_i \in S_i.$$

---

[3]As in Section 9.4, player i's best-response problem depends on s only through s_{-i}. However, it is notationally convenient to write it as a fucntion of s, rather than just s_{-i}.

Since f is supermodular in s_i and has increasing differences in (s_i, s_{-i}), and since S_i is a compact sublattice of some Euclidean space, it follows from Part 2 of Theorem 10.7 that the set of maximizers in this problem (i.e., player i's best-response correspondence $BR_i(\cdot)$) admits a greatest element $b_i^*(s)$ at each $s \in S$; and that $b_i^*(s)$ is nondecreasing in s. Therefore, so is the map $b^*: S \to S$, where

$$b^*(s) = (b_1^*(s), \ldots, b_n^*(s)).$$

Since each S_i is a compact sublattice, so is S. By Tarski's Fixed Point Theorem, b^* has a fixed point. Any fixed point of b^* is clearly a Nash equilibrium of the game. $\square$

10.4 A Proof of the Second-Derivative Characterization of Supermodularity

Our proof of Theorem 10.4 will rely on a characterization of supermodularity in terms of increasing differences that was proved in Topkis (1978). Some new notation and definitions are required.

Let $Z \subset \mathbb{R}^m$. For $z \in Z$, we will denote by (z_{-ij}, z_i', z_j') the vector z, but with z_i and z_j replaced by z_i' and z_j', respectively. A function $f: Z \to \mathbb{R}$ will be said to satisfy *increasing differences on Z* if for all $z \in Z$, for all distinct i and j in $\{1, \ldots, n\}$, and for all z_i', z_j' such that $z_i' \geq z_i$ and $z_j' \geq z_j$, it is the case that

$$f(z_{-ij}, z_i', z_j') - f(z_{-ij}, z_i', z_j) \geq f(z_{-ij}, z_i, z_j') - f(z_{-ij}, z_i, z_j).$$

In words, f has increasing differences on Z if it has increasing differences in each pair (z_i, z_j) when all other coordinates are held fixed at some value.

Theorem 10.12 *A function $f: Z \subset \mathbb{R}^m \to \mathbb{R}$ is supermodular on Z if and only if f has increasing differences on Z.*

Proof That supermodularity implies increasing differences on Z can be established by a slight modification of the proof of Part 2 of Theorem 10.3. The details are left to the reader.

To see the reverse implication (that increasing differences on Z implies supermodularity on Z), pick any z and z' in Z. We are required to show that

$$f(z) + f(z') \leq f(z \vee z') + f(z \wedge z').$$

If $z \geq z'$ or $z \leq z'$, this inequality trivially holds (in fact, we have an equality), so suppose z and z' are not comparable under $\geq$. For notational convenience, arrange the coordinates of z and z' so that

$$z \vee z' = (z'_1, \ldots, z'_k, z_{k+1}, \ldots, z_m)$$

$$z \wedge z' = (z_1, \ldots, z_k, z'_{k+1}, \ldots, z'_m).$$

(This rearrangement of the coordinates may obviously be accomplished without loss of generality.) Note that since z and z' are not comparable under $\geq$, we must have $0 < k < m$.

Now for $0 \leq i \leq j \leq m$, define

$$z^{i,j} = (z'_1, \ldots, z'_i, z_{i+1}, \ldots, z_j, z'_{j+1}, \ldots z'_m).$$

Then, we have

$$z^{0,k} = z \wedge z'$$
$$z^{k,m} = z \vee z'$$
$$z^{0,m} = z$$
$$z^{k,k} = z'.$$

Since f has increasing differences on Z, it is the case that for all $0 \leq i < k \leq j < m$,

$$f(z^{i+1,j+1}) - f(z^{i,j+1}) \geq f(z^{i+1,j}) - f(z^{i,j}).$$

Therefore, we have for $k \leq j < m$,

$$f(z^{k,j+1}) - f(z^{0,j+1}) = \sum_{i=0}^{k-1} [f(z^{i+1,j+1}) - f(z^{i,j+1})]$$

$$\geq \sum_{i=0}^{k-1} [f(z^{i+1,j}) - f(z^{i,j})]$$

$$= f(z^{k,j}) - f(z^{0,j}).$$

Since this inequality holds for all j satisfying $k \leq j < m$, it follows that the left-hand side is at its highest value at $j = m - 1$, while the right-hand side is at its lowest value when $j = k$. Therefore,

$$f(z^{k,m}) - f(z^{0,m}) \geq f(z^{k,k}) - f(z^{0,k}).$$

This is precisely the statement that

$$f(z \vee z') - f(z) \geq f(z') - f(z \wedge z').$$

Since z and z' were chosen arbitrarily, we have shown that f is supermodular on Z. Theorem 10.12 is proved. $\qquad\square$

We proceed with the proof of Theorem 10.4. Let f be a C^2 function on $Z \subset \mathbb{R}^m$. By Theorem 10.12, f is supermodular on Z if and only if for all $z \in Z$, for all distinct i and j, and for all $\epsilon > 0$ and $\delta > 0$, we have

$$f(z_{-ij}, z_i + \epsilon, z_j + \delta) - f(z_{-ij}, z_i + \epsilon, z_j) \geq f(z_{-ij}, z_i, z_j + \delta) - f(z_{-ij}, z_i, z_j).$$

Dividing both sides by the positive quantity δ and letting $\delta \downarrow 0$, we see that f is supermodular on Z if and only if for all $z \in Z$, for all distinct i and j, and for all $\epsilon > 0$,

$$\frac{\partial f}{\partial z_j}(z_{-ij}, z_i + \epsilon, z_j) \geq \frac{\partial f}{\partial z_j}(z_{-ij}, z_i, z_j).$$

Subtracting the right-hand side from the left-hand side, dividing by the positive quantity ϵ, and letting $\epsilon \downarrow 0$, f is seen to be supermodular on Z if and only if for all $z \in Z$, and for all distinct i and j, we have

$$\frac{\partial^2 f}{\partial z_i \partial z_j}(z) \geq 0.$$

Theorem 10.4 is proved.   □

10.5 Exercises

1. Show that the hyperplane $H = \{(x, y) \mid x - y = 1\}$ is a sublattice of $\mathbb{R}^2$.

2. Give an example of a nonempty compact sublattice in $\mathbb{R}^2$ which has at least two greatest elements, or show that no such example is possible.

3. Suppose a closed set X in $\mathbb{R}^2$ has the property that the meet of any two points from X is also in X. Suppose also that X is bounded above, i.e., there is $a \in \mathbb{R}^2$ such that $x \leq a$ for all $x \in X$. Is it true that X must have a greatest element? Why or why not?

4. Give an example of a set X in $\mathbb{R}^2$ with the property that the join of any two points in X is always in X, but there are at least two points x and y in X whose meet is not in X.

5. Let $C(S)$ be the set of all continuous functions on $S = [0, 1]$. For $f, g \in C(S)$, let $f \vee g$ and $f \wedge g$ be defined by

$$(f \vee g)(x) = \max\{f(x), g(x)\} \text{ and } (f \wedge g)(x) = \min\{f(x), g(x)\}.$$

Show that $f \vee g \in C(S)$ and $f \wedge g \in C(S)$, so $C(S)$ is a lattice.

6. Suppose in Part 3 of Theorem 10.7, we replaced the condition that f satisfies strictly increasing differences with the condition that f is strictly supermodular.

Will the result still hold that $\mathcal{D}^*$ is a nondecreasing correspondence? Why or why not?

7. Let $x \in S = [0, 1]$ and $\theta \in \Theta = \mathbb{R}_+$. In each of the following cases, determine if the given function is supermodular in (x, θ). In each case, determine also if the optimal action correspondence in the problem $\max\{f(x, \theta) \mid x \in S\}$ is nondecreasing in θ.

(a) $f(x, \theta) = x\theta - x^2\theta^2$.
(b) $f(x, \theta) = x\theta - x^2$.
(c) $f(x, \theta) = x/(1 + \theta)$.
(d) $f(x, \theta) = x(1 + \theta)$.
(e) $f(x, \theta) = x(\theta - x)$.

8. Prove Tarski's Fixed Point Theorem for the case where $S \subset \mathbb{R}$.

9. Show that Tarski's Fixed Point Theorem is false if "nondecreasing" is replaced by "nonincreasing." That is, give an example of a nonincreasing function from a compact lattice into itself that fails to have a fixed point.

11

Finite-Horizon Dynamic Programming

11.1 Dynamic Programming Problems

A *dynamic programming problem* is an optimization problem in which decisions have to be taken sequentially over several time periods. To make the problem non-trivial, it is usually assumed that periods are "linked" in some fashion, viz., that actions taken in any particular period affect the decision environment (and thereby, the reward possibilities) in all future periods. In practice, this is typically achieved by positing the presence of a "state" variable, representing the environment, which restricts the set of actions available to the decision-maker at any point in time, but which also moves through time in response to the decision-maker's actions. These twin features of the state variable provide the problem with "bite": actions that look attractive from the standpoint of immediate reward (for instance, a Carribean vacation) might have the effect of forcing the state variable (the consumer's wealth or savings) into values from which the continuation possibilities (future consumption levels) are not as pleasant. The modelling and study of this trade-off between current payoffs and future rewards is the focus of the theory of dynamic programming.

In this book, we focus on two classes of dynamic programming problems—Finite-Horizon Markovian Dynamic Programming Problems, which are the subject of this chapter, and Infinite-Horizon Stationary Discounted Dynamic Programming Problems, which we examine in the next chapter.

11.2 Finite-Horizon Dynamic Programming

A *Finite Horizon (Markovian) Dynamic Programming Problem* (henceforth FHDP) is defined by a tuple $\{S, A, T, (r_t, f_t, \Phi_t)_{t=1}^{T}\}$, where

1. S is the *state space* of the problem, with generic element s.
2. A is the *action space* of the problem, with generic element a.
3. T, a positive integer, is the *horizon* of the problem.

4. For each $t \in \{1, \dots, T\}$,

   (a) $r_t \colon S \times A \to \mathbb{R}$ is the period-t *reward function*,

   (b) $f_t \colon S \times A \to S$ is the period-t *transition function*, and

   (c) $\Phi_t \colon S \to P(A)$ is the period-t *feasible action correspondence*.

The FHDP has a simple interpretation. The decision-maker begins from some fixed *initial state* $s_1 = s \in S$. The set of actions available to the decision-maker at this state is given by the correspondence $\Phi_1(s_1) \subset A$. When the decision-maker chooses an action $a_1 \in \Phi_1(s)$, two things happen. First, the decision-maker receives an immediate reward of $r_1(s_1, a_1)$. Second, the state s_2 at the begining of period 2 is realized as $s_2 = f_1(s_1, a_1)$. At this new state, the set of feasible actions is given by $\Phi_2(s_2) \subset A$, and when the decision-maker chooses an action $a_2 \in \Phi_2(s_2)$, a reward of $r_2(s_2, a_2)$ is received, and the period-3 state s_3 is realized as $s_3 = f_2(s_2, a_2)$. The problem proceeds in this way till the terminal date T is reached. The objective is to choose a plan for taking actions at each point in time in order to maximize the sum of the per-period rewards over the horizon of the model, i.e., to solve

$$\text{Maximize} \quad \sum_{t=1}^{T} r_t(s_t, a_t)$$

$$\text{subject to} \quad s_1 = s \in S$$

$$s_t = f_{t-1}(s_{t-1}, a_{t-1}), \quad t = 2, \dots, T$$

$$a_t \in \Phi_t(s_t), \quad t = 1, \dots, T.$$

A cleaner way to represent this objective—and, as we explain, an analytically more advantageous one—is to employ the notion of a "strategy." We turn to this now.

11.3 Histories, Strategies, and the Value Function

A *strategy* for a dynamic programming problem is just a *contingency plan*, i.e., a plan that specifies what is to be done at each stage as a function of all that has transpired up to that point. In more formal language, a *t-history* η_t is a vector $\{s_1, a_1, \dots, s_{t-1}, a_{t-1}, s_t\}$ of the state s_τ in each period τ up to t, the action a_τ taken that period, and the period-t state s_t. Let $H_1 = S$, and for $t > 1$, let H_t denote the set of all possible t-histories η_t. Given a t-history η_t, we will denote by $s_t[\eta_t]$ the period-t state under the history η_t.

A *strategy* σ, for the problem, is a sequence $\{\sigma_t\}_{t=1}^{T}$, where for each t, $\sigma_t \colon H_t \to A$ specifies the action $\sigma_t(\eta_t) \in \Phi_t(s_t[\eta_t])$ to be taken in period t as a function of the history $\eta_t \in H_t$ up to t. The requirement that $\sigma_t(\eta_t)$ be an element of $\Phi_t(s_t[\eta_t])$ ensures that the feasibility of actions at all points is built into the definition of a strategy. Let Σ denote the set of all strategies σ for the problem.

Each strategy $\sigma \in \Sigma$ gives rise from each initial state $s \in S$ to a unique sequence of states and actions $\{s_t(\sigma, s), a_t(\sigma, s)\}$, and therefore, to a unique sequence of histories $\eta_t(\sigma, s)$, in the obvious recursive manner: we have $s_1(\sigma, s) = s$, and for $t = 1, \ldots, T$,

$$\eta_t(\sigma, s) = \{s_1(\sigma, s), a_1(\sigma, s), \ldots, s_t(\sigma, s)\}$$
$$a_t(\sigma, s) = \sigma_t[\eta_t(\sigma, s)]$$
$$s_{t+1}(\sigma, s) = f_t[s_t(\sigma, s), a_t(\sigma, s)].$$

Thus, given an initial state $s_1 = s \in S$, each strategy σ gives rise to a unique period-t reward $r_t(\sigma)(s)$ from s defined as

$$r_t(\sigma)(s) = r_t[s_t(\sigma, s), a_t(\sigma, s)].$$

The *total* reward under σ from the initial state s, denoted $W(\sigma)(s)$, is, therefore, given by

$$W(\sigma)(s) = \sum_{t=1}^{T} r_t(\sigma)(s).$$

Now, define the function $V: S \to \mathbb{R}$ by

$$V(s) = \sup_{\sigma \in \Sigma} W(\sigma)(s).$$

The function V is called the *value function* of the problem.[1] A strategy σ^* is said to be an *optimal strategy* for the problem if the payoff it generates from any initial state is the supremum over possible payoffs from that state, that is, if

$$W(\sigma^*)(s) = V(s), \quad \text{for all } s \in S.$$

In this notation, the objective of the decision-maker in our dynamic programming problem can be described as the problem of finding an optimal strategy. Writing the problem in this way has (at least) two big advantages over writing it as the problem of maximizing rewards over the set of feasible state-action sequences from each initial state.

The first advantage is a simple one. If we succeed in obtaining an optimal strategy, this strategy will enable us to calculate the optimal sequence of actions from *any* initial state. In particular, this will enable us to carry out "comparative dynamics" exercises, where we can examine the effect of a change in the value of the initial state (or some parameter of the problem) on the sequence of optimal actions and states.

The second advantage is deeper. In the formulation of dynamic programming problems we have given here, we have assumed that transitions are *deterministic*,

---

[1] The value function V in this problem is the exact analog of the maximized value function f^* that we examined in the context of parametric families of optimization problems. Indeed, the initial state s of the FHDP can be viewed precisely as parametrizing the problem.

i.e., that given any period-t state s_t and period-t action a_t, the period-$(t + 1)$ state is precisely determined as $f_t(s_t, a_t)$. In a variety of economic problems, it might be more realistic to replace this assumption with one where (s_t, a_t) determines a *probability distribution* over S, according to which the period-$(t + 1)$ state is realized. When the transition is allowed to be *stochastic* in this manner, it may be simply impossible to pick a sequence of actions *a priori*, since some of the actions in this sequence may turn out to be infeasible at the realized states. Moreover, even if infeasibility is not an issue, picking an *a priori* sequence of actions leaves us without any flexibility, in that it is not possible to vary continuation behavior based on the actual (i.e., realized) states. It is obvious that this is a serious shortcoming: it will rarely be the case that a single continuation action is optimal, regardless of which future state is realized. On the other hand, since a strategy specifies a contingency plan of action, its prescriptions do not suffer from such problems. We will not be dealing with the stochastic transitions case in this book, since the technical details involved are quite messy. Nonetheless, at a conceptual level, the techniques used to show existence are exactly the same as what we develop here for the deterministic case. By dealing with strategy spaces rather than sequences of actions, the methods we develop will continue to be applicable to the more general case.

11.4 Markovian Strategies

Any τ-history $\eta_\tau = (s_1, a_1, \ldots, s_\tau)$ in a given FHDP

$$\{S, A, T, (r_t, \Phi_t, f_t)_{t=1}^T\}$$

results in another FHDP, namely the $(T - \tau)$-period problem given by

$$\{S, A, T - \tau, (r_t^*, \Phi_t^*, f_t^*)_{t=1}^{T-\tau}\},$$

whose initial state is $s = s_\tau$, and where, for $t = 1, \ldots, T - \tau$, we have:

$$r_t^*(s, a) = r_{t+\tau}(s, a), \quad (s, a) \in S \times A$$
$$\Phi_t^*(s) = \Phi_{t+\tau}(s), \quad s \in S$$
$$f_t^*(s, a) = f_{t+\tau}(s, a), \quad (s, a) \in S \times A.$$

We shall call the problem $\{S, A, T - \tau, (r_t^*, \Phi_t^*, f_t^*)_{t=1}^{T-\tau}\}$ the $(T-\tau)$-*period continuation problem*, and, for notational simplicity, denote it by $\{S, A, T - \tau, (r_t, \Phi_t, f_t)_{t=\tau+1}^T\}$. Clearly, all τ-histories η_τ that end in s_τ result in the *same* continuation $(T-\tau)$-period problem. Therefore, at any point t in an FHDP, the current state s_t encapsulates all relevant information regarding continuation possibilities from period t onwards, such as the strategies that are feasible in the continuation and the consequent rewards that may be obtained.[2]

---

[2]Hence, the adjective "Markovian" to describe these problems.

Since continuation possibilities from a state are not affected by *how* one arrives at that state, it appears intuitively plausible that there is no gain to be made by conditioning actions on anything more than just the value of the current state and the time period in which this state was reached. (This last factor is obviously important; to calculate optimal continuations from a given state s requires knowledge of the number of time periods remaining, or, equivalently, what the current date is.) This leads us to the notion of a Markovian strategy.

A *Markovian strategy* is a strategy σ in which at each $t = 1, \ldots, T-1$, σ_t depends on the t-history η_t only through t and the value of the period-t state $s_t[\eta_t]$ under η_t. Such a strategy can evidently be represented simply by a sequence $\{g_1, \ldots, g_T\}$, where for each t, $g_t: S \to A$ specifies the action $g_t(s_t) \in \Phi_t(s_t)$ to be taken in period t, as a function of only the period-t state s_t.

If a Markovian strategy $\{g_1, \ldots, g_T\}$ is also an optimal strategy, it is called a *Markovian optimal strategy*. This terminology is standard, but is a little ambiguous; to avoid legitimate confusion, it should be stressed that a Markovian optimal strategy is a strategy that is optimal in the class of *all* strategies, and not just among Markovian strategies.

11.5 Existence of an Optimal Strategy

Let a strategy $\sigma = \{\sigma_1, \ldots, \sigma_T\}$ be given, and suppose $\{g_\tau, \ldots, g_T\}$ is a Markovian strategy for the $(T-\tau+1)$-period continuation problem. Then, we will use the notation

$$\{\sigma_1, \ldots, \sigma_{t-1}, g_t, \ldots, g_T\}$$

to represent the strategy in which the decision-maker acts according to the recommendations of σ for the first $(t-1)$ periods, and then switches to following the dictates of the strategy $\{g_t, \ldots, g_T\}$.

The key to proving the existence of an optimal strategy—indeed, of a Markovian optimal strategy—is the following lemma:

Lemma 11.1 *Let $\sigma = (\sigma_1, \ldots, \sigma_T)$ be an optimal strategy for the FHDP*

$$\{S, A, T, (r_t, f_t, \Phi_t)_{t=1}^T\}.$$

Suppose that for some $\tau \in \{1, \ldots, T\}$, the $(T-\tau+1)$-period continuation problem

$$\{S, A, T-\tau+1, (r_t, f_t, \Phi_t)_{t=\tau}^T\}$$

admits a Markovian optimal strategy $\{g_\tau, \ldots, g_T\}$. Then, the strategy

$$\{\sigma_1, \ldots, \sigma_{\tau-1}, g_\tau, \ldots, g_T\}$$

is an optimal strategy for the original problem.

Proof For notational ease, denote the strategy $\{\sigma_1, \ldots, \sigma_{\tau-1}, g_\tau, \ldots, g_T\}$ by γ. If the claim in the theorem were not true, then there would exist an initial state s of the T-period problem, such that the total payoffs under γ from the state s were strictly dominated by the total payoff from s under the optimal strategy σ, i.e., such that

$$W(\sigma)(s) > W(\gamma)(s).$$

Letting $r_t(\sigma)(s)$ and $r_t(\gamma)(s)$ denote the period-t rewards under σ and γ, respectively, from the initial state s, we have

$$W(\sigma)(s) = \sum_{t=1}^{T} r_t(\sigma)(s) = \sum_{t=1}^{\tau-1} r_t(\sigma)(s) + \sum_{t=\tau}^{T} r_t(\sigma)(s),$$

and

$$W(\gamma)(s) = \sum_{t=1}^{T} r_t(\gamma)(s) = \sum_{t=1}^{\tau-1} r_t(\gamma)(s) + \sum_{t=\tau}^{T} r_t(\gamma)(s).$$

By construction, $\sum_{t=1}^{\tau-1} r_t(\sigma)(s) = \sum_{t=1}^{\tau-1} r_t(\gamma)(s)$, since σ and γ are identical over the first $(\tau-1)$-periods. Therefore, for $W(\sigma)(s) > W(\gamma)(s)$ to hold, we must have

$$\sum_{t=\tau}^{T} r_t(\sigma)(s) > \sum_{t=\tau}^{T} r_t(\gamma)(s).$$

If we now let s_τ^* denote the common period-τ state under both γ and σ, this inequality states that from s_τ^*, the strategy $\{g_\tau, \ldots, g_T\}$ is strictly dominated by the continuation strategy $\{\sigma_\tau, \ldots, \sigma_T\}$. This is an obvious contradiction of the presumed optimality of $\{g_\tau, \ldots, g_T\}$ in the $(T-\tau+1)$-period problem: for, when beginning from the initial state s_τ^* in the $(T-\tau+1)$-period problem, one could simply behave "as if" the history $\eta_\tau(\sigma, s)$ had occurred, and follow the continuation strategy $\{\sigma_\tau, \ldots, \sigma_T\}$. This would result in a strictly larger reward from s_τ^* than from following $\{g_\tau, \ldots, g_T\}$. □

The importance of Lemma 11.1 arises from the fact that it enables us to solve for an optimal strategy by the method of *backwards induction*. That is, we first consider the one-period problem in which, from any $s \in S$, we solve

$$\text{Maximize } r_T(s, a) \text{ subject to } a \in \Phi_T(s).$$

Let $g_T^*(s)$ be a solution to this problem at the state s. By Lemma 11.1, the solution g_T^* can be used in the last period of an optimal strategy, without changing the total rewards. Now, *given* that we are going to use g_T^* in the last period, we can find the actions in the two-period problem beginning at period-$(T-1)$, that will be optimal for the two-period problem. This gives us an strategy pair (g_{T-1}^*, g_T^*) that is optimal for the two-period continuation problem beginning at period $T-1$. An induction argument now completes the construction of the optimal strategy. The formal details of this method are given below in Theorem 11.2. But first, since even the one-period problem will not have a solution unless minimal continuity and compactness conditions are met, we shall impose the following assumptions:

A1 For each t, r_t is continuous and bounded on $S \times A$.

A2 For each t, f_t is continuous on $S \times A$.

A3 For each t, Φ_t is a continuous, compact-valued correspondence on S.

Theorem 11.2 *Under A1–A3, the dynamic programming problem admits a Markovian optimal strategy. The value function $V_t(\cdot)$ of the $(T-t+1)$-period continuation problem satisfies for each $t \in \{1, \dots T\}$ and $s \in S$, the following condition, known as the "Bellman Equation," or the "Bellman Principle of Optimality:"*

$$V_t(s) = \max_{a \in \Phi_t(s)} \{r_t(s, a) + V_{t+1}[f_t(s, a)]\}.$$

Proof We begin with the last period. A strategy g_T for the one-period problem can be optimal if, and only if, at each s, $g_T(s)$ solves:

$$\max\{r_T(s, a) \mid a \in \Phi_T(s)\}.$$

Since r_T is continuous on $S \times A$, and Φ_T is a compact-valued continuous correspondence, the solution to this problem is well defined. The maximized value of the objective function is, of course, simply $V_T(s)$. Let $\Phi_T^*(s)$ denote the set of maximizers at s. By the Maximum Theorem, V_T is a continuous function on S, and Φ_T^* is a nonempty-valued usc correspondence from S into A.

Now, pick any function $g_T^*: S \to A$ such that $g_T^*(s) \in \Phi_T^*(s)$ for all $s \in S$. (Such a function is called a *selection* from Φ_T^*.) Then, at any initial state of the one-period problem, the function g_T^* recommends an action that is optimal from that state, so g_T^* is an optimal strategy for the one-period problem. Note that Φ_T^* may admit many selections, so the optimal strategy for the one-period problem may not be unique; however, all optimal strategies for this problem result in the payoff $V_T(s)$ from the initial state s.

Now pick any optimal strategy g_T^* for the one-period problem, and consider the two-period problem from the initial state s (i.e., when s is the state at the beginning of period $(T-1)$). If the action $a \in \Phi_{T-1}(s)$ is now taken, the immediate reward received is $r_{T-1}(s, a)$. The period-T state is then realized as $f_{T-1}(s, a)$. The maximum one-period reward from the state $f_{T-1}(s, a)$ in the continuation one-period problem is, by definition, $V_T[f_{T-1}(s, a)]$, which can be attained using the action recommended by g_T^* at this state. Thus, *given* that the action a is taken at state s in the first period of the two-period model, the maximum reward that can be obtained is

$$r_{T-1}(s, a) + V_T[f_{T-1}(s, a)].$$

It now follows that $\{g_{T-1}^*, g_T^*\}$ is an optimal strategy for the two-period problem if, and only if, at each $s \in S$, g_{T-1}^* solves

$$\max_{a \in \Phi_{T-1}(s)} \{r_{T-1}(s, a) + V_T[f_{T-1}(s, a)]\}.$$

Since f_{T-1} is continuous on $S \times A$ by assumption, and we have shown that V_T is continuous on S, it must be the case that $V_T[f_{T-1}(s, a)]$ is continuous in (s, a). Since r_{T-1} is also continuous on $S \times A$, the objective function in this problem is continuous on $S \times A$. By hypothesis, Φ_{T-1} is a continuous, compact-valued correspondence. Thus, invoking the Maximum Theorem again, we see that the maximum is well-defined, i.e., the correspondence of maximizers Φ_{T-1}^* is nonempty valued and usc, and the maximized value (which is, of course, just V_{T-1}) is continuous on S. Let g_{T-1}^* be any selection from Φ_{T-1}^*. By construction, then, (g_{T-1}^*, g_T^*) is an optimal strategy for the two-period problem. Since it is also a Markovian strategy, it is a Markovian optimal strategy for the two-period problem.

To show that there is a solution for any t, we use induction. Suppose that for some $t \in \{1, \ldots, T-1\}$, we have shown the following:

1. A solution (that is, a Markovian optimal strategy $\{g_{t+1}^*, \ldots, g_T^*\}$) exists for the $(T-t)$-period problem.
2. The value function V_{t+1} of the $(T-t)$-period problem is continuous on S.

We will show that these properties are also true for the $(T-t+1)$-period problem.

Suppose the initial state of the $(T-t+1)$-period problem (i.e., at the beginning of period t) is given by s. If the action $a \in \Phi_t(s)$ is taken, then an immediate reward of $r_t(s, a)$ is received; the state at the beginning of period t is then $f_t(s, a)$. The maximum one can receive in the continuation is, by definition, $V_{t+1}[f_t(s, a)]$, which can be obtained using $\{g_{t+1}^*, \ldots, g_T^*\}$. Thus, given the action a in period t, the maximum possible reward is

$$r_t(s, a) + V_{t+1}[f_t(s, a)].$$

It follows that g_t^* can be part of an optimal strategy in the $(T-t+1)$-period problem if, and only if, at each s, $g_t^*(s)$ solves:

$$\max_{a \in \Phi_t(s)} \{r_t(s, a) + V_{t+1}[f_t(s, a)]\}.$$

By hypothesis, r_t and f_t are both continuous in (s, a), and V_{t+1} is continuous on S. Therefore, the objective function in this problem is continuous on $S \times A$, and since Φ_t is a continuous compact-valued correspondence, a maximum exists at each s; the maximized value of the objective function (which is V_t) is continuous on S; and the correspondence of maximizers Φ_t^* is usc on S. Letting g_t^* denote any selection from Φ_t^*, we see that $\{g_t^*, \ldots, g_T^*\}$ is an optimal strategy for the $(T-t+1)$-period problem. The induction step is complete.

Finally, note that the Bellman Equation at each t has also been established in the course of proving the induction argument.   □

11.6 An Example: The Consumption–Savings Problem

We illustrate the use of backwards induction in this section in a simple finite-horizon dynamic optimization problem. A consumer faces a T-period planning horizon, where T is a finite positive integer. He has an initial wealth of $w \in \mathbb{R}_+$. If he begins period-t with a wealth of w_t, and consumes c_t ($w_t \geq c_t \geq 0$) that period, then his wealth at the beginning of the next period is $(w_t - c_t)(1 + r)$, where $r \geq 0$ is the interest rate. Consumption of c in any period gives the consumer utility of $u(c)$, where $u(\cdot)$ is a continuous, strictly increasing function on $\mathbb{R}_+$. The consumer's objective is to maximize utility over the T-period horizon.

We shall first set up the consumer's maximization problem as a dynamic programming problem. Then, assuming $u(c) = \sqrt{c}$, we shall obtain an exact solution.

The natural choice for the state space S is the set of possible wealth levels which is $\mathbb{R}_+$. Similarly, the natural choice for the action space A is the set of possible consumption levels, which is also $\mathbb{R}_+$.

The reward function r_t depends only on the consumption c in any period, and is given by $r_t(w, c) = u(c)$. The transition function f_t is given by $f_t(w, c) = (w - c)(1 + r)$. And, finally, the feasible action correspondence Φ_t is given by $\Phi_t(w) = [0, w]$ for all w.

Now suppose $u(c) = \sqrt{c}$. For ease of notation, let $k = (1 + r)$. In the last period, given a wealth level of w, the consumer solves:

$$\max_{c \in [0, w]} u(c).$$

It is easy to see that since $u(\cdot)$ is a strictly increasing function the unique solution at any w is to consume everything; thus, the unique optimal strategy for the one-period problem is $g_T(w) = w$ for all $w \in S$. The one-period value function V_T is, then,

$$V_T(w) = \sqrt{w}, \quad w \in S.$$

Now, consider the two-period problem starting from some level $w \in S$. The action $g_{T-1}(w)$ is part of an optimal strategy for the two-period problem if, and only if,

$g_{T-1}(w)$ solves

$$\max_{c \in [0,w]} \left\{ \sqrt{c} + V_T[k(w-c)] \right\}.$$

(Recall that $k = (1+r)$.) Thus, $g_{T-1}(w)$ must solve

$$\max_{c \in [0,w]} \left\{ \sqrt{c} + \sqrt{k(w-c)} \right\}.$$

This is a strictly convex optimization problem. The first-order conditions are, therefore, necessary and sufficient to identify a solution. A simple calculation reveals that there is a unique solution at each w, given by $w/(1+k)$. So, if g_{T-1} is to be part of an optimal strategy for the two-period problem, we must have

$$g_{T-1}(w) = \frac{w}{1+k}, \quad w \in S.$$

Substituting this into the maximization problem, we see also that the two-period value function V_{T-1} is given by

$$V_{T-1}(w) = (1+k)^{1/2} w^{1/2}, \quad w \in S.$$

Reworking this procedure for $t = 3$, $t = 4$, etc., is conceptually trivial, if a bit painful to carry out. When one actually does the calculations, a pattern begins to emerge: we obtain

$$V_t(w) = (1 + k + \cdots + k^{T-t})^{1/2} w^{1/2},$$

and

$$g_t(w) = \frac{w}{1 + k + \cdots + k^{T-t}}.$$

To check that these are correct expressions we use induction. Suppose that these are the forms for V_τ and g_τ for $\tau \in \{t+1, \ldots, T\}$. We will show that V_t and g_t also have these forms.

In period t, at the state w, the consumer solves:

$$\max_{c \in [0,w]} \{ \sqrt{c} + V_{t+1}[k(w-c)] \}$$

where $V_{t+1}[k(w-c)] = (1 + k + \cdots + k^{T-t-1})^{1/2} [k(w-c)]^{1/2}$, by the induction hypothesis. This is, once again, a strictly convex optimization problem, so $g_{T-t}(w)$ is uniquely determined by the solution. A simple calculation shows it is, in fact, given by

$$g_t(w) = \frac{w}{[1 + k + \cdots + k^{T-t}]}, \quad w \in S.$$

Substituting this back into the objective function of the problem, we obtain

$$V_t(w) = (1 + k + \cdots + k^{T-t})^{1/2} w^{1/2}, \quad w \in S.$$

The induction step is complete. □

11.7 Exercises

1. Redo the consumer's multiperiod utility maximization problem of Section 11.6 for each of the following specifications of the utility function:

   (a) $u(c) = c^\alpha, \alpha \in (0, 1)$.
   (b) $u(c) = c$.
   (c) $u(c) = c^\beta, \beta > 1$.

2. Consider the following problem of optimal harvesting of a natural resource. A firm (say, a fishery) begins with a given stock $y > 0$ of a natural resource (fish). In each period $t = 1, \ldots T$, of a finite horizon, the firm must decide how much of the resource to sell on the market that period. If the firm decides to sell x units of the resource, it receives a profit that period of $\pi(x)$, where $\pi \colon \mathbb{R}_+ \to \mathbb{R}$. The amount $(y - x)$ of the resource left unharvested grows to an available amount of $f(y - x)$ at the beginning of the next period, where $f \colon \mathbb{R}_+ \to \mathbb{R}_+$. The firm wishes to choose a strategy that will maximize the sum of its profits over the model's T-period horizon.

   (a) Set up the firm's optimization problem as a finite-horizon dynamic programming problem, i.e., describe precisely the state space S, the action space A, the period-t reward function feasible action r_t, etc.
   (b) Describe sufficient conditions on f and π under which an optimal strategy exists in this problem.
   (c) Assuming $\pi(x) = \log x$ and $f(x) = x^\alpha$ ($0 < \alpha \leq 1$), solve this problem for the firm's optimal strategy using backwards induction.

3. Given $w_1, w_2, \ldots, w_T \in \mathbb{R}_{++}$ and $c \in \mathbb{R}_{++}$ express the following problem as a dynamic programming problem, i.e., find S, A, r_t, f_t, and Φ_t, and solve it using backwards induction. The problem is:

$$\text{Maximize} \quad \sum_{t=1}^{T} s_t a_t^2$$

$$\text{subject to} \quad \sum_{t=1}^{T} a_t = c$$

$$a_t \geq 0, \ t = 1, \ldots, T.$$

4. Consider the following maximization problem:

$$\text{Maximize} \quad \sum_{t=1}^{T} a_t^{\delta_t}$$

$$\text{subject to} \quad \sum_{t=1}^{T} a_t = c$$

$$a_t \geq 0, \quad t = 1, \ldots, T$$

where $\delta_1, \ldots, \delta_T$ and c are given positive constants.

(a) Express this problem as a dynamic programming problem and solve it.

(b) Repeat this exercise with the constraints modified to

$$\prod_{t=1}^{T} a_t = c$$

$$a_t \geq 1, \quad t = 1, \ldots, T.$$

5. Express the following problem as a dynamic programming problem and solve it.

$$\text{Maximize} \quad \sum_{t=1}^{T} \frac{p_t s_t}{s_t + a_t}$$

$$\text{subject to} \quad \sum_{t=1}^{T} a_t = c$$

$$a_t \geq 0, \quad t = 1, \ldots, T$$

where p_t and s_t are parameters such that:

$$\sum_{t=1}^{T} p_t = 1$$

$$p_t \geq 0, \ s_t \geq 0, \quad t = 1, \ldots, T.$$

6. Let an $m \times n$ matrix A be given. Consider the problem of finding a path between entries a_{ij} in the matrix A which (i) starts at a_{11} and ends at a_{mn}, (ii) which moves only to the right or down, and (iii) which maximizes the sum of the entries a_{ij} encountered. Express this as a dynamic programming problem. Using backwards induction solve the problem when the matrix A is given by:

$$A = \begin{bmatrix} 4 & 9 & 3 & 6 & 3 \\ 5 & 6 & 6 & 4 & 4 \\ 6 & 7 & 1 & 1 & 0 \\ 4 & 3 & 5 & 1 & 9 \end{bmatrix}.$$

7. Describe the following problem in a dynamic programming framework, and solve it using backwards induction.

$$\text{Maximize} \quad \prod_{t=1}^{T} c_t$$

$$\text{subject to} \quad \sum_{t=1}^{T} c_t = c$$

$$c_t \geq 0.$$

8. A firm is faced with a choice of two technologies. The first (the *known technology*) results in the firm incurring a constant unit cost of c per unit of production. The second technology (the *unknown technology*) has associated with it an initial unit cost of production of $d > c$, but the cost of production declines over time as this technology is used owing to a "learning by doing" effect. Suppose that if the unknown technology has been used for t periods, the per-unit cost of production from using this for a $(t + 1)$-th period is given by $w(t)$, where

$$w(t) = d_0 + d_1 e^{-t}$$

where $d_0 < c$. (Note that we must have $d_0 + d_1 = d$, since $w(0) = d$.) Assume that the firm produces exactly one unit of output per period, and is interested in minimizing the sum of its costs of production over a T-period horizon.

(a) Express the optimization problem facing the firm as a dynamic programming problem, and write down the Bellman Equation.

(b) Does this problem have a solution for any T? Why or why not?

(c) As T increases, show that it becomes more likely that the firm will use the unknown technology in the following sense: if there exists an optimal strategy in the T-horizon model in which the firm uses the unknown technology in the first period, there exists an optimal strategy in the $(T + 1)$-horizon model in which the same statement is true.

(d) Fix any $T > 1$. Prove that if it is optimal for the firm to use the unknown technology in the first period, then it is optimal for the firm to stay with the unknown technology through the entire T-period horizon.

12

Stationary Discounted Dynamic Programming

The principal complication that arises in extending the results of the last chapter to dynamic programming problems with an *infinite* horizon is that infinite-horizon models lack a "last" period; this makes it impossible to use backwards induction techniques to derive an optimal strategy. In this chapter, we show that general conditions may, nonetheless, be described for the existence of an optimal strategy in such problems, although the process of actually deriving an optimal strategy is necessarily more complicated. A final section then studies the application of these results to obtaining and characterizing optimal strategies in the canonical model of dynamic economic theory: the one-sector model of economic growth.

12.1 Description of the Framework

A (deterministic) stationary discounted dynamic programming problem (henceforth, SDP) is specified by a tuple $\{S, A, \Phi, f, r, \delta\}$, where

1. S is the *state space,* or the set of environments, with generic element s. We assume that $S \subset \mathbb{R}^n$ for some n.
2. A is the *action space,* with typical element a. We assume that $A \subset \mathbb{R}^k$ for some k.
3. $\Phi: S \to P(A)$ is the *feasible action correspondence* that specifies for each $s \in S$ the set $\Phi(s) \subset A$ of actions that are available at s.
4. $f: S \times A \to S$ is the *transition function* for the state, that specifies for each current state-action pair (s, a) the next-period state $f(s, a) \in S$.
5. $r: S \times A \to \mathbb{R}$ is the *(one-period) reward function* that specifies a *reward* $r(s, a)$ when the action a is taken at the state s.
6. $\delta \in [0, 1)$ is the one-period *discount factor.*

The interpretation of this framework is similar to that of the finite-horizon model, the one important difference being the horizon of the model, which is assumed to be infinite here. An initial state $s_0 \in S$ is given. If the decision-maker takes an action a_0 in the set of actions $\Phi(s_0)$ that are feasible at this state, two things happen. First, the decision-maker receives an immediate reward of $r(s_0, a_0)$. Second, the state moves to its period-1 value $s_1 = f(s_0, a_0)$. The situation now repeats itself from s_1. The decision-maker is presumed to *discount* future rewards by the factor $\delta \in [0, 1)$; thus, if the action a_t is taken in period-t at the state s_t, the reward is deemed to be worth only $\delta^t r(s_t, a_t)$ today. As earlier, the aim of the decision-maker is to maximize the sum of the rewards over the model's (now infinite) horizon, i.e., to solve from any given initial state $s_0 \in S$:

$$\text{Maximize} \quad \sum_{t=0}^{\infty} \delta^t r(s_t, a_t)$$

$$\text{subject to} \quad s_{t+1} = f(s_t, a_t), \quad t = 0, 1, 2, \ldots$$
$$a_t \in \Phi(s_t), \quad\quad t = 0, 1, 2, \ldots$$

Once again, the notion of a "strategy" plays an important role in our analysis. We turn to a formal definition of this concept.

12.2 Histories, Strategies, and the Value Function

A *t-history* $h_t = \{s_0, a_0, \ldots, s_{t-1}, a_{t-1}, s_t\}$ for the SDP is a list of the state and action in each period up to $t - 1$, and the period-t state. Let $H_0 = S$, and for $t = 1, 2, \ldots$, let H_t denote the set of all possible t-histories. Denote by $s_t[h_t]$ the period-t state in the history h_t.

A *strategy* σ for the SDP is, as earlier, a contingency plan, which specifies an action for the decision-maker as a function of the history that has transpired. Formally, a strategy σ is a sequence of functions $\{\sigma_t\}_{t=0}^{\infty}$ such that for each $t = 0, 1, \ldots$, $\sigma_t \colon H_t \to A$ satisfies the feasibility requirement that $\sigma_t(h_t) \in \Phi(s_t[h_t])$. Let Σ denote the space of all strategies.

Fix a strategy σ. From each given initial state $s \in S$, the strategy σ determines a unique sequence of states and actions $\{s_t(\sigma, s), a_t(\sigma, s)\}$ as follows: $s_0(\sigma, s) = s$, and for $t = 0, 1, 2, \ldots$,

$$h_t(\sigma, s) = \{s_0(\sigma, s), a_0(\sigma, s), \ldots, s_t(\sigma, s)\}$$
$$a_t(\sigma, s) = \sigma_t(h_t(\sigma, s))$$
$$s_{t+1}(\sigma, s) = f(s_t(\sigma, s), a_t(\sigma, s)).$$

Thus, each strategy σ induces, from each initial state s, a period-t reward $r_t(\sigma)(s)$, where

$$r_t(\sigma)(s) = r[s_t(\sigma, s), a_t(\sigma, s)].$$

Let $W(\sigma)(s)$ denote the total discounted reward from s under the strategy σ:

$$W(\sigma)(s) = \sum_{t=0}^{\infty} \delta^t r_t(\sigma)(s).$$

The *value function* $V: S \to \mathbb{R}$ of the SDP is defined as

$$V(s) = \sup_{\sigma \in \Sigma} W(\sigma)(s).$$

A strategy σ^* is said to be an *optimal strategy* for the SDP if:

$$W(\sigma^*)(s) = V(s), \quad s \in S.$$

In words, an optimal strategy is one whose specifications yield a reward that cannot be beaten from any initial state.

12.3 The Bellman Equation

Simple examples show that several problems arise in the search for an optimal strategy unless we impose some restrictions on the structure of the SDP.

Problem 1 Two or more strategies may yield infinite total rewards from some initial states, yet may not appear equivalent from an intuitive standpoint. Consider the following example:

Example 12.1 Let $S = A = \mathbb{R}_+$, and let $\Phi(s) = [0, s]$ for $s \in S$. Define the transition and reward functions by

$$f(s, a) = 3(s - a), \quad (s, a) \in S \times A,$$

and

$$r(s, a) = a, \quad (s, a) \in S \times A.$$

Finally, let $\delta = 3/4$.

Suppose the initial state is $s_0 = 3$. It is easily checked that the sequence of actions $\{a_t\}$ given by $a_t = (4/3)^t$ is feasible from s_0.[1] For each t,

$$\delta^t r(s_t, a_t) = \left(\frac{3}{4}\right)^t \left(\frac{4}{3}\right)^t = 1,$$

so the total reward associated with this sequence is $1 + 1 + 1 + \ldots = +\infty$. On the other hand, the sequence of actions $\{a_t'\}$ defined by $a_t' = (3/2)(4/3)^t, t = 0, 1, 2, \ldots,$ is also feasible from $s_0 = 3$, and also yields infinite total reward. However, for each

---

[1] We are being sloppy here in the interests of brevity. What we mean formally is that there is a strategy σ in this SDP such that from the initial state s, the strategy σ results in the series of actions $\{a_t(\sigma, s)\} = \{(4/3)^t\}$.

$a_t' = (3/2)a_t$, and one gets the feeling that $\{a_t'\}$ is more "reasonable" as a possible solution than $\{a_t\}$. □

Problem 2 No optimal strategy may exist even if $\sum_{t=0}^{\infty} \delta^t r(s_t, a_t)$ converges for each feasible sequence $\{a_t\}$ from each initial state s. Consider the following example:

Example 12.2 Let $S = \{0\}$, $A = \{1, 2, 3, \ldots\}$, $\Phi(0) = A$, $f(0, a) = 0$, and $r(0, a) = (a-1)/a$. Let δ be any number in $(0, 1)$. It is easily seen that the supremum of the objective function over the space of feasible sequences of actions is $(1 - \delta)^{-1}$, but there is no feasible sequence $\{a_t\}$, such that $\sum_{t=0}^{\infty} \delta^t [(a_t - 1)/a_t] = (1 - \delta)^{-1}$.

□

The first problem can be overcome if we assume S and A to be compact sets and r to be continuous on $S \times A$. In this case, r is bounded on $S \times A$, so for any feasible action sequence, total reward is finite since $\delta < 1$. More generally, we may directly assume, as we shall, that r is bounded on $S \times A$:

Assumption 1 There is a real number K such that $|r(s, a)| \leq K$ for all $(s, a) \in S \times A$.

Assumption 1 is, by itself, sufficient to yield two useful conclusions.

Lemma 12.3 *Under Assumption 1, the value function V is well defined as a function from S to $\mathbb{R}$, even if an optimal strategy does not exist. Moreover, given any $s \in S$, and any $\epsilon > 0$, it is the case that there exists a strategy σ, depending possibly on ϵ and s, such that $W(\sigma)(s) \geq V(s) - \epsilon$.*

Proof Fix any s. Since r is bounded, it is the case that $|W(\sigma)(s)| \leq K/(1 - \delta)$ for any σ. Thus, $V(s) = \sup_\sigma W(\sigma)(s)$ must be finite, so $V : S \to \mathbb{R}$ is well defined. Pick any s and $\epsilon > 0$. If there were no strategy such that $W(\sigma)(s) \geq V(s) - \epsilon$, then we must have $W(\sigma)(s) \leq V(s) - \epsilon$, and so $V(s) = \sup_\sigma W(\sigma)(s) \leq V(s) - \epsilon$, which is absurd. □

Overcoming the second problem is, of course, the central issue: when does the SDP have a solution? The first step in examining the existence of a solution is the *Bellman Equation,* or the *Principle of Optimality.* Intuitively, the Bellman Equation is a statement of "dynamic consistency" of the optimal path—viz., that once on the path there is never a tendency to move away from it.

Theorem 12.4 (The Bellman Equation) *The value function V satisfies the following equation (the "Bellman Equation") at each $s \in S$:*

$$V(s) = \sup_{a \in \Phi(s)} \{r(s, a) + \delta V[f(s, a)]\}.$$

Proof Let $W: S \rightarrow \mathbb{R}$ be defined by

$$W(s) = \sup_{a \in \Phi(s)} \{r(s, a) + \delta V(f(s, a))\}.$$

We will show that $V = W$, by first showing $V(s) \leq W(s)$ for all s, and then $V(s) \geq W(s)$ for all s. Fix any $s \in S$.

Pick any $\epsilon > 0$. Let a be any action in $\Phi(s)$ and let $s' = f(s, a)$. Pick a strategy σ that satisfies $W(\sigma)(s') \geq V(s') - \epsilon/\delta$. As we have observed, such a strategy always exists by definition of V. Now the action a followed by the strategy σ is feasible from s, since a was chosen from $\Phi(s)$, and by definition all strategies specify only feasible actions. So

$$V(s) \geq r(s, a) + \delta W(\sigma)(f(s, a))$$
$$\geq r(s, a) + \delta V(f(s, a)) - \epsilon.$$

But a was picked arbitrarily; therefore, this holds for all $a \in \Phi(s)$. So

$$V(s) \geq \sup_{a \in \Phi(s)} \{r(s, a) + \delta V(f(s, a)) - \epsilon\}$$

or, since $\epsilon > 0$ was also arbitrary

$$V(s) \geq \sup_{a \in \Phi(s)} \{r(s, a) + \delta V(f(s, a))\}.$$

This completes step 1 of the proof.

Now fix an $s \in S$. Pick any $\epsilon > 0$. Let σ be a strategy that satisfies

$$W(\sigma)(s) \geq V(s) - \epsilon.$$

Let $a = \sigma_0(s)$, and $s_1 = f(s, a)$. Finally, let the continuation strategy specified by σ after the first period be denoted by $\sigma|_1$. Since the strategy $\sigma|_1$ is certainly a feasible continuation s_1, we must have

$$V(s_1) \geq W(\sigma|_1)(s_1).$$

We now have

$$V(s) - \epsilon \leq W(\sigma)(s)$$
$$= r(s, a) + \delta W(\sigma|_1)[f(s, a)]$$
$$\leq r(s, a) + \delta V(f(s, a)).$$

So

$$V(s) - \epsilon \leq \sup_{a \in \Phi(s)} \{r(s, a) + \delta V(f(s, a))\}.$$

Since ϵ is arbitrary, we have

$$V(s) \leq \sup_a \{r(s, a) + \delta V(f(s, a))\},$$

which completes the second step of the proof. $\qquad\qquad\qquad\qquad\square$

We shall use the Bellman Equation to identify a set of conditions under which the SDP has a solution. To do this, a technical digression is required.

12.4 A Technical Digression

12.4.1 Complete Metric Spaces and Cauchy Sequences

A metric space is a pair (X, d) where X is a vector space,[2] and $d: X \times X \to \mathbb{R}$ is a function satisfying the following conditions for all $x, y, z \in X$:

1. (Positivity) $d(x, y) \geq 0$, with equality if and only if $x = y$;
2. (Symmetry) $d(x, y) = d(y, x)$; and
3. (Triangle Inequality) $d(x, z) \leq d(x, y) + d(y, z)$.

A description of metric spaces and their properties may be found in Appendix C. We summarize here some of the properties that are important for this chapter.

The canonical example of a metric space is k-dimensional Euclidean space, $\mathbb{R}^k$, with the Euclidean metric. As we have seen in Chapter 1, the Euclidean metric meets the three conditions required in the definition of a metric.

A second example, and one of some importance for this chapter, is the space $C(S)$ of all continuous and bounded functions from $S \subset \mathbb{R}^n$ to $\mathbb{R}$, endowed with the "sup-norm metric" d, where d is defined by

$$d(f, g) = \sup_{y \in [0,1]} |f(y) - g(y)|, \qquad f, g \in C(S).$$

Since the absolute value $|f(y) - g(y)|$ is nonnegative, and is zero if and only if $f(y) = g(y)$, we have $d(f, g) \geq 0$, with equality if and only if $f(y) = g(y)$ for all y, i.e., if and only if $f = g$. Thus, the sup-norm metric meets the positivity condition. It is evidently symmetric. Finally, pick any $f, g, h \in C(S)$. For any $y \in S$, we have

$$|f(y) - h(y)| \leq |f(y) - g(y)| + |g(y) - h(y)|$$
$$\leq d(f, g) + d(g, h).$$

[2]Vector spaces are defined in Appendix C.

Since $y \in S$ was arbitrary,

$$d(f, h) = \sup |f(y) - h(y)| \leq d(f, g) + d(g, h),$$

and the sup-norm metric d meets the triangle inequality condition also. Thus, d is a metric on $C(S)$.

The definitions of a convergent sequence and a Cauchy sequence are generalized from $\mathbb{R}^n$ to abstract metric spaces in the obvious way. Given a sequence $\{x_n\}$ in a metric space (X, d), we say that $\{x_n\}$ converges to $x \in X$ (written $x_n \to x$) if it is the case that the sequence of real numbers $d(x_n, x)$ converges to zero, i.e., if for any $\epsilon > 0$, there is $n(\epsilon)$ such that for all $n \geq n(\epsilon)$, it is the case that $d(x_n, x) < \epsilon$.

A sequence $\{x_n\}$ in (X, d) is said to be a *Cauchy sequence* if for all $\epsilon > 0$, there is $n(\epsilon)$ such that for all $n, m \geq n(\epsilon)$, it is the case that $d(x_n, x_m) < \epsilon$.

A Cauchy sequence $\{x_n\}$ in (X, d) is said to *converge* if there is $x \in X$ such $d(x_n, x) \to 0$ as $n \to \infty$. (That the limit x be an element of X is an important part of the definition.)

As in $\mathbb{R}^n$ with the Euclidean metric, every convergent sequence in an abstract metric space is also a Cauchy sequence. Unlike $\mathbb{R}^n$, however, the converse is not always true. There exist metric spaces in which not all Cauchy sequences are convergent sequences. A simple example is the following: let X be the open interval $(0,1)$, and let d be the Euclidean metric on $\mathbb{R}$ restricted to $(0,1)$. Then, the sequence $\{x_n\}$ in X defined by $x_n = \frac{1}{n}$ for all n is a Cauchy sequence in X that does not converge: there is no $x \in X$ such that $\frac{1}{n} \to x$.

When a metric space has the property that all Cauchy sequences in the space converge, it is said to be a *complete* metric space.

12.4.2 Contraction Mappings

Let (X, d) be a metric space and $T: X \to X$. For notational convenience in what follows, we shall write Tx rather than $T(x)$ to denote the value of T at a point $x \in X$. The map T is said to be a *contraction* if there is $\rho \in [0, 1)$ such that

$$d(Tx, Ty) \leq \rho d(x, y), \quad x, y \in X.$$

Example 12.5 Let $X = [0, 1]$, d be the Euclidean metric restricted to $[0, 1]$. Let $T: X \to X$ be defined by $Tx = x/2$. Then, $d(Tx, Ty) = d(x/2, y/2) = d(x, y)/2$, so T is a contraction with $\rho = 1/2$. $\square$

A contraction mapping T on a metric space (X, d) must necessarily be continuous on that space. That is, it must be the case that for any sequence $y_n \to y$ in X, we have $T y_n \to T y$. This follows from applying the definition of a contraction: we have

$$d(T y_n, T y) \le \rho d(y_n, y) \to 0 \text{ as } n \to \infty.$$

The importance of contraction mappings for us arises from the following powerful result, which is also known as the Banach Fixed Point Theorem:

Theorem 12.6 (The Contraction Mapping Theorem) *Let (X, d) be a complete metric space, and $T: X \to X$ be a contraction. Then, T has a* unique *fixed point.*

Remark Observe that the theorem asserts two results under the stated conditions: (a) that a fixed point *exists*, and (b) that the fixed point is *unique*.   □

Proof Uniqueness of the fixed point is easy to prove. Suppose x and y were both fixed points of T, and $x \ne y$. Then, we must have $d(x, y) > 0$. Since x and y are both fixed points, we have $T x = x$ and $T y = y$, so $d(T x, T y) = d(x, y)$. On the other hand, since T is a contraction, we must also have $d(T x, T y) \le \rho d(x, y)$, and since we must have $\rho < 1$, this means $d(T x, T y) < d(x, y)$, a contradiction. Thus, T can have at most one fixed point.

It remains to be shown that T has at least one fixed point. Pick any $x \in X$, and let $T^2 x$ denote T evaluated at $T x$. By induction, define now $T^n x$ to be T evaluated at $T^{n-1} x$. Using the fact that T is a contraction, we will show that the sequence $\{T^n x\}$ is a Cauchy sequence in X.

To this end, note that $d(T^{n+1} x, T^n x) \le \rho d(T^n x, T^{n-1} x)$. It follows that $d(T^{n+1} x, T^n x) \le \rho^n d(T x, x)$. Therefore, if $m > n$, we have

$$d(T^m x, T^n x) \le d(T^m x, T^{m-1} x) + \cdots + d(T^{n+1} x, T^n x)$$
$$\le (\rho^{m-1} + \cdots + \rho^n) d(T x, x)$$
$$= (1 + \rho + \cdots + \rho^{m-n-1}) \rho^n d(T x, x)$$
$$\le [1 - \rho]^{-1} \rho^n d(T x, x).$$

Since x is fixed, $d(T x, x)$ is just a fixed number. Since $\rho < 1$, it follows that by taking n sufficiently large, we can make $d(T^m x, T^n x)$ as small as desired for any $m > n$. Therefore, $\{T^n x\}$ is a Cauchy sequence in X, and converges to a limit, say x^*.

We will show that x^* is a fixed point of T. Indeed, this is immediate: by the continuity of T, we have $\lim_n T(y_n) = T(\lim_n y_n)$ for any convergent sequence y_n, so

$$T x^* = T(\lim_n T^n x) = \lim_n T(T^n x) = \lim_n T^{n+1} x = x^*.$$

The theorem is proved.   □

It may be seen through examples that the conditions of the theorem cannot be weakened:

Example 12.7 (The definition of the contraction cannot be weakened to allow for $\rho = 1$.) Consider $\mathbb{R}_+$ with the Euclidean metric. This is a complete metric space. Let $T: \mathbb{R}_+ \to \mathbb{R}_+$ be defined by $T(x) = 1 + x$. Then $d(Tx, Ty) \leq d(x, y)$, but T has no fixed point. □

Indeed, an even more subtle result is true. It is not even sufficient that for each pair (x, y), there exists $\rho(x, y) < 1$ such that $d(Tx, Ty) < \rho(x, y)d(x, y)$. Equivalently, it is not sufficient that $d(Tx, Ty) < d(x, y)$ for all x, y. For an example, see the Exercises.

Example 12.8 (The completeness of X cannot be weakened.) Let $X = (0, 1)$ with the Euclidean metric. Let $T(x) = x/2$. Then T is a contraction, but X is not complete and T has no fixed point. □

12.4.3 Uniform Convergence

Let $S \subset \mathbb{R}^k$ and $\{f_n\}$ be a sequence of functions from S to $\mathbb{R}$. We say that the sequence $\{f_n\}$ *converges uniformly* to a limit function f if for all $\epsilon > 0$, there is an integer $N(\epsilon)$, such that for all $n \geq N(\epsilon)$, we have

$$|f_n(x) - f(x)| < \epsilon \quad \text{for all } x \in S.$$

In words, f_n converges uniformly to f if the distance between $f_n(x)$ and $f(x)$ can be made arbitrarily small simultaneously for all x, simply by taking n sufficiently large.

It is immediate from the definitions of uniform convergence and of the sup-norm that $\{f_n\}$ converges to f uniformly if and only if $\{f_n\}$ converges to f in the sup-norm metric, i.e., if and only if

$$\sup_{x \in S} |f_n(x) - f(x)| \to 0 \text{ as } n \to \infty.$$

We will use this observation shortly to prove an important property about $C(S)$, the space of continuous functions on S, endowed with the sup-norm. The following preliminary result, which is also of considerable independent interest, is needed first.

Theorem 12.9 (Uniform Convergence Theorem) *Let $S \subset \mathbb{R}^m$. Let $\{f_n\}$ be a sequence of functions from S to $\mathbb{R}$ such that $f_n \to f$ uniformly. If the functions f_n are all bounded and continuous, then f is also bounded and continuous.*

Proof Boundedness of f is obvious: since $f_n(x) \to f(x)$ for each x, if f is unbounded, then the functions f_n must also be. To show continuity of f at an arbitrary point $x \in S$ we need to show that for all $\epsilon > 0$, there is $\delta > 0$ such that $y \in S$ and $\|x - y\| < \delta$ implies $|f(x) - f(y)| < \epsilon$.

So let $\epsilon > 0$ be given. For any k, the triangle inequality implies

$$|f(x) - f(y)| \leq |f(x) - f_k(x)| + |f_k(x) - f_k(y)| + |f_k(y) - f(y)|.$$

Pick N sufficiently large so that for all $n \geq N$, $|f(z) - f_n(z)| < \epsilon/3$ for all $z \in S$. Since f_N is a continuous function, there is $\delta > 0$ such that $\|x - y\| < \delta$ implies $|f_N(x) - f_N(y)| < \epsilon/3$. Therefore, whenever $\|x - y\| < \delta$, we have

$$|f(x) - f(y)| \leq |f(x) - f_N(x)| + |f_N(x) - f_N(y)| + |f_N(y) - f(y)|$$
$$< \epsilon/3 + \epsilon/3 + \epsilon/3$$
$$= \epsilon.$$

The theorem is proved. $\qquad\qquad\qquad\qquad\qquad\qquad\qquad\qquad\qquad\qquad\qquad\qquad\qquad\square$

Our next result plays a significant role in establishing existence of an optimal strategy in stationary dynamic programming problems.

Theorem 12.10 *The space $C(S)$ of continuous, bounded real-valued functions on the set $S \subset \mathbb{R}^k$ is a complete metric space when endowed with the sup-norm metric.*

Proof Let $\{f_n\}$ be a Cauchy sequence in S. Pick any $x \in S$. Then, $\{f_n(x)\}$ is a Cauchy sequence in $\mathbb{R}$. Since $\mathbb{R}$ is complete, this Cauchy sequence converges to a limit. Call this limit $f(x)$. This defines a function $f: S \to \mathbb{R}$ such that $f_n(x) \to f(x)$ for each $x \in S$. We will first show that $\{f_n\}$ converges uniformly to f. This will establish, by the Uniform Convergence Theorem, that f is continuous on S.

Since $\{f_n\}$ is a Cauchy sequence in $C(S)$, it is the case that given any $\epsilon > 0$, there is $n(\epsilon)$ such that $m, n \geq n(\epsilon)$ implies

$$|f_n(x) - f_m(x)| < \epsilon, \quad x \in S.$$

Holding n fixed and letting $m \to \infty$, we obtain

$$|f_n(x) - f(x)| < \epsilon, \quad x \in S.$$

This says precisely that $\{f_n\}$ converges uniformly to S.

By the Uniform Convergence Theorem, f is a continuous function. Since uniform convergence is the same as sup-norm convergence, we have shown that an arbitrary Cauchy sequence in $C(S)$ converges in the sup-norm to a limit in $C(S)$. Thus, $C(S)$ is complete when endowed with the sup-norm. $\qquad\qquad\qquad\qquad\qquad\qquad\square$

We close this section with an important remark. It is necessary to distinguish uniform convergence from another notion of convergence in functional spaces —that of *pointwise convergence.* We say that a sequence of functions $\{f_n\}$ converges *pointwise* to a limit function f if for each fixed x the following condition holds: for all $\epsilon > 0$, there exists an integer $N(\epsilon)$, such that for all $n \geq N(\epsilon)$, $|f_n(x) - f(x)| \leq \epsilon$.

Clearly a function converges uniformly only if it converges pointwise. The converse, however, is not true. The key distinction is that in pointwise convergence we fix x first and see if the sequence of real numbers $\{f_n(x)\}$ converges to $f(x)$. On the other hand, uniform convergence requires not only that $f_n(x) \to f(x)$ for each x, but also (roughly speaking) that the "rate of convergence" of $f_n(x)$ to $f(x)$ be the same for all x. That is, for uniform convergence to hold, the same choice of $N(\epsilon)$ must make $|f_n(x) - f(x)| < \epsilon$ for all $n \geq N(\epsilon)$, *for all* x, whereas in the definition of pointwise convergence, the choice of $N(\epsilon)$ may depend on x. To illustrate this vital distinction, consider the following example.

Example 12.11 Let $\{f_n\}$ be a sequence of functions from $\mathbb{R}_+$ to $\mathbb{R}_+$, defined by

$$f_n(x) = \begin{cases} nx, & x \leq 1/n \\ 1, & x > 1/n. \end{cases}$$

Then, for each fixed $x > 0$, $f_n(x) \to 1$ as $n \to \infty$, while $f_n(0) = 0$ for all n, so f_n converges pointwise to f defined by $f(0) = 0$, $f(x) = 1$ for $x > 0$. However, f_n does not converge uniformly to f (if it did, f would be continuous by the uniform convergence theorem). □

12.5 Existence of an Optimal Strategy

We are now in a position to outline a set of assumptions on the SDP under which the existence of an optimal strategy can be guaranteed. We proceed in three stages. Recall that under Assumption 1, we have shown that the value function $V\colon S \to \mathbb{R}$ satisfies the Bellman Equation at all $s \in S$:

$$V(s) = \sup_{a \in \Phi(s)} \{r(s,a) + \delta V(f(s,a))\}.$$

In subsection 12.5.1, we establish that a strategy σ in the SDP is an optimal strategy if and only if the total payoff $W(\sigma)$ under σ also meets the Bellman Equation at each $s \in S$:

$$W(\sigma)(s) = \sup_{a \in \Phi(s)} \{r(s,a) + \delta W(\sigma)(f(s,a))\}.$$

In subsection 12.5.2, we identify a particularly useful class of strategies called *stationary strategies.* Finally, in subsection 12.5.3, we show that under suitable assumptions, there exists a stationary strategy π such that $W(\pi)$ meets the Bellman Equation, which completes the proof.

12.5.1 A Preliminary Result

Let $B(S)$ denote the set of all bounded functions from S to $\mathbb{R}$. Note that under Assumption 1, we have $V \in B(S)$. Endow $B(S)$ with the sup-norm metric, i.e., for $v, w \in B(S)$, let the distance $d(v, w)$ be given by

$$d(v, w) = \sup_{y \in S} |v(y) - w(y)|.$$

Lemma 12.12 *$B(S)$ is a complete metric space when endowed with the sup-norm metric.*

Proof Let $\{v_n\}$ be a Cauchy sequence in $B(S)$. Then, for each $y \in S$, $\{v_n(y)\}$ is a Cauchy sequence in $\mathbb{R}$. If we let $v(y)$ denote the limit of this sequence, we obtain a function $v: S \to \mathbb{R}$. Since $\{v_n\}$ is bounded for each n, v is bounded, it is the case that $v \in B(S)$. That $\{v_n\}$ converges uniformly to v is established along the lines of the proof of Theorem 12.10 on the completeness of $C(S)$ under the sup-norm metric. $\qquad\square$

Now, define a map T on $B(S)$ as follows: for $w \in B(S)$, let Tw be that function whose value at any $s \in S$ is specified by

$$Tw(s) = \sup_{a \in \Phi(s)} \{r(s, a) + \delta w(f(s, a))\}.$$

Since r and w are bounded by assumption, it follows that so is Tw, and therefore that $Tw \in B(S)$. So T maps $B(S)$ into itself. We first establish an important result concerning the fixed points of T.

Theorem 12.13 *V is the unique fixed point of the operator T. That is, if $w \in B(S)$ is any function satisfying*

$$w(s) = \sup_{a \in \Phi(s)} \{r(s, a) + \delta w(f(s, a))\}$$

at each $s \in S$, then we must have $w \equiv V$.

Proof That V is a fixed point of T is immediate from the definition of T and Theorem 12.4. We will show it is the only fixed point of T, by showing that T is a contraction on $B(S)$. Since $B(S)$ has been shown to be a complete metric space, the

Contraction Mapping Theorem will then imply that T has a unique fixed point on $B(S)$.

The proof that T is a contraction is simplified by the following lemma:

Lemma 12.14 (Contraction Mapping Lemma) *Let $L: B(S) \to B(S)$ be any map that satisfies*

1. *(Monotonicity) $w \geq v \Rightarrow Lw \geq Lv$.*
2. *(Discounting) There is $\beta \in [0, 1)$ such that $L(w + c) = Lw + \beta c$ for all $w \in B(S)$ and $c \in \mathbb{R}$.*

Then, L is a contraction.

Remark   Like most shorthand notation, the notation in the lemma is sloppy. First, $w \geq v$ means $w(s) \geq v(s)$ for all $s \in S$. Secondly, for $w \in B(S)$ and $c \in \mathbb{R}$, $w + c$ is the function which at any s assumes the value $w(s) + c$. Under this interpretation, it is clearly the case that whenever $w \in B(S)$, we also have $(w + c) \in B(S)$, so $L(w + c)$ is well defined.

Proof of the Contraction Mapping Lemma   Let $v, w \in B(S)$. Clearly for any $s \in S$, we have

$$w(s) - v(s) \leq \sup_{s \in S} |w(s) - v(s)| = \|w - v\|.$$

So $w(s) \leq v(s) + \|w - v\|$. Applying monotonicity and discounting in order, we now have

$$Lw(s) \leq L(v + \|w - v\|)(s) \leq Lv(s) + \beta\|w - v\|,$$

so that $[Lw(s) - Lv(s)] \leq \beta\|w - v\|$. Now, $v(s) - w(s) \leq \|w - v\|$, so going through the same procedure yields

$$Lv(s) \leq L(w + \|w - v\|)(s) \leq Lw(s) + \beta\|w - v\|,$$

or $[Lv(s) - Lw(s)] \leq \beta\|w - v\|$. Combining this with the previous inequality, we obtain

$$|Lw(s) - Lv(s)| \leq \beta\|w - v\|,$$

and so $\sup_{s \in S} |Lw(s) - Lv(s)| \leq \beta\|w - v\|$. Equivalently, $\|Lw - Lv\| \leq \beta\|w - v\|$. Since $\beta \in [0, 1)$, we are done. $\square$

To complete the proof of Theorem 12.13, we apply the Contraction Mapping Lemma to the mapping T. Note that T trivially satisfies monotonicity (a larger function can only give a higher supremum). Furthermore,

$$
\begin{aligned}
T(w + c)(s) &= \sup\{r(s, a) + \delta(w + c)(f(s, a))\} \\
&= \sup\{r(s, a) + \delta w(f(s, a)) + \delta c\} \\
&= Tw + \delta c.
\end{aligned}
$$

Since $\delta \in [0, 1)$ by hypothesis, T satisfies the discounting property also. Therefore, T is a contraction on $B(S)$, and the theorem is proved. $\square$

We can now establish the main result of this subsection.

Theorem 12.15 *Under Assumption 1, a strategy σ in the SDP is an optimal strategy if, and only if, $W(\sigma)$ satisfies the following equation at each $s \in S$:*

$$
W(\sigma)(s) = \sup_{a \in \Phi(s)} \{r(s, a) + \delta W(\sigma)(f(s, a))\}.
$$

Proof First, suppose that $W(\sigma)$ satisfies the given equation at each $s \in S$. Since r is bounded by Assumption 1, $W(\sigma)$ is evidently bounded. But then we must have $W(\sigma) = V$, since (by Theorem 12.13) V is the unique bounded function that satisfies this equation at all s. And, of course, $W(\sigma) = V$ says precisely that σ is an optimal strategy.

Now suppose σ is an optimal strategy. By definition of V, we must have $W(\sigma) = V$, so we certainly have

$$
W(\sigma)(s) = \sup_{a \in \Phi(s)} \{r(s, a) + \delta W(\sigma)(f(s, a))\},
$$

at all $s \in S$, as required. $\square$

By Theorem 12.15, the SDP will be solved if we can demonstrate the existence of a strategy σ such that $W(\sigma)$ satisfies the Bellman Equation at each $s \in S$. We do this in subsection 12.5.3 after first identifying an especially simple and attractive class of strategies.

12.5.2 Stationary Strategies

The aim of this section is to single out a particularly useful class of strategies, the class of *stationary strategies*. The definition of stationary strategies is motivated by the observation that any t-history $h_t = (s_1, a_1, \ldots, s_t)$ in a stationary dynamic programming problem $\{S, A, r, f, \Phi, \delta\}$ from the initial state $s = s_1$, simply results in the *same* stationary dynamic programming problem $\{S, A, r, f, \Phi, \delta\}$, but with initial state $s = s_t$. Intuitively, this appears to imply that there is no extra gain to be made by conditioning the strategy on anything more than the current state, and not even the date (i.e., the time period) on which this state was reached. A strategy which depends solely on the current state in this fashion is called a stationary Markovian strategy, or simply a stationary strategy.

For a more formal definition, a *Markovian strategy* σ for the SDP is defined to be a strategy where for each t, σ_t depends on h_t only through t and the period-t state under h_t, $s_t[h_t]$. Effectively, a Markovian strategy may be thought of as a sequence $\{\pi_t\}$ where for each t, π_t is a mapping from S to A satisfying $\pi_t(s) \in \Phi(s)$ for each s. The interpretation is that $\pi_t(s)$ is the action to be taken in period t, if the state at the beginning of period t is s.

A *stationary strategy* is a Markovian strategy $\{\pi_t\}$ which satisfies the further condition that $\pi_t = \pi_\tau (= \pi$, say) for all t and τ. Thus, in a stationary strategy, the action taken in any period t depends only on the state at the beginning of that period, and not even on the value of t. It is usual to denote such a strategy by $\pi^{(\infty)}$, but, for notational simplicity, we shall denote such a strategy simply by the function π.

Finally, a *stationary optimal strategy* is a stationary strategy that is also an optimal strategy.

12.5.3 Existence of an Optimal Strategy

We have already assumed that:

Assumption 1 r is bounded on $S \times A$.

We now add the following assumptions:

Assumption 2 r is continuous on $S \times A$.

Assumption 3 f is continuous on $S \times A$.

Assumption 4 Φ is a continuous, compact-valued correspondence on S.

Under Assumptions 1–4, we will show the existence of a stationary strategy π^* such that $W(\pi^*)$ meets the Bellman Principle of Optimality at all $s \in S$. Our derivation of this strategy is carried out in a series of three steps. The content of these steps is as follows:

Step 1 We first show that there is a unique *continuous* function $w^*: S \to \mathbb{R}$ such that w^* meets the Bellman Principle of Optimality at all $s \in S$:

$$w^*(s) = \max_{a \in \Phi(s)} \{r(s, a) + \delta w^*(f(s, a))\}.$$

Step 2 Define $G^*: S \to P(A)$ by

$$G^*(s) = \arg \max_{a \in \Phi(s)} \{w^*(s) = r(s, a) + \delta w^*(f(s, a))\}.$$

We show that G^* is well defined and admits a selection π^*, i.e., there is a function $\pi^*: S \to A$ satisfying $\pi^*(s) \in G^*(s)$ for all $s \in S$. The function π^* defines a stationary strategy which satisfies, by definition,

$$w^*(s) = r(s, \pi^*(s)) + \delta w^*[f(s, \pi^*(s))],$$

for all $s \in S$.

Step 3 Finally, we shall show that the total discounted reward $W(\pi^*)(s)$ under the stationary strategy π^* defined in Step 2, from the initial state s, satisfies

$$W(\pi^*)(s) = w^*(s).$$

By Step 1, therefore, $W(\pi^*)$ is a fixed point of the mapping T. Thus, by Theorem 12.15, π^* is a stationary optimal strategy.

Step 1

Let $C(S)$ be the space of all real-valued continuous functions on S. Endow $C(S)$ with the sup-norm metric. We have already seen that $C(S)$ is then a complete metric space. Now, define the function T on $C(S)$ as in subsection 12.5.1. That is, for $w \in C(S)$, let Tw be the function whose value at any $s \in S$ is given by:

$$Tw(s) = \max_{a \in \Phi(s)} \{r(s, a) + \delta w(f(s, a))\}.$$

Tw is evidently bounded on S since w and r are bounded functions. Moreover, since w is continuous and f is continuous, $w \circ f$ is continuous as the composition of continuous functions. By assumption, r is continuous on $S \times A$, therefore the expression in parentheses on the RHS is continuous on $S \times A$. For fixed s, $\Phi(s)$ is compact by hypothesis, so the maximum is well defined. The Maximum Theorem now implies that Tw is also continuous on S. Therefore:

Lemma 12.16 *T maps $C(S)$ into $C(S)$.*

For $w, v \in C(S)$, it is immediate from the definition of T that $w \geq v$ implies $Tw \geq Tv$, since a larger function can only give a larger maximum. Moreover, for any $w \in C(S)$ and $c \in \mathbb{R}$, we clearly have $(w + c) \in C(S)$, and, moreover, $T(w+c) = Tw + \delta c$. By mimicking the proof of the Contraction Mapping Lemma, it is easy to show that

Lemma 12.17 *$T: C(S) \to C(S)$ is a contraction.*

The following result, which obtains by combining these results, completes Step 1:

Lemma 12.18 *T has a unique fixed point $w^* \in C(S)$. That is, there is a unique $w^* \in C(S)$ that satisfies the following equation at each $s \in S$:*

$$w^*(s) = \max_{a \in \Phi(s)} \{r(s, a) + \delta w^*(f(s, a))\}.$$

Step 2

Define $G^*: S \to P(A)$ by

$$G^*(s) = \arg \max_{a \in \Phi(s)} \{r(s, a) + \delta w * (f(s, a)) = w^*(s)\}.$$

By the Maximum Theorem, G^* is a (nonempty-valued) usc correspondence. Thus, there is a function $\pi^*: S \to A$ such that for each $s \in S$, $\pi^*(s) \in G^*(s) \subset \Phi(s)$. The function π^* defines a stationary optimal strategy, that by definition satisfies at all $s \in S$,

$$w^*(s) = r(s, \pi^*(s)) + \delta w^*[f(s, \pi^*(s))]$$
$$\geq r(s, a) + \delta w^*[f(s, a)], \quad a \in \Phi(s).$$

This completes Step 2.

Step 3

Define π^* as in Step 2, and pick any initial state $s \in S$. Recall that $\{s_t(\pi^*, s), a_t(\pi^*, s)\}$ denotes the sequence of states and actions that result from s under π^*; and that $r_t(\pi^*)(s) = r[s_t(\pi^*, s), a_t(\pi^*, s)]$ is the period-t reward under π^* from s. For notational ease, let $s_t = s_t(\pi^*, s)$ and $a_t = a_t(\pi^*, s)$. By definition of $W(\pi^*)$, we have

$$W(\pi^*)(s) = \sum_{t=0}^{\infty} \delta^t r_t(\pi^*)(s).$$

On the other hand, by Step 2, we also have of L_π,

$$w^*(s) = r(s, \pi^*(s)) + \delta w^*[f(s, \pi^*(s))]$$
$$= r(s, \pi^*(s)) + \delta w^*(s_1)$$
$$= r(s, \pi^*(s)) + \delta r(s_1, a_1) + \delta^2 w^*[f(s_2)]$$
$$= r_0(\pi^*)(s) + \delta r_1(\pi^*)(s) + \delta^2 w^*[s_2(\pi^*, s)].$$

Iterating, we obtain for any integer T:

$$w^*(s) = \sum_{t=0}^{T-1} \delta^t r_t(\pi^*)(s) + \delta^T w^*[s_T(\pi^*, s)].$$

Since w^* is bounded and $\delta < 1$, letting $T \to \infty$ yields

$$w^*(s) = \sum_{t=0}^{\infty} r_t(\pi^*)(s),$$

so $w^* = W(\pi^*)$. Since Step 1 established that

$$w^*(s) = \max_{a \in \Phi(s)} \{r(s, a) + \delta w^*(f(s, a))\},$$

it follows that

$$W(\pi^*)(s) = \max_{a \in \Phi(s)} \{r(s, a) + \delta W(\pi^*)(f(s, a))\}.$$

By Theorem 12.15, this equation establishes that π^* is an optimal strategy. Since π^* is also stationary, we have shown that a stationary optimal strategy exists under Assumptions 1–4. We summarize in the following theorem.

Theorem 12.19 *Suppose the SDP $\{S, A, \Phi, f, r, \delta\}$ satisfies the following conditions:*

1. *$r: S \times A \to \mathbb{R}$ is continuous and bounded on $S \times A$.*
2. *$f: S \times A \to S$ is continuous on $S \times A$.*
3. *$\Phi: S \to P(A)$ is a compact-valued, continuous correspondence.*

   Then, there exists a stationary optimal policy π^*. Furthermore, the value function $V = W(\pi^*)$ is continuous on S, and is the unique bounded function that satisfies the Bellman Equation at each $s \in S$:

$$W(\pi^*)(s) = \max_{a \in \Phi(s)} \{r(s, a) + \delta W(\pi^*)(f(s, a))\}$$

$$= r(s, \pi^*(s)) + \delta W(\pi^*)[f(s, \pi * (s))].$$

12.6 An Example: The Optimal Growth Model

The one-sector model of optimal growth is a very popular framework in neoclassical economics. It studies the problem of a single agent (a "social planner") who maximizes discounted utility from consumption over an infinite horizon subject to technological constraints. It offers an excellent illustration of how convexity conditions can be combined with the continuity conditions on the primitives to provide a very sharp *characterization* of the solution.

12.6.1 The Model

The basic model of optimal growth is very simple. There is a single good (the metaphorical corn of neoclassical theory) which may be consumed or invested. The conversion of investment to output takes one period and is achieved through a *production function* $f: \mathbb{R}_+ \to \mathbb{R}_+$. Thus, if x_t denotes period-t investment, the output available in period-$(t + 1)$, denoted y_{t+1}, is given by $f(x_t)$. The agent begins with an initial endowment of $y = y_0 \in \mathbb{R}_{++}$. In each period $t = 0, 1, 2, \ldots$, the agent observes the available stock y_t and decides on the division of this stock between period-t consumption c_t and period-t investment x_t. Consumption of c_t in period t gives the consumer instantaneous utility of $u(c_t)$ where $u: \mathbb{R}_+ \to \mathbb{R}$ is a *utility function*. The agent discounts future utility by the discount factor $\delta \in [0, 1)$, and wishes to maximize total discounted utility from lifetime consumption. Thus, the problem is to solve:

$$\text{Maximize} \quad \sum_{t=0}^{\infty} \delta^t u(c_t)$$

$$\text{subject to} \quad y_0 = y$$
$$y_{t+1} = f(x_t), \quad t = 0, 1, 2, \ldots$$
$$c_t + x_t = y_t, \quad t = 0, 1, 2, \ldots$$
$$c_t, x_t \geq 0, \quad t = 0, 1, 2, \ldots.$$

The optimal growth model may be cast in a dynamic programming framework using the following definitions. Let $S^* = \mathbb{R}_+$ be the state space, and $A^* = \mathbb{R}_+$ be the action space. Let $\Phi(y) = [0, y]$ be the feasible action correspondence taking states $y \in S^*$ into the set of feasible actions $[0, y] \subset A^*$ at y. Let $r(y, c) = u(c)$ be the reward from taking the action $c \in \Phi(y)$ at the state $y \in S^*$. Finally, let $F(y, c) = f(y - c)$ be the transition function taking current state-action pairs (y, c) into future states $F(y, c)$. The tuple $\{S^*, A^*, \Phi, r, F, \delta\}$ now defines a stationary discounted dynamic programming problem, which represents the optimal growth model.

We are interested in several questions concerning this model. These include:

1. Under what conditions on u and f do optimal strategies *exist* in this model?
2. When is the optimal strategy *unique*?
3. What can one say about the dynamic implications of the optimal strategy? For instance, letting $\{y_t, c_t\}$ denote the evolution of state-action levels under the optimal strategy from an arbitrary initial state (i.e., stock level) y_0:

   (a) Will the sequences $\{y_t\}$ and $\{c_t\}$ be monotone, or will one (or both) exhibit cyclical tendencies?

(b) If the sequences are monotone, what are the properties of their limiting values y^* and c^*? In particular, are these limiting values independent of the initial state y_0 (that is, are the "long-run" implications of growth independent of where one starts)?

(c) Is it possible to use analogues of first-order conditions to characterize behavior on the optimal path?

In subsection 12.6.2 below, we tackle the question of existence of an optimal strategy. We show that under minimal continuity conditions, and a boundedness condition on f that enables compactification of the state space, it is possible to show that stationary optimal strategies exist.

The characterization of optimal strategies is taken up in subsection 12.6.3 under added strict convexity assumptions on f and u. We show that these assumptions carry several strong implications, including the following:[3]

1. If u is strictly concave, the optimal level of *savings* increases with stock levels. Therefore, the sequence of states $\{y_t\}$ that results from any initial state under the optimal plan is monotone, and converges to a limiting value y^*.[4]

2. If f and u are both strictly concave:

   (a) The optimal consumption sequence $\{c_t\}$ from any initial state is also monotone, and converges to a limit c^*.

   (b) The limiting values y^* and c^* are independent of the initial state; curiously, they are even independent of the properties of the utility function u, and depend only on the properties of the technology f and the discount factor δ.[5]

   (c) The right-hand side of the Bellman Equation is strictly concave in y and c, so a unique maximizing action exists for each y. As a consequence, the optimal strategy is *unique*.

   (d) If f and u are also continuously differentiable, then the optimal path may also be characterized using a dynamic analogue of first-order conditions known as the *Ramsey–Euler Equations*.

12.6.2 Existence of Optimal Strategies

We cannot directly appeal to Theorem 12.19 to establish existence of optimal strategies in this problem, because u may be unbounded on $\mathbb{R}_+$. Rather than impose

---

[3] The order in which results are listed here is not the order in which they are proved. Some of the results listed later here—such as the Ramsey–Euler Equation—are used to prove some of those listed earlier (such as the monotonicity of the sequence $\{c_t\}$).

[4] It must be emphasized that this result does not depend on f having any convexity properties.

[5] This is true only of the limiting values y^* and c^*. The path by which $\{y_t\}$ and $\{c_t\}$ converge to y^* and c^* does depend on u.

boundedness on the framework as an assumption, we consider a more natural and plausible restriction which will ensure that we may, without loss of generality, restrict S^* and A^* to compact intervals in $\mathbb{R}_+$, thereby obtaining boundedness of u from its continuity.

Assumption 1 The production function f satisfies the following conditions:

1. (No free production) $f(0) = 0$.
2. (Continuity and Monotonicity) f is continuous and nondecreasing on $\mathbb{R}_+$.
3. (Unproductivity at high investment levels) There is $\bar{x} > 0$ such that $f(x) \leq x$ for all $x \geq \bar{x}$.

Parts 1 and 2 of this assumption are self-explanatory. Part 3 can be justified as a version of diminishing marginal returns.

We assume that the initial state y_0 lies in some compact interval $[0, \hat{y}]$ of $\mathbb{R}_+$. Define $y^* = \max\{\bar{x}, \hat{y}\}$. Then, by Assumption 1, if $y \in [0, y^*]$, we have $f(x) \in [0, y^*]$ for all $x \in [0, y]$, and we may, without loss of generality, restrict analysis to $[0, y^*]$. We now set

$$S = A = [0, y^*].$$

Secondly, we make the usual continuity assumption on the reward function:

Assumption 2 $u: \mathbb{R}_+ \to \mathbb{R}$ is continuous on $\mathbb{R}_+$.

The tuple $\{S, A, \Phi, r, F, \delta\}$ now meets the requisite compactness and continuity conditions to guarantee existence of an optimal strategy, and we have:

Theorem 12.20 *There is a stationary optimal strategy* $g: S \to A$ *in the optimal growth problem under Assumptions 1 and 2. The value function V is continuous on S and satisfies the Bellman Equation at each $y \in S$:*

$$V(y) = \max_{c \in [0, y]} \{u(c) + \delta V[f(y - c)]\}$$
$$= u(g(y)) + \delta V[f(y - g(y))].$$

12.6.3 Characterization of Optimal Strategies

What more can we say about this problem without making additional assumptions? Consider two different initial states y and y' with $y < y'$. Let $c = g(y)$ be an optimal action at y. Then, c is a feasible (but not necessarily optimal) action at y', since

$$\Phi(y') = [0, y'] \supset [0, y] = \Phi(y).$$

Moreover, since f is nondecreasing, consuming c at y' results in a period-1 stock level of $f(y' - c) \geq f(y - c)$. Thus, in the continuation also, the optimal action at $f(y - c)$ will be feasible (but not necessarily optimal) at $f(y' - c)$. It follows by induction that the entire sequence of actions $\{c_t\}$ that results from y under the optimal strategy g is feasible (but not necessarily optimal) from y'. Therefore:[6]

Theorem 12.21 $V: S \to \mathbb{R}$ *is nondecreasing on S.*

Without additional structure, it is not possible to further characterize the solution; we proceed therefore to make assumptions of increasing degrees of restrictiveness on the structure.

Assumption 3 $u: \mathbb{R}_+ \to \mathbb{R}$ is strictly increasing on $\mathbb{R}_+$.

Assumption 4 $u: \mathbb{R}_+ \to \mathbb{R}$ is strictly concave on $\mathbb{R}_+$.

Note that under Assumptions 1–3, Theorem 12.21 can be strengthened to the statement that V is a strictly increasing function. When Assumptions 1–3 are combined with the curvature condition in Assumption 4, we obtain a very strong conclusion: namely, that the marginal propensity to save must be nonnegative. That is, if the stock level increases from y to y', then the optimal level of *savings* that results at y' must be at least as large as the optimal level of savings that results at y.

More formally, let $\xi(y) = y - g(y)$ denote the optimal *savings* (or *investment*) at y under the optimal strategy g. Since choosing the consumption level c at y is equivalent to choosing the investment level $x = y - c$, we must have

$$V(y) = \max_{x \in [0, y]} \{u(y - x) + \delta V[f(x)]\}.$$

Theorem 12.22 *Under Assumptions 1–4, ξ is nondecreasing on S. That is, y, $y' \in S$ with $y < y'$ implies $\xi(y) \leq \xi(y')$.*

Proof Suppose not. Then, there exist y, $y' \in S$ with $y < y'$ and $\xi(y) > \xi(y')$. For ease of notation, let x and x' denote $\xi(y)$ and $\xi(y')$, respectively.

---

[6]An alternative, and somewhat lengthier, way to prove this result is to consider the set $C^*(S)$ of bounded, continuous, and nondecreasing functions on S with the sup-norm. This space is complete, and a simple argument shows that the map T^* defined on $C^*(S)$ by

$$T^*w(y) = \max\{u(c) + \delta w[f(y - c)] \mid c \in [0, y]\}$$

is a contraction that maps $C^*(S)$ into itself. (We use the monotonicity of w and f to show that T^*w is a nondecreasing function on S.) Therefore, T^* has a unique fixed point V^*. Since $V^* \in C^*(S)$, V^* must be continuous. But V is the unique continuous function that satisfies the Bellman Equation. Therefore, we must have $V^* = V$, so V is nondecreasing.

Since $y' > y \geq x$, x is a feasible level of savings at y'. Similarly, since $y \geq x$, and $x > x'$ by hypothesis, x' is a feasible level of savings at y. Since x and x' are the *optimal* savings levels at y and y', respectively, we must have

$$V(y) = u(y - x) + \delta V(f(x))$$
$$\geq u(y - x') + \delta V(f(x')).$$
$$V(y') = u(y' - x') + \delta V(f(x'))$$
$$\geq u(y' - x) + \delta V(f(x)).$$

From these inequalities we obtain:

$$u(y - x) - u(y - x') \geq \delta[V(f(x')) - V(f(x))] \geq u(y' - x) - u(y' - x'),$$

and so

$$u(y - x') - u(y - x) \leq u(y' - x') - u(y' - x).$$

But $(y - x')$ and $(y - x)$ are the same distance apart as $(y' - x')$ and $(y' - x)$. However, $y < y'$, and u is increasing and *strictly* concave, which means we must have $u(y-x') - u(y-x) > u(y'-x') - u(y'-x)$, a contradiction. This establishes the theorem. $\qquad\Box$

We now make an additional convexity assumption. Assumptions 1–5 describe the framework known as the *concave one-sector growth model.*

Assumption 5 f is concave on $\mathbb{R}_+$.

Note that we do not (yet) require strict concavity of f. Nonetheless, this is now sufficient to prove two strong results: the concavity of the value function V, and using this, the *uniqueness* of the optimal strategy g. The second result is an especially significant one.

Theorem 12.23 *Under Assumptions 1–5, V is concave on S.*

Proof Let $y, y' \in S$ with $y \neq y'$. Pick $\lambda \in (0, 1)$ and let $y_\lambda = \lambda y + (1 - \lambda)y'$. We need to show that

$$V(y_\lambda) \geq \lambda V(y) + (1 - \lambda)V(y').$$

Let $\{c_t\}$ and $\{c_t'\}$ be the optimal consumption sequences from y and y' respectively, and let $\{y_t\}$ and $\{y_t'\}$ denote the respective sequences of stock levels that arise. Of course, we have

$$c_t \leq y_t \text{ and } c_t' \leq y_t'$$

for all t. Now define for $t = 0, 1, 2, \ldots,$

$$c_t^\lambda = \lambda c_t + (1 - \lambda)c_t'.$$

We will establish that the sequence $\{c_t^\lambda\}$ is a feasible consumption sequence from y_λ. Let $\{x_t^*\}$ denote the sequence of investment levels that will arise if $\{c_t^\lambda\}$ is followed from y_λ. The feasibility of $\{c_t^\lambda\}$ from y_λ will be established if we can show that $y_\lambda \geq c_0^\lambda$ and for $t = 0, 1, 2, \ldots,$

$$f(x_t^*) \geq c_{t+1}^\lambda.$$

The first of the required inequalities holds since

$$y_\lambda = \lambda y + (1 - \lambda)y' \geq \lambda c_0 + (1 - \lambda)c_0 = c_0^\lambda.$$

Using $x_0^* = y_\lambda - c_0^\lambda$ and the concavity of f, we also have

$$
\begin{aligned}
f(x_0^*) &= f[\lambda(y - c_0) + (1 - \lambda)(y' - c_0')] \\
&\geq \lambda f(y - c_0) + (1 - \lambda)f(y' - c_0') \\
&\geq \lambda c_1 + (1 - \lambda)c_1' \\
&= c_1^\lambda.
\end{aligned}
$$

The obvious induction argument now completes this step.

Since $\{c_t^\lambda\}$ is a feasible, but not necessarily optimal, consumption sequence from y_λ, and since $u[\lambda c_t + (1 - \lambda)c_t'] \geq \lambda u(c_t) + (1 - \lambda)u(c_t')$ for each t, we have

$$
\begin{aligned}
V(y_\lambda) &\geq \sum_{t=0}^{\infty} \delta^t u(c_t^\lambda) \\
&= \sum_{t=0}^{\infty} \delta^t u[\lambda c_t + (1 - \lambda)c_t'] \\
&\geq \lambda \sum_{t=0}^{\infty} \delta^t u(c_t) + (1 - \lambda) \sum_{t=0}^{\infty} \delta^t u(c_t') \\
&= \lambda V(y) + (1 - \lambda)V(y'),
\end{aligned}
$$

which completes the proof.   □

Theorem 12.24 *Under Assumptions 1–5, the correspondence of maximizers G of the Bellman Equation is single-valued on S. Therefore, there is a unique optimal strategy g, and g is a continuous function on S.*

Proof By hypothesis, u is strictly concave and f is concave. By Theorem 12.23, V inherits this concavity. Thus, the RHS of the Bellman Equation

$$\{u(c) + \delta V[f(y - c)]\}$$

is strictly concave as a function of c. The single-valuedness of G follows. As a single-valued correspondence, G admits a unique selection g; since G is a usc correspondence, g must be a continuous function. $\qquad\square$

It is very important to emphasize that this result shows the uniqueness of the optimal strategy itself, not just that there is a unique *stationary* optimal strategy. We leave it as an exercise to the reader to explain why this is the case.[7]

Finally, we add the following differentiability assumptions and obtain the *differentiable concave model*:

Assumption 6 u is C^1 on $\mathbb{R}_{++}$ with $\lim_{c \downarrow 0} u'(c) = \infty$.

Assumption 7 f is C^1 on $\mathbb{R}_{++}$ with $\lim_{x \downarrow 0} f'(x) > 1/\delta$.

Assumption 8 f is strictly concave on $\mathbb{R}_+$.

The assumptions that $u'(0) = +\infty$ and $f'(0) > \delta^{-1}$ are called the *Inada conditions* on u and f, respectively. They ensure essentially that the agent will try to keep consumption levels strictly positive in all periods. If consumption in period-t is positive and in period-$(t + 1)$ is zero, the agent can gain in total utility by transferring a "small" amount from period-t to period-$(t + 1)$: the fall in marginal utility in period t will be more than compensated for the gain in marginal utility in period $(t + 1)$. However, this argument is not quite complete, since f may be so "unproductive" as to make transferring any amount across periods unattractive. The Inada assumption on f rules out this possibility. The following result formalizes these ideas:

Theorem 12.25 *Under Assumptions 1–7, it is the case that for all $y > 0$, we have $0 < g(y) < y$, i.e., the solution to the model is "interior."*

Remark It is important to note that the proof of this result makes no use of the concavity of f. $\qquad\square$

---

[7] The following is a sketch of the required arguments. We have seen that a strategy π in a dynamic programming problem is optimal if and only if the payoff $W(\pi)$ under π satisfies the Bellman Equation. Therefore, the actions prescribed by π at any state must solve the Bellman Equation. Since V is the only solution to the Bellman Equation, it follows that if there is a unique action maximizing the right-hand side of the Bellman Equation, then there is also a unique optimal strategy.

Proof Pick any $y > 0$. Let $x = y - g(y)$ be the optimal investment at y, and $x' = y' - g(y')$ be the optimal investment at $y' = g(y - g(y))$, i.e., in the period following y. Then x must solve the following two-period maximization problem:

$$\max_{z \in [0, y]} \{u(y - z) + \delta u(f(z) - x')\}.$$

The reason is simple: suppose x was dominated in this problem by some z. Then, by consuming $(y - z)$ at the state y, and $f(z) - x'$ at the state $f(z)$, the utility over the first two periods beginning from y is strictly larger than following the prescriptions of the optimal plan in these two periods. But in either case, the investment at the end of the second period is x'; therefore, the continuation possibilities after the second period are the same in either case. This means x could not have been an optimal investment level at y, a contradiction.

Now, if it were not true that the solution x to this two-period maximization problem lies in $(0, y)$, then we must have $x = 0$ or $x = y$.

Case 1: $(x = 0)$

The first-order conditions for a maximum in this case are:

$$\delta u'(f(x) - x') f'(x) \leq u'(y - x).$$

If $x = 0$, then $f(x) = 0$, so $x' = 0$. But these conditions then reduce to the contradiction

$$+\infty = \delta u'(0) f'(0) \leq u'(y) < u'(0) = +\infty.$$

Case 2: $(x = y)$

In this case, the FOC's are (using $x = y$)

$$\delta u'(f(y) - x') f'(y) \geq u'(0).$$

This is not possible unless $x' = f(y)$. But $x' = f(y)$ would similarly be impossible as an optimal choice unless $x'' = f(y')$, where $y'' = f(x')$, and $x'' = y'' - g(y'')$, and so on. Thus the only way this situation can arise is if on the entire path from y, we have zero consumption. But this is evidently suboptimal since u is strictly increasing. □

Thus, Cases 1 and 2 are both impossible, and the result is established. □

As an immediate consequence of Theorem 12.25, we obtain the *Ramsey–Euler Equation*, the first-order condition for optimality in the one-sector growth model:

Theorem 12.26 (Ramsey–Euler Equation) *Suppose Assumptions 1–7 are met. Let $y > 0$, and $y^* = f(y - g(y))$. Then, g satisfies*

$$u'[g(y)] = \delta u'[g(y^*)]f'[y - g(y)].$$

Proof We have shown that at each y, $g(y)$ must solve

$$\max_{c \in [0,y]} \{u(c) + \delta u[f(y - c) - x']\},$$

and that the solution to this problem is interior. The Ramsey–Euler Equation is simply the first-order condition for an interior optimal solution to this problem. □

Remark The Ramsey–Euler Equation is often expressed more elegantly as follows. Let $y > 0$ be any given initial state, and let $\{c_t\}$ and $\{x_t\}$ denote the optimal consumption and savings sequences that arise from y. Then, it must be the case that at each t:

$$u'(c_t) = \delta u'(c_{t+1})f'(x_t).$$ □

Using the Ramsey–Euler Equation, it is now an easy task to show that the sequence of *consumption* levels from any initial state must also be monotone:

Theorem 12.27 *Under Assumptions 1–7, g is increasing on S. That is, $y > \hat{y}$ implies $g(y) > g(\hat{y})$.*

Proof For notational ease, let $c = g(y)$ and $\hat{c} = g(\hat{y})$. Let y_1 and $\hat{y}_1$ denote, respectively, the output levels that result from y and $\hat{y}$ one period hence, i.e., $y_1 = f(y - c)$ and $\hat{y}_1 = f(\hat{y} - \hat{c})$. Finally, let $c_1 = g(y_1)$ and $\hat{c}_1 = g(\hat{y}_1)$. By the Ramsey –Euler equation, we have

$$u'(c) = \delta u'(c_1)f'(y - c)$$
$$u'(\hat{c}) = \delta u'(\hat{c}_1)f'(\hat{y} - \hat{c}).$$

Therefore,

$$\left(\frac{u'(c)}{u'(\hat{c})}\right) = \left(\frac{u'(c_1)f'(y - c)}{u'(\hat{c}_1)f'(\hat{y} - \hat{c})}\right).$$

Suppose $c \leq \hat{c}$. Then, since u is strictly concave, $u'(c) \geq u'(\hat{c})$. Moreover, $y - c > \hat{y} - \hat{c}$, so $f'(y - c) < f'(\hat{y} - \hat{c})$. Therefore, we must have $u'(c_1) > u'(\hat{c}_1)$, or $c_1 < \hat{c}_1$.

In summary, we have shown that if $y > \hat{y}$ and $c \leq \hat{c}$, then these inequalities are repeated in the next period also; that is, $y_1 > \hat{y}_1$ and $c_1 < \hat{c}_1$. Iterating on this argument, it is seen that the sequence of consumption levels from y is dominated in every period by the sequence of consumption levels from y'. This means the total utility from y is strictly smaller than that from y', a contradiction to the fact that V is strictly increasing. $\square$

Finally, define a *steady state* under the optimal policy g to be a state $y \in S$ with the property that

$$y = f(y - g(y)).$$

That is, y is a steady state under the optimal policy, if, whenever the initial state is y, the system remains at y forever under the optimal policy. Also define the *golden-rule* state y_δ^* to be equal to $f(x_\delta^*)$ where x_δ^* is the unique solution to

$$\delta f'(x) = 1.$$

Finally, define the *golden-rule consumption level* c_δ^* to be that value of c that would make y_δ^* a steady state, i.e.,

$$c_\delta^* = y_\delta^* - x_\delta^*.$$

Note that y_δ^*, x_δ^*, and c_δ^* are all independent of the utility function u, and depend only on f and the value of δ.

Theorem 12.28 *Given any $y \in S$, define the sequence of states $\{y_t(y)\}_{t=0}^{\infty}$ from y under the optimal policy g as $y_0(y) = y$, and for $t \geq 0$, $y_{t+1}(y) = f[y_t(y) - g(y_t(y))]$. Let $\{c_t(y)\}$ denote the corresponding sequence of consumption levels. Then,*

$$y_t(y) \rightarrow y_\delta^* \text{ and } c_t(y) \rightarrow c_\delta^*.$$

Proof For notational ease, fix y and suppress all dependence on y. Since the investment function ξ is nondecreasing on S, and since f is also a nondecreasing function, the sequence $\{y_t\}$ is a monotone sequence. Since g is nondecreasing, the sequence $\{c_t\}$ is also monotone. Therefore, both the sequences have limits, denoted, say, y^* and c^*. Since $y_{t+1} = f(y_t - c_t)$ for all t, we must have

$$y^* = f(y^* - c^*)$$

by the continuity of f. Moreover, since

$$u'(c_t) = \delta u'(c_{t+1}) f'(y_t - c_t),$$

the continuous differentiability of f and u implies that in the limit $u'(c^*) = \delta u'(c^*) f'(y^* - c^*)$, or

$$1 = \delta f'(y^* - c^*).$$

Thus, y^* and c^* are also solutions to the two equations that define y_δ^* and c_δ^*. Since these solutions are unique, we are done. □

12.7 Exercises

1. Let (x_n) be a Cauchy sequence. Show that if (x_n) has a convergent subsequence then the sequence is itself convergent.

2. Determine whether or not the following subsets of $\mathbb{R}$ are complete:

    (a) $[0, 1]$
    (b) $\mathbb{Q}$
    (c) $\mathbb{Q}^c$, the set of irrational numbers
    (d) $\mathbb{N}$
    (e) $\{1, 1/2, 1/3, \ldots, 1/n, \ldots\}$
    (f) $\{1, 1/2, 1/3, \ldots, 1/n, \ldots\} \cup \{0\}$
    (g) $[-1, 2)$

3. Let $f: \mathbb{R} \to \mathbb{R}$ be defined as $f(x) = ax + b$. What are the values of $a, b \in \mathbb{R}$ that make f a contraction?

4. Let $X = (1, \infty)$. Let $f: X \to \mathbb{R}$ be given by

$$f(x) = \frac{1}{2}\left(x + \frac{a}{x}\right).$$

    (a) Show that if $a \in (1, 3)$, then f maps X into itself, i.e., $f(x) \in X$ for all $x \in X$.
    (b) Show that f is actually a contraction if $a \in (1, 3)$. Find the fixed point as a function of a for each a.
    (c) What about $a = 1$ or $a = 3$?
    (d) Is X complete?

5. Let $f: \mathbb{R} \to \mathbb{R}$ be defined by

$$f(x) = \begin{cases} x - \frac{1}{2}e^x, & x \le 0 \\ -\frac{1}{2} + \frac{1}{2}x, & x > 0. \end{cases}$$

    Show that f satisfies the condition that $|f(x) - f(y)| < |x - y|$ for all $x, y \in \mathbb{R}$, but that f has no fixed points.

6. Let X be a finite set, and $f_n: X \to \mathbb{R}$. Suppose f_n converges pointwise to f, i.e., for each $x \in X$, $f_n(x) \to f(x)$. Show that f_n converges uniformly to f.

7. Let $X = [0, 1]$. For $n \in \mathbb{N}$ define $f_n \colon X \to \mathbb{R}$ by

$$f_n(x) = \begin{cases} nx, & x \leq 1/n \\ 1, & x > 1/n. \end{cases}$$

(a) Show that f_n converges pointwise to f where f is given by

$$f(x) = \begin{cases} 0, & x = 0 \\ 1, & x > 0 \end{cases}$$

i.e., show that for each $x \in X$, $f_n(x) \to f(x)$.

(b) Let d be the sup-norm metric. What is $d(f_n, f)$? Show that $d(f_n, f)$ does not converge to 0, i.e., f_n does not converge uniformly to f.

8. Let $X = [0, 1]$ and let for each $n \in \mathbb{N}$ define $f_n \colon X \to \mathbb{R}$ as

$$f_n(x) = x^n.$$

Show that f_n converges pointwise to $f \colon X \to \mathbb{R}$ defined by

$$f(x) = \begin{cases} 0, & x < 1 \\ 1, & x = 1. \end{cases}$$

Does f_n converge uniformly to f?

9. For each $n \in \mathbb{N}$ let $f_n \colon \mathbb{R} \to \mathbb{R}$ be defined by

$$f(x) = \begin{cases} 1 - \frac{1}{n}|x|, & |x| < n \\ 0, & |x| \geq n. \end{cases}$$

Show that f_n converges pointwise to the constant function $f(x) = 1$. Does f_n converge uniformly to f?

10. Let $X \subseteq \mathbb{R}_+$ be a compact set and let $f \colon X \to X$ be a continuous and increasing function. Prove that f has a fixed point.

11. Let $X = [0, 1]$, and $f \colon X \to X$ be an increasing but not necessarily continuous function. Must f have a fixed point?

12. If $f \colon \mathbb{R} \to \mathbb{R}$ and $g \colon \mathbb{R} \to \mathbb{R}$ are both contraction mappings, what can we say about $f \circ g$?

13. Is it possible to have two discontinuous functions whose composition is a contraction mapping?

14. If $f \colon \mathbb{R} \to \mathbb{R}$ is a differentiable contraction mapping, what can we say about the value of $df(x)/dx$?

15. A function $F \colon X \to Y$ is said to be an *onto* function, if for any $y \in Y$, there is some $x \in X$ such that $f(x) = y$. Show that the mapping $f(x) = (1 - x)^{1/2}$ is an onto mapping from $[0, 1]$ to $[0, 1]$. Find the fixed points of this mapping.

16. Let a mapping of the interval $[0, 1]$ onto itself be defined by $f(x) = 4x - 4x^2$.

    (a) Sketch the graph of the function and the diagonal line $y = x$.
    (b) Is the mapping one-to-one in the interval?
    (c) Find the fixed points of the mapping.

17. Give an example of a mapping of the interval $[0, 1]$ into itself having precisely two fixed points, namely 0 and 1. Can such a function be a contraction mapping?

18. Give an example of an onto function of the open interval $(0, 1)$ into itself having no fixed points.

19. Let $X = [0, 1]$. Find an function $f: X \to X$ which has 0 as its only fixed point, or show that no such example is possible.

20. Let $S \subset \mathbb{R}^n$. Let $BU(S)$ be the set of all bounded upper-semicontinuous functions w mapping S into $\mathbb{R}$. Give $BU(S)$ the sup-norm metric and show that $BU(S)$ is a complete metric space under this metric.

21. Let $S = \{0, 1\}$, $A = \mathbb{R}_+$, and $\Phi(s) = A$ for any $s \in S$. Let the state transition function be given by

$$f(s, a) = \begin{cases} 0 & \text{if } s = 0 \text{ or } a < 1/2 \\ 1 & \text{if } s = 1 \text{ and } a \geq 1/2. \end{cases}$$

Let $r: S \times A \to \mathbb{R}$ be given by

$$r(s, a) = \begin{cases} -a & \text{if } s = 0 \\ 1 - a & \text{if } s = 1. \end{cases}$$

    (a) Show that f is *not* continuous on $S \times A$.
    (b) Suppose $\delta = 0$, i.e., the future is worthless. Then, the problem is simply to maximize $r(s, a)$ for each $s \in S$. What is the solution? What is $V(0)$? $V(1)$?
    (c) Suppose $\delta \in (0, 1)$. Show that a solution exists. Find the solution as a function of δ.
    (d) What "should" the solution be for $\delta = 1$?
    (e) Suppose that f is modified to

$$f(s, a) = \begin{cases} 0 & \text{if } s = 0 \text{ or } a \leq 1/2 \\ 1 & \text{if } s = 1 \text{ and } a > 1/2. \end{cases}$$

Does a solution exist for all $\delta \in (0, 1)$? Why or why not?

22. A wholesaler faces a known demand of k units per period for its product, at a given price p. At any given time, a maximum of $l \in \mathbb{N}$ ($l > k$) units of the product can be ordered from the manufacturer at a cost of c per unit. There is also a fixed cost $I > 0$ of placing the order. Ordered amounts are delivered instantly. Any amount of the product that remains unsold in a given period can be stored

at a cost of s per unit. Assuming that the wholesaler discounts future profits by a factor $\delta \in (0, 1)$, and has an initial stock of x units of the product, describe the optimization problem as a stationary dynamic programming problem, and write down the Bellman Equation. Is it possible to assert the existence of an optimal strategy? Why or why not?

23. Consider the one-sector model of optimal growth. Suppose the only restrictions we place on the utility function $u: \mathbb{R}_+ \to \mathbb{R}$ and the production function $f: \mathbb{R}_+ \to \mathbb{R}_+$ are:

(a) u and f are both continuous on $\mathbb{R}_+$.

(b) $f(x) \in [0, 1]$ for all $x \in [0, 1]$.

Let $S = [0, 1]$. Suppose the problem admits *free disposal*. That is, the agent can decide on the amount c_t of consumption and x_t of investment out of the available stock y_t, and costlessly dispose the remaining quantity $y_t - c_t - x_t$. Then, given a discount factor $\delta \in (0, 1)$, the agent solves:

$$\text{Maximize} \quad \sum_{t=0}^{\infty} \delta u(c_t)$$

$$\text{subject to} \quad y_0 = y \in S$$
$$y_{t+1} = f(x_t)$$
$$c_t + x_t \leq y_t$$
$$c_t, x_t \geq 0.$$

(a) Does this problem have a solution? Why or why not?

(b) Describe the Bellman Equation for this problem.

(c) Show that the value function in (b) is nondecreasing on S.

24. Suppose that in the optimal growth problem we had $u(c) = c^{\alpha}$, $\alpha \in 0, 1$ and $f(x) = x$. Solve for the optimal policy g with $S = [0, 1]$ and $\delta \in (0, 1)$.
Hint 1: Use the FOC's for the problem.
Hint 2: g is linear, i.e., $g(y) = ay$ for some constant a. Solve for a.

25. Redo the last question, assuming $f(x) = x^{\alpha}$ for $\alpha \in (0, 1]$, and $u(c) = \log c$. (Note that $\log c$ is unbounded at 0, so our sufficient conditions for the existence of an optimal strategy do not apply here. Nonetheless, it turns out that the Bellman Equation does hold, and a solution can be calculated using this equation. The value function V has the form $V(y) = A + B \log y$. Using this on both sides of the Bellman Equation, solve for A and B, and thereby for an optimal policy.)

26. Consider the following optimization problem:

$$\text{Maximize } \sum_{t=0}^{\infty} u(a_t)$$

$$\text{subject to } \sum_{t=0}^{\infty} a_t \leq s$$

$$a_t \geq 0.$$

This problem, which is a dynamic programming problem with $\delta = 1$, is known as the "cake-eating" problem. We begin with a cake of size s, and have to allocate this cake to consumption in each period of an infinite horizon.

(a) Show that the problem may be rewritten as a dynamic programming problem. That is, describe formally the state and action spaces, the reward function, the transition function, and the feasible action correspondence.

(b) Show that if $u: A \to \mathbb{R}$ is increasing and *linear*, i.e., $u(a) = ka$ for some $k > 0$, then the problem always has at least one solution. Find a solution.

(c) Show that if $u: A \to \mathbb{R}$ is increasing and *strictly* concave, then the problem has no solution.

(d) What happens to part (c) if we assume $0 < \delta < 1$, i.e., if the objective function is given by $\sum_{t=0}^{\infty} \delta^t u(c_t)$?

27. In each period $t = 0, 1, 2, \ldots$, of an infinite horizon, a fishery must decide on the quantity q of fish to be caught for selling in the market that period. (All fish caught must be sold.) The firm obtains a constant price p per unit of fish it sells. Catching fish requires effort by the firm. In each period t, the firm must decide on its effort level $e_t \in [0, 1]$ that it wishes to expend in this direction. The total catch q_t is then determined as a function $q_t = h(e_t, y_t)$ of the effort level e_t the firm expends and the number of fish y_t in the lake that period. Assume that $h : [0, 1] \times \mathbb{R}_+ \to \mathbb{R}_+$ is a continuous function satisfying $h(e, y) \in [0, y]$ for all $y \in \mathbb{R}_+$, $e \in [0, 1]$. Expending an effort level e_t in period t also results in a cost to the firm of $c(e_t)$, where $c: [0, 1] \to \mathbb{R}_+$ is continuous.
Lastly, the population of fish $y_t - q_t$ not caught in period t grows to a population y_{t+1} in period $t + 1$ according to a growth function f, as

$$y_{t+1} = f(y_t - q_t).$$

Assume that (i) $f: \mathbb{R}_+ \to \mathbb{R}_+$ is a continuous function, (ii) $f(0) = 0$ (no fish in the lake this period implies no fish next period), and (iii) f maps $[0, \bar{x}]$ into $[0, \bar{x}]$ for some $\bar{x} > 0$. Assume also that the initial stock of fish is $y_0 \in [0, \bar{x}]$. Finally, assume that the firm discounts future profit levels by a factor $\delta \in [0, 1)$. Set up the dynamic programming problem faced by the firm. Show that this problem admits a stationary optimal policy. Describe the Bellman Equation.

28. A firm's income in any period t depends on the level of capital stock x_t that it has that period, and the amount of investment i_t it undertakes that period, and is given by $g(x_t) - h(i_t)$, where g and h are continuous functions. The capital stock next period is then given by $\beta x_t + i_t$, where $\beta \in (0, 1)$ is a depreciation factor. In no period is investment allowed to exceed $b > 0$, where b is some fixed level. Investment is allowed to be negative but cannot be smaller than $-\beta x$, where x is the capital stock of that period. The firm discounts future income by $\delta \in (0, 1)$. Given that the firm begins with an initial capital stock of $x_0 > 0$, show that the dynamic programming problem facing the firm has a solution, and describe the Bellman Equation. Explain all your steps clearly.

Appendix A

Set Theory and Logic: An Introduction

This appendix discusses the basic rules of set theory and logic. For a more leisurely and detailed discussion of this material, we refer the reader to Halmos (1960), or the excellent introductory chapter of Munkres (1975).

A.1 Sets, Unions, Intersections

We adopt the naïve point of view regarding set theory. That is, we shall assume that what is meant by a set is intuitively clear. Throughout this chapter, we shall denote sets by capital letters such as A, B, X, and Y, and elements of these sets by lowercase letters such as a, b, x, and y. That an object a belongs to a set A is denoted by

$$a \in A.$$

If a is *not* an element of A, we shall write

$$a \notin A.$$

If A is the set of all elements from some collection X which also satisfy some property Π, we will write this as

$$A = \{x \in X \mid x \text{ satisfies the property } \Pi\}.$$

If X is understood, then we will write this as simply

$$A = \{x \mid x \text{ satisfies the property } \Pi\}.$$

It may be that there is no $x \in X$ that satisfies the property Π. For instance, there is no real number x that satisfies the property that $x^2 + 1 = 0$. In such a case, A will contain no elements at all. A set which contains no elements will be called the *empty set*, denoted $\emptyset$.

If every element of a set B is also an element of a set A, we shall say that B is a *subset* of A, and write

$$B \subset A.$$

We will also say in this case that A is a *superset* of B, and denote the relationship $B \subset A$ alternatively by

$$A \supset B.$$

The set B will be said to be a *proper subset* of A if $B \subset A$, and there is some $x \in A$ with $x \notin B$. In words, B is a proper subset of A if every element of B is also in A, but A contains at least one element that is not in B.

Two sets A and B are said to be *equal*, written $A = B$, if every element of A is also an element of B, and *vice versa*. That is, $A = B$ if we have both

$$A \subset B \quad \text{and} \quad B \subset A.$$

If two sets A and B are *not* equal, we will write this as $A \neq B$. Note that B is a proper subset of A if and only if we have $B \subset A$ and $B \neq A$.

The *union* of two sets A and B, denoted $A \cup B$, is the set which consists of all elements which are either in A or in B (or both):

$$A \cup B = \{x \mid x \in A \text{ or } x \in B\}.$$

The *intersection* of two sets A and B, denoted $A \cap B$, is the set which consists of all elements which belong to both A *and* B:

$$A \cap B = \{x \mid x \in A \text{ and } x \in B\}.$$

If $A \subset X$, *the complement of A in X*, denoted A^c, is defined as

$$A^c = \{x \in X \mid x \notin A\}.$$

If the reference set X is understood, as it usually is in applications,[1] we will omit the words "in X," and refer to A^c as simply the complement of A.

A.2 Propositions: Contrapositives and Converses

Given two propositions P and Q, the statement "If P, then Q" is interpreted as the statement that if the proposition P is true, then the statement Q is also true. We

---

[1] For instance, by the expression "the complement of the negative reals," one usually means the complement of the negative reals *in* $\mathbb{R}$, which is the set of nonnegative reals.

denote this by

$$P \Rightarrow Q.$$

We will also say in this case that "P implies Q."

We stress the point that $P \Rightarrow Q$ only says that if P is true, then Q is also true. It has nothing to say about the case where P is *not* true; in this case, Q could be either true or false. For example, if P is the statement $x > 0$ and Q is the statement that $x^2 > 0$, then it is certainly true that

$$P \Rightarrow Q,$$

since the square of a positive number is positive. However, Q can be true even if P is not true, since the square of a negative number is also positive.

Given a statement of the form "if P, then Q," its *contrapositive* is the statement that "if Q is not true, then P is not true." If we let $\sim Q$ denote the statement that Q is *not* true (we will simply call this "not Q," for short), then the contrapositive of the statement

$$P \Rightarrow Q$$

is the statement

$$\sim Q \Rightarrow \sim P.$$

For example, the contrapositive of the statement

$$\text{If } x \text{ is positive, then } x^3 \text{ is positive}$$

is the statement

$$\text{If } x^3 \text{ is not positive, then } x \text{ is not positive.}$$

A statement and its contrapositive are logically equivalent. That is, if the statement is true, then the contrapositive is also true, while if the statement is false, so is the contrapositive. This is easy to see. Suppose, first, that $P \Rightarrow Q$ is true. Then, if Q is false, P must also be false: if P were true, then, by $P \Rightarrow Q$, Q would have to be true, and a statement cannot be both true and false. Thus, if $P \Rightarrow Q$ holds, then $\sim Q \Rightarrow \sim P$ also holds. Now, suppose $P \Rightarrow Q$ is false. The only way this can happen is if P were true and Q were false. But this is precisely the statement that $\sim Q \Rightarrow \sim P$ is not true. Therefore, if $P \Rightarrow Q$ is false, so is $\sim Q \Rightarrow \sim P$.

An important implication of the logical equivalence of a statement and its contra-positive is the following: if we are required to prove that $P \Rightarrow Q$, the result can be regarded as established if we show that $\sim Q \Rightarrow \sim P$.

The *converse* of the statement $P \Rightarrow Q$ is the statement that

$$Q \Rightarrow P,$$

that is, the statement that "if Q, then P."

There is no logical relationship between a statement and its converse. As we have seen, if P is the proposition that $x > 0$ and Q is the proposition that $x^2 > 0$, then it is certainly true that

$$P \Rightarrow Q,$$

but the converse

$$Q \Rightarrow P$$

is false: x could be negative and still satisfy $x^2 > 0$.

If a statement and its converse both hold, we express this by saying that "P if and only if Q," and denote this by

$$P \Leftrightarrow Q.$$

For example, if P is the proposition that $x > 0$ and Q is the proposition that $x^3 > 0$, we have $P \Leftrightarrow Q$.

A.3 Quantifiers and Negation

There are two kinds of logical quantifiers, the *universal* or "for all" quantifier, and the *existential* or "there exists" quantifier. The former is used to denote that a property Π holds *for every* element a in some set A; the latter to denote that the property holds for *at least one* element a in the set A.

The *negation* of a proposition P is its denial $\sim P$. If the proposition P involves a universal quantifier, then its negation involves an existential quantifier: to deny the truth of a universal statement requires us to find just one case where the statement fails. For instance, let A be some set and let $\Pi(a)$ be some property defined for elements $a \in A$. Suppose P is the proposition of the form

For all $a \in A$, property $\Pi(a)$ holds.

Then, P is false if there is just a single element $a \in A$ for which the property $\Pi(a)$ does not hold. Thus, the negation of P is the proposition

There exists $a \in A$ such that property $\Pi(a)$ does not hold.

Similarly, the negation of an existential quantifier involves a universal quantifier: to deny that there is at least one case where the proposition holds requires us to show that the proposition fails in every case. That is, if Q is a proposition of the form

There exists $b \in B$ such that property $\Pi'(b)$ holds,

its negation is the proposition

For all $b \in B$, property $\Pi'(b)$ does not hold.

As a concrete example, consider the following. Given a real number x, let $\Pi(x)$ be the property that $x^2 > 0$. Let P be the proposition that "Property $\Pi(x)$ holds for every real number x." In the language of quantifiers, we would express P as

For every $x \in \mathbb{R}$, $x^2 > 0$.

P is evidently negated if there is at least one real number whose square is not strictly positive. So the negation $\sim P$ is the statement

There is $x \in \mathbb{R}$ such that $x^2 \not> 0$.

When multiple quantifiers are involved in a statement, the situation gets a little more complicated. If all the quantifiers in a given proposition are of the same type (i.e., they are all universal, or are all existential) the order of the quantifiers is immaterial. For instance, the statement

For all $x \in \mathbb{R}$, for all $y \in \mathbb{R}$, $(x + y)^2 = x^2 + 2xy + y^2$,

is the same as the statement

For all $y \in \mathbb{R}$, for all $x \in \mathbb{R}$, $(x + y)^2 = x^2 + 2xy + y^2$.

However, the order of the quantifiers becomes significant if quantifiers of different types are involved. The statement

For every $x > 0$, there exists $y > 0$ such that $y^2 = x$

is most definitely not the same as the statement that

There exists $y > 0$ such that for all $x > 0$, $y^2 = x$.

In fact, while the first statement is true (it asserts essentially that every positive real number has a positive square root), the second is false (it claims that a single fixed real number.is the square root of every positive number).

The importance of the order of quantifiers makes it necessary to exercise caution in forming the negation of statements with multiple quantifiers, since the negation will also involve the use of multiple quantifiers. To elaborate, let $\Pi(a, b)$ denote a property defined on elements a and b in sets A and B, respectvely. Consider the statement P

> For every $a \in A$, there exists $b \in B$ such that $\Pi(a, b)$ holds.

The statement P will be falsified if there is even one $a \in A$ for which the property $\Pi(a, b)$ fails to hold, no matter what we take for the value of $b \in B$. Thus, the negation of P is the statement $\sim P$ defined by

> There exists $a \in A$ such that for all $b \in B$, $\Pi(a, b)$ fails.

We reiterate the importance of the order of quantifiers in forming this negation. The negation of P is *not* the statement

> For every $b \in B$, there exists $a \in A$ such that $\Pi(a, b)$ fails.

A.4 Necessary and Sufficient Conditions

The study of optimization theory involves the use of conditions that are called *necessary conditions* and *sufficient conditions*. These are implications of the form $P \Rightarrow Q$ and $Q \Rightarrow P$ that were discussed in the previous section. There is, however, one point that bears elaboration. Necessary and sufficient conditions in optimization theory are usually derived under some subsidiary hypotheses on the problem, and their validity depends on these hypotheses holding. Moreover, these hypotheses need not be the same; that is, the necessary conditions may be derived under one set, while the sufficient conditions may use another. We discuss some aspects of this issue here.

We begin with a definition of *necessary conditions* in the abstract. Suppose an implication of the form

$$P \Rightarrow Q$$

is valid. Then, Q is said to be a *necessary condition* for P. The reason for this terminology is apparent: if $P \Rightarrow Q$ holds, and P is to be true, then Q must necessarily also be true.

In optimization theory, P is usually taken to be a statement of the form

> P: x^* is a maximum of a function f on a constraint set $\mathcal{D}$.

Under some subsidiary hypotheses on f and $\mathcal{D}$, we then try to identify implications Q of x^* being a maximum point. Any such implication Q, that arises from the assumption that x^* is a maximum, is a *necessary condition* for an optimum, whenever the subsidiary hypotheses used in this derivation hold.

This is the approach we take in Chapters 4 through 6 of this book. In Chapter 4, for instance, we make the following subsidiary hypotheses, that we shall call H_1 here:

H_1: $\mathcal{D}$ is open, and f is differentiable on $\mathcal{D}$.[2]

We then show that if the proposition P (that x^* is a maximum of f on $\mathcal{D}$) is true, then the proposition Q must be true, where Q states that

$$Q: \quad Df(x^*) = 0.$$

Thus, the condition that $Df(x^*) = 0$ is a necessary condition for f to have a maximum at x^*, provided H_1 holds.

For a definition of sufficient conditions in the abstract, suppose that a statement of the form

$$Q \Rightarrow P$$

is true. Then, Q is said to be a *sufficient condition* for P. In words, since the truth of Q must imply the truth of P, it is enough for P to be true that Q is true.

Sufficient conditions come in many forms in optimization theory. In one, we take P to be a statement of the form

$$P: \quad x^* \text{ is a maximum of } f \text{ on } \mathcal{D}.$$

The objective now is to find, under some subsidiary hypotheses on the problem, a set of conditions Q such that whenever the conditions in Q are met at the point x^*, P is always true. Such conditions are called *sufficient conditions* for the point x^* to be a maximum.

This is the route we follow in Chapters 7 and 8 of this book. In Chapter 7, for instance, one of the results assumes the subsidiary hypotheses H_2 that

H_2: $\mathcal{D}$ is convex and open, and f is concave and differentiable on $\mathcal{D}$.

It is then shown that if proposition Q that

$$Q: \quad Df(x^*) = 0$$

holds, then proposition P is also true. That is, the condition $Df(x^*) = 0$ is a *sufficient condition* for a maximum at x^* provided H_2 holds.

An alternative class of sufficient conditions that optimization theory studies involves the statement P^* that

$$P^*: \quad \text{There exists a maximum of } f \text{ on } \mathcal{D}.$$

The objective is then to find a set of conditions Q^* on f and $\mathcal{D}$ such that proposition P^* is true. Such conditions Q^*, in the context of optimization theory, are called *sufficient conditions for the existence of a maximum*. These are the conditions that Chapter 3 and the chapters on dynamic programming are primarily concerned with.

---

[2]The actual conditions we assume are weaker than this.

In Chapter 3, for instance, we show that if Q^* is the set of conditions that

$$Q^*: \quad \mathcal{D} \text{ is a compact set in } \mathbb{R}^n \text{ and } f \text{ is continuous on } \mathcal{D}$$

then it is true that $Q^* \Rightarrow P^*$, i.e., that a solution exists in the maximization problem. A condition Q is said to be both *necessary* and *sufficient* for P if it is the case that

$$P \Leftrightarrow Q.$$

In this case, P and Q are equivalent in the sense that either both are true, or both are false. Thus, identifying the truth of P is the same thing as identifying the truth of Q.

In some sense, this equivalence makes conditions that are necessary and sufficient an ideal set of conditions for working with in optimization theory. However, as should be apparent from the two examples above, necessary conditions often require far weaker subsidiary hypotheses on the problem than sufficient conditions. Therefore, necessary conditions derived under a given set of subsidiary hypotheses are unlikely to also be sufficient under those hypotheses. For instance, the condition that $Df(x^*) = 0$ is necessary for x^* to be a maximum under H_1, but it is not sufficient under H_1. Sufficiency of this condition requires the stronger hypotheses contained in H_2.

On the other hand, since the subsidiary hypotheses used in deriving sufficient conditions are typically stronger than those used to prove that the same conditions are necessary, it *is* possible that sufficient conditions derived under a given set of hypotheses may also be necessary under the same hypotheses. For instance, it is apparent that whenever H_2 is met, H_1 is also met. Therefore, we have the following result: the proposition Q that

$$Q: \quad Df(x^*) = 0$$

is necessary and sufficient for the proposition P that

$$P: \quad x^* \text{ is a maximum of } f \text{ on } \mathcal{D}$$

provided H_2 holds.

Appendix B

The Real Line

There are many methods for obtaining the real number system from the rational number system. We describe one in this appendix, which "constructs" the real number system as (appropriately defined) limits of Cauchy sequences of rational numbers. An alternative constructive approach—the method of Dedekind cuts—is described in Rudin (1976). A third approach, which is axiomatic, rather than constructive, may be found in Apostol (1967), Bartle (1964), or Royden (1968).

Our presentation in this appendix, which is based on Strichartz (1982), is brief and relatively informal. For omitted proofs and greater detail than we provide here, we refer the reader to Hewitt and Stromberg (1965), or Strichartz (1982).

B.1 Construction of the Real Line

We use the following notation: $\mathbb{N}$ will denote the set of natural numbers and $\mathbb{Z}$ the set of all integers:

$$\mathbb{N} = \{1, 2, 3, \ldots\}$$
$$\mathbb{Z} = \{\ldots, -2, -1, 0, 1, 2, \ldots\}.$$

$\mathbb{Q}$ will denote the set of rational numbers:

$$\mathbb{Q} = \left\{ x \mid x = \frac{p}{q}, \ p, q \in \mathbb{Q}, \ q \neq 0 \right\}.$$

It is assumed throughout this appendix that the reader is familiar with handling rational numbers, and with the rules for addition ($+$) and multiplication ($\cdot$) of such numbers. It can be shown that under these operations, the rational numbers form a *field*; that is, for all rationals a, b, and c in $\mathbb{Q}$, the following conditions are met:

1. Addition is commutative: $a + b = b + a$.
2. Addition is associative: $(a + b) + c = a + (b + c)$.

323

3. Multiplication is commutative: $a \cdot b = b \cdot a$.
4. Multiplication is associative: $(a \cdot b) \cdot c = a \cdot (b \cdot c)$.
5. Multiplication distributes over addition: $a \cdot (b + c) = a \cdot b + a \cdot c$.
6. 0 is the additive identity: $0 + a = a$.
7. 1 is the multiplicative identity: $1 \cdot a = a$.
8. Every rational has a negative: $a + (-a) = 0$.
9. Every non-zero rational has an inverse: $a \cdot \dfrac{1}{a} = 1$.

A rational p/q (with $q \neq 0$) is *positive* if p and q are both positive; it is *negative* if p is positive and q negative, or q is positive and p negative; and it is zero if $p = 0$. Every rational is either positive, negative, or zero. The rationals are also ordered: for every two distinct rationals a and b, we have either $a > b$ (if $a - b$ is positive) or $b > a$ (if $a - b$ is negative). Finally, the rationals satisfy the *triangle inequality*: if x and y are any rationals, we have

$$|x + y| \leq |x| + |y|,$$

where $|x|$ denote the absolute value of a rational x, i.e., $|x| = x$, if $x \geq 0$, and $|x| = -x$, otherwise.

The need to extend the rational number system arises from the observation that there are objects such as $\sqrt{2}$ that are easy to describe (say, as the solution to $x^2 = 2$), and that intuitively "should" form part of a reasonable number system, but that are not part of the rational number system. The real number system attempts to extend the rational number system to close such holes, but also in a manner which ensures that the field properties of the rationals and the order relation ($>$) are also extended to the reals.

Two simple and intuitive ideas underlie the construction of the reals that we present here. The first is that although objects such as $\sqrt{2}$ are not rational, they are capable of being approximated arbitrarily closely by rational numbers. For example, the sequence of rational numbers

$$1.4, \ 1.41, \ 1.414, \ 1.4142, \ \ldots$$

when squared, results in the following sequence, which gets closer and closer to 2:

$$1.96, \ 1, 9881, \ 1.999396, \ 1.99996164, \ \ldots.$$

The second idea central to our construction is that the approximating sequence of rationals cannot be unique. For instance, the sequences

$$1.4, \ 1.41, \ 1.414, \ 1.4142, \ 1, 41421, \ \ldots$$
$$1.5, \ 1.42, \ 1.415, \ 1.4143, \ 1.41422, \ \ldots$$

both approximate $\sqrt{2}$, the first sequence from "below" (each term in the sequence is strictly smaller than $\sqrt{2}$), and the second from "above" (each term is strictly larger than $\sqrt{2}$).

To sum up, the idea is to regard real numbers as limits of sequences of rational numbers, but with the caveat that two sequences of rationals are to be regarded as equivalent (i.e., as defining the same real number) if they are themselves getting closer together, the farther one goes out in the sequence. We formalize these ideas now.

Let $|a|$ denote the absolute value of a rational number a, and let $|a - b|$ denote the distance between two rationals a and b. A sequence of rational numbers $\{x_n\}$ is called a *Cauchy sequence* if it is the case that for all natural numbers $n \in \mathbb{N}$, there exists an integer $m(n)$, such that for all $k, l \geq m(n)$, we have

$$|x_k - x_l| < \frac{1}{n}.$$

In words, a Cauchy sequence of rationals is one where the distance between terms in the tail of the sequence gets smaller, the farther one goes out in the sequence.

Two Cauchy sequences of rationals $\{x_n\}$ and $\{y_n\}$ will be called *equivalent* if for all natural numbers $n \in \mathbb{N}$, there exists $m(n)$ such that for all $k \geq m(n)$, we have

$$|x_k - y_k| < \frac{1}{n}.$$

We write this as $\{x_n\} \sim \{y_n\}$. In words, equivalent Cauchy sequences are those whose terms are getting closer together, the farther we go out in the sequences. Intuitively, if two Cauchy sequences are equivalent, they can be viewed as approximating the same real number.

It is easy to show that $\sim$ is, in fact, an equivalence relationship: it is reflexive ($\{x_n\} \sim \{x_n\}$), and symmetric ($\{x_n\} \sim \{y_n\}$ implies $\{y_n\} \sim \{x_n\}$). It is also transitive: that is, $\{x_n\} \sim \{y_n\}$ and $\{y_n\} \sim \{z_n\}$ implies $\{x_n\} \sim \{z_n\}$. We leave the proof of the transitivity of $\sim$ as an exercise to the reader.

An equivalence class $\mathcal{C}$ of a Cauchy sequence of rationals is a collection of Cauchy sequences of rationals such that if $\{x_n\} \in \mathcal{C}$ and $\{y_n\} \in \mathcal{C}$, then $\{x_n\} \sim \{y_n\}$. At an intuitive level, all members of a given equivalence class may be viewed as approximating the same real number. Thus, we may as well identify each equivalence class with a real number, and this is, in fact, our definition:

Definition B.1 The set of all equivalence classes of Cauchy sequences of rationals, denoted $\mathbb{R}$, is called the *real number system*. A typical element of $\mathbb{R}$, denoted x, is called a *real number*.

In keeping with the intuition underlying this definition, we will also say that if $\{x_n\}$ is an element of the equivalence class $x \in \mathbb{R}$, then $\{x_n\}$ *converges to x*, or that x is the *limit* of the sequence $\{x_n\}$.

B.2 Properties of the Real Line

We now turn to an examination of the properties possessed by the real line, when it is defined as in the previous section. We are especially interested in examining whether the reals also constitute a field, and whether they can be ordered. The first question requires us to first define the notion of addition and multiplication for arbitrary real numbers. The following result shows that one may proceed to do this in the obvious manner.

Lemma B.2 *Let $\{x_n\}$ and $\{x'_n\}$ be Cauchy sequences of rationals in the equivalence class $x \in \mathbb{R}$, and let $\{y_n\}$ and $\{y'_n\}$ be Cauchy sequences of rationals in the equivalence class $y \in \mathbb{R}$. Then:*

1. *$\{x_n + y_n\}$ and $\{x'_n + y'_n\}$ are both Cauchy sequences of rationals. Moreover, they are equivalent sequences.*
2. *$\{x_n \cdot y_n\}$ and $\{x'_n \cdot y'_n\}$ are both Cauchy sequences of rationals. Moreover, they are equivalent sequences.*

Proof Left as an exercise.   □

In view of this lemma, we may simply define the sum $(x + y)$ of two real numbers x and y in $\mathbb{R}$ as the equivalence class of $\{x_n + y_n\}$, where $\{x_n\}$ converges to x (i.e., $\{x_n\}$ is in the equivalence class of x) and $\{y_n\}$ converges to y. Similarly, the product $x \cdot y$ can be defined as the equivalence class of $\{x_n \cdot y_n\}$. With addition and multiplication defined thus, our next result states that one of the properties desirable in $\mathbb{R}$ is, in fact, true. The proof of this result is omitted.

Theorem B.3 *The real numbers form a field.*

Now, let $\{x_n\}$ be any Cauchy sequence of rationals converging to $x \in \mathbb{R}$. Then, x is said to be *positive* if there is $n \in \mathbb{N}$ and $m(n)$ such that

$$x_k \geq \frac{1}{n}, \quad k \geq m(n).$$

The number x is *negative* if $-x$ is positive. Under these definitions, it can be shown that the real numbers inherit another important property of the rationals:

Theorem B.4 *Every real number is positive, negative, or zero. The sum and product of positive numbers is positive, while the product of a negative and positive number is negative.*

Proof Omitted. □

When the notion of positivity on a field satisfies the conditions of this theorem, the field is called an *ordered field*. Thus, the reals, like the rationals, are an ordered field.

The notion of a positive number can be used to define the notion of absolute values for real numbers. Given any $x \in \mathbb{R}$, the *absolute value* of x, denoted $|x|$, is defined by

$$|x| = \begin{cases} x, & x \geq 0 \\ -x, & x < 0. \end{cases}$$

We can also define inequalities for real numbers: given x and y in $\mathbb{R}$, we say that $x > y$ if $x - y > 0$, that $x < y$ if $y - x > 0$, etc. Finally, we define the (Euclidean) distance between two real numbers x and y, to be the absolute value $|x - y|$ of their difference. The following simple result comes in handy surprisingly often:

Lemma B.5 *Let x and $y \in \mathbb{R}$ be the limits of the Cauchy sequences of rationals $\{x_n\}$ and $\{y_n\}$, respectively. If $x_n \geq y_n$ for each n, then $x \geq y$.*

Proof If not, then $x < y$, so $x - y < 0$. Since $x - y$ is the limit of $x_n - y_n$, there must then exist $m \in \mathbb{N}$ such that $x_n - y_n < -\frac{1}{m}$ for all large n. This contradicts the assumption that $x_n \geq y_n$ for all n. □

Theorem B.6 (Triangle inequality for real numbers) *Let x and y be real numbers. Then,*

$$|x + y| \leq |x| + |y|.$$

Proof Let $\{x_k\}$ and $\{y_k\}$ be sequences of rationals converging to x and y, respectively. By definition, the Cauchy sequence of rationals $\{x_k + y_k\}$ converges to $x + y$. By the triangle inequality for rationals,

$$|x_k + y_k| \leq |x_k| + |y_k|,$$

for each k. Taking limits as $k \to \infty$, and using Lemma B.5, the theorem is proved. □

There is another important property of the real line: it is the case that there are rational numbers arbitrarily close to any real number. This fact is expressed by saying that the rationals are *dense* in the reals.[1]

Theorem B.7 (Denseness of Rationals) *Given any real number x and any $n \in \mathbb{N}$, there exists a rational number $y \in \mathbb{Q}$ such that $|x - y| \le \frac{1}{n}$.*

Proof Let $\{x_n\}$ be a Cauchy sequence of rationals converging to x. Then, given n, there exists $m(n)$ such that

$$|x_k - x_l| < \frac{1}{n}, \quad k, l \ge m(n).$$

Define $y = x_{m(n)}$. Then, $|x_k - y| < \frac{1}{n}$ for all k, so taking limits as $k \to \infty$, and using Lemma B.5, we obtain $|x_y| \le \frac{1}{n}$. □

Extending the definition for rational numbers in the obvious manner, we say that a sequence of real numbers $\{x_n\}$ converges to a *limit* $x \in \mathbb{R}$ if it is the case that for all $\epsilon > 0$, there is $n(\epsilon)$ such that for all $n \ge n(\epsilon)$, we have

$$|x_n - x| < \epsilon.$$

We also say that $\{x_n\}$ is a *Cauchy sequence* if for all $\epsilon > 0$, there is $n(\epsilon)$ such that for all $k, l \ge n(\epsilon)$, we have

$$|x_k - x_l| < \epsilon.$$

Note that these definitions are meaningful, since we have defined inequalities between any two real numbers.

Our last result is particularly important because it shows that if we do to the reals what we did to the rationals, no new numbers are created: the limits of Cauchy sequences of real numbers are also only real numbers. This fact is expressed as saying that the real line $\mathbb{R}$ is *complete*.[2]

Theorem B.8 (Completeness of $\mathbb{R}$) *A sequence of real numbers $\{x_n\}$ has a limit if and only if it is a Cauchy sequence.*

Proof It is easy to see that if a sequence $\{x_n\}$ converges to a limit x, then $\{x_n\}$ must be a Cauchy sequence. We leave the details to the reader as an exercise.

So suppose that $\{x_n\}$ is a Cauchy sequence of real numbers. We are to show that there is $x \in \mathbb{R}$ such that $x_n \to x$.

[1] For a definition of denseness in the context of abstract metric spaces, see Appendix C.
[2] For a definition of completeness in the context of abstract metric spaces, see Appendix C.

Since each x_n is a real number, there is a rational number y_n arbitrarily close to it. In particular, we can choose a sequence $\{y_n\}$ of rationals such that for each n, we have

$$|x_n - y_n| < \frac{1}{n}.$$

It is not very difficult to show that since $\{x_n\}$ is a Cauchy sequence, $\{y_n\}$ is also a Cauchy sequence. Once again, we leave the details to the reader as an exercise. Since $\{y_n\}$ is a Cauchy sequence of rationals, it converges to a limit $x \in \mathbb{R}$.

We will show that $x = \lim_{n\to\infty} x_n$ also. To this end, note that for any n, we have

$$|x - x_n| \leq |x - y_n| + |y_n - x_n| \leq |x - y_n| + \frac{1}{n}.$$

Since $\{y_n\}$ converges to x, it is the case that $|x - y_n|$ can be made arbitrarily small for all n sufficiently large. Since this also true of the term $\frac{1}{n}$, it follows that $\{x_n\}$ converges to x. $\qquad\square$

Appendix C

Structures on Vector Spaces

This appendix provides a brief introduction to vector spaces, and the structures (inner product, norm, metric, and topology) that can be placed on them. It also describes an abstract context for locating the results of Chapter 1 on the topological structure on $\mathbb{R}^n$. The very nature of the material discussed here makes it impossible to be either comprehensive or complete; rather, the aim is simply to give the reader a flavor of these topics. For more detail than we provide here, and for omitted proofs, we refer the reader to the books by Bartle (1964), Munkres (1975), or Royden (1968).

C.1 Vector Spaces

A *vector space over* $\mathbb{R}$ (henceforth, simply vector space) is a set V, on which are defined two operators "addition," which specifies for each x and y in V, an element $x + y$ in V; and "scalar multiplication," which specifies for each $a \in \mathbb{R}$ and $x \in V$, an element ax in V. These operators are required to satisfy the following axioms for all $x, y, z \in V$ and $a, b \in \mathbb{R}$:

1. Addition satisfies the commutative group axioms:

    (a) Commutativity: $x + y = y + x$.
    (b) Associativity: $x + (y + z) = (x + y) + z$.
    (c) Existence of zero: There is an element 0 in V such that $x + 0 = x$.
    (d) Existence of additive inverse: For every $x \in V$, there is $(-x) \in V$ such that $x + (-x) = 0$.

2. Scalar multiplication is

    (a) Associative: $(ab)x = a(bx)$, and
    (b) Distributive: $a(x + y) = ax + ay$, and $(a + b)x = ax + bx$.

Throughout, the letters a, b, c, etc. will denote scalars while x, y, z, will denote elements of V.

Standard examples of vector spaces V, that we will use for illustrative purposes throughout this chapter, include the following:

Example C.1 Let $V = \mathbb{R}^n$. Define addition and scalar multiplication on V in the usual way: for $x = (x_1, \ldots, x_n)$ and $y = (y_1, \ldots, y_n)$ in V, and $a \in \mathbb{R}$, let

$$x + y = (x_1 + y_1, \ldots, x_n + y_n)$$
$$ax = (ax_1, \ldots, ax_n).$$

It is an elementary matter to check that addition and scalar multiplication so defined meet all of the requisite axioms to make $\mathbb{R}^n$ a vector space over $\mathbb{R}$. $\square$

Example C.2 Let V be the space of bounded sequences in $\mathbb{R}$. A typical element of V is a sequence $x = (x_1, x_2, \ldots)$ which has the property that

$$\sup_{i \in \mathbb{N}} |x_i| < \infty,$$

where $|x_i|$ is the absolute value of x_i. Define addition and scalar multiplication on V as follows: for $x = (x_1, x_2, \ldots)$ and $y = (y_1, y_2, \ldots)$ in V, and $a \in \mathbb{R}$, let

$$x + y = (x_1 + y_1, x_2 + y_2, \ldots)$$
$$ax = (ax_1, ax_2, \ldots).$$

Then, V is a vector space. $\square$

Example C.3 Let $C([0, 1])$ denote the space of all continuous functions from $[0, 1]$ to $\mathbb{R}$:

$$C([0, 1]) = \{f : [0, 1] \to \mathbb{R} \mid f \text{ is continuous on } [0, 1]\}.$$

Let $V = C([0, 1])$. Define addition and scalar multiplication on V as follows: for f, g in V and $a \in \mathbb{R}$, let $(f + g)$ and af be the functions in V, whose values at any $\xi \in [0, 1]$ are given respectively by

$$(f + g)(\xi) = f(\xi) + g(\xi)$$
$$(af)(\xi) = af(\xi).$$

Once again, it is a simple matter to verify that all relevant axioms are met, so $C([0, 1])$ defines a vector space over $\mathbb{R}$. $\square$

Many different structures can be placed on V. We will examine four of these (inner product spaces, normed spaces, metric spaces, and topological spaces) below. The four we examine are successive generalizations in that every inner product space generates a normed space, every normed space a metric space, and every metric space a topological space. The reverse containments need not always be true; thus, for instance, there exist topological spaces that are not generated by any metric space, and metric spaces that are not generated by any normed space.

C.2 Inner Product Spaces

The most restrictive structure on V that we shall study is that of the *inner product*. An inner product on V is a function $\langle \cdot, \cdot \rangle$ from $V \times V$ to $\mathbb{R}$ that satisfies the following conditions for all $x, y \in V$:

1. Symmetry: $\langle x, y \rangle = \langle y, x \rangle$.
2. Bilinearity: $\langle ax+by, z \rangle = \langle ax, z \rangle + \langle by, z \rangle$, and $\langle x, ay+bz \rangle = \langle x, ay \rangle + \langle x, bz \rangle$.
3. Positivity: $\langle x, x \rangle \geq 0$, $\langle x, x \rangle = 0$ iff $x = 0$.

An *inner product space* is a pair $(V, \langle \cdot, \cdot \rangle)$, where V is a vector space over $\mathbb{R}$, and $\langle \cdot, \cdot \rangle$ is an inner product on V.

Typical examples of inner product spaces include the following:

Example C.4 Let $V = \mathbb{R}^n$, with addition and scalar multiplication defined as in Example C.1. For $x, y \in \mathbb{R}^n$, let

$$\langle x, y \rangle = x \cdot y = \sum_{i=1}^{n} x_i y_i.$$

We have seen in Chapter 1 that $\langle \cdot, \cdot \rangle$ defined in this way satisfies the conditions of symmetry, positivity, and bilinearity. Thus, $\langle x, y \rangle = \sum_{i=1}^{n} x_i y_i$ defines an inner product over $V = \mathbb{R}^n$, the *Euclidean inner product*. □

Example C.5 Let $V = C([0, 1])$, with addition and scalar multiplication defined as in Example C.3. For $f, g \in V$, let

$$\langle f, g \rangle = \int_0^1 f(\xi)g(\xi)d\xi.$$

It is immediate that the symmetry condition is met. To check positivity, note that

$$\langle f, f \rangle = \int f(\xi)f(\xi)d\xi$$
$$= \int (f(\xi))^2 d\xi.$$

This last term is always nonnegative, since $(f(\xi))^2 \geq 0$ for all ξ, and the integral of a function which only takes on nonnegative values is nonnegative. Finally,

$$\langle af + bg, h \rangle = \int (af(\xi) + bg(\xi))h(\xi)d\xi$$

$$= \int af(\xi)h(\xi)d\xi + \int bg(\xi)h(\xi)d\xi$$

$$= \langle af, h \rangle + \langle bg, h \rangle,$$

so bilinearity also holds. Therefore, $\langle f, g \rangle = \int f(\xi)g(\xi)d\xi$ defines an inner product over $V = C([0, 1])$. $\square$

It is important to note that more than one inner product can be defined on the same vector space V. For instance, let $V = \mathbb{R}^2$, and let a_1 and a_2 be strictly positive numbers. Then, it can be verified that

$$\langle x, y \rangle = a_1 x_1 y_1 + a_2 x_2 y_2$$

defines an inner product on V. Unless $a_1 = a_2 = 1$, this is not the Euclidean inner product on $\mathbb{R}^2$.

We close this section with a statement of a very useful result regarding inner products:

Theorem C.6 (Cauchy–Schwartz Inequality) *Let $\langle ., . \rangle$ be an inner product on V. Then,*

$$\langle x, y \rangle \leq \langle x, x \rangle^{1/2} \langle y, y \rangle^{1/2}$$

for all $x, y \in V$.

Proof The proof of the Cauchy–Schwartz inequality for the Euclidean inner product in $\mathbb{R}^n$ (see Chapter 1, Theorem 1.2), relied only on the three properties defining an inner product, and not on the specific definition of the Euclidean inner product itself. The current result may, therefore, be established by mimicking that proof, with the obvious changes. $\square$

C.3 Normed Spaces

A notion less restrictive (in a sense to be made precise) than the inner product is that of a *norm*. A norm is a function $\| \cdot \| : V \to \mathbb{R}$ that satisfies the following requirements for all $x, y \in V$:

1. Positivity: $\|x\| \geq 0$, $\|x\| = 0$ iff $x = 0$.

2. Homogeneity: $\|ax\| = \|a\| \cdot \|x\|$.
3. Triangle Inequality: $\|x + y\| \le \|x\| + \|y\|$.

An *normed space* is a pair $(V, \|\cdot\|)$, where V is a vector space, and $\|\cdot\|$ is a norm on V. Standard examples of normed spaces include the following:

Example C.7 Let $V = \mathbb{R}^n$, and let $p \ge 1$ be any real number. Define $\|\cdot\|_p : V \to \mathbb{R}$ by

$$\|x\|_p = \left(\sum_{i=1}^{n} |x_i|^p\right)^{1/p},$$

where $|x_i|$ denotes the absolute value of x_i.

It is easy to see that $\|\cdot\|$ satisfies homogeneity. It also satisfies positivity since $|x_i|$, and, hence, $|x_i|^p$, is nonnegative for each i. Finally, that $\|\cdot\|_p$ satisfies the triangle inequality is a consequence of an inequality known as the *Minkowski inequality*. For a general statement of Minkowski's inequality, we refer the reader to Royden (1968, p.114). In the special context of $\mathbb{R}^n$, the Minkowski inequality states that

$$\|x + y\|^p \le \|x\|^p + \|y\|^p,$$

which is precisely the triangle inequality.

Therefore, for any $p \ge 1$, $\|\cdot\|_p$ defines a norm over $\mathbb{R}^n$, the so-called *p-norm* on $\mathbb{R}^n$.   □

Note that, as with inner products, Example C.7 shows that many different norms can be placed on the same vector space. Examples C.8 and C.9 below, which define various norms on the space $C([0, 1])$, reiterate this point.

When $p = 2$, the p-norm $\|\cdot\|_p$ on $\mathbb{R}^n$ is called the *Euclidean norm*. As $p \to \infty$ we obtain the *sup-norm*

$$\|x\|_\infty = \|x\|_{\text{sup}} = \sup_{i=1,\dots,n} |x_i|.$$

Example C.8 Let $V = C([0, 1])$, with addition and scalar multiplication defined as in Example C.3. For $f \in V$ and $p \ge 1$, let

$$\|f\|_p = \left(\int_0^1 |f(\xi)|^p d\xi\right)^{1/p}.$$

As in the earlier example, it is easy to check that the positivity and homogeneity conditions are met by $\|\cdot\|_p$. The triangle inequality is again a consequence of the Minkowski inequality (see Royden, 1968, p.114).   □

Example C.9 Let $V = C([0, 1])$. For $f \in V$, let

$$\|f\| = \sup_{\xi \in [0,1]} |f(\xi)|.$$

Since f is continuous and $[0, 1]$ is compact, $\|f\|$ is well defined and finite for every $f \in V$. It is evident that $\|\cdot\|$ meets the positivity and homogeneity conditions required of a norm. To see that it meets the triangle inequality, note that for any f and g in V, and any $\xi \in [0, 1]$, we have

$$|f(\xi) + g(\xi)| \leq |f(\xi) + g(\xi)$$
$$\leq \|f\| + \|g\|,$$

where the first inequality is just the triangle inequality for the absolute value of real numbers, and the second inequality follows from the definition of $\|\cdot\|$. Taking the supremum of $|f(\xi) + g(\xi)|$ over ξ, we now obtain

$$\|f + g\| \leq \|f\| + \|g\|,$$

and the triangle inequality is also met. Thus, $\|\cdot\|$ is a norm on $C([0, 1])$, the *sup-norm*.
□

The following results relate norms and inner products. The first result shows that every inner product on V generates a norm on V. The second result shows that if a norm is generated by an inner product, it has to satisfy a certain property. It is an easy matter to construct norms (even on $\mathbb{R}^n$) that do *not* satisfy this property, so a corollary of this result is that the concept of a norm is less restrictive than that of the inner product.

Theorem C.10 *Let $\langle \cdot, \cdot \rangle$ be an inner product on V. Let $\|x\| = \langle x, x \rangle^{1/2}$. Then, $\|\cdot\|$ is a norm on V.*

Proof Immediate.
□

Theorem C.11 (Parallelogram Law) *If $\|\cdot\|$ is a norm generated by an inner product, then it satisfies the following equation for all x, $y \in V$:*

$$\|x + y\|^2 + \|x - y\|^2 = 2(\|x\|^2 + \|y\|^2).$$

Proof Omitted. See, e.g., Bartle (1964, p.58).
□

It is actually true that the parallelogram law characterizes norms and their associated inner products. If a norm $\|\cdot\|$ satisfies the parallelogram law, then the following relationship, called the *polarization identity*

$$\langle x, y \rangle = \frac{1}{4} \left(\|x + y\|^2 - \|x - y\|^2 \right)$$

defines an inner product from the norm, and the norm defined by this inner product must coincide with the original norm. We leave the details as an exercise.

C.4 Metric Spaces

C.4.1 Definitions

A *metric* on V is a function $d: V \times V \rightarrow \mathbb{R}$ that satisfies the following conditions for all $x, y, z \in V$:

1. Positivity: $d(x, y) \geq 0$, with equality iff $x = y$.
2. Symmetry: $d(x, y) = d(y, x)$.
3. Triangle Inequality: $d(x, z) \leq d(x, y) + d(y, z)$.

A *metric space* is a vector space V with a metric d on V, and is usually denoted (V, d). Standard examples of metric spaces include the following:

Example C.12 Let $V = \mathbb{R}^n$. Define the metric d_p on V by

$$d_p(x, y) = \|x - y\|_p,$$

where $\| \cdot \|_p$ is the p-norm of the previous section. It follows from Theorem C.14 below that d_p is a metric on $\mathbb{R}^n$. Since d_p is generated by the p-norm, it is called the *p-metric* on $\mathbb{R}^n$.   □

When $p = 2$, the p-metric d_p on $\mathbb{R}^n$ is called the *Euclidean metric*. As $p \rightarrow \infty$, we obtain the *sup-norm metric* d_∞:

$$d_\infty(x, y) = \sup_{i \in \{1, \dots n\}} |x_i - y_i|.$$

Example C.13 Let $V = C([0, 1])$. Define the metric d_p on V by

$$d_p(f, g) = \left(\int_0^1 |f(x) - g(x)|^p dx \right)^{1/p}$$

Then, d_p is generated by the p-norm on $C([0, 1])$, and it follows from Theorem C.14 below that d_p is a metric on $C([0, 1])$.   □

Just as every inner product generates a norm, it is also true that every norm generates a metric:

Theorem C.14 *Let $\| \cdot \|$ be a norm on V. Define d by $d(x, y) = \|x - y\|$, $x, y \in V$.*
Then, d is a metric on V.

Proof Immediate from the properties of the norm. $\square$

On the other hand, there do exist metrics even on $\mathbb{R}^n$, which are not generated by any norm. An example of such a metric is the "discrete metric" ρ on $\mathbb{R}$ defined by

$$\rho(x, y) = \begin{cases} 1, & x \neq y, \\ 0, & x = y. \end{cases}$$

Thus, the concept of a metric space is less restrictive than that of a normed space.

C.4.2 Sets and Sequences in Metric Spaces

Let a metric space (V, d) be given. Given a sequence $\{x_n\}$ in V, we will say that $\{x_n\}$ converges to the limit $x \in V$ (written $x_n \to x$) in the metric d, if it is the case that

$$d(x_n, x) \to 0 \text{ as } n \to \infty.$$

Note that convergence depends on the metric d. For instance, the sequence $\{x_n\} = \{1/n\}$ converges in the Euclidean metric to the point 0, but not so in the discrete metric. (In the discrete metric, the only convergent sequences are constant sequences.) In the interests of expositional cleanliness, however, we will drop the constant references to the underlying metric d in the sequel. Thus, for instance, we will simply say that "$x_n \to x$" rather than "$x_n \to x$ in the metric d."

A point $x \in V$ is said to be a *limit-point* of a sequence $\{x_n\}$, if there exists a subsequence $\{x_{k(n)}\}$ of $\{x_n\}$ such that $x_{k(n)} \to x$. Note that x is a limit point of $\{x_n\}$ if and only for all $r > 0$, it is the case that there are infinitely many indices n for which $d(x_n, x) < r$.

A sequence $\{x_n\}$ in V is said to be a *Cauchy sequence* if for all $\epsilon > 0$, there is $n(\epsilon)$ such that for all $m, n > n(\epsilon)$, we have $d(x_m, x_n) < \epsilon$.

Every convergent sequence in a metric space (V, d) must obviously be a Cauchy sequence, but the converse is not always true. For instance, suppose $V = (0, 1)$ and the metric d on V is defined by $d(x, y) = |x - y|$ for $x, y \in V$. Then, $\{x_n\} = \{1/n\}$ is a Cauchy sequence in V, but that does not converge (there is no $x \in V$ such that $x_n \to x$). A metric space (V, d) in which every Cauchy sequence converges is called *complete*.

The *open ball* of radius r and center x in (V, d), denoted $B(x, r)$, is defined by

$$B(x, r) = \{y \in V \mid d(x, y) < r\}.$$

A set $X \subset V$ is said to be *open in V*, or simply *open* if it is the case that for any $x \in X$, there is $r > 0$ such that $B(x, r) \subset A$.

As with convergent sequences, it must be stressed that whether or not a subset X of V is open depends on the particular metric being used. For instance, while not all subsets of $\mathbb{R}$ are open in the Euclidean metric, *every* subset X of $\mathbb{R}$ is open under the discrete metric on $\mathbb{R}$. To see this, pick any $X \subset \mathbb{R}$ and any $x \in X$. If $r \in (0, 1)$, then from the definition of the discrete metric, the open ball $B(x, r)$ with center x and radius r consists of only the point x. Since $x \in X$, we have shown that there exists $r > 0$ such that $B(x, r) \subset X$. Since $x \in X$ was arbitrary, we have shown that X is an open subset of $\mathbb{R}$ under the discrete metric.

A set $X \subset V$ is said to be *closed in V*, or simply closed, if X^c is open, where X^c, the complement of X in V, that is the set defined by

$$\{y \in V \mid y \notin X\}.$$

It is easy to mimic the steps of Theorem 1.20 in Chapter 1 to establish that

Theorem C.15 *The set $X \subset V$ is closed if and only if for all sequences $\{x_k\}$ in X such that $\{x_k\}$ converges to some $x \in X$, it is the case that $x \in X$.*

The set $X \subset V$ is *compact* if every sequence of points in X contains a convergent subsequence. That is, X is compact if for all sequences $\{x_n\}$ in X, there is a subsequence $\{x_{n(k)}\}$ of $\{x_n\}$, and a point $x \in X$, such that

$$\lim_{k \to \infty} x_{n(k)} = x.$$

Furthermore, a set $X \subset V$ is said to be *bounded* if X is completely contained in some open ball around 0, that is, if there is $r > 0$ such that $X \subset B(0, r)$.

As in $\mathbb{R}^n$ with the Euclidean metric, the following properties hold for arbitrary metric spaces also. The proofs are omitted:

Theorem C.16 *Let A be an arbitrary index set. If X_α is an open set in V for each $\alpha \in A$, then so is $\cup_{\alpha \in A} X_\alpha$.*

Theorem C.17 *Let A be an arbitrary index set. If Y_α is a closed set in V for each $\alpha \in A$, then so is $\cap_{\alpha \in A} Y_\alpha$.*

Theorem C.18 *Let F be a finite index set. If X_ϕ is an open set in V for every $\phi \in F$, then so is $\cap_{\phi \in F} X_\phi$.*

Theorem C.19 *Let F be a finite index set. If Y_ϕ is a closed set in V for every $\phi \in F$, then so is $\cup_{\phi \in F} Y_\phi$.*

Theorem C.20 *A set $Z \subset V$ is compact if and only if every open cover of Z has a finite subcover. That is, Z is compact if and only if whenever $(X_\alpha)_{\alpha \in A}$ is an arbitrary family of open sets satisfying $Z \subset \cup_{\alpha \in A} X_\alpha$, there is a finite subfamily $(X_\phi)_{\phi \in F}$ such that $Z \subset \cup_{\phi \in F} X_\phi$.*

However, not all properties that hold in $\mathbb{R}^n$ under the Euclidean metric hold for general metric spaces. For instance, an important result in $\mathbb{R}^n$ is that a set Z is compact if and only if it is closed and bounded. However, in arbitrary metric spaces, it is possible for a set to be closed and bounded without the set being compact. Here is an example:

Example C.21 As in Example C.2, let V be the space of bounded sequences in $\mathbb{R}$. Let $\| \cdot \|$ denote the sup-norm on V, i.e., for $x = (x_1, x_2, \ldots) \in V$, let

$$\|x\| = \sup_{i \in \mathbb{N}} |x_i|,$$

and let d denote the corresponding metric:

$$d(x, y) = \|x - y\| = \sup_{i \in \mathbb{N}} |x_i - y_i|.$$

Let e_i be the element of V that contains a 1 in the i-th place, and zeros elsewhere. Note that for any i and j with $i \neq j$, we have $d(e_i, e_j) = 1$. Let

$$X = \{e_i \mid i = 1, 2, \ldots\}.$$

The set X is bounded since $\|e_i\| = 1$ for all i. Since $d(e_i, e_j) = 1$ for all $i \neq j$, X contains no convergent sequences, so it is (vacuously) closed. However, the sequence $\{e_i\}$ is a sequence in X with no convergent subsequence, so X is not compact. $\qquad\Box$

C.4.3 Continuous Functions on Metric Spaces

Given metric spaces (V_1, d_1) and (V_2, d_2), a function $f : V_1 \to V_2$ is said to be *continuous* at the point $v \in V_1$, if it is the case that for all sequences $\{v_n\}$ in V_1 with $v_n \to v$, it is the case that $f(v_n) \to f(v)$. Equivalently, f is continuous at v if for all sequences $\{v_n\}$ in V_1,

$$d_1(v_n, v) \to 0 \text{ implies } d_2(f(v_n), f(v)) \to 0.$$

The function f is said to be continuous *on V_1* if f is continuous at each $v \in V_1$.

By using virtually the same arguments as in the proof of Theorem 1.49 in Chapter 1, it can be shown that

Theorem C.22 *Let* $f: V_1 \to V_2$, *where* (V_1, d_1) *and* (V_2, d_2) *are metric spaces. Then, f is continuous at* $v \in V_1$ *if and only if for all open sets* $U_2 \subset V_2$ *such that* $f(v) \in U_2$, *there is an open set* $U_1 \subset V_1$ *such that* $v \in U_1$, *and* $f(x) \in U_2$ *for all* $x \in U_1$.

As an immediate corollary of this result, we get the result that a function is continuous if and only if "the inverse image of every open set is open":

Corollary C.23 *A function* $f: V_1 \to V_2$ *is continuous on* V_1 *if and only if for all open sets* $U_2 \subset V_1$, $f^{-1}(U_2) = \{x \in U_1 \mid f(x) \in U_2\}$ *is an open set in* V_1.

C.4.4 Separable Metric Spaces

A point $x \in V$ is said to be a *limit point* of a set $X \subset V$ if for all $r > 0$, there is $z \in V, z \neq x$, such that

$$z \in B(x, r) \cap V,$$

that is, if the open ball $B(x, r)$ contains a point of X different from x.

The closure in V of a set $X \subset V$ is the set X together with all the limit points of X. We will denote the closure of X by $\mathrm{cl}(X)$. Note that we have $\mathrm{cl}(X) = X$ if and only if the set X is itself closed.

A set $W \subset V$ is said to be *dense* in V if the closure of W contains V, that is, if $\mathrm{cl}(W) \supset V$. Every set is dense in itself. However, as we have shown in Appendix B, every real number arises as the limit of some Cauchy sequence of rational numbers, so the closure of the rationals $\mathbb{Q}$ is the entire real line $\mathbb{R}$. Thus, a dense subset of a set X could be very "small" in relation to X.

A metric space (V, d) is said to be *separable* if it possesses a countable dense set, that is, there exists a countable subset W of V such that $\mathrm{cl}(W) = V$. For example, the set of rationals $\mathbb{Q}$ is countable and is dense in $\mathbb{R}$, so $\mathbb{R}$ is separable.

The following result gives us an equivalent way of identifying separability. It comes in handy frequently in applications.

Theorem C.24 *A metric space* (V, d) *is separable if and only if there is a countable family of open sets* $\{Z_n\}$ *such that for any open* $Z \subset V$, *it is the case that* $Z = \cup_{n \in N(Z)} Z_n$, *where* $N(Z) = \{n \mid Z_n \subset Z\}$.

Proof See Royden (1968, Chapter 7, p.130).   □

C.4.5 Subspaces

Let (V, d) be a metric space, and let $W \subset V$. Define a metric d_W on W by $d_W(x, y) = d(x, y)$ for $x, y \in W$. That is, d_W is just the metric d restricted to W. The space (W, d_W) is then called a *(metric) subspace* of (V, d).

Let (W, d_W) be a subspace of (V, d). A set $X \subset W$ is said to be *open in W* if there exists an open set $Y \subset V$ such that $X = Y \cap W$. If W is itself open in V, then a subset X of W is open in W if and only if it is open in V.

For example, consider the interval $W = [0, 1]$ with the metric $d_W(x, y) = |x - y|$ for $x, y \in W$. Then, (W, d_W) is a subspace of the real line with the Euclidean metric. The set $(\frac{1}{2}, 1]$ is open in W since $(\frac{1}{2}, 1] = (\frac{1}{2}, \frac{3}{2}) \cap W$ and $(\frac{1}{2}, \frac{3}{2})$ is open in $\mathbb{R}$.

The following result relates separability of (V, d) to separability of the subspace (W, d_W):

Theorem C.25 *Every subspace of a separable metric space is itself separable.*

Proof Let (V, d) be a separable metric space, and let (W, d_W) be a subspace of (V, d). Since V is separable, there exists, by Theorem C.24, a countable collection of open sets $(Z_n)_{n \in \mathbb{N}}$ such that every open set in V can be expressed as the union of sets from this collection. Define the family $(Y_n)_{n \in \mathbb{N}}$ by $Y_n = Z_n \cap W$. Then, Y_n is open in W for each n. Now suppose a set X is open in W. Then, there exists a set X' open in V such that $X = X' \cap W$. Therefore, there exists $K \subset \mathbb{N}$ and such that

$$X' \subset \cup_{i \in K} Z_i.$$

It follows that

$$X \subset \cup_{i \in K} Y_i.$$

Thus, we have shown that an arbitrary open set in W can be expressed as the union of open sets drawn from the countable collection $(Y_n)_{n \in \mathbb{N}}$. By Theorem C.24, W is separable. $\square$

Finally, our last result of this section relates the notions of "completeness" and "closedness" of a metric space:

Theorem C.26 *If (W, d_W) is complete, then it is closed. On the other hand, if W is a closed subset of V, and V is complete then (W, d_W) is also complete.*

Proof Left as an exercise. $\square$

C.5 Topological Spaces

C.5.1 Definitions

Unlike a metric space (V, d) which uses the metric d to determine which classes of sets are open, and which are closed or compact, a *topological space* takes as the defining primitive on a vector space V, the notion of *open sets*. Formally, a topological space (V, τ) is a vector space V and a collection τ of subsets of V that satisfy

1. $\emptyset, V \in \tau$.

2. $O_1, O_2 \in \tau$ implies $O_1 \cap O_2 \in \tau$.

3. For any index set A, $O_\alpha \in \tau$ for $\alpha \in A$ implies $\cup_{\alpha \in A} O_\alpha \in \tau$.

The sets in τ are called the "open sets" of V (under τ); τ itself is called a *topology* on V.

As we have seen in the previous subsection, if the open sets of V are identified using a metric d on V, then the collection of open sets generated by d will have the three properties required above. Thus, every metric space (V, d) gives rise to a topological space (V, τ). If a topological space (V, τ) is generated by a metric space (V, d) in this manner, then the topological space is said to be *metrizable*.

It is possible that two different metric spaces (V, d_1) and (V, d_2) give rise to the same topological space (V, τ), since two different metrics may generate the same class of open sets (see the Exercises). Thus, even if a topological space is metrizable, there may not be a unique metric space associated with it. It is also possible that a topological space is *not* metrizable. For instance:

Example C.27 Let V be any vector space consisting of at least two points. Define τ to be the two-point set $\tau = \{\emptyset, V\}$. Then, it is easily verified that τ meets the three conditions required of a topology (τ is called the *trivial topology* on V). We leave it as an exercise to the reader to verify that there cannot exist a metric d on V such that the only open sets of V under d are $\emptyset$ and V itself.[1]   □

Thus, a topological space is a generalization of the concept of a metric space.

Finally, a small point. Even if a topological space is metrizable, the topology could be quite "large." For instance, under the topology generated on V by the discrete metric (the *discrete topology*), *every* point of V, and therefore *every* subset of V, is open.

---

[1] If there were such a metric, it must satisfy $d(x, y) = 0$ for all x and y in V, but this violates the condition required of a metric that $d(x, y) > 0$ if $x \neq y$.

C.5.2 Sets and Sequences in Topological Spaces

A sequence $\{x_n\}$ in a topological space (V, τ) is said to *converge* to a limit $x \in V$ if for all open sets $O \in \tau$ such that $x \in O$, there exists N such that for all $n \geq N$, $x_n \in O$.

A set $X \subset V$ is *closed* if A^c is open (i.e., if $A^c \in \tau$). It is easy to show the following properties:

Theorem C.28 *Let (V, τ) be a topological space. Then, $\emptyset$ and V are both closed.*

Theorem C.29 *Let (V, τ) be a topological space. Let $(X_\phi)_{\phi \in F}$ be a collection of closed sets in V, where F is a finite index set. Then, $\cup_{\phi \in F} X_\phi$ is also closed.*

Theorem C.30 *Let (V, τ) be a topological space. Let $(X_\alpha)_{\alpha \in A}$ be a collection of closed sets in V, where A is an arbitrary index set. Then, $\cap_{\alpha \in A} X_\alpha$ is also closed.*

A subset W of a topological space (V, τ) is said to be *compact* if every open cover of W has a finite subcover. It is not very hard to see that if (V, τ) is metrizable, then a set W is compact in the sequential sense (i.e., every sequence in W contains a convergent subsequence) if and only if it is topologically compact (every open cover of W has a finite subcover). If a topological space is not metrizable, this is no longer true.[2]

C.5.3 Continuous Functions on Topological Spaces

Let (V, τ) and (V', τ') be topological spaces, and let $f: V \to V'$. Then, f is said to be *continuous* at $x \in V$ if for all $O' \in \tau'$ such that $f(x) \in O'$ it is the case that $f^{-1}(O') \in \tau$. Further, f is continuous on V if for all $O' \in \tau'$, we have $f^{-1}(O') \in \tau$.

It is easy to see that if (V, τ) and (V', τ') are metrizable spaces, then a function is continuous at x in the topological sense given above, if and only if f is sequentially continuous at x (i.e., for all sequences $x_n \to x$ we have $f(x_n) \to f(x)$). We leave it to the reader to examine if this remains true if (V, τ) and/or (V', τ') are not metrizable.

C.5.4 Bases

A *base* at x for a topological (V, τ) is a collection of open sets $\mathcal{B}_x \subset \tau$ such that

$$(O \in \tau, x \in O) \text{ implies there is } B \in \mathcal{B}_x \text{ such that } x \in B \subset O.$$

---

[2]In a sense this is analogous to the result that while closed and bounded sets in $\mathbb{R}$ are compact, this is not true in general metric spaces.

In words, B_x is a base for (V, τ) at x, if every open set containing x is a superset of some set in the base that also contains x.

For example, suppose (V, τ) is a metrizable topological space with metric d. Pick any $x \in V$, and define B_x by

$$B_x = \{B \mid B = B(x, r) \text{ for some } r > 0\},$$

where, of course, $B(x, r)$ represents the open ball with center x and radius r in the metric d. Since the metric d gives rise to the topology τ, it follows from the definition of an open set in metric spaces that B_x forms a base at x. Thus, the concept of a base at x is simply the topological analogue of the metric space notion of the open balls $B(x, r)$ around x.

A *base for a topological space* (V, τ) is a collection $B \subset \tau$ of open sets such that B is a base at x for each $x \in V$. It is easy to see that

Proposition C.31 *Let B be a base for (V, τ). Then, $O \in \tau$ if and only if for each $x \in O$, there is $B \in B$ such that $x \in B \subset O$.*

Proof Necessity (the "only if" part) follows from the definition of a base B for (V, τ). To see sufficiency, suppose $O \subset V$ is such that if $x \in O$, then there is $B \in B$ with $x \in B \subset O$. Then, we must have

$$O = \cup\{B \in B \mid B \subset O\}.$$

Therefore, O is the union of open sets, and must be open. That is, $O \in \tau$. □

A base B is said to be a *countable* base if it contains countably many sets. A topological space (V, τ) is said to be *first-countable*, or to satisfy the *first axiom of countability*, if for each point x, there exists a countable base B_x at x. It is said to be *second-countable*, or to satisfy the *second axiom of countability*, if it has a countable base B.

The following result relates separability to the notion of a countable base.

Theorem C.32 *Let (V, τ) be a metrizable topological space with metric d. Then,*

1. *(V, τ) is first-countable.*
2. *(V, τ) is second-countable if and only if the metric space (V, d) is separable.*

Proof If at each $x \in V$, we take the open balls $B(x, r)$ for *rational* $r > 0$, then the collection B_x of all such open balls forms a base at x which is countable. Thus, every metric space is first-countable, which proves Part 1. Part 2 is an immediate consequence of Theorem C.24. □

C.6 Exercises

1. Show that if a norm $\| \cdot \|$ on a vector space V is generated by an inner product $\langle \cdot, \cdot \rangle$, then the polarization identity holds, i.e., show that for all x and y in V, we have

$$\langle x, y \rangle = \frac{1}{4}(\|x + y\|^2 - \|x - y\|^2).$$

   Hint: This follows by expanding $\langle x \pm y, x \pm y \rangle = \|x \pm y\|^2$.

2. Using the polarization identity, prove the Parallelogram Law.

3. Of all the p-norms on $\mathbb{R}^n$, only one is generated by an inner product—the Euclidean ($p = 2$) norm. Show that, for example, $| \cdot |_1$ is not generated by an inner product. One way to do this is to show that the Parallelogram Law is violated for some pair x and y.

4. Let d_1 and d_2 be metrics on a vector space V. Define d_1 and d_2 to be *equivalent* if there exist constants c_1 and c_2 in $\mathbb{R}$ such that for all $x, y \in V$, we have

$$d_1(x, y) \leq c_2 d_2(x, y)$$

$$d_2(x, y) \leq c_1 d_1(x, y).$$

   Show that if d_1 and d_2 are equivalent metrics on V, then the following hold:

   (a) A sequence $\{x_n\}$ in V converges to a limit x in (V, d_1) if and only if $\{x_n\}$ converges to x in (V, d_2).

   (b) A set $X \subset V$ is open under d_1 if and only if it is open under d_2.

5. Give an example of two metrics d_1 and d_2 on a vector space V, that generate the same open sets but are not equivalent.

6. Which of the metrics induced by the p-norms $\| \cdot \|_p$ on $\mathbb{R}^2$ are equivalent?

7. Is the equivalence of metrics a transitive relationship? That is, is it true that if d_1 is equivalent to d_2, and d_2 is equivalent to d_3, then d_1 is equivalent to d_3?

8. Show that the discrete metric on $\mathbb{R}$ does, in fact, meet the three properties required of a metric.

9. Which subsets of $\mathbb{R}$ are closed sets in the discrete metric? Which are compact?

10. Prove that under the discrete metric, (V, d) is separable if and only if V is countable.

11. Let (V_1, d_1) denote $\mathbb{R}$ with the discrete metric and (V_2, d_2) denote $\mathbb{R}$ with the Euclidean metric. Let $\mathcal{F}$ denote the class of continuous functions from V_1 to V_2; $\mathcal{G}$ the class of continuous functions from V_1 to V_1, and $\mathcal{H}$ the class of continuous functions from V_2 to V_2. Compare $\mathcal{F}, \mathcal{G}$, and $\mathcal{H}$. Which is the largest set (in terms of containment)? Which is the second largest?

12. How does the class of continuous functions on $\mathbb{R}^n$ under the sup-norm metric compare to those on $\mathbb{R}^n$ under the Euclidean metric. (Assume in both cases that the functions map $\mathbb{R}^n$ into $\mathbb{R}$, and that the range space $\mathbb{R}$ is given the Euclidean metric.)

13. (The p-adic metric) Fix a prime p. Any rational r can be written as $r = p^{-n}(\frac{a}{b})$ where n, a, b, are integers and p does not divide a or b. Let $|r|_p = p^n$. This, the p-adic "valuation," is not a norm. For r, q, rational, let the p-adic metric be defined by $d(r, q) = |r - q|_p$. Show that the p-adic valuation obeys $|q|_p + |r|_p \le \max\{|q|_p, |r|_p\}$. Use this to show that the p-adic metric satisfies the triangle inequality. Verify the other requirements for a metric. Finally, show that if $r \in B(q, e)$ then $B(q, e) \subset B(r, e)$. It follows that $B(q, e) = B(r, e)$, so every point in an open ball around r in the p-adic metric is also the center point of the ball!

14. Let V be a vector space. Suppose V is given the discrete topology. Which subsets of V are compact?

15. Let V be a vector space. Suppose V is given the discrete topology. Which functions $f: V \to \mathbb{R}$ are continuous on V, if $\mathbb{R}$ is given the Euclidean topology?

16. Let (X, d_1) and (X_2, d_2) be metric spaces. Let $Z = X \times Y$. Define a metric (the *product metric*) on Z by

$$d[(x, y), (x', y')] = (d_1(x, x')^2 + d_2(y, y')^2)^{1/2}.$$

Show that the product metric is, in fact, a metric.

17. Let (V, τ) and (V', τ') be topological spaces, and let $W = V \times V'$. The *product topology* τ_W on W is defined as the topology that takes as open, sets of the form

$$O \times O', \quad O \in \tau, \ O' \in \tau',$$

and completes the topology by taking the finite intersection and arbitrary union of all such sets. Show that if (V, τ) and (V', τ') are topological spaces that are metrizable (with metrics d and d', say), then the product metric defines the product topolgy.

18. A set $X \subset V$ in a topological space (V, τ) is said to be *sequentially compact* if every sequence of points in X contains a susequence converging to a point of X.

   (a) Show that if (V, τ) is a metrizable space (say, with metric d), then X is sequentially compact if and only if it is compact, that is, if and only if every open cover of X contains a finite subcover.

   (b) Give an example of a nonmetrizable topological space (V, τ) in which there is a sequentially compact set that is not compact.

19. Show that if (V, τ) and (V', τ') are metrizable topological spaces, then a function $f: V \to V'$ is continuous at a point x in the topological sense if and only if it is sequentially continuous at x, i.e., if and only if for all sequences $x_n \to x$, we have $f(x_n) \to f(x)$. Is this true if (V, τ) and/or (V', τ') are not metrizable?

20. Let $V = [0, 1]$. Let τ be the collection of sets consisting of $\emptyset$, V, and all subsets of V whose complements are finite sets. Show that τ is a topology for V. Show also that (V, τ) is not first-countable.

Bibliography

Apostol, T. (1967) *Calculus*, Second Edition, Blaiswell, Waltham, Mass.

Arrow, K.J. and A.C. Enthoven (1961) Quasi-Concave Programming, *Econometrica* 29(4), 779–800.

Arrow, K.J., L. Hurwicz, and H. Uzawa (1958) (Eds.) *Studies in Linear and Non-Linear Programming*, Stanford University Press, Stanford, Calif.

Bank, B., *et al.* (1983) *Nonlinear Parametric Optimization*, Birkhäuser-Verlag, Boston and Basel.

Bartle, R.G. (1964) *Elements of Real Analysis*, Wiley, New York.

Berge, C. (1963) *Topological Spaces*, Macmillan, New York.

Billingsley, P. (1978) *Probability and Measure*, Wiley, New York.

Birkhoff, G. (1967) *Lattice Theory*, American Mathematical Society, Providence, R.I.

Blackwell, D. (1964) Memoryless Strategies in Finite-Stage Dynamic Programming, *Annals of Mathematical Statistics* 35, 863–865.

Blackwell, D. (1965) Discounted Dynamic Programming, *Annals of Mathematical Statistics* 36, 225–235.

Debreu, G. (1952) Definite and Semidefinite Quadratic Forms, *Econometrica* 20(2), 295–300.

Debreu, G. (1959) *Theory of Value*, Wiley, New York.

Fenchel, W. (1953) *Convex Cones, Sets, and Functions*, mimeograph, Princeton, N.J.

Fudenberg, D. and J. Tirole (1990) *Game Theory*, MIT Press, Cambridge, Mass.

Halmos, P.R. (1961) *Naïve Set Theory*, Van Nostrand, Princeton, N.J.

Hewitt, E. and K. Stromberg (1965) *Real and Abstract Analysis*, Springer-Verlag, Berlin and New York.

Hildenbrand, W. (1974) *Core and Equilibria of a Large Economy*, Princeton University Press, Princeton, N.J.

Hurwicz, L. (1958) Programming in Linear Spaces, in *Studies in Linear and Non-Linear Programming* (K. Arrow, L. Hurwicz, and H. Uzawa, Eds.), Stanford University Press, Stanford, Calif.

Johnston, J. (1984) *Econometric Methods*, McGraw-Hill International, Singapore.

Milgrom, P. and J. Roberts (1990) Rationalizability, Learning, and Equilibrium in Games with Strategic Complementarities, *Econometrica* 58(6), 1255–1278.

Munkres, J.R. (1964) *Elementary Linear Algebra*, Addison-Wesley, Reading, Mass.

Munkres, J.R. (1975) *Topology: A First Course*, Prentice–Hall International, Englewood Cliffs, N.J.

Parthsarathy, T. (1973) Discounted, Positive, and Noncooperative Stochastic Games, *International Journal of Game Theory* 2, 25–37.

Royden, H.L. (1968) *Real Analysis*, Macmillan, New York.

Rudin, W. (1976) *Principles of Mathematical Analysis*, Third Edition, McGraw-Hill International Editions, Singapore.

Samuelson, P.A. (1947) *Foundations of Economic Analysis*, Harvard University Press, Cambridge, Mass.

Smart, D. (1974) *Fixed-Point Theorems*, Cambridge University Press, Cambridge and New York.

Strichartz, R. (1982) *The Way of Analysis*, Vols. I and II, mimeograph, Department of Mathematics, Cornell University, Ithaca, N.Y.

Takayama, A. (1985) *Mathematical Economics*, Second Edition, Cambridge University Press, Cambridge and New York.

Tarski, A. (1955) A Lattice-Theoretic Fixed-Point Theorem and Its Applications, *Pacific Journal of Mathematics* 5, 285–308.

Topkis, D. (1978) Minimizing a Submodular Function on a Lattice, *Operations Research* 26(2), 305–321.

Topkis, D. (1995) Comparative Statics of the Firm, *Journal of Economic Theory* 67(2), 370–401.

Vives, X. (1990) Nash Equilibrium with Strategic Complementarities, *Journal of Mathematical Economics* 19(3), 305–321.

Index

C^1, 44
C^2, 49
$\mathbb{N}$, 2, 323
$\mathbb{Q}$, 2, 323
$\mathbb{R}$, 2, 325
$\mathbb{R}^n$, 2
  completeness of, 12, 328
$\mathbb{Z}$, 2, 323
e_i, 117

absolute value, 2, 324, 327
action set, 243
adjoint, 39
Apostol, T., 323
arg max, 76
arg min, 76
Arrow, K.J., 208
associative, 323, 324, 330
attainable values, 75

backwards induction, 273, 276
Banach Fixed Point Theorem, 288
Bartle, R.G., 1, 323, 330
base, 343
  countable, 344
Bellman Equation, 88, 274, 276, 283–286, 291,
  298, 301, 302, 304
Bellman principle of optimality, 274, 284, 295
Bertrand oligopoly, 262
best-response, 244, 263
bilinearity, 332
Birkhoff, G., 255
bordered
  hessian, *see* hessian, bordered
  matrix, *see* matrix, bordered
bounded set, *see* set, bounded
Brouwer Fixed Point Theorem, 244, 246
budget correspondence, 240–242
budget set, 79, 92, 113, 128, 158

Cartesian product, 69
Cauchy criterion, 11
Cauchy sequence, 11–14, 287, 323, 325, 326, 328,
  329
  defined, 11
  equivalent, 13, 325
  limit of, 12
Cauchy–Schwartz inequality, 4–6, 66, 333
closed ball, 22
closed graph, 233
closed set, *see* set, closed
closure, *see* set, closure of
cofactor, 38
commutative, 323, 324, 330
compact set, *see* set, compact
compactification, 94, 300
comparative dynamics, 270
complement, *see* set, complement of
complementary slackness, 147, 149, 154
concave function, *see* function, concave
constraint
  effective, 145–147, 148, 156–159, 162, 163, 165
  equality, 86, 112, 128
  inequality, 87, 112, 113, 128, 145, 158
  relaxation of, 116
constraint qualification
  under equality constraints, 115–116, 122–127,
    130, 132
  under inequality constraints, 147, 148, 149,
    152–154, 161, 162
constraint set, 74
consumer theory, 128
consumption–leisure choice, 81, 98
consumption–savings problem, 276
continuously differentiable, 44–45, 172
  twice, 49
contraction mapping, 287–289, 302
Contraction Mapping Lemma, 293, 296
Contraction Mapping Theorem, 288
contrapositive, 316–318

351

convergence
   pointwise, *see* pointwise convergence
   uniform, *see* uniform convergence
converse, 316–318
convex
   function, *see* function, convex
   set, *see* set, convex
convexity, 86–88, 237, 253, 263, 298, 300
   and optimization theory, 185–198
   and the Kuhn–Tucker Theorem, 187–189,
      194–198
   and unconstrained optimization, 187
   strict, 172
correspondence, 224–234, 261
   closed, 229
   closed-graph, 229
   closed-valued, 228, 229
   compact-valued, 228, 229, 231, 233, 235, 237,
      240, 245, 274, 298
   constant, 228, 260
   continuous, 235, 237, 240, 274, 298
      defined, 226
   convex graph, 229, 238
   convex-valued, 228, 237–240, 245, 246
   defined, 225
   graph of, 228
   lower-inverse, 230
   lower-semicontinuous (lsc), 236; characterized,
      230, 232; defined, 226
   nonempty-valued, 245, 246, 274
   single-valued, 225, 233, 237
   upper-inverse, 229
   upper-semicontinuous (usc), 231, 235, 237, 239,
      246, 297; characterized, 230, 231; defined,
      226
cost minimization, 80, 94, 121, 128, 130, 133, 157,
   161
cover, 28
critical point, 102, 121–124, 126, 128, 129, 131,
   150, 151, 153–157, 162, 190, 216
cyclical, 299

Debreu, G., 120
Dedekind cuts, 323
demand correspondence, 240, 242
demand curve, 80, 262
DeMorgan's laws, 25, 26
denseness of rationals, 328
derivative, *see* function, derivative of
determinant, *see* matrix, determinant of
deterministic, 271
differentiability, 86
diminishing marginal product, 173
diminishing marginal utility, 173
directional derivative, *see* function, directional
   derivative of
discount factor, 281, 282, 300
distributive, 330
dynamic programming, 88, 268, 322
   finite-horizon, 88, 268–278; optimal strategy in,
     272–276

infinite-horizon, 88, 281–298; optimal strategy
   in, 291–298

endowment, 81, 83
Enthoven, A.C., 208
epigraph, *see* function: epigraph of
equality-constrained optimization, 112–142
Euclidean inner product, 4–5, 332
   bilinearity of, 4
   defined, 4
   positivity of, 4
   properties of, 4
   symmetry of, 4
Euclidean metric, 2, 6–67, 336
   and triangle inequality, 6
   defined, 6
   positivity of, 6
   properties of, 6
   relation to norm, 6
   symmetry of, 6
Euclidean norm, 5–6, 334
   and triangle inequality, 5
   defined, 5
   homogeneity of, 5
   positivity of, 5
   properties of, 5
   relation to inner product, 5
Euclidean space, 1, 2, 264
expected utility, 82
expenditure minimization, 79, 80, 95, 97

field, 323, 326
   ordered, 327
finite subcover, 28
finite-horizon dynamic programming, 88, 268–278
first-countable, 344
first-order conditions, 101, 117, 122, 145, 172, 187,
   203, 277, 300
   for unconstrained maximum, 137
   for unconstrained optima, 101, 104–110
   under equality constraints, 114, 117
   under inequality constraints, 147
fixed point, 244, 245, 288
   unique, 288
fixed point theorem, 244, 263, 288
free disposal, 80
function
   C^1, 44, 45
   C^2, 49, 50, 52
   concave, 87, 172–185, 187, 203, 237, 239, 242;
     continuity properties of, 177–179; defined,
     174; differentiability properties of,
     179–183; second derivative of, 183–185
   continuous, 1, 41–43, 71, 90, 237, 239, 242, 244
   convex, 87, 172–185, 203; defined, 174
   decreasing, 89
   derivative of, 43–45, 114; higher order, 50;
     second, 49–50
   differentiable, 1, 43–50, 116
   directional derivative of, 48–49, 72
   epigraph of, 174

image of, 75
increasing, 89, 239
inverse, 65
jointly continuous, 72
lower-semicontinuous (lsc), 234
nondecreasing, 263
nonincreasing, 263
one-to-one, 65
onto, 65
partial derivative of, 46–48
quasi-concave, 87, 203–213, 239; defined, 204;
    derivative of, 210, 216–217; properties of,
    209–210; second derivative of, 211,
    217–220
quasi-convex, 87, 203–213; defined, 204;
    properties of 209–210
separately continuous, 72
strictly concave, 173, 176, 186, 190, 237, 239,
    243
strictly convex, 173, 176
strictly increasing, 76, 208
strictly quasi-concave, 205, 213, 239
strictly quasi-convex, 205
strictly supermodular, 256
subgraph of, 174
supermodular, 255, 264–266
upper-semicontinuous (usc), 234

games, 243
    strictly supermodular, 262
    supermodular, 262, 263
global maximum, 101, 104
global minimum, 104
golden rule, 308
greatest element, 255, 259, 260, 264
growth model, 298–309
    concave, 303
    differentiable concave, 305
    optimal strategies in, 300–309

Halmos, P.R., 315
hessian, 49, 73, 120
    bordered, 120
Hewitt, E., 323
history, 269
homogeneity, 334
hyperplane, 56–60, 255
    separating, 56–60
    supporting, 56

Implicit Function Theorem, 56, 65, 66, 136, 138
Inada conditions, 305
increasing differences, 253, 255–258, 264
    strictly, 256, 258, 260
index, 24
index set, 24
    arbitrary, 24
    finite, 24
indirect utility function, 240, 242

inequality-constrained optimization, 145, 168, 187,
    189
inf, *see* infimum
infimum, 14–17, 68, 78, 89, 234
    defined, 14
    relation to minimum, 17
infinite-horizon dynamic programming, 88,
    281–298
inner product, 2, 4, 6, 59, 330, 332–333
    Euclidean, *see* Euclidean inner product
    relation to norm, 335
inner product space, 332
integer, 2
interest rate, 276
Intermediate Value Theorem, 60
    for the derivative, 61
    in $\mathbb{R}^n$, 63
intersection, *see* sets, intersection of
inverse
    of function, *see* function, inverse
    of matrix, *see* matrix, inverse
Inverse Function Theorem, 56, 65
inverse image, 42
irrational number, 1, 2

Johnston, J., 1
join, 254, 255

Kakutani Fixed Point Theorem, 244, 246
Kuhn–Tucker first-order conditions, 147, 152, 185,
    188, 203, 214, 216
Kuhn–Tucker multipliers, 148–150
Kuhn–Tucker Theorem, *see* Theorem of Kuhn and
    Tucker

labor supply, 81
Lagrange's Theorem, *see* Theorem of Lagrange
Lagrangean
    under equality constraints, 121, 123–128, 130
    under inequality constraints, 150, 151, 155, 157,
        159, 189
Lagrangean method
    under equality constraints, 121–123, 126, 127,
        133
    under inequality constraints, 150–151
Lagrangean multipliers, 116, 117, 121
    and shadow price, 117
lattices, 254–255
least element, 255
lim inf, 18–21, 67, 68
    defined, 19
    properties of, 19–21
limit, *see* sequence, limit of
limit point, *see* sequence, limit point of
lim sup, 18–21, 67, 68
    defined, 19
    properties of, 19–21
linearly dependent, 33, 34
linearly independent, 34

local maximum, *see* maximum, local
local minimum, *see* minimum, local
local optimum, *see* optimum, local
logic, 315
lower bound, 14
lower-contour set, 204
lower-semicontinuous correspondence, *see* correspondence, lower-semicontinuous
lower-semicontinuous function, *see* function, lower-semicontinuous
lsc, *see* correspondence, lower-semicontinuous; function, lower-semicontinuous

Markovian, 268, 271
Markovian strategy, *see* strategy, Markovian
matrix, 1, 30–41
    adjoint, 39
    bordered, 120
    cofactor, 38
    column rank, 34
    determinant of, 35–38, 70, 120; and rank, 38; calculation of, 39–41; defined, 36; properties of, 37
    diagonal, 32
    full rank, 35
    identity, 33
    indefinite, 51
    inverse, 38–39, 70; calculation of, 38–39; properties of, 39
    lower-triangular, 33
    negative definite, 50–55, 73, 103, 104, 140
    negative semidefinite, 50–55, 73, 103, 104, 139
    nonnegative definite, 51
    nonpositive definite, 51
    positive definite, 50–55, 73, 103, 104
    positive semidefinite, 50–55, 73, 103, 104
    product, 31
    rank, 33–35
    rank of, 114
    row rank, 34
    square, 32
    sum, 30
    symmetric, 32
    transpose, 31, 33
    upper-triangular, 33
maximixer, 224
maximization problem, 75, 76, 224
    convex, 173
    existence of solution to, 90–92, 190
    quasi-convex, 205
    solution to, 75
    strictly convex, 173
    under inequality constraints, 151
maximizer, 75, 76, 186, 264, 274
maximum, 16–17, 68
    defined, 16
    global, 122–124, 126, 127, 130, 161, 186, 213
    local, 101, 102, 104; 114, 117, 118, 136, 146, 151, 165, 186, 213
    relation to supremum, 17

strict local, 103, 140
unconstrained, 100
unconstrained local, 101
Maximum Theorem, 88, 224, 225, 235–237, 240, 296, 297
    applications of, 240–247
    under convexity, 88, 225, 237–240
Mean Value Theorem, 61–63
    in $\mathbb{R}^n$, 63
meet, 254, 255
metric, 2, 4, 6, 330
    Euclidean, *see* Euclidean metric
    relation to norm, 336
    relation to topology, 342
    sup-norm, 286, 292, 336
metric space, 2, 328, 336–341
    bounded set in, 338
    Cauchy sequence in, 337
    closed set in, 338
    closure of set in, 340
    complete, 12, 286–287, 290, 292, 337
    continuous functions on, 339
    convergence in, 337
    convergent sequence in, 337
    dense subset of, 340
    open ball in, 337
    open set in, 338
    separable, 340, 344
    sequence in, 337
    subspace of, 341
metrizable space, 343
Milgrom, P., 262
minimization problem, 75, 76, 224
    convex, 173
    existence of solution to, 90–92
    quasi-convex, 205
    solution to, 75
    strictly convex, 173
minimizer, 75, 76
minimum, 16–17, 68
    defined, 16
    global, 122, 127, 132, 151
    local, 102, 104, 114, 117, 118, 136, 146
    relation to infimum, 17
    strict local, 103, 131
    unconstrained, 100
Minkowski inequality, 334
mixed constraints, 113, 145, 164–165
mixed strategies, 243
monotone, 299, 300
Munkres, J.R., 1, 315, 330

Nash equilibrium, 243, 244, 246, 263, 264
necessary conditions, 85, 86, 91, 95, 102, 103, 112, 114, 118, 123, 145, 185, 188, 277, 320–322
negation, 318, 320
negative definite, 50–55
negative semidefinite, 50–55
norm, 2, 4, 6, 330, 333–336
    Euclidean, *see* Euclidean norm

relation to inner product, 335
relation to metric, 336
normal form games, 243
normed space, 334

objective function, 74, 94, 164, 253, 278
open ball, 22
open cover, 28, 231, 343
open set, *see* set, open
optimal strategy, *see* strategy, optimal
optimization, 1, 74
optimization problem, 76, 258
    convex, 173
    defined, 74
    equality constrained, 113, 121
    existence of solution to, 90–92, 190
    existence of solutions, 85, 86
    inequality constrained, 113
    parametric, 77
    quasi-convex, 205
    solution to, 75, 76
    strictly convex, 173, 186, 277
    uniqueness of solution, 85, 172, 186
    with mixed constraints, 113
optimization theory
    objectives of, 85
optimum
    global, 86, 87, 122, 123, 127, 172, 203
    interior, 100
    local, 86, 122, 136, 145, 172
    unconstrained, 100, 187

Parallelogram Law, 335
parameter space, 224
parametric continuity, 85, 87, 224, 235–239
parametric maximization problem
    defined, 77
    solution to, 77
parametric minimization problem
    defined, 77
    solution to, 77
parametric monotonicity, 85, 88, 253, 258–261, 263
parametric optimization problem, 77, 85, 224
    defined, 77
Pareto optimum, 82, 93, 134
partial derivative, *see* function, partial derivative of
payoff function, 243
permutation, 35, 120
    even, 36
    inversions in, 36
    odd, 36
players, 243
pointwise convergence, 291
portfolio, 81
portfolio selection, 81, 98
positive definite, 50–55
positive semidefinite, 50–55
positivity, 332, 333, 336
producer theory, 128
production function, 80, 130, 299

Cobb–Douglas, 94
    linear, 94, 133
profit maximization, 80, 97
public finance, 83, 84
public goods, 83, 98

quadratic form, 1, 118, 120
    defined, 50
    negative definite, 50–55
    negative semidefinite, 50–55
    positive definite, 50–55
    positive semidefinite, 50–55
quantifier
    existential, 318, 319
    universal, 318, 319
quasi-concave function, *see* function, quasi-concave
quasi-convex function, *see* function, quasi-convex
quasi-convexity, 87, 203, 205
    and convexity, 205–209
    and optimization theory, 213–216
    and the Theorem of Kuhn and Tucker, 214–215,
        220–221

Ramsey–Euler Equation, 300, 306
rank of matrix, *see* matrix, rank
rational number, 1, 2
real line, 1
real number, 325
real number system, 325
reward function, 243, 269, 281
Roberts, J., 262
Royden, H.L., 323, 330, 334
Rudin, W., 1, 46, 61–63, 65, 66, 323

second-countable, 344
second-order conditions, 101, 128
    for unconstrained optima, 103–110
    under equality constraints, 117–121
securities, 81
separable, *see* metric space, separable
separating hyperplane, *see* hyperplane, separating
separation theorems, 56–60
sequence
    bounded, 7
    convergence of, 7–9
    convergent, 7, 67, 287
    defined, 7
    limit of, 7, 326
    limit point of, 10, 19, 67
    monotone, 17–18
    monotone decreasing, 17
    monotone increasing, 17
    nondecreasing, 17
    nonincreasing, 17
    unbounded, 7
set
    bounded, 2, 23, 68–70, 93
    closed, 2, 22–93; defined, 22; properties of,
        25–26; sum of, 27
    closure of, 57, 59, 69
    compact, 2, 23, 59, 68–69, 89, 90, 93, 94, 128;

(*cont.*)

defined, 23; finite intersection property, 70; nested sequences of, 27; nonempty intersection property, 26; properties of, 23, 26–29; sum of, 27

complement of, 24, 316

connected, 68

convex, 23–24, 57, 59, 60, 63, 68, 70, 87, 172, 173, 190, 204, 237, 244; defined, 23; properties of, 29; sum of, 29

empty, 315

interior of, 100

open, 22–136; defined, 22; properties of, 25–26

proper subset of, 316

subset of, 316

superset of, 316

set theory, 315

sets

intersection of, 24–26, 316

union of, 24–26, 316

shadow price, 117

Slater's condition, 188–190

social planner, 298

stationary

dynamic programming, *see* dynamic programming, infinite horizon

strategy, *see* strategy, stationary

steady state, 308

stochastic, 271

strategy, 269, 282

Markovian, 271–272, 295

Markovian optimal, 272, 274, 275

optimal, 270, 272, 274, 277, 283, 284

stationary, 292, 294–296

stationary optimal, 295, 296, 298, 301

strategy set, 243

Strichartz, R., 323

strict local maximum, *see* maximum, strict local

strict local minimum, *see* minimum, strict local

strictly concave function, *see* function, strictly concave

strictly convex function, *see* function, strictly convex

Stromberg, K., 323

subcollection, 24

arbitrary, 24

finite, 24

subcover, 28, 231

subgraph, *see* function, subgraph of

sublattice, 254, 255, 261

compact, 255, 259, 263, 264

noncompact, 255

submatrix, 119, 120, 135

subsequence, 67, 235, 241

defined, 10

limit of, 10

subset, *see* set, subset of

subspace, 341

sufficient conditions, 85, 87, 91, 95, 102, 103, 114, 118, 147, 185, 253, 277, 320–322

sup, *see* supremum

sup-norm, 334

sup-norm metric, *see* metric, sup-norm

supermodular, 255

strictly, 256

supermodularity, 88, 253, 255–258

characterization of, 264–266

superset, *see* set, superset of

supporting hyperplane, *see* hyperplane, supporting

supremum, 14–17, 68, 78, 89, 234

defined, 14

relation to maximum, 17

symmetry, 332, 336

t-history, 269, 271, 272, 282, 295

Tarski Fixed Point Theorem, 263

taxation, 84

Taylor's Theorem, 62, 65, 140, 141

in $\mathbb{R}^n$, 63, 64

Theorem of Kuhn and Tucker, 87, 145, 165, 168, 189

cookbook procedure for using, 150

proof of, 165–168

statement of, 145

under convexity, 187–189, 194–198

under quasi-convexity, 214–215, 220–221

Theorem of Lagrange, 86, 112–142, 145, 165, 166

cookbook procedure for using, 121–127

proof of, 135–137

statement of, 114

Topkis, D., 264

topological space, 2, 342–344

base for, 344

closed set in, 343

compact set in, 343

convergence in, 343

metrizable, 344

sequences in, 343

topology, 2, 330, 342

discrete, 342

nonmetrizable, 342

relation to metric, 342

trivial, 342

transition function, 269, 281

triangle inequality, 324, 327, 334, 336

uniform convergence, 289–291

Uniform Convergence Theorem, 289, 291

union, *see* sets, union of

upper bound, 14

upper-contour set, 204

upper-semicontinuous correspondence, *see* correspondence, upper-semicontinuous

upper-semicontinuous function, *see* function, upper-semicontinuous

usc, *see* correspondence, upper-semicontinuous; function, upper-semicontinuous

utility function, 78, 81, 92, 128, 133, 158, 240, 276, 299, 300

Cobb–Douglas, 79, 203

weighted, 83, 93, 134

utility maximization, 78, 79, 81, 84, 92, 121, 123, 128, 133, 157, 261

value function, 78, 269, 270, 274, 276, 277, 283–285, 301
  maximized, 78, 224
  minimized, 78
vector space, 2, 330–332

Vives, X., 262

Weierstrass Theorem, 52, 57, 86, 90–97, 123, 127–129, 132, 133, 234
  Generalized, 234
  in applications, 92–96
  proof of, 96–97
  statement of, 90